Race, Class, and Gender in the United States

An Integrated Study

Race, Class, and Gender in the United States

An Integrated Study

SIXTH EDITION

Paula S. Rothenberg
William Paterson University of New Jersey

Worth Publishers

Publisher: Catherine Woods
Executive Editor: Valerie Raymond
Executive Marketing Manager: Renée Altier
Production Editor: Margaret Comaskey
Production Manager: Barbara Anne Seixas
Art Director and *Cover Designer:* Barbara Reingold
Interior Designer: Paul Lacy
Cover Researcher: Vikii Wong
Cover Art: Magdalena Abakanowicz, *7 Dancing Figures,* 2001-02.
© Magadalena Abakanowicz; courtesy Marlborough Gallery, New York
Composition: TSI Graphics Inc.
Printing and Binding: R. R. Donnelley & Sons Company

Library of Congress Control Number: 2003105073
ISBN-13: 978-0-7167-5515-9
ISBN-10: 0-7167-5515-7

Printed in the United States of America

Sixth Printing

Worth Publishers
41 Madison Avenue
New York, NY 10010
www.worthpublishers.com

Contents

PART VI HOW IT HAPPENED:
RACE AND GENDER ISSUES IN U.S. LAW 435

Preface

As did its predecessors, this new edition undertakes the study of issues of race, gender, and sexuality within the context of class. Part I of the book introduces these issues by simultaneously examining the ways in which each has been socially constructed and by examining the social construction of difference or hierarchy itself, which underlies all of them. Part II takes an in-depth look at racism, sexism, heterosexism, and class privilege and introduces the concepts of patriarchy and white privilege. Designed both to focus on the similarities and differences between and among these forms of oppression and to emphasize the ways in which they intersect, the structure of this book continually explores the interlocking nature of these systems as they work in combination, affecting virtually every aspect of life in U.S. society today.

One of the greatest impediments to teaching this material to college-age students is the belief held by some that discrimination based on race, gender, sexual orientation, or class is a thing of the past. A surprising number are convinced that unfair treatment, if it ever existed, has largely been eliminated, while another group believes that if unfair treatment exists, it is white people or white men who are currently disadvantaged. Part III of the text, "Discrimination in Everyday Life," speaks directly to this misconception. Using newspaper accounts of individual and institutional discrimination, all new to this edition, this section makes a compelling case for the continuing existence of unfair and unequal treatment based on people's race/ethnicity, class, gender, sexual orientation, or some combination of them. It is guaranteed to produce some lively classroom discussion.

There are new articles in virtually every section of the book, as well as two articles from previous editions that have been reinstated and six articles from the last edition that have been updated by their authors especially for the new edition. New articles include "Disability and the Justification of Inequality in American History" by Douglas C. Baynton; a discussion of aversive racism by John F. Dovidio and Samuel L. Gaertner; "Yes, I Follow Islam, but I'm Not a Terrorist," by Nada El Sawy; and "Masked Racism," by Angela Davis. Among those revised and updated for this edition are Gregory Mantsios's piece on class in America; Holly Sklar's "Imagine a Country"; and the charts and graphs from the National Committee on Pay Equity. This means that, once again, the statistics in this text are as up to date as humanly possible.

New articles and essays consider the ways in which changing U.S. demographics and recent immigration history have complicated both racial and ethnic categories, as well as the relationships between and among groups within those categories. And several readings compare and contrast the successes and failures of various racial and ethnic groups and their causes. By broadening the consideration of issues of ethnicity and race, this edition reflects some of the ways in which this discourse is changing during the first part of the new century. Additional attention is also paid to examining both white-skin privilege and class privilege and making them more visible to readers who are sometimes reluctant to recognize that the flip side of discrimination is privilege.

Throughout the book, issues of gender are framed in inclusive terms to include attention to the socialization of men and boys as well as that of women and girls. Attention is also paid to some of the ways in which male socialization is related to misogyny and homophobia, and a number of articles make clear that male privilege has its price. On the other hand, a number of articles go beyond "victimology," to present positive accounts of the experiences of individuals and groups as they proudly claim identities that were previously viewed by many as problematic.

Finally, Part VIII, "Making A Difference: Social Activism," the concluding section of the book, has been substantially revised. It now focuses even more concretely on the ways in which people who care about issues of inequality, privilege, and injustice can and are making a difference. Included are articles that talk very specifically about student activism, including the United Students Against Sweatshops campaign and student involvement in the Taco Bell boycott. I think that faculty who use the book will find that this section allows them to end their courses in a very positive way. This is important, because students who study social problems often end up feeling overwhelmed by the extent and severity of those problems. The new articles in the last section leave students with an understanding that ordinary people acting on their principles really can make a difference.

Organization and Structure

Individual instructors may wish to modify the order of presentation of readings to conform to their own vision of how this complex and challenging material is best presented. The articles included in the sixth edition provide considerable flexibility in this respect. For example, the Gregory Mantsios article on class that appears in Part II could easily be used early in Part IV to frame the discussion of the economics of race, class, and gender in the United States. The piece by Evelyn Alsultany, "Los Intersticios," in Part V might well be used in conjunction with essays in Parts I and II to illustrate the ways in which identity is constructed and contextualized. Douglas Baynton's essay, "Disability and the Justification of Inequality in American History," can be combined with selections 79 and 80 to provide a mini-unit on disability issues. Articles that focus on male socialization and men's experience might be grouped together for a special section on the social construction of masculinity. These include the Michael Kimmel essay in Part I, the Allan Johnson piece in Part II, "The Loneliest Athletes" in Part III, and the Don Sabo, Tommi Avicolli, Libby Copeland, June Jordan, and Kate Bornstein pieces in Part V, as well as "White Lies" and "Pulling Train" in Part VII and the Michael Bronski piece in Part VIII.

I continue to place the historical materials in Part VI, fairly late in the book, because I continue to believe that students are more likely to read and digest this material after their interest has been captured by the more contemporary readings. To my mind, this ordering helps students see that history holds answers to perplexing contemporary questions rather than simply providing background for them. Other instructors will undoubtedly prefer to use the historical material earlier. Countless other reorderings will emerge from the contents, depending on each instructor's own vision for the course being taught. I think this flexibility is one of the strong points of a collection that is genuinely interdisciplinary and inclusive.

In this new edition I have tried to continue to enlarge the scope of vision and deepen the analysis that prompted the book in the first place. I have been helped by conversations with faculty and students throughout the country who have shared their experiences in using the text with me. The fact that so many have found the book useful confirms my own belief that these topics are an essential part of a liberal education today. To me, it is unthinkable that students graduating from college in the twenty-first century would fail to grapple with issues of diversity, difference, and inequality in the course of their studies. This book is intended to facilitate that process. To that end, I welcome suggestions and comments from students and faculty and others who use the text. I can be reached at rothenbergp@wpunj.edu.

Acknowledgments

Many people contributed to this book. First, I owe a profound debt to the old 12th Street study group, with whom I first studied black history and first came to understand the centrality of the issue of race. I am also indebted to the group's members, who provided me with a lasting example of what it means to commit one's life to the struggle for justice for all people.

Next, I owe an equally profound debt to my friends and colleagues who are part of the New Jersey Project on Inclusive Scholarship, Curriculum, and Teaching and to friends, colleagues, and students at William Paterson University who been involved in the various race and gender projects we have carried out for some years now. I have learned a great deal from all of them. I am especially grateful to J. Samuel Jordan and Leslie Agard-Jones: colleagues, teachers, and friends.

Many other people contributed to this new edition by helping me track down articles or information or by discussing various topics with me. In particular I would like to thank Naomi Miller, Steve Shalom, Greg Mantsios, Joan Griscom, Holly Sklar, Judy Baker, Helena Farrell, Kelly Mayhew, Robert Jersen, Carolyn

Jacobson of the National Committee on Pay Equity, and Paula Ettelbrick, formerly Legislative Counsel for the Empire State Pride Agenda. I continue to be grateful to Arlene Hirschfelder and Dennis White of the Association of American Indian Affairs and Marion Saviola of the Center for Independence of the Disabled, New York City, for their help.

I am also grateful to the following reviewers: Ann Baker (George Mason University), Susan Cavin (New York University), Michel Coconis (Grand Valley State University), Elizabeth Cramer (Virginia Commonwealth University), Nandi Crosby (California State University, Chico), David Goldstein-Shirley (University of Washington, Bothell), Laura Y. Liu (Rutgers University), Ann Lucas (San Jose State University), Keith Osajima (University of the Redlands), Ralph Pyle (Michigan State University), Salome Raheim (University of Iowa), Margaret Villanueva (St. Cloud University), and Abby Wilkerson (George Washington University).

Additional thanks to the faculty and students, too numerous to name, at the many colleges and universities where I have lectured during the past several years. Their generous sharing of bibliographies, articles, insights, and questions has enriched this book immeasurably. The same is true of the e-mail I have received from faculty and students around the country who have shared with me their response to the text.

This new edition has benefited greatly from the professional contributions of many people at Worth Publishers. In particular, I would like to thank my editor, Valerie Raymond, for her help and support and other members of the terrific team at Worth for the care and concern they have shown throughout the editorial, production, and promotion process. These include Paul Stenis, Renée Altier, Barbara Seixas, Nancy Walker, and Laura Hanrahan. My thanks also to Margaret Comaskey for her infinite attention to detail and high standards and to Diane Kraut, who carefully gathered the permissions.

Finally, I want to thank my partner, Greg Mantsios, and our now-grown children, Alexi Mantsios and Andrea Mantsios, for their insight, humor, and passion for social justice—all of which have left their mark on this edition.

Paula S. Rothenberg

About the Author

Paula S. Rothenberg is Director of the New Jersey Project on Inclusive Scholarship, Curriculum, and Teaching and a professor at the William Paterson University of New Jersey. She attended the University of Chicago and received her undergraduate degree from New York University, where she also did her graduate work. Rothenberg has lectured and consulted on multicultural and gender issues and curriculum transformation at hundreds of colleges and universities throughout the country. Her articles and essays appear in journals and anthologies across the disciplines, and many have been widely reprinted. Rothenberg is editor of *White Privilege: Essential Readings on the Other Side of Racism* (Worth, 2002); co-editor of *Creating an Inclusive College Curriculum: A Teaching Sourcebook from the New Jersey Project* (Teachers College Press, 1996); as well as co-editor of several highly successful college text anthologies, including *Feminist Frameworks* (McGraw-Hill, 1978, 1984, 1993). Her political memoir, *Invisible Privilege: A Memoir About Race, Class, and Gender*, was published by the University Press of Kansas in 2000.

Introduction

It is impossible to make sense out of either the past or the present without using race, class, gender, and sexuality as central categories of description and analysis. Ironically, many of us are the products of an educational system that has taught us *not* to use these categories and, hence, taught us *not* to see the differences in power and privilege that surround us. As a result, things that some people identify as clear examples of sexism or racism, appear to others to be simply "the way things are." Understandably, this often makes conversation difficult and frustrating. A basic premise of this book is that much of what passes for a neutral perspective across the disciplines and in cultural life already "smuggles in" elements of class, race, and gender bias and distortion. Because the so-called "neutral" point of view is so pervasive, it is often difficult to identify. One of the goals of this text is to help the reader learn to recognize some of the ways in which issues of race, class, and gender are embedded in ordinary discourse and daily life. Learning to identify and employ race, class, and gender as fundamental categories of description and analysis is essential if we wish to understand our own lives and the lives of others.

Beginning the Study

Beginning our study together makes apparent some immediate differences from other academic enterprises. Whereas students and faculty in an introductory literature or chemistry class do not begin the semester with deeply felt and firmly entrenched attitudes toward the subject, almost every student in a course that deals with issues of race, class, gender, and sexuality enters the room on the first day with strong feelings, and almost every faculty member does so as well. This can have either very good or very bad consequences. Under the best conditions and if we acknowledge them head-on, these feelings can provide the basis for a passionate and personal study of the topics and can make this course something out of the ordinary, one that has real long-term meaning for both students and teachers. But if we fail to find a way to channel these feelings positively, they are likely to function as obstacles that prevent the study from ever beginning in earnest. For this reason, it is important to acknowledge the existence of these feelings and devise some ground rules for classroom interactions, rules that help create an atmosphere that encourages candid and respectful dialogue.

Approaching this material presents many challenges. Racism, sexism, heterosexism, and class privilege are all systems of oppression with their own particular history and their own intrinsic logic (or illogic); for this reason, it is important to explore each of these systems in its own right. At the same time, these systems operate in conjunction with each other to form an enormously complex set of interlocking and self-perpetuating relations of domination and subordination. It is essential that we understand the ways in which these systems overlap and intersect and play off each other. For purposes of analysis it may be necessary to talk as if it were possible to abstract race or sexuality from, say, gender and class, and subject it to exclusive scrutiny for a time, even though such distinctions are never possible in reality. When we engage in this kind of abstraction, we should never lose sight of the fact that any particular woman or man has an ethnic background, class location, age, sexual orientation, religious orientation, gender, and so forth, and all these characteristics are inseparable from the person and from each other. Always, the particular combination of these identities shapes the individual and locates him or her in society.

It is also true that in talking about racism, sexism, and heterosexism within the context of class, we may have to make generalizations about the experience of different groups of people, even as we affirm that each individual is unique. For example, in order to highlight similarities in the experiences of some individuals, this book often talks about "people of color" or "women of color," even though these terms are somewhat problematic. When I refer to "women" in this book instead of "white women" or "women of color," it is usually in order to focus on the particular experiences or the legal status of women qua women. In doing so, I use language in much the same way that one might write a guide to "the anatomy of the cat." There is no such thing as "the cat" any more than there is "a woman" or there are "people of color." Yet for the purposes of discussion and analysis, it is often necessary to make artificial distinctions in order to focus on particular aspects of experience that may not be separable in reality. Language both mirrors reality and helps to structure it. No wonder, then, that it is so difficult to use our language in ways that adequately address our topics.

Structure of the Book

This book begins with an examination of the ways in which race, class, gender, and sexuality have been socially constructed in the United States as "difference" in the form of hierarchy. Part I treats the idea of difference itself as a social construct, one that underlies and grounds racism, sexism, class privilege, and homophobia. Each of the authors included would agree that while some of these differences may appear to be "natural" or given in nature, they are in fact socially constructed and the meanings and values associated with these differences create a hierarchy of power and privilege that, precisely because it does appear to be "natural," is used to rationalize inequality. Part II introduces the concept of "oppression" in order to examine racism, sexism, heterosexism, and class privilege as interlocking *systems* of oppression that insure advantages for some and diminished opportunities for others. Part III provides us with concrete examples of how these systems of oppression operate in contemporary society. Through the use of newspaper stories we get a firsthand look at the kinds of discrimination faced by members of groups subject to unequal and discriminatory treatment.

What exactly does it mean to claim that someone or some group of people is "different"? What kind of evidence might be offered to support this claim? What does it mean to construct differences? And how does society treat people who are categorized in this way? The readings in Parts I, II, and III of this book are intended to initiate a dialogue about the ways in which U.S. society constructs difference and the social, political, and personal consequences that flow from that construction. These readings encourage us to think about the meaning of racism, sexism, heterosexism, and class privilege and how these systems intersect.

Defining racism and sexism is always a volatile undertaking. Most of us have fairly strong feelings about race and gender relations and have a stake in the way those relations are portrayed and analyzed. Definitions, after all, are powerful. They can focus attention on certain aspects of reality and make others disappear. They may even end up assigning blame or responsibility for the phenomena under consideration. Parts I, II, and III are intended to initiate this process of definition. The readings allow us to discuss the ways in which we have been taught to think about race, class, and gender difference and to examine how these differences manifest themselves in daily life. The project of this entire volume is to carry this enterprise further, deepening our understanding of these phenomena, their manifestations, and their intersections.

Part IV provides statistics and analyses that demonstrate the impact of race, class, and gender difference on people's lives. Whereas previous selections depended primarily on narrative to define, describe, and illustrate discrimination and oppression, the material in Part IV presents current data, much of it drawn from U.S. government sources, that document the ways in which socially constructed differences mean real differences in opportunity, expectations, and treatment. These differences are brought to life in the articles, poems, and stories in Part V, which offer a glimpse into the lives of women and men of different ethnic and class backgrounds, expressing their sexuality and cultures in a variety of ways. Although many selections are highly personal, each points beyond the individual's experience to social policy or practice or culturally conditioned attitudes.

When people first begin to recognize the enormous toll that racism, sexism, heterosexism, and class privilege take on our lives, they often are overwhelmed. How can we reconcile our belief that the United States extends liberty and justice and equal opportunity for all with the reality presented in these pages? How did it happen? At this point we must turn to history.

Part VI highlights important aspects of the history of subordinated groups in the United States by focusing on historical documents that address race and gender issues in U.S. law since the beginning of the Republic. When these documents are read in the context of the earlier material describing race, gender, and class differences in contemporary society, history becomes a way of using the past to make sense of the present. Focusing on the legal status of women of all colors and men of color allows us to telescope hundreds of years of history into manageable size, while still providing the historical information needed to make sense of contemporary society.

Our survey of racism and sexism in the United States, past and present, has shown that these phenomena can assume different forms in different contexts. For some, the experiences that Richard Wright describes in "The Ethics of Living Jim Crow" (Part I) are still all too real today; but for others they reflect a crude, blatant racism that seems incompatible with contemporary life. How then are racism, sexism, homophobia, and class privilege perpetuated in contemporary society? Why do these divisions and the accompanying differences in opportunity and achievement continue? How are they reproduced? Why is it so difficult to recognize the reality that lies behind a rhetoric of equality of opportunity and justice for all? Part VII offers some suggestions.

A classic essay on sex-role conditioning draws an important distinction between discrimination (which frustrates choices already made) and the force of a largely unconscious gender-role ideology (which compromises one's ability to choose).* In Part VII, our discussion of stereotypes, violence, ideology, and social control is concerned with analyzing how the way we conceive of others—and, equally important, the way we come to conceive of ourselves—helps perpetuate racism, sexism, heterosexism, and class privilege. The discussion moves beyond the specificity of stereotypes; it analyzes how modes of conceptualizing reality itself are conditioned by forces that are not always obvious. Racism, sexism, and classism are not only systems of oppression that provide advantages and privileges to some; not simply identifiable attitudes, policies, and practices that affect individuals' lives— racism, sexism, heterosexism, and classism operate on a basic level to structure what we come to think of as "reality." In this way, they limit our possibilities and personhood. They cause us to internalize beliefs that distort our perspective and expectations and make it more difficult to identify the origins of unequal and unjust distribution of resources. We grow up being taught that the prevailing hierarchy in society is natural and inevitable, perhaps even desirable, and so we fail to identity the unequal distribution itself as a problem.

Finally, Part VIII offers some very specific suggestions about how to interrupt the cycle of oppression and bring about social change. Some of the selections suggest things that individuals can do in the course of their everyday life in order to make a difference and others provide examples of people working together to organize to bring about social change. Among the latter are accounts of campus initiatives that have attracted students at colleges and universities across the nation. They provide dramatic examples of the difference that students can make when they use their collective power in the interests of social justice.

*Sandra L. Bem and Daryl Bem. "Homogenizing the American Woman," in *Beliefs, Attitudes, and Human Affairs* by D. J. Bem (Monterey, CA: Brooks/Cole, 1970), pp. 89–99.

PART I

The Social Construction of Difference: Race, Class, Gender, and Sexuality

EVERY SOCIETY GRAPPLES WITH THE QUESTION of how to distribute its wealth, power, resources, and opportunity. In some cases the distribution is relatively egalitarian and in others it is dramatically unequal. Those societies that tend toward a less egalitarian distribution have adopted various ways to apportion privilege; some have used age, others have used ancestry. United States society, like many others, places a priority on sex, race, and class. To this end, race and gender difference have been portrayed as unbridgeable and immutable. Men and women have been portrayed as polar opposites with innately different abilities and capacities. The very personality traits that were considered positive in a man were seen as signs of dysfunction in a woman, and the qualities that were praised in women were often ridiculed in men. In fact, until very recently, introductory psychology textbooks provided a description of neurosis in a woman that was virtually identical with their description of a healthy male personality.

Race difference has been similarly portrayed. White-skinned people of European origins have viewed themselves as innately superior in intelligence and ability to people with darker skin or different physical characteristics. As both the South Carolina Slave Code of 1712 and the Dred Scott Decision in Part VI make clear, "Negroes" were believed to be members of a different and lesser race. Their enslavement, like the genocide carried out against Native Americans, was justified based on this assumed difference. In the Southwest, Anglo landowners claimed that "Orientals" and Mexicans were naturally suited to perform certain kinds of brutal, sometimes crippling, farm labor to which whites were "physically unable to adapt."[1] Women from various Asian populations have been said to be naturally suited to the tedious and precise labor required in the electronics industry (an appeal to supposedly innate race and gender difference).

Class status, too, has been correlated with supposed differences in innate ability and moral worth. Property qualifications for voting have been used not only to prevent African Americans from exercising the right to vote, but to exclude poor whites as well. From the beginnings of U.S. society, being a person of property was considered an indication of superior intelligence and character. The most dramatic expression of this belief is found in Calvinism, which taught that success in business was a sign of being in God's grace and, similarly, that being poor was a punishment inflicted by the Almighty.

In Part I we begin with a different premise. All the readings in this section argue that, far from reflecting natural and innate differences among people, the categories of gender, race, and class are themselves socially constructed. Rather than being "given" in nature, they reflect culturally constructed differences that maintain the prevailing distribution of power and privilege in a society, and they change in relation to changes in social, political, and economic life.

At first this may seem to be a strange claim. On the face of it, whether a person is male or female or a member of a particular race seems to be a straightforward question of biology. But like most differences that are alleged to be "natural" and "immutable," or unchangeable, the categories of race and gender are far more complex than they might seem. While it is true that most (though, as Judith Lorber points out in Selection 5, not all) of us are born unambiguously "male" or "female" as defined by our chromosomes or genitalia, the meaning of being a man or a woman differs from culture to culture and within each society. It is this difference in connotation or meaning that theorists point to when they claim that gender is socially constructed.

Social scientists distinguish between "sex," which is, in fact, a biologically based category, and "gender," which refers to the particular set of socially constructed meanings that are associated with each sex. These are seen to vary over time and place so that what is understood as "naturally" masculine or feminine behavior in one society may be the exact opposite of what is considered "natural" for women or men in another culture. Furthermore, while it is true that most societies have sex-role stereotypes that identify certain jobs or activities as appropriate for women and others for men, and claim that these divisions reflect "natural" differences in ability and/or interest, there is little consistency in what kinds of tasks have been so categorized. Whereas in many cultures strenuous physical activity is considered to be more appropriate to men than to women, in one society where women are responsible for such labor the heaviest loads are described as being "so heavy only a woman can lift it." In some societies it is women who are responsible for agricultural labor, and in others it is men. Even within cultures that claim that women are unsuited for heavy manual labor, some women (usually women of color and poor, white working women) have always been expected and required to perform back-breaking physical work—on plantations, in factories, on farms, in commercial laundries, and in their homes. The actual lives of real women and real men throughout history stand in sharp contrast to the images of masculinity and femininity that have been constructed by society and then rationalized as reflecting innate differences between the sexes.

In addition to pointing out the enormous differences in how societies have defined what is "naturally" feminine or masculine, and using these disparities to challenge the notion of an innate masculine or feminine nature, some theorists, such as Ruth Hubbard, Judith Lorber, and Michael Kimmel talk about the social construction of gender to make an even more profoundly challenging claim. They argue that the notion of difference itself is constructed and suggest that the claim that women and men are naturally and profoundly different reflects a political and social decision rather than a distinction given in nature. Anthropologist Gayle Rubin explains it this way:

> Gender is a socially imposed division of the sexes. . . . Men and women are, of course, different. But they are not as different as day and night, earth and sky, yin and yang, life and death. In fact from the standpoint of nature, men and women are closer to each other than either is to anything else—for instance mountains, kangaroos, or coconut palms. The idea that men and women are more different from one another than either is from anything else must come from somewhere other than nature.[2]

In fact, we might go on to argue, along with Rubin, that "far from being an expression of natural differences, exclusive gender identity is the suppression of natural similarities."[3] Boys and girls, women and men are under enormous pressure from the earliest ages to conform to sex-role stereotypes that divide basic human attributes between the two sexes. In Selection 5, Judith Lorber argues that differences between women and men are never merely differences but are constructed hierarchically so that women are always portrayed as different in the sense of being deviant and deficient. Central to this construction of difference is the social construction of sexuality, a process Ruth Hubbard, Jonathan Ned Katz, and Michael Kimmel analyze in Selections 6, 7, and 8. If they are correct, in a society where parents thought of their job as raising "human beings" instead of "boys" and "girls," we would likely find all people sharing a wide range of human attributes. In such a society, the belief that men and women naturally occupy two mutually exclusive categories would not structure social, political, and economic life.

The idea of race has been socially constructed in similar ways. The claim that race is a social construction takes issue with the once popular belief that people were born into different races with innate, biologically based differences in intellect, temperament, and character. The idea of ethnicity, in contrast to race, focuses on the shared social/cultural experiences and heritages of various groups and divides or categorizes them according to these shared experiences and traits. The important difference here is that those who talk of race and racial identity believe that they are dividing people according to biological or genetic similarities and differences, whereas those who talk of ethnicity simply point to commonalities that are understood as social, not biological, in origin.

Contemporary historian Ronald Takaki suggests that in the United States, "race . . . has been a social construction that has historically set apart racial minorities from European immigrant groups."[4] Michael Omi and Howard Winant, authors of Selection 1, would agree. They maintain that race is more a political categorization than a biological or scientific category. They point to the relatively arbitrary way in which the category has been constructed and suggest that changes in the meaning and use of racial distinctions can be correlated with economic and political changes in U.S. society. Dark-skinned men and women from Spain were once classified as "white" along with fair-skinned immigrants from England and Ireland, whereas early Greek immigrants were often classified as "Orientals" and subjected to the same discrimination that Chinese and Japanese immigrants experienced under the laws of California and other western states. In South Africa, Japanese immigrants were categorized as "white," not "black" or "colored," presumably because the South African economy depended on trade with Japan. In contemporary U.S. society, dark-skinned Latin people are often categorized as "black" by individuals who continue to equate something called "race" with skin color. In Selection 3, Pem Davidson Buck argues that whiteness and white privilege were constructed historically along with race difference in order to divide working people from each other and in this way protect the wealth and power of a small, privileged elite. In Selection 4, entitled "How Jews Became White Folks," Karen Brodkin provides a detailed account of the specific ways in which the status and classifications of one group, Jewish immigrants to the United States, changed over time as a result of and in relation to economic, political, and social changes in our society.

The claim that race is a social construction is not meant to deny the obvious differences in skin color and physical characteristics that people manifest. It simply sees these differences on a continuum of diversity rather than as reflecting innate genetic differences among peoples. Scientists have long argued that all human beings are descended from a common stock. Some years ago the United Nations published a pictorial essay called *The Family of Man*. It included numerous photographs of people from all over the world and challenged readers to survey the enormous diversity among the people depicted and point out where one race ended and the other began. Of course, it was impossible to do so. The photographs did not reflect sharply distinguished races but simply diversity on one and the same continuum.

The opening line of the autobiographical account by Richard Wright (Selection 2) provides another opportunity to think about the ways in which race is socially constructed. Wright begins his account by announcing, "My first lesson in how to live as a Negro came when I was quite small." Although it is true that Wright was born with dark skin, an unambiguous physical characteristic, it was for others to define the meaning of being black. As Wright's selection makes clear, in the South during the early 1900s it was primarily whites who defined what it meant to be a "Negro." They did so by making clear what behavior would be acceptable and what behavior would provoke violence, perhaps even death. In Part VII of this book, William Chafe draws an analogy between the way in which (white) women and black men have been socialized in this country under the threat of violence to conform to rigid race and gender roles. The irony is that when this socialization is successful, its results are used to support the claim that sex and race stereotypes are valid and reflect innate differences.

Writing about racism, Algerian-born French philosopher Albert Memmi once explained that racism consists of stressing a difference between individuals or populations. The difference can be real or imagined and in itself doesn't entail racism (or, by analogy, sexism). It is not difference itself that leads to subordination, but the interpretation of difference. It is the assigning of a value to a particular difference in a way that discredits an individual or group to the advantage of another that transforms mere difference into deficiency.[5] In this country, both race and gender difference have been carefully constructed as hierarchy. This means that in the United States, women are not merely described as different than men, but also that difference is understood to leave them deficient. The same is true of race. People of color are not merely described as different from white people, but that difference too is understood as deviance from an acceptable norm—even as pathology—and in both cases difference is used to rationalize racism and sexism.

In Selection 8, Michael Kimmel argues that homophobia is "intimately interwoven with both sexism and racism." According to Kimmel, the ideal of masculinity that prevails in U.S. society today is one that reflects the needs and interests of capitalism. It effectively defines "women, nonwhite men, nonnative-born men, homosexual men" as "other" and deficient, and in this way renders members of all these groups as well as large numbers of white working-class and middle-class men powerless in contemporary society. Our understanding of the ways in which race and gender difference has been constructed is further enriched by Douglas Baynton's analysis in Selection 9. Baynton argues that the idea of disability has functioned historically to justify unequal treatment for women and minority groups as well as justifying inequality for disabled people themselves. In his essay, he explores the ways in which the *concept* of disability has been used at different moments in history to disenfranchise various groups in U.S. society and to justify discrimination against them.

The social construction of class is analogous but not identical to that of race and gender. Differences between rich and poor, which result from particular ways of structuring the economy, are socially constructed as innate differences among people. They are then used to rationalize or justify the unequal distribution of wealth and power that results from economic decisions made to perpetuate privilege. In addition, straightforward numerical differences in earnings are rarely the basis for conferring class status. For example, school teachers and college professors are usually considered to have a higher status than plumbers and electricians even though the latters' earnings are often significantly higher. Where people are presumed to fit into the class hierarchy has less to do with clear-cut numerical categories than it does with the socially constructed superiority of those who perform mental labor (i.e., work with their heads) over those who perform manual labor (i.e., work with their hands). In addition, the status of various occupations and the class position they imply often changes depending on whether the occupation is predominately female or male and according to its racial composition as well.

Equally significant, differences in wealth and family income have been overladen with value judgments and stereotypes to the extent that identifying someone as a member of the middle class, working class, or underclass carries implicit statements about his or her moral character and ability. As Herbert Gans suggests in Selection 10, various ways of classifying and portraying poor people in this country have been used to imply that their poverty reflected a personal failure rather than a social problem for which society as a whole might be held responsible. In the nineteenth century, proponents of Calvinism and social Darwinism maintained that being poor in itself indicated that an individual was morally flawed and thus deserved his or her poverty—again relieving society of any responsibility for social ills.

Finally, class difference can be said to be socially constructed in a way that parallels the construction of race and gender as difference. In this respect, U.S. society is organized in such a way as to make hierarchy or class itself appear natural and inevitable. We grade and rank children from their earliest ages and claim to be sorting them according to something called natural ability. The tracking that permeates our system of education both reflects and creates the expectation that there are A people, B people, C people, and so forth. Well before high school, children come to define themselves and others in just this way and accept this kind of classification as natural. Consequently, quite apart from accepting the particular mythology or ideology of class difference prevailing at any given moment (i.e., "the poor are lazy and worthless" versus "the poor are meek and humble and will inherit the earth"), we come to think it natural and inevitable that there should be class differences in the first place. In the final essay in Part I, Jean Baker Miller asks and answers the question "What do people do to people who are different from them and why?"

NOTES

1. Ronald Takaki, *A Different Mirror: Multicultural American History* (Boston: Little, Brown, 1993), p. 321.

2. Gayle Rubin, "The Traffic in Women," in *Toward an Anthropology of Women,* Rayna R. Reiter, ed. (New York: Monthly Review Press, 1975), p. 179.

3. Ibid., p. 180.

4. Takaki, *Different Mirror.*

5. Albert Memmi, *Dominated Man* (Boston: Beacon Press, 1968).

Racial Formations

Michael Omi and Howard Winant

In 1982–83, Susie Guillory Phipps unsuccessfully sued the Louisiana Bureau of Vital Records to change her racial classification from black to white. The descendant of an eighteenth-century white planter and a black slave, Phipps was designated "black" in her birth certificate in accordance with a 1970 state law which declared anyone with at least one-thirty-second "Negro blood" to be black. The legal battle raised intriguing questions about the concept of race, its meaning in contemporary society, and its use (and abuse) in public policy. Assistant Attorney General Ron Davis defended the law by pointing out that some type of racial classification was necessary to comply with federal record-keeping requirements and to facilitate programs for the prevention of genetic diseases. Phipps's attorney, Brian Begue, argued that the assignment of racial categories on birth certificates was unconstitutional and that the one-thirty-second designation was inaccurate. He called on a retired Tulane University professor who cited research indicating that most whites have one-twentieth "Negro" ancestry. In the end, Phipps lost. The court upheld a state law which quantified racial identity, and in so doing affirmed the legality of assigning individuals to specific racial groupings.[1]

The Phipps case illustrates the continuing dilemma of defining race and establishing its meaning in institutional life. Today, to assert that variations in human physiognomy are racially based is to enter a constant and intense debate. *Scientific* interpretations of race have not been alone in sparking heated controversy; *religious* perspectives have done so as well.[2] Most centrally, of course, race has been a matter of *political* contention. This has been particularly true in the United States, where the concept of race has varied enormously over time without ever leaving the center stage of US history.

What Is Race?

Race consciousness, and its articulation in theories of race, is largely a modern phenomenon. When European explorers in the New World "discovered" people who looked different than themselves, these "natives" challenged then existing conceptions of the origins of the human species, and raised disturbing questions as to whether *all* could be considered in the same "family of man."[3] Religious debates flared over the attempt to reconcile the Bible with the existence of "racially distinct" people. Arguments took place over creation itself, as theories of polygenesis questioned whether God had made only one species of humanity ("monogenesis"). Europeans wondered if the natives of the New World were indeed human beings with redeemable souls. At stake were not only the prospects for conversion, but the types of treatment to be accorded them. The expropriation of property, the denial of political rights, the introduction of slavery and other forms of coercive labor, as well as outright extermination, all presupposed a worldview which distinguished Europeans—children of God, human beings, etc.—from "others." Such a worldview was needed to explain why some should be "free" and others enslaved, why some had rights to land and property while others did not. Race, and the interpretation of racial differences, was a central factor in that worldview.

In the colonial epoch science was no less a field of controversy than religion in attempts to comprehend the concept of race and its meaning. Spurred on by the classificatory scheme of living organisms devised by Linnaeus in *Systema Naturae*, many scholars in the eighteenth and nineteenth centuries dedicated themselves to the identification and ranking of variations in humankind. Race was thought of as a *biological* concept, yet its precise definition was the subject of debates which, as we have noted, continue to rage today. Despite efforts ranging from Dr. Samuel Morton's studies of cranial capacity[4] to contemporary attempts to base racial classification on shared gene pools,[5] the concept of race has defied biological definition. . . .

Attempts to discern the *scientific meaning* of race continue to the present day. Although most physical anthropologists and biologists have abandoned the quest for a scientific basis to determine racial categories, controversies have recently flared in the area of genetics and educational psychology. For instance, an essay by Arthur Jensen which argued that hereditary factors shape intelligence not only revived the "nature or nurture" controversy, but raised highly volatile questions about racial equality itself.[6] Clearly the attempt to establish a *biological* basis of race has not been swept into the dustbin of history, but is being resurrected in various scientific arenas. All such attempts seek to remove the concept of race from fundamental social, political, or economic determination. They suggest instead that the truth of race lies in the terrain of innate characteristics, of which skin color and other physical attributes provide only the most obvious, and in some respects most superficial, indicators.

Race as a Social Concept

The social sciences have come to reject biologistic notions of race in favor of an approach which regards race as a *social* concept. Beginning in the eighteenth century, this trend has been slow and uneven, but its direction clear. In the nineteenth century Max Weber discounted biological explanations for racial conflict and instead highlighted the social and political factors which engendered such conflict.[7] The work of pioneering cultural anthropologist Franz Boas was crucial in refuting the scientific racism of the early twentieth century by rejecting the connection between race and culture, and the assumption of a continuum of "higher" and "lower" cultural groups. Within the contemporary social science literature, race is assumed to be a variable which is shaped by broader societal forces.

Race is indeed a pre-eminently *sociohistorical* concept. Racial categories and the meaning of race are given concrete expression by the specific social relations and historical context in which they are embedded. Racial meanings have varied tremendously over time and between different societies.

In the United States, the black/white color line has historically been rigidly defined and enforced. White is seen as a "pure" category. Any racial intermixture makes one "nonwhite." In the movie *Raintree County*, Elizabeth Taylor describes the worst of fates to befall whites as "havin' a little Negra blood in ya'—just one little teeny drop and a person's all Negra."[8] This thinking flows from what Marvin Harris has characterized as the principle of *hypo-descent*:

> By what ingenious computation is the genetic tracery of a million years of evolution unraveled and each man [*sic*] assigned his proper social box? In the United States, the mechanism employed is the rule of hypo-descent. This descent rule requires Americans to believe that anyone who is known to have had a Negro ancestor is a Negro. We admit nothing in between. . . . "Hypo-descent" means affiliation with the subordinate rather than the superordinate group in order to avoid the ambiguity of intermediate identity. . . . The rule of hypo-descent is, therefore, an invention, which we in the United States have made in order to keep biological facts from intruding into our collective racist fantasies.[9]

The Susie Guillory Phipps case merely represents the contemporary expression of this racial logic.

By contrast, a striking feature of race relations in the lowland areas of Latin America since the abolition of slavery has been the relative absence of sharply defined racial groupings. No such rigid descent rule characterizes racial identity in many Latin American societies. Brazil, for example, has historically had less rigid conceptions of race, and thus a variety of "intermediate" racial categories exist. Indeed, as Harris notes, "One of the most striking consequences of the Brazilian system of racial identification is that parents and children and even brothers and sisters are frequently accepted as representatives of quite opposite racial types."[10] Such a possibility is incomprehensible within the logic of racial categories in the US.

To suggest another example: the notion of "passing" takes on new meaning if we compare various American cultures' means of assigning racial identity. In the United States, individuals who are actually "black" by the logic of hypo-descent have attempted to skirt the discriminatory barriers imposed by law and custom by attempting to "pass" for white.[11] Ironically, these same individuals would not be able to pass for "black" in many Latin American societies.

Consideration of the term "black" illustrates the diversity of racial meanings which can be found among different societies and historically within a given society. In contemporary British politics the term "black" is used to refer to all non-whites. Interestingly this designation has not arisen through the racist discourse of groups such as the National Front. Rather, in political and cultural movements, Asian as well as Afro-Caribbean youth are adopting the term as an expression of self-identity.[12] The wide-ranging meanings of "black" illustrate the manner in which racial categories are shaped politically.[13]

The meaning of race is defined and contested throughout society, in both collective action and personal practice. In the process, racial categories themselves are formed, transformed, destroyed and re-formed. We use the term *racial formation* to refer to the process by which social, economic and political forces determine the content and importance of racial categories, and by which they are in turn shaped by racial meanings. Crucial to this formulation is the treatment of race as a *central axis* of social relations which cannot be subsumed under or reduced to some broader category or conception.

Racial Ideology and Racial Identity

The seemingly obvious, "natural" and "common sense" qualities which the existing racial order exhibits themselves testify to the effectiveness of the racial formation process in constructing racial meanings and racial identities.

One of the first things we notice about people when we meet them (along with their sex) is their race. We utilize race to provide clues about *who* a person is. This fact is made painfully obvious when we encounter someone whom we cannot conveniently racially categorize—someone who is, for example, racially "mixed" or of an ethnic/racial group with which we are not familiar. Such an encounter becomes a source of discomfort and momentarily a crisis of racial meaning. Without a racial identity, one is in danger of having no identity.

Our compass for navigating race relations depends on preconceived notions of what each specific racial group looks like. Comments such as, "Funny, you don't look black," betray an underlying image of what black should be. We also become disoriented when people do not act "black," "Latino," or indeed "white." The content of such stereotypes reveals a series of unsubstantiated beliefs about who these groups are and what "they" are like.[14]

In US society, then, a kind of "racial etiquette" exists, a set of interpretative codes and racial meanings which operate in the interactions of daily life. Rules shaped by our perception of race in a comprehensively racial society determine the "presentation of self,"[15] distinctions of status, and appropriate modes of conduct. "Etiquette" is not mere universal adherence to the dominant group's rules, but a more dynamic combination of these rules with the values and beliefs of subordinated groupings. This racial "subjection" is quintessentially ideological.

Everybody learns some combination, some version, of the rules of racial classification, and of their own racial identity, often without obvious teaching or conscious inculcation. Race becomes "common sense"—a way of comprehending, explaining and acting in the world.

Racial beliefs operate as an "amateur biology," a way of explaining the variations in "human nature."[16] Differences in skin color and other obvious physical characteristics supposedly provide visible clues to differences lurking underneath. Temperament, sexuality, intelligence, athletic ability, aesthetic preferences and so on are presumed to be fixed and discernible from the palpable mark of race. Such diverse questions as our confidence and trust in others (for example, clerks or salespeople, media figures, neighbors), our sexual preferences and romantic images, our tastes in music, films, dance, or sports, and our very ways of talking, walking, eating and dreaming are ineluctably shaped by notions of race. Skin color "differences" are thought to explain perceived differences in intellectual, physical and artistic temperaments, and to justify distinct treatment of racially identified individuals and groups.

The continuing persistence of racial ideology suggests that these racial myths and stereotypes cannot be exposed as such in the popular imagination. They are, we think, too essential, too integral, to the maintenance of the US social order. Of course, particular meanings, stereotypes and myths can change, but the presence of a *system* of racial meanings and stereotypes, of racial ideology, seems to be a permanent feature of US culture.

Film and television, for example, have been notorious in disseminating images of racial minorities which establish for audiences what people from these groups look like, how they behave, and "who they are."[17] The power of the media lies not only in their ability to reflect the dominant racial ideology, but in their capacity to shape that ideology in the first place. D. W. Griffith's epic *Birth of a Nation*, a sympathetic treatment of the rise of the Ku Klux Klan during Reconstruction, helped to generate, consolidate and "nationalize" images of blacks which had been more disparate (more regionally specific, for example) prior to the film's appearance.[18] In US television, the necessity to define characters in the briefest and most condensed manner has led to the perpetuation of racial caricatures, as racial stereotypes serve as shorthand for scriptwriters, directors and actors, in commercials, etc. Television's tendency to address the "lowest common denominator" in order to render programs "familiar" to an enormous and diverse audience leads it regularly to assign and reassign racial characteristics to particular groups, both minority and majority.

These and innumerable other examples show that we tend to view race as something fixed and immutable—something rooted in "nature." Thus we mask the historical construction of racial categories, the shifting meaning of race, and the crucial role of politics and ideology in shaping race relations. Races do not emerge full-blown. They are the results of diverse historical practices and are continually subject to challenge over their definition and meaning.

Racialization: The Historical Development of Race

In the United States, the racial category of "black" evolved with the consolidation of racial slavery. By the end of the seventeenth century, Africans whose specific identity was Ibo, Yoruba, Fulani, etc. were rendered "black" by an ideology of exploitation based on racial logic—the establishment and maintenance of a "color line." This of course did not occur overnight. A period of indentured servitude which was not rooted in racial logic preceded the consolidation of racial slavery. With slavery, however, a racially based understanding of society was set in motion which resulted in the shaping of a specific *racial* identity not only for the slaves but for the European settlers as well. Winthrop Jordan has observed: "From the initially common term *Christian*, at mid-century there was a marked shift toward the terms *English* and *free*. After about 1680, taking the colonies as a whole, a new term of self-identification appeared—*white*."[19]

We employ the term *racialization* to signify the extension of racial meaning to a previously racially unclassified relationship, social practice or group. Racialization is an ideological process, an historically specific one. Racial ideology is constructed from pre-existing conceptual (or, if one prefers, "discursive") elements and emerges from the struggles of competing political projects and ideas seeking to articulate similar elements differently. An account of racialization processes that avoids the pitfalls of US ethnic history[20] remains to be written.

Particularly during the nineteenth century, the category of "white" was subject to challenges brought about by the influx of diverse groups who were not of the same Anglo-Saxon stock as the founding immigrants. In the nineteenth century, political and ideological struggles emerged over the classification of Southern Europeans, the Irish and Jews, among other "non-white" categories.[21] Nativism was only effectively curbed by the institutionalization of a racial order that drew the color line *around*, rather than *within*, Europe.

By stopping short of racializing immigrants from Europe after the Civil War, and by subsequently allowing their assimilation, the American racial order was reconsolidated in the wake of the tremendous challenge placed before it by the abolition of racial slavery.[22] With the end of Reconstruction in 1877, an effective program for limiting the emergent class struggles of the later nineteenth century was forged: the definition of the working class *in racial terms*—as "white." This was not accomplished by any legislative decree or capitalist maneuvering to divide the working class, but rather by white workers themselves. Many of them were recent immigrants, who organized on racial lines as much as on traditionally defined class lines.[23] The Irish on the West Coast, for example, engaged in vicious anti-Chinese race-baiting and committed many pogrom-type assaults on Chinese in the course of consolidating the trade union movement in California.

Thus the very political organization of the working class was in important ways a racial project. The legacy of racial conflicts and arrangements shaped the definition of interests and in turn led to the consolidation of institutional patterns (e.g., segregated unions, dual labor markets, exclusionary legislation) which perpetuated the color line *within* the working class. Selig Perlman, whose study of the development of the labor movement is fairly sympathetic to this process, notes that:

> The political issue after 1877 was racial, not financial, and the weapon was not merely the ballot, but also "direct action"—violence. The anti-Chinese agitation in California, culminating as it did in the Exclusion Law passed by Congress in 1882, was doubtless the most important single factor in the history of American labor, for without it the entire country might have been overrun by Mongolian [*sic*] labor and *the labor movement might have become a conflict of races instead of one of classes.*[24]

More recent economic transformations in the US have also altered interpretations of racial identities and meanings. The automation of southern agriculture and the augmented labor demand of the postwar boom transformed blacks from a largely rural, impoverished labor force to a largely urban, working-class group by 1970.[25] When boom became bust and liberal welfare statism moved rightwards, the majority of blacks came to be seen, increasingly, as part of the "underclass," as state "dependents." Thus the particularly deleterious effects on blacks of global and national economic shifts (generally rising unemployment rates, changes in the employment structure away from reliance on labor intensive work, etc.) were explained once again in the late 1970s and 1980s (as they had been in the 1940s and mid-1960s) as the result of defective black cultural norms, of familial disorganization, etc.[26] In this way new racial attributions, new racial myths, are affixed to "blacks."[27] Similar changes in racial identity are presently affecting Asians and Latinos, as such economic forces as increasing Third World impoverishment and indebtedness fuel immigration and high interest rates, Japanese competition spurs resentments, and US jobs seem to fly away to Korea and Singapore.[28] . . .

Once we understand that race overflows the boundaries of skin color, super-exploitation, social stratification, discrimination and prejudice, cultural domination and cultural resistance, state policy (or of any other particular social relationship we list), once we recognize the racial dimension present to some degree in *every* identity, institution and social practice in the United States—once we have done this, it becomes possible to speak of *racial formation*. This recognition is hard-won; there is a continuous temptation to think of race as an *essence*, as something fixed, concrete and objective, as (for example) one of the categories just enumerated. And there is also an opposite temptation: to see it as a mere illusion, which an ideal social order would eliminate.

In our view it is crucial to break with these habits of thought. The effort must be made to understand race as *an unstable and "decentered" complex of social meanings constantly being transformed by political struggle.* . . .

NOTES

1. *San Francisco Chronicle*, 14 September 1982, 19 May 1983. Ironically, the 1970 Louisiana law was enacted to supersede an old Jim Crow statute which relied on the idea of "common report" in determining an infant's race. Following Phipps's unsuccessful attempt to change her classification and have the law declared unconstitutional, a legislative effort arose which culminated in the repeal of the law. See *San Francisco Chronicle*, 23 June 1983.

2. The Mormon church, for example, has been heavily criticized for its doctrine of black inferiority.

3. Thomas F. Gossett notes:

> Race theory . . . had up until fairly modern times no firm hold on European thought. On the other hand, race theory and race prejudice were by no means unknown at the time when the English colonists came to North America. Undoubtedly, the age of exploration led many to speculate on race differences at a period when neither Europeans nor Englishmen were prepared to make allowances for vast cultural diversities. Even though race theories had not then secured wide acceptance or even sophisticated formulation, the first contacts of the Spanish with the Indians in the Americas can now be recognized as the beginning of a struggle between conceptions of the nature of primitive peoples which has not yet been wholly settled. (Thomas F. Gossett, *Race: The History of an Idea in America* [New York: Schocken Books, 1965], p. 16).

Winthrop Jordan provides a detailed account of early European colonialists' attitudes about color and race in *White Over Black: American Attitudes Toward the Negro, 1550–1812* (New York: Norton, 1977 [1968]), pp. 3–43.

4. Pro-slavery physician Samuel George Morton (1799–1851) compiled a collection of 800 crania from all parts of the world which formed the sample for his studies of race. Assuming that the larger the size of the cranium translated into greater intelligence, Morton established a relationship between race and skull capacity. Gossett reports that:

> In 1849, one of his studies included the following results: The English skulls in his collection proved to be the largest, with an average cranial capacity of 96 cubic inches. The Americans and Germans were rather poor seconds, both with cranial capacities of 90 cubic inches. At the bottom of the list were the Negroes with 83 cubic inches, the Chinese with 82, and the Indians with 79. (Ibid., p. 74).

On Morton's methods, see Stephen J. Gould, "The Finagle Factor," *Human Nature* (July 1978).

5. Definitions of race founded upon a common pool of genes have not held up when confronted by scientific research which suggests that the differences *within* a given human population are greater than those *between* populations. See L. L. Cavalli-Sforza, "The Genetics of Human Populations," *Scientific American* (September 1974), pp. 81–9.

6. Arthur Jensen, "How Much Can We Boost IQ and Scholastic Achievement?" *Harvard Educational Review*, vol. 39 (1969), pp. 1–123.

7. Ernst Moritz Manasse, "Max Weber on Race," *Social Research*, vol. 14 (1947), pp. 191–221.

8. Quoted in Edward D. C. Campbell, Jr., *The Celluloid South: Hollywood and the Southern Myth* (Knoxville: University of Tennessee Press, 1981), pp. 168–70.

9. Marvin Harris, *Patterns of Race in the Americas* (New York: Norton, 1964), p. 56.

10. Ibid., p. 57.

11. After James Meredith had been admitted as the first black student at the University of Mississippi, Harry S. Murphy announced that he, and not Meredith, was the first black student to attend "Ole Miss." Murphy described himself as black but was able to pass for white and spent nine months at the institution without attracting any notice (ibid., p. 56).

12. A. Sivanandan, "From Resistance to Rebellion: Asian and Afro-Caribbean Struggles in Britain," *Race and Class*, vol. 23, nos. 2–3 (Autumn–Winter 1981).

13. Consider the contradictions in racial status which abound in the country with the most rigidly defined racial categories—South Africa. There a race classification agency is employed to adjudicate claims for upgrading of official racial identity. This is particularly necessary for the "coloured" category. The apartheid system considers Chinese as "Asians" while the Japanese are accorded the status of "honorary whites." This logic nearly detaches race from any grounding in skin color and other physical attributes and nakedly exposes race as a juridical category subject to economic, social and political influences. (We are indebted to Steve Talbot for clarification of some of these points.)

14. Gordon W. Allport, *The Nature of Prejudice* (Garden City, New York: Doubleday, 1958), pp. 184–200.

15. We wish to use this phrase loosely, without committing ourselves to a particular position on such social psychological approaches as symbolic interactionism, which are outside the scope of this study. An interesting study on this subject is S. M. Lyman and W. A. Douglass, "Ethnicity: Strategies of Individual and Collective Impression Management," *Social Research*, vol. 40, no. 2 (1973).

16. Michael Billig, "Patterns of Racism: Interviews with National Front Members," *Race and Class*, vol. 20, no. 2 (Autumn 1978), pp. 161–79.

17. "Miss San Antonio USA Lisa Fernandez and other Hispanics auditioning for a role in a television soap opera did not fit the Hollywood image of real Mexicans and had to darken their faces before filming." Model Aurora Garza said that their faces were bronzed with powder because they looked too white. "'I'm a real Mexican [Garza said] and very dark anyway. I'm even darker right now because I have a tan. But they kept wanting me to make my face darker and darker'" (*San Francisco Chronicle*, 21 September 1984). A similar dilemma faces Asian American actors who feel that Asian character lead roles inevitably go to white actors who make themselves up to be Asian. Scores of Charlie Chan films, for example, have been made with white leads (the last one was the 1981 *Charlie Chan and the Curse of the Dragon Queen*). Roland Winters, who played in six Chan features, was asked by playwright Frank Chin to explain the logic of casting a white man in the role of Charlie Chan: "'The only thing I can think of is, if you want to cast a homosexual in a show, and you get a homosexual, it'll be awful. It won't be funny . . . and maybe there's something there . . .'" (Frank Chin, "Confessions of the Chinatown Cowboy," *Bulletin of Concerned Asian Scholars*, vol. 4, no. 3 [Fall 1972]).

18. Melanie Martindale-Sikes, "Nationalizing 'Nigger' Imagery Through 'Birth of a Nation'," paper prepared for the 73rd Annual Meeting of the American Sociological Association, 4–8 September 1978, in San Francisco.

19. Winthrop D. Jordan, op. cit., p. 95; emphasis added.

20. Historical focus has been placed either on particular racially defined groups or on immigration and the "incorporation" of ethnic groups. In the former case the characteristic

ethnicity theory pitfalls and apologetics such as functionalism and cultural pluralism may be avoided, but only by sacrificing much of the focus on race. In the latter case, race is considered a manifestation of ethnicity.

21. The degree of antipathy for these groups should not be minimized. A northern commentator observed in the 1850s: "An Irish Catholic seldom attempts to rise to a higher condition than that in which he is placed, while the Negro often makes the attempt with success." Quoted in Gossett, op. cit., p. 288.

22. This analysis, as will perhaps be obvious, is essentially DuBoisian. Its main source will be found in the monumental (and still largely unappreciated) *Black Reconstruction in the United States, 1860–1880* (New York: Atheneum, 1977 [1935]).

23. Alexander Saxton argues that:

North Americans of European background have experienced three great racial confrontations: with the Indian, with the African, and with the Oriental. Central to each transaction has been a totally one-sided preponderance of power, exerted for the exploitation of nonwhites by the dominant white society. In each case (but especially in the two that began with systems of enforced labor), white workingmen have played a crucial, yet ambivalent, role. They have been both exploited and exploiters. On the one hand, thrown into competition with nonwhites as enslaved or "cheap" labor, they suffered economically; on the other hand, being white, they benefited by that very exploitation which was compelling the nonwhites to work for low wages or for nothing. Ideologically they were drawn in opposite directions. *Racial identification cut at right angles to class consciousness.* (Alexander Saxton, *The Indispensable Enemy: Labor and the Anti-Chinese Movement in California* (Berkeley and Los Angeles: University of California Press, 1971), p. 1; emphasis added.)

24. Selig Perlman, *The History of Trade Unionism in the United States* (New York: Augustus Kelley, 1950), p. 52; emphasis added.

25. Whether southern blacks were "peasants" or rural workers is unimportant in this context. Sometime during the 1960s blacks attained a higher degree of urbanization than whites. Before World War II most blacks had been rural dwellers and nearly 80 percent lived in the South.

26. See George Gilder, *Wealth and Poverty* (New York: Basic Books, 1981); Charles Murray, *Losing Ground* (New York: Basic Books, 1984).

27. A brilliant study of the racialization process in Britain, focused on the rise of "mugging" as a popular fear in the 1970s, is Stuart Hall *et al., Policing the Crisis* (London: Macmillan, 1978).

28. The case of Vincent Chin, a Chinese American man beaten to death in 1982 by a laid-off Detroit auto worker and his stepson who mistook him for Japanese and blamed him for the loss of their jobs, has been widely publicized in Asian American communities. On immigration conflicts and pressures, see Michael Omi, "New Wave Dread: Immigration and Intra–Third World Conflict," *Socialist Review,* no. 60 (November–December 1981).

The Ethics of Living Jim Crow:
An Autobiographical Sketch

Richard Wright

I

My first lesson in how to live as a Negro came when I was quite small. We were living in Arkansas. Our house stood behind the railroad tracks. Its skimpy yard was paved with black cinders. Nothing green ever grew in that yard. The only touch of green we could see was far away, beyond the tracks, over where the white folks lived. But cinders were good enough for me and I never missed the green growing things. And anyhow cinders were fine weapons. You could always have a nice hot war with huge black cinders. All you had to do was crouch behind the brick pillars of a house with your hands full of gritty ammunition. And the first woolly black head you saw pop out from behind another row of pillars was your target. You tried your very best to knock it off. It was great fun.

I never fully realized the appalling disadvantages of a cinder environment till one day the gang to which I belonged found itself engaged in a war with the white boys who lived beyond the tracks. As usual we laid down our cinder barrage, thinking that this would wipe the white boys out. But they replied with a steady bombardment of broken bottles. We doubled our cinder barrage, but they hid behind trees, hedges, and the sloping embankments of their lawns. Having no such fortifications, we retreated to the brick pillars of our homes. During the retreat a broken milk bottle caught me behind the ear, opening a deep gash which bled profusely. The sight of blood pouring over my face completely demoralized our ranks. My fellow-combatants left me standing paralyzed in the center of the yard, and scurried for their homes. A kind neighbor saw me and rushed me to a doctor, who took three stitches in my neck.

I sat brooding on my front steps, nursing my wound and waiting for my mother to come from work. I felt that a grave injustice had been done me. It was all right to throw cinders. The greatest harm a cinder could do was leave a bruise. But broken bottles were dangerous; they left you cut, bleeding, and helpless.

When night fell, my mother came from the white folks' kitchen. I raced down the street to meet her. I could just feel in my bones that she would understand. I knew she would tell me exactly what to do next time. I grabbed her hand and babbled out the whole story. She examined my wound, then slapped me.

"How come yuh didn't hide?" she asked me. "How come yuh awways fightin'?"

I was outraged, and bawled. Between sobs I told her that I didn't have any trees or hedges to hide behind. There wasn't a thing I could have used as a trench. And you couldn't throw very far when you were hiding behind the brick pillars of a house. She grabbed a barrel stave, dragged me home, stripped me naked, and beat me till I had a fever of one hundred and two. She would smack my rump with the stave, and, while the skin was still smarting, impart to me gems of Jim Crow wisdom. I was never to throw cinders any more. I was never to fight any more wars. I was never, never, under any conditions, to fight *white* folks again. And they were absolutely right in clouting me with the broken milk bottle. Didn't I know she was working hard every day in the hot kitchens of the white folks to make money to take care of me? When was I ever going to learn to be a good boy? She couldn't be bothered with my fights. She finished by telling me that I ought to be thankful to God as long as I lived that they didn't kill me.

All that night I was delirious and could not sleep. Each time I closed my eyes I saw monstrous white faces suspended from the ceiling, leering at me.

From that time on, the charm of my cinder yard was gone. The green trees, the trimmed hedges, the cropped lawns grew very meaningful, became a symbol. Even today when I think of white folks, the hard, sharp outlines of white houses surrounded by trees, lawns, and hedges are present somewhere in the background of my mind. Through the years they grew into an overreaching symbol of fear.

It was a long time before I came in close contact with white folks again. We moved from Arkansas to Mississippi. Here we had the good fortune not to live behind the railroad tracks, or close to white neighborhoods. We lived in the very heart of the local Black Belt. There were black churches and black preachers; there were black schools and black teachers; black groceries and black clerks. In fact, everything was so solidly black that for a long time I did not even think of white folks, save in remote and vague terms. But this could not last forever. As one grows older one eats more. One's clothing costs more. When I finished grammar school I had to go to work. My mother could no longer feed and clothe me on her cooking job.

There is but one place where a black boy who knows no trade can get a job, and that's where the houses and faces are white, where the trees, lawns, and hedges are green. My first job was with an optical company in Jackson, Mississippi. The morning I applied I stood straight and neat before the boss, answering all his questions with sharp yessirs and nosirs. I was very careful to pronounce my *sirs* distinctly, in order that he might know that I was polite, that I knew where I was, and that I knew he was a *white* man. I wanted that job badly.

He looked me over as though he were examining a prize poodle. He questioned me closely about my schooling, being particularly insistent about how much mathematics I had had. He seemed very pleased when I told him I had had two years of algebra.

"Boy, how would you like to try to learn something around here?" he asked me.

"I'd like it fine, sir," I said, happy. I had visions of "working my way up." Even Negroes have those visions.

"All right," he said. "Come on."

I followed him to the small factory.

"Pease," he said to a white man of about thirty-five, "this is Richard. He's going to work for us."

Pease looked at me and nodded.

I was then taken to a white boy of about seventeen.

"Morrie, this is Richard, who's going to work for us."

"Whut yuh sayin' there, boy!" Morrie boomed at me.

"Fine!" I answered.

The boss instructed these two to help me, teach me, give me jobs to do, and let me learn what I could in my spare time.

My wages were five dollars a week.

I worked hard, trying to please. For the first month I got along O.K. Both Pease and Morrie seemed to like me. But one thing was missing. And I kept thinking about it. I was not learning anything and nobody was volunteering to help me. Thinking they had forgotten that I was to learn something about the mechanics of grinding lenses, I asked Morrie one day to tell me about the work. He grew red.

"Whut yuh tryin' t' do, nigger, get smart?" he asked.

"Naw; I ain' tryin' t' git smart," I said.

"Well, don't, if yuh know whut's good for yuh!"

I was puzzled. Maybe he just doesn't want to help me, I thought. I went to Pease.

"Say, are yuh crazy, you black bastard?" Pease asked me, his gray eyes growing hard.

I spoke out, reminding him that the boss had said I was to be given a chance to learn something.

"Nigger, you think you're white, don't you?"

"Naw, sir!"

"Well, you're acting mighty like it!"

"But, Mr. Pease, the boss said . . ."

Pease shook his fist in my face.

"This is a *white* man's work around here, and you better watch yourself!"

From then on they changed toward me. They said good-morning no more. When I was just a bit slow in performing some duty, I was called a lazy black son-of-a-bitch.

Once I thought of reporting all this to the boss. But the mere idea of what would happen to me if Pease and Morrie should learn that I had "snitched" stopped me. And after all the boss was a white man, too. What was the use?

The climax came at noon one summer day. Pease called me to his workbench. To get to him I had to go between two narrow benches and stand with my back against a wall.

"Yes, sir," I said.

"Richard, I want to ask you something," Pease began pleasantly, not looking up from his work.

"Yes, sir," I said again.

Morrie came over, blocking the narrow passage between the benches. He folded his arms, staring at me solemnly.

I looked from one to the other, sensing that something was coming.

"Yes, sir," I said for the third time.

Pease looked up and spoke very slowly.

"Richard, Mr. Morrie here tells me you called me *Pease*."

I stiffened. A void seemed to open up in me. I knew this was the show-down.

He meant that I had failed to call him Mr. Pease. I looked at Morrie. He was gripping a steel bar in his hands. I opened my mouth to speak, to protest, to assure Pease that I had never called him simply *Pease*, and that I had never had any intentions of doing so, when Morrie grabbed me by the collar, ramming my head against the wall.

"Now, be careful, nigger!" snarled Morrie, baring his teeth. "*I heard yuh call 'im Pease!* 'N' if yuh say yuh didn't, yuh're callin' me a *lie*, see?" He waved the steel bar threateningly.

If I had said: No, sir, Mr. Pease, I never called you *Pease*, I would have been automatically calling Morrie a liar. And if I had said: Yes, sir, Mr. Pease, I called you *Pease*, I would have been pleading guilty to having uttered the worst insult that a Negro can utter to a southern white man. I stood hesitating, trying to frame a neutral reply.

"Richard, I asked you a question!" said Pease. Anger was creeping into his voice.

"I don't remember calling you *Pease*, Mr. Pease," I said cautiously. "And if I did, I sure didn't mean . . ."

"You black son-of-a-bitch! You called me *Pease*, then!" he spat, slapping me till I bent sideways over a bench. Morrie was on top of me, demanding:

"Didn't yuh call 'im *Pease*? If yuh say yuh didn't, I'll rip yo' gut string loose with this bar, yuh black granny dodger! Yuh can't call a white man a lie 'n' git erway with it, you black son-of-a-bitch!"

I wilted. I begged them not to bother me. I knew what they wanted. They wanted me to leave.

"I'll leave," I promised. "I'll leave right *now*."

They gave me a minute to get out of the factory. I was warned not to show up again, or tell the boss.

I went.

When I told the folks at home what had happened, they called me a fool. They told me that I must never again attempt to exceed my boundaries. When you are working for white folks, they said, you got to "stay in your place" if you want to keep working.

II

My Jim Crow education continued on my next job, which was portering in a clothing store. One morning, while polishing brass out front, the boss and his twenty-year-old son got out of their car and half dragged and half kicked a Negro woman into the store. A policeman standing at the corner looked on, twirling his night-stick. I watched out of the corner of my eye, never slackening the strokes of my chamois upon the brass. After a few minutes, I heard shrill screams coming from the rear of the store. Later the woman stumbled out, bleeding, crying, and holding her stomach. When she reached the end of the block, the policeman grabbed her and accused her of being drunk. Silently, I watched him throw her into a patrol wagon.

When I went to the rear of the store, the boss and his son were washing their hands at the sink. They were chuckling. The floor was bloody and strewn with wisps of hair and clothing. No doubt I must have appeared pretty shocked, for the boss slapped me reassuringly on the back.

"Boy, that's what we do to niggers when they don't want to pay their bills," he said, laughing.

His son looked at me and grinned.

"Here, hava cigarette," he said.

Not knowing what to do, I took it. He lit his and held the match for me. This was a gesture of kindness, indicating that even if they had beaten the poor old woman, they would not beat me if I knew enough to keep my mouth shut.

"Yes, sir," I said, and asked no questions.

After they had gone, I sat on the edge of a packing box and stared at the bloody floor till the cigarette went out.

That day at noon, while eating in a hamburger joint, I told my fellow Negro porters what had happened. No one seemed surprised. One fellow, after swallowing a huge bite, turned to me and asked:

"Huh! Is tha' all they did t' her?"

"Yeah. Wasn't tha' enough?" I asked.

"Shucks! Man, she's a lucky bitch!" he said, burying his lips deep into a juicy hamburger. "Hell, it's a wonder they didn't lay her when they got through."

III

I was learning fast, but not quite fast enough. One day, while I was delivering packages in the suburbs, my bicycle tire was punctured. I walked along the hot, dusty road, sweating and leading my bicycle by the handle-bars.

A car slowed at my side.

"What's the matter, boy?" a white man called.

I told him my bicycle was broken and I was walking back to town.

"That's too bad," he said, "Hop on the running board."

He stopped the car. I clutched hard at my bicycle with one hand and clung to the side of the car with the other.

"All set?"

"Yes, sir," I answered. The car started.

It was full of young white men. They were drinking. I watched the flask pass from mouth to mouth.

"Wanna drink, boy?" one asked.

I laughed as the wind whipped my face. Instinctively obeying the freshly planted precepts of my mother, I said:

"Oh, no!"

The words were hardly out of my mouth before I felt something hard and cold smash me between the eyes. It was an empty whisky bottle. I saw stars, and fell backwards from the speeding car into the dust of the road, my feet becoming entangled in the steel spokes of my bicycle. The white men piled out and stood over me.

"Nigger, ain' yuh learned no better sense'n tha' yet?" asked the man who hit me. "Ain't yuh learned t' say *sir* t' a white man yet?"

Dazed, I pulled to my feet. My elbows and legs were bleeding. Fists doubled, the white man advanced, kicking my bicycle out of the way.

"Aw, leave the bastard alone. He's got enough," said one.

They stood looking at me. I rubbed my shins, trying to stop the flow of blood. No doubt they felt a sort of contemptuous pity, for one asked:

"Yuh wanna ride t' town now, nigger? Yuh reckon yuh know enough t' ride now?"

"I wanna walk," I said, simply.

Maybe it sounded funny. They laughed.

"Well, walk, yuh black son-of-a-bitch!"

When they left they comforted me with:

"Nigger, yuh sho better be damn glad it wuz us yuh talked t' tha' way. Yuh're a lucky bastard, 'cause if yuh'd said tha' t' somebody else, yuh might've been a dead nigger now."

IV

Negroes who have lived South know the dread of being caught alone upon the streets in white neighborhoods after the sun has set. In such a simple situation as this the plight of the Negro in America is graphically symbolized. While white strangers may be in these neighborhoods trying to get home, they can pass unmolested. But the color of a Negro's skin makes him easily recognizable, makes him suspect, converts him into a defenseless target.

Late one Saturday night I made some deliveries in a white neighborhood. I was pedaling my bicycle back to the store as fast as I could, when a police car, swerving toward me, jammed me into the curbing.

"Get down and put up your hands!" the policemen ordered.

I did. They climbed out of the car, guns drawn, faces set, and advanced slowly.

"Keep still!" they ordered.

I reached my hands higher. They searched my pockets and packages. They seemed dissatisfied when they could find nothing incriminating. Finally, one of them said:

"Boy, tell your boss not to send you out in white neighborhoods after sundown."

As usual, I said:

"Yes, sir."

V

My next job was a hall-boy in a hotel. Here my Jim Crow education broadened and deepened. When the bell-boys were busy, I was often called to assist them. As many of the rooms in the hotel were occupied by prostitutes, I was constantly called to carry them liquor and cigarettes. These women were nude most of the time. They did not bother about clothing, even for bell-boys. When you went into their rooms, you were supposed to take their nakedness for granted, as though it startled you no more than a blue vase or a red rug. Your presence awoke in them no sense of shame, for you were not regarded as human. If they were alone, you could steal sidelong glimpses at them. But if they were receiving men, not a flicker of your eyelids could show. I remember one incident vividly. A new woman, a huge, snowy-skinned blonde, took a room on my floor. I was sent to wait upon her. She was in bed with a thick-set man; both were nude and uncovered. She said she wanted some liquor and slid out of bed and waddled across the floor to get her money from a dresser drawer. I watched her.

"Nigger, what in hell you looking at?" the white man asked me, raising himself upon his elbows.

"Nothing," I answered, looking miles deep into the blank wall of the room.

"Keep your eyes where they belong, if you want to be healthy!" he said.

"Yes, sir."

VI

One of the bell-boys I knew in this hotel was keeping steady company with one of the Negro maids. Out of a clear sky the police descended upon his home and arrested him, accusing him of bastardy. The poor boy swore he had had no intimate relations with the girl. Nevertheless, they forced him to marry her. When the child arrived, it was found to be much lighter in complexion than either of the two supposedly legal parents. The white men around the hotel made a great joke of it. They spread the rumor that some white cow must have scared the poor girl while she was carrying the baby. If you were in their presence when this explanation was offered, you were supposed to laugh.

VII

One of the bell-boys was caught in bed with a white prostitute. He was castrated and run out of town. Immediately after this all the bell-boys and hall-boys were called together and warned. We were given to understand that the boy who had been castrated was a "mighty, mighty lucky bastard." We were impressed with the fact that next time the management of the hotel would not be responsible for the lives of "trouble-makin' niggers." We were silent.

VIII

One night, just as I was about to go home, I met one of the Negro maids. She lived in my direction, and we fell in to walk part of the way home together. As we passed the white night-watchman, he slapped the maid on her buttock. I turned around, amazed. The watchman looked at me with a long, hard, fixed-under stare. Suddenly he pulled his gun and asked:

"Nigger, don't yuh like it?"

I hesitated.

"I asked yuh don't yuh like it?" he asked again, stepping forward.

"Yes, sir," I mumbled.

"Talk like it, then!"

"Oh, yes sir!" I said with as much heartiness as I could muster.

Outside, I walked ahead of the girl, ashamed to face her. She caught up with me and said:

"Don't be a fool! Yuh couldn't help it!"

This watchman boasted of having killed two Negroes in self-defense.

Yet, in spite of all this, the life of the hotel ran with an amazing smoothness. It would have been impossible for a stranger to detect anything. The maids, the hall-boys, and the bell-boys were all smiles. They had to be.

IX

I had learned my Jim Crow lessons so thoroughly that I kept the hotel job till I left Jackson for Memphis. It so happened that while in Memphis I applied for a job at a branch of the optical company. I was hired. And for some reason, as long as I worked there, they never brought my past against me.

Here my Jim Crow education assumed quite a different form. It was no longer brutally cruel, but subtly cruel. Here I learned to lie, to steal, to dissemble. I learned to play that dual role which every Negro must play if he wants to eat and live.

For example, it was almost impossible to get a book to read. It was assumed that after a Negro had imbibed what scanty schooling the state furnished he had no further need for books. I was always borrowing books from men on the job. One day I mustered enough courage to ask one of the men to let me get books from the library in his name. Surprisingly, he consented. I cannot help but think that he consented because he was a Roman Catholic and felt a vague sympathy for Negroes, being himself an object of hatred. Armed with a library card, I obtained books in the following manner: I would write a note to the librarian, saying: "Please let this nigger boy have the following books." I would then sign it with the white man's name.

When I went to the library, I would stand at the desk, hat in hand, looking as unbookish as possible. When I received the books desired I would take them home. If the books listed in the note happened to be out, I would sneak into the lobby and forge a new one. I never took any chances guessing with the white librarian about what the fictitious white man would want to read. No doubt if any of the white patrons had suspected that some of the volumes they enjoyed had been in the home of a Negro, they would not have tolerated it for an instant.

The factory force of the optical company in Memphis was much larger than that in Jackson, and more urbanized. At least they liked to talk, and would engage the Negro help in conversation whenever possible. By this means I found that many subjects were taboo from the white man's point of view. Among the topics they did not like to discuss with Negroes were the following: American white women; the Ku Klux Klan; France, and how Negro soldiers fared while there; French women; Jack Johnson; the entire northern part of the United States; the Civil War; Abraham Lincoln; U. S. Grant; General Sherman; Catholics; the Pope; Jews; the Republican Party; slavery; social equality; Communism; Socialism; the 13th and 14th Amendments to the Constitution; or any topic calling for positive knowledge or manly self-assertion on the part of the Negro. The most accepted topics were sex and religion.

There were many times when I had to exercise a great deal of ingenuity to keep out of trouble. It is a southern custom that all men must take off their hats when they enter an elevator. And especially did this apply to us blacks with rigid force. One day I stepped into an elevator with my arms full of packages. I was forced to ride with my hat on. Two white men stared at me coldly. Then one of them very kindly lifted my hat and placed it upon my armful of packages. Now the most accepted response for a Negro to make under such circumstances is to look at the white man out of the corner of his eye and grin. To have said: "Thank you!" would have made the white man *think* that you *thought* you were receiving from him a personal service. For such an act I have seen Negroes take a blow in the mouth. Finding the first alternative distasteful, and the second dangerous, I hit upon an acceptable course of action which fell safely between these two poles. I immediately—no sooner than my hat was lifted—pretended that my packages were about to spill, and appeared deeply distressed with keeping them in my arms. In this fashion I evaded having to acknowledge his service, and, in spite of adverse circumstances, salvaged a slender shred of personal pride.

How do Negroes feel about the way they have to live? How do they discuss it when alone amongst themselves? I think this question can be answered in a single sentence. A friend of mine who ran an elevator once told me:

"Lawd, man! Ef it wuzn't fer them polices 'n' them ol' lynch-mobs, there wouldn't be nothin' but uproar down here!"

3

Constructing Race, Creating White Privilege

Pem Davidson Buck

Constructing Race

Improbable as it now seems, since Americans live in a society where racial characterization and self-definition appear to be parts of nature, in the early days of colonization before slavery was solidified and clearly distinguished from other forms of forced labor, Europeans and Africans seem not to have seen their physical differences in that way.[1] It took until the end of the 1700s for ideas about race to develop until they resembled those we live with today. Before Bacon's Rebellion, African and European indentured servants made love with each other, married each other, ran away with each other, lived as neighbors, liked or disliked each other according to individual personality. Sometimes they died or were punished together for resisting or revolting. And masters had to free both Europeans and Africans if they survived to the end of their indentures. Likewise, Europeans initially did not place all Native Americans in a single racial category. They saw cultural, not biological, differences among Native Americans as distinguishing one tribe from another and from themselves.

Given the tendency of slaves, servants, and landless free Europeans and Africans to cooperate in rebellion, the elite had to "teach Whites the value of whiteness" in order to divide and rule their labor force.[2] After Bacon's Rebellion they utilized their domination of colonial legislatures that made laws and of courts that administered them, gradually building a racial strategy based on the earlier tightening and lengthening of African indenture. Part of this process was tighter control of voting. Free property-owning blacks, mulattos, and Native Americans, all identified as *not* of European ancestry, were denied the vote in 1723.[3]

To keep the racial categories separate, a 1691 law increased the punishment of European women who married African or Indian men; toward the end of the 1600s a white woman could be whipped or enslaved for marrying a Black. Eventually enslavement for white women was abolished because it transgressed the definition of slavery as black. The problem of what to do with white women's "black" children was eventually partially solved by the control of white women's reproduction to prevent the existence of such children. The potentially "white" children of black women were defined out of existence; they were "black" and shifted from serving a thirty-year indenture to being slaves. To facilitate these reproductive distinctions and to discourage the intimacy that can lead to solidarity and revolts, laws were passed requiring separate quarters for black and white laborers. Kathleen Brown points out that the control of women's bodies thus became critical to the maintenance of whiteness and to the production of slaves.[4] At the same time black men were denied the rights of colonial masculinity as property ownership, guns, and access to white women were forbidden. Children were made to inherit their mother's status, freeing European fathers from any vestiges of responsibility for their offspring born to indentured or enslaved African mothers. This legal shift has had a profound effect on the distribution of wealth in the United States ever since; slaveholding fathers were some of the richest men in the country, and their wealth, distributed among *all* their children, would have created a significant wealthy black segment of the population.

At the same time a changing panoply of specific laws molded European behavior into patterns that made slave revolt and cross-race unity more and more difficult.[5] These laws limited, for instance, the European right to teach slaves to read. Europeans couldn't use slaves in skilled jobs, which were reserved for Europeans. Europeans had to administer prescribed punishment for slave "misbehavior" and were expected to participate in patrolling at night. They did not have the legal right to befriend Blacks. A white servant who ran away with a Black was subject to additional punishment beyond that for simply running away. European rights to free their slaves were also curtailed.

Built into all this, rarely mentioned but nevertheless basic to the elite's ability to create and maintain whiteness, slavery, and exploitation, was the use of force against both Blacks and Whites. Fear kept many Whites from challenging, or even questioning, the system. It is worth quoting Lerone Bennett's analysis of how the differentiation between black and white was accomplished:

> The whole system of separation and subordination rested on official state terror. The exigencies of the situation required men to kill some white people to keep them white and to kill many blacks to keep them black. In the North and South, men and women were maimed, tortured, and murdered in a comprehensive campaign of mass conditioning. The severed heads of black and white rebels were impaled on poles

along the road as warnings to black people and white people, and opponents of the status quo were starved to death in chains and roasted slowly over open fires. Some rebels were branded; others were castrated. This exemplary cruelty, which was carried out as a deliberate process of mass education, was an inherent part of the new system.[6]

Creating White Privilege

White privileges were established. The "daily exercise of white personal power over black individuals had become a cherished aspect of Southern culture," a critically important part of getting Whites to "settle for being white."[7] Privilege encouraged Whites to identify with the big slaveholding planters as members of the same "race." They were led to act on the belief that all Whites had an equal interest in the maintenance of whiteness and white privilege, and that it was the elite—those controlling the economic system, the political system, and the judicial system— who ultimately protected the benefits of being white.[8]

More pain could be inflicted on Blacks than on Whites.[9] Whites alone could bear arms; Whites alone had the right of self-defense. White servants could own livestock; Africans couldn't. It became illegal to whip naked Whites. Whites but not Africans had to be given their freedom dues at the end of their indenture. Whites were given the right to beat any Blacks, even those they didn't own, for failing to show proper respect. Only Whites could be hired to force black labor as overseers. White servants and laborers were given lighter tasks and a monopoly, for a time, on skilled jobs. White men were given the right to control "their" women without elite interference; Blacks as slaves were denied the right to family at all, since family would mean that slave husbands, not owners, controlled slave wives. In 1668, all free African women were defined as labor, for whom husbands or employers had to pay a tithe, while white women were defined as keepers of men's homes, not as labor; their husbands paid no tax on them. White women were indirectly given control of black slaves and the right to substitute slave labor for their own labor in the fields.

Despite these privileges, landless Whites, some of them living in "miserable huts," might have rejected white privilege if they saw that in fact it made little *positive* difference in their lives, and instead merely protected them from the worst *negative* effects of elite punishment and interference, such as were inflicted on those of African descent.[10] After all, the right to whip someone doesn't cure your own hunger or landlessness. By the end of the Revolutionary War unrest was in the air. Direct control by the elite was no longer politically or militarily feasible. Rebellions and attempted rebellions had been fairly frequent in the hundred years following Bacon's Rebellion.[11] They indicated the continuing depth of landless European discontent. Baptist ferment against the belief in the inherent superiority of the upper classes simply underscored the danger.[12]

So landless Europeans had to be given some *material* reason to reject those aspects of their lives that made them similar to landless Africans and Native Americans, and to focus instead on their similarity to the landed Europeans—to accept whiteness as their defining characteristic. Landless Europeans' only real similarity to the elite was their European ancestry itself, so that ancestry had to be given real significance: European ancestry was identified with upward mobility and the right to use the labor of the non-eligible in their upward climb. So, since land at that time was the source of upward mobility, land had to be made available, if only to a few.

Meanwhile, Thomas Jefferson advocated the establishment of a solid white Anglo-Saxon yeoman class of small farmers, who, as property owners, would acquire a vested interest in law and order and reject class conflict with the elite. These small farmers would, by upholding "law and order," support and sometimes administer the legal mechanisms—jails, workhouses and poorhouses, and vagrancy laws—that would control other Whites who would remain a landless labor force. They would support the legal and illegal mechanisms controlling Native Americans, Africans, and poor Whites, becoming a buffer class between the elite and those they most exploited, disguising the elite's continuing grip on power and wealth. . . .

The Psychological Wage

The initial construction of whiteness had been based on a material benefit for Whites: land, or the apparently realistic hope of land. By the 1830s and 1840s, most families identified by their European descent had had several generations of believing their whiteness was real. But its material benefit had faded. Many Whites were poor, selling their labor either as farm renters or as industrial workers, and they feared wage slavery, no longer certain they were much freer than slaves.[13] But this time, to control unrest, the elite had no material benefits they were willing to part with. Nor were employers willing to raise wages. Instead, politicians and elites emphasized whiteness as a benefit in itself.

The work of particular white intellectuals, who underscored the already existing belief in white superiority and the worries about white slavery, was funded by elites and published in elite-owned printing houses.[14] These intellectuals provided fodder for newspaper discussions, speeches, scientific analysis, novels, sermons, songs, and blackface minstrel shows in which white superiority was phrased as if whiteness in and of itself was naturally a benefit, despite its lack of material advantage. This sense of superiority allowed struggling northern Whites to look down their noses at free Blacks and at recent immigrants, particularly the Irish. This version of whiteness was supposed to make up for their otherwise difficult situation, providing them with a "psychological wage" instead of cash—a bit like being employee of the month and given a special parking place instead of a raise.

Many Whites bought into the psychological wage, expressing their superiority over non-Whites and defining them, rather than the capitalists, as the enemy. They focused, often with trade union help, on excluding Blacks and immigrants from skilled trades and better-paying jobs. Employers cooperated in confining Blacks and immigrants to manual labor and domestic work, making a clear definition of the work suitable for white men.[15] Native white men began shifting away from defining themselves by their landowning freedom and independence. Instead they accepted their dependence on capitalists and the control employers exercised over their lives, and began to define themselves by their class position as skilled "mechanics" working for better wages under better working conditions than other people. They became proud of their productivity, which grew with the growing efficiency of industrial technology, and began using it to define whiteness—and manhood. The ethnic of individual hard work gained far wider currency. Successful competition in the labor marketplace gradually became a mark of manhood, and "white man's work" became the defining characteristic of whiteness.[16] Freedom was equated with the right to own and sell your own labor, as opposed to slavery, which allowed neither right. Independence was now defined not only by property ownership but also by possession of skill and tools that allowed wage-earning men to acquire status as a head of household controlling dependents.[17]

This redefinition of whiteness was built as much on changing gender as on changing class relationships.[18] Many native white men and women, including workers, journalists, scientists, and politicians, began discouraging married women from working for wages, claiming that true women served only their own families. Despite this claim—the cult of domesticity, or of true womanhood—many wives of working class men actually did work outside the home. They were less likely to do so in those cases where native men were able, through strikes and the exclusion of women, immigrants, and free Blacks, to create an artificial labor shortage. Such shortages gave native working class men the leverage to force employers to pay them enough to afford a non-earning wife. Women in the families of such men frequently did "stay home" and frequently helped to promote the idea that people who couldn't do the same were genetically or racially or culturally inferior.

But native Whites whose wages actually weren't sufficient struggled on in poverty. If a native woman worked for wages, particularly in a factory, the family lost status. Many female factory workers were now immigrants rather than native Whites. Many had no husband or had husbands whose wages, when they could get work, came nowhere near supporting a family.[19] It is no wonder immigrant women weren't particularly "domestic." Such families didn't meet the cultural requirements for white privilege—male "productivity" in "white man's work" and dependent female "domesticity." These supposed white virtues became a bludgeon with which to defend white privilege and to deny it to not-quite-Whites and not-Whites, helping to construct a new working class hierarchy. This new hierarchy reserved managerial and skilled jobs for "productive" native Whites. So, for the price of reserving better jobs for some native Whites, the capitalist class gained native white consent to their own loss of independence and to keeping most of the working class on abysmally low wages.

In the South, where there was less industry, the psychological wage slowly developed an additional role. It was used not only to gain consent to oppressive industrial relations, but also to convince poor farming Whites to support Southern elites in their conflict with Northern elites. Du Bois points out that by the Civil War

> . . . it became the fashion to pat the disenfranchised poor white man on the back and tell him after all he was white and that he and the planters had a common object in keeping the white man superior. This virus increased bitterness and relentless hatred, and after the war it became a chief ingredient in the division of the working class in the Southern States.[20]

REFERENCES

1. My discussion of the construction of race and racial slavery is deeply indebted to Lerone Bennett, *The Shaping of Black America* (New York: Penguin Books, 1993 [1975]), 1–109. See also Theodore Allen, *Invention of the White Race*, vol. II, *The Origin of Racial Oppression in Anglo-America* (New York: Verso, 1997), 75–109; Audrey Smedley, *Race in North America: Origin and Evolution of a Worldview* (Boulder: Westview Press, 1993), 100–1, 109, 142–3, 198; Kathleen Brown, *Good Wives, Nasty Wenches, and Anxious Patriarchs: Gender, Race, and Power in Colonial Virginia* (Chapel Hill: University of North Carolina Press, 1996), 107–244; bell hooks, *Ain't I a Woman: Black Women and Feminism* (Boston: South End Press, 1981), 15–51.

2. Bennett, *Shaping of Black America*, 74–5.

3. Allen, *Invention*, vol. II, 241.

4. Brown, *Good Wives*, pays particular attention to control of women's bodies and status in producing slavery and race (see especially 181, 129–33, 116); also see Allen, *Invention*, vol. II, 128–35, 146–7, 177–88; Bennett, *Shaping of Black America*, 75.

5. For this section see Bennett, *Shaping of Black America*, 72; Edmund Morgan, *American Slavery, American Freedom: The Ordeal of Colonial Virginia* (New York: W. W. Norton and Co, 1975), 311–3; Allen, *Invention*, vol. II, 249–53.

6. Bennett, *Shaping of Black America*, 73–4.

7. The first quote is from Smedley, *Race in North America*, 224; the second is from David Roediger, *The Wages of Whiteness: Race and the Making of the American Working Class* (New York: Verso, 1991), 6.

8. Allen, *Invention*, vol. II, 162, 248–53, emphasizes that elites invented white supremacy to protect their own interests, although working-class Whites did much of the "dirty work" of oppression.

9. Morgan, *American Slavery*, 312–3. On white privileges see Ronald Takaki, *A Different Mirror: A History of Multicultural America* (Boston: Little, Brown, 1993), 67–8; Allen, *Invention*, vol. II, 250–3; Brown, *Good Wives*, 180–3.

10. The quote is from Allen, *Invention*, vol. II, 256, citing a contemporary traveler.

11. Howard Zinn, *A People's History of the United States* (New York: HarperCollins, 1995, 2nd ed.), 58.

12. Smedley, *Race in North America*, 174–5.

13. Bennett, *Shaping of Black America*, 10, 44–5.

14. Allen, *Invention*, vol. I, 109.

15. On runaways see Morgan, *American Slavery, American Freedom*, 217; Smedley, *Race*, 103–5; Bennett, *Shaping of Black America*, 55.

16. On the tendency to make common cause, see Allen, *Invention*, vol. II, 148–58; Bennett, *Shaping of Black America*, 19–22, 74. On increasing anger and landlessness see Allen, *Invention*, vol. II, 208–9, 343 n. 33; Ronald Takaki, *A Different Mirror: A History of Multicultural America* (Boston: Little, Brown, 1993), 62.

17. Berkeley is quoted in Takaki, *Different Mirror*, 63.

18. On Bacon's Rebellion see Takaki, *Different Mirror*, 63–5; Morgan, *American Slavery, American Freedom*, 254–70; Allen, *Invention*, vol. II, 163–5, 208–17, 239; Brown, *Good Wives*, 137–86. Although interpretations of the rebellion vary widely, it does seem clear that the frightening aspect of the rebellion for those who controlled the drainage system was its dramatic demonstration of the power of a united opposition to those who monopolized land, labor, and trade with Native Americans.

19. Allan Kulikoff, *Tobacco and Slaves: The Development of Southern Cultures in the Chesapeake 1680–1800* (Chapel Hill: University of North Carolina Press, 1986), 77, 104–17.

20. Morgan, *American Slavery, American Freedom*, 271–9.

4

How Jews Became White Folks
and What That Says about Race in America

Karen Brodkin

> The American nation was founded and developed by the Nordic race, but if a few
> more million members of the Alpine, Mediterranean and Semitic races are poured
> among us, the result must inevitably be a hybrid race of people as worthless and futile
> as the good-for-nothing mongrels of Central America and Southeastern Europe.
> KENNETH ROBERTS, "WHY EUROPE LEAVES HOME"

It is clear that Kenneth Roberts did not think of my ancestors as white, like him.
The late nineteenth century and early decades of the twentieth saw a steady stream
of warnings by scientists, policymakers, and the popular press that "mongreliza-
tion" of the Nordic or Anglo-Saxon race—the real Americans—by inferior
European races (as well as by inferior non-European ones) was destroying the fabric of the nation.

I continue to be surprised when I read books that indicate that America once
regarded its immigrant European workers as something other than white, as biologically different. My parents are not surprised; they expect anti-Semitism to be
part of the fabric of daily life, much as I expect racism to be part of it. They came
of age in the Jewish world of the 1920s and 1930s, at the peak of anti-Semitism in
America.[1] They are rightly proud of their upward mobility and think of themselves as pulling themselves up by their own bootstraps. I grew up during the
1950s in the Euro-ethnic New York suburb of Valley Stream, where Jews were
simply one kind of white folks and where ethnicity meant little more to my generation than food and family heritage. Part of my ethnic heritage was the belief that
Jews were smart and that our success was due to our own efforts and abilities, reinforced by a culture that valued sticking together, hard work, education, and deferred gratification.

I am willing to affirm all those abilities and ideals and their contribution to
Jews' upward mobility, but I also argue that they were still far from sufficient to ac-

count for Jewish success. I say this because the belief in a Jewish version of Horatio Alger has become a point of entry for some mainstream Jewish organizations to adopt a racist attitude against African Americans especially and to oppose affirmative action for people of color.[2] Instead I want to suggest that Jewish success is a product not only of ability but also of the removal of powerful social barriers to its realization.

It is certainly true that the United States has a history of anti-Semitism and of beliefs that Jews are members of an inferior race. But Jews were hardly alone. American anti-Semitism was part of a broader pattern of late-nineteenth-century racism against all southern and eastern European immigrants, as well as against Asian immigrants, not to mention African Americans, Native Americans, and Mexicans. These views justified all sorts of discriminatory treatment, including closing the doors, between 1882 and 1927, to immigration from Europe and Asia. This picture changed radically after World War II. Suddenly, the same folks who had promoted nativism and xenophobia were eager to believe that the Euro-origin people whom they had deported, reviled as members of inferior races, and prevented from immigrating only a few years earlier, were now model middle-class white suburban citizens.[3]

It was not an educational epiphany that made those in power change their hearts, their minds, and our race. Instead, it was the biggest and best affirmative action program in the history of our nation, and it was for Euromales. That is not how it was billed, but it is the way it worked out in practice. I tell this story to show the institutional nature of racism and the centrality of state policies to creating and changing races. Here, those policies reconfigured the category of whiteness to include European immigrants. There are similarities and differences in the ways each of the European immigrant groups became "whitened." I tell the story in a way that links anti-Semitism to other varieties of anti-European racism because this highlights what Jews shared with other Euro-immigrants.

Euroraces

The U.S. "discovery" that Europe was divided into inferior and superior races began with the racialization of the Irish in the mid-nineteenth century and flowered in response to the great waves of immigration from southern and eastern Europe that began in the late nineteenth century. Before that time, European immigrants—including Jews—had been largely assimilated into the white population. However, the 23 million European immigrants who came to work in U.S. cities in the waves of migration after 1880 were too many and too concentrated to absorb. Since immigrants and their children made up more than 70 percent of the population of most of the country's largest cities, by the 1890s urban America had taken on a distinctly southern and eastern European immigrant flavor. Like the Irish in Boston and New York, their urban concentrations in dilapidated neighborhoods put them cheek by jowl next to the rising elites and the middle class with whom they shared public space and to whom their working-class ethnic communities were particularly visible.

The Red Scare of 1919 clearly linked anti-immigrant with anti-working-class sentiment—to the extent that the Seattle general strike by largely native-born workers was blamed on foreign agitators. The Red Scare was fueled by an economic depression, a massive postwar wave of strikes, the Russian Revolution, and another influx of postwar immigration. . . .

Not surprisingly, the belief in European races took root most deeply among the wealthy, U.S.-born Protestant elite, who feared a hostile and seemingly inassimilable working class. By the end of the nineteenth century, Senator Henry Cabot Lodge pressed Congress to cut off immigration to the United States; Theodore Roosevelt raised the alarm of "race suicide" and took Anglo-Saxon women to task for allowing "native" stock to be outbred by inferior immigrants. In the early twentieth century, these fears gained a great deal of social legitimacy thanks to the efforts of an influential network of aristocrats and scientists who developed theories of eugenics—breeding for a "better" humanity—and scientific racism.

Key to these efforts was Madison Grant's influential *The Passing of the Great Race*, published in 1916. Grant popularized notions developed by William Z. Ripley and Daniel Brinton that there existed three or four major European races, ranging from the superior Nordics of northwestern Europe to the inferior southern and eastern races of the Alpines, Mediterraneans, and worst of all, Jews, who seemed to be everywhere in his native New York City. Grant's nightmare was race-mixing among Europeans. For him, "the cross between any of the three European races and a Jew is a Jew." He didn't have good things to say about Alpine or Mediterranean "races" either. For Grant, race and class were interwoven: the upper class was racially pure Nordic; the lower classes came from the lower races.[4]

Far from being on the fringe, Grant's views were well within the popular mainstream. Here is the *New York Times* describing the Jewish Lower East Side of a century ago:

> The neighborhood where these people live is absolutely impassable for wheeled vehicles other than their pushcarts. If a truck driver tries to get through where their pushcarts are standing they apply to him all kinds of vile and indecent epithets. The driver is fortunate if he gets out of the street without being hit with a stone or having a putrid fish or piece of meat thrown in his face. This neighborhood, peopled almost entirely by the people who claim to have been driven from Poland and Russia, is the eyesore of New York and perhaps the filthiest place on the western continent. It is impossible for a Christian to live there because he will be driven out, either by blows or the dirt and stench. Cleanliness is an unknown quantity to these people. They cannot be lifted up to a higher plane because they do not want to be. If the cholera should ever get among these people, they would scatter its germs as a sower does grain.[5]

Such views were well within the mainstream of the early-twentieth-century scientific community.[6] Madison Grant and eugenicist Charles B. Davenport organized the Galton Society in 1918 in order to foster research, promote eugenics, and restrict immigration.[7] . . .

By the 1920s, scientific racism sanctified the notion that real Americans were white and that real whites came from northwest Europe. Racism by white workers in the West fueled laws excluding and expelling the Chinese in 1882. Widespread racism led to closing the immigration door to virtually all Asians and most Europeans between 1924 and 1927, and to deportation of Mexicans during the Great Depression.

Racism in general, and anti-Semitism in particular, flourished in higher education. Jews were the first of the Euro-immigrant groups to enter college in significant numbers, so it was not surprising that they faced the brunt of discrimination there. The Protestant elite complained that Jews were unwashed, uncouth, unrefined, loud, and pushy. Harvard University President A. Lawrence Lowell, who was also a vice president of the Immigration Restriction League, was open about his opposition to Jews at Harvard. The Seven Sister schools had a reputation for "flagrant discrimination." . . .

Columbia's quota against Jews was well known in my parents' community. My father is very proud of having beaten it and been admitted to Columbia Dental School on the basis of his skill at carving a soap ball. Although he became a teacher instead because the tuition was too high, he took me to the dentist every week of my childhood and prolonged the agony by discussing the finer points of tooth-filling and dental care. My father also almost failed the speech test required for his teaching license because he didn't speak "standard," i.e., nonimmigrant, nonaccented English. For my parents and most of their friends, English was the language they had learned when they went to school, since their home and neighborhood language was Yiddish. They saw the speech test as designed to keep all ethnics, not just Jews, out of teaching.

There is an ironic twist to this story. My mother always urged me to speak well, like her friend Ruth Saronson, who was a speech teacher. Ruth remained my model for perfect diction until I went away to college. When I talked to her on one of my visits home, I heard the New York accent of my version of "standard English," compared to the Boston academic version.

My parents believe that Jewish success, like their own, was due to hard work and a high value placed on education. They attended Brooklyn College during the Depression. My mother worked days and went to school at night; my father went during the day. Both their families encouraged them. More accurately, their families expected it. Everyone they knew was in the same boat, and their world was made up of Jews who were advancing just as they were. The picture for New York—where most Jews lived—seems to back them up. In 1920, Jews made up 80 percent of the students at New York's City College, 90 percent of Hunter College, and before World War I, 40 percent of private Columbia University. By 1934, Jews made up almost 24 percent of all law students nationally and 56 percent of those in New York City. Still, more Jews became public school teachers, like my parents and their friends, than doctors or lawyers. Indeed, Ruth Jacknow Markowitz has shown that "my daughter, the teacher" was, for parents, an aspiration equivalent to "my son, the doctor."[8]

How we interpret Jewish social mobility in this milieu depends on whom we compare them to. Compared with other immigrants, Jews were upwardly mobile. But compared with nonimmigrant whites, that mobility was very limited and circumscribed. The existence of anti-immigrant, racist, and anti-Semitic barriers kept the Jewish middle class confined to a small number of occupations. Jews were excluded from mainstream corporate management and corporately employed professions, except in the garment and movie industries, in which they were pioneers. Jews were almost totally excluded from university faculties (the few who made it had powerful patrons). Eastern European Jews were concentrated in small businesses, and in professions where they served a largely Jewish clientele. . . .

My parents' generation believed that Jews overcame anti-Semitic barriers because Jews are special. My answer is that the Jews who were upwardly mobile were special among Jews (and were also well placed to write the story). My generation might well respond to our parents' story of pulling themselves up by their own bootstraps with "But think what you might have been without the racism and with some affirmative action!" And that is precisely what the post-World War II boom, the decline of systematic, public, anti-Euro racism and anti-Semitism, and governmental affirmative action extended to white males let us see.

Whitening Euro-ethnics

By the time I was an adolescent, Jews were just as white as the next white person. Until I was eight, I was a Jew in a world of Jews. Everyone on Avenue Z in Sheepshead Bay was Jewish. I spent my days playing and going to school on three blocks of Avenue Z, and visiting my grandparents in the nearby Jewish neighborhoods of Brighton Beach and Coney Island. There were plenty of Italians in my neighborhood, but they lived around the corner. They were a kind of Jew, but on the margins of my social horizons. Portuguese were even more distant, at the end of the bus ride, at Sheepshead Bay. The *shul*, or temple, was on Avenue Z, and I begged my father to take me like all the other fathers took their kids, but religion wasn't part of my family's Judaism. Just how Jewish my neighborhood was hit me in first grade, when I was one of two kids to go to school on Rosh Hashanah. My teacher was shocked—she was Jewish too—and I was embarrassed to tears when she sent me home. I was never again sent to school on Jewish holidays. We left that world in 1949 when we moved to Valley Stream, Long Island, which was Protestant and Republican and even had farms until Irish, Italian, and Jewish ex-urbanites like us gave it a more suburban and Democratic flavor.

Neither religion nor ethnicity separated us at school or in the neighborhood. Except temporarily. During my elementary school years, I remember a fair number of dirt-bomb (a good suburban weapon) wars on the block. Periodically, one of the Catholic boys would accuse me or my brother of killing his god, to which we'd reply, "Did not," and start lobbing dirt bombs. Sometimes he'd get his friends from Catholic school and I'd get mine from public school kids on the block, some of whom were Catholic. Hostilities didn't last for more than a couple of hours and punctuated an otherwise friendly relationship. They ended by our junior high years, when other things became more important. Jews, Catholics, and Protestants, Italians, Irish, Poles, "English" (I don't remember hearing WASP as a kid), were mixed up on the block and in school. We thought of ourselves as middle class and very enlightened because our ethnic backgrounds seemed so irrelevant to high school culture. We didn't see race (we thought), and racism was not part of our peer consciousness. Nor were the immigrant or working-class histories of our families.

As with most chicken-and-egg problems, it is hard to know which came first. Did Jews and other Euro-ethnics become white because they became middle-class? That is, did money whiten? Or did being incorporated into an expanded version of whiteness open up the economic doors to middle-class status? Clearly, both tendencies were at work.

Some of the changes set in motion during the war against fascism led to a more inclusive version of whiteness. Anti-Semitism and anti-European racism lost respectability. The 1940 Census no longer distinguished native whites of native parentage from those, like my parents, of immigrant parentage, so Euro-immigrants and their children were more securely white by submersion in an expanded notion of whiteness.[9]

Theories of nurture and culture replaced theories of nature and biology. Instead of dirty and dangerous races that would destroy American democracy, immigrants became ethnic groups whose children had successfully assimilated into the mainstream and risen to the middle class. In this new myth, Euro-ethnic suburbs like mine became the measure of American democracy's victory over racism. Jewish mobility became a new Horatio Alger story. In time and with hard work, every ethnic group would get a piece of the pie, and the United States would be a nation with equal opportunity for all its people to become part of a prosperous middle-class majority. And it seemed that Euro-ethnic immigrants and their children were delighted to join middle America.

This is not to say that anti-Semitism disappeared after World War II, only that it fell from fashion and was driven underground. . . .

Although changing views on who was white made it easier for Euro-ethnics to become middle class, economic prosperity also played a very powerful role in the whitening process. The economic mobility of Jews and other Euro-ethnics derived ultimately from America's postwar economic prosperity and its enormously expanded need for professional, technical, and managerial labor, as well as on government assistance in providing it.

The United States emerged from the war with the strongest economy in the world. Real wages rose between 1946 and 1960, increasing buying power a hefty 22 percent and giving most Americans some discretionary income. American manufacturing, banking, and business services were increasingly dominated by large corporations, and these grew into multinational corporations. Their organizational centers lay in big, new urban headquarters that demanded growing numbers of clerical, technical, and managerial workers. The postwar period was a historic moment for real class mobility and for the affluence we have erroneously come to believe was the American norm. It was a time when the old white and the newly white masses became middle class.[10]

The GI Bill of Rights, as the 1944 Serviceman's Readjustment Act was known, is arguably the most massive affirmative action program in American history. It was created to develop needed labor force skills and to provide those who had them with a lifestyle that reflected their value to the economy. The GI benefits that were ultimately extended to 16 million GIs (of the Korean War as well) included priority in jobs—that is, preferential hiring, but no one objected to it then—financial support during the job search, small loans for starting up businesses, and most important, low-interest home loans and educational benefits, which included tuition and living expenses. This legislation was rightly regarded as one of the most revolutionary postwar programs. I call it affirmative action because it was aimed at and disproportionately helped male, Euro-origin GIs.[11] . . .

Education and Occupation

It is important to remember that, prior to the war, a college degree was still very much a "mark of the upper class," that colleges were largely finishing schools for Protestant elites. Before the postwar boom, schools could not begin to accommodate the American masses. Even in New York City before the 1930s, neither the public schools nor City College had room for more than a tiny fraction of potential immigrant students.[12]

Not so after the war. The almost 8 million GIs who took advantage of their educational benefits under the GI Bill caused "the greatest wave of college building in American history." White male GIs were able to take advantage of their educational benefits for college and technical training, so they were particularly well positioned to seize the opportunities provided by the new demands for professional, managerial, and technical labor.

> It has been well documented that the GI educational benefits transformed American higher education and raised the educational level of that generation and generations to come. With many provisions for assistance in upgrading their educational attainments, veterans pulled ahead of nonveterans in earning capacity. In the long run it was the nonveterans who had fewer opportunities.[13]

. . . Even more significantly, the postwar boom transformed America's class structure—or at least its status structure—so that the middle class expanded to encompass most of the population. Before the war, most Jews, like most other Americans, were part of the working class, defined in terms of occupation, education, and income. Already upwardly mobile before the war relative to other immigrants, Jews floated high on this rising economic tide, and most of them entered the middle class. The children of other immigrants did too. Still, even the high tide missed some Jews. As late as 1973, some 15 percent of New York's Jews were poor or near poor, and in the 1960s, almost 25 percent of employed Jewish men remained manual workers.[14]

The reason I refer to educational and occupational GI benefits as affirmative action programs for white males is because they were decidedly not extended to African Americans or to women of any race. Theoretically they were available to all veterans; in practice women and black veterans did not get anywhere near their share. Women's Army and Air Force units were initially organized as auxiliaries, hence not part of the military. When that status was changed, in July 1943, only those who reenlisted in the armed forces were eligible for veterans' benefits. Many women thought they were simply being demobilized and returned home. The majority remained and were ultimately eligible for veterans' benefits. But there was little counseling, and a social climate that discouraged women's careers and independence cut down on women's knowledge and sense of entitlement. The Veterans Administration kept no statistics on the number of women who used their GI benefits.[15]

The barriers that almost completely shut African American GIs out of their benefits were even more formidable. In Neil Wynn's portrait, black GIs anticipated starting new lives, just like their white counterparts. Over 43 percent hoped to return to school, and most expected to relocate, to find better jobs in new lines of work. The exodus from the South toward the North and West was particularly large. So it was not a question of any lack of ambition on the part of African American GIs. White male privilege was shaped against the backdrop of wartime racism and postwar sexism.

During and after the war, there was an upsurge in white racist violence against black servicemen, in public schools, and by the Ku Klux Klan. It spread to California and New York. The number of lynchings rose during the war, and in 1943 there were antiblack race riots in several large northern cities. Although there was a wartime labor shortage, black people were discriminated against when it came to well-paid defense industry jobs and housing. In 1946, white riots against African Americans occurred across the South and in Chicago and Philadelphia.

Gains made as a result of the wartime civil rights movement, especially in defense-related employment, were lost with peacetime conversion, as black workers were the first to be fired, often in violation of seniority. White women were also laid off, ostensibly to make room for jobs for demobilized servicemen, and in the long run women lost most of the gains they had made in wartime. We now know that women did not leave the labor force in any significant numbers but, instead, were forced to find inferior jobs, largely nonunion, part-time, and clerical.[16]

The military, the Veterans Administration, the U.S. Employment Services (USES), and the Federal Housing Administration effectively denied African American GIs access to their benefits and to new educational, occupational, and residential opportunities. Black GIs who served in the thoroughly segregated armed forces during World War II served under white officers. African American soldiers were given a disproportionate share of dishonorable discharges, which denied them veterans' rights under the GI Bill. Between August and November 1946, for example, 21 percent of white soldiers and 39 percent of black soldiers were dishonorably discharged. Those who did get an honorable discharge then faced the Veterans Administration and the USES. The latter, which was responsible for job placements, employed very few African Americans, especially in the South. This meant that black veterans did not receive much employment information and that the offers they did receive were for low-paid and menial jobs. "In one survey of 50 cities, the movement of blacks into peacetime employment was found to be lagging far behind that of white veterans: in Arkansas ninety-five percent of the placements made by the USES for Afro-Americans were in service or unskilled jobs."[17] African Americans were also less likely than whites, regardless of GI status, to gain new jobs commensurate with their wartime jobs. For example, in San Francisco, by 1948, black Americans "had dropped back halfway to their prewar employment status."[18]

Black GIs faced discrimination in the educational system as well. Despite the end of restrictions on Jews and other Euro-ethnics, African Americans were not welcome in white colleges. Black colleges were overcrowded, but the combination of segregation and prejudice made for few alternatives. About 20,000 black veterans attended college by 1947, most in black colleges, but almost as many, 15,000, could not gain entry. Predictably, the disproportionately few African Americans who did gain access to their educational benefits were able, like their white counterparts, to become doctors and engineers, and to enter the black middle class.[19]

Suburbanization

In 1949, ensconced in Valley Stream, I watched potato farms turn into Levittown and Idlewild (later Kennedy) airport. This was the major spectator sport in our first years on Long Island. A typical weekend would bring various aunts, uncles, and cousins out from the city. After a huge meal, we'd pile into the car—itself a novelty—to look at the bulldozed acres and comment on the matchbox construction. During the week, my mother and I would look at the houses going up within walking distance.

Bill Levitt built a basic, 900–1,000 square foot, somewhat expandable house for a lower-middle-class and working-class market on Long Island, and later in

Pennsylvania and New Jersey. Levittown started out as 2,000 units of rental housing at $60 a month, designed to meet the low-income housing needs of returning
war vets, many of whom, like my Aunt Evie and Uncle Julie, were living in
Quonset huts. By May 1947, Levitt and Sons had acquired enough land in
Hempstead Township on Long Island to build 4,000 houses, and by the next
February, he had built 6,000 units and named the development after himself. After
1948, federal financing for the construction of rental housing tightened, and Levitt
switched to building houses for sale. By 1951, Levittown was a development of
some 15,000 families.[20]

At the beginning of World War II, about one-third of all American families
owned their houses. That percentage doubled in twenty years. Most Levittowners
looked just like my family. They came from New York City or Long Island; about
17 percent were military, from nearby Mitchell Field; Levittown was their first
house, and almost everyone was married. Three-quarters of the 1947 inhabitants
were white collar, but by 1950 more blue-collar families had moved in, so that by
1951, "barely half" of the new residents were white collar, and by 1960 their occupational profile was somewhat more working class than for Nassau County as a
whole. By this time too, almost one-third of Levittown's people were either foreign-
born or, like my parents, first-generation U.S.-born.[21]

The Federal Housing Administration (FHA) was key to buyers and builders
alike. Thanks to the FHA, suburbia was open to more than GIs. People like us
would never have been in the market for houses without FHA and Veterans
Administration (VA) low-down-payment, low-interest, long-term loans to young
buyers. . . .

The FHA believed in racial segregation. Throughout its history, it publicly and
actively promoted restrictive covenants. Before the war, these forbade sales to Jews
and Catholics as well as to African Americans. The deed to my house in Detroit
had such a covenant, which theoretically prevented it from being sold to Jews or
African Americans. Even after the Supreme Court outlawed restrictive covenants
in 1948, the FHA continued to encourage builders to write them in against
African Americans. FHA underwriting manuals openly insisted on racially homogeneous neighborhoods, and their loans were made only in white neighborhoods.
I bought my Detroit house in 1972, from Jews who were leaving a largely African
American neighborhood. By that time, restrictive covenants were a dead letter, but
block busting by realtors was replacing it.

With the federal government behind them, virtually all developers refused to
sell to African Americans. Palo Alto and Levittown, like most suburbs as late as
1960, were virtually all white. Out of 15,741 houses and 65,276 people, averaging
4.2 people per house, only 220 Levittowners, or 52 households, were "nonwhite."
In 1958, Levitt announced publicly, at a press conference held to open his New
Jersey development, that he would not sell to black buyers. This caused a furor because the state of New Jersey (but not the U.S. government) prohibited discrimination in federally subsidized housing. Levitt was sued and fought it. There had been

a white riot in his Pennsylvania development when a black family moved in a few years earlier. In New Jersey, he was ultimately persuaded by township ministers to integrate. . . .

The result of these policies was that African Americans were totally shut out of the suburban boom. An article in *Harper's* described the housing available to black GIs.

> On his way to the base each morning, Sergeant Smith passes an attractive air-conditioned, FHA-financed housing project. It was built for service families. Its rents are little more than the Smiths pay for their shack. And there are half-a-dozen vacancies, but none for Negroes.[22]

Where my family felt the seductive pull of suburbia, Marshall Berman's experienced the brutal push of urban renewal. In the Bronx, in the 1950s, Robert Moses's Cross-Bronx Expressway erased "a dozen solid, settled, densely populated neighborhoods like our own. . . . [S]omething like 60,000 working- and lower-middle-class people, mostly Jews, but with many Italians, Irish, and Blacks thrown in, would be thrown out of their homes. . . . For ten years, through the late 1950s and early 1960s, the center of the Bronx was pounded and blasted and smashed."[23]

Urban renewal made postwar cities into bad places to live. At a physical level, urban renewal reshaped them, and federal programs brought private developers and public officials together to create downtown central business districts where there had formerly been a mix of manufacturing, commerce, and working-class neighborhoods. Manufacturing was scattered to the peripheries of the city, which were ringed and bisected by a national system of highways. Some working-class neighborhoods were bulldozed, but others remained. In Los Angeles, as in New York's Bronx, the postwar period saw massive freeway construction right through the heart of old working-class neighborhoods. In East Los Angeles and Santa Monica, Chicana/o and African American communities were divided in half or blasted to smithereens by the highways bringing Angelenos to the new white suburbs, or to make way for civic monuments like Dodger Stadium.[24]

Urban renewal was the other side of the process by which Jewish and other working-class Euro-immigrants became middle class. It was the push to suburbia's seductive pull. The fortunate white survivors of urban renewal headed disproportionately for suburbia, where they could partake of prosperity and the good life. . . .

If the federal stick of urban renewal joined the FHA carrot of cheap mortgages to send masses of Euro-Americans to the suburbs, the FHA had a different kind of one-two punch for African Americans. Segregation kept them out of the suburbs, and redlining made sure they could not buy or repair their homes in the neighborhoods in which they were allowed to live. The FHA practiced systematic redlining. This was a practice developed by its predecessor, the Home Owners Loan Corporation (HOLC), which in the 1930s developed an elaborate neighborhood rating system that placed the highest (green) value on all-white, middle-class neighborhoods, and the lowest (red) on racially nonwhite or mixed and working-class neighborhoods. High ratings meant high property values. The idea was that low property values in redlined neighborhoods made them bad investments. The FHA was, after all, created by and for banks and the housing industry. Redlining warned banks not to lend there, and the FHA would not insure mortgages in such neighborhoods. Redlining created a self-fulfilling prophesy.

> With the assistance of local realtors and banks, it assigned one of the four ratings to every block in every city. The resulting information was then translated into the appropriate color [green, blue, yellow, or red] and duly recorded on secret "Residential Security Maps" in local HOLC offices. The maps themselves were placed in elaborate "City Survey Files," which consisted of reports, questionnaires, and workpapers relating to current and future values of real estate.[25]

The FHA's and VA's refusal to guarantee loans in redlined neighborhoods made it virtually impossible for African Americans to borrow money for home improvement or purchase. Because these maps and surveys were quite secret, it took the civil rights movement to make these practices and their devastating consequences public. As a result, those who fought urban renewal, or who sought to make a home in the urban ruins, found themselves locked out of the middle class. They also faced an ideological assault that labeled their neighborhoods slums and called them slumdwellers.[26]

Conclusion

The record is very clear. Instead of seizing the opportunity to end institutionalized racism, the federal government did its level best to shut and double-seal the postwar window of opportunity in African Americans' faces. It consistently refused to combat segregation in the social institutions that were key to upward mobility in education, housing, and employment. Moreover, federal programs that were themselves designed to assist demobilized GIs and young families systematically discriminated against African Americans. Such programs reinforced white/nonwhite racial distinctions even as intrawhite racialization was falling out of fashion. This other side of the coin, that white men of northwest European ancestry and white men of southeastern European ancestry were treated equally in theory and in practice with regard to the benefits they received, was part of the larger postwar whitening of Jews and other eastern and southern Europeans.

The myth that Jews pulled themselves up by their own bootstraps ignores the fact that it took federal programs to create the conditions whereby the abilities of Jews and other European immigrants could be recognized and rewarded rather than denigrated and denied. The GI Bill and FHA and VA mortgages, even though they were advertised as open to all, functioned as a set of racial privileges. They were privileges because they were extended to white GIs but not to black GIs. Such privileges were forms of affirmative action that allowed Jews and other Euro-American men to become suburban homeowners and to get the training that allowed them—but much less so women vets or war workers—to become professionals, technicians, salesmen, and managers in a growing economy. Jews and other white ethnics' upward mobility was due to programs that allowed us to float on a rising economic tide. To African Americans, the government offered the cement boots of segregation, redlining, urban renewal, and discrimination.

Those racially skewed gains have been passed across the generations, so that racial inequality seems to maintain itself "naturally," even after legal segregation ended. Today, I own a house in Venice, California, like the one in which I grew up in Valley Stream, and my brother until recently owned a house in Palo Alto much like an Eichler house. Both of us are where we are thanks largely to the postwar benefits our parents received and passed on to us, and to the educational benefits we received in the 1960s as a result of affluence and the social agitation that developed from the black Freedom Movement. I have white, African American, and Asian American colleagues whose parents received fewer or none of America's postwar benefits and who expect never to own a house despite their considerable academic achievements. Some of these colleagues who are a few years younger than I also carry staggering debts for their education, which they expect to have to repay for the rest of their lives.

Conventional wisdom has it that the United States has always been an affluent land of opportunity. But the truth is that affluence has been the exception and that real upward mobility has required massive affirmative action programs. . . .

NOTES

1. Gerber 1986; Dinnerstein 1987, 1994.

2. On the belief in Jewish and Asian versions of Horatio Alger, see Steinberg 1989, chap. 3; Gilman 1996. On Jewish culture, see Gordon 1964; see Sowell 1981 for an updated version.

3. Not all Jews are white or unambiguously white. It has been suggested, for example, that Hasidim lack the privileges of whiteness. Rodriguez (1997, 12, 15) has begun to unpack the claims of white Jewish "amenity migrants" and the different racial meanings of Chicano claims to a crypto-Jewish identity in New Mexico. See also Thomas 1996 on African American Jews.

4. M. Grant 1916; Ripley 1923; see also Patterson 1997; M. Grant, quoted in Higham 1955, 156.

5. *New York Times*, 30 July 1893, "East Side Street Vendors," reprinted in Schoener 1967, 57–58.

6. Gould 1981; Higham 1955; Patterson 1997, 108–115.

7. It was intended, as Davenport wrote to the president of the American Museum of Natural History, Henry Fairfield Osborne, as "an anthropological society . . . with a central governing body, self-elected and self-perpetuating, and very limited in members, and also

confined to native Americans [*sic*] who are anthropologically, socially and politically sound, no Bolsheviki need apply" (Barkan 1992, 67–68).

8. Steinberg 1989, 137, 227; Markowitz 1993.

9. This census also explicitly changed the Mexican race to white (U.S. Bureau of the Census 1940, 2:4).

10. Nash et al. 1986, 885–886.

11. On planning for veterans, see F. J. Brown 1946; Hurd 1946; Mosch 1975; "Post-war Jobs for Veterans" 1945; Willenz 1983.

12. Willenz 1983, 165.

13. Nash et al. 1986, 885; Willenz 1983, 165. On mobility among veterans and non veterans, see Havighurst et al. 1951.

14. Steinberg 1989, 89–90.

15. Willenz 1983, 20–28, 94–97. I thank Nancy G. Cattell for calling my attention to the fact that women GIs were ultimately eligible for benefits.

16. Willenz 1983, 168; Dalfiume 1969, 133–134; Wynn 1976, 114–116; Anderson 1981; Milkman 1987.

17. Nalty and MacGregor 1981, 218, 60–61.

18. Wynn 1976, 114, 116.

19. On African Americans in the U.S. military, see Foner 1974; Dalfiume 1969; Johnson 1967; Binkin and Eitelberg 1982; Nalty and MacGregor 1981. On schooling, see Walker 1970, 4–9.

20. Hartman (1975, 141–142) cites massive abuses in the 1940s and 1950s by builders under the Section 608 program in which "the FHA granted extraordinarily liberal concessions to lackadaisically supervised private developers to induce them to produce rental housing rapidly in the postwar period." Eichler (1982) indicates that things were not that different in the subsequent FHA-funded home-building industry.

21. Dobriner 1963, 91, 100.

22. Quoted in Foner 1974, 195.

23. Berman 1982, 292.

24. On urban renewal and housing policies, see Greer 1965; Hartman 1975; Squires 1989. On Los Angeles, see Pardo 1990; Cockroft 1990.

25. Jackson 1985, 197. These ideas from the real estate industry were "codified and legitimated in 1930s work by University of Chicago sociologist Robert Park and real estate professor Homer Hoyt" (Ibid., 198–199).

26. See Gans 1962.

REFERENCES

Anderson, Karen. 1981. *Wartime Women*. Westport, Conn.: Greenwood.

Barkan, Elazar. 1992. *The Retreat of Scientific Racism: Changing Concepts of Race in Britain and the United States Between the World Wars*. New York: Cambridge University Press.

Berman, Marshall. 1982. *All That Is Solid Melts into Air: The Experience of Modernity*. New York: Simon and Schuster.

Binkin, Martin, and Mark J. Eitelberg. 1982. *Blacks and the Military*. Washington, D.C.: Brookings Institution.

Brown, Francis J. 1946. *Educational Opportunities for Veterans*. Washington, D.C.: Public Affairs Press American Council on Public Affairs.

Cockcroft, Eva. 1990. *Signs from the Heart: California Chicano Murals*. Venice, Calif.: Social and Public Art Resource Center.

Dalfiume, Richard M. 1969. *Desegregation of the U.S. Armed Forces: Fighting on Two Fronts, 1939–1953*. Columbia: University of Missouri Press.

Dinnerstein, Leonard, 1987. *Uneasy at Home: Anti-Semitism and the American Jewish Experience*. New York: Columbia University Press.

———. 1994. *Anti-Semitism in America*. New York: Oxford University Press.

Dobriner, William. M. 1963. *Class in Suburbia*. Englewood Cliffs, N.J.: Prentice-Hall.

Eichler, Ned. 1982. *The Merchant Builders*. Cambridge, Mass.: MIT Press.

Foner, Jack. 1974. *Blacks and the Military in American History: A New Perspective*. New York: Praeger Publishers.

Gans, Herbert. 1962. *The Urban Villagers*. New York: Free Press of Glencoe.

Gerber, David, ed. 1986. *Anti-Semitism in American History*. Urbana: University of Illinois Press.

Gilman, Sander. 1996. *Smart Jews: The Construction of the Image of Jewish Superior Intelligence*. Lincoln: University of Nebraska Press.

Gordon, Milton. 1964. *Assimilation in American Life: The Role of Race, Religion and National Origins*. New York: Oxford University Press.

Gould, Stephen J. 1981. *The Mismeasure of Man*. New York: Norton.

Grant, Madison. 1916. *The Passing of the Great Race: Or the Racial Basis of European History*. New York: Charles Scribner.

Greer, Scott. 1965. *Urban Renewal and American Cities*. Indianapolis: Bobbs-Merrill.

Hartman, Chester. 1975. *Housing and Social Policy*. Englewood Cliffs, N.J.: Prentice-Hall.

Havighurst, Robert J., John W. Baughman, Walter H. Eaton, and Ernest W. Burgess. 1951. *The American Veteran Back Home: A Study of Veteran Readjustment*. New York: Longmans, Green and Co.

Higham, John. 1955. *Strangers in the Land*. New Brunswick, N.J.: Rutgers University Press.

Hurd, Charles. 1946. *The Veterans' Program: A Complete Guide to Its Benefits, Rights and Options*. New York: McGraw-Hill Book Company.

Jackson, Kenneth T. 1985. *Crabgrass Frontier: The Suburbanization of the United States*. New York: Oxford University Press.

Johnson, Jesse J. 1967. *Ebony Brass: An Autobiography of Negro Frustration Amid Aspiration*. New York: The William Frederick Press.

Markowitz, Ruth Jacknow. 1993. *My Daughter, the Teacher: Jewish Teachers in the New York City Schools*. New Brunswick, N.J.: Rutgers University Press.

Milkman, Ruth. 1987. *Gender at Work: The Dynamics of Job Segregation by Sex During World War II*. Urbana: University of Illinois Press.

Mosch, Theodore R. 1975. *The GI Bill: A Breakthrough in Educational and Social Policy in the United States*. Hicksville, N.Y.: Exposition Press.

Nalty, Bernard C., and Morris J. MacGregor, eds. 1981. *Blacks in the Military: Essential Documents*. Wilmington, Del.: Scholarly Resources, Inc.

Nash, Gary B., Julie Roy Jeffrey, John R. Howe, Allen F. Davis, Peter J. Frederick, and Allen M. Winkler. 1986. *The American People: Creating a Nation and a Society*. New York: Harper and Row.

Pardo, Mary. 1990. "Mexican-American Women Grassroots Community Activists: 'Mothers of East Los Angeles'." *Frontiers* 11, 1:1–7.

Patterson, Thomas C. 1997. *Inventing Western Civilization*. New York: Monthly Review Press.

"Postwar Jobs for Veterans." 1945. *The Annals of the American Academy of Political and Social Science* 238 (March).

Ripley, William Z. 1923. *The Races of Europe: A Sociological Study*. New York: Appleton.

Rodriguez, Sylvia. 1997. "Tourism, Whiteness, and the Vanishing Anglo." Paper presented at the conference "Seeing and Being Seen: Tourism in the American West." Center for the American West, Boulder, Colorado, 2 May.

Schoener, Allon. 1967. *Portal to America: The Lower East Side 1870–1925*. New York: Holt, Rinehart, and Winston.

Sowell, Thomas. 1981. *Ethnic America: A History*. New York: Basic Books.

Squires, Gregory D., ed. 1989. *Unequal Partnerships: The Political Economy of Urban Redevelopment in Postwar America*. New Brunswick, N.J.: Rutgers University Press.

Steinberg, Stephen. 1989. *The Ethnic Myth: Race, Ethnicity and Class in America*. 2d ed. Boston: Beacon Press.

Thomas, Laurence Mordekhai. 1996. "The Soul of Identity: Jews and Blacks." In *People of the Book*, ed. S. F. Fishkin and J. Rubin-Dorsky. Madison: University of Wisconsin Press, 169–186.

U.S. Bureau of the Census. 1940. *Sixteenth Census of the United States*, V.2. Washington, D.C.: U.S. Government Printing Office.

Walker, Olive. 1970. "The Windsor Hills School Story." *Integrated Education: Race and Schools* 8, 3:4–9.

Willenz, June A. 1983. *Women Veterans: America's Forgotten Heroines*. New York: Continuum.

Wynn, Neil A. 1976. *The Afro-American and the Second World War*. London: Paul Elek.

"Night to His Day":
The Social Construction of Gender

Judith Lorber

Talking about gender for most people is the equivalent of fish talking about water. Gender is so much the routine ground of everyday activities that questioning its taken-for-granted assumptions and presuppositions is like thinking about whether the sun will come up.[1] Gender is so pervasive that in our society we assume it is bred into our genes. Most people find it hard to believe that gender is constantly created and re-created out of human interaction, out of social life, and is the texture and order of that social life. Yet gender, like culture, is a human production that depends on everyone constantly "doing gender" (West and Zimmerman 1987).

And everyone "does gender" without thinking about it. Today, on the subway, I saw a well-dressed man with a year-old child in a stroller. Yesterday, on a bus, I saw a man with a tiny baby in a carrier on his chest. Seeing men taking care of small children in public is increasingly common—at least in New York City. But both men were quite obviously stared at—and smiled at, approvingly. Everyone was doing gender—the men who were changing the role of fathers and the other passengers, who were applauding them silently. But there was more gendering going on that probably fewer people noticed. The baby was wearing a white crocheted cap and white clothes. You couldn't tell if it was a boy or a girl. The child in the stroller was wearing a dark blue T-shirt and dark print pants. As they started to leave the train, the father put a Yankee baseball cap on the child's head. Ah, a boy, I thought. Then I noticed the gleam of tiny earrings in the child's ears, and as they got off, I saw the little flowered sneakers and lace-trimmed socks. Not a boy after all. Gender done.

Gender is such a familiar part of daily life that it usually takes a deliberate disruption of our expectations of how women and men are supposed to act to pay attention to how it is produced. Gender signs and signals are so ubiquitous that we usually fail to note them—unless they are missing or ambiguous. Then we are uncomfortable until we have successfully placed the other person in a gender status; otherwise, we feel socially dislocated. . . .

For the individual, gender construction starts with assignment to a sex category on the basis of what the genitalia look like at birth.[2] Then babies are dressed or adorned in a way that displays the category because parents don't want to be constantly asked whether their baby is a girl or a boy. A sex category becomes a gender status through naming, dress, and the use of other gender markers. Once a child's gender is evident, others treat those in one gender differently from those in the other, and the children respond to the different treatment by feeling different and behaving differently. As soon as they can talk, they start to refer to themselves as members of their gender. Sex doesn't come into play again until puberty, but by that time, sexual feelings and desires and practices have been shaped by gendered norms and expectations. Adolescent boys and girls approach and avoid each other in an elaborately scripted and gendered mating dance. Parenting is gendered, with different expectations for mothers and for fathers, and people of different genders work at different kinds of jobs. The work adults do as mothers and fathers and as low-level workers and high-level bosses, shapes women's and men's life experiences, and these experiences produce different feelings, consciousness, relationships, skills—ways of being that we call feminine or masculine.[3] All of these processes constitute the social construction of gender.

Gendered roles change—today fathers are taking care of little children, girls and boys are wearing unisex clothing and getting the same education, women and men are working at the same jobs. Although many traditional social groups are quite strict about maintaining gender differences, in other social groups they seem to be blurring. Then why the one-year-old's earrings? Why is it still so important to mark a child as a girl or a boy, to make sure she is not taken for a boy or he for a girl? What would happen if they were? They would, quite literally, have changed places in their social world.

To explain why gendering is done from birth, constantly and by everyone, we have to look not only at the way individuals experience gender but at gender as a social institution. As a social institution, gender is one of the major ways that human beings organize their lives. Human society depends on a predictable division of labor, a designated allocation of scarce goods, assigned responsibility for children and others who cannot care for themselves, common values and their systematic transmission to new members, legitimate leadership, music, art, stories, games, and other symbolic productions. One way of choosing people for the different tasks of society is on the basis of their talents, motivations, and competence—their demonstrated achievements. The other way is on the basis of gender, race, ethnicity—ascribed membership in a category of people. Although societies vary in the extent to which they use one or the other of these ways of allocating people to work and to carry out other responsibilities, every society uses gender and age grades. Every society classifies people as "girl and boy children," "girls and boys ready to be married," and "fully adult women and men," constructs similarities among them and differences between them, and assigns them to different roles and responsibilities. Personality characteristics, feelings, motivations, and ambitions flow from these different life experiences so that the members of these different groups become different kinds of people. The process of gendering and its outcome are legitimated by religion, law, science, and the society's entire set of values. . . .

Western society's values legitimate gendering by claiming that it all comes from physiology—female and male procreative differences. But gender and sex are not equivalent, and gender as a social construction does not flow automatically from genitalia and reproductive organs, the main physiological differences of females and males. In the construction of ascribed social statuses, physiological differences such as sex, stage of development, color of skin, and size are crude markers. They are not the source of the social statuses of gender, age grade, and race. Social statuses are carefully constructed through prescribed processes of teaching, learning, emulation, and enforcement. Whatever genes, hormones, and biological evolution contribute to human social institutions is materially as well as qualitatively transformed by social practices. Every social institution has a material base, but culture and social practices transform that base into something with qualitatively different patterns and constraints. The economy is much more than producing food and goods and distributing them to eaters and users; family and kinship are not the equivalent of having sex and procreating; morals and religions cannot be equated with the fears and ecstasies of the brain; language goes far beyond the sounds produced by tongue and larynx. No one eats "money" or "credit"; the concepts of "god" and "angels" are the subjects of theological disquisitions; not only words but objects, such as their flag, "speak" to the citizens of a country.

Similarly, gender cannot be equated with biological and physiological differences between human females and males. The building blocks of gender are *socially constructed statuses*. Western societies have only two genders, "man" and "woman." Some societies have three genders—men, women, and *berdaches* or *hijras* or *xaniths*. Berdaches, hijras, and xaniths are biological males who behave, dress, work, and are treated in most respects as social women; they are therefore not men, nor are they female women; they are, in our language, "male women."[4] There are African and American Indian societies that have a gender status called *manly hearted women*—biological females who work, marry, and parent as men; their social status is "female men" (Amadiume 1987; Blackwood 1984). They do not have to behave or dress as men to have the social responsibilities and prerogatives of husbands and fathers; what makes them men is enough wealth to buy a wife.

Modern Western societies' *transsexuals* and *transvestites* are the nearest equivalent of these crossover genders, but they are not institutionalized as third genders (Bolin 1987). Transsexuals are biological males and females who have sex-change operations to alter their genitalia. They do so in order to bring their physical anatomy in congruence with the way they want to live and with their own sense of gender identity. They do not become a third gender; they change genders. Transvestites are males who live as women and females who live as men but do not intend to have sex-change surgery. Their dress, appearance, and mannerisms fall within the range of what is expected from members of the opposite gender, so that they "pass." They also change genders, sometimes temporarily, some for most of their lives. Transvestite women have fought in wars as men soldiers as recently as the nineteenth century; some married women, and others went back to being women and married men once the war was over.[5] Some were discovered when their wounds were treated; others not until they died. In order to work as a jazz musician, a man's occupation, Billy Tipton, a woman, lived most of her life as a man. She died recently at seventy-four, leaving a wife and three adopted sons for whom she was husband and father, and musicians with whom she had played and traveled, for whom she was "one of the boys" (*New York Times* 1989).[6] There have been many other such occurrences of women passing as men to do more prestigious or lucrative men's work (Matthaei 1982, 192–93).[7]

Genders, therefore, are not attached to a biological substratum. Gender boundaries are breachable, and individual and socially organized shifts from one gender to another call attention to "cultural, social, or aesthetic dissonances" (Garber 1992, 16). These odd or deviant or third genders show us what we ordinarily take for granted—that people have to learn to be women and men. . . .

For Individuals, Gender Means Sameness

Although the possible combinations of genitalia, body shapes, clothing, mannerisms, sexuality, and roles could produce infinite varieties in human beings, the social institution of gender depends on the production and maintenance of a limited number of gender statuses and of making the members of these statuses similar to each other. Individuals are born sexed but not gendered, and they have to be taught to be masculine or feminine.[8] As Simone de Beauvoir said: "One is not born, but rather becomes, a woman . . . ; it is civilization as a whole that produces this creature . . . which is described as feminine." (1953, 267).

Children learn to walk, talk, and gesture the way their social group says girls and boys should. Ray Birdwhistell, in his analysis of body motion as human communication, calls these learned gender displays *tertiary* sex characteristics and argues that they are needed to distinguish genders because humans are a weakly dimorphic species—their only sex markers are genitalia (1970, 39–46). Clothing, paradoxically, often hides the sex but displays the gender.

In early childhood, humans develop gendered personality structures and sexual orientations through their interactions with parents of the same and opposite gender. As adolescents, they conduct their sexual behavior according to gendered scripts. Schools, parents, peers, and the mass media guide young people into gendered work and family roles. As adults, they take on a gendered social status in their society's stratification system. Gender is thus both ascribed and achieved (West and Zimmerman 1987). . . .

Gender norms are inscribed in the way people move, gesture, and even eat. In one African society, men were supposed to eat with their "whole mouth, wholeheartedly, and not, like women, just with the lips, that is halfheartedly, with reservation and restraint" (Bourdieu [1980] 1990, 70). Men and women in this society learned to walk in ways that proclaimed their different positions in the society:

The manly man . . . stands up straight into the face of the person he approaches, or wishes to welcome. Ever on the alert, because ever threatened, he misses nothing of what happens around him. . . . Conversely, a well brought-up woman . . . is expected to walk with a slight stoop, avoiding every misplaced movement of her body, her head or her arms, looking down, keeping her eyes on the spot where she will next put her foot, especially if she happens to have to walk past the men's assembly. (70)

. . . For human beings there is no essential femaleness or maleness, femininity or masculinity, womanhood or manhood, but once gender is ascribed, the social order constructs and holds individuals to strongly gendered norms and expectations. Individuals may vary on many of the components of gender and may shift genders temporarily or permanently, but they must fit into the limited number of gender statuses their society recognizes. In the process, they re-create their society's version of women and men: "If we do gender appropriately, we simultaneously sustain, reproduce, and render legitimate the institutional arrangements. . . . If we fail to do gender appropriately, we as individuals—not the institutional arrangements—may be called to account (for our character, motives, and predispositions)" (West and Zimmerman 1987, 146).

The gendered practices of everyday life reproduce a society's view of how women and men should act (Bourdieu [1980] 1990). Gendered social arrangements are justified by religion and cultural productions and backed by law, but the most powerful means of sustaining the moral hegemony of the dominant gender ideology is that the process is made invisible; any possible alternatives are virtually unthinkable (Foucault 1972; Gramsci 1971).[9]

For Society, Gender Means Difference

The pervasiveness of gender as a way of structuring social life demands that gender statuses be clearly differentiated. Varied talents, sexual preferences, identities, personalities, interests, and ways of interacting fragment the individual's bodily and social experiences. Nonetheless, these are organized in Western cultures into two and only two socially and legally recognized gender statuses, "man" and "woman."[10] In the social construction of gender, it does not matter what men and women actually do; it does not even matter if they do exactly the same thing. The social institution of gender insists only that what they do is *perceived* as different.

If men and women are doing the same tasks, they are usually spatially segregated to maintain gender separation, and often the tasks are given different job titles as well, such as executive secretary and administrative assistant (Reskin 1988). If the differences between women and men begin to blur, society's "sameness taboo" goes into action (Rubin 1975, 178). At a rock and roll dance at West Point in 1976, the year women were admitted to the prestigious military academy for the first time, the school's administrators "were reportedly perturbed by the sight of mirror-image couples dancing in short hair and dress gray trousers," and a rule was established that women cadets could dance at these events only if they wore skirts (Barkalow and Raab 1990, 53).[11] Women recruits in the U.S. Marine Corps are required to wear makeup—at a minimum, lipstick and eye shadow—and they have to take classes in makeup, hair care, poise, and etiquette. This feminization is part of a deliberate policy of making them clearly distinguishable from men Marines. Christine Williams quotes a twenty-five-year-old woman drill instructor as saying: "A lot of the recruits who come here don't wear makeup; they're tomboyish or athletic. A lot of them have the preconceived idea that going into the military means they can still be a tomboy. They don't realize that you are a *Woman* Marine" (1989, 76–77).[12]

If gender differences were genetic, physiological, or hormonal, gender bending and gender ambiguity would occur only in hermaphrodites, who are born with chromosomes and genitalia that are not clearly female or male. Since gender differences are socially constructed, all men and all women can enact the behavior of the other, because they know the other's social script: " 'Man' and 'woman' are at once empty and overflowing categories. Empty because they have no ultimate, transcendental meaning. Overflowing because even when they appear to be fixed, they still contain within them alternative, denied, or suppressed definitions." (Scott 1988, 49). . . .

For one transsexual man-to-woman, the experience of living as a woman changed his/her whole personality. As James, Morris had been a soldier, foreign correspondent, and mountain climber; as Jan, Morris is a successful travel writer. But socially, James was superior to Jan, and so Jan developed the "learned helplessness" that is supposed to characterize women in Western society:

> We are told that the social gap between the sexes is narrowing, but I can only report that having, in the second half of the twentieth century, experienced life in both roles, there seems to me no aspect of existence, no moment of the day, no contact, no arrangement, no response, which is not different for men and for women. The very tone of voice in which I was now addressed, the very posture of the person next in the queue, the very feel in the air when I entered a room or sat at a restaurant table, constantly emphasized my change of status.
>
> And if other's responses shifted, so did my own. The more I was treated as woman, the more woman I became. I adapted willy-nilly. If I was assumed to be incompetent at reversing cars, or opening bottles, oddly incompetent I found myself becoming. If a case was thought too heavy for me, inexplicably I found it so myself. . . . Women treated me with a frankness which, while it was one of the happiest discoveries of my metamorphosis, did imply membership of a camp, a faction, or at least a school of thought; so I found myself gravitating always towards the female, whether in sharing a railway compartment or supporting a political cause. Men treated me more and more as junior, . . . and so, addressed every day of my life as an inferior, involuntarily, month by month I accepted the condition. I discovered that even now men prefer women to be less informed, less able, less talkative, and certainly less self-centered than they are themselves; so I generally obliged them. (1975, 165–66)[13]

Gender as Process, Stratification, and Structure

As a social institution, gender is a process of creating distinguishable social statuses for the assignment of rights and responsibilities. As part of a stratification system that ranks these statuses unequally, gender is a major building block in the social structures built on these unequal statuses.

As a *process*, gender creates the social differences that define "woman" and "man." In social interaction throughout their lives, individuals learn what is expected, see what is expected, act and react in expected ways, and thus simultaneously construct and maintain the gender order: "The very injunction to be a given gender takes place through discursive routes: to be a good mother, to be a heterosexually desirable object, to be a fit worker, in sum, to signify a multiplicity of guarantees in response to a variety of different demands all at once" (Butler 1990, 145). Members of a social group neither make up gender as they go along nor exactly replicate in rote fashion what was done before. In almost every encounter, human beings produce gender, behaving in the ways they learned were appropriate for their status, or resisting or rebelling against these norms. Resistance and rebellion have altered gender norms, but so far they have rarely eroded the statuses.

Gendered patterns of interaction acquire additional layers of gendered sexuality, parenting, and work behaviors in childhood, adolescence, and adulthood. Gendered norms and expectations are enforced through informal sanctions of gender-inappropriate behavior by peers and by formal punishment or threat of punishment by those in authority should behavior deviate too far from socially imposed standards for women and men. . . .

As part of a *stratification* system, gender ranks men above women of the same race and class. Women and men could be different but equal. In practice, the process of creating difference depends to a great extent on differential evaluation. As Nancy Jay (1981) says: "That which is defined, separated out, isolated from all else is A and pure. Not-A is necessarily impure, a random catchall, to which nothing is external except A and the principle of order that separates it from Not-A" (45). From the individual's point of view, whichever gender is A, the other is Not-A; gender boundaries tell the individual who is like him or her, and all the rest are unlike. From society's point of view, however, one gender is usually the touchstone, the normal, the dominant, and the other is different, deviant, and subordinate. In Western society, "man" is A, "wo-man" is Not-A. (Consider what a society would be like where woman was A and man Not-A.)

The further dichotomization by race and class constructs the gradations of a heterogeneous society's stratification scheme. Thus, in the United States, white is A, African American is Not-A; middle class is A, working class is Not-A, and "African-American women occupy a position whereby the inferior half of a series of these dichotomies converge" (Collins 1990, 70). The dominant categories are the hegemonic ideals, taken so for granted as the way things should be that white is not ordinarily thought of as a race, middle class as a class, or men as a gender. The characteristics of these categories define the Other as that which lacks the valuable qualities the dominants exhibit.

In a gender-stratified society, what men do is usually valued more highly than what women do because men do it, even when their activities are very similar or the same. In different regions of southern India, for example, harvesting rice is men's work, shared work, or women's work: "Wherever a task is done by women it is considered easy, and where it is done by [men] it is considered difficult" (Mencher 1988, 104). A gathering and hunting society's survival usually depends on the nuts, grubs, and small animals brought in by the women's foraging trips, but when the men's hunt is successful, it is the occasion for a celebration. Conversely, because they are the superior group, white men do not have to do the "dirty work," such as housework; the most inferior group does it, usually poor women of color (Palmer 1989). . . .

Societies vary in the extent of the inequality in social status of their women and men members, but where there is inequality, the status "woman" (and its attendant behavior and role allocations) is usually held in lesser esteem than the status "man." Since gender is also intertwined with a society's other constructed statuses of differential evaluation—race, religion, occupation, class, country of origin, and so on—men and women members of the favored groups command more power, more prestige, and more property than the members of the disfavored groups. Within many social groups, however, men are advantaged over women. The more economic resources, such as education and job opportunities, are available to a group, the more they tend to be monopolized by men. In poorer groups that have few resources (such as working-class African Americans in the United States), women and men are more nearly equal, and the women may even outstrip the men in education and occupational status (Almquist 1987).

As a *structure*, gender divides work in the home and in economic production, legitimates those in authority, and organizes sexuality and emotional life (Connell 1987, 91–142). As primary parents, women significantly influence children's psychological development and emotional attachments, in the process reproducing gender. Emergent sexuality is shaped by heterosexual, homosexual, bisexual, and sadomasochistic patterns that are gendered—different for girls and boys, and for women and men—so that sexual statuses reflect gender statuses.

When gender is a major component of structured inequality, the devalued genders have less power, prestige, and economic rewards than the valued genders. In countries that discourage gender discrimination, many major roles are still gendered; women still do most of the domestic labor and child rearing, even while doing full-time paid work; women and men are segregated on the job and each does work considered "appropriate"; women's work is usually paid less than men's work. Men dominate the positions of authority and leadership in government, the military, and the law; cultural productions, religions, and sports reflect men's interests.

In societies that create the greatest gender difference, such as Saudi Arabia, women are kept out of sight behind walls or veils, have no civil rights, and often create a cultural and emotional world of their own (Bernard 1981). But even in societies with less rigid gender boundaries, women and men spend much of their time with people of their own gender because of the way work and family are organized. This spatial separation of women and men reinforces gendered differentness, identity, and ways of thinking and behaving (Coser 1986).

Gender inequality—the devaluation of "women" and the social domination of "men"—has social functions and a social history. It is not the result of sex, procreation, physiology, anatomy, hormones, or genetic predispositions. It is produced and maintained by identifiable social processes and built into the general social structure and individual identities deliberately and purposefully. The social order as we know it in Western societies is organized around racial ethnic, class, and gender inequality. I contend, therefore, that the continuing purpose of gender as a modern social institution is to construct women as a group to be the subordinates of men as a group. The life of everyone placed in the status "woman" is "night to his day—that has forever been the fantasy. Black to his white. Shut out of his system's space, she is the repressed that ensures the system's functioning" (Cixous and Clément [1975] 1986, 67).

NOTES

1. Gender is, in Erving Goffman's words, an aspect of *Felicity's Condition:* "any arrangement which leads us to judge an individual's . . . acts not to be a manifestation of strangeness. Behind Felicity's Condition is our sense of what it is to be sane" (1983, 27). Also see Bem 1993; Frye 1983, 17–40; Goffman 1977.

2. In cases of ambiguity in countries with modern medicine, surgery is usually performed to make the genitalia more clearly male or female.

3. See Butler 1990 for an analysis of how doing gender *is* gender identity.

4. On the hijras of India, see Nanda 1990; on the xaniths of Oman, Wikan 1982, 168–86; on the American Indian berdaches, W. L. Williams 1986. Other societies that have similar institutionalized third-gender men are the Koniag of Alaska, the Tanala of Madagascar, the Mesakin of Nuba, and the Chukchee of Siberia (Wikan 1982, 170).

5. Durova 1989; Freeman and Bond 1992; Wheelwright 1989.

6. Gender segregation of work in popular music still has not changed very much, according to Groce and Cooper 1990, despite considerable androgyny in some very popular figures. See Garber 1992 on the androgyny. She discusses Tipton on pp. 67–70.

7. In the nineteenth century, not only did these women get men's wages, but they also "had male privileges and could do all manner of things other women could not: open a bank account, write checks, own property, go anywhere unaccompanied, vote in elections" (Faderman 1991, 44).

8. For an account of how a potential man-to-woman transsexual learned to be feminine, see Garfinkel 1967, 116–85, 285–88. For a gloss on this account that points out how, throughout his encounters with Agnes, Garfinkel failed to see how he himself was constructing his own masculinity, see Rogers 1992.

9. The concepts of moral hegemony, the effects of everyday activities (praxis) on thought and personality, and the necessity of consciousness of these processes before political change can occur are all based on Marx's analysis of class relations.

10. Other societies recognize more than two categories, but usually no more than three or four (Jacobs and Roberts 1989).

11. Carol Barkalow's book has a photograph of eleven first-year West Pointers in a math class, who are dressed in regulation pants, shirts, and sweaters, with short haircuts. The caption challenges the reader to locate the only woman in the room.

12. The taboo on males and females looking alike reflects the U.S. military's homophobia (Bérubé 1989). If you can't tell those with a penis from those with a vagina, how are you going to determine whether their sexual interest is heterosexual or homosexual unless you watch them having sexual relations?

13. See Bolin 1988, 149–50, for transsexual men-to-women's discovery of the dangers of rape and sexual harassment. Devor's "gender blenders" went in the opposite direction. Because they found that it was an advantage to be taken for men, they did not deliberately cross-dress, but they did not feminize themselves either (1989, 126–40).

REFERENCES

Almquist, Elizabeth M. 1987. Labor market gendered inequality in minority groups. *Gender & Society* 1:400–14.

Amadiume, Ifi. 1987. *Male daughters, female husbands: Gender and sex in an African society.* London: Zed Books.

Barkalow, Carol, with Andrea Raab. 1990. *In the men's house.* New York: Poseidon Press.

Bem, Sandra Lipsitz. 1993. *The lenses of gender: Transforming the debate on sexual inequality.* New Haven: Yale University Press.

Bernard, Jessie. 1981. *The female world.* New York: Free Press.

Bérubé, Allan. 1989. Marching to a different drummer: Gay and lesbian GIs in World War II. In Duberman, Vicinus, and Chauncey.

Birdwhistell, Ray L. 1970. *Kinesics and context: Essays on body motion communication.* Philadelphia: University of Pennsylvania Press.

Blackwood, Evelyn. 1984. Sexuality and gender in certain Native American tribes: The case of cross-gender females. *Signs: Journal of Women in Culture and Society* 10:27–42.

Bolin, Anne. 1987. Transsexualism and the limits of traditional analysis. *American Behavioral Scientist* 31:41–65.

_____. 1988. *In search of Eve: Transsexual rites of passage.* South Hadley, Mass.: Bergin & Garvey.

Bourdieu, Pierre. [1980] 1990. *The logic of practice.* Stanford, Calif.: Stanford University Press.

Butler, Judith. 1990. *Gender trouble: Feminism and the subversion of identity.* New York and London: Routledge.

Cixous, Hélène, and Catherine Clément. [1975] 1986. *The newly born woman,* translated by Betsy Wing. Minneapolis: University of Minnesota Press.

Collins, Patricia Hill. 1990. *Black feminist thought: Knowledge, consciousness, and the politics of empowerment.* Boston: Unwin Hyman.

Connell, R.[Robert] W. 1987. *Gender and power: Society, the person, and sexual politics.* Stanford, Calif.: Stanford University Press.

Coser, Rose Laub. 1986. Cognitive structure and the use of social space. *Sociological Forum* 1:1–26.

De Beauvoir, Simone. 1953. *The second sex*, translated by H. M. Parshley. New York: Knopf.

Devor, Holly. 1989. *Gender blending: Confronting the limits of duality*. Bloomington: Indiana University Press.

Duberman, Martin Bauml, Martha Vicinus, and George Chauncey, Jr. (eds.). 1989. *Hidden from history: Reclaiming the gay and lesbian past*. New York: New American Library.

Durova, Nadezhda. 1989. *The cavalry maiden: Journals of a Russian officer in the Napoleonic Wars*, translated by Mary Fleming Zirin. Bloomington: Indiana University Press.

Dwyer, Daisy, and Judith Bruce (eds.). 1988. *A home divided: Women and income in the Third World*. Palo Alto, Calif.: Stanford University Press.

Faderman, Lillian. 1991. *Odd girls and twilight lovers: A history of lesbian life in twentieth-century America*. New York: Columbia University Press.

Foucault, Michel. 1972. *The archeology of knowledge and the discourse on language*, translated by A.M. Sheridan Smith. New York: Pantheon.

Freeman, Lucy, and Alma Halbert Bond. 1992. *America's first woman warrior: The courage of Deborah Sampson*. New York: Paragon.

Frye, Marilyn. 1983. *The politics of reality: Essays in feminist theory*. Trumansburg, N.Y.: Crossing Press.

Garber, Marjorie. 1992. *Vested interests: Cross-dressing and cultural anxiety*. New York and London: Routledge.

Garfinkel, Harold. 1967. *Studies in ethnomethodology*. Englewood Cliffs, N.J.: Prentice-Hall.

Goffman, Erving. 1977. The arrangement between the sexes. *Theory and Society* 4:301–33.

_____. 1983. Felicity's condition. *American Journal of Sociology* 89:1–53.

Gramsci, Antonio. 1971. *Selections from the prison notebooks*, translated and edited by Quintin Hoare and Geoffrey Nowell Smith. New York: International Publishers.

Groce, Stephen B., and Margaret Cooper. 1990. Just me and the boys? Women in local-level rock and roll. *Gender & Society* 4:220–29.

Jacobs, Sue-Ellen, and Christine Roberts. 1989. Sex, sexuality, gender, and gender variance. In *Gender and anthropology*, edited by Sandra Morgen. Washington, D.C.: American Anthropological Association.

Jay, Nancy. 1981. Gender and dichotomy. *Feminist Studies* 7:38–56.

Matthaei, Julie A. 1982. *An economic history of women's work in America*. New York: Schocken.

Mencher, Joan. 1988. Women's work and poverty: Women's contribution to household maintenance in South India. In Dwyer and Bruce.

Morris, Jan. 1975. *Conundrum*. New York: Signet.

Nanda, Serena. 1990. *Neither man nor woman: The hijras of India*. Belmont, Calif.: Wadsworth.

New York Times. 1989. Musician's death at 74 reveals he was a woman. 2 February.

Palmer, Phyllis. 1989. *Domesticity and dirt: Housewives and domestic servants in the United States, 1920–1945*. Philadelphia: Temple University Press.

Reskin, Barbara F. 1988. Bringing the men back in: Sex differentiation and the devaluation of women's work. *Gender & Society* 2:58–81.

Rogers, Mary F. 1992. They were all passing: Agnes, Garfinkel, and company. *Gender & Society* 6:169–91.

Rubin, Gayle. 1975. The traffic in women: Notes on the political economy of sex. In *Toward an anthropology of women*, edited by Rayna R[app] Reiter. New York: Monthly Review Press.

Scott, Joan Wallach. 1988. *Gender and the politics of history*. New York: Columbia University Press.

West, Candace, and Don Zimmerman. 1987. Doing gender. *Gender & Society* 1:125–51.

Wheelwright, Julie. 1989. *Amazons and military maids: Women who cross-dressed in pursuit of life, liberty and happiness*. London: Pandora Press.

Wikan, Unni. 1982. *Behind the veil in Arabia: Women in Oman*. Baltimore, Md.: Johns Hopkins University Press.

Williams, Christine L. 1989. *Gender differences at work: Women and men in nontraditional occupations*. Berkeley: University of California Press.

Williams, Walter L. 1986. *The spirit and the flesh: Sexual diversity in American Indian culture*. Boston: Beacon Press.

6

The Social Construction of Sexuality

Ruth Hubbard

There is no "natural" human sexuality. This is not to say that our sexual feelings are "unnatural" but that whatever feelings and activities our society interprets as sexual are channeled from birth into socially acceptable forms of expression.

Western thinking about sexuality is based on the Christian equation of sexuality with sin, which must be redeemed through making babies. To fulfill the Christian mandate, sexuality must be intended for procreation, and thus all forms of sexual expression and enjoyment other than heterosexuality are invalidated. Actually, for most Christians nowadays just plain heterosexuality will do, irrespective of whether it is intended to generate offspring.

From Ruth Hubbard, *The Politics of Women's Biology*. Copyright © 1991 by Rutgers, The State University. Reprinted by permission of Rutgers University Press.

These ideas about sexuality set up a major contradiction in what we tell children about sex and procreation. We teach them that sex and sexuality are about becoming mommies and daddies and warn them not to explore sex by themselves or with playmates of either sex until they are old enough to have babies. Then, when they reach adolescence and the entire culture pressures them into heterosexual activity, whether they themselves feel ready for it or not, the more "enlightened" among us tell them how to be sexually (meaning heterosexually) active without having babies. Surprise: It doesn't work very well. Teenagers do not act "responsibly"—teenage pregnancies and abortions are on the rise and teenage fathers do not acknowledge and support their partners and babies. Somewhere we forget that we have been telling lies. Sexuality and procreation are not linked in societies like ours. On the contrary, we expect youngsters to be heterosexually active from their teens on but to put off having children until they are economically independent and married, and even then to have only two or, at most, three children.

Other contradictions: This society, on the whole, accepts Freud's assumption that children are sexual beings from birth and that society channels their polymorphously perverse childhood sexuality into the accepted forms. Yet we expect our children to be asexual. We raise girls and boys together more than is done in many societies while insisting that they must not explore their own or each other's sexual parts or feelings.

What if we acknowledged the separation of sexuality from procreation and encouraged our children to express themselves sexually if they were so inclined? What if we, further, encouraged them to explore their own bodies as well as those of friends of the same and the other sex when they felt like it? They might then be able to feel at home with their sexuality, have some sense of their own and other people's sexual needs, and know how to talk about sexuality and procreation with their friends and sexual partners before their ability to procreate becomes an issue for them. In this age of AIDS and other serious sexually transmitted infections, such a course of action seems like essential preventive hygiene. Without the embarrassment of unexplored and unacknowledged sexual needs, contraceptive needs would be much easier to confront when they arise. So, of course, would same-sex love relationships.

Such a more open and accepting approach to sexuality would make life easier for children and adolescents of either sex, but it would be especially advantageous for girls. When a boy discovers his penis as an organ of pleasure, it is the same organ he is taught about as his organ of procreation. A girl exploring her pleasurable sensations finds her clitoris, but when she is taught about making babies, she hears about the functions of the vagina in sex and birthing. Usually, the clitoris goes unmentioned, and she doesn't even learn its name until much later. Therefore for boys there is an obvious link between procreation and their own pleasurable, erotic explorations; for most girls, there isn't.

Individual Sexual Scripts

Each of us writes our own sexual script out of the range of our experiences. None of this script is inborn or biologically given. We construct it out of our diverse life situations, limited by what we are taught or what we can imagine to be permissible and correct. There is no unique female sexual experience, no male sexual experience, no unique heterosexual, lesbian, or gay male experience. We take the experiences of different people and sort and lump them according to socially significant categories. When I hear generalizations about *the* sexual experience of some particular group, exceptions immediately come to mind. Except that I refuse to call them exceptions: They are part of the range of our sexual experiences. Of course, the similar circumstances in which members of a particular group find themselves will give rise to group similarities. But we tend to exaggerate them when we go looking for similarities within groups or differences between them.

This exaggeration is easy to see when we look at the dichotomy between "the heterosexual" and "the homosexual." The concept of "the homosexual," along with many other human typologies, originated toward the end of the nineteenth century. Certain kinds of behavior stopped being attributed to particular persons and came to define them. A person who had sexual relations with someone of the same sex became a certain kind of person, a "homosexual"; a person who had sexual relations with people of the other sex, a different kind, a "heterosexual."

This way of categorizing people obscured the hitherto accepted fact that many people do not have sexual relations exclusively with persons of one or the other sex. (None of us has sex with a kind of person; we have sex with a person.) This categorization created the stereotypes that were popularized by the sex reformers, such as Havelock Ellis and Edward Carpenter, who biologized the "difference." "The homosexual" became a person who is different by nature and therefore should not be made responsible for his or her so-called deviance. This definition served the purpose of the reformers (although the laws have been slow to change), but it turned same-sex love into a medical problem to be treated by doctors rather than punished by judges—an improvement, perhaps, but not acceptance or liberation. . . .

Toward a Nondeterministic Model of Sexuality

. . . Some gay men and lesbians feel that they were born "different" and have always been homosexual. They recall feeling strongly attracted to members of their own sex when they were children and adolescents. But many women who live with men and think of themselves as heterosexual also had strong affective and erotic ties to girls and women while they were growing up. If they were now in loving relationships with women, they might look back on their earlier loves as proof that they were always lesbians. But if they are now involved with men, they may be tempted to devalue their former feelings as "puppy love" or "crushes."

Even within the preferred sex, most of us feel a greater affinity for certain "types" than for others. Not any man or woman will do. No one has seriously suggested that something in our innate makeup makes us light up in the presence of only certain women or men. We would think it absurd to look to hormone levels or any other simplistic biological cause for our preference for a specific "type" within a sex. In fact, scientists rarely bother to ask what in our psychosocial experience shapes these kinds of tastes and preferences. We assume it must have something to do with our relationship to our parents or with other experiences, but we do not probe deeply unless people prefer the "wrong" sex. Then, suddenly, scientists begin to look for specific causes.

Because of our recent history and political experiences, feminists tend to reject simplistic, causal models of how our sexuality develops. Many women who have thought of themselves as heterosexual for much of their life and who have been married and have had children have fallen in love with a woman (or women) when they have had the opportunity to rethink, refeel, and restructure their lives.

The society in which we live channels, guides, and limits our imagination in sexual as well as other matters. Why some of us give ourselves permission to love people of our own sex whereas others cannot even imagine doing so is an interesting question. But I do not think it will be answered by measuring our hormone levels or by trying to unearth our earliest affectional ties. As women begin to speak freely about our sexual experiences, we are getting a varied range of information with which we can reexamine, reevaluate, and change ourselves. Lately, increasing numbers of women have begun to acknowledge their "bisexuality"—the fact that they can love women and men in succession or simultaneously. People fall in love with individuals, not with a sex. Gender need not be a significant factor in our choice, although for some of us it may be.

7

The Invention of Heterosexuality

Jonathan Ned Katz

Heterosexuality is old as procreation, ancient as the lust of Eve and Adam. That first lady and gentleman, we assume, perceived themselves, behaved, and felt just like today's heterosexuals. We suppose that heterosexuality is unchanging, universal, essential: ahistorical.

Contrary to that common sense conjecture, the concept of heterosexuality is only one particular historical way of perceiving, categorizing, and imagining the social relations of the sexes. Not ancient at all, the idea of heterosexuality is a modern invention, dating to the late nineteenth century. The heterosexual belief, with its metaphysical claim to eternity, has a particular, pivotal place in the social universe of the late nineteenth and twentieth centuries that it did not inhabit earlier. This essay traces the historical process by which the heterosexual idea was created as ahistorical and taken-for-granted. . . .

By not studying the heterosexual idea in history, analysts of sex, gay and straight, have continued to privilege the "normal" and "natural" at the expense of the "abnormal" and "unnatural." Such privileging of the norm accedes to its domination, protecting it from questions. By making the normal the object of a thoroughgoing historical study we simultaneously pursue a pure truth and a sex-radical and subversive goal: we upset basic preconceptions. We discover that the heterosexual, the normal, and the natural have a history of changing definitions. Studying the history of the term challenges its power.

Contrary to our usual assumption, past Americans and other peoples named, perceived, and socially organized the bodies, lusts, and intercourse of the sexes in

I'm grateful to Lisa Duggan, Judith Levine, Sharon Thompson, Carole S. Vance, and Jeffrey Weeks for comments on a recent version of this manuscript, and to Manfred Herzer and his editor, John DeCecco, for sharing, prepublication, Herzer's most recent research on Kertbeny. I'm also indebted to John Gagnon, Philip Greven, and Catharine R. Stimpson for bravely supporting my (unsuccessful) attempts to fund research for a full-length study of heterosexual history.

ways radically different from the way we do. If we care to understand this vast past sexual diversity, we need to stop promiscuously projecting our own hetero and homo arrangement. Though lip-service is often paid to the distorting, ethnocentric effect of such conceptual imperialism, the category heterosexuality continues to be applied uncritically as a universal analytical tool. Recognizing the time-bound and culturally-specific character of the heterosexual category can help us begin to work toward a thoroughly historical view of sex. . . .

Before Heterosexuality: Early Victorian True Love, 1820–1860

In the early nineteenth-century United States, from about 1820 to 1860, the heterosexual did not exist. Middle-class white Americans idealized a True Womanhood, True Manhood, and True Love, all characterized by "purity"—the freedom from sensuality.[1] Presented mainly in literary and religious texts, this True Love was a fine romance with no lascivious kisses. This ideal contrasts strikingly with late nineteenth- and twentieth-century American incitements to a hetero sex.*

Early Victorian True Love was only realized within the mode of proper procreation, marriage, the legal organization for producing a new set of correctly gendered women and men. Proper womanhood, manhood, and progeny—not a normal male-female eros—was the main product of this mode of engendering and of human reproduction.

The actors in this sexual economy were identified as manly men and womanly women and as procreators, not specifically as erotic beings or heterosexuals. Eros did not constitute the core of a heterosexual identity that inhered, democratically, in both men and women. True Women were defined by their distance from lust. True Men, though thought to live closer to carnality, and in less control of it, aspired to the same freedom from concupiscence.

Legitimate natural desire was for procreation and a proper manhood or womanhood; no heteroerotic desire was thought to be directed exclusively and naturally toward the other sex; lust in men was roving. The human body was thought of as a means towards procreation and production; penis and vagina were instruments of reproduction, not of pleasure. Human energy, thought of as a closed and severely limited system, was to be used in producing children and in work, not wasted in libidinous pleasures.

---

*Some historians have recently told us to revise our idea of sexless Victorians: their experience and even their ideology, it is said, were more erotic than we previously thought. Despite the revisionists, I argue that "purity" was indeed the dominant, early Victorian, white middle-class standard. For the debate on Victorian sexuality see John D'Emilio and Estelle Freedman, *Intimate Matters: A History of Sexuality in America* (New York: Harper & Row, 1988), p. xii.

The location of all this engendering and procreative labor was the sacred sanctum of early Victorian True Love, the home of the True Woman and True Man—a temple of purity threatened from within by the monster masturbator, an archetypal early Victorian cult figure of illicit lust. The home of True Love was a castle far removed from the erotic exotic ghetto inhabited most notoriously then by the prostitute, another archetypal Victorian erotic monster. . . .

Late Victorian Sex-Love: 1860–1892

"Heterosexuality" and "homosexuality" did not appear out of the blue in the 1890s. These two eroticisms were in the making from the 1860s on. In late Victorian America and in Germany, from about 1860 to 1892, our modern idea of an eroticized universe began to develop, and the experience of a heterolust began to be widely documented and named. . . .

In the late nineteenth-century United States, several social factors converged to cause the eroticizing of consciousness, behavior, emotion, and identity that became typical of the twentieth-century Western middle class. The transformation of the family from producer to consumer unit resulted in a change in family members' relation to their own bodies; from being an instrument primarily of work, the human body was integrated into a new economy, and began more commonly to be perceived as a means of consumption and pleasure. Historical work has recently begun on how the biological human body is differently integrated into changing modes of production, procreation, engendering, and pleasure so as to alter radically the identity, activity, and experience of that body.[2]

The growth of a consumer economy also fostered a new pleasure ethic. This imperative challenged the early Victorian work ethic, finally helping to usher in a major transformation of values. While the early Victorian work ethic had touted the value of economic production, that era's procreation ethic had extolled the virtues of human reproduction. In contrast, the late Victorian economic ethic hawked the pleasures of consuming, while its sex ethic praised an erotic pleasure principle for men and even for women.

In the late nineteenth century, the erotic became the raw material for a new consumer culture. Newspapers, books, plays, and films touching on sex, "normal" and "abnormal," became available for a price. Restaurants, bars, and baths opened, catering to sexual consumers with cash. Late Victorian entrepreneurs of desire incited the proliferation of a new eroticism, a commoditized culture of pleasure.

In these same years, the rise in power and prestige of medical doctors allowed these upwardly mobile professionals to prescribe a healthy new sexuality. Medical men, in the name of science, defined a new ideal of male-female relationships that included, in women as well as men, an essential, necessary, normal eroticism. Doctors, who had earlier named and judged the sex-enjoying woman a "nymphomaniac," now began to label women's *lack* of sexual pleasure a mental disturbance, speaking critically, for example, of female "frigidity" and "anesthesia."*

By the 1880s, the rise of doctors as a professional group fostered the rise of a new medical model of Normal Love, replete with sexuality. The new Normal Woman and Man were endowed with a healthy libido. The new theory of Normal Love was the modern medical alternative to the old Cult of True Love. The doctors prescribed a new sexual ethic as if it were a morally neutral, medical description of health. The creation of the new Normal Sexual had its counterpart in the invention of the late Victorian Sexual Pervert. The attention paid the sexual abnormal created a need to name the sexual normal, the better to distinguish the average him and her from the deviant it.

Heterosexuality: The First Years, 1892–1900

In the periodization of heterosexual American history suggested here, the years 1892 to 1900 represent "The First Years" of the heterosexual epoch, eight key years in which the idea of the heterosexual and homosexual were initially and tentatively formulated by U.S. doctors. The earliest-known American use of the word "heterosexual" occurs in a medical journal article by Dr. James G. Kiernan of Chicago, read before the city's medical society on March 7, 1892, and published that May—portentous dates in sexual history.[3] But Dr. Kiernan's heterosexuals were definitely not exemplars of normality. Heterosexuals, said Kiernan, were defined by a mental condition, "psychical hermaphroditism." Its symptoms were "inclinations to both sexes." These heterodox sexuals also betrayed inclinations "to abnormal methods of gratification," that is, techniques to insure pleasure without procreation. Dr. Kiernan's heterogeneous sexuals did demonstrate "traces of the normal sexual appetite" (a touch of procreative desire). Kiernan's normal sexuals were implicitly defined by a monolithic other-sex inclination and procreative aim. Significantly, they still lacked a name.

Dr. Kiernan's article of 1892 also included one of the earliest-known uses of the word "homosexual" in American English. Kiernan defined "Pure homosexuals" as persons whose "general mental state is that of the opposite sex." Kiernan thus defined homosexuals by their deviance from a gender norm. His heterosexuals displayed a double deviance from both gender and procreative norms.

Though Kiernan used the new words heterosexual and homosexual, an old procreative standard and a new gender norm coexisted uneasily in his thought. His

---

*This reference to females reminds us that the invention of heterosexuality had vastly different impacts on the histories of women and men. It also differed in its impact on lesbians and heterosexual women, homosexual and heterosexual men, the middle class and working class, and on different religious, racial, national, and geographic groups.

word heterosexual defined a mixed person and compound urge, abnormal because they wantonly included procreative and non-procreative objectives, as well as same-sex and different-sex attractions.

That same year, 1892, Dr. Krafft-Ebing's influential *Psychopathia Sexualis* was first translated and published in the United States.[4] But Kiernan and Krafft-Ebing by no means agreed on the definition of the heterosexual. In Krafft-Ebing's book, "hetero-sexual" was used unambiguously in the modern sense to refer to an erotic feeling for a different sex. "Homo-sexual" referred unambiguously to an erotic feeling for a "same sex." In Krafft-Ebing's volume, unlike Kiernan's article, heterosexual and homosexual were clearly distinguished from a third category, a "psycho-sexual hermaphroditism," defined by impulses toward both sexes.

Krafft-Ebing hypothesized an inborn "sexual instinct" for relations with the "opposite sex," the inherent "purpose" of which was to foster procreation. Krafft-Ebing's erotic drive was still a reproductive instinct. But the doctor's clear focus on a different-sex versus same-sex sexuality constituted a historic, epochal move from an absolute procreative standard of normality toward a new norm. His definition of heterosexuality as other-sex attraction provided the basis for a revolutionary, modern break with a centuries-old procreative standard.

It is difficult to overstress the importance of that new way of categorizing. The German's mode of labeling was radical in referring to the biological sex, masculinity or femininity, and the pleasure of actors (along with the procreant purpose of acts). Krafft-Ebing's heterosexual offered the modern world a new norm that came to dominate our idea of the sexual universe, helping to change it from a mode of human reproduction and engendering to a mode of pleasure. The heterosexual category provided the basis for a move from a production-oriented, procreative imperative to a consumerist pleasure principle—an institutionalized pursuit of happiness. . . .

Only gradually did doctors agree that heterosexual referred to a normal, "other-sex" eros. This new standard-model heterosex provided the pivotal term for the modern regularization of eros that paralleled similar attempts to standardize masculinity and femininity, intelligence, and manufacturing.[5] The idea of heterosexuality as the master sex from which all others deviated was (like the idea of the master race) deeply authoritarian. The doctors' normalization of a sex that was hetero proclaimed a new heterosexual separatism—an erotic apartheid that forcefully segregated the sex normals from the sex perverts. The new, strict boundaries made the emerging erotic world less polymorphous—safer for sex normals. However, the idea of such creatures as heterosexuals and homosexuals emerged from the narrow world of medicine to become a commonly accepted notion only in the early twentieth century. In 1901, in the comprehensive *Oxford English Dictionary*, "heterosexual" and "homosexual" had not yet made it.

The Distribution of the Heterosexual Mystique: 1900–1930

In the early years of this heterosexual century the tentative hetero hypothesis was stabilized, fixed, and widely distributed as the ruling sexual orthodoxy: The Heterosexual Mystique. Starting among pleasure-affirming urban working-class youths, southern blacks, and Greenwich-Village bohemians as defensive subculture, heterosex soon triumphed as dominant culture.[6]

In its earliest version, the twentieth-century heterosexual imperative usually continued to associate heterosexuality with a supposed human "need," "drive," or "instinct" for propagation, a procreant urge linked inexorably with carnal lust as it had not been earlier. In the early twentieth century, the falling birth rate, rising divorce rate, and "war of the sexes" of the middle class were matters of increasing public concern. Giving vent to heteroerotic emotions was thus praised as enhancing baby-making capacity, marital intimacy, and family stability. (Only many years later, in the mid-1960s, would heteroeroticism be distinguished completely, in practice and theory, from procreativity and male-female pleasure sex justified in its own name.)

The first part of the new sex norm—hetero—referred to a basic gender divergence. The "oppositeness" of the sexes was alleged to be the basis for a universal, normal, erotic attraction between males and females. The stress on the sexes' "oppositeness," which harked back to the early nineteenth century, by no means simply registered biological differences of females and males. The early twentieth-century focus on physiological and gender dimorphism reflected the deep anxieties of men about the shifting work, social roles, and power of men over women, and about the ideals of womanhood and manhood. That gender anxiety is documented, for example, in 1897, in *The New York Times'* publication of the Reverend Charles Parkhurst's diatribe against female "andromaniacs," the preacher's derogatory, scientific-sounding name for women who tried to "minimize distinctions by which manhood and womanhood are differentiated."[7] The stress on gender difference was a conservative response to the changing social-sexual division of activity and feeling which gave rise to the independent "New Woman" of the 1880s and eroticized "Flapper" of the 1920s.

The second part of the new hetero norm referred positively to sexuality. That novel upbeat focus on the hedonistic possibilities of male-female conjunctions also reflected a social transformation—a revaluing of pleasure and procreation, consumption and work in commercial, capitalist society. The democratic attribution of a normal lust to human females (as well as males) served to authorize women's enjoyment of their own bodies and began to undermine the early Victorian idea of the pure True Woman—a sex-affirmative action still part of women's struggle. The twentieth-century Erotic Woman also undercut nineteenth-century feminist assertion of women's moral superiority, cast suspicions of lust on women's passionate romantic friendships with women, and asserted the presence of a menacing female monster, "the lesbian."[8] . . .

In the perspective of heterosexual history, this early twentieth-century struggle for the more explicit depiction of an "opposite-sex" eros appears in a curious new light. Ironically, we find sex-conservatives, the social purity advocates of censorship and repression, fighting against the depiction not just of sexual perversity but also of the new normal heterosexuality. That a more open depiction of normal sex had to be defended against forces of propriety confirms the claim that heterosexuality's predecessor, Victorian True Love, had included no legitimate eros. . . .

The Heterosexual Steps Out: 1930–1945

In 1930, in *The New York Times*, heterosexuality first became a love that dared to speak its name. On April 30th of that year, the word "heterosexual" is first known to have appeared in *The New York Times Book Review*. There, a critic described the subject of André Gide's *The Immoralist* proceeding "from a heterosexual liaison to a homosexual one." The ability to slip between sexual categories was referred to casually as a rather unremarkable aspect of human possibility. This is also the first known reference by *The Times* to the new hetero/homo duo.[9]

The following month the second reference to the hetero/homo dyad appeared in *The New York Times Book Review*, in a comment on Floyd Dell's *Love in the Machine Age*. This work revealed a prominent antipuritan of the 1930s using the dire threat of homosexuality as his rationale for greater heterosexual freedom. *The Times* quoted Dell's warning that current abnormal social conditions kept the young dependent on their parents, causing "infantilism, prostitution and homosexuality." Also quoted was Dell's attack on the "inculcation of purity" that "breeds distrust of the opposite sex." Young people, Dell said, should be "permitted to develop normally to heterosexual adulthood." "But," *The Times* reviewer emphasized, "such a state already exists, here and now." And so it did. Heterosexuality, a new gender-sex category, had been distributed from the narrow, rarified realm of a few doctors to become a nationally, even internationally, cited aspect of middle-class life.[10] . . .

Heterosexual Hegemony: 1945–1965

The "cult of domesticity" following World War II—the reassociation of women with the home, motherhood, and child-care; men with fatherhood and wage work outside the home—was a period in which the predominance of the hetero norm went almost unchallenged, an era of heterosexual hegemony. This was an age in which conservative mental-health professionals reasserted the old link between heterosexuality and procreation. In contrast, sex-liberals of the day strove, ultimately with success, to expand the heterosexual ideal to include within the boundaries of normality a wider-than-ever range of nonprocreative, premarital, and extramarital behaviors. But sex-liberal reform actually helped to extend and secure the dominance of the heterosexual idea, as we shall see when we get to Kinsey.

The postwar sex-conservative tendency was illustrated in 1947, in Ferdinand Lundberg and Dr. Marnia Farnham's book, *Modern Woman: The Lost Sex.* Improper masculinity and femininity was exemplified, the authors decreed, by "engagement in heterosexual relations . . . with the complete intent to see to it that they do not eventuate in reproduction."[11] Their procreatively defined heterosex was one expression of a postwar ideology of fecundity that, internalized and enacted dutifully by a large part of the population, gave rise to the postwar baby boom.

The idea of the feminine female and masculine male as prolific breeders was also reflected in the stress, specific to the late 1940s, on the homosexual as sad symbol of "sterility"—that particular loaded term appears incessantly in comments on homosex dating to the fecund forties.

In 1948, in *The New York Times Book Review,* sex liberalism was in ascendancy. Dr. Howard A. Rusk declared that Alfred Kinsey's just published report on *Sexual Behavior in the Human Male* had found "wide variations in sex concepts and behavior." This raised the question: "What is 'normal' and 'abnormal'?" In particular, the report had found that "homosexual experience is much more common than previously thought," and "there is often a mixture of both homo and hetero experience."[12]

Kinsey's counting of orgasms indeed stressed the wide range of behaviors and feelings that fell within the boundaries of a quantitative, statistically accounted heterosexuality. Kinsey's liberal reform of the hetero/homo dualism widened the narrow, old hetero category to accord better with the varieties of social experience. He thereby contradicted the older idea of a monolithic, qualitatively defined, natural procreative act, experience, and person.[13]

Though Kinsey explicitly questioned "whether the terms 'normal' and 'abnormal' belong in a scientific vocabulary," his counting of climaxes was generally understood to define normal sex as majority sex. This quantified norm constituted a final, society-wide break with the old qualitatively defined reproductive standard. Though conceived of as purely scientific, the statistical definition of the normal as the-sex-most-people-are-having substituted a new, quantitative moral standard for the old, qualitative sex ethic—another triumph for the spirit of capitalism.

Kinsey also explicitly contested the idea of an absolute, either/or antithesis between hetero and homo persons. He denied that human beings "represent two discrete populations, heterosexual and homosexual." The world, he ordered, "is not to be divided into sheep and goats." The hetero/homo division was not nature's doing: "Only the human mind invents categories and tries to force facts into separated pigeon-holes. The living world is a continuum."[14]

With a wave of the taxonomist's hand, Kinsey dismissed the social and historical division of people into heteros and homos. His denial of heterosexual and homosexual personhood rejected the social reality and profound subjective force of a historically constructed tradition which, since 1892 in the United States, had cut the sexual population in two and helped to establish the social reality of a hetero-sexual and homosexual identity.

On the one hand, the social construction of homosexual persons has led to the development of a powerful gay liberation identity politics based on an ethnic group model. This has freed generations of women and men from a deep, painful, socially induced sense of shame, and helped to bring about a society-wide liberal-ization of attitudes and responses to homosexuals.[15] On the other hand, contesting the notion of homosexual and heterosexual persons was one early, partial resis-tance to the limits of the hetero/homo construction. Gore Vidal, rebel son of Kinsey, has for years been joyfully proclaiming:

> there is no such thing as a homosexual or a heterosexual person. There are only homo- or heterosexual acts. Most people are a mixture of impulses if not practices, and what anyone does with a willing partner is of no social or cosmic significance.
>
> So why all the fuss? In order for a ruling class to rule, there must be arbitrary prohibitions. Of all prohibitions, sexual taboo is the most useful because sex in-volves everyone. . . . we have allowed our governors to divide the population into two teams. One team is good, godly, straight; the other is evil, sick, vicious.[16]

Heterosexuality Questioned: 1965–1982

By the late 1960s, anti-establishment counterculturalists, fledgling feminists, and homosexual-rights activists had begun to produce an unprecedented critique of sexual repression in general, of women's sexual repression in particular, of mar-riage and the family—and of some forms of heterosexuality. This critique even found its way into *The New York Times*.

In March 1968, in the theater section of that paper, freelancer Rosalyn Regelson cited a scene from a satirical review brought to New York by a San Francisco troupe:

> a heterosexual man wanders inadvertently into a homosexual bar. Before he realizes his mistake, he becomes involved with an aggressive queen who orders a drink for him. Being a broadminded liberal and trying to play it cool until he can back out of the situation gracefully, he asks, "How do you like being a ah homosexual?" To which the queen drawls drily, "How do you like being ah whatever it is you are?"

Regelson continued:

> The Two Cultures in confrontation. The middle-class liberal, challenged today on many fronts, finds his last remaining fixed value, his heterosexuality, called into question. The theater . . . recalls the strategies he uses in dealing with this ultimate threat to his world view.[17]

Heterosexual History: Out of the Shadows

Our brief survey of the heterosexual idea suggests a new hypothesis. Rather than naming a conjunction old as Eve and Adam, heterosexual designates a word and concept, a norm and role, an individual and group identity, a behavior and feeling, and a peculiar sexual-political institution particular to the late nineteenth and twentieth centuries.

Because much stress has been placed here on heterosexuality as word and concept, it seems important to affirm that heterosexuality (and homosexuality) came into existence before it was named and thought about. The formulation of the heterosexual idea did not create a heterosexual experience or behavior; to suggest otherwise would be to ascribe determining power to labels and concepts. But the titling and envisioning of heterosexuality did play an important role in consolidating the construction of the heterosexual's social existence. Before the wide use of the word "heterosexual," I suggest, women and men did not mutually lust with the same profound, sure sense of normalcy that followed the distribution of "heterosexual" as universal sanctifier.

According to this proposal, women and men make their own sexual histories. But they do not produce their sex lives just as they please. They make their sexualities within a particular mode of organization given by the past and altered by their changing desire, their present power and activity, and their vision of a better world. That hypothesis suggests a number of good reasons for the immediate inauguration of research on a historically specific heterosexuality.

The study of the history of the heterosexual experience will forward a great intellectual struggle still in its early stages. This is the fight to pull heterosexuality, homosexuality, and all the sexualities out of the realm of nature and biology [and] into the realm of the social and historical. Feminists have explained to us that anatomy does not determine our gender destinies (our masculinities and femininities). But we've only recently begun to consider that *biology does not settle our erotic fates.* The common notion that biology determines the object of sexual desire, or that physiology and society together cause sexual orientation, are determinisms that deny the break existing between our bodies and situations and our desiring. Just as the biology of our hearing organs will never tell us why we take pleasure in Bach or delight in Dixieland, our female or male anatomies, hormones, and genes will never tell us why we yearn for women, men, both, other, or none. That is because desiring is a self-generated project of individuals within particular historical cultures. Heterosexual history can help us see the place of values and judgments in the construction of our own and others' pleasures, and to see how our erotic tastes—our aesthetics of the flesh—are socially institutionalized through the struggle of individuals and classes.

The study of heterosexuality in time will also help us to recognize the *vast historical diversity of sexual emotions and behaviors*—a variety that challenges the monolithic heterosexual hypothesis. John D'Emilio and Estelle Freedman's

Intimate Matters: A History of Sexuality in America refers in passing to numerous substantial changes in sexual activity and feeling: for example, the widespread use of contraceptives in the nineteenth century, the twentieth-century incitement of the female orgasm, and the recent sexual conduct changes by gay men in response to the AIDS epidemic. It's now a commonplace of family history that people in particular classes feel and behave in substantially different ways under different historical conditions.[18] Only when we stop assuming an invariable essence of heterosexuality will we begin the research to reveal the full variety of sexual emotions and behaviors.

The historical study of the heterosexual experience can help us *understand the erotic relationships of women and men in terms of their changing modes of social organization.* Such modal analysis actually characterizes a sex history well underway.[19] This suggests that the eros-gender-procreation system (the social ordering of lust, femininity and masculinity, and baby-making) has been linked closely to a society's particular organization of power and production. To understand the subtle history of heterosexuality we need to look carefully at correlations between (1) society's organization of eros and pleasure; (2) its mode of engendering persons as feminine or masculine (its making of women and men); (3) its ordering of human reproduction; and (4) its dominant political economy. This General Theory of Sexual Relativity proposes that substantial historical changes in the social organization of eros, gender, and procreation have basically altered the activity and experience of human beings within those modes.[20]

A historical view locates heterosexuality and homosexuality in time, helping us distance ourselves from them. This distancing can help us formulate new questions that clarify our long-range sexual-political goals: What has been and is the social function of sexual categorizing? Whose interests have been served by the division of the world into heterosexual and homosexual? Do we dare not draw a line between those two erotic species? Is some sexual naming socially necessary? Would human freedom be enhanced if the sex-biology of our partners in lust was of no particular concern, and had no name? In what kind of society could we all more freely explore our desire and our flesh?

As we move [into the year 2000], a new sense of the historical making of the heterosexual and homosexual suggests that these are ways of feeling, acting, and being with each other that we can together unmake and radically remake according to our present desire, power, and our vision of a future political-economy of pleasure.

REFERENCES

1. Barbara Welter, "The Cult of True Womanhood: 1820–1860," *American Quarterly*, vol. 18 (Summer 1966); Welter's analysis is extended here to include True Men and True Love.

2. See, for example, Catherine Gallagher and Thomas Laqueur, eds., "The Making of the Modern Body: Sexuality and Society in the Nineteenth Century," *Representations*, no. 14 (Spring 1986) (republished, Berkeley: University of California Press, 1987).

3. Dr. James G. Kiernan, "Responsibility in Sexual Perversion," *Chicago Medical Recorder*, vol. 3 (May 1892), pp. 185–210.

4. R. von Krafft-Ebing, *Psychopathia Sexualis, with Especial Reference to Contrary Sexual Instinct: A Medico-Legal Study*, trans. Charles Gilbert Chaddock (Philadelphia: F. A. Davis, 1892), from the 7th and revised German ed. Preface, November 1892.

5. For the standardization of gender see Lewis Terman and C. C. Miles, *Sex and Personality, Studies in Femininity and Masculinity* (New York: McGraw Hill, 1936). For the standardization of intelligence see Lewis Terman, *Stanford-Binet Intelligence Scale* (Boston: Houghton Mifflin, 1916). For the standardization of work, see "scientific management" and "Taylorism" in Harry Braverman, *Labor and Monopoly Capital: The Degradation of Work in the Twentieth Century* (New York: Monthly Review Press, 1974).

6. See D'Emilio and Freedman, *Intimate Matters*, pp. 194–201, 231, 241, 295–96; Ellen Kay Trimberger, "Feminism, Men, and Modern Love: Greenwich Village, 1900–1925," in *Powers of Desire: The Politics of Sexuality*, ed. Ann Snitow, Christine Stansell, Sharon Thompson (New York: Monthly Review Press, 1983), pp. 131–52; Kathy Peiss, "'Charity Girls' and City Pleasures: Historical Notes on Working Class Sexuality, 1880–1920," in *Powers of Desire*, pp. 74–87; and Mary P. Ryan, "The Sexy Saleslady: Psychology, Heterosexuality, and Consumption in the Twentieth Century," in her *Womanhood in America*, 2nd ed. (New York: Franklin Watts, 1979), pp. 151–82.

7. [Rev. Charles Parkhurst], "Woman. Calls Them Andromaniacs. Dr. Parkhurst So Characterizes Certain Women Who Passionately Ape Everything That Is Mannish. Woman Divinely Preferred. Her Supremacy Lies in Her Womanliness, and She Should Make the Most of It—Her Sphere of Best Usefulness the Home," *The New York Times*, May 23, 1897, p. 16:1.

8. See Lisa Duggan, "The Social Enforcement of Heterosexuality and Lesbian Resistance in the 1920s," in *Class, Race, and Sex: The Dynamics of Control*, ed. Amy Swerdlow and Hanah Lessinger (Boston: G. K. Hall, 1983), pp. 75–92; Rayna Rapp and Ellen Ross, "The Twenties Backlash: Compulsory Heterosexuality, the Consumer Family, and the Waning of Feminism," in *Class, Race, and Sex*; Christina Simmons, "Companionate Marriage and the Lesbian Threat," *Frontiers*, vol. 4, no. 3 (Fall 1979), pp. 54–59; and Lillian Faderman, *Surpassing the Love of Men* (New York: William Morrow, 1981).

9. Louis Kronenberger, review of André Gide, *The Immoralist*, *New York Times Book Review*, April 20, 1930, p. 9.

10. Henry James Forman, review of Floyd Dell, *Love in the Machine Age* (New York: Farrar & Rinehart), *New York Times Book Review*, September 14, 1930, p. 9.

11. Ferdinand Lundberg and Dr. Marnia F. Farnham, *Modern Woman: The Lost Sex* (New York: Harper, 1947).

12. Dr. Howard A. Rusk, *New York Times Book Review*, January 4, 1948, p. 3.

13. Alfred Kinsey, Wardell B. Pomeroy, Clyde E. Martin, *Sexual Behavior in the Human Male* (Philadelphia: W. B. Saunders, 1948), pp. 199–200.

14. Kinsey, *Sexual Behavior*, pp. 637, 639.

15. See Steven Epstein, "Gay Politics, Ethnic Identity: The Limits of Social Constructionism," *Socialist Review* 93/93 (1987), pp. 9–54.

16. Gore Vidal, "Someone to Laugh at the Squares With" [Tennessee Williams], *New York Review of Books*, June 13, 1985; reprinted in his *At Home: Essays, 1982–1988* (New York: Random House, 1988), p. 48.

17. Rosalyn Regelson, "Up the Camp Staircase," *The New York Times*, March 3, 1968, Section II, p. 1:5.

18. D'Emilio and Freedman, *Intimate Matters*, pp. 57–63, 268, 356.

19. Ryan, *Womanhood*; John D'Emilio, "Capitalism and Gay Identity," in *Powers of Desire*, pp. 100–13; Jeffrey Weeks, *Coming Out: Homosexual Politics in Britain from the Nineteenth Century to the Present* (London: Quartet Books, 1977); D'Emilio and Freedman, *Intimate Matters*; Katz, "Early Colonial Exploration, Agriculture, and Commerce: The Age of Sodomitical Sin, 1607–1740," *Gay/Lesbian Almanac*, pp. 23–65.

20. This tripartite system is intended as a revision of Gayle Rubin's pioneering work on the social-historical orgainization of eros and gender. See "The Traffic in Women: Notes on the Political-Economy of Sex," in *Toward an Anthropology of Women*, ed. Rayna R. Reiter (New York: Monthly Review Press, 1975), pp. 157–210, and "Thinking Sex: Notes for a Radical Theory of the Politics of Sexuality," in *Pleasure and Danger: Exploring Female Sexuality*, ed. Carole S. Vance (Boston: Routledge & Kegan Paul, 1984), pp. 267–329.

8

Masculinity as Homophobia
Fear, Shame, and Silence in the Construction of Gender Identity

Michael S. Kimmel

We think of manhood as eternal, a timeless essence that resides deep in the heart of every man. We think of manhood as a thing, a quality that one either has or doesn't have. We think of manhood as innate, residing in the particular biological composition of the human male, the result of androgens or the possession of a penis. We think of manhood as a transcendent tangible property that each man

From *Theorizing Masculinities*, Harry Brod and Michael Kaufman, eds., pp. 119–141. Copyright © 1994. Reprinted by permission of Sage Publications, Inc. I am grateful to Tim Beneke, Harry Brod, Michael Kaufman, Iona Mara-Drita, and Lillian Rubin for comments on earlier versions of the chapter.

must manifest in the world, the reward presented with great ceremony to a young novice by his elders for having successfully competed an arduous initiation ritual. . . .

In this chapter, I view masculinity as a constantly changing collection of meanings that we construct through our relationships with ourselves, with each other, and with our world. Manhood is neither static nor timeless; it is historical. Manhood is not the manifestation of an inner essence; it is socially constructed. Manhood does not bubble up to consciousness from our biological makeup; it is created in culture. Manhood means different things at different times to different people. We come to know what it means to be a man in our culture by setting our definitions in opposition to a set of "others"—racial minorities, sexual minorities, and, above all, women. . . .

Classical Social Theory as a Hidden Meditation of Manhood

Begin this inquiry by looking at four passages from that set of texts commonly called classical social and political theory. You will, no doubt, recognize them, but I invite you to recall the way they were discussed in your undergraduate or graduate courses in theory:

> The bourgeoisie cannot exist without constantly revolutionizing the instruments of production, and thereby the relations of production, and with them the whole relations of society. Conservation of the old modes of production in unaltered form, was, on the contrary, the first condition of existence for all earlier industrial classes. Constant revolutionizing of production, uninterrupted disturbance of all social conditions, everlasting uncertainty and agitation distinguish the bourgeois epoch from all earlier ones. All fixed, fast-frozen relations, with their train of ancient and venerable prejudices and opinions are swept away, all new-formed ones become antiquated before they can ossify. All that is solid melts into air, all that is holy is profaned, and man is at last compelled to face with sober senses, his real conditions of life, and his relation with his kind. (Marx & Engels, 1848/1964)

> An American will build a house in which to pass his old age and sell it before the roof is on; he will plant a garden and rent it just as the trees are coming into bearing; he will clear a field and leave others to reap the harvest; he will take up a profession and leave it, settle in one place and soon go off elsewhere with his changing desires. . . . At first sight there is something astonishing in this spectacle of so many lucky men restless in the midst of abundance. But it is a spectacle as old as the world; all that is new is to see a whole people performing in it. (Tocqueville, 1835/1967)

> Where the fulfillment of the calling cannot directly be related to the highest spiritual and cultural values, or when, on the other hand, it need not be felt simply as economic compulsion, the individual generally abandons the attempt to justify it at all. In the field of its highest development, in the United States, the pursuit of

wealth, stripped of its religious and ethical meaning, tends to become associated with purely mundane passions, which often actually give it the character of sport. (Weber, 1905/1966)

We are warned by a proverb against serving two masters at the same time. The poor ego has things even worse: it serves three severe masters and does what it can to bring their claims and demands into harmony with one another. These claims are always divergent and often seem incompatible. No wonder that the ego so often fails in its task. Its three tyrannical masters are the external world, the super ego and the id. . . . It feels hemmed in on three sides, threatened by three kinds of danger, to which, if it is hard pressed, it reacts by generating anxiety. . . . Thus the ego, driven by the id, confined by the super ego, repulsed by reality, struggles to master its economic task of bringing about harmony among the forces and influences working in and upon it; and we can understand how it is that so often we cannot suppress a cry: "Life is not easy!" (Freud, "The Dissection of the Psychical Personality," 1933/1966)

If your social science training was anything like mine, these were offered as descriptions of the bourgeoisie under capitalism, of individuals in democratic societies, of the fate of the Protestant work ethic under the ever rationalizing spirit of capitalism, or of the arduous task of the autonomous ego in psychological development. Did anyone ever mention that in all four cases the theorists were describing men? Not just "man" as in generic mankind, but a particular type of masculinity, a definition of manhood that derives its identity from participation in the marketplace, from interaction with other men in that marketplace—in short, a model of masculinity for whom identity is based on homosocial competition? Three years before Tocqueville found Americans "restless in the midst of abundance," Senator Henry Clay had called the United States "a nation of self-made men."

What does it mean to be "self-made"? What are the consequences of self-making for the individual man, for other men, for women? It is this notion of manhood—rooted in the sphere of production, the public arena, a masculinity grounded not in land ownership or in artisanal republican virtue but in successful participation in marketplace competition—this has been the defining notion of American manhood. Masculinity must be proved, and no sooner is it proved that it is again questioned and must be proved again—constant, relentless, unachievable, and ultimately the quest for proof becomes so meaningless than it takes on the characteristic, as Weber said, of a sport. He who has the most toys when he dies wins. . . .

Masculinity as History and the History of Masculinity

The idea of masculinity expressed in the previous extracts in the product of historical shifts in the grounds on which men rooted their sense of themselves as men. To argue that cultural definitions of gender identity are historically specific goes only so far; we have to specify exactly what those models were. In my historical inquiry into the development of these models of manhood[1] I chart the fate of two models for manhood at the turn of the 19th century and the emergence of a third in the first few decades of that century.

In the late 18th and early 19th centuries, two models of manhood prevailed. The *Genteel Patriarch* derived his identity from landownership. Supervising his estate, he was refined, elegant, and given to casual sensuousness. He was a doting and devoted father, who spent much of his time supervising the estate and with his family. Think of George Washington or Thomas Jefferson as examples. By contrast, the *Heroic Artisan* embodied the physical strength and republican virtue that Jefferson observed in the yeoman farmer, independent urban craftsman, or shopkeeper. Also a devoted father, the Heroic Artisan taught his son his craft, bringing him through ritual apprenticeship to status as master craftsman. Economically autonomous, the Heroic Artisan also cherished his democratic community, delighting in the participatory democracy of the town meeting. Think of Paul Revere at his pewter shop, shirtsleeves rolled up, a leather apron—a man who took pride in his work.

Heroic Artisans and Genteel Patriarchs lived in casual accord, in part because their gender ideals were complementary (both supported participatory democracy and individual autonomy, although patriarchs tended to support more powerful state machineries and also supported slavery) and because they rarely saw one another: Artisans were decidedly urban and the Genteel Patriarchs ruled their rural estates. By the 1830s, though, this casual symbiosis was shattered by the emergence of a new vision of masculinity, *Marketplace Manhood*.

Marketplace Man derived his identity entirely from his success in the capitalist marketplace, as he accumulated wealth, power, status. He was the urban entrepreneur, the businessman. Restless, agitated, and anxious, Marketplace Man was an absentee landlord at home and an absent father with his children, devoting himself to his work in an increasingly homosocial environment—a male-only world in which he pits himself against other men. His efforts at self-making transform the political and economic spheres, casting aside the Genteel Patriarch as an anachronistic feminized dandy—sweet, but ineffective and outmoded, and transforming the Heroic Artisan into a dispossessed proletarian, a wage slave.

As Tocqueville would have seen it, the coexistence of the Genteel Patriarch and the Heroic Artisan embodied the fusion of liberty and equality. Genteel Patriarchy was the manhood of the traditional aristocracy, the class that embodied the virtue of liberty. The Heroic Artisan embodied democratic community, the solidarity of the urban shopkeeper or craftsman. Liberty and democracy, the patriarch and the artisan, could, and did, coexist. But Marketplace Man is capitalist man, and he makes both freedom and equality problematic, eliminating the freedom of the aristocracy and proletarianizing the equality of the artisan. In one sense, American history has been an effort to restore, retrieve, or reconstitute the virtues of Genteel Patriarchy and Heroic Artisanate as they were being transformed in the capitalist marketplace.

Marketplace Manhood was a manhood that required proof, and that required the acquisition of tangible goods as evidence of success. It reconstituted itself by the exclusion of "others"—women, nonwhite men, nonnative-born men, homosexual men—and by terrified flight into a pristine mythic homosocial Eden where men could, at last, be real men among other men. The story of the ways in which Marketplace Man becomes American Everyman is a tragic tale, a tale of striving to live up to impossible ideals of success leading to chronic terrors of emasculation, emotional emptiness, and a gendered rage that leave a wide swath of destruction in its wake.

Masculinities as Power Relations

Marketplace Masculinity describes the normative definition of American masculinity. It describes his characteristics—aggression, competition, anxiety—and the arena in which those characteristics are deployed—the public sphere, the marketplace. If the marketplace is the arena in which manhood is tested and proved, it is a gendered arena, in which tensions between women and men and tensions among different groups of men are weighted with meaning. These tensions suggest that cultural definitions of gender are played out in a contested terrain and are themselves power relations.

All masculinities are not created equal; or rather, we are all *created* equal, but any hypothetical equality evaporates quickly because our definitions of masculinity are not equally valued in our society. One definition of manhood continues to remain the standard against which other forms of manhood are measured and evaluated. Within the dominant culture, the masculinity that defines white, middle class, early middle-aged, heterosexual men is the masculinity that sets the standards for other men, against which other men are measured and, more often than not, found wanting. Sociologist Erving Goffman (1963) wrote that in America, there is only "one complete, unblushing male":

> a young, married, white, urban, northern heterosexual, Protestant father of college education, fully employed, of good complexion, weight and height, and a recent record in sports. Every American male tends to look out upon the world from this perspective. . . . Any male who fails to qualify in any one of these ways is likely to view himself . . . as unworthy, incomplete, and inferior. (p. 128)

This is the definition that we will call "hegemonic" masculinity, the image of masculinity of those men who hold power, which has become the standard in psychological evaluations, sociological research, and self-help and advice literature for teaching young men to become "real men" (Connell, 1987). The hegemonic definition of manhood is a man *in* power, a man *with* power, and a man *of* power. We equate manhood with being strong, successful, capable, reliable, in control. The very definitions of manhood we have developed in our culture maintain the power that some men have over other men and that men have over women.

Our culture's definition of masculinity is thus several stories at once. It is about the individual man's quest to accumulate those cultural symbols that denote manhood, signs that he has in fact achieved it. It is about those standards being used against women to prevent their inclusion in public life and their consignment to a devalued private sphere. It is about the differential access that different types of men have to those cultural resources that confer manhood and about how each of these groups then develop their own modifications to preserve and claim their manhood. It is about the power of these definitions themselves to serve to maintain the real-life power that men have over women and that some men have over other men.

This definition of manhood has been summarized cleverly by psychologist Robert Brannon (1976) into four succinct phrases:

1. "No Sissy Stuff!" One may never do anything that even remotely suggests femininity. Masculinity is the relentless repudiation of the feminine.
2. "Be a Big Wheel." Masculinity is measured by power, success, wealth, and status. As the current saying goes, "He who has the most toys when he dies wins."
3. "Be a Sturdy Oak." Masculinity depends on remaining calm and reliable in a crisis, holding emotions in check. In fact, proving you're a man depends on never showing your emotions at all. Boys don't cry.
4. "Give 'em Hell." Exude an aura of manly daring and aggression. Go for it. Take risks.

These rules contain the elements of the definition against which virtually all American men are measured. Failure to embody these rules, to affirm the power of the rules and one's achievement of them is a source of men's confusion and pain. Such a model is, of course, unrealizable for any man. But we keep trying, valiantly and vainly, to measure up. American masculinity is a relentless test.[2] The chief test is contained in the first rule. Whatever the variations by race, class, age, ethnicity, or sexual orientation, being a man means "not being like women." This notion of anti-femininity lies at the heart of contemporary and historical conceptions of manhood, so that masculinity is defined more by what one is not rather than who one is.

Masculinity as the Flight From the Feminine

Historically and developmentally, masculinity has been defined as the flight from women, the repudiation of femininity. . . .

The drive to repudiate the mother as the indication of the acquisition of masculine gender identity has three consequences for the young boy. First, he pushes away his real mother, and with her the traits of nurturance, compassion, and tenderness she may have embodied. Second, he suppresses those traits in himself, because they will reveal his incomplete separation from mother. His life becomes a lifelong project to demonstrate that he possesses none of his mother's traits. Masculine identity is born in the renunciation of the feminine, not in the direct affirmation of the masculine, which leaves masculine gender identity tenuous and fragile.

Third, as if to demonstrate the accomplishment of these first two tasks, the boy also learns to devalue all women in his society, as the living embodiments of those traits in himself he has learned to despise. Whether or not he was aware of it, Freud also described the origins of sexism—the systematic devaluation of women—in the desperate efforts of the boy to separate from mother. We may *want* "a girl just like the girl that married dear old Dad," as the popular song had it, but we certainly don't want to *be like* her.

This chronic uncertainty about gender identity helps us understand several obsessive behaviors. Take, for example, the continuing problem of the school-yard bully. Parents remind us that the bully is the *least* secure about his manhood, and so he is constantly trying to prove it. But he "proves" it by choosing opponents he is absolutely certain he can defeat; thus the standard taunt to a bully is to "pick on someone your own size." He can't, though, and after defeating a smaller and weaker opponent, which he was sure would prove his manhood, he is left with the empty gnawing feeling that he has not proved it after all, and he must find another opponent, again one smaller and weaker, that he can again defeat to prove it to himself.[3] . . .

When does it end? Never. To admit weakness, to admit frailty or fragility, is to be seen as a wimp, a sissy, not a real man. But seen by whom?

Masculinity as a Homosocial Enactment

Other men: We are under the constant careful scrutiny of other men. Other men watch us, rank us, grant our acceptance into the realm of manhood. Manhood is demonstrated for other men's approval. It is other men who evaluate the performance. Literary critic David Leverenz (1991) argues that "ideologies of manhood have functioned primarily in relation to the gaze of male peers and male authority" (p. 769). Think of how men boast to one another of their accomplishments—from their latest sexual conquest to the size of the fish they caught—and how we constantly parade the markers of manhood—wealth, power, status, sexy women—in front of other men, desperate for their approval.

That men prove their manhood in the eyes of other men is both a consequence of sexism and one of its chief props. "Women have, in men's minds, such a low place on the social ladder of this country that it's useless to define yourself in terms of a woman," noted playwright David Mamet. "What men need is men's approval." Women become a kind of currency that men use to improve their ranking on the masculine social scale. (Even those moments of heroic conquest of women carry, I believe, a current of homosocial evaluation.) Masculinity is a *homosocial* enactment. We test ourselves, perform heroic feats, take enormous risks, all because we want other men to grant us our manhood. . . .

Masculinity as Homophobia

. . . That nightmare from which we never seem to awaken is that those other men will see that sense of inadequacy, they will see that in our own eyes we are not who we are pretending to be. What we call masculinity is often a hedge against being revealed as a fraud, an exaggerated set of activities that keep others from seeing through us, and a frenzied effort to keep at bay those fears within ourselves. Our real fear "is not fear of women but of being ashamed or humiliated in front of other men, or being dominated by stronger men" (Leverenz, 1986, p. 451).

This, then, is the great secret of American manhood: *We are afraid of other men.* Homophobia is a central organizing principle of our cultural definition of manhood. Homophobia is more than the irrational fear of gay men, more than the fear that we might be perceived as gay. "The word 'faggot' has nothing to do with homosexual experience or even with fears of homosexuals," writes David Leverenz (1986). "It comes out of the depths of manhood: a label of ultimate contempt for anyone who seems sissy, untough, uncool" (p. 455). Homophobia is the fear that other men will unmask us, emasculate us, reveal to us and the world that we do not measure up, that we are not real men. We are afraid to let other men see that fear. Fear makes us ashamed, because the recognition of fear in ourselves is proof to ourselves that we are not as manly as we pretend, that we are, like the young man in a poem by Yeats, "one that ruffles in a manly pose for all his timid heart." Our fear is the fear of humiliation. We are ashamed to be afraid.

Shame leads to silence—the silences that keep other people believing that we actually approve of the things that are done to women, to minorities, to gays and lesbians in our culture. The frightened silence as we scurry past a woman being hassled by men on the street. That furtive silence when men make sexist or racist jokes in a bar. That clammy-handed silence when guys in the office make gay-bashing jokes. Our fears are the sources of our silences, and men's silence is what keeps the system running. This might help to explain why women often complain that their male friends or partners are often so understanding when they are alone and yet laugh at sexist jokes or even make those jokes themselves when they are out with a group.

The fear of being seen as a sissy dominates the cultural definitions of manhood. It starts so early. "Boys among boys are ashamed to be unmanly," wrote one educator in 1871 (cited in Rotundo, 1993, p. 264). I have a standing bet with a friend that I can walk onto any playground in America where 6-year-old boys are happily playing and by asking one question, I can provoke a fight. That question is simple: "Who's a sissy around here?" Once posed, the challenge is made. One of two things is likely to happen. One boy will accuse another of being a sissy, to which that boy will respond that he is not a sissy, that the first boy is. They may have to fight it out to see who's lying. Or a whole group of boys will surround one boy and all shout "He is! He is!" That boy will either burst into tears and run home crying, disgraced, or he will have to take on several boys at once, to prove that he's not a sissy. (And what will his father or older brothers tell him if he chooses to run home crying?) It will be some time before he regains any sense of self-respect.

Violence is often the single most evident marker of manhood. Rather it is the willingness to fight, the desire to fight. The origin of our expression that one has a chip on one's shoulder lies in the practice of an adolescent boy in the country or small town at the turn of the century, who would literally walk around with a chip of wood balanced on his shoulder—a signal of his readiness to fight with anyone who would take the initiative of knocking the chip off (see Gorer, 1964, p. 38; Mead, 1965).

As adolescents, we learn that our peers are a kind of gender police, constantly threatening to unmask us as feminine, as sissies. One of the favorite tricks when I was an adolescent was to ask a boy to look at his fingernails. If he held his palm toward his face and curled his fingers back to see them, he passed the test. He'd look at his nails "like a man." But if he held the back of his hand away from his face, and looked at his fingernails with arm outstretched, he was immediately ridiculed as sissy.

As young men we are constantly riding those gender boundaries, checking the fences we have constructed on the perimeter, making sure that nothing even remotely feminine might show through. The possibilities of being unmasked are everywhere. Even the most seemingly insignificant thing can pose a threat or activate that haunting terror. On the day the students in my course "Sociology of Men and Masculinities" were scheduled to discuss homophobia and male-male friendships, one student provided a touching illustration. Noting that it was a beautiful day, the first day of spring after a brutal northeast winter, he decided to wear shorts to class. "I had this really nice pair of new Madras shorts," he commented. "But then I thought to myself, these shorts have lavender and pink in them. Today's class topic is homophobia. Maybe today is not the best day to wear these shorts."

Our efforts to maintain a manly front cover everything we do. What we wear. How we talk. How we walk. What we eat. Every mannerism, every movement contains a coded gender language. Think, for example, of how you would answer the question: How do you "know" if a man is homosexual? When I ask this question in classes or workshops, respondents invariably provide a pretty standard list of stereotypically effeminate behaviors. He walks a certain way, talks a certain way, acts a certain way. He's very emotional; he shows his feelings. One woman commented that she "knows" a man is gay if he really cares about her; another said she knows he's gay if he shows no interest in her, if he leaves her alone.

Now alter the question and imagine what heterosexual men do to make sure no one could possibly get the "wrong idea" about them. Responses typically refer to the original stereotypes, this time as a set of negative rules about behavior. Never dress that way. Never talk or walk that way. Never show your feelings or get emotional. Always be prepared to demonstrate sexual interest in women that you meet, so it is impossible for any woman to get the wrong idea about you. In this sense, homophobia, the fear of being perceived as gay, as not a real man, keeps men exaggerating all the traditional rules of masculinity, including sexual predation with women. Homophobia and sexism go hand in hand. . . .

Homophobia as a Cause of Sexism, Heterosexism, and Racism

Homophobia is intimately interwoven with both sexism and racism. The fear—sometimes conscious, sometimes not—that others might perceive us as homosexual propels men to enact all manner of exaggerated masculine behaviors and attitudes to make sure that no one could possibly get the wrong idea about us. One of the centerpieces of that exaggerated masculinity is putting women down, both by excluding them from the public sphere and by the quotidian put-downs in speech and behaviors that organize the daily life of the American man. Women and gay men become the "other" against which heterosexual men project their identities, against whom they stack the decks so as to compete in a situation in which they will always win, so that by suppressing them, men can stake a claim for their own manhood. Women threaten emasculation by representing the home, workplace, and familial responsibility, the negation of fun. Gay men have historically played the role of the consummate sissy in the American popular mind because homosexuality is seen as an inversion of normal gender development. There have been other "others." Through American history, various groups have represented the sissy, the non-men against whom American men played out their definitions of manhood, often with vicious results. In fact, these changing groups provide an interesting lesson in American historical development.

At the turn of the 19th century, it was Europeans and children who provided the contrast for American men. The "true American was vigorous, manly, and direct, not effete and corrupt like the supposed Europeans," writes Rupert Wilkinson (1986). "He was plain rather than ornamented, rugged rather than luxury seeking, a liberty loving common man or natural gentleman rather than an aristocratic oppressor or servile minion" (p. 96). The "real man" of the early 19th century was neither noble nor serf. By the middle of the century, black slaves had replaced the effete nobleman. Slaves were seen as dependent, helpless men, incapable of defending their women and children, and therefore less than manly. Native Americans were cast as foolish and naive children, so they could be infantalized as the "Red Children of the Great White Father" and therefore excluded from full manhood.

By the end of the century, new European immigrants were also added to the list of the unreal men, especially the Irish and Italians, who were seen as too passionate and emotionally volatile to remain controlled sturdy oaks, and Jews, who were seen as too bookishly effete and too physically puny to truly measure up. In the mid-20th century, it was also Asians—first the Japanese during the Second World War, and more recently, the Vietnamese during the Vietnam War—who have served as unmanly templates against which American men have hurled their gendered rage. Asian men were seen as small, soft, and effeminate—hardly men at all.

Such a list of "hyphenated" Americans—Italian-, Jewish-, Irish-, African-, Native-, Asian-, gay—composes the majority of American men. So manhood is only possible for a distinct minority, and the definition has been constructed to prevent the others from achieving it. Interestingly, this emasculation of one's enemies has a flip side—and one that is equally gendered. These very groups that have historically been cast as less than manly were also, often simultaneously, cast as hypermasculine, as sexually aggressive, violent rapacious beasts, against whom "civilized" men must take a decisive stand and thereby rescue civilization. Thus black men were depicted as rampaging sexual beasts, women as carnivorously carnal, gay men as sexually insatiable, southern European men as sexually predatory and voracious, and Asian men as vicious and cruel torturers who were immorally disinterested in life itself, willing to sacrifice their entire people for their whims. But whether one saw these groups as effeminate sissies or as brutal savages, the terms with which they were perceived were gendered. These groups become the "others," the screens against which traditional conceptions of manhood were developed. . . .

Power and Powerlessness in the Lives of Men

I have argued that homophobia, men's fear of other men, is the animating condition of the dominant definition of masculinity in America, that the reigning definition of masculinity is a defensive effort to prevent being emasculated. In our efforts to suppress or overcome those fears, the dominant culture exacts a tremendous price from those deemed less than fully manly: women, gay men, nonnative-born men, men of color. This perspective may help clarify a paradox in men's lives, a paradox in which men have virtually all the power and yet do not feel powerful (see Kaufman, 1993).

Manhood is equated with power—over women, over other men. Everywhere we look, we see the institutional expression of that power—in state and national legislatures, on the boards of directors of every major U.S. corporation or law firm, and in every school and hospital administration. . . .

When confronted with the analysis that men have all the power, many men react incredulously. "What do you mean, men have all the power?" they ask. "What are you talking about? My wife bosses me around. My kids boss me around. My boss bosses me around. I have no power at all! I'm completely powerless!"

Men's feelings are not the feelings of the powerful, but of those who see themselves as powerless. These are the feelings that come inevitably from the discontinuity between the social and the psychological, between the aggregate analysis that reveals how men are in power as a group and the psychological fact that they do not feel powerful as individuals. They are the feelings of men who were raised to believe themselves entitled to feel that power, but do not feel it. No wonder many men are frustrated and angry. . . .

Why, then, do American men feel so powerless? Part of the answer is because we've constructed the rules of manhood so that only the tiniest fraction of men come to believe that they are the biggest of wheels, the sturdiest of oaks, the most virulent repudiators of femininity, the most daring and aggressive. We've managed to disempower the overwhelming majority of American men by other means—such as discriminating on the basis of race, class, ethnicity, age, or sexual preference. . . .

Others still rehearse the politics of exclusion, as if by clearing away the playing field of secure gender identity of any that we deem less than manly—women, gay men, nonnative-born men, men of color—middle-class, straight, white men can re-ground their sense of themselves without those haunting fears and that deep shame that they are unmanly and will be exposed by other men. This is the manhood of racism, of sexism, of homophobia. It is the manhood that is so chronically insecure that it trembles at the idea of lifting the ban on gays in the military, that is so threatened by women in the workplace that women become the targets of sexual harassment, that is so deeply frightened of equality that it must ensure that the playing field of male competition remains stacked against all newcomers to the game.

Exclusion and escape have been the dominant methods American men have used to keep their fears of humiliation at bay. The fear of emasculation by other men, of being humiliated, of being seen as a sissy, is the leitmotif in my reading of the history of American manhood. Masculinity has become a relentless test by which we prove to other men, to women, and ultimately to ourselves, that we have successfully mastered the part. The restlessness that men feel today is nothing new in American history; we have been anxious and restless for almost two centuries. Neither exclusion nor escape has ever brought us the relief we've sought, and there is no reason to think that either will solve our problems now. Peace of mind, relief from gender struggle, will come only from a politics of inclusion, not exclusion, from standing up for equality and justice, and not by running away.

NOTES

1. Much of this work is elaborated in *Manhood: The American Quest* (in press).

2. Although I am here discussing only American masculinity, I am aware that others have located this chronic instability and efforts to prove manhood in the particular cultural and economic arrangements of Western society. Calvin, after all, inveighed against the disgrace "for men to become effeminate," and countless other theorists have described the mechanics of manly proof. (see, for example, Seidler, 1994.)

3. Such observations also led journalist Heywood Broun to argue that most of the attacks against feminism came from men who were shorter than 5 ft. 7 in. "The man who, whatever his physical size, feels secure in his own masculinity and in his own relation to life is rarely resentful of the opposite sex" (cited in Symes, 1930, p. 139).

REFERENCES

Brannon, R. (1976). The male sex role—and what it's done for us lately. In R. Brannon & D. David (Eds.), *The forty-nine percent majority* (pp. 1–40). Reading, MA: Addison-Wesley.

Connell, R. W. (1987). *Gender and power*. Stanford, CA: Stanford University Press.

Freud, S. (1933/1966). *New introductory lectures on psychoanalysis* (L. Strachey, Ed.). New York: Norton.

Goffman, E. (1963). *Stigma*. Englewood Cliffs, NJ: Prentice Hall.

Gorer, G. (1964). *The American people: A study in national character*. New York: Norton.

Kaufman, M. (1993). *Cracking the armour: Power and pain in the lives of men*. Toronto: Viking Canada.

Leverenz, D. (1986). Manhood, humiliation and public life: Some stories. *Southwest Review, 71*, Fall.

Leverenz, D. (1991). The last real man in America: From Natty Bumppo to Batman. *American Literary Review, 3*.

Marx, K., & F. Engels. (1848/1964). The communist manifesto. In R. Tucker (Ed.), *The Marx-Engels reader*. New York: Norton.

Mead, M. (1965). *And keep your powder dry*. New York: William Morrow.

Rotundo, E. A. (1993). *American manhood: Transformations in masculinity from the revolution to the modern era*. New York: Basic Books.

Seidler, V. J. (1994). *Unreasonable men: Masculinity and social theory*. New York: Routledge.

Symes, L. (1930). The new masculinism. *Harper's Monthly, 161*, January.

Tocqueville, A. de. (1835/1967). *Democracy in America*. New York: Anchor.

Weber, M. (1905/1966). *The Protestant ethic and the spirit of capitalism*. New York: Charles Scribner's.

Wilkinson, R. (1986). *American tough: The tough-guy tradition and American character*. New York: Harper & Row.

9

Disability and the Justification of Inequality in American History

Douglas C. Baynton

Since the social and political revolutions of the eighteenth century, the trend in western political thought has been to refuse to take for granted inequalities between persons or groups. Differential and unequal treatment has continued, of course, but it has been considered incumbent on modern societies to produce a

From *The New Disability History*, Paul K. Longmore and Lauri Umansky, eds. Copyright © 2000 NYU Press. Reprinted by permission of the publisher.

rational explanation for such treatment. In recent decades, historians and other scholars in the humanities have studied intensely and often challenged the ostensibly rational explanations for inequalities based on identity—in particular, gender, race, and ethnicity. Disability, however, one of the most prevalent justifications for inequality, has rarely been the subject of historical inquiry.

Disability has functioned historically to justify inequality for disabled people themselves, but it has also done so for women and minority groups. That is, not only has it been considered justifiable to treat disabled people unequally, but the *concept* of disability has been used to justify discrimination against other groups by attributing disability to them. Disability was a significant factor in the three great citizenship debates of the nineteenth and early twentieth centuries: women's suffrage, African American freedom and civil rights, and the restriction of immigration. When categories of citizenship were questioned, challenged, and disrupted, disability was called on to clarify and define who deserved, and who was deservedly excluded from, citizenship. Opponents of political and social equality for women cited their supposed physical, intellectual, and psychological flaws, deficits, and deviations from the male norm. These flaws—irrationality, excessive emotionality, physical weakness—are in essence mental, emotional, and physical disabilities, although they are rarely discussed or examined as such. Arguments for racial inequality and immigration restrictions invoked supposed tendencies to feeble-mindedness, mental illness, deafness, blindness, and other disabilities in particular races and ethnic groups. Furthermore, disability figured prominently not just in arguments *for* the inequality of women and minorities but also in arguments *against* those inequalities. Such arguments took the form of vigorous denials that the groups in question actually had these disabilities; they were not disabled, the argument went, and therefore were not proper subjects for discrimination. Rarely have oppressed groups denied that disability is an adequate justification for social and political inequality. Thus, while disabled people can be considered one of the minority groups historically assigned inferior status and subjected to discrimination, disability has functioned for all such groups as a sign of and justification for inferiority. . . .

The metaphor of the natural versus the monstrous was a fundamental way of constructing social reality in Edmund Burke's time. By the late nineteenth and early twentieth centuries, however, the concept of the natural was to a great extent displaced or subsumed by the concept of normality.[1] Since then, normality has been deployed in all aspects of modern life as a means of measuring, categorizing, and managing populations (and resisting such management). Normality is a complex concept, with an etiology that includes the rise of the social sciences, the science of statistics, and industrialization with its need for interchangeable parts and interchangeable workers. It has been used in a remarkable range of contexts and with a bewildering variety of connotations. The natural and the normal both are ways of establishing the universal, unquestionable good and right. Both are also ways of establishing social hierarchies that justify the denial of legitimacy and certain rights to individuals or groups. Both are constituted in large part by being set in opposition to culturally variable notions of disability—just as the natural was meaningful in relation to the monstrous and the deformed, so are the cultural meanings of the normal produced in tandem with disability. . . .[2]

As an evolutionary concept, normality was intimately connected to the western notion of progress. By the mid-nineteenth century, nonwhite races were routinely connected to people with disabilities, both of whom were depicted as evolutionary laggards or throwbacks. As a consequence, the concept of disability, intertwined with the concept of race, wsa also caught up in ideas of evolutionary progress. Physical or mental abnormalities were commonly depicted as instances of atavism, reversions to earlier stages of evolutionary development. Down's syndrome, for example, was called Mongolism by the doctor who first identified it in 1866 because he believed the syndrome to be the result of a biological reversion by Caucasians to the Mongol racial type. Teachers of the deaf at the end of the century spoke of making deaf children more like "normal" people and less like savages by forbidding them the use of sign language, and they opposed deaf marriages with a rhetoric of evolutionary progress and decline. . . .

Disability arguments were prominent in justifications of slavery in the early to mid-nineteenth century and of other forms of unequal relations between white and black Americans after slavery's demise. The most common disability argument for slavery was simply that African Americans lacked sufficient intelligence to participate or compete on an equal basis in society with white Americans. This alleged deficit was sometimes attributed to physical causes, as when an article on the "diseases and physical peculiarities of the negro race" in the *New Orleans Medical and Surgical Journal* helpfully explained, "It is the defective hematosis, or atmospherization of the blood, conjoined with a deficiency of cerebral matter in the cranium, and an excess of nervous matter distributed to the organs of sensation and assimilation, that is the true cause of that debasement of mind, which has rendered the people of Africa unable to take care of themselves." Diseases of blacks were commonly attributed to "inferior organisms and constitutional weaknesses," which were claimed to be among "the most pronounced race characteristics of the American negro." While the supposedly higher intelligence of "mulattos" compared to "pure" blacks was offered as evidence for the superiority of whites, those who argued against "miscegenation" claimed to the contrary that the products of "race-mixing" were themselves less intelligent and less healthy than members of either race in "pure" form.[3] A medical doctor, John Van Evrie of New York, avowed that the "disease and disorganization" in the "abnormal," "blotched, deformed" offspring of this "monstrous" act "could no more exist beyond a given period than any other physical degeneration, no more than tumors, cancers, or other abnormal growths or physical disease can become permanent." Some claimed greater "corporeal vigor" for "mixed offspring" but a deterioration in "moral and intellectual endowments," while still others saw greater intelligence but "frailty," "less stamina," and "inherent physical weakness."[4]

A second line of disability argument was that African Americans, because of their inherent physical and mental weaknesses, were prone to become disabled under conditions of freedom and equality. A New York medical journal reported that deafness was three times more common and blindness twice as common among free blacks in the North compared to slaves in the South. John C. Calhoun, senator from South Carolina and one of the most influential spokesmen for the slave states, thought it a powerful argument in defense of slavery that the "number of deaf and dumb, blind, idiots, and insane, of the negroes in the States that have changed the ancient relation between the races" was seven times higher than in the slave states.[5]

While much has been written about the justification of slavery by religious leaders in the South, more needs to be said about similar justifications by medical doctors. Dr. Samuel Cartwright, in 1851, for example, described two types of mental illness to which African Americans were especially subject. The first, Drapetomania, a condition that caused slaves to run away—"as much a disease of the mind as any other species of mental alienation"—was common among slaves whose masters had "made themselves too familiar with them, treating them as equals." The need to submit to a master was built into the very bodies of African Americans, in whom "we see 'genu flexit' written in the physical structure of his knees, being more flexed or bent, than any other kind of man." The second mental disease peculiar to African Americans, Dysaesthesia Aethiopis—a unique ailment differing "from every other species of mental disease, as it is accompanied with physical signs or lesions of the body"—resulted in a desire to avoid work and generally to cause mischief. It was commonly known to overseers as "rascality." Its cause, similar to that of Drapetomania, was a lack of firm governance, and it was therefore far more common among free blacks than among slaves—indeed, nearly universal among them—although it was a "common occurrence on badly-governed plantations" as well.[6]

Dr. Van Evrie also contributed to this line of thought when he wrote in the 1860s that education of African Americans came "at the expense of the body, shortening the existence" and resulted in bodies "dwarfed or destroyed" by the unnatural exertion. "An 'educated negro,' like a 'free negro,' is a social monstrosity, even more unnatural and repulsive than the latter." He argued further that, since they belonged to a race inferior by nature, *all* blacks were necessarily inferior to (nearly) *all* whites. It occasionally happened that a particular white person might not be superior to all black people because of a condition that "deforms or blights individuals; they may be idiotic, insane, or otherwise incapable." But these unnatural exceptions to the rule were "the result of human vices, crimes, or ignorance, immediate or remote." Only disability might lower a white person in the scale of life to the level of being of a marked race.[7] . . .

Daryl Michael Scott has described how both conservatives and liberals have long used an extensive repertory of "damage imagery" to describe African Americans. Conservatives "operated primarily from within a biological framework and argued for the innate inferiority of people of African descent" in order to justify social and political exclusion. Liberals maintained that social conditions were responsible for black inferiority and used damage imagery to argue for inclusion and rehabilitation; but regardless of their intentions, Scott argues, liberal damage imagery "reinforced the belief system that made whites feel superior in the first place." Both the "contempt and pity" of conservatives and liberals—a phrase that equally well describes historically prevalent attitudes toward disabled people—

framed Americans of African descent as defective. Scott cites the example of Charles S. Johnson, chair of the social science department and later president of Fisk University, who told students in a 1928 speech that "the sociologists classify Negroes with cripples, persons with recognized physical handicaps." Like Johnson, Scott is critical of the fact that "African Americans were often lumped with the 'defective,' 'delinquent,' and dependent classes." This is obviously a bad place to be "lumped." Scott does not ask, however, why that might be the case[8] The attribution of disease or disability to racial minorities has a long history. Yet, while many have pointed out the injustice and perniciousness of attributing these qualities to a racial or ethnic group, little has been written about why these attributions are such powerful weapons for inequality, why they were so furiously denied and condemned by their targets, and what this tells us about our attitudes toward disability.

During the long-running debate over women's suffrage in the nineteenth and early twentieth centuries, one of the rhetorical tactics of suffrage opponents was to point to the physical, intellectual, and psychological flaws of women, their frailty, irrationality, and emotional excesses. By the late nineteenth century, these claims were sometimes expressed in terms of evolutionary progress; like racial and ethnic minorities, women were said to be less evolved than white men, their disabilities a result of lesser evolutionary development. Cynthia Eagle Russett has noted that "women and savages, together with idiots, criminals, and pathological monstrosities [those with congenital disabilities] were a constant source of anxiety to male intellectuals in the late nineteenth century."[9] What all shared was an evolutionary inferiority, the result of arrested development or atavism.

Paralleling the arguments made in defense of slavery, two types of disability argument were used in opposition to women's suffrage: that women had disabilities that made them incapable of using the franchise responsibly, and that because of their frailty women would become disabled if exposed to the rigors of political participation. The American anti-suffragist Grace Goodwin, for example, pointed to the "great temperamental disabilities" with which women had to contend: "woman lacks endurance in things mental. . . . She lacks nervous stability. The suffragists who dismay England are nervesick women." The second line of argument, which was not incompatible with the first and often accompanied it, went beyond the claim that women's flaws made them incapable of exercising equal political and social rights with men to warn that if women were given those rights, disability would surely follow. This argument is most closely identified with Edward Clarke, author of *Sex in Education; or, A Fair Chance for Girls*. Clarke's argument chiefly concerned education for women, though it was often applied to suffrage as well. Clarke maintained that overuse of the brain among young women was in large part responsible for the "numberless pale, weak, neuralgic, dyspeptic, hysterical, menorraghic, dysmenorrhoeic girls and women" of America. The result of excessive education in this country was "bloodless female faces, that suggest consumption, scrofula, anemia, and neuralgia." An appropriate education designed for their frail constitutions would ensure "a future secure from neuralgia, uterine disease, hysteria, and other derangements of the nervous system."[10]

Similarly, Dr. William Warren Potter, addressing the Medical Society of New York in 1891, suggested that many a mother was made invalid by inappropriate education: "her reproductive organs were dwarfed, deformed, weakened, and diseased, by artificial causes imposed upon her during their development."[11] Dr. A. Lapthorn Smith asserted in *Popular Science Monthly* that educated women were increasingly "sick and suffering before marriage and are physically disabled from performing physiological functions in a normal manner." Antisuffragists likewise warned that female participation in politics invariably led to "nervous prostration" and "hysteria," while Dr. Almroth E. Wright noted the "fact that there is mixed up with the woman's movement much mental disorder." A prominent late nineteenth-century neurophysiologist, Charles L. Dana, estimated that enfranchising women would result in a 25 percent increase in insanity among them and "throw into the electorate a mass of voters of delicate nervous stability . . . which might do injury to itself without promoting the community's good." The answer for Clarke, Potter, and others of like mind was special education suited to women's special needs. As with disabled people today, women's social position was treated as a medical problem that necessitated separate and special care. Those who wrote with acknowledged authority on the "woman question" were doctors. As Clarke wrote, the answer to the "problem of woman's sphere . . . must be obtained from physiology, not from ethics or metaphysics."[12] . . .

Disability figured not just in arguments *for* the inequality of women and minorities but also in arguments *against* those inequalities. Suffragists rarely challenged the notion that disability justified political inequality and instead disputed the claim that women suffered from these disabilities. Their arguments took three forms: one, women were not disabled and therefore deserved the vote; two, women were being erroneously and slanderously classed with disabled people, with those who were legitimately denied suffrage; and three, women were not naturally or inherently disabled but were *made* disabled by inequality—suffrage would ameliorate or cure these disabilities. . . .

Ethnicity also has been defined by disability. One of the fundamental imperatives in the initial formation of American immigration policy at the end of the nineteenth century was the exclusion of disabled people. Beyond the targeting of disabled people, the concept of disability was instrumental in crafting the image of the undesirable immigrant. The first major federal immigration law, the Act of 1882, prohibited entry to any "lunatic, idiot, or any person unable to take care of himself or herself without becoming a public charge." Those placed in the categories "lunatic" and "idiot" were automatically excluded. The "public charge" provision was intended to encompass people with disabilities more generally and was left to the examining officer's discretion. The criteria for excluding disabled people were steadily tightened as the eugenics movement and popular fears about the decline of the national stock gathered strength. The Act of 1891 replaced the phrase "*unable* to take care of himself or herself without becoming a public charge," with "*likely* to become a public charge." The 1907 law then denied entry to anyone judged "mentally or physically defective, such mental or physical defect being of a nature which *may affect* the ability of such alien to earn a living." These changes considerably lowered the threshold for exclusion and expanded the latitude of immigration officials to deny entry.[13]

The category of persons *automatically* excluded was also steadily expanded. In 1903, people with epilepsy were added and, in addition to those judged insane, "persons who have been insane within five years previous [or] who have had two or more attacks of insanity at any time previously." This was reduced to one "attack" in the 1917 law; the classification of "constitutional psychopathic inferiority" was also added, which inspection regulations described as including "various unstable individuals on the border line between sanity and insanity . . . and persons with abnormal sex instincts."[14] This was the regulation under which, until recently, gays and lesbians were excluded. One of the significant factors in lifting this ban, along with other forms of discrimination against gays and lesbians, was the decision by the American Psychiatric Association in 1973 to remove homosexuality from its list of mental illnesses. That is, once gays and lesbians were declared not to be disabled, discrimination became less justifiable.

Legislation in 1907 added "imbeciles" and "feeble-minded persons" to the list, in addition to "idiots," and regulations for inspectors directed them to exclude persons with "any mental abnormality whatever . . . which justifies the statement that the alien is mentally defective." These changes encompassed a much larger number of people and again granted officials considerably more discretion to judge the fitness of immigrants for American life. Fiorello H. LaGuardia, who worked his way through law school as an interpreter at Ellis Island, later wrote that "over fifty percent of the deportations for alleged mental disease were unjustified," based as they often were on "ignorance on the part of the immigrants or the doctors and the inability of the doctors to understand the particular immigrant's norm, or standard."[15]

The detection of physical disabilities was a major aspect of the immigration inspector's work. The Regulations for the medical inspection of immigrants in 1917 included a long list of diseases and disabilities that could be cause for exclusion, among them arthritis, asthma, bunions, deafness, deformities, flat feet, heart disease, hernia, hysteria, poor eyesight, poor physical development, spinal curvature, vascular disease of the heart, and varicose veins. . . .

In short, the exclusion of disabled people was central to the laws and the work of the immigration service. As the Commissioner General of Immigration reported in 1907, "The exclusion from this country of the morally, mentally, and physically deficient is the principal object to be accomplished by the immigration laws." Once the laws and procedures limiting the entry of disabled people were firmly established and functioning well, attention turned to limiting the entry of undesirable ethnic groups. Discussion on this topic often began by pointing to the general public agreement that the laws excluding disabled people had been a positive, if insufficient, step. In 1896, for example, Francis Walker noted in the *Atlantic Monthly* that the necessity of "straining out" immigrants who were "deaf, dumb, blind, idiotic, insane, pauper, or criminal" was "now conceded by men of all shades of opinion"; indeed there was a widespread "resentment at the attempt of such persons to impose themselves upon us." As one restrictionist wrote, the need to exclude the disabled was "self evident."[16]

For the more controversial business of defining and excluding undesirable ethnic groups, however, restrictionists found the *concept* of disability to be a powerful tool. That is, while people with disabilities constituted a distinct category of persons unwelcome in the United States, the charge that certain ethnic groups were mentally and physically deficient was instrumental in arguing for *their* exclusion. The belief that discriminating on the basis of disability was justifiable in turn helped justify the creation of immigration quotas based on ethnic origin. The 1924 Immigration Act instituted a national quota system that severely limited the numbers of immigrants from southern and eastern Europe, but long before that, disabilities stood in for nationality. Superintendents of institutions, philanthropists, immigration reformers, and politicians had been warning for decades before 1924 that immigrants were disproportionately prone to be mentally defective—up to half the immigrants from southern and eastern Europe were feebleminded, according to expert opinion.[17] Rhetoric about "the slow-witted Slav," the "neurotic condition of our Jewish immigrants," and, in general, the "degenerate and psychopathic types, which are so conspicuous and numerous among the immigrants," was pervasive in the debate over restriction.[18] The laws forbidding entry to the feebleminded were motivated in part by the desire to limit immigration from inferior nations, and conversely, it was assumed that the 1924 act would reduce the number of feebleminded immigrants. The issues of ethnicity and disability were so intertwined in the immigration debate as to be inseparable. . . .

Historians have scrutinized the attribution of mental and physical inferiority based on race and ethnicity, but only to condemn the slander. With their attention confined to ethnic stereotypes, they have largely ignored what the attribution of disability might also tell us about attitudes toward disabled people. Racial and ethnic prejudice is exposed while prejudice against people with disabilities is passed over as insignificant and understandable. As a prominent advocate of restriction wrote in 1930, "The necessity of the exclusion of the crippled, the blind, those who are likely to become public charges, and, of course, those with a criminal record is self evident."[19] The necessity has been treated as self-evident by historians as well, so much so that even the possibility of discrimination against people with disabilities in immigration law has gone unrecognized. In historical accounts, disability is present but rendered invisible or insignificant. While it is certain that immigration restriction rests in good part on a fear of "strangers in the land," in John Higham's phrase, American immigration restriction at the turn of the century was also clearly fueled by a fear of *defectives* in the land.

Still today, women and other groups who face discrimination on the basis of identity respond angrily to accusations that they might be characterized by physical, mental, or emotional disabilities. Rather than challenging the basic assumptions behind the hierarchy, they instead work to remove themselves from the negatively marked categories—that is, to disassociate themselves from those people who "really are" disabled—knowing that such categorization invites discrimination. For example, a recent proposal in Louisiana to permit pregnant women to use parking spaces reserved for people with mobility impairments was opposed by women's organizations. A lobbyist for the Women's Health Foundation said, "We've spent a long time trying to dispel the myth that pregnancy is a disability, for obvious reasons of discrimination." She added, "I have no problem with it being a courtesy, but not when a legislative mandate provides for pregnancy in the same way as for disabled persons."[20] To be associated with disabled people or with the accommodations accorded disabled people is stigmatizing. . . .

This common strategy for attaining equal rights, which seeks to distance one's own group from imputations of disability and therefore tacitly accepts the idea that disability is a legitimate reason for inequality, is perhaps one of the factors responsible for making discrimination against people with disabilities so persistent and the struggle for disability rights so difficult. . . .

Disability is everywhere in history, once you begin looking for it, but conspicuously absent in the histories we write. When historians do take note of disability, they usually treat it merely as personal tragedy or an insult to be deplored and a label to be denied, rather than as a cultural construct to be questioned and explored. Those of us who specialize in the history of disability, like the early historians of other minority groups, have concentrated on writing histories of disabled people and the institutions and laws associated with disability. This is necessary and exciting work. It is through this work that we are building the case that disability is culturally constructed rather than natural and timeless—that disabled people have a history, and a history worth studying. Disability, however, more than an identity, is a fundamental element in cultural signification and indispensable for *any* historian seeking to make sense of the past. It may well be that all social hierarchies have drawn on culturally constructed and socially sanctioned notions of disability. If this is so, then there is much work to do. It is time to bring disability from the margins to the center of historical inquiry.

NOTES

1. Ian Hacking, *The Taming of Chance* (Cambridge and New York: Cambridge University Press, 1990), 160–66. See also Georges Canguilhem, *The Normal and the Pathological* (New York: Zone Books, 1989); Douglas C. Baynton, *Forbidden Signs: American Culture and the Campaign against Sign Language* (Chicago: University of Chicago Press, 1996), chaps. 5–6.

2. Francois Ewald, "Norms Discipline, and the Law," *Representations* 30 (Spring 1990): 146, 149–150, 154; Lennard Davis, *Enforcing Normalcy: Disability, Deafness, and the Body* (London: Verso, 1995); Baynton, *Forbidden Signs*, chaps. 5 and 6.

3. Samuel A. Cartwright, "Report on the Diseases and Physical Peculiarities of the Negro Race," *New Orleans Medical and Surgical Journal* 7 (May 1851): 693; George M. Fredrickson, *The Black Image in the White Mind* (New York: Harper and Row, 1971), 250–51; J. C. Nott, "The Mulatto a Hybrid," *American Journal of Medical Sciences* (July 1843), quoted in Samuel Forry, "Vital Statistics Furnished by the Sixth Census of the

United States," *New York Journal of Medicine and the Collateral Sciences* 1 (September 1843): 151–53.

4. John H. Van Evrie, *White Supremacy and Negro Subordination, or Negroes a Subordinate Race* (New York: Van Evrie, Horton, & Co., 1868), 153–55; Forry, "Vital Statistics," 159; Paul B. Barringer, *The American Negro: His Past and Future* (Raleigh: Edwards & Broughton, 1900), 10.

5. Cited in Forry, "Vital Statistics," 162–63. John C. Calhoun, "Mr. Calhoun to Mr. Pakenham," in Richard K. Cralle, ed., *The works of John C. Calhoun* (New York: D. Appleton, 1888), 5:337.

6. Cartwright, "Report," 707–10. See also Thomas S. Szasz, "The Sane Slave: A Historical Note on the use of Medical Diagnosis as Justificatory Rhetoric," *American Journal of Psychotherapy* 25 (1971): 228–39.

7. Van Evrie, *White Supremacy*, 121, 181, 221. Van Evrie notes in his preface that the book was completed "about the time of Mr. Lincoln's election" and was therefore originally an argument in favor of the continuation of slavery but presently constituted an argument for its restoration.

8. Daryl Michael Scott, *Contempt and Pity: Social Policy and the Image of the Damaged Black Soul, 1880–1996* (Chapel Hill: University of North Carolina Press, 1997), xi–xvii; 12, 208 n. 52.

9. Cynthia Eagle Russett, *Sexual Science: The Victorian Construction of Womanhood* (Cambridge, Mass.: Harvard University Press, 1989), 63. See also Lois N. Magner, "Darwinism and the Woman Question: The Evolving Views of Charlotte Perkins Gilman," in Joanne Karpinski, *Critical Essays on Charlotte Perkins Gilman* (New York: G. K. Hall, 1992), 119–20.

10. Grace Duffield Goodwin, *Anti-Suffrage: Ten Good Reasons* (New York: Duffield and Co., 1913), 91–92 (in Smithsonian Institution Archives, Collection 60—Warshaw Collection, "Women," Box 3). Edward Clarke, *Sex in Education; or, A Fair Chance for Girls* (1873; reprint, New York: Arno Press, 1972), 18, 22, 62.

11. William Warren Potter, "How Should Girls Be Educated? A Public Health Problem for Mothers, Educators, and Physicians," *Transactions of the Medical Society of the State of New York* (1891): 48, quoted in Martha H. Verbrugge, *Able Bodied Womanhood: Personal Health and Social Change in Nineteenth-Century Boston* (Oxford and New York: Oxford University Press, 1988), 121.

12. A. Lapthorn Smith, "Higher Education of Women and Race Suicide," *Popular Science Monthly* (March 1905), reprinted in Louise Michele Newman, ed., *Men's Ideas/Women's Realities: Popular Science, 1870–1915* (New York: Pergamon Press, 1985), 149; Almroth E. Wright quoted in Mara Mayor, "Fears and Fantasies of the Anti-Suffragists," *Connecticut Review* 7 (April 1974): 67; Charles L. Dana quoted in Jane Jerome Camhi, *Women against Women: American Anti-Suffragism, 1880–1920* (New York: Carlson Publishing Co., 1994), 18; Clarke, *Sex in Education*, 12.

13. *United States Statutes at Large* (Washington, D.C.: Government Printing Office, 1883), 22:214. *United States Statutes at Large* (Washington, D.C.: Government Printing Office, 1891), 26:1084; *United States Statutes at Large* (Washington, D.C.: Government Printing Office, 1907), 34:899. Emphases added.

14. *United States Statutes at Large* (Washington, D.C.: Government Printing Office, 1903), 32:1213; United States Public Health Service, *Regulations Governing the Medical Inspection of Aliens* (Washington, D.C.: Government Printing Office, 1917), 28–29.

15. *Statutes* (1907), 34:899; United States Public Health Service, *Regulations*, 30–31; Fiorello H. LaGuardia, *The Making of an Insurgent: An Autobiography, 1882–1919* (1948; reprint, New York: Capricorn, 1961), 65.

16. U.S. Bureau of Immigration, *Annual Report of the Commissioner of Immigration* (Washington, D.C.: Government Printing Office, 1907), 62; Francis A. Walker, "Restriction of Immigration," *Atlantic Monthly* 77 (June 1896): 822; Ellsworth Eliot, Jr., M.D., "Immigration," in Madison Grant and Charles Steward Davison, eds., *The Alien in Our Midst, or Selling Our Birthright for a Mess of Industrial Pottage* (New York: Galton Publishing Co., 1930), 101.

17. See James W. Trent, Jr., *Inventing the Feeble Mind: A History of Mental Retardation in the United States* (Berkeley: University of California Press, 1994), 166–69.

18. Thomas Wray Grayson, "The Effect of the Modern Immigrant on Our Industrial Centers" in *Medical Problems of Immigration* (Easton, Penn.: American Academy of Medicine, 1913), 103, 107–9.

19. Ellsworth Eliot, Jr., M.D., "Immigration," in Grant and Davison, *Alien in Our Midst,* 101.

20. Heather Salerno, "Mother's Little Dividend: Parking," *Washington Post* (September 16, 1997): A1.

10

Deconstructing the Underclass

Herbert Gans

A Matter of Definition?

Buzzwords for the undeserving poor are hardly new, for in the past the poor have been termed paupers, rabble, white trash, and the dangerous classes. Today, however, Americans do not use such harsh terms in their public discourse, whatever people may say to each other in private. Where possible, euphemisms are employed, and if they are from the academy, so much the better. A string of

From *Journal of the American Planning Association* 271 (Summer 1990). Reprinted by permission of the *Journal of the American Planning Association.*

these became popular in the 1960s; the most famous is Oscar Lewis's anthropological concept *culture of poverty*, a term that became his generation's equivalent of underclass.

When Gunnar Myrdal invented or reinvented the term underclass in his 1962 book *Challenge to Affluence*, he used the word as a purely economic concept, to describe the chronically unemployed, underemployed, and underemployables being created by what we now call the post-industrial economy. He was thinking of people being driven to the margins, or entirely out, of the modern economy, here and elsewhere; but his intellectual and policy concern was with reforming that economy, not with changing or punishing the people who were its victims.

Some other academics, this author included, used the term with Myrdal's definition in the 1960s and 1970s. However, gradually the users shifted from Myrdal's concern with unemployment to poverty, so that by the late 1970s social scientists had begun to identify the underclass with acute or persistent poverty rather than joblessness. Around the same time a very different definition of the underclass also emerged that has become the most widely used, and is also the most dangerous.

That definition has two novel elements. The first is racial, for users of this definition see the underclass as being almost entirely black and Hispanic. Second, it adds a number of behavioral patterns to an economic definition—and almost always these patterns involve behavior thought to be undeserving by the definers.

Different definers concentrate on somewhat different behavior patterns, but most include antisocial or otherwise harmful behavior, such as crime. Many definers also focus on various patterns that are *deviant* or aberrant from what they consider middle class norms, but that in fact are not automatically or always harmful, such as common law marriage. Some definers even measure membership in the underclass by deviant answers to public opinion poll questions. . . .

In the past five years the term's diverse definitions have remained basically unchanged, although the defining attempt itself has occasioned a very lively, often angry, debate among scholars. Many researchers have accepted much or all of the now-dominant behavioral definition; some have argued for a purely economic one, like Myrdal's; and some—this author included—have felt that the term has taken on so many connotations of undeservingness and blameworthiness that it has become hopelessly polluted in meaning, ideological overtone and implications, and should be dropped—with the issues involved studied via other concepts. Basically the debate has involved positions usually associated with the Right and the Left, partisans of the former arguing that the underclass is the product of the unwillingness of the black poor to adhere to the American work ethic, among other cultural deficiencies, and the latter claiming that the underclass is a consequence of the development of the post-industrial economy, which no longer needs the unskilled poor.

The debate has swirled in part around William J. Wilson, the University of Chicago sociologist and author of *The Truly Disadvantaged* (1987), who is arguably the most prominent analyst of the underclass in the 1980s. He focuses entirely on the black underclass and insists that this underclass exists mainly because of large-scale and harmful changes in the labor market, and its resulting spatial concentration as well as the isolation of such areas from the more affluent parts of the black community. One of his early definitions also included a reference to aberrant behavior patterns, although his most recent one, offered in November 1989, centers around the notion of "weak attachment to the labor force," an idea that seems nearly to coincide with Myrdal's, especially since Wilson attributes that weakness to faults in the economy rather than in the jobless.

Wilson's work has inspired a lot of new research, not only about the underclass but about poverty in general, and has made poverty research funding, public and private, available again after a long drought. Meanwhile, various scholars have tried to resolve or reorient the political debate, but without much luck, for eventually the issue always boils down to whether the fault for being poor and the responsibility for change should be assigned more to poor people or more to the economy and the state. At the same time, journalistic use of the so-called behavioral definition of the underclass has increased—and so much so that there is a danger of researchers and policy analysts being carried along by the popularity of this definition of the term in the public discourse. . . .

The Power of Buzzwords and Labels

The behavioral definition of the underclass, which in essence proposes that some very poor people are somehow to be selected for separation from the rest of society and henceforth treated as especially undeserving, harbors many dangers—for their civil liberties and ours, for example, for democracy, and for the integration of society. But the rest of this essay will concentrate on what seem to me to be the major dangers for planners. The *first* danger of the term is its unusual power as a buzzword. It is a handy euphemism; while it seems inoffensively technical on the surface, it hides within it all the moral opprobrium Americans have long felt toward those poor people who have been judged to be undeserving. Even when it is being used by journalists, scholars, and others as a technical term, it carries with it this judgmental baggage. . . .

A *second* and related danger of the term is its use as a racial codeword that subtly hides anti-black and anti-Hispanic feelings. A codeword of this kind fits in with the tolerant public discourse of our time, but it also submerges and may further repress racial—and class—antagonisms that continue to exist, yet are sometimes not expressed until socio-political boiling points are reached. Racial and class codewords—and codewords of any kind—get in the way of planners, however, because the citizenry may read codewords even though planners are writing analytical concepts.

A *third* danger of the term is its flexible character. Given the freedom of definition available in a democracy, anyone can decide, or try to persuade others, that yet additional people should be included in the underclass. For example, it is conceivable that in a city, region, or country with a high unemployment rate, powerless competitors for jobs, such as illegal immigrants or even legal but recently arrived workers, might be added to the list of undeserving people. . . .

The *fourth* danger of the term, a particularly serious one, is that it is a synthesizing notion—or what William Kornblum has more aptly called a lumping one—that covers a number of different people. Like other synthesizing notions that have moved far beyond the researchers' journals, it has also become a stereotype. Stereotypes are lay generalizations that are necessary in a very diversified society, and are useful when they are more or less accurate. When they are not, however, or when they are also judgmental terms, they turn into *labels*, to be used by some people to judge, and usually to stigmatize, other people, often those with less power or prestige. . . .

Insofar as poor people keep up with the labels the rest of society sticks on them, they are aware of the latest one. We do not all know the "street-level" consequences of stigmatizing labels, but they cannot be good. One of the likely, and most dangerous, consequences of labels is that they can become self-fulfilling prophecies. People publicly described as members of the underclass may begin to feel that they *are* members of such a class and are therefore unworthy in a new way. At the least, they now have to fight against yet another threat to their self-respect, not to mention another reason for feeling that society would just as soon have them disappear.

More important perhaps, people included in the underclass are quickly treated accordingly in their relations with the private and public agencies in which, like the rest of us, they are embedded—from workplaces, welfare agencies, and schools to the police and the courts. We know from social research that teachers with negative images of their pupils do not expect them to succeed and thus make sure, often unconsciously, that they do not; likewise, boys from single parent families who are picked up by the police are often thought to be wild and therefore guilty because they are assumed to lack male parental control. We know also that areas associated with the underclass do not get the same level of services as more affluent areas. After all, these populations are not likely to protest. . . .

Social Policy Implications

The remaining dangers are more directly relevant for planners, other policy researchers, and policy makers. The most general one, and the *fifth* on my list, is the term's interference with antipoverty policy and other kinds of planning. This results in part from the fact that underclass is a quite distinctive synthesizing term that lumps together a variety of highly diverse people who need different kinds of help. Categorizing them all with one term, and a buzzword at that, can be disastrous, especially if the political climate should demand that planners formulate a single "underclass policy." Whether one thinks of the poorest of the poor as having problems or as making problems for others, or both, they cannot be planned for with a single policy. For example, educational policies to prevent young people from dropping out of school, especially the few good ones in poor areas, have nothing to do with housing policies for dealing with various kinds of homelessness and the lack of affordable dwellings. Such policies are in turn different from programs to reduce street crime, and from methods of discouraging the very poor from escaping into the addictions of drugs, alcohol, mental illness, or pentecostal religion—which has its own harmful side effects. To be sure, policies relevant to one problem may have positive overlaps for another, but no single policy works for all the problems of the different poverty-stricken populations. Experts who claim one policy can do it all, like education, are simply wrong.

This conclusion applies even to jobs and income grant policies. Although it is certain that all of the problems blamed on the people assigned to the underclass would be helped considerably by policies to reduce sharply persistent joblessness and poverty, *and generally before other programs are implemented,* these policies also have limits. While all poor people need economic help, such help will not alone solve other problems some of them have or make for others. Although the middle class does not mug, neither do *the* poor; only a small number of poor male youngsters and young adults do so. Other causal factors are also involved, and effective antipoverty planning has to be based on some understanding of these factors and how to overcome them. Lumping concepts like the underclass can only hurt this effort.

A related or *sixth* danger stems from the persuasive capacity of concepts or buzzwords. These terms may become so *reified* through their use that people think they represent actual groups or aggregates, and may also begin to believe that being in what is, after all, an imaginary group is a *cause* of the characteristics included in its definition. Sometimes journalists and even scholars—especially those of conservative bent—appear to think that becoming very poor and acting in antisocial or deviant ways is an *effect* of being in the underclass. When the underclass becomes a causal term, however, especially on a widespread basis, planners, as well as politicians and citizens, are in trouble; sooner or later, someone will argue that the only policy solution is to lock up everyone described as an underclass member.

Similar planning problems develop if and when the reification of a term leads to its being assigned *moral* causality. Using notions that blame victims may help the blamers to feel better by blowing off the steam of righteous indignation, but it does not eliminate the problems very poor people have or make. Indeed, those who argue that all people are entirely responsible for what they do sidestep the morally and otherwise crucial issue of determining how much responsibility should be assigned to people who lack resources, who are therefore under unusual stress, and who lack effective choices in many areas of life in which even moderate income people can choose relatively freely. . . .

The *seventh* danger of the term, and one also particularly salient for planners, stems from the way the underclass has been analyzed. As already noted, some researchers have tried to identify underclass neighborhoods. Planners must be especially sensitive to the dangers of the underclass neighborhood notion, because, once statistically defined "neighborhoods," or even sets of adjacent census tracts, are marked with the underclass label, the politicians who make the basic land use decisions in the community may propose a variety of harmful policies, such as moving all of a city's homeless into such areas, or declaring them ripe for urban renewal because of the undeservingness of the population. Recall that this is how much of the federal urban renewal of the 1950s and 1960s was justified. In addition, neighborhood policies generally rest on the assumption that people inside the boundaries of such areas are more homogeneous than they in fact are, and that they remain inside boundaries that are more often nothing but lines on a map. Since very poor people tend to suffer more from public policies than they benefit, and since they have fewer defenses than more affluent people against harmful policies, "neighborhood policies" may hurt more often than they will help.

A related danger—and my *eighth*—stems from William J. Wilson's "concentration and isolation" hypotheses. Wilson argues that the economic difficulties of the very poorest blacks are compounded by the fact that as the better-off blacks move out, the poorest are more and more concentrated, having only other very poor people, and the few institutions that minister to them, as neighbors. This concentration causes social isolation, among other things, Wilson suggests, because the very poor are now isolated from access to the people, job networks, role models, institutions, and other connections that might help them escape poverty.

Wilson's hypotheses, summarized all too briefly here, are now being accepted as dogma by many outside the research community. Fortunately, they are also being tested in a number of places, but until they are shown to be valid, planners should probably go slowly with designing action programs—especially programs to reduce concentration. In the minimal-vacancy housing markets in which virtually all poor people live, such a policy might mean having to find a new, and surely more costly, dwelling unit, or having to double up with relatives, or in some cases being driven into shelters or into the streets. Even if working- and middle-class areas were willing to accept relocatees from deconcentrated areas, a response that seems unlikely, the relocatees could not afford to live in such areas—although many would flourish if they had the money to do so. Meanwhile, the dysfunctions of dispersal may be as bad as those of overconcentration, not because the latter has any virtues, but because, until an effective jobs-and-income-grants program has gone into operation, requiring very poor people to move away from the neighborly support structures they *do* have may deprive them of their only resources.

While it may be risky to attempt deconcentration at this stage, it is worth trying to reduce isolation. One form of isolation, the so-called urban-suburban mismatch between jobless workers residing in cities and available suburban jobs, is already being attacked again, which is all to the good. Perhaps something has been learned from the failures of the 1960s to reduce the mismatch. We must bear in mind, however, that in some or perhaps many cases the physical mismatch is only a cover for class and racial discrimination, and the widespread unwillingness of white suburban employers—and white workers—to have black coworkers. . . .

The *ninth* danger is inherent in the concept of an underclass. While it assumes that the people assigned to the underclass are poor, the term itself sidesteps issues of poverty. It also permits analysts to ignore the dramatic recent increases in certain kinds of poverty, or persisting poverty, and hence the need for resuming effective antipoverty programs. For example, terms like underclass make it easier for conservative researchers to look at the homeless mainly as mentally ill or the victims of rent control, and frees them of any need to discuss the disappearance of jobs, SROs [single-room occupancies], and other low income housing.

Indeed, to the extent that the underclass notion is turned into a synonym for the undeserving poor, the political conditions for reinstituting effective antipoverty policy are removed. If the underclass is undeserving, then the government's responsibility is limited to beefing up the courts and other punitive agencies and institutions that try to isolate the underclass and protect the rest of society from it. Conversely, the moral imperative to help the poor through the provision of jobs and income grants is reduced. Describing the poor as undeserving has long been an effective if immoral short-term approach to tax reduction. . . .

NOTES

I am grateful to Michael Katz for his helpful comments on an earlier draft of this essay.

Kornblum, William. 1984. Lumping the Poor: What *Is* the Underclass. *Dissent*. September: 295–302.

Lewis, Oscar. 1969. The Culture of Poverty. In *On Understanding Poverty*, edited by Daniel P. Moynihan. New York: Basic.

Myrdal, Gunnar. 1962. *The Challenge to Affluence*. New York: Pantheon.

Wilson, William J. 1987. *The Truly Disadvantaged: The Inner City, the Underclass, and Public Policy*. Chicago: University of Chicago Press.

Domination and Subordination

Jean Baker Miller

What do people do to people who are different from them and why? On the individual level, the child grows only via engagement with people very different from her/himself. Thus, the most significant difference is between the adult and the child. At the level of humanity in general, we have seen massive problems around a great variety of differences. But the most basic difference is the one between women and men.

On both levels it is appropriate to pose two questions. When does the engagement of difference stimulate the development and the enhancement of both parties to the engagement? And, conversely, when does such a confrontation with difference have negative effects: When does it lead to great difficulty, deterioration, and distortion and to some of the worst forms of degradation, terror, and violence—both for individuals and for groups—that human beings can experience? It is clear that "mankind" in general, especially in our Western tradition but in some others as well, does not have a very glorious record in this regard.

It is not always clear that in most instances of difference there is also a factor of inequality—inequality of many kinds of resources, but fundamentally of status and power. One useful way to examine the often confusing results of these confrontations with difference is to ask: What happens in situations of inequality? What forces are set in motion? While we will be using the terms "dominant" and "subordinate" in the discussion, it is useful to remember that flesh and blood women and men are involved. Speaking in abstractions sometimes permits us to accept what we might not admit to on a personal level.

Temporary Inequality

Two types of inequality are pertinent for present purposes. The first might be called temporary inequality. Here, the lesser party is *socially* defined as unequal. Major examples are the relationships between parents and children, teachers and

From Jean Baker Miller, *Toward a New Psychology of Women.* © 1976, 1986 by Jean Baker Miller. Reprinted by permission of Beacon Press, Boston.

students, and, possibly, therapists and clients. There are certain assumptions in these relationships which are often not made explicit, nor, in fact, are they carried through. But they are the social structuring of the relationship.

The "superior" party presumably has more of some ability or valuable quality, which she/he is supposed to impart to the "lesser" person. While these abilities vary with the particular relationship, they include emotional maturity, experience in the world, physical skills, a body of knowledge, or the techniques for acquiring certain kinds of knowledge. The superior person is supposed to engage with the lesser in such a way as to bring the lesser member up to full parity; that is, the child is to be helped to become the adult. Such is the overall task of this relationship. The lesser, the child, is to be given to, by the person who presumably has more to give. Although the lesser party often also gives much to the superior, these relationships are *based in service* to the lesser party. That is their *raison d'être.*

It is clear, then, that the paramount goal is to end the relationship; that is, to end the relationship of inequality. The period of disparity is meant to be temporary. People may continue their association as friends, colleagues, or even competitors, but not as "superior" and "lesser." At least this is the goal.

The reality is that we have trouble enough with this sort of relationship. Parents or professional institutions often tip toward serving the needs of the donor instead of those of the lesser party (for example, schools can come to serve teachers or administrators, rather than students). Or the lesser person learns how to be a good "lesser" rather than how to make the journey from lesser to full stature. Overall, we have not found very good ways to carry out the central task: to foster the movement from unequal to equal. In childrearing and education we do not have an adequate theory and practice. Nor do we have concepts that work well in such other unequal so-called "helping" relationships as healing, penology, and rehabilitation. Officially, we say we want to do these things, but we often fail.

We have a great deal of trouble deciding on how many rights "to allow" to the lesser party. We agonize about how much power the lesser party shall have. How much can the lesser person express or act on her or his perceptions when these definitely differ from those of the superior? Above all, there is great difficulty in maintaining the conception of the lesser person *as a person of as much intrinsic worth as the superior.*

A crucial point is that power is a major factor in all of these relationships. But power alone will not suffice. Power exists and it has to be taken into account, not denied. The superiors hold all the real power, but power will not accomplish *the task.* It will not bring the unequal party up to equality.

Our troubles with these relationships may stem from the fact that they exist within the context of a second type of inequality that tends to overwhelm the ways we learn to operate in the first kind. The second type molds the very ways we perceive and conceptualize what we are doing in the first, most basic kind of relationships.

The second type of inequality teaches us how to enforce inequality, but not how to make the journey from unequal to equal. Most importantly, its consequences are kept amazingly obscure—in fact they are usually denied. . . . However, the underlying notion is that this second type has determined, and still determines, the only ways we can think and feel in the first type.

Permanent Inequality

In these relationships, some people or groups of people are defined as unequal by means of what sociologists call ascription; that is, your birth defines you. Criteria may be race, sex, class, nationality, religion, or other characteristics ascribed at birth. Here, the terms of the relationships are very different from those of temporary inequality. There is, for example, no notion that superiors are present primarily to help inferiors, to impart to them their advantages and "desirable" characteristics. There is no assumption that the goal of the unequal relationship is to end the inequality; in fact, quite the reverse. A series of other governing tendencies are in force, and occur with great regularity. . . . While some of these elements may appear obvious, in fact there is a great deal of disagreement and confusion about psychological characteristics brought about by conditions as obvious as these.

Dominants

Once a group is defined as inferior, the superiors tend to label it as defective or substandard in various ways. These labels accrete rapidly. Thus, blacks are described as less intelligent than whites, women are supposed to be ruled by emotion, and so on. In addition, the actions and words of the dominant group tend to be destructive of the subordinates. All historical evidence confirms this tendency. And, although they are much less obvious, there are destructive effects on the dominants as well. The latter are of a different order and are much more difficult to recognize.

Dominant groups usually define one or more acceptable roles for the subordinate. Acceptable roles typically involve providing services that no dominant group wants to perform for itself (for example, cleaning up the dominant's waste products). Functions that a dominant group prefers to perform, on the other hand, are carefully guarded and closed to subordinates. Out of the total range of human possibilities, the activities most highly valued in any particular culture will tend to be enclosed within the domain of the dominant group; less valued functions are relegated to the subordinates.

Subordinates are usually said to be unable to perform the preferred roles. Their incapacities are ascribed to innate defects or deficiencies of mind or body, therefore immutable and impossible of change or development. It becomes difficult for dominants even to imagine that subordinates are capable of performing the preferred activities. More importantly, subordinates themselves can come to find it difficult to believe in their own ability. The myth of their inability to fulfill wider or more valued roles is challenged only when a drastic event disrupts the usual arrangements. Such disruptions usually arise from outside the relationship itself. For instance, in the emergency situation of World War II, "incompetent" women suddenly "manned" the factories with great skill.

It follows that subordinates are described in terms of, and encouraged to develop, personal psychological characteristics that are pleasing to the dominant group. These characteristics form a certain familiar cluster: submissiveness, passivity, docility, dependency, lack of initiative, inability to act, to decide, to think, and the like. In general, this cluster includes qualities more characteristic of children than adults—immaturity, weakness, and helplessness. If subordinates adopt these characteristics they are considered well-adjusted.

However, when subordinates show the potential for, or even more dangerously have developed other characteristics—let us say intelligence, initiative, assertiveness—there is usually no room available within the dominant framework for acknowledgement of these characteristics. Such people will be defined as at least unusual, if not definitely abnormal. There will be no opportunities for the direct application of their abilities within the social arrangements. (How many women have pretended to be dumb!)

Dominant groups usually impede the development of subordinates and block their freedom of expression and action. They also tend to militate against stirrings of greater rationality or greater humanity in their own members. It was not too long ago that "nigger lover" was a common appellation, and even now men who "allow their women" more than the usual scope are subject to ridicule in many circles.

A dominant group, inevitably, has the greatest influence in determining a culture's overall outlook—its philosophy, morality, social theory, and even its science. The dominant group, thus, legitimizes the unequal relationship and incorporates it into society's guiding concepts. The social outlook, then, obscures the true nature of this relationship—that is, the very existence of inequality. The culture explains the events that take place in terms of other premises, premises that are inevitably false, such as racial or sexual inferiority. While in recent years we have learned about many such falsities on the larger social level, a full analysis of the psychological implications still remains to be developed. In the case of women, for example, despite overwhelming evidence to the contrary, the notion persists that women are meant to be passive, submissive, docile, secondary. From this premise, the outcome of therapy and encounters with psychology and other "sciences" are often determined.

Inevitably, the dominant group is the model for "normal human relationships." It then becomes "normal" to treat others destructively and to derogate them, to obscure the truth of what you are doing, by creating false explanations, and to oppose actions toward equality. In short, if one's identification is with the dominant group, it is "normal" to continue in this pattern. Even though most of us do not like to think of ourselves as either believing in, or engaging in, such dominations, it is, in fact, difficult for a member of a dominant group to do otherwise. But to keep on doing these things, one need only behave "normally."

It follows from this that dominant groups generally do not like to be told about or even quietly reminded of the existence of inequality. "Normally" they can avoid awareness because their explanation of the relationship becomes so well integrated *in other terms*; they can even believe that both they and the subordinate group share the same interests and, to some extent, a common experience. If pressed a bit, the familiar rationalizations are offered: the home is "women's natural place," and we know "what's best for them anyhow."

Dominants prefer to avoid conflict—open conflict that might call into question the whole situation. This is particularly and tragically so, when many members of the dominant group are not having an easy time of it themselves. Members of a dominant group, or at least some segments of it, such as white working-class men (who are themselves also subordinates), often feel unsure of their own narrow toehold on the material and psychological bounties they believe they desperately need. What dominant groups usually cannot act on, or even see, is that the situation of inequality in fact deprives them, particularly on the psychological level.

Clearly, inequality has created a state of conflict. Yet dominant groups will tend to suppress conflict. They will see any questioning of the "normal" situation as threatening; activities by subordinates in this direction will be perceived with alarm. Dominants are usually convinced that the way things are is right and good, not only for them but especially for the subordinates. All morality confirms this view, and all social structure sustains it.

It is perhaps unnecessary to add that the dominant group usually holds all of the open power and authority and determines the ways in which power may be acceptably used.

Subordinates

What of the subordinates' part in this? Since dominants determine what is normal for a culture, it is much more difficult to understand subordinates. Initial expressions of dissatisfaction and early actions by subordinates always come as a surprise; they are usually rejected as atypical. After all, dominants *knew* that all women needed and wanted was a man around whom to organize their lives. Members of the dominant group do not understand why "they"—the first to speak out—are so upset and angry.

The characteristics that typify the subordinates are even more complex. A subordinate group has to concentrate on basic survival. Accordingly, direct, honest reaction to destructive treatment is avoided. Open, self-initiated action in its own self-interest must also be avoided. Such actions can, and still do, literally result in death for some subordinate groups. In our own society, a woman's direct action can result in a combination of economic hardship, social ostracism, and psychological isolation—and even the diagnosis of a personality disorder. Any one of these consequences is bad enough. . . .

It is not surprising then that a subordinate group resorts to disguised and indirect ways of acting and reacting. While these actions are designed to accommodate and please the dominant group, they often, in fact, contain hidden defiance and "put ons." Folk tales, black jokes, and women stories are often based on how the wily peasant or sharecropper outwitted the rich landowner, boss, or husband. The essence of the story rests on the fact that the overlord does not even know that he has been made a fool of.

One important result of this indirect mode of operation is that members of the dominant group are denied an essential part of life—the opportunity to acquire self-understanding through knowing their impact on others. They are thus deprived of "consensual validation," feedback, and a chance to correct their actions and expressions. Put simply, subordinates won't tell. For the same reasons, the dominant group is deprived also of valid knowledge about the subordinates. (It is particularly ironic that the societal "experts" in knowledge about subordinates are usually members of the dominant group.)

Subordinates, then, know much more about the dominants than vice versa. They have to. They become highly attuned to the dominants, able to predict their reactions of pleasure and displeasure. Here, I think, is where the long story of "feminine intuition" and "feminine wiles" begins. It seems clear that these "mysterious" gifts are in fact skills, developed through long practice, in reading many small signals, both verbal and nonverbal.

Another important result is that subordinates often know more about the dominants than they know about themselves. If a large part of your fate depends on accommodating to and pleasing the dominants, you concentrate on them. Indeed, there is little purpose in knowing yourself. Why should you when your knowledge of the dominants determines your life? This tendency is reinforced by many other restrictions. One can know oneself only through action and interaction. To the extent that their range of action or interaction is limited, subordinates will lack a realistic evaluation of their capacities and problems. Unfortunately, this difficulty in gaining self-knowledge is even further compounded.

Tragic confusion arises because subordinates absorb a large part of the untruths created by the dominants; there are a great many blacks who feel inferior to whites, and women who still believe they are less important than men. This internalization of dominant beliefs is more likely to occur if there are few alternative concepts at hand. On the other hand, it is also true that members of the subordinate group have certain experiences and perceptions that accurately reflect the truth about themselves and the injustice of their position. Their own more truthful concepts are bound to come into opposition with the mythology they have absorbed from the dominant group. An inner tension between the two sets of concepts and their derivations is almost inevitable.

From a historical perspective, despite the obstacles, subordinate groups have tended to move toward greater freedom of expression and action, although this progress varies greatly from one circumstance to another. There were always some slaves who revolted; there were some women who sought greater development or self-determination. Most records of these actions are not preserved by the dominant culture, making it difficult for the subordinate group to find a supporting tradition and history.

Within each subordinate group, there are tendencies for some members to imitate the dominants. This imitation can take various forms. Some may try to treat their fellow subordinates as destructively as the dominants treat them. A few may develop enough of the qualities valued by the dominants to be partially accepted into their fellowship. Usually they are not wholly accepted, and even then only if they are willing to forsake their own identification with fellow subordinates. "Uncle Toms" and certain professional women have often been in this position. (There are always a few women who have won the praise presumably embodied in the phrase "she thinks like a man.")

To the extent that subordinates move toward freer expression and action, they will expose the inequality and throw into question the basis for its existence. And they will make the inherent conflict an open conflict. They will then have to bear the burden and take the risks that go with being defined as "troublemakers." Since this role flies in the face of their conditioning, subordinates, especially women, do not come to it with ease.

What is immediately apparent from studying the characteristics of the two groups is that mutually enhancing interaction is not probable between unequals. Indeed, conflict is inevitable. The important questions, then, become: Who defines the conflict? Who sets the terms? When is conflict overt or covert? On what issues is the conflict fought? Can anyone win? Is conflict "bad," by definition? If not, what makes for productive or destructive conflict?

Suggestions for Further Reading

Alba, Richard D. *Ethnic Identity: The Transformation of White American Identity*. New Haven: Yale University Press, 1990.

Berkhofer, Robert F., Jr. *The White Man's Indian: Images of the American Indian from Columbus to the Present*. New York: Vintage, 1978.

Connell, R. W. *Masculinities*. Berkeley: University of California Press, 1995.

De Beauvoir, Simone. *The Second Sex*. New York: Alfred A. Knopf, 1952.

Doty, William G. *The Myths of Masculinity*. New York: Crossroad Publishing, 1993.

Epstein, Cynthia Fuchs. *Deceptive Distinctions: Sex, Gender, and the Social Order*. New Haven: Yale University Press; New York: Russell Sage Foundation, 1988.

Frankenberg, Ruth. *White Women, Race Matters*. Minneapolis: University of Minnesota Press, 1993.

Gould, Stephen. *The Mismeasure of Man*. New York: W. W. Norton, 1984.

Gregory, Steven, and Roger Sanjek, eds. *Race*. New Brunswick, NJ: Rutgers University Press, 1994.

Hubbard, Ruth. *The Politics of Women's Biology*. New Brunswick, NJ: Rutgers University Press, 1990.

Katz, Jonathan Ned. *The Invention of Heterosexuality*. New York: Dutton, 1995.

Kimmel, Michael. *Manhood in America: A Cultural History*. New York: Free Press, 1997.

Lopez, Ian F. Haney. *White By Law: The Legal Construction of Race*. New York: New York University Press, 1997.

Lorber, Judith. *Paradoxes of Gender*. New Haven: Yale University Press, 1995.

Lowe, M., and R. Hubbard, eds. *Women's Nature: Rationalizations of Inequality*. New York: Pergamon Press, 1983.

Memmi, Albert. *Dominated Man*. Boston: Beacon Press, 1969.

Montague, M. F. Ashley. *Man's Most Dangerous Myth*. New York: Harper & Row, 1952.

Omi, Michael, and Howard Winant. *Racial Formations in the United States*. New York: Routledge and Kegan Paul, 1986.

Sanday, Peggy R. *Female Power and Male Dominance: On the Origins of Sexual Inequality*. New York: Cambridge University Press, 1981.

Williams, Gregory Howard. *Life on the Color Line*. New York: Dutton, 1995.

PART II

Understanding Racism, Sexism, Heterosexism, and Class Privilege

IN PART II, WE SPEND SOME TIME ANALYZING SYSTEMS of oppression and examining the relations of dominance and subordination they incorporate almost seamlessly into daily life. Racism, sexism, heterosexism, and class privilege are systems of advantage that provide those with the "right" race, sex, sexual orientation, and class (or some combination of these) with opportunities and rewards that are unavailable to other individuals and groups in society. Sometimes they work in isolation from each other but most often they operate in combination to create a system of advantage and disadvantage that enhances the life chances of some while limiting the life chances of others.

The construction of difference as deviance or deficiency underlies the systems of oppression that determine how power, privilege, wealth, and opportunity are distributed. We are surrounded by differences every day but our society chooses to place a value on only some of them. By valuing the characteristics and lifestyles of certain individuals or groups and devaluing those of others, society constructs some of its members as "other." These "others" are understood to be less deserving, less intelligent, even less human. Once this happens, it is possible to distribute wealth, opportunity, and justice unequally without appearing to be unfair. The social construction of race, class, gender, and sexuality as difference—where being white, male, European, heterosexual, and prosperous is the norm and everyone else is considered less able and less worthy—lies at the heart of racism, sexism, heterosexism, and classism.

Some people are uncomfortable with words like "racism," "sexism," and "oppression," which seem to them highly charged and unnecessarily accusatory. They prefer to talk about discrimination and prejudice. However, those who wish to emphasize the complex, pervasive, and self-perpetuating nature of the system of beliefs, policies, practices, and attitudes that enforce the relations of subordination and domination in our society find the term discrimination too narrow and too limited to do so effectively. Words like racism, sexism, and oppression are more appropriate because they capture the comprehensive nature of the systems being studied. In Selection 18, Marilyn Frye does a good job of explaining the meaning of "oppression" in the course of using that concept to convey the pervasive nature of sexism. Frye uses the metaphor of a bird cage to illustrate how a system of oppression, in this case sexism, imprisons its victims through a set of interlocking impediments to motion. Taken alone, none of the barriers seems very powerful or threatening; taken together they are unyielding. They constitute a cage that appears light and airy, masking the fact that its occupants are trapped as completely as if they were in a sealed vault.

Racism and sexism are systems of advantage based on race and sex. In the United States racism perpetuates an interlocking system of institutions, attitudes, privileges, and rewards that work to the benefit of white people just as sexism works to the advantage of men. In Selection 12 Beverley Daniels Tatum elaborates on this definition of racism (originally offered by David Wellman in his book *Portraits of White Racism*) and discusses the resistance some of those of us who are white feel toward acknowledging both the existence of racism and the advantages it bestows on us. As Tatum observes, many prefer to define racism in terms of racial prejudice, because by adopting this definition it is possible to say that people of color as well as white people can be racist. For many people in this society, being able to say so seems to satisfy a deep emotional need. Confronted with behavior or speech that is hateful, they wish to use the strongest words they can to condemn and deplore it. Once racism is defined as a system of advantages based on race, it is no longer possible to attribute racism to people of color because clearly they do not systematically benefit from racism, only white people do. This, of course, does not deny that people of all colors are capable of hateful and hurtful behavior, nor does it prevent us from taking them to task for their prejudice. But it does mean that we will reserve the term "racism" to refer specifically to the comprehensive system of advantages that work to the benefit of white people in the United States. For more on this important and provocative distinction, you will want to turn directly to the essay by Tatum.

In Selection 13, John Dovidio and Samuel Gaertner take a closer look at the nature of contemporary prejudice in U.S. society and offer a nuanced account of the way in which racism is often expressed and perpetuated. The authors describe a kind of subtle racism that is practiced by many white people who sincerely believe that they are not prejudiced. The purpose of their study is not to assign blame so much as it is to call attention to this serious but subtle kind of unconscious bias, which is partially responsible for the persistence of racism in our society.

Rita Chaudhry Sethi (Selection 14) reminds us how easy it is, in certain parts of the United States, to think of racial conflict in black and white terms. Sethi rejects this simplistic racial paradigm because it leaves no room for the racism that Asian Americans experience. According to Sethi, white America constructs Asian Americans as a model minority and Asian Americans themselves and for their own reasons tend to minimize anti-Asian discrimination as well. As a result, the racism that Asian Americans experience in the United States is often rendered invisible or trivialized. Sethi's project is to uncover the hidden racism directed against Asians and by doing so to broaden the use of the term. Although she does not argue the point directly, unlike Tatum, Sethi seems willing to use the term "racism" to describe certain behavior and attitudes that occur within and among communities of color.

In Selection 16, Manning Marable further deepens our understanding of racism. While Tatum tends to focus on broad interpersonal issues and Sethi is concerned with cultural conflict, Marable's focus is on the conditions under which people of color live in contemporary U.S. society and the forms of social control used to keep the prevailing hierarchy in place. In the course of his discussion, he draws parallels between racism and sexism as systems of domination and looks at the nature of what he calls the "new racism" we are now encountering.

The term "sexism" refers to the oppression of women by men in a society that is largely patriarchal. As defined by Allan Johnson in Selection 17, a patriarchal society is male-dominated, male-identified, and male-centered. In such a society, every institution and aspect of culture contrives to rationalize and perpetuate the dominance of men and the subordination of women. Marilyn Frye's article asks us to look closely at examples of some seemingly innocent but oppressive social rituals that perpetuate these relations of domination. She takes as her paradigm or model the "male door-opening ritual" and argues that its meaning and implications go far beyond the conscious intentions of the man who opens the door. The point is that sexism and racism can be perpetuated by people who are just trying to be nice. As you think about her example, remember that Frye is analyzing the implications of a social practice, not looking at any individual's motives for carrying out that ritual.

The use of the term "heterosexism" parallels the other two and, according to Suzanne Pharr in Selection 19, creates the assumption that the world is and must be heterosexual at the same time that it rationalizes the existing distribution of power and privilege that flows from this assumption. In her essay Pharr argues that economics, violence, and homophobia, or fear of lesbians and gays, are the most effective weapons of sexism and makes it clear that homophobia and heterosexism are oppressive of all women, not just those of us who are not exclusively heterosexual. For more current statistics on economic inequality (which continue to support Pharr's claims), take a look at the material in Part IV of this book.

Finally, "class privilege" refers to the system of advantages that continues to insure that wealth, power, opportunity, and privilege go hand in hand. In Selection 21, Greg Mantsios explores some of the myths about class that mislead people about their real-life chances and documents the impact of class position on daily life. While many in the United States are oblivious to the full force of class privilege, the statistics in this article suggest that the class position of one's family, not hard work, intelligence, or determination, is probably the single most significant determinant of future success. This gap between people's beliefs about what it takes to succeed and the tremendous role that class privilege plays in determining who is successful provides a dramatic illustration of the effectiveness of systems of oppression both in terms of perpetuating the current systems of advantage and in rendering their continuing operation invisible to so many.

These are strong and disturbing claims and they are likely to provoke equally strong reactions from many people reading this introduction. Some will feel angry, others will feel depressed and discouraged, some will feel uncomfortable, others will be skeptical, and some will simply feel confused. This is understandable. If what you have just read is true, then things in the United States are neither as fair nor as equitable as most of us would like them to be. If some people, as these definitions suggest, have more than their share, then others have less than they deserve, and each of us must wonder where we will stand in the final computation. Further, many readers who are white and working class or middle class will be hard pressed to imagine what kind of privilege they exercise. They look at their own lives and the lives of their parents and friends and see people who have worked very hard for everything they have achieved. The idea that they are privileged may seem very foreign to them. The same will be true for other readers as well. Heterosexism, class privilege, male privilege? "What have these abstract and politically charged terms got to do with me?" they ask. "I work hard, try to get ahead, wish others well, and feel more like a victim myself than a victimizer." This understandable response underscores how effectively the systems of oppression we are discussing function in contemporary society to rationalize the hierarchy they create, often making its operation invisible both to those who benefit from it and to those who are shortchanged by it. In addition, it points to the complicated and ambiguous nature of privilege, which means that a single individual can be privileged in some respects at the very same time he or she is disadvantaged in other respects. Let us examine these two points in more detail.

Many people who are privileged fail to realize that this is the case because the systems of oppression we are studying so effectively make the current distribution of privilege and power appear almost "natural." In addition, some of us, including those of us who are disadvantaged, grow up believing things about ourselves and others that make our life choices and opportunities or lack of the same seem inevitable or deserved. In many cases, people with privileges have enjoyed them so long that they have simply come to take them for granted. Instead of recognizing them as special benefits that come with, for example, white skin, they just assume that these privileges are things to which they have a right. (For more on this topic see Peggy McIntosh's essay, Selection 20, which does an excellent job of examining how white privilege works.)

In other cases, privilege may be difficult to identify and acknowledge because the individual is privileged in some respects but not in others. For example, those who are privileged by virtue of their sex or sexual orientation may be disadvantaged in other respects, say by virtue of their race/ethnicity or their class position or both. The disadvantages they experience in some areas may seem so unfair and so egregious that they prevent them from recognizing the privileges they nonetheless enjoy. For example, a poor white, single mother who receives public assistance and who feels very much at the mercy of an unfair and inhumane system might still be able to call upon her white skin privilege or her heterosexual privilege in certain situations, and yet be oblivious to that privilege because she feels so disadvantaged in other respects. A working class or lower middle class white male who has trouble stretching his paycheck to cover all his expenses may be so preoccupied with his financial situation that he doesn't recognize the male privilege and white skin privilege from which he nonetheless benefits—privileges that may not feel at all like privileges to him because he takes them for granted and regards them as "natural" and "normal." And finally, since most people are basically decent and fair, those of us who are privileged are often simply reluctant to acknowledge that we have unfair advantages over others because that would require that we reevaluate our sense of who we are and what we have accomplished in our lives.

As should by now be clear, each of the thinkers whose work is included in Part II shares the belief that the various systems of oppression operate in relation to each other, forming an interlocking system of advantages and disadvantages that rationalize and preserve the prevailing distribution of power and privilege in society. As you read these articles, try to keep an open mind about this claim. If these thinkers are correct, they have something important to tell us about this society and the forces that will be in place as each of us goes about creating our own future. Reading some of this material may make some people temporarily uncomfortable, but failing to grapple with it may leave us all the more vulnerable to the forces that play a compelling role in determining the life chances of the individuals and groups that make up our society.

Defining Racism: *"Can We Talk?"*

Beverley Daniels Tatum

Early in my teaching career, a White student I knew asked me what I would be teaching the following semester. I mentioned that I would be teaching a course on racism. She replied, with some surprise in her voice, "Oh, is there still racism?" I assured her that indeed there was and suggested that she sign up for my course. Fifteen years later, after exhaustive media coverage of events such as the Rodney King beating, the Charles Stuart and Susan Smith cases, the O. J. Simpson trial, the appeal to racial prejudices in electoral politics, and the bitter debates about affirmative action and welfare reform, it seems hard to imagine that anyone would still be unaware of the reality of racism in our society. But in fact, in almost every audience I address, there is someone who will suggest that racism is a thing of the past. There is always someone who hasn't noticed the stereotypical images of people of color in the media, who hasn't observed the housing discrimination in their community, who hasn't read the newspaper articles about documented racial bias in lending practices among well-known banks, who isn't aware of the racial tracking pattern at the local school, who hasn't seen the reports of rising incidents of racially motivated hate crimes in America—in short, someone who hasn't been paying attention to issues of race. But if you are paying attention, the legacy of racism is not hard to see, and we are all affected by it.

The impact of racism begins early. Even in our preschool years, we are exposed to misinformation about people different from ourselves. Many of us grew up in neighborhoods where we had limited opportunities to interact with people different from our own families. When I ask my college students, "How many of you grew up in neighborhoods where most of the people were from the same racial group as your own?" almost every hand goes up. There is still a great deal of social segregation in our communities. Consequently, most of the early information we receive about "others"—people racially, religiously, or socioeconomically different from ourselves—does not come as the result of firsthand experience. The secondhand information we do receive has often been distorted, shaped by cultural stereotypes, and left incomplete.

Some examples will highlight this process. Several years ago one of my students conducted a research project investigating preschoolers' conceptions of Native Americans.[1] Using children at a local day care center as her participants, she asked these three- and four-year-olds to draw a picture of a Native American. Most children were stumped by her request. They didn't know what a Native American was. But when she rephrased the question and asked them to draw a picture of an Indian, they readily complied. Almost every picture included one central feature: feathers. In fact, many of them also included a weapon—a knife or tomahawk—and depicted the person in violent or aggressive terms. Though this group of children, almost all of whom were White, did not live near a large Native American population and probably had had little if any personal interaction with American Indians, they all had internalized an image of what Indians were like. How did they know? Cartoon images, in particular the Disney movie *Peter Pan*, were cited by the children as their number-one source of information. At the age of three, these children already had a set of stereotypes in place. Though I would not describe three-year-olds as prejudiced, the stereotypes to which they have been exposed become the foundation for the adult prejudices so many of us have.

Sometimes the assumptions we make about others come not from what we have been told or what we have seen on television or in books, but rather from what we have *not* been told. The distortion of historical information about people of color leads young people (and older people, too) to make assumptions that may go unchallenged for a long time. Consider this conversation between two White students following a discussion about the cultural transmission of racism:

"Yeah, I just found out that Cleopatra was actually a Black woman."

"What?"

The first student went on to explain her newly learned information. The second student exclaimed in disbelief, "That can't be true. Cleopatra was beautiful!"

What had this young woman learned about who in our society is considered beautiful and who is not? Had she conjured up images of Elizabeth Taylor when she thought of Cleopatra? The new information her classmate had shared and her own deeply ingrained assumptions about who is beautiful and who is not were too incongruous to allow her to assimilate the information at that moment.

Omitted information can have similar effects. For example, another young woman, preparing to be a high school English teacher, expressed her dismay that she had never learned about any Black authors in any of her English courses. How was she to teach about them to her future students when she hadn't learned about them herself? A White male student in the class responded to this discussion with frustration in his response journal, writing "It's not my fault that Blacks don't write books." Had one of his elementary, high school, or college teachers ever told him that there were no Black writers? Probably not. Yet because he had never been exposed to Black authors, he had drawn his own conclusion that there were none.

Stereotypes, omissions, and distortions all contribute to the development of prejudice. *Prejudice* is a preconceived judgment or opinion, usually based on limited information. I assume that we all have prejudices, not because we want them, but simply because we are so continually exposed to misinformation about others. Though I have often heard students or workshop participants describe someone as not having "a prejudiced bone in his body," I usually suggest that they look again. Prejudice is one of the inescapable consequences of living in a racist society. Cultural racism—the cultural images and messages that affirm the assumed superiority of Whites and the assumed inferiority of people of color—is like smog in the air. Sometimes it is so thick it is visible, other times it is less apparent, but always, day in and day out, we are breathing it in. None of us would introduce ourselves as "smog-breathers" (and most of us don't want to be described as prejudiced), but if we live in a smoggy place, how can we avoid breathing the air? If we live in an environment in which we are bombarded with stereotypical images in the media, are frequently exposed to the ethnic jokes of friends and family members, and are rarely informed of the accomplishments of oppressed groups, we will develop the negative categorizations of those groups that form the basis of prejudice.

People of color as well as Whites develop these categorizations. Even a member of the stereotyped group may internalize the stereotypical categories about his or her own group to some degree. In fact, this process happens so frequently that it has a name, *internalized oppression*. Some of the consequences of believing the distorted messages about one's own group will be discussed in subsequent chapters.

Certainly some people are more prejudiced than others, actively embracing and perpetuating negative and hateful images of those who are different from themselves. When we claim to be free of prejudice, perhaps what we are really saying is that we are not hatemongers. But none of us is completely innocent. Prejudice is an integral part of our socialization, and it is not our fault. Just as the preschoolers my student interviewed are not to blame for the negative messages they internalized, we are not at fault for the stereotypes, distortions, and omissions that shaped our thinking as we grew up.

To say that it is not our fault does not relieve us of responsibility, however. We may not have polluted the air, but we need to take responsibility, along with others, for cleaning it up. Each of us needs to look at our own behavior. Am I perpetuating and reinforcing the negative messages so pervasive in our culture, or am I seeking to challenge them? If I have not been exposed to positive images of marginalized groups, am I seeking them out, expanding my own knowledge base for myself and my children? Am I acknowledging and examining my own prejudices, my own rigid categorizations of others, thereby minimizing the adverse impact they might have on my interactions with those I have categorized? Unless we engage in these and other conscious acts of reflection and reeducation, we easily repeat the process with our children. We teach what we were taught. The unexamined prejudices of the parents are passed on to the children. It is not our fault, but it is our responsibility to interrupt this cycle.

Racism: A System of Advantage Based on Race

Many people use the terms *prejudice* and *racism* interchangeably. I do not, and I think it is important to make a distinction. In his book *Portraits of White Racism*, David Wellman argues convincingly that limiting our understanding of racism to prejudice does not offer a sufficient explanation for the persistence of racism. He defines racism as a "system of advantage based on race."[2] In illustrating this definition, he provides example after example of how Whites defend their racial advantage—access to better schools, housing, jobs—even when they do not embrace overtly prejudicial thinking. Racism cannot be fully explained as an expression of prejudice alone.

This definition of racism is useful because it allows us to see that racism, like other forms of oppression, is not only a personal ideology based on racial prejudice, but a *system* involving cultural messages and institutional policies and practices as well as the beliefs and actions of individuals. In the context of the United States, this system clearly operates to the advantage of Whites and to the disadvantage of people of color. Another related definition of racism, commonly used by antiracist educators and consultants, is "prejudice plus power." Racial prejudice when combined with social power—access to social, cultural, and economic resources and decision-making—leads to the institutionalization of racist policies and practices. While I think this definition also captures the idea that racism is more than individual beliefs and attitudes, I prefer Wellman's definition because the idea of systematic advantage and disadvantage is critical to an understanding of how racism operates in American society.

In addition, I find that many of my White students and workshop participants do not feel powerful. Defining racism as prejudice plus power has little personal relevance. For some, their response to this definition is the following: "I'm not really prejudiced, and I have no power, so racism has nothing to do with me." However, most White people, if they are really being honest with themselves, can see that there are advantages to being White in the United States. Despite the current rhetoric about affirmative action and "reverse racism," every social indicator, from salary to life expectancy, reveals the advantages of being White.[3]

The systematic advantages of being White are often referred to as White privilege. In a now well-known article, "White Privilege: Unpacking the Invisible Knapsack," Peggy McIntosh, a White feminist scholar, identified a long list of societal privileges that she received simply because she was White.[4] She did not ask for them, and it is important to note that she hadn't always noticed that she was receiving them. They included major and minor advantages. Of course she enjoyed greater access to jobs and housing. But she also was able to shop in department stores without being followed by suspicious salespeople and could always find appropriate hair care products and makeup in any drugstore. She could send her child to school confident that the teacher would not discriminate against him on the basis of race. She could also be late for meetings, and talk with her mouth full, fairly confident that these behaviors would not be attributed to the fact that she was

White. She could express an opinion in a meeting or in print and not have it labeled the "White" viewpoint. In other words, she was more often than not viewed as an individual, rather than as a member of a racial group.

This article rings true for most White readers, many of whom may have never considered the benefits of being White. It's one thing to have enough awareness of racism to describe the ways that people of color are disadvantaged by it. But this new understanding of racism is more elusive. In very concrete terms, it means that if a person of color is the victim of housing discrimination, the apartment that would otherwise have been rented to that person of color is still available for a White person. The White tenant is, knowingly or unknowingly, the beneficiary of racism, a system of advantage based on race. The unsuspecting tenant is not to blame for the prior discrimination, but she benefits from it anyway.

For many Whites, this new awareness of the benefits of a racist system elicits considerable pain, often accompanied by feelings of anger and guilt. These uncomfortable emotions can hinder further discussion. We all like to think that we deserve the good things we have received, and that others, too, get what they deserve. Social psychologists call this tendency a "belief in a just world."[5] Racism directly contradicts such notions of justice.

Understanding racism as a system of advantage based on race is antithetical to traditional notions of an American meritocracy. For those who have internalized this myth, this definition generates considerable discomfort. It is more comfortable simply to think of racism as a particular form of prejudice. Notions of power or privilege do not have to be addressed when our understanding of racism is constructed in that way.

The discomfort generated when a systemic definition of racism is introduced is usually quite visible in the workshops I lead. Someone in the group is usually quick to point out that this is not the definition you will find in most dictionaries. I reply, "Who wrote the dictionary?" I am not being facetious with this response. Whose interests are served by a "prejudice only" definition of racism? It is important to understand that the system of advantage is perpetuated when we do not acknowledge its existence.

Racism: For Whites Only?

Frequently someone will say, "You keep talking about White people. People of color can be racist, too." I once asked a White teacher what it would mean to her if a student or parent of color accused her of being racist. She said she would feel as though she had been punched in the stomach or called a "low-life scum." She is not alone in this feeling. The word *racist* holds a lot of emotional power. For many White people, to be called racist is the ultimate insult. The idea that this term might only be applied to Whites becomes highly problematic for after all, can't people of color be "low-life scum" too?

Of course, people of any racial group can hold hateful attitudes and behave in racially discriminatory and bigoted ways. We can all cite examples of horrible hate crimes which have been perpetrated by people of color as well as Whites. Hateful behavior is hateful behavior no matter who does it. But when I am asked, "Can people of color be racist?" I reply, "The answer depends on your definition of racism." If one defines racism as racial prejudice, the answer is yes. People of color can and do have racial prejudices. However, if one defines racism as a system of advantage based on race, the answer is no. People of color are not racist because they do not systematically benefit from racism. And equally important, there is no systematic cultural and institutional support or sanction for the racial bigotry of people of color. In my view, reserving the term *racist* only for behaviors committed by Whites in the context of a White-dominated society is a way of acknowledging the ever-present power differential afforded Whites by the culture and institutions that make up the system of advantage and continue to reinforce notions of White superiority. (Using the same logic, I reserve the word *sexist* for men. Though women can and do have gender-based prejudices, only men systematically benefit from sexism.)

Despite my best efforts to explain my thinking on this point, there are some who will be troubled, perhaps even incensed, by my response. To call the racially motivated acts of a person of color acts of racial bigotry and to describe similar acts committed by Whites as racist will make no sense to some people, including some people of color. To those, I will respectfully say, "We can agree to disagree." At moments like these, it is not agreement that is essential, but clarity. Even if you don't like the definition of racism I am using, hopefully you are now clear about what it is. If I also understand how you are using the term, our conversation can continue—despite our disagreement.

Another provocative question I'm often asked is "Are you saying all Whites are racist?" When asked this question, I again remember that White teacher's response, and I am conscious that perhaps the question I am really being asked is, "Are you saying all Whites are bad people?" The answer to that question is of course not. However, all White people, intentionally or unintentionally, do benefit from racism. A more relevant question is what are White people as individuals doing to interrupt racism? For many White people, the image of a racist is a hood-wearing Klan member or a name-calling Archie Bunker figure. These images represent what might be called *active racism*, blatant, intentional acts of racial bigotry and discrimination. *Passive racism* is more subtle and can be seen in the collusion of laughing when a racist joke is told, of letting exclusionary hiring practices go unchallenged, of accepting as appropriate the omissions of people of color from the curriculum, and of avoiding difficult race-related issues. Because racism is so ingrained in the fabric of American institutions, it is easily self-perpetuating.[6] All that is required to maintain it is business as usual.

I sometimes visualize the ongoing cycle of racism as a moving walkway at the airport. Active racist behavior is equivalent to walking fast on the conveyor belt. The person engaged in active racist behavior has identified with the ideology of

White supremacy and is moving with it. Passive racist behavior is equivalent to standing still on the walkway. No overt effort is being made, but the conveyor belt moves the bystanders along to the same destination as those who are actively walking. Some of the bystanders may feel the motion of the conveyor belt, see the active racists ahead of them, and choose to turn around, unwilling to go to the same destination as the White supremacists. But unless they are walking actively in the opposite direction at a speed faster than the conveyor belt—unless they are actively antiracist—they will find themselves carried along with the others.

So, not all Whites are actively racist. Many are passively racist. Some, though not enough, are actively antiracist. The relevant question is not whether all Whites are racist, but how we can move more White people from a position of active or passive racism to one of active antiracism. The task of interrupting racism is obviously not the task of Whites alone. But the fact of White privilege means that Whites have greater access to the societal institutions in need of transformation. To whom much is given, much is required.

It is important to acknowledge that while all Whites benefit from racism, they do not all benefit equally. Other factors, such as socioeconomic status, gender, age, religious affiliation, sexual orientation, mental and physical ability, also play a role in our access to social influence and power. A White woman on welfare is not privileged to the same extent as a wealthy White heterosexual man. In her case, the systematic disadvantages of sexism and classism intersect with her White privilege, but the privilege is still there. This point was brought home to me in a 1994 study conducted by a Mount Holyoke graduate student, Phyllis Wentworth.[7] Wentworth interviewed a group of female college students, who were both older than their peers and were the first members of their families to attend college, about the pathways that led them to college. All of the women interviewed were White, from working-class backgrounds, from families where women were expected to graduate from high school and get married or get a job. Several had experienced abusive relationships and other personal difficulties prior to coming to college. Yet their experiences were punctuated by "good luck" stories of apartments obtained without a deposit, good jobs offered without experience or extensive reference checks, and encouragement provided by willing mentors. While the women acknowledged their good fortune, none of them discussed their Whiteness. They had not considered the possibility that being White had worked in their favor and helped give them the benefit of the doubt at critical junctures. This study clearly showed that even under difficult circumstances, White privilege was still operating.

It is also true that not all people of color are equally targeted by racism. We all have multiple identities that shape our experience. I can describe myself as a light-skinned, well-educated, heterosexual, able-bodied, Christian African American woman raised in a middle-class suburb. As an African American woman, I am systematically disadvantaged by race and by gender, but I systematically receive benefits in the other categories, which then mediate my experience of racism and sexism. When one is targeted by multiple isms—racism, sexism, classism, heterosexism, ableism, anti-Semitism, ageism—in whatever combination, the effect is intensified. The particular combination of racism and classism in many communities of color is life-threatening. Nonetheless, when I, the middle-class Black mother of two sons, read another story about a Black man's unlucky encounter with a White police officer's deadly force, I am reminded that racism by itself can kill.

NOTES

1. C. O'Toole, "The effect of the media and multicultural education on children's perceptions of Native Americans" (senior thesis, Department of Psychology and Education, Mount Holyoke College, South Hadley, MA, May 1990).

2. For an extended discussion of this point, see David Wellman, *Portraits of White racism* (Cambridge: Cambridge University Press, 1977), ch. 1.

3. For specific statistical information, see R. Farley, "The common destiny of Blacks and Whites: Observations about the social and economic status of the races," pp. 197–233 in H. Hill and J. E. Jones, Jr. (Eds.), *Race in America: The struggle for equality* (Madison: University of Wisconsin Press, 1993).

4. P. McIntosh, "White privilege: Unpacking the invisible knapsack," *Peace and Freedom* (July/August 1989): 10–12.

5. For further discussion of the concept of "belief in a just world," see M. J. Lerner, "Social psychology of justice and interpersonal attraction," in T. Huston (Ed.), *Foundations of interpersonal attraction* (New York: Academic Press, 1974).

6. For a brief historical overview of the institutionalization of racism and sexism in our legal system, see "Part V: How it happened: Race and gender issues in U.S. law," in P. S. Rothenberg (Ed.), *Race, class, and gender in the United States: An integrated study*, 3d ed. (New York: St. Martin's Press, 1995).

7. P. A. Wentworth, "The identity development of non-traditionally aged first-generation women college students: An exploratory study" (master's thesis, Department of Psychology and Education, Mount Holyoke College, South Hadley, MA, 1994).

13

On the Nature of Contemporary Prejudice
The Causes, Consequences, and Challenges of Aversive Racism

John F. Dovidio
Samuel L. Gaertner

Race relations in the United States are better now than ever before. Or are they? On one hand, the dramatic positive impact of the civil rights legislation of the 1960s is undeniable. Before this legislation, in many parts of the country, it was customary for whites to limit the freedom of blacks (e.g., limiting blacks to the back of buses), to demand deference from blacks (e.g., requiring blacks to give up their seats to whites on buses), and to restrict residential, educational, and employment opportunities for blacks. Under the civil rights legislation, discrimination and segregation became no longer simply immoral, but also illegal. As a consequence, black Americans currently have greater access to political, social, and economic opportunities than ever before in our history. On the other hand, there are new signals of deteriorating race relations. Symptoms of racial tension, which emerged in the 1960s, are reappearing. As the 1990s began, riots in Miami, Tampa, New Jersey, Washington, D.C., and Los Angeles reflected large-scale and violent racial unrest. Over the past 5 years, over 300 colleges have reported significant racial incidents and protests. In the first 6 months of 1996, there were 27 suspicious fires, presumed to be racially motivated arson, across the South

From "On the Nature of Contemporary Prejudice," in *Confronting Racism: The Problem and the Responses,* Jennifer L. Eberhardt and Susan T. Fiske, eds. Copyright © 1998. Reprinted by permission of Sage Publications, Inc.

AUTHOR'S NOTE: The work presented in this chapter was supported by NIMH Grant MH-48721. We express our appreciation to Jennifer Eberhardt and Susan Fiske for their thoughtful comments on earlier versions of the chapter. Correspondence regarding this chapter should be addressed to John F. Dovidio, Department of Psychology, Colgate University, Hamilton, NY 13346.

(Morganthau, 1996). The majority of blacks in the United States today have a profound distrust of the police and the legal system, and about a third are overtly distrustful of whites in general (Anderson, 1996). Middle-class blacks are very worried about the future for blacks and for the nation (Hochschild, 1995). . . .

Racial Attitudes in the United States

Across time, the attitudes of whites toward minorities, in general, and blacks, in particular, are becoming less negative and more accepting. Negative stereotypes are declining. For example, in 1933, 75% of white respondents described blacks as lazy; in 1993, that figure declined to just 5% (Dovidio, Brigham, Johnson, & Gaertner, 1996). White America is also becoming more accepting of black leaders. In 1958, the majority of whites reported that they would not be willing to vote for a well-qualified black presidential candidate; in 1994, over 90% said that they would (Davis & Smith, 1994). In addition, the increase in tolerance of white Americans extends beyond blacks to other racial and ethnic minority groups as well (American National Election Survey, 1995).

Despite these encouraging trends in the intergroup attitudes of white Americans, there are still reasons for concern. One reason is that, across a variety of surveys and polls, 10%–15% of the white population still expresses the old-fashioned, overt form of bigotry. These respondents consistently describe blacks as innately less intelligent than whites, say that they will not vote for a well-qualified presidential candidate simply because of that person's race, and oppose programs designed to ensure full integration and equal opportunity. Another reason for concern is that a substantial portion of the white population expresses merely racial tolerance but not true openness to or enthusiasm for full racial equality. A third reason for concern, which is our current focus, is that there is also evidence that many of the people who are part of the 85%–90% of the white population who say and probably believe that they are not prejudiced may nonetheless be practicing a modern, subtle form of bias.

We believe that the existence of this subtle form of bias helps to account, in part, for the persistence of racism in our society. In a 1988 nationwide poll (Gelman, 1988), 25% of the black respondents said that they believed that white people "want to hold" black people down; 44% of all respondents said that they believed that society is holding blacks down. In a more recent poll, 32% of blacks reported that discrimination is the primary obstacle to achieving equality in the United States (Anderson, 1996). Furthermore, despite dramatic improvements in whites' expressed racial attitudes over time, racial disparities persist in the United States. Gaps between black and white Americans in physiological areas (e.g., infant mortality, life expectancy) and economic areas (e.g., employment, income, poverty) have continued to exist; and, in many cases, these disparities have actually increased over the past 30 years (Hacker, 1995).

Aversive Racism

Over the past 20 years, we, with a number of our colleagues, have investigated a prevalent type of modern racial bias, called *aversive racism* (Dovidio & Gaertner, 1991; Gaertner & Dovidio, 1986; Gaertner et al., 1997; Kovel, 1970). In contrast to "old-fashioned" racism, which is expressed directly and openly, aversive racism represents a subtle, often unintentional, form of bias that characterizes many white Americans who possess strong egalitarian values and who believe that they are non-prejudiced. Aversive racists also possess negative racial feelings and beliefs of which they are unaware or that they try to dissociate from their nonprejudiced self-images. The negative feelings that aversive racists have for blacks do not reflect open hostility or hate. Instead, their reactions involve discomfort, uneasiness, disgust, and sometimes fear. That is, they find blacks "aversive," while, at the same time, they find any suggestion that they might be prejudiced aversive as well. . . .

The aversive racism framework helps to identify when discrimination against blacks and other minority groups will or will not occur. The ambivalence involving both positive and negative feelings that aversive racists experience creates psychological tension that leads to behavioral instability. Thus, unlike the consistent and overt pattern of discrimination that might be expected from old-fashioned racists, aversive racists sometimes discriminate (manifesting their negative feelings) and sometimes do not (reflecting their egalitarian beliefs). Our research has provided a framework for understanding this pattern of discrimination.

Because aversive racists consciously recognize and endorse egalitarian values—they truly want to be fair and just people—they will not discriminate in situations in which they recognize that discrimination would be obvious to others and themselves. Specifically, we propose that when people are presented with a situation in which the appropriate response is clear, in which right and wrong is clearly defined, aversive racists will not discriminate against blacks. Wrongdoing, which would directly threaten their nonprejudiced self-image, would be too obvious. Because aversive racists still possess negative feelings, however, these negative feelings will eventually be expressed, but they will be expressed in subtle, indirect, and rationalizable ways. For instance, discrimination will occur when appropriate (and thus inappropriate) behavior is not obvious or when an aversive racist can justify or rationalize a negative response on the basis of some factor other than race. Under these circumstances, aversive racists may discriminate, but in a way that insulates them from ever having to believe that their behavior was racially motivated.

Aversive racists may be identified by a constellation of characteristic responses to racial issues and interracial situations. First, aversive racists, in contrast to old-fashioned racists, endorse fair and just treatment of all groups. Second, despite their conscious good intentions, aversive racists unconsciously harbor negative feelings towards blacks, and thus try to avoid interracial interaction. Third, when interracial interaction is unavoidable, aversive racists experience anxiety and discomfort, and consequently they try to disengage from the interaction as quickly as possible. As we noted earlier, the negative feelings that aversive racists have toward blacks involve discomfort rather than hostility or hatred. Fourth, because part of the discomfort that aversive racists experience is due to a concern about acting inappropriately and appearing prejudiced, aversive racists strictly adhere to established rules and codes of behavior in the interracial situations that they cannot avoid. They also frequently assert that they are color-blind; if they do not see race, then it follows that no one can accuse them of being racist. Finally, their negative feelings will get expressed, but in subtle, rationalizable ways that may ultimately disadvantage minorities or unfairly benefit the majority group. . . .

Subtle, Rationalizable Bias

Because of the ambivalence that characterizes their attitudes toward blacks, aversive racists' interracial behavior is more variable than that of old-fashioned racists. In this section, we illustrate support for our framework concerning how aversive racism operates. We first examine spontaneous reactions to blacks, and then we compare the effects of aversive racism to old-fashioned racism in more deliberative decisions.

Reactions in an Emergency

In one of the early tests of our framework (Gaertner & Dovidio, 1977), we tried to take advantage of a naturally occurring event and model it in the laboratory. The event was the Kitty Genovese incident, which occurred in New York City in 1964. Kitty Genovese was returning home one evening. As she entered the parking lot of her building, a man drove up, jumped out of his car, and began to stab her. She screamed. Lights went on in her building. The brutal attack continued for 45 minutes, but no one intervened or even called the police. After he was sure she was dead, the assailant calmly got into his car and drove away.

We know so much about this case because when the police arrived a short time later, they found that there were 38 witnesses who watched the event from beginning to end. How could it happen that none of these people helped, either directly or indirectly? One explanation that psychologists have developed concerns the bystander's sense of responsibility (Darley & Latané, 1968). When a person is the only witness to an emergency, that bystander bears 100% of the responsibility for helping and 100% of the guilt and blame for not helping. The appropriate behavior in this situation, helping, is clearly defined. If, however, a person witnesses an emergency but believes that somebody else is around who can help or will help, then that bystander's personal responsibility is less clearly defined. Under these circumstances, the bystander could rationalize not helping by coming to believe that someone else will intervene. Of course, if everyone believes that someone else will help, no one will intervene. That presumably was what occurred in the Kitty Genovese incident. . . .

We predicted that when people were the only witness to the emergency, aversive racists would not discriminate against the black victim. In this situation, appropriate behavior is clearly defined. Not to help a black victim could easily be interpreted, by oneself or others, as racial bias. We predicted, however, that because aversive racists have unconscious negative feelings toward blacks, they would discriminate when they could justify their behavior on the basis of some factor other than race—such as the belief that someone else would help the victim. Specifically, we expected that blacks would be helped less than whites only when white bystanders believed that there were other witnesses to the emergency.

The results of the study supported our predictions. When white bystanders were the only witnesses to the emergency, they helped very frequently and equivalently for black and white victims. In fact, they even helped black victims somewhat more often than white victims (95% vs. 83%, respectively). There was no evidence of old-fashioned racism. In contrast, when white bystanders were given an opportunity to rationalize not helping on the basis of the belief that one of the two other witnesses could intervene, they were less likely to help, particularly when the victim was African American. When participants believed that there were two other bystanders, they helped the black victim half as often as they helped the white victim (38% vs. 75%). If this situation were real, the white victim would have died 25% of the time; the black victim would have died 62% of the time. As we hypothesized, the nature of the situation determines whether discrimination does or does not occur. This principle applies in more considered decision-making situations, often with equally severe consequences for blacks. Next we consider the roles of subtle and overt biases in juridic decisions.

Is Justice Color-Blind?

Traditionally, blacks and whites have not been treated equally under the law. Across time and locations in the United States, blacks have been more likely to be convicted of crimes, and, if convicted, sentenced to longer terms for similar crimes, particularly if the victim is white (see Johnson, 1985; Nickerson, Mayo, & Smith, 1986). In addition, blacks are more likely to receive the death penalty (General Accounting Office, 1990). Baldus, Woodsworth, and Pulaski (1990) examined over 2,000 murder cases in Georgia and found that a death sentence was returned in 22% of the cases in which black defendants were convicted of killing a white victim, but in only 8% of the cases in which the defendant and the victim were white. Although differences in judicial outcomes have tended to persist, paralleling the trends in overt expressions of bias, racial disparities in sentencing are declining over time, and the effects are becoming more indirect (Nickerson et al., 1986).

Although the influence of old-fashioned racism in juridic judgments may be waning, aversive racism appears to have a continuing, subtle influence. That is, bias does occur, but mainly when it can be justified on the basis of some other—ostensibly nonrace-related—basis. For example, in a laboratory simulation study,

Johnson, Whitestone, Jackson, and Gatto (1995) examined the effect of the introduction of inadmissible evidence, which was damaging to a defendant's case, on whites' judgments of a black or white defendant's guilt. No differences in judgments of guilt occurred as a function of defendant race when all the evidence presented was admissible. Consistent with the aversive racism framework, however, the presentation of inadmissible evidence increased judgment of guilt when the defendant was black, but not when the defendant was white. Furthermore, suggesting the unconscious or unintentional nature of the bias, participants' self-reports indicated that they believed that the inadmissible evidence had less effect on their decisions when the defendant was black than when the defendant was white. Johnson et al. (1995) conclude that these results "are clearly consistent with the modern racism perspective, which suggests that discriminatory behavior will occur only when it can be justified on nonracial grounds" (p. 896). . . .

Recently, we have also found laboratory evidence of direct and indirect patterns of racial discrimination among whites scoring high and low in self-reported prejudice in recommending the death penalty (Dovidio, Smith, Donnella, & Gaertner, 1997). High- and low-prejudice-scoring white college students read a summary of facts associated with a case in which the offender was found guilty of murdering a white police officer following a robbery. The race of the defendant, black or white, was systematically varied. After reading the case and before making a decision, participants viewed five other jurors on videotape individually presenting their decisions to vote for the death penalty in the case. In half of the conditions, all of these jurors were white; in the other half of the conditions, the second juror presenting a decision was a black male student. The main measure of interest was how strongly the participant subsequently recommended the death penalty. . . .

As predicted, high-prejudice-scoring whites showed a straightforward pattern of bias against black defendants: Regardless of the other jurors, they gave generally stronger recommendations for the death penalty for black defendants than for white defendants. Low-prejudice-scoring white participants, in contrast, demonstrated a more complicated pattern of responses. Their strongest recommendations for the death penalty occurred when the defendant was black and a black juror advocated the death penalty. Under these conditions, in which their response could not necessarily be interpreted as racial bias, low-prejudice whites were as discriminating as high-prejudice whites. When, however, all of the jurors were white and thus their responses could potentially be attributed to racial antipathy, low-prejudice scoring whites exhibited the strongest recommendations *against* the death penalty when the defendant was black. Consistent with the aversive racism framework, aversive racism is expressed subtly, indirectly, and in rationalizable ways. Although the bias may be subtle, the consequences may still be of great consequence, potentially influencing life or death decisions. In the next section of the chapter, we examine how aversive racism is reflected in the conscious and nonconscious manifestations of attitudes and beliefs about blacks.

Bias in Words and Thought

We believe that aversive racism has relevance to the way that whites express their racial attitudes. When we ask people directly, as in surveys, "Do you support integration?" "Would you vote for a well-qualified black presidential candidate?" the socially acceptable answer is very obvious to people. To say anything but "yes" could be interpreted by other people and oneself as racial bias. As a consequence, we believe that many of the nationwide surveys overrepresent the racially tolerant response.

Blacks Are Not Worse Than Whites, But . . .

To examine how aversive racism relates to questionnaire or survey responses, we conducted an experiment in which we asked people on 1 to 7 scales (e.g., good to bad) to describe blacks and whites (Dovidio & Gaertner, 1991). These white respondents demonstrated no racial difference in their evaluative ratings. A biased response (e.g., "bad") is obvious, and respondents consistently rated both blacks and whites on the positive ends of the scales. When, however, we varied the instrument slightly by placing positive and negative characteristics in separate scales (e.g., bad, from *not at all* to *extremely*), we found that bias does exist, but in a subtle form. Although the ratings of blacks and whites on the negative scales showed no racial bias, the ratings on the positive scales did reveal a significant difference. Whereas blacks were not rated more negatively than whites, whites were evaluated more positively than blacks. Apparently, aversive racists resist believing that blacks are bad or even that they are worse than whites, remarks easily interpreted as racial bias. Subtle bias is displayed, however, in respondents' willingness to believe that whites are better than blacks. Again, this is not the old-fashioned, overt type of bias associated with the belief about black inferiority. Instead, it is a modern, subtle form of bias that reflects a belief about white superiority. . . .

The identification of aversive racists who say that they are not prejudiced, but who have these unconscious negative associations, is important to our understanding of contemporary racism. For example, in a recent study (Dovidio, 1995), unconscious racial attitudes were used to predict and understand the development of conflict in interracial communication. The study examined the possibility that whites and blacks attend to different aspects in social interactions. A black person and a white person first interacted and then completed questionnaires that asked how friendly they felt they behaved during the conversation and how friendly their partner acted. In general, whites' perceptions of their own friendliness correlated with their self-reported prejudice scores: Those who said they were less prejudiced said that they behaved in a more friendly manner with the black partner in the subsequent interaction. These perceptions were apparently guided by the conscious attitudes of whites; at this level, they seemed to be behaving consistently. In contrast, the perceptions of black partners about the friendliness of these same white participants were more strongly associated with the whites' response latency measure of bias (see also Fazio et al., 1995). That is, in assessing how friendly the white person was, blacks may have been considering not only the overt, consciously controlled behavior of the partner, but also concentrating on the nonconscious behaviors (such as eye contact, nonverbal expression of discomfort) that whites were unable to monitor or control. These findings suggest that although whites may intend to convey a positive and friendly attitude to their black partner and believe that they have succeeded, in the same interaction the black partner may be attuned to the negative or mixed messages inadvertently sent by whites (see Devine, Evett, & Vasquez-Suson, 1996). These unintended messages can produce a very different, potentially conflicting, perspective that can contribute to racial tension and distrust. . . .

What does all this have to do with behavior? If the decisions that people make are biased in systematic ways, they will have biased outcomes for minorities and nonminorities. Attitudes translate into the way people think, and the way people think translates into the way people behave, sometimes as discrimination. In the next section we consider a relatively unique prediction of the aversive racism framework—that more bias is expressed toward higher status blacks. Regarding discrimination, it may also be that it is not that blacks are worse than whites, but that whites are better than blacks.

Higher Status, Greater Bias

We investigated the relationship between status and bias in the context of an important decision for our participants (Kline & Dovidio, 1982). We recruited participants to help us make admissions decisions for their university. Because students believed that their decisions would have direct implications for them, partially determining who would attend their college, we hypothesized that bias against blacks would be expressed, but in subtle ways (Dovidio & Mullen, 1992). Participants were presented with information about an applicant whose qualifications were systematically varied. Some participants evaluated a poorly qualified applicant, some rated a moderately qualified candidate, and others judged a highly qualified applicant. In addition, the race of the applicant was manipulated by a photograph attached to the file. The central question concerned how this picture would affect students' admissions decisions.

Discrimination against the black applicant occurred, but, as expected, it did not occur equally in all conditions. Participants rated the poorly qualified black and white applicants equally low. They showed some bias when they evaluated the moderately qualified white applicant slightly higher than the comparable black candidate. Discrimination against the black applicant was most apparent, however, when the applicants were highly qualified. Consistent with our other studies, there was no bias on the "low" end: Poorly qualified black applicants were not rated worse than poorly qualified white applicants. As in the previous studies, discrimination occurred at the "high" end. Although white participants evaluated the highly qualified black applicant very positively, they judged the highly qualified white applicant, with exactly the same credentials, as even better. . . .

[In another study,] white male undergraduates were introduced to a black or white male confederate who was presented as either the participant's supervisor or subordinate. In addition, the confederate was described as being higher or lower than the participant in an intellectual ability that was relevant to the dyad's task. The dependent measure was an incidental helping task, picking up pencils that the confederate "accidentally" knocked to the floor.

Overall, participants helped black partners more than white partners. The effect of race, however, was moderated by status and ability. Specifically, the results indicated that relative status, rather than relative ability was the primary determinant of helping behavior toward blacks. Black supervisors were helped less than black subordinates, whereas white supervisors were helped somewhat more than white subordinates. Relative ability, in contrast, did not affect prosocial behavior toward blacks. In general, high- and low-ability blacks were helped equally often, whereas high-ability white partners were helped more frequently than were low-ability white partners. Thus, ability, not status, was instrumental in determining helping toward whites, but status, not ability, was the major factor influencing prosocial behavior toward blacks. Given that there were no significant effects involving participants' self-reports of prejudice, it seems that even well-intentioned whites will respond negatively to a black supervisor compared to a black subordinate, regardless of apparent qualifications.

How could people in this experiment rationalize not responding positively to competent blacks? Subjects' postexperimental evaluations of their partners revealed that their behaviors may have been mediated by perceptions of relative intelligence (competence). Although participants' ratings indicated that they accepted high-ability white partners as being somewhat more intelligent than themselves, the ratings revealed that participants described even high-ability black partners as significantly less intelligent than themselves. Blacks may be regarded as intelligent, but not as intelligent as whites. It therefore appears that although whites may accept that a black person is intelligent on an absolute dimension, white participants are reluctant to believe that a black person is higher or equal in intelligence compared to themselves. . . .

Across organizations as diverse as the armed forces, federal government, and Fortune 1000 companies, we find data consistent with our prediction of greater racial disparities at higher-status levels. In addition, these patterns persist over the past decade. Within the Navy, for example, blacks represent 13% of the force, but only 5% of the officers and 1.5% of the admirals. Furthermore, these differences cannot be accounted for by vastly different backgrounds. A recent study by the General Accounting Office (1995) found that, over a recent 5-year period, the success rate of blacks who qualified for promotions was systematically below the rate of whites across all of the military services. Consistent with our model, the disparities in promotion rates tended to increase with higher ranks for enlisted personnel and up through ranks equivalent to Major for officers (Hudson, 1995). We have also examined patterns of disparities for various segments of federal employees and found evidence consistent with our model: Blacks are generally less well represented in higher grades (e.g., GS 16-18) than in lower grades. Furthermore, these disparities have remained relatively stable across time. A study of industry provides independent evidence of the "glass ceiling effect" for minorities (Federal Glass Ceiling Commission, 1995). Representations of minorities consistently decline with higher occupational status. Fewer than 1% of the top-level executives in Fortune 1000 industrial and Fortune 500 service firms are black. Independent research reveals that not only are blacks promoted less frequently than whites, they have less access to training and development opportunities (Greenhaus, Parasuraman, & Wormley, 1990). . . .

Conclusion

In summary, despite apparent consistent improvements in expressed racial attitudes over time, aversive racism continues to exert a subtle but pervasive influence on the lives of black Americans. This bias is expressed in indirect and rationalizable ways that restrict opportunities for blacks while insulating aversive racists from ever having to confront their prejudices. It is an elusive phenomenon: When aversive racists monitor their interracial behaviors, they do not discriminate. In fact, they may respond even more favorably to blacks than to whites as a way of reaffirming their nonprejudiced self-images. When they are not conscious of their actions, however, bias is subtly expressed, usually in ways that can be justified on the basis of some factor other than race. Although the expression of bias may be more subtle, the consequences of aversive racism are comparable to that of old-fashioned racism—the restriction of opportunity to other groups and support for a system that is believed to be fair in principle but that perpetuates the social and economic advantages of the majority group over minority groups.

Even though these negative feelings, which aversive racists harbor toward blacks, may be unconscious and rooted in normal processes, this does not imply that this bias is either excusable or immutable. Having the potential for bias is not an acceptable excuse for being biased. In addition, what is unconscious can, with increased awareness and commitment, be made conscious and replaced by truly egalitarian beliefs and feelings. Racial bias, whether subtle or blatant, is inconsistent with standards of fairness and justice. The unfulfilled potential of human lives as well as the expense of violence and other crimes that arise out of disaffection with the system and personal despair, make racism costly to both blacks and whites. Thus, recognition of this subtle racism may be an essential step in moving a significant segment of white America from feeling nonprejudiced to actually being nonprejudiced.

REFERENCES

American National Election Survey Studies 1948–1994. (1995). Ann Arbor, MI: Interuniversity Consortium for Political and Social Research.

Anderson, J. (1996, April 29/May 6). Black and blue. *New Yorker,* 62–64.

Baldus, D., Woodsworth, G., & Pulaski, C. (1990). *Equal justice and the death penalty: A legal and empirical analysis.* Boston: Northeastern University Press.

Darley, J. M., & Latané, B. (1968). Bystander intervention in emergencies: Diffusion of responsibility. *Journal of Personality and Social Psychology,* 8, 377–383.

Davis, J. A., & Smith, T. W. (1994). *General social surveys, 1972–1994: Cumulative codebook.* Chicago: National Opinion Research Center.

Devine, P. G., Evett, S. R., & Vasquez-Suson, K. A. (1996). Exploring the interpersonal dynamics of intergroup contact. In R. M. Sorrentino & E. T. Higgins (Eds.), *Handbook of motivation and cognition: The interpersonal context* (Vol. 3, pp. 423–464). New York: Guilford.

Dovidio, J. F. (1995, August). *Stereotypes, prejudice, and discrimination: Automatic and controlled processes.* Paper presented at the annual meeting of the American Psychological Society, New York.

Dovidio, J. F., Brigham, J. C., Johnson, B. T., & Gaertner, S. L. (1996). Stereotyping, prejudice, and discrimination: Another look. In N. Macrae, C. Stangor, & M. Hewstone (Eds.), *Foundations of stereotypes and stereotyping* (pp. 276–319). New York: Guilford.

Dovidio, J. F., & Gaertner, S. L. (1991). Changes in the nature and expression of racial prejudice. In H. Knopke, J. Norrell, & R. Rogers (Eds.), *Opening doors: An appraisal of race relations in contemporary America* (pp. 201–241). Tuscaloosa: University of Alabama Press.

Dovidio, J. F., & Mullen, B. (1992). *Race, physical handicap, and response amplification.* Unpublished manuscript, Colgate University, Hamilton, NY.

Dovidio, J. F., Smith, J. K., Donnella, A. G., & Gaertner, S. L. (1997). Racial attitudes and the death penalty. *Journal of Applied Social Psychology,* 27, 1468–1487.

Fazio, R. H., Jackson, J. R., Dunton, B. C., & Williams, C. J. (1995). Variability in automatic activation as an unobtrusive measure of racial attitudes: A bona fide pipeline? *Journal of Personality and Social Psychology,* 69, 1013–1027.

Federal Glass Ceiling Commission. (1995). *Good for business: Making full use of the nation's human capital.* Washington, DC: Government Printing Office.

Gaertner, S. L., & Dovidio, J. F. (1977). The subtlety of white racism, arousal, and helping behavior. *Journal of Personality and Social Psychology,* 35, 691–707.

Gaertner, S. L., & Dovidio, J. F. (1986). The aversive form of racism. In J. F. Dovidio & S. L. Gaertner (Eds.), *Prejudice, discrimination, and racism* (pp. 61–89). Orlando, FL: Academic Press.

Gaertner, S. L., Dovidio, J. F., Banker, B., Rust, M., Nier, J., Mottola, G., & Ward, C. (1997). Does racism necessarily mean antiblackness? Aversive racism and pro-whiteness. In M. Fine, L. Powell, L. Weis, & M. Wong (Eds.), *Off white* (pp. 167–178). London: Routledge.

Gelman, D. (1988, March 7). Black and white in America. *Newsweek, 111,* 24–43.

General Accounting Office. (1990). *Death penalty sentencing: Research indicates patterns of racial disparities* (GAO/GGD-90-57). Washington, DC: Author.

General Accounting Office. (1995). *Military equal opportunity: Certain trends in racial and gender data may warrant further analysis* (GAO/NSIAD Report No. 96-17). Washington, DC: Author.

Greenhaus, J. H., Parasuraman, S., & Wormley, W. M. (1990). Effects of race on organizational experiences, job performance evaluations, and career outcomes. *Academy of Management Journal, 33*(1), 64–86.

Hacker, A. (1995). *Two nations: Black and white, separate, hostile, unequal.* New York: Ballantine.

Hochschild, J. L. (1995). *Facing up to the American dream: Race, class, and the soul of the nation.* Princeton, NJ: Princeton University Press.

Hudson, N. (1995, December 4). Study: Races differ in promotion rates. *Navy Times,* p. 8.

Johnson, J. D., Whitestone, E., Jackson, L. E., & Gatto, L. (1995). Justice is still not color-blind: Differential racial effects of exposure to inadmissible evidence. *Personality and Social Psychology Bulletin, 21,* 893–898.

Johnson, S. L. (1985). Black innocence and the white jury. *Michigan Law Review, 83,* 1611–1708.

Kline, B. B., & Dovidio, J. F. (1982, April). *Effects of race, sex, and qualifications on predictions of a college applicant's performance.* Paper presented at the annual meeting of the Eastern Psychological Association, Baltimore, MD.

Kovel, J. (1970). *White racism: A psychohistory.* New York: Pantheon.

Morganthau, T. (1996, June 24). Fires in the night. *Newsweek, 127,* 28–38.

Nickerson, S., Mayo, C., & Smith, A. (1986). Racism in the courtroom. In J. F. Dovidio & S. L. Gaertner (Eds.), *Prejudice, discrimination, and racism* (pp. 255–278). Orlando, FL: Academic Press.

14

Smells Like Racism

Rita Chaudhry Sethi

When I started my first job after college, Steve Riley, an African American activist, asked me: "So, how do you feel being black?" I confessed, "I am not black." "In America," Steve responded, "if you're not white, you're black."

U.S. discourse on racism is generally framed in these simplistic terms: the stark polarity of black/white conflict. As it is propagated, it embraces none of the true complexities of racist behavior. Media sensationalism, political expedience, intellectual laziness, and legal constraints conspire to narrow the scope of cognizable racism. What remains is a pared-down image of racism, one that delimits the definition of its forms, its perpetrators, and, especially, its victims. Divergent

experiences are only included in the hierarchy of racial crimes when they sufficiently resemble the caricature. Race-based offenses that do not conform to this
model are permitted to exist and fester without remedy by legal recourse, collective retribution, or even moral indignation.

Asians' experiences exist in the penumbra of actionable racial affronts. Our
cultural, linguistic, religious, national, and color differences do not, as one might
imagine, form the basis for a modified paradigm of racism; rather, they exist on the
periphery of offensiveness. The racial insults we suffer are usually trivialized; our
reactions are dismissed as hypersensitivity or regarded as a source of amusement.
The response to a scene where a Korean-owned store is being destroyed with a bat
in the 1993 film *Falling Down* (a xenophobic and racist diatribe on urban life)[1] reflects how mainstream America/American culture responds to the phenomenon of
anti-Asian violence:

> There was, in the theater where I saw the film, a good deal of appreciative laughter
> and a smattering of applause during this scene, which of course flunks the most ob-
> vious test of comparative racism: imagine a black or an Orthodox Jew, say, in that
> Korean's place and you imagine the theater's screen being ripped from the walls.
> Asians, like Arabs, remain safe targets for the movies' casual racism.[2]

The perpetuation of the caricature of racism is attributable to several complex and symbiotic causes. First, Asians often do not ascribe racist motivation to
the discrimination they suffer, or they have felt that they could suffer the injustice of racial intolerance, in return for being later compensated by the fruits of
economic success. Second, many Asians do not identify with other people of
color. Sucheta Mazumdar posits that South Asians exclude themselves from efforts at political mobilization because of their rigid self-perception as Aryan, not
as people of color.[3]

The final and most determinative factor, however, is the perspective that excludes the experiences of Asians (and other people of color) from the rubric of
racism. Whites would deny us our right to speak out against majority prejudice,
partially because it tarnishes their image of Asians as "model" minorities; other
people of color would deny us the same because of monopolistic sentiments that
they alone endure real racism.

For example, a poll conducted by *The Wall Street Journal* and NBC News revealed that "most American voters thought that Asian Americans did not suffer discrimination" but in fact received too many "special advantages."[4] Similarly, when
crimes against Asians were on the rise in housing projects in San Francisco, the
Housing Authority was loathe to label the crimes as racially motivated, despite the
clear racial bias involved.[5] The deputy director of the Oakland Housing Authority's
response to the issue was: "There may be some issues of race in it, but it's largely
an issue of people who don't speak English feeling very isolated and not having a
support structure to deal with what's happening to them."[6]

Other minorities reject Asian claims of racial victimization by pointing to economic privilege or perceived whiteness.[7] Such rejections even occur among different Asian groups. Chinese Americans in San Francisco attempted to classify Indians as white for the purposes of the California Minority Business Enterprise Statute: "If you are a white, male buyer in the City, all else being equal, would you buy from another Caucasian [i.e., Indian] or from a person of the Mongolian race?"[8]

The perspective of some people of color that there is a monopoly on oppression is debilitating to an effort at cross-ethnic coalition building. Our experiences are truly distinct, and our battles will in turn be unique; but if we are to achieve a community, we must begin to educate ourselves about our common denominator as well as our different histories and struggles. Ranking and diminishing relative subjugation and discrimination will only subvert our goal of unity. Naheed Islam expresses this sentiment in part of a poem addressed to African American women:

> Ah Sister! What have they done to us! Separated, segregated, unable to love one another, to cross the color line. I am not trying to cash in on your chains. I have my own. The rape, plunder, pain of dislocation is not yours alone. We have different histories, different voices, different ways of expressing our anger, but they used the same bullets to reach us all.[9]

The combination of white America refusing to acknowledge anti-Asian discrimination, and minority America minimizing anti-Asian discrimination, foists a formidable burden upon Asians: to combat our own internalized racial alienation, and to fight extrinsic racial classifications by both whites and other minority groups. It also renders overly simplistic those suggestions that if South Asians simply became "sufficiently politicized" they could overcome fragmentation in the struggle by people of color.[10]

As activists, a narrow-minded construct of racism impairs our political initiatives to use racism as a banner that unites all people of color in a common struggle.[11] The mainstream use of the word "racism" does not embrace Asian experiences, and we are not able to include ourselves in a definition that minimizes our encounters with racism. Participation in an antiracism campaign, therefore, is necessarily limited to those involved in a battle against racism that fits within the confines of the black/white paradigm, and conversely relegates anti-Asian racism to a lesser realm in terms of both exposure and horribleness.

We need to be more sophisticated in our analysis of racism, and less equivocal in our condemnation. In doing so, we will expand the base of opposition against anti-Asian racism, and forge an alliance against all its myriad forms. The first step in this process is for Asians to apply a racial analysis to our lives. This involves developing a greater understanding of how racism has operated socially and institutionally in this country against ourselves and other people of color, as well as acknowledging our own complicity; and secondly, accepting ourselves as people of color, with a shared history of being targeted as visibly Other. Only then can we act in solidarity with other efforts at ending racism.

Anti-Asian Racism: Fashioning a More Inclusive Paradigm

Racism takes on manifold creative and insidious expressions. Intra-racism, racism among different racial communities, and internalized racism all complicate an easy understanding of the phenomenon. My project here is to uncover shrouded racism perpetrated against Asians, particularly South Asians, in an attempt to broaden the use of the term.

Accent

It is only since 1992 that the Courts have begun to realize the legitimacy of discrimination based upon accent.[12] Immigrants, primarily those not of European descent,[13] suffer heightened racism because of their accents, including job discrimination and perpetual taunting and caricaturization. This is a severe and pervasive form of racism that is often not acknowledged as racist, or even offensive. Even among Asians there is a high degree of denial about the accent discrimination that is attributable to race. In a letter to the *New York Times*, an Asian man blithely encouraged immigrants to maintain their accents, without acknowledging the potential discrimination that we face, though he personally was "linguistically gifted" with an "American accent." The man wrote, "Fellow immigrants, don't worry about the way you speak until Peter Jennings eliminates his Canadian accent."[14]

Accent discrimination is linked directly to American jingoism, and its accompanying virulently anti-immigrant undertones. In the aforementioned movie *Falling Down*, the protagonist has the following exchange with a Korean grocer:

Mr. Lee: Drink eighty-five cent. You pay or go.

Foster: This "fie," I don't understand a "fie." There's a "v" in the word. It's "fie-vah." You don't got "v's" in China?

Mr. Lee: Not Chinese. I'm Korean.

Foster: Whatever. You come to my country, you take my money, you don't even have the grace to learn my language?[15]

A person's accent is yet another symbol of otherness, but it is one that even U.S.-born minorities do not regard as a target for race-based discrimination. Language is implicitly linked with race, and must be treated as such.

Subversive Stereotyping

The myths that are built based on the commonality of race are meant to depersonalize and simplify people. To many, the Indian persona is that of a greedy, unethical, cheap immigrant. This stereotype is reflected in popular culture, where its appearance gives it credibility, thereby reinforcing the image. In the television comedy *The Simpsons*, a purportedly politically sensitive program, one of the characters is a South Asian owner of a convenience store. In one episode, in an effort to make a sale, he says, "I'll sell you expired baby food for a nickel off." Similarly, in the program *Star Trek: Deep Space Nine*, an alien race called the Firengi (Hindi for foreigner) are proprietors and sleazy entrepreneurs who take advantage of any opportunity for wealth, regardless of the moral cost.[16]

These constructs are reified in everyday life as people respond to Indians as if they have certain inherent qualities. Indian physicians, for example, are perceived as shoddy practitioners, who are greedy and disinterested in the health of their patients. In successful medical malpractice suits, Indian doctors are routinely required to pay higher penalties.[17] Similarly, in the now-famous "East Side Butcher" case, where an Indian doctor was convicted of performing illegal abortions, there was no racial analysis despite the fact that no one had been prosecuted for that crime in New York State since the early 1980s despite the fact that hundreds of illegal abortions are performed annually.[18] Another Indian doctor, less than two weeks later, was found guilty of violations in her mammography practice and fined the largest amount in New York State history in such a case. One can not help but wonder if these convictions were, at least in part, motivated by the stereotype of the Indian immigrant.[19]

The Onus

A white, liberal woman once asked my friend Ritu if she wasn't being overly sensitive for taking offense when people put their feet near her face (a high insult in Indian culture), when she could not fairly expect people to understand her culture. The onus is always on us, as outsiders, to explain and justify our culture while also being expected to know and understand majority culture.[20] Constant cultural slights about cows, bindis, and Gandhi are deemed appropriate by the majority while we are expected to subjugate expression of our culture to an understanding and acceptance of American culture. As another example, the swastika is an extremely common, ancient Hindu symbol. However, Hindus cannot wear or display the swastika in America because of Hitler's appropriation of it, and the expectation that we suppress our cultural symbols in an attempt to understand the affront to Jewish Americans. The assumption that it is our normative responsibility to make our culture secondary is racist because it suggests that one culture should be more free to express itself than another.

Religious Fanaticism

Eastern religions are commonly perceived as fraudulent, cultish, and fanatical; they are rarely perceived as equally legitimate as the spiritual doctrines of the Judeo-Christian tradition. The story of immaculate conception is accepted as plausible, while the multiarmed, multiheaded God is an impossible fantasy. Hinduism is portrayed as Hare Krishnas chanting with shaved heads and orange robes; and Islam is characterized as a rigid, violent, military religion. These hyperbolic characterizations are responsible for the fear of religion that causes local communities to refuse to permit places of worship in their neighborhoods.[21]

Western appropriation of Hindu terms reflects the perception of religion as charlatanical; the words have been reshaped through their use in the English language with an edge of irreverence or disbelief.

	Hindi Meaning	**English Use**
1. Guru	Religious teacher	Purported head; self-designated leader
2. Nirvana	Freedom from endless cycle of rebirth	Psychedelic ecstasy; drug-induced high
3. Pundit	Religious scholar	One with claimed knowledge
4. Mantra	A meditative tool; repetition of word or phrase	Mindless chant

Similarly, during times of political crisis (the 1991 Persian Gulf War; the February 1993 World Trade Center bombing), Islam has been the object of derision as a dangerous and destructive religion. After the suspects from the World Trade Center bombing were identified as Muslims, the media, the FBI, and mainstream America responded with gross anti-Muslim rhetoric. A professor in Virginia pointed out the ignorant conflation of the entire Muslim population into one extremist monolith:

> Not all Islamic revivalists are Islamic fundamentalists, and not all Islamic fundamentalists are political activists, and not all Islamic political activists are radical and prone to violence.[22]

Muslims have linked these characterizations of their religion to racial demonization.[23] The *New York Post* carried a headline entitled "The Face of Hate" with the face of a dark-skinned, bearded man of South Asian or Middle Eastern descent (the accused bomber). Similarly, the *New York Times* described the work of courtroom artists: "the defendant's beakish nose, hollow cheeks, cropped beard and the sideways tilt of his head."[24] In an Op-Ed piece in the *New York Times*, one Muslim responded to this description: "Such racial stereotyping serves nothing except to feed an existing hate and fear."[25]

Indicia of Culturalness

Indicia that identify us as Other are generally used as vehicles for discrimination; with East Asians, eye-shape provides the target for racial harassment. South Asians' unique attributes are warped for use as racist artillery: attire (we are towel heads and wear loin cloths and sheets); costume (we are dot-heads); and odor (we are unclean and smelly). Nila Gupta has written about the power of smell, and its identification of South Asians as targets for racist behavior:[26]

> it is spring
> she walks a strong walk
> but they are waiting
> for her in the air
> they can't smell curry and oil poori and dahl for breakfast
> scents they are trained to hate
> confusion
> like hunting dogs after prey
> enraged
> thrown off the scent
> by a river
> enraged
> was she trying to pass?

Gupta's poem recounts a moment of racial discrimination as it is manifested in the degradation of cultural characteristics. When we explore racism, and its effect upon different ethnic and cultural groups, we must also examine the unique ways that specific groups experience racism, and the more neutral proxies and buzz-words used to signify race.

Class Conflicts/Economic Envy

Racism and economic tension are inextricable because race discrimination against Asians has often been manifested as class competition, and vice versa. Since the early 1800s, when Asians became a source of cheap labor for the railroads, we have been an economic threat. As Asians have more recently been portrayed as the prosperous minority, the favored child of America, there has inevitably been sibling rivalry. When auto workers beat up Vincent Chin, was it Japanese competition in the auto industry or unbridled racism that motivated the murderers? When African Americans targeted Korean-owned stores in the riots in Los Angeles after the Rodney King verdict, was it the economic hardship of the inner city and perceived Asian advantages or was it simply racism? The answer is that race and class are inseparable because of the inherent difficulty in identifying the primary or motivating factor; any racial analysis must consider economic scapegoating as an avenue for racial harassment and racial victimization as an excuse for expressing economic tensions.

Conceptual and Perspective Differences

When an immigrant perspective clashes with a white American perspective, the conflict should be considered a racial one. Values such as individuality, privacy, confrontation, competition, and challenging the status quo are considered positive and healthy; however, these components of the liberal state are not necessarily virtues elsewhere. When Hawaiian children do not respond to competitive models of teaching, but thrive in group activities; and when Punjabi children defer to authority, rather than challenge their teachers out of intellectual "curiosity," they are harmed by their inability to function in an essentially and uniquely "American" world. Identifying the differences in perspective and lifestyle between Asian immigrants and Americans will help in recognizing arenas in which we will be at a cultural/racial disadvantage.[27]

A Case Study in Anti-Asian Racism: The Dotbusters of Jersey City

In early fall of 1986, Asian Indians in New Jersey were the targets of racial terrorism. Houses and businesses were vandalized, and graffitied with racial slurs, women had their saris pulled, Indians on the street were harassed and assaulted, and a 28-year-old man was beaten into a coma. The *Jersey Journal* received and printed a letter from a group calling themselves the Dotbusters threatening all Asian Indians in Jersey City, and promising to drive them out of Jersey City. Teenagers in Dickinson High School were found with Dotbuster IDs. In spite of the obvious danger to the community, the police were unresponsive and denied that any Indians should truly be concerned.

The most heinous incident was the murder of Navroze Mody, a 30-year-old Citicorp executive. Navroze was bludgeoned to death with bricks by a group of young Latinos. Long after he had lost consciousness, he was repeatedly propped up and beaten further. His white companion was not touched. Four of the eleven attackers were indicted for manslaughter; two of the indicted were also accused of assaulting two Indian students two weeks before killing Navroze.

Despite the context in which the murder occurred, the incident was not generally perceived as racist in motive by the mainstream, the press, or the Indian community. The ways that Indians were targeted made it convenient to try to find other names for their encounters with racism. Their experiences were unrecognizable as the caricature of racism, and there was a collective refusal to be expansive and open-minded in interpreting what was happening.

The tone for the general characterization of the crime as not racially motivated was set by Hudson County prosecutor Paul DePascale, assigned to Mody's case. Although he conceded that: "There was no apparent motive for the assault other than the fact that the victim was an Asian American,"[28] he refused to pursue criminal charges for racial bias.[29]

The press, a reflection of mainstream sentiment, was reluctant to label the crime as racial in nature. Even *The Village Voice*, a liberal newspaper, carried a story asking above the headline: "Was his [Navroze Mody's] murder racially motivated?"[30] One newspaper accepted the racial motive by qualifying it as a "new" racism/"new" bigotry. The defendants' supporters saw no racial animus against Indians in the crime, inquiring instead: "Do you think there would be justice if it was the other way around? If the Indian were alive and the Puerto Rican dead?"[31]

Indians-at-large were mystified about the source of the anti-Asian wave of violence and found it difficult to accept as pure racism. People looked for other potential justifications and alternative labels.[32] One community leader remarked, "We pay our taxes," and characterized the Indian community as "faultless immigrants" in an effort to distinguish Asian Indians from African Americans and Latinos.[33] A second-generation Indian lawyer characterized such attacks as "national origin" discrimination, rather than racism.[34] Such denial prevented Asian Indians from making the obvious connection to other groups victimized because of their race.

The uncommonness of the anti-Indian discrimination obfuscated the real racism that rested at its core. Economic envy was the most obvious nonracial analysis proffered for escalating crimes against Asians. One Jersey City resident commented: "I've been in this country all my life and they come here and plop down $200,000 for a house."[35] Part of the infamous Dotbuster letter contained similar comments to journalist Ronald Leir: "You say that Indians are good businessmen. Well I suppose if I had 15 people living in my apartment I'd be able to save money too."[36]

Another major source of attack was traditional Indian attire. According to one community leader: "The number two factor for racism is that we look different."[37] Similarly, the hate group, the Dotbusters, takes its name from the cosmetic dot, or bindi, worn by many Indian women on their foreheads.

Finally, Indian languages and residential clustering create a sense of exclusive cohesiveness that threatens Jersey City's non-Asian communities. Anything that represented the insular-seeming culture was the object of harrassment and hatred. Indian religion and cuisine were mocked, and Indians were repeatedly characterized as smelly (due to the lingering scents of cooking spice).

Despite the heinousness of the crime, the Mody case, and anti-Indian violence, did not receive sufficient public attention or outrage. During the same time that the case was being tried, the Howard Beach case[38] was in the headlines of all major newspapers. Of the four Howard Beach attackers, three received manslaughter convictions; of the eleven attackers in the Mody case, three were convicted of aggravated assault, and one of simple assault. Perhaps it was because Asian Indians did not know how to employ the political system that the verdicts returned did not fit the crimes committed. Perhaps it was because the attackers were also minorities. But the main reason why justice was not served was because the racism that Indians were enduring did not fit the neat, American paradigm for racial violence.

In 1993, we can no longer see the world in black and white, where "those who don't fit the color scheme become shadows."[39] Lessons from our battles with bigotry should convince us that our understanding of it and the machinery we have built to fight it are hopelessly obsolete. Denying the richness of our community of people of color ultimately undermines the objective of unity, and hampers our political work combating racism. During the late '80s, the left fought to find a common ground for people of color to coalesce; however, it is now the time to refine our collective mission to truly encompass the range of diversity among us. Any movement forged upon the principles of equality and tolerance can only be legitimate if it represents its margins.

NOTES

1. While the film generated much debate about the possible ironic intent of its stereotyping, the reactions of moviegoers showed that the irony was lost on most audiences.
2. Godfrey Cheshire, complete citation for article not available.
3. Mazumdar, Sucheta, "Race and Racism: South Asians in the United States," *Frontiers of Asian American Studies.*
4. Polner, Murray, "Asian-Americans Say They Are Treated Like Foreigners," *The New York Times*, March 7, 1993, Section B, p. 1.
5. Racial slurs were rampant (including "Go home, Chinaman" and accent harassment) and tension between the Asian and African American community was worsening. The fact that the perpetrators were African American might have contributed to the general reluctance to characterize these crimes as racially motivated. Again, this reflects an inability, or an unwillingness, to intellectually digest racism between non-white races, as it falls outside of the narrow black/white paradigm.
6. Chin, Steven A., "Asians Terrorized in Housing Projects," *San Francisco Examiner*, January 17, 1993, p. B1.
7. Witness this morsel of divisiveness: In Miami, where large Latino and African American populations coexist, a Cuban woman was sworn in as State Attorney General. Many in the African American community were dismayed by this decision, and responded by stripping Cubans of their "rank" as a minority. One black lawyer commented: "Cubans are really 'white people whose native language is Spanish'" and others agreed that Cuban Americans should be "disqualified because they have higher income levels than other minorities." Certainly there is complexity in this conflict; however, the net result is that people who could be in alliance based on race are divided. Rohter, Larry, "Black-Cuban Rift Extends to Florida Law School," *The New York Times*, March 19, 1993, p. B16L.
8. Transcript of San Francisco Board of Supervisors Special Session of Economic and Social Policy Committee, April 30, 1991.
9. Islam, Naheed, "Untitled," from *Smell This*, an official publication of The Center for Racial Education, Berkeley, CA, 1991.

10. Mazumdar, *supra* at p. 36.

11. Here, and throughout this chapter, I am operating within the constructs of our existing political reality. I am not addressing the normative question of whether people of color should be in coalition against racism, but given that it has been our primary organizing principle, how can we be more effective and inclusive?

12. Interestingly, the case was brought by the EEOC while under the tenure of Joy Cherian, a naturalized Indian. The Commission's 1980 guidelines covering this type of discrimination were written by an Indian, and the case was brought by an Indian plaintiff. Is that what it takes to obtain recognition of the racism that we experience?

13. The Executive Assistant for the Commissioner noted: "If an employer has an applicant who speaks with a French accent . . . or with an English accent, they say, 'How cute.' But if he speaks with a Hispanic accent they say, 'What's wrong with this guy?'"

14. Letter to the editor from Yan Hong Krompacky, "Immigrants, Don't Be in Such a Hurry to Shed Your Accents," *The New York Times*, March 4, 1993.

15. Foster then proceeds to demolish Mr. Lee's grocery store with a bat, in much the same way that Japanese cars were hatefully demolished just before Vincent Chin's death.

16. That such stereotypes exist in two programs that are perceived as being among the more progressive on television is itself indicative of the continuing denial that anti-Asian racism exists.

17. According to several medical malpractice attorneys.

18. This was exacerbated further by the fact that Dr. Hayat's sentence was so severe that even the District Attorney's Office had expected less and was "pleasantly surprised." Perez-Pena, Richard, "Prison Term for Doctor Convicted in Abortions," *The New York Times*, June 15, 1993, p. B1.

19. These stereotypes find expression everywhere. I was haggling for a pair of earrings in Times Square, and the vendor asked me if I was Indian. When I replied that I was, he responded, "Oh, I should have guessed. Indians don't want to take anything out of their pockets."

20. In an effort to better integrate into American culture, and mend relations with ethnic groups in New York City, Korean grocers are taking seminars to learn to smile more frequently, supposedly rare in their culture. *The New York Times*, March 22, 1993.

21. "It's the Hindus! Circle the Zoning Laws." Viewpoint by Bob Weiner, *Newsday*, April 26, 1993, p. 40.

22. Steinfeld, Peter, "Many Varieties of Fundamentalism," *The New York Times*, no date. An even better response was: [the World Trade bomber suspect's] "variety of fundamentalism was not any more representative of Islam than the people in Waco are representative of [mainstream] Christianity." *Id.*

23. Op Ed Letter to Editor, "Don't Let Trade Center Blast Ignite Witch Hunt," March 23, 1993.

24. "Surprises in a Crowded Courtroom," Moustafa Bayami, March 5, 1993.

25. *Ibid.*

26. Gupta, Nila, "So She Could Walk," from *The Best of Fireweed*; Women's Press, Canada (1986).

27. Many Asians find themselves in low-ranking jobs in the corporate world because their skills have little application in the old boy cultural network. This is due in part to different concepts of authority and competition, as much as it is pure racial bigotry. My point is that the two should be viewed together to truly understand the full flourish of racism.

28. Vicente, Raul Jr., "Cops Arrest Two as Dotbusters," *Gold Coast*, March 24–March 31, 1988, p. 4.

29. His failure to label this as a racially motivated crime may in fact be racially motivated. In March of 1988 there was opposition by the Inter Departmental Minority Police Action Council in Jersey City to his appointment as the city's acting police director because of alleged discrimination against a black woman officer. "Minority Cops Blast Director," *Gold Coast*, March 31, 1988, p. 7.

30. "Racial Terror on The Gold Coast," *The Village Voice*, January 26, 1988.

31. *Jersey Journal*, March 1, 1988.

32. The collective denial precluded group solutions. Around the same time in Elmhurst 25 African American and Indian families were "preyed" upon in Queens. However, Indians were uninterested in forging an alliance with the African American community to fight ongoing racial harassment. Pais, Arthur, "Long Island Families Were Apathetic and Tearful When Harassed," *India Abroad*, July 31, 1987, p. 1.

33. Walt, Vivienne, "A New Racism Gets Violent in New Jersey," *Newsday*, April 6, 1988, p. 5.

34. Spoken at the Strategy Session for the case of Dr. Kaushal Sharan, March 28, 1993, by a representative of the *Indian American Magazine*.

35. Walt, Vivienne, "A New Racism Gets Violent in New Jersey," *Newsday*, April 6, 1988, p. 5.

36. Letter to *Jersey Journal* on August 5, 1987.

37. Walt, Vivienne, "A New Racism Gets Violent in New Jersey," *Newsday*, April 6, 1988, p. 5.

38. A 1986 attack by white youths in Queens where a group of African Americans were stranded; one person died when he was chased onto a highway by the mob.

39. Zia, Helen, "Another American Racism," *The New York Times*, letter to the editor.

15

Racial Relations Becoming More Complex across Country

Jonathan Tilove

HOUSTON   As a trouble-shooter with the U.S. Justice Department, Efrain Martinez negotiates racial peace in and around America's fourth-largest city.

There are, of course, the classic black-and-white or brown-and-white conflicts. But often now, it is blacks and browns who are butting heads over jobs and power. And increasingly, Martinez finds himself mediating disputes involving peoples who barely existed here 20 years ago.

The Houston area, for example, has one of the nation's largest Vietnamese communities, and over the years Martinez, in his sotto voce style, has defused violent confrontations between Vietnamese fishermen and the Ku Klux Klan, between Vietnamese merchants and black customers and between Vietnamese and Latino residents of the same condominium.

In the past year, he even brokered a truce between Vietnamese and Chinese members of the board of a new Tao temple, prompting one member of the board to gush, "You a hero. You stop a war."

Nationally, and especially in those cities like Houston that are magnets for immigrants, race and ethnic relations are becoming more complexly contentious. In part it is simple math: Greater diversity yields more diverse points of conflict. But a wealth of survey research indicates that inter-minority hostilities and negative attitudes often are more pronounced than those that exist between whites and minorities, though the more polite white attitudes may be as much a function of more affluent distance as meaningful commitment.

Still, Asians in Los Angeles are far more likely than whites to view most blacks and Hispanics as unintelligent, while most Hispanics and Asians—but only a minority of whites—think blacks prefer welfare to self-sufficiency. In New York City, Hispanics and Asians are more likely than whites to think blacks provoke hostility.

In return, blacks more than whites in both New York and Los Angeles consider Asians difficult to get along with. In Houston, blacks rate their relationship with Asians as worse than their relationship with whites.

From *The Star-Ledger* (December 26, 1996). Reprinted by permission of Newhouse News Services, Washington, DC.

"If we posit the original Rodney King question—'Can we all get along?'—the answer is a resounding no," says James Johnson Jr., a professor of business, sociology and geography at the University of North Carolina at Chapel Hill, and the former director of the Center for the Study of Urban Poverty at UCLA.

"I think we're really headed toward more intolerance," says Johnson, who is black.

Diversity's Effect

Not everyone is so sure.

University of Houston sociologist Nestor Rodriguez says it remains to be seen whether Houston's transformation from a city that was more than half Anglo (which is what they call whites here) in 1980, to one that will be 29 percent Anglo, 25 percent black, 39 percent Hispanic and 7 percent Asian by the year 2000, will prove its doing or undoing.

"I have a sense of Houston becoming better," says Rodriguez. He takes hope from the fact that his survey this year of Houston's black and Hispanic communities discovered black ambivalence—rather than one-sided anger—about immigration and people speaking Spanish at work.

Houston, with the largest black population and largest Hispanic immigrant population of any city in the South, has enjoyed relative racial calm. People variously credit its size and sprawl, its deep-seated conservatism and the almost small-town relationships of the leaders of its various racial and ethnic communities. They also credit the deft capacity of the oligarchy that has always run America's freest enterprise city to accommodate as necessary to keep a lid on.

"Our city fathers have always been tremendously successful at smelling a rat, calling it a rat, and driving the rat away," says Barbara Lange, a black woman who serves on the board of the Houston Inter-Ethnic Forum, formed to foster city-wide dialogue on these issues.

Rodriguez thinks Johnson's pessimism is premature, a consequence of looking at race relations through the fractured prism of Los Angeles.

But Johnson says that is not a prism but a window on the future.

"Los Angeles is the cutting edge and leading end of this wave of things to come," he warns.

That whites should now express the most benign racial attitudes of any group may be the final irony for a nation whose racial order was built on bedrock notions of white supremacy, a legacy that still heavily conditions the way new immigrants encounter and evaluate blacks. But there is a logical explanation.

Tolerance of the Affluent

A 1994 National Conference [of Christians and Jews] survey conducted nationally by Louis Harris confirmed that minorities were more likely to stereotype one another than whites were. But, it noted a complementary pattern: "The affluent are more tolerant."

It may be a function of education and sophistication. But it may also be that affluent whites living in comfortable suburbs or gated communities, with children ensconced in good public or private schools, can afford greater tolerance.

One in five whites exited Houston's city limits in the 1980s. Only about one in 10 students in the Houston Independent School District are white. In his annual survey of ethnic relations in Houston, Rice University sociologist Stephen Klineberg discovered that whites are increasingly likely to support principles of ethnic tolerance, and yet oppose government programs designed to support greater social and economic equality.

"Anglos don't support educating minorities of any color," says Rosemary Covalt, a Hispanic activist deeply involved in school politics. Instead, she says, "Anglos play blacks against Hispanics and Hispanics against blacks."

Yet Covalt acknowledges that most of her scrapes are with blacks over control of the schools, and those fights can be quite ugly, though she finds them more satisfying than contending with Anglo reserve.

"Anglos don't vent. They can't, they won't, they don't," says Covalt, though she was pleased to hear cries of white anger emanating from the affluent suburb of Kingwood when it was recently annexed by the city of Houston. "I've never seen so many angry Anglos in my life," says a delighted Covalt.

Dynamics of Friction

Efrain Martinez sketches out Houston's new racial dynamics on a paper napkin. At the top he writes "Heaven," and underlines it. Just below the line he writes, "whites," and at the very bottom of the napkin, he writes, "Hispanics."

"And here," he says, placing his pen point mid-napkin, "are blacks." He explains that many Hispanics see blacks standing between them and their share of public jobs and political power.

The friction with Hispanics is understandable, says Michael Harris, a popular black radio talk host on KCOH in Houston, who often uses his show to foster interethnic dialogue. "They are fighting for the same things we are fighting for. White people have the whole pie."

In the private sector, blacks see immigrants taking jobs that once might have been theirs. The fundamental problem, says Klineberg, is that immigrants are arriving in a city "increasingly unable to produce enough well-paid jobs for the workers who are already here."

The story of South Central Los Angeles, says James Johnson, is immigrants settling in a black community from which the good, industrial jobs have vanished. The employers that remain prefer cheaper, more pliant Hispanic immigrant labor for jobs at the bottom of the economy. And ethnic networks keep those jobs "in the family."

Even a term like "Hispanic immigrant labor," though, obscures more than it illuminates.

At the day labor site in the heavily immigrant neighborhood of Gulfton, more than 200 men gather daily in search of landscaping or construction jobs. Most all the laborers are Hispanic but, says Gonzalo Fernandez, a neighborhood organizer who helps at the site, there are distinct differences among them.

He explains: "The Guatemalans more easily agree to low wages. They come from the most conflicted area of Guatemala, they suffered a lot and they don't want to put up more of a fight than they already put up with in their home country. The Hondurans get the most frustrated because they don't want to work for less than $6 or $7."

As opposed to the black–Hispanic competition, the Asian–black (and sometimes Asian–Latino) relationship in Houston or New York or Los Angeles is often defined by the merchant–customer interaction, which Queens College sociologist Pyong Gap Min says is made to order for negative stereotyping.

Min, the author of a new book, *Caught in the Middle: Korean Merchants in America's Multiethnic Cities,* says those Korean merchants, most arriving from middle-class backgrounds in a thoroughly homogenous country, suddenly find themselves working in poor, black communities with high levels of violence, family breakup and other problems.

Min's New York City survey found that most Korean merchants believed that black people were generally less intelligent, less honest and more criminally oriented than white people.

That same survey found that nearly two-thirds of native-born blacks in New York thought the Korean businesses drained resources from their community, and that about one in five blacks thought Koreans to be a "rude and nasty people."

In Houston, as well, says Rodney Penn, head of Houston's Black United Front, relations at the corner store are defining. "That's the face of the Asian community," he says.

Helping Asian Merchants

Glenda Joe, a chain-smoking Asian-American activist (she is of Irish and Chinese descent) with a blond streak and a Texas twang, wrote a handbook detailing how Asian merchants can get along better with black customers.

"They may not come from a culture where the customer is always right," explains Joe, who grew up working at her father's store in the black community. He knew all about extending credit and developing friendships.

But Victoria Hyonchu Kwon, who has written a book about Koreans in Houston, says it is a very hard-working, insular, self-sufficient community and, as a rule they are just not that interested in getting to know poor black people, or any other non-Koreans for that matter.

Most searing on the psyche of the immigrant community, of course, are the many occasions on which Asian businesses in the black community have been robbed in Houston and other cities, with sometimes fatal consequences.

"Everybody knows someone who has been killed," says Joe.

Dr. Tinh Van Tran, the president of the Vietnamese Community of Houston and Vicinity, who has worked closely with Efrain Martinez resolving many disputes involving his people, recalls a recent occasion when he slowed down to pick up some hitchhikers who were black.

As he slowed, though, Tran recalls, "my mind remembered that my adopted sister got robbed, got beaten." The assailant was black. "I put my foot on the accelerator," he says, acknowledging the unfairness.

Joe Feagin, a leading scholar on race and racism, says immigrants arrive with a melange of home-grown and imported prejudices.

"Latin Americans have a great deal of racism and discrimination against darker-skinned people, Indians and those of African descent, even though their whole ideology is that they don't," he says.

But, he says, you don't have to have lived a day in the United States to have already been deeply influenced by the racial images promulgated in its media.

For example, Feagin says, a Taiwanese graduate student of his at the University of Florida interviewed people in rural Taiwan and found, "They had negative attitudes toward African-Americans even though they hadn't met one. They pick it up from American media."

And, on their arrival in America, Feagin says existing racist tendencies "are immediately reinforced."

"That is the trend," says the Rev. Alcides Alvarenga, the young Salvadoran pastor of a mission church in Gulfton. "We tend to adopt [white American] attitudes and prejudices."

But, he adds, "we do not condone that."

In the end, this attention to skin color and racial identity can be especially vexing for those who don't fit any of the conventional categories.

Romulo and Eva Sandoval are Garifunas from Honduras, the descendants of the survivors of a ship-wrecked slave ship on its way from Africa to the New World.

In Honduras, they say, their racial and ethnic identity was not particularly problematic. But in Houston, they find themselves caught in the middle of the racial crossfire.

White Americans mostly see them as black. That means that at their mostly white church some people assume that they must have become associated with the church through an affiliated drug abuse program. A woman asks Eva, a very well-educated and well-spoken English teacher, whether she works at K-Mart or Wal-Mart. The well-meaning pastor takes pains to inform parishioners that the Sandovals are from good Honduran families.

At the same time, Romulo says, American-born blacks view them as "not really black." And Eva recalls how two Mexican-American women who were her best friends in college heartbreakingly left her out of their wedding parties.

Eva's older sister came to Texas when she was two. "Ask her race and she says, 'black.'" Eva arrived when she was seven. "I'm just Hispanic."

"I find myself being very lonely," says Eva. "I think I have the best of both worlds but when I try to find someone like me I can't find anybody. Have you read that story. 'The Man Without a Country'? Sometimes I feel like that."

16

Racism and Sexism

Manning Marable

What is racism? How does the system of racial discrimination that people of color experience today differ from the type of discrimination that existed in the period of Jim Crow, or legal racial segregation? How is the rich spectrum of cultural groups affected by practices of discrimination within America's "democratic society" today? What parallels can be drawn between sexism, racism, and other types of intolerance, such as anti-Semitism, anti-Arabism, homophobia, and handicapism? What kinds of national and international strategies are needed for a multicultural democracy in the whole of American society and throughout the Western world? And finally, what do we need to do to not just see beyond our differences, but to realize our commonalities and deepen each other's efforts to seize our full freedom and transform the nature of society?

Let's begin with point one: Racism is the system of ignorance, exploitation, and power used to oppress African Americans, Latinos, Asians, Pacific Americans, Native Americans, and other people on the basis of ethnicity, culture, mannerisms, and color. Point two: When we try to articulate an agenda of multicultural democracy, we run immediately into the stumbling block of stereotypes—the device at the heart of every form of racism today. Stereotypes are at work when people are not viewed as individuals with unique cultural and social backgrounds, with different religious traditions and ethnic identities, but as two-dimensional

This article appeared as "Racism and Multicultural Democracy" in Chester Hartman, ed., *Double Exposure: Poverty and Race in America.* Copyright 1977 M. E. Sharpe. Reprinted by permission of the author.

characters bred from the preconceived attitudes, half-truths, ignorance, and fear of closed minds. When seen through a stereotype, a person isn't viewed as a bona fide human being, but as an object onto which myths and half-truths are projected.

There are many ways that we see stereotypes degrade people, but perhaps most insidious is the manner in which stereotypes deny people their own history. In a racist society like our own, people of color are not viewed as having their own history or culture. Everything must conform to the so-called standards of white bourgeois society. Nothing generated by people of color is accepted as historically original, dynamic, or creative. This even applies to the way in which people of color are miseducated about their own history. Indeed, the most insidious element of stereotypes is how people who are oppressed themselves begin to lose touch with their own traditions of history, community, love, celebration, struggle, and change.

In the 1980s we saw a proliferation of racist violence, most disturbingly on college campuses. Why the upsurge of racism? Why was it occurring in the 1980s, and why does this disease continue to spread into the 1990s? How is it complicit with other systemic crises we now face within the political, economic, and social structures of our society?

First, we need to be clear about how we recognize racism. Racism is never accidental within a social structure or institution. It is the systematic exploitation of people of color in the process of production and labor, the attempt to subordinate our cultural, social, educational, and political life. The key concepts here are subordinate and systemic. The dynamics of racism attempt to inflict a subordinate position for people of color.

Racism in the 1990s means lower pay for equal work. It means a process that sustains inequality within the income structure of this country. Institutional racism in America's economic system today means that the rhetoric of equal opportunity in the marketplace remains, in effect, a hoax for most people of color. Between 1973 and 1993, the real average earnings for young Hispanic males age eighteen to twenty-nine declined by 27 percent. For African American males in this age group, the decline was a devastating 48 percent.

Pushing Drugs

What else intensifies racism and inequality in the 1990s? Drugs. We are witnessing the complete disintegration of America's inner cities, the home of millions of Latinos and Blacks. We see the daily destructive impact of gang violence inside our neighborhoods and communities, which is directly attributable to the fact that for twenty years the federal government has done little to address the crisis of drugs inside the ghetto and the inner city. For people of color, crack addiction has become part of the new urban slavery, a method of disrupting lives and regulating masses of young people who would otherwise be demanding jobs, adequate health care, better schools, and control of their own communities. Is it accidental that this insidious cancer has been unleashed within the very poorest urban neighborhoods, and that the police concentrate on petty street dealers rather than on those who actually control and profit from the drug traffic? How is it possible that thousands and thousands of pounds of illegal drugs can be transported throughout the country, in airplanes, trucks, and automobiles, to hundreds of central distribution centers with thousands of employees, given the ultra-high-tech surveillance and intelligence capacity of law enforcement officers? How, unless crack presents a systemic form of social control?

The struggle we have now is not simply against the system. It's against the kind of insidious violence and oppressive behavior that people of color carry out against each other. What I'm talking about is the convergence between the utility of a certain type of commodity—addictive narcotics—and economic and social problems that are confronting the system. That is, the redundancy, the unemployment of millions of people of color, young women and men, living in our urban centers. The criminal justice system represents one type of social control. Crack and addictive narcotics represent another. If you're doing organizing within the Black community, it becomes impossible to get people and families to come out to your community center when there are crack houses all around the building. It becomes impossible to continue political organizing when people are afraid for their own lives. This is the new manifestation of racism in which we see a form of social control existing in our communities, the destruction of social institutions, and the erosion of people's ability to fight against the forms of domination that continuously try to oppress them.

Women's Freedom

How do we locate the connections between racism and sexism? There are many direct parallels, both in theory and in practice, between these two systems of domination. A good working definition of sexism is the subordination of women's social, cultural, political, and educational rights as human beings and the unequal distribution of power and resources between women and men based on gender. Sexism is a subsocial dynamic, like racism, in that the dynamic is used to subordinate one part of the population to another.

How does sexism function in the economic system? Women experience it through the lack of pay equity—the absence of equal pay for comparable work performed by women and men on the job. Sexism exists in the stratification of the vocational hierarchy by gender, which keeps women disproportionately at the bottom. The upper levels of the corporations are dominated by white wealthy males, as is the ownership of productive forces and property. Women consequently have less income mobility and frequently are defined as "homemakers," a vocation for which there is absolutely no financial compensation, despite sixty to eighty hours of work per week.

Sexism within cultural and social institutions means the domination of males in decision-making positions. Males control the majority of newspapers, the film industry, radio, and television. Sexist stereotypes of both males and females are thus perpetuated through the dominant cultural institutions, advertising and broadcast media.

In political institutions, sexism translates into an unequal voice and influence within the government. The overwhelming majority of seats in the Congress, state legislatures, courts, and city councils are controlled by white men. The United States has one of the lowest percentages of women represented within its national legislature among Western democratic societies.

And finally, like racism, the wire that knots sexist mechanisms together, that perpetuates women's inequality within the fabric of the social institution, is violence. Rape, spouse abuse, and sexual harassment on the job are all essential to the perpetuation of a sexist society. For the sexist, violence is the necessary and logical part of an unequal, exploitative relationship. Rape and sexual harassment are therefore not accidental to the structure of gender relations within a sexist order. This is why progressives must first target the issue of violence against women, in the struggle for human equality and a nonsexist environment. This is why we must fight for women's right to control their own bodies.

Sexism and racism combine with class exploitation to produce a three-edged mode of oppression for women of color. Economically, African American, Latina, and Native American women are far below white women in terms of income, job security, and job mobility. The median income of a Black woman who is also a single parent with children is below twelve thousand dollars annually. One-third of all Black people live below the federal government's poverty line. And more than three-quarters of that number are Black women and their children.

Black and Latina women own virtually no sizable property; they head no major corporations; they only rarely are the heads of colleges and universities; they possess no massive real estate holdings; they are not on the Supreme Court; few are in the federal court system; they are barely represented in Congress; and they represent tiny minorities in state legislatures or in the leadership of both major parties. Only a fractional percentage of the attorneys and those involved in the criminal justice system are African American women. It is women of color, not white women, who are overwhelmingly harassed by police, arrested without cause, and who are the chief victims of all types of crimes.

Sexism and racism are not perpetuated biologically like a disease or drug addiction; both behaviors are learned within a social framework and have absolutely no ground in hereditary biology. They are perpetuated by stereotypes, myths, and irrational fears that are rooted in a false sense of superiority. Both sexism and racism involve acts of systemic coercion—job discrimination, legal domination, and political underrepresentation. And both sexism and racism may culminate in acts of physical violence.

Education

What are some other characteristics of the new racism we are now encountering? What we see in general is a duplicitous pattern that argues that African Americans and other people of color are moving forward, whereas their actual material conditions are being pushed back. Look at America's education system. The number of doctoral degrees being granted to Blacks, for example, is falling. The Reagan administration initiated budget cuts in education, replacing government grants with loans, and deliberately escalated unemployment for low-income people, making it difficult to afford tuition at professional schools. Between 1981 and 1995, the actual percentage of young African American adults between the ages eighteen and twenty-six enrolled in colleges and universities declined by more than 20 percent. A similar crisis is occurring in our public school systems. In many cities, the dropout rate for nonwhite high school students exceeds 40 percent. Across the United States, more than fifteen hundred teenagers of color drop out of school every day. And many of those who stay in school do not receive adequate training to prepare them for the realities of today's high-tech labor market.

Despite the curricular reforms of the 1970s and 1980s, American education retains a character of elitism and cultural exclusivity. The overwhelming majority of faculty at American colleges are white males: less than 5 percent of all college faculty today are African Americans. The basic pattern of elitism and racism in colleges conforms to the dynamics of Third World colonialism. At nearly all white academic institutions, the power relationship between whites as a group and people of color is unequal. Authority is invested in the hands of a core of largely white male administrators, bureaucrats, and influential senior faculty. The board of trustees or regents is dominated by white, conservative, affluent males. Despite the presence of academic courses on minorities, the vast majority of white students take few or no classes that explore the heritage or cultures of non-Western peoples or domestic minorities. Most courses in the humanities and social sciences focus narrowly on topics or issues from the Western capitalist experience and minimize the centrality and importance of non-Western perspectives. Finally, the university or college divorces itself from the pressing concerns, problems, and debates that relate to Blacks, Hispanics, or even white working-class people. Given this structure and guiding philosophy, it shouldn't surprise us that many talented nonwhite students fail to achieve in such a hostile environment.

The Color of Our Prisons

The racial oppression that defines U.S. society today is most dramatically apparent in the criminal justice system and the prisons. Today, about half the inmates in prisons and jails, more than 750,000 people, are African Americans. One-quarter of all African American males in their twenties today are in prison, on probation or parole, or awaiting trial. According to a 1991 survey, about one-third of all prisoners were unemployed at the time of their arrest, while two-thirds of all prisoners have less than a high-school-level education and few marketable skills. The prisons of our country have become vast warehouses for the poor and unemployed, for low-wage workers and the poorly educated, and, most especially, for Latino and African American males.

Toward a Multicultural Democracy

So what do we need in this country? How do we begin to redefine the nature of democracy? Not as a thing, but as a process. Democracy is a dynamic concept. African Americans twenty-five years ago did not have the right to eat in many restaurants, we couldn't sit down in the front seats of buses or planes, we couldn't vote in the South, we weren't allowed to use public toilets or drink from water fountains marked "For Whites Only." All of that changed through struggle, commitment, and an understanding that democracy is not something you do once every four years when you vote. It's something that you live every single day.

17

Patriarchy

Allan Johnson

What is patriarchy? A society is patriarchal to the degree that it is *male-dominated*, *male-identified*, and *male-centered*. It also involves as one of its key aspects the oppression of women. Patriarchy is male-dominated in that positions of authority—political, economic, legal, religious, educational, military, domestic—are generally reserved for men. Heads of state, corporate CEOs and board members, religious leaders, school principals, members of legislatures at all levels of government, senior law partners, tenured full professors, generals and admirals, and even those identified as "head of household" all tend to be male under patriarchy. When a woman finds her way into such positions, people tend to be struck by the exception to the rule, and wonder how she'll measure up against a man in the same position. It's a test we rarely apply to men ("I wonder if he'll be as good a president as a woman would be") except, perhaps, on those rare occasions when men venture into the devalued domestic and other "caring" work most women do. Even then, men's failure to measure up can be interpreted as a sign of superiority, a trained incapacity that actually protects their privileged status ("You change the diaper, I'm no good at that sort of thing").

From *The Gender Knot: Unraveling Our Patriarchal Legacy*. Reprinted by permission of Temple University Press. © 1997 by Allan G. Johnson. All rights reserved.

In the simplest sense, male dominance creates power differences between men and women. It means, for example, that men can claim larger shares of income and wealth. It means they can shape culture in ways that reflect and serve men's collective interests by, for example, controlling the content of films and television shows, passing laws that allow husbands to rape their wives, or adjudicating rape and sexual harassment cases in ways that put the victim rather than the defendant on trial. Male dominance also promotes the idea that men are superior to women. In part this occurs because we don't distinguish between the superiority of *positions* in a hierarchy and the kinds of people who usually occupy them.[1] This means that if superior positions are occupied by men, it's a short leap to the idea that *men* must be superior. If presidents, generals, legislators, priests, popes, and corporate CEOs are all men (with a few token women as exceptions to prove the rule), then men as a group become identified with superiority even though most men aren't powerful in their individual lives. In this sense, *every* man's standing in relation to women is enhanced by the male monopoly over authority in patriarchal societies.

Patriarchal societies are *male-identified* in that core cultural ideas about what is considered good, desirable, preferable, or normal are associated with how we think about men and masculinity. The simplest example of this is the still widespread use of male pronouns and nouns to represent people in general. When we routinely refer to human beings as "man" or to doctors as "he," we construct a symbolic world in which men are in the foreground and women in the background, marginalized as outsiders and exceptions to the rule.[2] (This practice can back people into some embarrassingly ridiculous corners, as in the anthropology text that described man as a "species that breast-feeds his young.") But male identification amounts to much more than this, for it also takes men and men's lives as the standard for defining what is normal. The idea of a career, for example, with its 60-hour weeks, is defined in ways that assume the career-holder has something like a wife at home to perform the vital support work of taking care of children, doing laundry, and making sure there's a safe, clean, comfortable haven for rest and recuperation from the stress of the competitive male-dominated world. Since women generally don't have wives, they find it harder to identify with and prosper within this male-identified model.

Another aspect of male identification is the cultural description of masculinity and the ideal man in terms that closely resemble the core values of society as a whole. These include qualities such as control, strength, efficiency, competitiveness, toughness, coolness under pressure, logic, forcefulness, decisiveness, rationality, autonomy, self-sufficiency, and control over any emotion that interferes with other core values (such as invulnerability).[3] These male-identified qualities are associated with the work valued most in most patriarchal societies—such as business, politics, war, athletics, law, and medicine—because this work has been organized in ways that require such qualities for success. In contrast, qualities such as inefficiency, cooperation, mutuality, equality, sharing, compassion, caring, vulnerability, a readiness to negotiate and compromise, emotional expressiveness, and intuitive and other nonlinear ways of thinking are all devalued *and* culturally associated with femininity and femaleness.

Of course, femaleness isn't devalued entirely. Women are often prized for their beauty as objects of male sexual desire, for example, but as such they are often possessed and controlled in ways that ultimately devalue them. There is also a powerful cultural romanticizing of women in general and mothers in particular, but it is a tightly focused sentimentality (as on Mother's Day or Secretaries' Day) that has little effect on how women are regarded and treated on a day-to-day basis. And, like all sentimentality, it doesn't have much weight when it comes to actually doing something to support women's lives by, for example, providing effective and affordable child day-care facilities for working mothers, or family leave policies that allow working women to attend to the caring functions for which we supposedly value them so highly.

Because patriarchy is male-identified, when most women look out on the world they see themselves reflected as women in a few narrow areas of life such as "caring" occupations (teaching, nursing, child care) and personal relationships. To see herself as a leader, for example, a woman must first get around the fact that leadership itself has been gendered through its identification with maleness and masculinity as part of patriarchal culture. While a man might have to learn to see himself as a manager, a woman has to be able to see herself as a *woman* manager who can succeed in spite of the fact that she isn't a man. As a result, any woman who dares strive for standing in the world beyond the sphere of caring relationships must choose between two very different cultural images of who she is and ought to be. For her to assume real public power—as in politics, corporations, or her church—she must resolve a contradiction between her culturally based identity as a woman, on the one hand, and the male-identified *position* that she occupies on the other. For this reason, the more powerful a woman is under patriarchy, the more "unsexed" she becomes in the eyes of others as her female cultural identity recedes beneath the mantle of male-identified power and the masculine images associated with it. With men the effect is just the opposite: the more powerful they are, the more aware we are of their maleness. Power looks sexy on men but not on women.

But for all the pitfalls and limitations, some women do make it to positions of power. What about Margaret Thatcher, Queen Elizabeth I, Catherine the Great, Indira Gandhi, and Golda Meir? Doesn't their power contradict the idea that patriarchy is male-dominated? The answer is that patriarchy can accommodate a limited number of powerful women so long as the society retains its essential patriarchal character, especially in being male-identified.[4] Although some individual women have wielded great power, it has always been in societies organized on a patriarchal model. Each woman was surrounded by powerful men—generals, cabinet ministers, bishops, and wealthy aristocrats or businessmen—whose collective interests she supported and without whom she could not have ruled as she did. And not one of these women could have achieved and held her position without embracing core patriarchal values. Indeed, part of what makes these women stand out as so exceptional is their ability to embody values culturally defined as masculine: they've been tougher, more decisive, more aggressive, more calculating, and more emotionally controlled than most men around them.[5] These women's power, however, has nothing to do with whether women in general are subordinated under patriarchy. It also doesn't mean that putting more women in positions of authority will by itself do much for women unless we also change the patriarchal character of the systems in which they operate. . . .

Since patriarchy identifies power with men, the vast majority of men who aren't powerful but are instead dominated by other men can still feel some connection with the *idea* of male dominance and with men who *are* powerful. It is far easier, for example, for an unemployed working-class man to identify with male leaders and their displays of patriarchal masculine toughness than it is for women of any class. When upper-class U.S. President George Bush "got tough" with Saddam Hussein, for example, men of all classes could identify with his acting out of basic patriarchal values. In this way, male identification gives even the most lowly placed man a cultural basis for feeling some sense of superiority over the othe wise most highly placed woman (which is why a construction worker can feel within his rights as a man when he sexually harasses a well-dressed professional woman who happens to walk by).[6] . . .

In addition to being male-dominated and male-identified, patriarchy is *male-centered*, which means that the focus of attention is primarily on men and what they do. Pick up any newspaper or go to any movie theater and you'll find stories primarily about men and what they've done or haven't done or what they have to say about either. With rare exceptions, women are portrayed as along for the ride, fussing over their support work of domestic labor and maintaining love relationships, providing something for men to fight over, or being foils that reflect or amplify men's heroic struggle with the human condition. If there's a crisis, what we see is what men did to create it and how men dealt with it.

If you want a story about heroism, moral courage, spiritual transformation, endurance, or any of the struggles that give human life its deepest meaning and significance, men and masculinity are usually the terms in which you must see it. (To see what I mean, make a list of the twenty most important movies you've ever seen and count how many focus on men as the central characters whose experience forms the point of the story.) Male experience is what patriarchal culture offers to represent *human* experience and the enduring themes of life, even when these are most often about women in the actual living of them. . . .

A male center of focus is everywhere. Research makes clear, for example, what most women probably already know: that men dominate conversations by talking more, interrupting more, and controlling content.[7] When women suggest ideas in business meetings, they often go unnoticed until a man makes the same suggestion and receives credit for it (or, as a cartoon caption put it, "Excellent idea Ms. Jones. Perhaps one of the men would like to suggest it"). In classrooms at all levels of schooling, boys and men command center stage and receive the lion's share of attention.[8] Even when women gather together, they must often resist the ongoing assumption that no situation can be complete or even entirely real unless a man is there to take the center position. How else do we understand the experience of groups of women who go out for drinks and conversation and are approached by men who ask, "Are you ladies alone?" . . .

Women and Patriarchy

At the heart of patriarchy is the oppression of women, which takes several forms. Historically, for example, women have been excluded from major institutions such as church, state, universities, and the professions. Even when they've been allowed to participate, it's generally been at subordinate, second-class levels. . . .

Because patriarchy is male-identified and male-centered, women and the work they do tends to be devalued, if not made invisible. In their industrial capitalist form, for example, patriarchal cultures do not define the unpaid domestic work that women do as real work, and if women do something, it tends to be valued less than when men do it. As women's numbers in male-dominated occupations increase, the prestige and income that go with them tend to decline, a pattern found in a variety of occupations, from telephone operator and secretary to psychotherapist.[9] Like many minorities, women are routinely repressed in their development as human beings through neglect and discrimination in schools[10] and in occupational hiring, development, promotion, and rewards. Anyone who doubts that patriarchy is an oppressive system need only spend some time with the growing literature documenting not only economic, political, and other institutionalized sexism, but pervasive violence, from pornography to the everyday realities of wife battering, sexual harassment, and sexual assault.[11] . . .

The power of patriarchy is also reflected in its ability to absorb the pressures of superficial change as a defense against deeper challenges. Every social system has a certain amount of "give" in it that allows some change to occur, and in the process leaves deep structures untouched and even invisible. Indeed, the "give" plays a critical part in maintaining the status quo by fostering illusions of fundamental change and acting as a systemic shock absorber. It keeps us focused on symptoms while root causes go unnoticed and unremarked; and it deflects the power we need to take the risky deeper journey that leads to the heart of patriarchy and our involvement in it. . . .

We'd Rather Not Know

We're as stuck as we are primarily because we can't or won't acknowledge the roots of patriarchy and our involvement in it. We show no enthusiasm for going deeper than a surface obsession with sex and gender. We resist even saying the word "patriarchy" in polite conversation. We act as if patriarchy weren't there, because the realization that it does exist is a door that swings only one way and we can't go back again to not knowing. We're like a family colluding in silence over dark secrets of damage and abuse, or like "good and decent Germans" during the Holocaust who "never knew" anything terrible was being done. We cling to the illusion that everything is basically all right, that bad things don't happen to good people, that good people can't participate in the production of evil, and that if we only leave things alone they'll stay pretty much as they are and, we often like to think, always have been.

Many women, of course, do dare to see and speak the truth, but they are always in danger of being attacked and discredited in order to maintain the silence. Even those who would never call themselves feminists often know there is something terribly wrong with the structures of dominance and control that are so central to life in modern societies and without which we think we cannot survive. The public response to feminism has been ferociously defensive precisely because feminism touches such a deep nerve of truth and the denial that keeps us from it. If feminism were truly ridiculous, it would be ignored. But it isn't ridiculous, and so it provokes a vigorous backlash.

We shouldn't be too hard on ourselves for hanging on to denial and illusions about patriarchy. Letting go is risky business, and patriarchy is full of smoke and mirrors that make it difficult to see what has to be let go of. It's relatively easy to accept the idea of patriarchy as male-dominated and male-identified, for example, and even as male-centered. Many people, however, have a much harder time seeing women as oppressed.[12] This is a huge issue that sparks a lot of arguments, and for that reason it will take several chapters to do it justice. Still, it's worthwhile outlining a basic response here.

The reluctance to see women as oppressed has several sources. The first is that many women enjoy race or class privilege and it's difficult for many to see them as oppressed without, as Sam Keen put it, insulting "truly oppressed" groups such as the lower classes or racial minorities.[13] How, for example, can we count upper-class women among the oppressed and lower-class men among their oppressors?

Although Keen's objection has a certain logic to it, it rests on a confusion between the position of women and men as groups and as individuals. To identify "female" as an oppressed status under patriarchy doesn't mean that every woman suffers its consequences to an equal degree, just as living in a racist society doesn't mean that every person of color suffers equally or that every white person shares equally in the benefits of race privilege. Living in patriarchy does mean, however, that every woman must come to grips with an inferior gender *position* and that whatever she achieves will be *in spite of* that position. With the exception of child care and other domestic work and a few paid occupations related to it, women in almost every field of adult endeavor must labor under the presumption that they are inferior to men, that they are interlopers from the margins of society who must justify their participation. Men may have such experiences because of their race, ethnicity, or other minority standing, but rarely if ever because they're men.

It is in this sense that patriarchies are male-dominated even though most individual men may not *feel* dominant, especially in relation to other men. This is a crucial insight that rests on the fact that when we talk about societies, words like "dominance" and "oppression" describe relations between categories of people such as whites and Hispanics, lower and upper classes, or women and men. How dominance and oppression actually play out among individuals is another issue. Sexism, for example, is an ideology, a set of ideas that promote male privilege in part by portraying women as inferior to men. But depending on other social factors such as race, class, or age, individual men will vary in their ability to take advantage of sexism and the benefits it produces. We can make a similar argument about women and the price they pay for belonging to a subordinate group. Upper-class women, for example, are insulated to some degree from the oppressive effects of being women under patriarchy, such as discrimination in the workplace. Their class privilege, however, exists *in spite of* their subordinate standing as women, which they can never completely overcome, especially in relation to husbands.[14] No woman is immune, for example, to the cultural devaluing of women's bodies as sexual objects to be exploited in public and private life, or the ongoing threat of sexual and domestic violence. To a rapist, the most powerful woman in the land is first and foremost a woman, and this more than anything else culturally marks her as a potential victim.

Along with not seeing women as oppressed, we resist seeing men as a privileged oppressor group. This is especially true of men who are aware of their own suffering, who often argue that men and women are both oppressed because of their gender and that neither oppresses the other. Undoubtedly men do suffer because of their participation in patriarchy, but it isn't because men are oppressed *as men.* For women, gender oppression is linked to a cultural devaluing of femaleness itself. Women are subordinated and treated as inferior because they are culturally defined as inferior *as women,* just as many racial and ethnic minorities are devalued simply because they aren't considered to be white. Men, however, do not suffer because maleness is devalued as an oppressed status in relation to some higher, more powerful one. Instead, to the extent that men suffer as men—and not because they're also poor or a racial or ethnic minority—it's because they belong to the dominant gender group in a system of gender oppression, which both privileges them and exacts a price in return.

A key to understanding this is that a group cannot oppress itself. A group can inflict injury on itself, and its members can suffer from their position in society. But if we say that a group can oppress or persecute *itself* we turn the concept of social oppression into a mere synonym for socially caused suffering, which it isn't.[15] Oppression is a social phenomenon that happens between different groups in a society; it is a system of social inequality through which one group is positioned to dominate and benefit from the exploitation and subordination of another. This means not only that a group cannot oppress itself, but also that it cannot be oppressed *by society.* Oppression is a relation that exists *between groups,* not between groups and society as a whole.

To understand oppression, then, we must distinguish it from suffering that has other social roots. Even the massive suffering inflicted on men through the horrors of war is not an oppression of men *as men,* because there is no system in which a group of non-men enforces and benefits from men's suffering. The systems that control the machinery of war are themselves patriarchal, which makes it impossible for them to oppress men as men. Warfare *does* oppress racial and ethnic minorities and the poor, who are often served up as cannon fodder by privileged classes whose interests war most often serves. Some 80 percent of all U.S. troops who served in Vietnam, for example, were from working- and lower-class backgrounds.[16] But this oppression is based on race and class, not gender. . . . If war made men truly disposable *as men*, we wouldn't find monuments and cemeteries in virtually every city and town in the United States dedicated to fallen soldiers (with no mention of their race or class), or endless retrospectives on the fiftieth anniversary of every milestone in World War II.

Rather than devalue or degrade patriarchal manhood, warfare celebrates and affirms it. As I write this on the fiftieth anniversary of the Normandy invasion, I can't help but feel the power of the honor and solemn mourning accorded the casualties of war, the deep respect opponents often feel for one another, and the countless monuments dedicated to men killed while trying to kill other men whose names, in turn, are inscribed on still more monuments.[17] But these ritual remembrances do more than sanctify sacrifice and tragic loss, they also sanctify war itself and the patriarchal institutions that promote it. Military leaders whose misguided orders, blunders, and egomaniacal schemes brought death to tens of thousands, for example, earn not ridicule, disgust, and scorn but a curious historical immunity framed in images of noble tragedy and heroic masculine endeavor. In stark contrast to massive graveyards of honored dead, the memorials, the annual speeches and parades, there are no monuments to the millions of women and children caught in the slaughter and bombed, burned, starved, raped, and left homeless. An estimated nine out of ten wartime casualties are civilians, not soldiers, and these include a huge proportion of children and women,[18] but there are no great national cemeteries devoted to *them*. War, after all, is a man's thing.

Perhaps one of the deepest reasons for denying the reality of women's oppression is that we don't want to admit that a real basis for conflict exists between men and women. We don't want to admit it because, unlike other groups involved in social oppression, such as whites and blacks, females and males really need each other, if only as parents and children. This can make us reluctant to see how patriarchy puts us at odds regardless of what we want or how we feel about it. Who wants to consider the role of gender oppression in everyday married and family life? Who wants to know how dependent we are on patriarchy as a system, how deeply our thoughts, feelings, and behavior are embedded in it? Men resist seeing the oppression of their mothers, wives, sisters, and daughters because we've participated in it, benefited from it, and developed a vested interest in it. . . .

We can move toward a clearer and more critical awareness of what patriarchy is about, of what gets in the way of working to end it, and new ways for all of us— men in particular—to participate in its long evolutionary process of turning into something else. Patriarchy is our collective legacy, and there's nothing we can do about that or the condition in which we received it. But we can do a lot about what we pass on to those who follow us.

NOTES

1. See Marilyn French, *Beyond Power: On Men, Women, and Morals* (New York: Summit Books, 1985), 303.

2. There is a lot of research that shows how such uses of language affect people's perceptions. See, for example, Mykol C. Hamilton, "Using Masculine Generics: Does Generic 'He' Increase Male Bias in the User's Imagery?" *Sex Roles* 19, nos. 11/12 (1988): 785–799; Wendy Martyna, "Beyond the 'He/Man' Approach: The Case for Nonsexist Language," *Signs* 5 (1980): 482–493; Casey Miller and Kate Swift, *Words and Women*, updated ed. (New York: HarperCollins, 1991); and Joseph W. Schneider and Sally L. Hacker, "Sex Role Imagery in the Use of the Generic 'Man' in Introductory Texts: A Case in the Sociology of Sociology," *American Sociologist* 8 (1973): 12–18.

3. Note that I'm *not* describing actual men and women here, but cultural *ideas* about men and women under patriarchy. As concepts, masculinity and femininity play a complex role in patriarchal societies.

4. Just as a white-racist society can accommodate a certain number of powerful people of color so long as they do not challenge white privilege and the institutions that support it.

5. See, for example, Carole Levin's *The Heart and Stomach of a King: Elizabeth I and the Politics of Sex and Power* (Philadelphia: University of Pennsylvania Press, 1994).

6. See Carol Brooks Gardner, *Passing By: Gender and Public Harassment* (Berkeley: University of California Press, 1995).

7. For more on gender and interaction, see Robin Lakoff, *Language and Woman's Place* (New York: Harper and Row, 1975) and *Talking Power: The Politics of Language in Our Lives* (New York: Basic Books, 1990). See also Deborah Tannen, *Conversational Style: Analyzing Talk among Friends* (Norwood, N.J.: Ablex, 1984); idem, *You Just Don't Understand: Women and Men in Conversation* (New York: William Morrow, 1990).

8. See American Association of University Women, *How Schools Shortchange Girls* (Washington, D.C.: American Association of University Women, 1992); and Myra Sadker and David M. Sadker, *Failing at Fairness: How America's Schools Cheat Girls* (New York: Charles Scribner's Sons, 1994).

9. See Paula England and D. Dunn, "Evaluating Work and Comparable Worth," *Annual Review of Sociology* 14 (1988): 227–248.

10. See American Association of University Women, *How Schools Shortchange Girls*; and Sadker and Sadker, *Failing at Fairness*.

11. See Susan Brownmiller, *Against Our Will: Men, Women, and Rape* (New York: Simon and Schuster, 1975); Andrea Dworkin, *Woman Hating* (New York: E. P. Dutton, 1974); Susan Faludi, *Backlash: The Undeclared War Against American Women* (New York: Crown Publishers, 1991); Marilyn French, *The War Against Women* (New York: Summit Books, 1992); Gardner, *Passing By*; Diana E. H. Russell, *Rape in Marriage* (New York: Macmillan, 1982); idem, *Sexual Exploitation: Rape, Child Sexual Abuse, and Workplace Harassment* (Beverly Hills, Calif.: Sage Publications, 1984); Medical News and Perspectives, *Journal of the American Medical Association* 264, no. 8 (1990): 939; Laura Lederer, ed., *Take Back the Night: Women on Pornography* (New York: William Morrow, 1980); Diana E. H. Russell, ed., *Making Violence Sexy: Feminist Views on Pornography* (New York: Teachers College Press, 1993); and Catharine MacKinnon, *Only Words* (Cambridge: Harvard University Press, 1993).

12. For more on this, see Marilyn Frye, *The Politics of Reality: Essays in Feminist Theory* (Freedom, Calif.: Crossing Press, 1983).

13. Sam Keen, *Fire in the Belly: On Being a Man* (New York: Bantam, 1991), 203.

14. See, for example, Susan A. Ostrander, *Women of the Upper Class* (Philadelphia: Temple University Press, 1984).

15. See Frye, *Politics of Reality*, 1–16.

16. Christian G. Appy, *Working-Class War: American Combat Soldiers in Vietnam* (Chapel Hill: University of North Carolina Press, 1993).

17. It is useful to note that in thirteenth-century Europe peasants were not allowed to participate in battle, since the nobility's monopoly over the tools and skills of warfare was its main basis for power and domination over land and peasants. Although knights undoubtedly suffered considerably from their endless wars with one another, one could hardly argue that their obligation to fight rendered them an oppressed group. Whatever price they paid for their dominance, the concept of oppression is not the word to describe it. For a lively history of this era, see Barbara Tuchman, *A Distant Mirror* (New York: Alfred A. Knopf, 1978).

18. Save the Children. Study results reported in *The Boston Globe*, 17 November 1994, 23.

18

Oppression

Marilyn Frye

It is a fundamental claim of feminism that women are oppressed. The word "oppression" is a strong word. It repels and attracts. It is dangerous and dangerously fashionable and endangered. It is much misused, and sometimes not innocently.

The statement that women are oppressed is frequently met with the claim that men are oppressed too. We hear that oppressing is oppressive to those who oppress as well as to those they oppress. Some men cite as evidence of their oppression their much-advertised inability to cry. It is tough, we are told, to be masculine. When the stresses and frustrations of being a man are cited as evidence that oppressors are oppressed by their oppressing, the word "oppression" is being stretched to meaninglessness; it is treated as though its scope includes any and all human experience of limitation or suffering, no matter the cause, degree or consequence. Once such usage has been put over on us, then if ever we deny that any person or group is oppressed, we seem to imply that we think they never suffer and have no feelings. We are accused of insensitivity, even of bigotry. For women, such accusation is particularly intimidating, since sensitivity is one of the few virtues that has been assigned to us. If we are found insensitive, we may fear we have no redeeming traits at all and perhaps are not real women. Thus are we silenced before we begin: the name of our situation drained of meaning and our guilt mechanisms tripped.

But this is nonsense. Human beings can be miserable without being oppressed, and it is perfectly consistent to deny that a person or group is oppressed without denying that they have feelings or that they suffer.

We need to think clearly about oppression, and there is much that mitigates against this. I do not want to undertake to prove that women are oppressed (or that men are not), but I want to make clear what is being said when we say it. We need this word, this concept, and we need it to be sharp and sure.

The root of the word "oppression" is the element "press." *The press of the crowd; pressed into military service; to press a pair of pants; printing press; press the button.* Presses are used to mold things or flatten them or reduce them in bulk, sometimes to reduce them by squeezing out the gases or liquids in them. Something pressed is something caught between or among forces and barriers which are so related to each other that jointly they restrain, restrict or prevent the thing's motion or mobility. Mold. Immobilize. Reduce.

The mundane experience of the oppressed provides another clue. One of the most characteristic and ubiquitous features of the world as experienced by oppressed people is the double bind—situations in which options are reduced to a very few and all of them expose one to penalty, censure or deprivation. For example, it is often a requirement upon oppressed people that we smile and be cheerful. If we comply, we signal our docility and our acquiescence in our situation. We need not, then, be taken note of. We acquiesce in being made invisible, in our occupying no space. We participate in our own erasure. On the other hand, anything but the sunniest countenance exposes us to being perceived as mean, bitter, angry or dangerous. This means, at the least, that we may be found "difficult" or unpleasant to work with, which is enough to cost one one's livelihood; at worst, being seen as mean, bitter, angry or dangerous has been known to result in rape, arrest, beating and murder. One can only choose to risk one's preferred form and rate of annihilation.

Another example: It is common in the United States that women, especially younger women, are in a bind where neither sexual activity nor sexual inactivity is all right. If she is heterosexually active, a woman is open to censure and punishment for being loose, unprincipled or a whore. The "punishment" comes in the form of criticism, snide and embarrassing remarks, being treated as an easy lay by men, scorn from her more restrained female friends. She may have to lie and hide her behavior from her parents. She must juggle the risks of unwanted pregnancy and dangerous contraceptives. On the other hand, if she refrains from heterosexual activity, she is fairly constantly harassed by men who try to persuade her into it and pressure her to "relax" and "let her hair down"; she is threatened with labels like "frigid," "uptight," "man-hater," "bitch" and "cocktease." The same parents who would be disapproving of her sexual activity may be worried by her inactivity because it suggests she is not or will not be popular, or is not sexually normal. She may be charged with lesbianism. If a woman is raped, then if she has been heterosexually active she is subject to the presumption that she liked it (since her activity is presumed to show that she likes sex), and if she has not been heterosexually active, she is subject to the presumption that she liked it (since she is supposedly "repressed and frustrated"). Both heterosexual activity and heterosexual nonactivity are likely to be taken as proof that you wanted to be raped, and hence, of course, weren't *really* raped at all. You can't win. You are caught in a bind, caught between systematically related pressures.

Women are caught like this, too, by networks of forces and barriers that expose one to penalty, loss or contempt whether one works outside the home or not, is on welfare or not, bears children or not, raises children or not, marries or not, stays married or not, is heterosexual, lesbian, both or neither. Economic necessity; confinement to racial and/or sexual job ghettos; sexual harassment; sex discrimination; pressures of competing expectations and judgments about *women, wives* and *mothers* (in the society at large, in racial and ethnic subcultures and in one's own mind); dependence (full or partial) on husbands, parents or the state; commitment to political ideas; loyalties to racial or ethnic or other "minority" groups; the demands of self-respect and responsibilities to others. Each of these factors exists in complex tension with every other, penalizing or prohibiting all of the apparently available options. And nipping at one's heels, always, is the endless pack of little things. If one dresses one way, one is subject to the assumption that one is advertising one's sexual availability; if one dresses another way, one appears to "not care about oneself" or to be "unfeminine." If one uses "strong language," one invites categorization as a whore or slut; if one does not, one invites categorization as a "lady"—one too delicately constituted to cope with robust speech or the realities to which it presumably refers.

The experience of oppressed people is that the living of one's life is confined and shaped by forces and barriers which are not accidental or occasional and hence avoidable, but are systematically related to each other in such a way as to catch one between and among them and restrict or penalize motion in any direction. It is the experience of being caged in: all avenues, in every direction, are blocked or booby-trapped.

Cages. Consider a birdcage. If you look very closely at just one wire in the cage, you cannot see the other wires. If your conception of what is before you is determined by this myopic focus, you could look at that one wire, up and down the length of it, and be unable to see why a bird would not just fly around the wire any time it wanted to go somewhere. Furthermore, even if, one day at a time, you myopically inspected each wire, you still could not see why a bird would have trouble going past the wires to get anywhere. There is no physical property of any one wire, *nothing* that the closest scrutiny could discover, that will reveal how a bird could be inhibited or harmed by it except in the most accidental way. It is only when you step back, stop looking at the wires one by one, microscopically, and take a macroscopic view of the whole cage, that you can see why the bird does not go anywhere; and then you will see it in a moment. It will require no great subtlety of mental powers. It is perfectly *obvious* that the bird is surrounded by a network of systematically related barriers, no one of which would be the least hindrance to its flight, but which, by their relations to each other, are as confining as the solid walls of a dungeon.

It is now possible to grasp one of the reasons why oppression can be hard to see and recognize: one can study the elements of an oppressive structure with great care and some good will without seeing the structure as a whole, and hence without seeing or being able to understand that one is looking at a cage and that there are people there who are caged, whose motion and mobility are restricted, whose lives are shaped and reduced.

The arresting of vision at a microscopic level yields such common confusion as that about the male door-opening ritual. This ritual, which is remarkably wide-spread across classes and races, puzzles many people, some of whom do and some of whom do not find it offensive. Look at the scene of the two people approaching a door. The male steps slightly ahead and opens the door. The male holds the door open while the female glides through. Then the male goes through. The door closes after them. "Now how," one innocently asks, "can those crazy womenslibbers say that is oppressive? The guy *removed* a barrier to the lady's smooth and unruffled progress." But each repetition of this ritual has a place in a pattern, in fact in several patterns. One has to shift the level of one's perception in order to see the whole picture.

The door-opening pretends to be a helpful service, but the helpfulness is false. This can be seen by noting that it will be done whether or not it makes any practical sense. Infirm men and men burdened with packages will open doors for able-bodied women who are free of physical burdens. Men will impose themselves awkwardly and jostle everyone in order to get to the door first. The act is not determined by convenience or grace. Furthermore, these very numerous acts of un-needed or even noisome "help" occur in counterpoint to a pattern of men not being helpful in many practical ways in which women might welcome help. What *women* experience is a world in which gallant princes charming commonly make a fuss about being helpful and providing small services when help and services are of little or no use, but in which there are rarely ingenious and adroit princes at hand when substantial assistance is really wanted either in mundane affairs or in situations of threat, assault or terror. There is no help with the (his) laundry; no help typing a report at 4:00 A.M.; no help in mediating disputes among relatives or children. There is nothing but advice that women should stay indoors after dark, be chaperoned by a man, or when it comes down to it, "lie back and enjoy it."

The gallant gestures have no practical meaning. Their meaning is symbolic. The door-opening and similar services provided are services which really are needed by people who are for one reason or another incapacitated—unwell, burdened with parcels, etc. So the message is that women are incapable. The detachment of the acts from the concrete realities of what women need and do not need is a vehicle for the message that women's actual needs and interests are unimportant or irrelevant. Finally, these gestures imitate the behavior of servants toward masters and thus mock women, who are in most respects the servants and caretakers of men. The message of the false helpfulness of male gallantry is female dependence, the invisibility or insignificance of women, and contempt for women.

One cannot see the meanings of these rituals if one's focus is riveted upon the individual event in all its particularity, including the particularity of the individual man's present conscious intentions and motives and the individual woman's conscious perception of the event in the moment. It seems sometimes that people take a deliberately myopic view and fill their eyes with things seen microscopically in order not to see macroscopically. At any rate, whether it is deliberate or not, people can and do fail to see the oppression of women because they fail to see macroscopically and hence fail to see the various elements of the situation as systematically related in larger schemes.

As the cageness of the birdcage is a macroscopic phenomenon, the oppressiveness of the situations in which women live our various and different lives is a macroscopic phenomenon. Neither can be *seen* from a microscopic perspective. But when you look macroscopically you can see it—a network of forces and barriers which are systematically related and which conspire to the immobilization, reduction and molding of women and the lives we live.

19

Homophobia as a Weapon of Sexism

Suzanne Pharr

Patriarchy—an enforced belief in male dominance and control—is the ideology and sexism the system that holds it in place. The catechism goes like this: Who do gender roles serve? Men and the women who seek power from them. Who suffers from gender roles? Women most completely and men in part. How are gender roles maintained? By the weapons of sexism: economics, violence, homophobia.

Why then don't we ardently pursue ways to eliminate gender roles and therefore sexism? It is my profound belief that all people have a spark in them that yearns for freedom, and the history of the world's atrocities—from the Nazi concentration

From *Homophobia: A Weapon of Sexism*. Published by Chardon Press, Inverness, CA, copyright © 1988. Distributed by the Women's Project, 2224 Main St., Little Rock, AR 72206. Reprinted by permission of the Women's Project.

camps to white dominance in South Africa to the battering of women—is the story of attempts to snuff out that spark. When that spark doesn't move forward to full flame, it is because the weapons designed to control and destroy have wrought such intense damage over time that the spark has been all but extinguished.

Sexism, that system by which women are kept subordinate to men, is kept in place by three powerful weapons designed to cause or threaten women with pain and loss. . . .

We have to look at economics not only as the root cause of sexism but also as the underlying, driving force that keeps all the oppressions in place. In the United States, our economic system is shaped like a pyramid, with a few people at the top, primarily white males, being supported by large numbers of unpaid or low-paid workers at the bottom. When we look at this pyramid, we begin to understand the major connection between sexism and racism because those groups at the bottom of the pyramid are women and people of color. We then begin to understand why there is such a fervent effort to keep those oppressive systems (racism and sexism and all the ways they are manifested) in place to maintain the unpaid and low-paid labor.

As in most other countries, in the United States, income is unequally distributed. However, among the industrialized countries of the world, the U.S. has the most unequal distribution of income of all. (See *The State of Working America 2000/2001*, p. 388.) What's more, over the past 30 plus years, income distribution has become even more unequal. In an OpEd piece distributed by Knight/Rider/Tribune NewsService, Holly Sklar reports that poverty rates in 2001 were higher than in the 1970s and the top 5% of households got richer at the expense of everyone else. According to the U.S. Census bureau, there were 33 million poor in the U.S. in 2001 and median pretax income fell for all households except those in the top 5%. In other words, income inequality increased dramatically. In 1967, the wealthiest 5% of households had 17.5% of the income and by 2001 they had increased their share to 22.4%, while the bottom fifth had to make do with 3.5% of aggregate income, down from 4% in 1967 (September 30, 2002). And wealth is even more unequally distributed than income. According to U.S. government figures for 1997, the wealthiest 10% of U.S. families own more than 72% of the total wealth, with 39% of the total wealth concentrated in the hands of the wealthiest 1%. In contrast, the bottom 40% of the population owns less than 1%.

In order for this top-heavy system of economic inequity to maintain itself, the 90 percent on the bottom must keep supplying cheap labor. A very complex, intricate system of institutionalized oppressions is necessary to maintain the status quo so that the vast majority will not demand its fair share of wealth and resources and bring the system down. Every institution—schools, banks, churches, government, courts, media, etc.—as well as individuals must be enlisted in the campaign to maintain such a system of gross inequity.

What would happen if women gained the earning opportunities and power that men have? What would happen if these opportunities were distributed equitably, no matter what sex one was, no matter what race one was born into, and no matter where one lived? What if educational and training opportunities were equal? Would women spend most of our youth preparing for marriage? Would marriage be based on economic survival for women? What would happen to issues of power and control? Would women stay with our batterers? If a woman had economic independence in a society where women had equal opportunities, would she still be thought of as owned by her father or husband?

Economics is the great controller in both sexism and racism. If a person can't acquire food, shelter, and clothing and provide them for children, then that person can be forced to do many things in order to survive. The major tactic, worldwide, is to provide unrecompensed or inadequately recompensed labor for the benefit of those who control wealth. Hence, we see women performing unpaid labor in the home or filling low-paid jobs, and we see people of color in the lowest-paid jobs available.

The method is complex: limit educational and training opportunities for women and for people of color and then withhold adequate paying jobs with the excuse that people of color and women are incapable of filling them. Blame the economic victim and keep the victim's self-esteem low through invisibility and distortion within the media and education. Allow a few people of color and women to succeed among the profitmakers so that blaming those who don't "make it" can be intensified. Encourage those few who succeed in gaining power now to turn against those who remain behind rather than to use their resources to make change for all. Maintain the myth of scarcity—that there are not enough jobs, resources, etc., to go around—among the middle class so that they will not unite with laborers, immigrants, and the unemployed. The method keeps in place a system of control and profit by a few and a constant source of cheap labor to maintain it.

If anyone steps out of line, take her/his job away. Let homelessness and hunger do their work. The economic weapon works. And we end up saying, "I would do this or that—be openly who I am, speak out against injustice, work for civil rights, join a labor union, go to a political march, etc.—if I didn't have this job. I can't afford to lose it." We stay in an abusive situation because we see no other way to survive. . . .

Violence against women is directly related to the condition of women in a society that refuses us equal pay, equal access to resources, and equal status with males. From this condition comes men's confirmation of their sense of ownership of women, power over women, and assumed right to control women for their own means. Men physically and emotionally abuse women because they *can*, because they live in a world that gives them permission. Male violence is fed by their sense of their *right* to dominate and control, and their sense of superiority over a group of people who, because of gender, they consider inferior to them.

It is not just the violence but the threat of violence that controls our lives. Because the burden of responsibility has been placed so often on the potential victim, as women we have curtailed our freedom in order to protect ourselves from violence. Because of the threat of rapists, we stay on alert, being careful not to walk in isolated places, being careful where we park our cars, adding incredible security measures to our homes—massive locks, lights, alarms, if we can afford them—and we avoid places where we will appear vulnerable or unprotected while the abuser walks with freedom. Fear, often now so commonplace that it is unacknowledged, shapes our lives, reducing our freedom. . . .

Part of the way sexism stays in place is the societal promise of survival, false and unfulfilled as it is, that women will not suffer violence if we attach ourselves to a man to protect us. A woman without a man is told she is vulnerable to external violence and, worse, that there is something wrong with her. When the male abuser calls a woman a lesbian, he is not so much labeling her a woman who loves women as he is warning her that by resisting him, she is choosing to be outside society's protection from male institutions and therefore from wide-ranging, unspecified, ever-present violence. When she seeks assistance from woman friends or a battered women's shelter, he recognizes the power in woman bonding and fears loss of her servitude and loyalty: the potential loss of his control. The concern is not affectional/sexual identity: the concern is disloyalty and the threat is violence.

The threat of violence against women who step out of line or who are disloyal is made all the more powerful by the fact that women do not have to do anything—they may be paragons of virtue and subservience—to receive violence against our lives: the violence still comes. It comes because of the woman-hating that exists throughout society. Chance plays a larger part than virtue in keeping women safe. Hence, with violence always a threat to us, women can never feel completely secure and confident. Our sense of safety is always fragile and tenuous.

Many women say that verbal violence causes more harm than physical violence because it damages self-esteem so deeply. Women have not wanted to hear battered women say that the verbal abuse was as hurtful as the physical abuse: to acknowledge that truth would be tantamount to acknowledging that *virtually every woman is a battered woman*. It is difficult to keep strong against accusations of being a bitch, stupid, inferior, etc., etc. It is especially difficult when these individual assaults are backed up by a society that shows women in textbooks, advertising, TV programs, movies, etc. as debased, silly, inferior, and sexually objectified, and a society that gives tacit approval to pornography. When we internalize these messages, we call the result "low self-esteem," a therapeutic individualized term. It seems to me we should use the more political expression: when we internalize these messages, we experience *internalized sexism*, and we experience it in common with all women living in a sexist world. The violence against us is supported by a society in which woman-hating is deeply imbedded.

In "Eyes on the Prize," a 1987 Public Television documentary about the Civil Rights Movement, an older white woman says about her youth in the South that it was difficult to be anything different from what was around her when there was no vision for another way to be. Our society presents images of women that say it is appropriate to commit violence against us. Violence is committed against women because we are seen as inferior in status and in worth. It has been the work of the women's movement to present a vision of another way to be.

Every time a woman gains the strength to resist and leave her abuser, we are given a model of the importance of stepping out of line, of moving toward freedom.

And we all gain strength when she says to violence, "Never again!" Thousands of women in the last fifteen years have resisted their abusers to come to this country's 1100 battered women's shelters. There they have sat down with other women to share their stories, to discover that their stories again and again are the same, to develop an analysis that shows that violence is a statement about power and control, and to understand how sexism creates the climate for male violence. Those brave women are now a part of a movement that gives hope for another way to live in equality and peace.

Homophobia works effectively as a weapon of sexism because it is joined with a powerful arm, heterosexism. Heterosexism creates the climate for homophobia with its assumption that the world is and must be heterosexual and its display of power and privilege as the norm. Heterosexism is the systemic display of homophobia in the institutions of society. Heterosexism and homophobia work together to enforce compulsory heterosexuality and that bastion of patriarchal power, the nuclear family. The central focus of the rightwing attack against women's liberation is that women's equality, women's self-determination, women's control of our own bodies and lives will damage what they see as the crucial societal institution, the nuclear family. The attack has been led by fundamentalist ministers across the country. The two areas they have focused on most consistently are abortion and homosexuality, and their passion has led them to bomb women's clinics and to recommend deprogramming for homosexuals and establishing camps to quarantine people with AIDS. To resist marriage and/or heterosexuality is to risk severe punishment and loss.

It is not by chance that when children approach puberty and increased sexual awareness they begin to taunt each other by calling these names: "queer," "faggot," "pervert." It is at puberty that the full force of society's pressure to conform to heterosexuality and prepare for marriage is brought to bear. Children know what we have taught them, and we have given clear messages that those who deviate from standard expectations are to be made to get back in line. The best controlling tactic at puberty is to be treated as an outsider, to be ostracized at a time when it feels most vital to be accepted. Those who are different must be made to suffer loss. It is also at puberty that misogyny begins to be more apparent, and girls are pressured to conform to societal norms that do not permit them to realize their full potential. It is at this time that their academic achievements begin to decrease as they are coerced into compulsory heterosexuality and trained for dependency upon a man, that is, for economic survival.

There was a time when the two most condemning accusations against a woman meant to ostracize and disempower her were "whore" and "lesbian." The sexual revolution and changing attitudes about heterosexual behavior may have led to some lessening of the power of the word *whore*, though it still has strength as a threat to sexual property and prostitutes are stigmatized and abused. However, the word *lesbian* is still fully charged and carries with it the full threat of loss of power and privilege, the threat of being cut asunder, abandoned, and left outside society's protection.

To be a lesbian is to be *perceived* as someone who has stepped out of line, who has moved out of sexual/economic dependence on a male, who is woman-identified. A lesbian is perceived as someone who can live without a man, and who is therefore (however illogically) against men. A lesbian is perceived as being outside the acceptable, routinized order of things. She is seen as someone who has no societal institutions to protect her and who is not privileged to the protection of individual males. Many heterosexual women see her as someone who stands in contradiction to the sacrifices they have made to conform to compulsory heterosexuality. A lesbian is perceived as a threat to the nuclear family, to male dominance and control, to the very heart of sexism.

Gay men are perceived also as a threat to male dominance and control, and the homophobia expressed against them has the same roots in sexism as does homophobia against lesbians. Visible gay men are the objects of extreme hatred and fear by heterosexual men because their breaking ranks with male heterosexual solidarity is seen as a damaging rent in the very fabric of sexism. They are seen as betrayers, as traitors who must be punished and eliminated. In the beating and killing of gay men we see clear evidence of this hatred. When we see the fierce homophobia expressed toward gay men, we can begin to understand the ways sexism also affects males through imposing rigid, dehumanizing gender roles on them. The two circumstances in which it is legitimate for men to be openly physically affectionate with one another are in competitive sports and in the crisis of war. For many men, these two experiences are the highlights of their lives, and they think of them again and again with nostalgia. War and sports offer a cover of all-male safety and dominance to keep away the notion of affectionate openness being identified with homosexuality. When gay men break ranks with male roles through bonding and affection outside the arenas of war and sports, they are perceived as not being "real men," that is, as being identified with women, the weaker sex that must be dominated and that over the centuries has been the object of male hatred and abuse. Misogyny gets transferred to gay men with a vengeance and is increased by the fear that their sexual identity and behavior will bring down the entire system of male dominance and compulsory heterosexuality.

If lesbians are established as threats to the status quo, as outcasts who must be punished, homophobia can wield its power over all women through lesbian baiting. Lesbian baiting is an attempt to control women by labeling us as lesbians because our behavior is not acceptable, that is, when we are being independent, going our own way, living whole lives, fighting for our rights, demanding equal pay, saying no to violence, being self-assertive, bonding with and loving the company of women, assuming the right to our bodies, insisting upon our own authority, making changes that include us in society's decision-making; lesbian baiting occurs when women are called lesbians because we resist male dominance and control. And it has little or nothing to do with one's sexual identity.

To be named as lesbian threatens all women, not just lesbians, with great loss. And any woman who steps out of role risks being called a lesbian. To understand how this is a threat to all women, one must understand that any woman can be called a lesbian and there is no real way she can defend herself: there is no way to credential one's sexuality. ("The Children's Hour," a Lillian Hellman play, makes this point when a student asserts two teachers are lesbians and they have no way to disprove it.) She may be married or divorced, have children, dress in the most feminine manner, have sex with men, be celibate—but there are lesbians who do all those things. *Lesbians look like all women and all women look like lesbians.* There is no guaranteed method of identification, and as we all know, sexual identity can be kept hidden. (The same is true for men. There is no way to prove their sexual identity, though many go to extremes to prove heterosexuality.) Also, women are not necessarily born lesbian. Some seem to be, but others become lesbians later in life after having lived heterosexual lives. Lesbian baiting of heterosexual women would not work if there were a definitive way to identify lesbians (or heterosexuals).

We have yet to understand clearly how sexual identity develops. And this is disturbing to some people, especially those who are determined to discover how lesbian and gay identity is formed so that they will know where to start in eliminating it. (Isn't it odd that there is so little concern about discovering the causes of heterosexuality?) There are many theories: genetic makeup, hormones, socialization, environment, etc. But there is no conclusive evidence that indicates that heterosexuality comes from one process and homosexuality from another.

We do know, however, that sexual identity can be in flux, and we know that sexual identity means more than just the gender of people one is attracted to and has sex with. To be a lesbian has as many ramifications as for a woman to be heterosexual. It is more than sex, more than just the bedroom issue many would like to make it: it is a woman-centered life with all the social interconnections that entails. Some lesbians are in long-term relationships, some in short-term ones, some date, some are celibate, some are married to men, some remain as separate as possible from men, some have children by men, some by alternative insemination, some seem "feminine" by societal standards, some "masculine," some are doctors, lawyers and ministers, some laborers, housewives and writers: what all share in common is a sexual/affectional identity that focuses on women in its attractions and social relationships.

If lesbians are simply women with a particular sexual identity who look and act like all women, then the major difference in living out a lesbian sexual identity as opposed to a heterosexual identity is that as lesbians we live in a homophobic world that threatens and imposes damaging loss on us for *being who we are*, for choosing to live whole lives. Homophobic people often assert that homosexuals have the choice of not being homosexual; that is, we don't have to act out our sexual identity. In that case, I want to hear heterosexuals talk about their willingness not to act out their sexual identity, including not just sexual activity but heterosexual social interconnections and heterosexual privilege. It is a question of wholeness. It is very difficult for one to be denied the life of a sexual being, whether expressed in sex or in physical affection, and to feel complete, whole. For our loving relationships with humans feed the life of the spirit and enable us to overcome our basic isolation and to be interconnected with humankind.

If, then, any woman can be named a lesbian and be threatened with terrible losses, what is it she fears? Are these fears real? Being vulnerable to a homophobic world can lead to these losses:

- *Employment.* The loss of job leads us right back to the economic connection to sexism. This fear of job loss exists for almost every lesbian except perhaps those who are self-employed or in a business that does not require societal approval. Consider how many businesses or organizations you know that will hire and protect people who are openly gay or lesbian.
- *Family.* Their approval, acceptance, love.
- *Children.* Many lesbians and gay men have children, but very, very few gain custody in court challenges, even if the other parent is a known abuser. Other children may be kept away from us as though gays and lesbians are abusers. There are written and unwritten laws prohibiting lesbians and gays from being foster parents or from adopting children. There is an irrational fear that children in contact with lesbians and gays will become homosexual through influence or that they will be sexually abused. Despite our knowing that 95 percent of those who sexually abuse children are heterosexual men, there are no policies keeping heterosexual men from teaching or working with children, yet in almost every school system in America, visible gay men and lesbians are not hired through either written or unwritten law.
- *Heterosexual privilege and protection.* No institutions, other than those created by lesbians and gays—such as the Metropolitan Community Church, some counseling centers, political organizations such as the National Gay and Lesbian Task Force, the National Coalition of Black Lesbians and Gays, the Lambda Legal Defense and Education Fund, etc.—affirm homosexuality and offer protection. Affirmation and protection cannot be gained from the criminal justice system, mainline churches, educational institutions, the government.
- *Safety.* There is nowhere to turn for safety from physical and verbal attacks because the norm presently in this country is that it is acceptable to be overtly homophobic. Gay men are beaten on the streets; lesbians are kidnapped and "deprogrammed." The National Gay and Lesbian Task Force, in an extended study, has documented violence against lesbians and gay men and noted the inadequate response of the criminal justice system. One of the major differences between homophobia/heterosexism and racism and sexism is that because of the Civil Rights Movement and the women's movement racism and sexism are expressed more covertly (though with great harm); because there has not been a major, visible lesbian and gay movement, it is permissible to be overtly homophobic in any institution or public forum. Churches spew forth homophobia in the same way they did racism prior to the Civil Rights Movement. Few laws are in place to protect lesbians and gay men, and the criminal justice system is wracked with homophobia.

- *Mental health.* An overtly homophobic world in which there is full permission to treat lesbians and gay men with cruelty makes it difficult for lesbians and gay men to maintain a strong sense of well-being and self-esteem. Many lesbians and gay men are beaten, raped, killed, subjected to aversion therapy, or put in mental institutions. The impact of such hatred and negativity can lead one to depression and, in some cases, to suicide. The toll on the gay and lesbian community is devastating.
- *Community.* There is rejection by those who live in homophobic fear, those who are afraid of association with lesbians and gay men. For many in the gay and lesbian community, there is a loss of public acceptance, a loss of allies, a loss of place and belonging.
- *Credibility.* This fear is large for many people: the fear that they will no longer be respected, listened to, honored, believed. They fear they will be social outcasts.

The list goes on and on. But any one of these essential components of a full life is large enough to make one deeply fear its loss. A black woman once said to me in a workshop, "When I fought for Civil Rights, I always had my family and community to fall back on even when they didn't fully understand or accept what I was doing. I don't know if I could have borne losing them. And you people don't have either with you. It takes my breath away."

What does a woman have to do to get called a lesbian? Almost anything, sometimes nothing at all, but certainly anything that threatens the status quo, anything that steps out of role, anything that asserts the rights of women, anything that doesn't indicate submission and subordination. Assertiveness, standing up for oneself, asking for more pay, better working conditions, training for and accepting a non-traditional (you mean a man's?) job, enjoying the company of women, being financially independent, being in control of one's life, depending first and foremost upon oneself, thinking that one can do whatever needs to be done, but above all, working for the rights and equality of women.

In the backlash to the gains of the women's liberation movement, there has been an increased effort to keep definitions man-centered. Therefore, to work on behalf of women must mean to work against men. To love women must mean that one hates men. A very effective attack has been made against the word *feminist* to make it a derogatory word. In current backlash usage, *feminist* equals *man-hater* which equals *lesbian*. This formula is created in the hope that women will be frightened away from their work on behalf of women. Consequently, we now have women who believe in the rights of women and work for those rights while from fear deny that they are feminists, or refuse to use the word because it is so "abrasive."

So what does one do in an effort to keep from being called a lesbian? She steps back into line, into the role that is demanded of her, tries to behave in such a way that doesn't threaten the status of men, and if she works for women's rights, she begins modifying that work. When women's organizations begin doing significant social change work, they inevitably are lesbian-baited; that is, funders or institutions or community members tell us that they can't work with us because of our "man-hating attitudes" or the presence of lesbians. We are called too strident, told we are making enemies, not doing good. . . .

In my view, homophobia has been one of the major causes of the failure of the women's liberation movement to make deep and lasting change. (The other major block has been racism.) We were fierce when we set out but when threatened with the loss of heterosexual privilege, we began putting on brakes. Our best-known nationally distributed women's magazine was reluctant to print articles about lesbians, began putting a man on the cover several times a year, and writing articles about women who succeeded in a man's world. We worried about our image, our being all right, our being "real women" despite our work. Instead of talking about the elimination of sexual gender roles, we stepped back and talked about "sex role stereotyping" as the issue. Change around the edges for middle-class white women began to be talked about as successes. We accepted tokenism and integration, forgetting that equality for all women, for all people — and not just equality of white middle-class women with white men — was the goal that we could never put behind us.

But despite backlash and retreats, change is growing from within. The women's liberation movement is beginning to gain strength again because there are women who are talking about liberation for all women. We are examining sexism, racism, homophobia, classism, anti-Semitism, ageism, ableism, and imperialism, and we see everything as connected. This change in point of view represents the third wave of the women's liberation movement, a new direction that does not get mass media coverage and recognition. It has been initiated by women of color and lesbians who were marginalized or rendered invisible by the white heterosexual leaders of earlier efforts. The first wave was the 19th and early 20th century campaign for the vote; the second, beginning in the 1960s, focused on the Equal Rights Amendment and abortion rights. Consisting of predominantly white middle-class women, both failed in recognizing issues of equality and empowerment for all women. The third wave of the movement, multi-racial and multi-issued, seeks the transformation of the world for us all. We know that we won't get there until everyone gets there; that we must move forward in a great strong line, hand in hand, not just a few at a time.

We know that the arguments about homophobia originating from mental health and Biblical/religious attitudes can be settled when we look at the sexism that permeates religious and psychiatric history. The women of the third wave of the women's liberation movement know that *without the existence of sexism, there would be no homophobia.*

Finally, we know that as long as the word *lesbian* can strike fear in any woman's heart, then work on behalf of women can be stopped; the only successful work against sexism must include work against homophobia.

White Privilege:
Unpacking the Invisible Knapsack

Peggy McIntosh

Through work to bring materials from Women's Studies into the rest of the curriculum, I have often noticed men's unwillingness to grant that they are overprivileged, even though they may grant that women are disadvantaged. They may say they will work to improve women's status, in the society, the university, or the curriculum, but they can't or won't support the idea of lessening men's. Denials which amount to taboos surround the subject of advantages which men gain from women's disadvantages. These denials protect male privilege from being fully acknowledged, lessened or ended.

Thinking through unacknowledged male privilege as a phenomenon, I realized that since hierarchies in our society are interlocking, there was most likely a phenomenon of white privilege which was similarly denied and protected. As a white person, I realized I had been taught about racism as something which puts others at a disadvantage, but had been taught not to see one of its corollary aspects, white privilege, which puts me at an advantage.

I think whites are carefully taught not to recognize white privilege, as males are taught not to recognize male privilege. So I have begun in an untutored way to ask what it is like to have white privilege. I have come to see white privilege as an invisible package of unearned assets which I can count on cashing in each day, but about which I was "meant" to remain oblivious. White privilege is like an invisible weightless knapsack of special provisions, maps, passports, codebooks, visas, clothes, tools and blank checks.

Describing white privilege makes one newly accountable. As we in Women's Studies work to reveal male privilege and ask men to give up some of their power, so one who writes about having white privilege must ask, "Having described it, what will I do to lessen or end it?"

After I realized the extent to which men work from a base of unacknowledged privilege, I understood that much of their oppressiveness was unconscious. Then I remembered the frequent charges from women of color that white women whom they encounter are oppressive. I began to understand why we are justly seen as oppressive, even when we don't see ourselves that way. I began to count the ways in which I enjoy unearned skin privilege and have been conditioned into oblivion about its existence.

My schooling gave me no training in seeing myself as an oppressor, as an unfairly advantaged person, or as a participant in a damaged culture. I was taught to see myself as an individual whose moral state depended on her individual moral will. My schooling followed the pattern my colleague Elizabeth Minnich has pointed out: whites are taught to think of their lives as morally neutral, normative, and average, and also ideal, so that when we work to benefit others, this is seen as work which will allow "them" to be more like "us."

I decided to try to work on myself at least by identifying some of the daily effects of white privilege in my life. I have chosen those conditions which I think in my case *attach somewhat more to skin-color privilege* than to class, religion, ethnic status, or geographical location, though of course all these other factors are intricately intertwined. As far as I can see, my African American co-workers, friends and acquaintances with whom I come into daily or frequent contact in this particular time, place, and line of work cannot count on most of these conditions.

1. I can if I wish arrange to be in the company of people of my race most of the time.
2. If I should need to move, I can be pretty sure of renting or purchasing housing in an area which I can afford and in which I would want to live.
3. I can be pretty sure that my neighbors in such a location will be neutral or pleasant to me.
4. I can go shopping alone most of the time, pretty well assured that I will not be followed or harassed.
5. I can turn on the television or open to the front page of the paper and see people of my race widely represented.
6. When I am told about our national heritage or about "civilization," I am shown that people of my color made it what it is.
7. I can be sure that my children will be given curricular materials that testify to the existence of their race.
8. If I want to, I can be pretty sure of finding a publisher for this piece on white privilege.
9. I can go into a music shop and count on finding the music of my race represented, into a supermarket and find the staple foods which fit with my cultural traditions, into a hairdresser's shop and find someone who can cut my hair.
10. Whether I use checks, credit cards, or cash, I can count on my skin color not to work against the appearance of financial reliability.
11. I can arrange to protect my children most of the time from people who might not like them.

12. I can swear, or dress in secondhand clothes, or not answer letters, without having people attribute these choices to the bad morals, the poverty, or the illiteracy of my race.
13. I can speak in public to a powerful male group without putting my race on trial.
14. I can do well in a challenging situation without being called a credit to my race.
15. I am never asked to speak for all the people of my racial group.
16. I can remain oblivious of the language and customs of persons of color who constitute the world's majority without feeling in my culture any penalty for such oblivion.
17. I can criticize our government and talk about how much I fear its policies and behavior without being seen as a cultural outsider.
18. I can be pretty sure that if I ask to talk to "the person in charge," I will be facing a person of my race.
19. If a traffic cop pulls me over or if the IRS audits my tax return, I can be sure I haven't been singled out because of my race.
20. I can easily buy posters, postcards, picture books, greeting cards, dolls, toys, and children's magazines featuring people of my race.
21. I can go home from most meetings of organizations I belong to feeling somewhat tied in, rather than isolated, out-of-place, outnumbered, un-heard, held at a distance, or feared.
22. I can take a job with an affirmative action employer without having co-workers on the job suspect that I got it because of my race.
23. I can choose public accommodation without fearing that people of my race cannot get in or will be mistreated in the places I have chosen.
24. I can be sure that if I need legal or medical help, my race will not work against me.
25. If my day, week, or year is going badly, I need not ask of each negative episode or situation whether it has racial overtones.
26. I can choose blemish cover or bandages in "flesh" color and have them more or less match my skin.

I repeatedly forgot each of the realizations on this list until I wrote it down. For me white privilege has turned out to be an elusive and fugitive subject. The pressure to avoid it is great, for in facing it I must give up the myth of meritocracy. If these things are true, this is not such a free country; one's life is not what one makes it; many doors open for certain people through no virtues of their own.

In unpacking this invisible knapsack of white privilege, I have listed conditions of daily experience which I once took for granted. Nor did I think of any of these perquisites as bad for the holder. I now think that we need a more finely differentiated taxonomy of privilege, for some of these varieties are only what one would want for everyone in a just society, and others give license to be ignorant, oblivious, arrogant and destructive.

I see a pattern running through the matrix of white privilege, a pattern of assumptions which were passed on to me as a white person. There was one main piece of cultural turf; it was my own turf, and I was among those who could control the turf. *My skin color was an asset for any move I was educated to want to make.* I could think of myself as belonging in major ways, and of making social systems work for me. I could freely disparage, fear, neglect, or be oblivious to anything outside of the dominant cultural forms. Being of the main culture, I could also criticize it fairly freely.

In proportion as my racial group was being made confident, comfortable, and oblivious, other groups were likely being made inconfident, uncomfortable, and alienated. Whiteness protected me from many kinds of hostility, distress, and violence, which I was being subtly trained to visit in turn upon people of color.

For this reason, the word "privilege" now seems to me misleading. We usually think of privilege as being a favored state, whether earned or conferred by birth or luck. Yet some of the conditions I have described here work to systematically overempower certain groups. Such privilege simply *confers dominance* because of one's race or sex.

I want, then, to distinguish between earned strength and unearned power conferred systemically. Power from unearned privilege can look like strength when it is in fact permission to escape or to dominate. But not all of the privileges on my list are inevitably damaging. Some, like the expectation that neighbors will be decent to you, or that your race will not count against you in court, should be the norm in a just society. Others, like the privilege to ignore less powerful people, distort the humanity of the holders as well as the ignored groups.

We might at least start by distinguishing between positive advantages which we can work to spread, and negative types of advantages which unless rejected will always reinforce our present hierarchies. For example, the feeling that one belongs within the human circle, as Native Americans say, should not be seen as privilege for a few. Ideally it is an *unearned entitlement.* At present, since only a few have it, it is an unearned advantage for them. This paper results from a process of coming to see that some of the power which I originally saw as attendant on being a human being in the U.S. consisted in *unearned advantage* and *conferred dominance.*

I have met very few men who are truly distressed about systemic, unearned male advantage and conferred dominance. And so one question for me and others like me is whether we will be like them, or whether we will get truly distressed, even outraged, about unearned race advantage and conferred dominance and if so, what we will do to lessen them. In any case, we need to do more work in identifying how they actually affect our daily lives. Many, perhaps most, of our white students in the U.S. think that racism doesn't affect them because they are not people of color; they do not see "whiteness" as a racial identity. In addition, since race and sex are not the only advantaging systems at work, we need similarly to examine the daily experience of having age advantage, or ethnic advantage, or physical ability, or advantage related to nationality, religion, or sexual orientation.

Difficulties and dangers surrounding the task of finding parallels are many. Since racism, sexism, and heterosexism are not the same, the advantaging associated with them should not be seen as the same. In addition, it is hard to disentangle aspects of unearned advantage which rest more on social class, economic class, race, religion, sex and ethnic identity than on other factors. Still, all of the oppressions are interlocking, as the Combahee River Collective Statement of 1977 continues to remind us eloquently.

One factor seems clear about all of the interlocking oppressions. They take both active forms which we can see and embedded forms which as a member of the dominant group one is taught not to see. In my class and place, I did not see myself as a racist because I was taught to recognize racism only in individual acts of meanness by members of my group, never in invisible systems conferring unsought racial dominance on my group from birth.

Disapproving of the systems won't be enough to change them. I was taught to think that racism could end if white individuals changed their attitudes. [But] a "white" skin in the United States opens many doors for whites whether or not we approve of the way dominance has been conferred on us. Individual acts can palliate, but cannot end, these problems.

To redesign social systems we need first to acknowledge their colossal unseen dimensions. The silences and denials surrounding privilege are the key political tool here. They keep the thinking about equality or equity incomplete, protecting unearned advantage and conferred dominance by making these taboo subjects. Most talk by whites about equal opportunity seems to me now to be about equal opportunity to try to get into a position of dominance while denying that *systems* of dominance exist.

It seems to me that obliviousness about white advantage, like obliviousness about male advantage, is kept strongly inculturated in the United States so as to maintain the myth of meritocracy, the myth that democratic choice is equally available to all. Keeping most people unaware that freedom of confident action is there for just a small number of people props up those in power, and serves to keep power in the hands of the same groups that have most of it already.

Though systemic change takes many decades, there are pressing questions for me and I imagine for some others like me if we raise our daily consciousness on the perquisites of being light-skinned. What will we do with such knowledge? As we know from watching men, it is an open question whether we will choose to use unearned advantage to weaken hidden systems of advantage, and whether we will use any of our arbitrarily-awarded power to try to reconstruct power systems on a broader base.

21

Class in America—2003

Gregory Mantsios

People in the United States don't like to talk about class. Or so it would seem. We don't speak about class privileges, or class oppression, or the class nature of society. These terms are not part of our everyday vocabulary, and in most circles they are associated with the language of the rhetorical fringe. Unlike people in most other parts of the world, we shrink from using words that classify along economic lines or that point to class distinctions: phrases like "working class," "upper class," and "ruling class" are rarely uttered by Americans.

For the most part, avoidance of class-laden vocabulary crosses class boundaries. There are few among the poor who speak of themselves as lower class; instead, they refer to their race, ethnic group, or geographic location. Workers are more likely to identify with their employer, industry, or occupational group than with other workers, or with the working class.[1]

Neither are those at the other end of the economic spectrum likely to use the word "class." In her study of thirty-eight wealthy and socially prominent women, Susan Ostrander asked participants if they considered themselves members of the upper class. One participant responded, "I hate to use the word 'class.' We are responsible, fortunate people, old families, the people who have something."

Another said, "I hate [the term] upper class. It is so non-upper class to use it. I just call it 'all of us,' those who are wellborn."[2]

It is not that Americans, rich or poor, aren't keenly aware of class differences— those quoted above obviously are; it is that class is not in the domain of public discourse. Class is not discussed or debated in public because class identity has been stripped from popular culture. The institutions that shape mass culture and define the parameters of public debate have avoided class issues. In politics, in primary and secondary education, and in the mass media, formulating issues in terms of class is unacceptable, perhaps even un-American.

There are, however, two notable exceptions to this phenomenon. First, it is acceptable in the United States to talk about "the middle class." Interestingly enough, such references appear to be acceptable precisely because they mute class

The author wishes to thank Herbert Fair and Margarita Colon for their assistance in updating this article. Copyright © Gregory Mantsios. Reprinted by permission of the author.

differences. References to the middle class by politicians, for example, are designed to encompass and attract the broadest possible constituency. Not only do references to the middle class gloss over differences, but these references also avoid any suggestion of conflict or exploitation.

This leads us to the second exception to the class-avoidance phenomenon. We are, on occasion, presented with glimpses of the upper class and the lower class (the language used is "the wealthy" and "the poor"). In the media, these presentations are designed to satisfy some real or imagined voyeuristic need of "the ordinary person." As curiosities, the ground-level view of street life and the inside look at the rich and the famous serve as unique models, one to avoid and one to aspire to. In either case, the two models are presented without causal relation to each other: one is not rich because the other is poor.

Similarly, when social commentators or liberal politicians draw attention to the plight of the poor, they do so in a manner that obscures the class structure and denies class exploitation. Wealth and poverty are viewed as one of several natural and inevitable states of being: differences are only differences. One may even say differences are the American way, a reflection of American social diversity.

We are left with one of two possibilities: either talking about class and recognizing class distinctions are not relevant to U.S. society, or we mistakenly hold a set of beliefs that obscure the reality of class differences and their impact on people's lives.

Let us look at four common, albeit contradictory, beliefs about the United States.

Myth 1: The United States is fundamentally a classless society. Class distinctions are largely irrelevant today, and whatever differences do exist in economic standing, they are—for the most part—insignificant. Rich or poor, we are all equal in the eyes of the law, and such basic needs as health care and education are provided to all regardless of economic standing.

Myth 2: We are, essentially, a middle-class nation. Despite some variations in economic status, most Americans have achieved relative affluence in what is widely recognized as a consumer society.

Myth 3: We are all getting richer. The American public as a whole is steadily moving up the economic ladder, and each generation propels itself to greater economic well-being. Despite some fluctuations, the U.S. position in the global economy has brought previously unknown prosperity to most, if not all, Americans.

Myth 4: Everyone has an equal chance to succeed. Success in the United States requires no more than hard work, sacrifice, and perseverance: "In America, anyone can become a millionaire; it's just a matter of being in the right place at the right time."

In trying to assess the legitimacy of these beliefs, we want to ask several important questions. Are there significant class differences among Americans? If these differences do exist, are they getting bigger or smaller, and do these differences have a significant impact on the way we live? Finally, does everyone in the United States really have an equal opportunity to succeed?

The Economic Spectrum

Let's begin by looking at difference. An examination of available data reveals that variations in economic well-being are, in fact, immense. Consider the following:

- The wealthiest 1 percent of the American population holds 38 percent of the total national wealth. That is, they own well over one-third of all the consumer durables (such as houses, cars, and stereos) and financial assets (such as stocks, bonds, property, and savings accounts). The richest 20 percent of Americans hold 83 percent of the total household wealth in the country.[3]
- Approximately 241,000 Americans, or approximately three quarters of 1 percent of the adult population, earn more than $1 million **annually,** with many of these individuals earning over $10 million and some earning over $100 million. It would take the average American, earning $34,000 per year, more than 65 **lifetimes** to earn $100 million.[4]

Affluence and prosperity are clearly alive and well in certain segments of the U.S. population. However, this abundance is in contrast to the poverty and despair that is also prevalent in the United States. At the other end of the spectrum:

- Approximately 12 percent of the American population—that is, nearly one of every eight people in this country—live below the official poverty line (calculated in 2001 at $9,214 for an individual and $17,960 for a family of four).[5] Among the poor are over 2.3 million homeless, including nearly 1 million homeless children.[6]
- Approximately one out of every five children in the United States under the age of six lives in poverty.[7]

The contrast between rich and poor is sharp, and with nearly one-third of the American population living at one extreme or the other, it is difficult to argue that we live in a classless society. Big-payoff reality shows, celebrity salaries, and multimillion dollar lotteries notwithstanding, evidence suggests that the level of inequality in the United States is getting higher. Census data show the gap between the rich and the poor to be the widest since the government began collecting information in 1947[8] and that this gap is continuing to grow. While four out of five households in the United States saw their share of net worth fall between 1992 and 2000, households in the top fifth of the population saw their share increase from 59 percent to 63 percent.[9]

Nor is such a gap between rich and poor representative of the rest of the industrialized world. In fact, the United States has by far the most unequal distribution of household income.[10] The income gap between rich and poor in the United States (measured as the percentage of total income held by the wealthiest 20 percent of the population versus the poorest 20 percent) is approximately 11 to 1, one of the highest ratios in the industrialized world. The ratio in Japan and Germany, by contrast, is 4 to 1.[11]

Reality 1: There are enormous differences in the economic standing of American citizens. A sizable proportion of the U.S. population occupies opposite ends of the economic spectrum. In the middle range of the economic spectrum:

- Sixty percent of the American population holds less than 6 percent of the nation's wealth.[12]
- While the real income of the top 1 percent of U.S. families skyrocketed by 59 percent during the economic boom of the late 1990s, the income of the middle fifth of the population grew only slightly and its share of income (15 percent of the total compared to 48 percent of the total for the wealthiest fifth), actually declined during this same period.[13]
- Regressive changes in governmental tax policies and the weakening of labor unions over the last quarter century have led to a significant rise in the level of inequality between the rich and the middle class. Between 1979 and 2000, the gap in household income between the top fifth and middle fifth of the population rose by 31 percent.[14] During the economic boom of the 1990s, four out of five Americans saw their share of net worth decline, while the top fifth saw their share increase from 59 percent to 63 percent.[15] One prominent economist described economic growth in the United States as a "spectator sport for the majority of American families."[16] Economic decline, on the other hand, is much more "inclusive," with layoffs impacting hardest on middle- and lower-income families—those with fewer resources to fall back on.

The level of inequality is sometimes difficult to comprehend fully by looking at dollar figures and percentages. To help his students visualize the distribution of income, the well-known economist Paul Samuelson asked them to picture an income pyramid made of children's blocks, with each layer of blocks representing $1,000. If we were to construct Samuelson's pyramid today, the peak of the pyramid would be much higher than the Eiffel Tower, yet almost all of us would be within six feet of the ground.[17] In other words, the distribution of income is heavily skewed; a small minority of families take the lion's share of national income, and the remaining income is distributed among the vast majority of middle-income and low-income families. Keep in mind that Samuelson's pyramid represents the distribution of income, not wealth. The distribution of wealth is skewed even further.

Reality 2: The middle class in the United States holds a very small share of the nation's wealth and that share is declining steadily. The gap between rich and poor and between rich and the middle class is larger than it has ever been.

American Life-Styles

At last count, nearly 33 million Americans across the nation lived in unrelenting poverty.[18] Yet, as political scientist Michael Harrington once commented, "America has the best dressed poverty the world has ever known."[19] Clothing disguises much of the poverty in the United States, and this may explain, in part, its middle-class image. With increased mass marketing of "designer" clothing and with shifts in the nation's economy from blue-collar (and often better-paying) manufacturing jobs to white-collar and pink-collar jobs in the service sector, it is becoming increasingly difficult to distinguish class differences based on appearance.[20] The dress-down environment prevalent in the high-tech industry (what one author refers to as the "no-collars movement") has reduced superficial distinctions even further.[21]

Beneath the surface, there is another reality. Let's look at some "typical" and not-so-typical life-styles.

American Profile

Name: Harold S. Browning

Father: manufacturer, industrialist

Mother: prominent social figure in the community

Principal child-rearer: governess

Primary education: an exclusive private school on Manhattan's Upper East Side

Note: a small, well-respected primary school where teachers and administrators have a reputation for nurturing student creativity and for providing the finest educational preparation

Ambition: "to become President"

Supplemental tutoring: tutors in French and mathematics

Summer camp: sleep-away camp in northern Connecticut

Note: camp provides instruction in the creative arts, athletics, and the natural sciences

Secondary education: a prestigious preparatory school in Westchester County

Note: classmates included the sons of ambassadors, doctors, attorneys, television personalities, and well-known business leaders

After-school activities: private riding lessons

Ambition: "to take over my father's business"

High-school graduation gift: BMW

Family activities: theater, recitals, museums, summer vacations in Europe, occasional winter trips to the Caribbean

Note: as members of and donors to the local art museum, the Brownings and their children attend private receptions and exhibit openings at the invitation of the museum director

Higher education: an Ivy League liberal arts college in Massachusetts

Major: economics and political science

After-class activities: debating club, college newspaper, swim team

Ambition: "to become a leader in business"

First full-time job (age 23):	assistant manager of operations, Browning Tool and Die, Inc. (family enterprise)
Subsequent employment:	*3 years*—executive assistant to the president, Browning Tool and Die
	Responsibilities included: purchasing (materials and equipment), personnel, and distribution networks
	4 years—advertising manager, Lackheed Manufacturing (home appliances)
	3 years—director of marketing and sales, Comerex, Inc. (business machines)
Present employment (age 38):	executive vice president, SmithBond and Co. (digital instruments)
	Typical daily activities: review financial reports and computer printouts, dictate memoranda, lunch with clients, initiate conference calls, meet with assistants, plan business trips, meet with associates
	Transportation to and from work: chauffeured company limousine
	Annual salary: $315,000
	Ambition: "to become chief executive officer of the firm, or one like it, within the next five to ten years"
Present residence:	eighteenth-floor condominium on Manhattan's Upper West Side, eleven rooms, including five spacious bedrooms and terrace overlooking river
	Interior: professionally decorated and accented with elegant furnishings, valuable antiques, and expensive artwork
	Note: building management provides doorman and elevator attendant; family employs au pair for children and maid for other domestic chores
Second residence:	farm in northwestern Connecticut, used for weekend retreats and for horse breeding (investment/hobby)
	Note: to maintain the farm and cater to the family when they are there, the Brownings employ a part-time maid, groundskeeper, and horse breeder

Harold Browning was born into a world of nurses, maids, and governesses. His world today is one of airplanes and limousines, five-star restaurants, and luxurious living accommodations. The life and life-style of Harold Browning is in sharp contrast to that of Bob Farrell.

American Profile

Name:	Bob Farrell
Father:	machinist
Mother:	retail clerk
Principal child-rearer:	mother and sitter
Primary education:	a medium-size public school in Queens, New York, characterized by large class size, outmoded physical facilities, and an educational philosophy emphasizing basic skills and student discipline
	Ambition: "to become President"
Supplemental tutoring:	none
Summer camp:	YMCA day camp
	Note: emphasis on team sports, arts and crafts
Secondary education:	large regional high school in Queens
	Note: classmates included the sons and daughters of carpenters, postal clerks, teachers, nurses, shopkeepers, mechanics, bus drivers, police officers, salespersons
	After-school activities: basketball and handball in school park
	Ambition: "to make it through college"
	High-school graduation gift: $500 savings bond
Family activities:	family gatherings around television set, bowling, an occasional trip to the movie theater, summer Sundays at the public beach
Higher education:	a two-year community college with a technical orientation
	Major: electrical technology
	After-school activities: employed as a part-time bagger in local supermarket
	Ambition: "to become an electrical engineer"
First full-time job (age 19):	service-station attendant
	Note: continued to take college classes in the evening
Subsequent employment:	mail clerk at large insurance firm; manager trainee, large retail chain
Present employment (age 38):	assistant sales manager, building supply firm
	Typical daily activities: demonstrate products, write up product orders, handle customer complaints, check inventory
	Transportation to and from work: city subway

Annual salary:	$39,261
	Ambition: "to open up my own business"
	Additional income: $6,100 in commissions from evening and weekend work as salesman in local men's clothing store
Present residence:	the Farrells own their own home in a working-class neighborhood in Queens

Bob Farrell and Harold Browning live very differently: the life-style of one is privileged; that of the other is not so privileged. The differences are class differences, and these differences have a profound impact on the way they live. They are differences between playing a game of handball in the park and taking riding lessons at a private stable; watching a movie on television and going to the theater; and taking the subway to work and being driven in a limousine. More important, the difference in class determines where they live, who their friends are, how well they are educated, what they do for a living, and what they come to expect from life.

Yet, as dissimilar as their life-styles are, Harold Browning and Bob Farrell have some things in common; they live in the same city, they work long hours, and they are highly motivated. More important, they are both white males.

Let's look at someone else who works long and hard and is highly motivated. This person, however, is black and female.

	American Profile
Name:	Cheryl Mitchell
Father:	janitor
Mother:	waitress
Principal child-rearer:	grandmother
Primary education:	large public school in Ocean Hill-Brownsville, Brooklyn, New York
	Note: rote teaching of basic skills and emphasis on conveying the importance of good attendance, good manners, and good work habits; school patrolled by security guards
	Ambition: "to be a teacher"
Supplemental tutoring:	none
Summer camp:	none
Secondary education:	large public school in Ocean Hill-Brownsville
	Note: classmates included sons and daughters of hairdressers, groundskeepers, painters, dressmakers, dishwashers, domestics
	After-school activities: domestic chores, part-time employment as babysitter and housekeeper

Ambition:	"to be a social worker"
	High-school graduation gift: corsage
Family activities:	church-sponsored socials
Higher education:	one semester of local community college
	Note: dropped out of school for financial reasons
First full-time job (age 17):	counter clerk, local bakery
Subsequent employment:	file clerk with temporary-service agency, supermarket checker
Present employment (age 38):	nurse's aide at a municipal hospital
	Typical daily activities: make up hospital beds, clean out bedpans, weigh patients and assist them to the bathroom, take temperature readings, pass out and collect food trays, feed patients who need help, bathe patients, and change dressings
	Annual salary: $15,820
	Ambition: "to get out of the ghetto"
Present residence:	three-room apartment in the South Bronx, needs painting, has poor ventilation, is in a high-crime area
	Note: Cheryl Mitchell lives with her four-year-old son and her elderly mother

When we look at the lives of Cheryl Mitchell, Bob Farrell, and Harold Browning, we see life-styles that are very different. We are not looking, however, at economic extremes. Cheryl Mitchell's income as a nurse's aide puts her above the government's official poverty line.[22] Below her on the income pyramid are 33 million poverty-stricken Americans. Far from being poor, Bob Farrell has an annual income as an assistant sales manager that puts him well above the median income level—that is, more than 50 percent of the U.S. population earns less money than Bob Farrell.[23] And while Harold Browning's income puts him in a high-income bracket, he stands only a fraction of the way up Samuelson's income pyramid. Well above him are the 241,000 individuals whose annual salary exceeds $1 million. Yet Harold Browning spends more money on his horses than Cheryl Mitchell earns in a year.

Reality 3: Even ignoring the extreme poles of the economic spectrum, we find enormous class differences in the life-styles among the haves, the have-nots, and the have-littles.

Class affects more than life-style and material well-being. It has a significant impact on our physical and mental well-being as well.

Researchers have found an inverse relationship between social class and health. Lower-class standing is correlated to higher rates of infant mortality, eye and ear disease, arthritis, physical disability, diabetes, nutritional deficiency, respiratory disease, mental illness, and heart disease.[24] In all areas of health, poor people do not share the same life chances as those in the social class above them. Furthermore, lower-class standing is correlated with a lower quality of treatment for illness and disease. The results of poor health and poor treatment are borne out in the life expectancy rates within each class. Researchers have found that the higher your class standing, the higher your life expectancy. Conversely, they have also found that within each age group, the lower one's class standing, the higher the death rate; in some age groups, the figures are as much as two and three times as high.[25]

Reality 4: From cradle to grave, class standing has a significant impact on our chances for survival.

The lower one's class standing, the more difficult it is to secure appropriate housing, the more time is spent on the routine tasks of everyday life, the greater is the percentage of income that goes to pay for food and other basic necessities, and the greater is the likelihood of crime victimization.[26] Class can accurately predict chances for both survival and success.

Class and Educational Attainment

School performance (grades and test scores) and educational attainment (level of schooling completed) also correlate strongly with economic class. Furthermore, despite some efforts to make testing fairer and schooling more accessible, current data suggest that the level of inequity is staying the same or getting worse.

In his study for the Carnegie Council on Children twenty-five years ago, Richard De Lone examined the test scores of over half a million students who took the College Board exams (SATs). His findings were consistent with earlier studies that showed a relationship between class and scores on standardized tests; his conclusion: "the higher the student's social status, the higher the probability that he or she will get higher grades."[27] Fifteen years after the release of the Carnegie report, College Board surveys reveal data that are no different: test scores still correlate strongly with family income.

Average Combined Scores by Income (400 to 1600 scale)[28]

Family Income	Median Score
More than $100,000	1130
$80,000 to $100,000	1082
$70,000 to $80,000	1058
$60,000 to $70,000	1043
$50,000 to $60,000	1030
$40,000 to $50,000	1011
$30,000 to $40,000	986
$20,000 to $30,000	954
$10,000 to $20,000	907
less than $10,000	871

These figures are based on the test results of 1,302,903 SAT takers in 1999.

A little more than twenty years ago, researcher William Sewell showed a positive correlation between class and overall educational achievement. In comparing the top quartile (25 percent) of his sample to the bottom quartile, he found that students from upper-class families were twice as likely to obtain training beyond high school and four times as likely to attain a postgraduate degree. Sewell concluded: "Socioeconomic background . . . operates independently of academic ability at every stage in the process of educational attainment."[29]

Today, the pattern persists. There are, however, two significant changes. On the one hand, the odds of getting into college have improved for the bottom quartile of the population, although they still remain relatively low compared to the top. On the other hand, the chances of completing a college degree have deteriorated markedly for the bottom quartile. Researchers estimate the chances of completing a four-year college degree (by age 24) to be nineteen times as great for the top 25 percent of the population as it is for the bottom 25 percent.[30]

Reality 5: Class standing has a significant impact on chances for educational achievement.

Class standing, and consequently life chances, are largely determined at birth. Although examples of individuals who have gone from rags to riches abound in the mass media, statistics on class mobility show these leaps to be extremely rare. In fact, dramatic advances in class standing are relatively infrequent. One study showed that fewer than one in five men surpass the economic status of their fathers.[31] For those whose annual income is in six figures, economic success is due in large part to the wealth and privileges bestowed on them at birth. Over 66 percent of the consumer units with incomes of $100,000 or more have inherited assets. Of these units, over 86 percent reported that inheritances constituted a substantial portion of their total assets.[32]

Economist Harold Wachtel likens inheritance to a series of Monopoly games in which the winner of the first game refuses to relinquish his or her cash and commercial property for the second game. "After all," argues the winner, "I accumulated my wealth and income by my own wits." With such an arrangement, it is not difficult to predict the outcome of subsequent games.[33]

Reality 6: All Americans do not have an equal opportunity to succeed. Inheritance laws ensure a greater likelihood of success for the offspring of the wealthy.

Spheres of Power and Oppression

When we look at society and try to determine what it is that keeps most people down—what holds them back from realizing their potential as healthy, creative, productive individuals—we find institutional forces that are largely beyond individual control. Class domination is one of these forces. People do not choose to be poor or working class; instead, they are limited and confined by the opportunities afforded or denied them by a social and economic system. The class structure in the United

States is a function of its economic system: capitalism, a system that is based on private rather than public ownership and control of commercial enterprises. Under capitalism, these enterprises are governed by the need to produce a profit for the owners, rather than to fulfill collective needs. Class divisions arise from the differences between those who own and control corporate enterprise and those who do not.

Racial and gender domination are other forces that hold people down. Although there are significant differences in the way capitalism, racism, and sexism affect our lives, there are also a multitude of parallels. And although class, race, and gender act independently of each other, they are at the same time very much interrelated.

On the one hand, issues of race and gender cut across class lines. Women experience the effects of sexism whether they are well-paid professionals or poorly paid clerks. As women, they face discrimination and male domination, as well as catcalls and stereotyping. Similarly, a wealthy black man faces racial oppression, is subjected to racial slurs, and is denied opportunities because of his color. Regardless of their class standing, women and members of minority races are constantly dealing with institutional forces that are holding them down precisely because of their gender, the color of their skin, or both.

On the other hand, the experiences of women and minorities are differentiated along class lines. Although they are in subordinate positions vis-à-vis white men, the particular issues that confront women and minorities may be quite different depending on their position in the class structure.

Power is incremental, and class privileges can accrue to individual women and to individual members of a racial minority. At the same time, class-oppressed men, whether they are white or black, have privileges afforded them as men in a sexist society. Similarly, class-oppressed whites, whether they are men or women, benefit from white privilege in a racist society. Spheres of power and oppression divide us deeply in our society, and the schisms between us are often difficult to bridge.

Whereas power is incremental, oppression is cumulative, and those who are poor, black, and female are often subject to all of the forces of class, race, and gender discrimination simultaneously. This cumulative situation is what is meant by the double and triple jeopardy of women and minorities.

Furthermore, oppression in one sphere is related to the likelihood of oppression in another. If you are black and female, for example, you are much more likely to be poor or working class than you would be as a white male. Census figures show that the incidence of poverty varies greatly by race and gender.

Chances of Being Poor in America[34]

White male/ female	White female head*	Hispanic male/ female	Hispanic female head*	Black male/ female	Black female head*
1 in 10	1 in 5	1 in 5	1 in 3	1 in 5	1 in 3

*Persons in families with female householder, no husband present.

In other words, being female and being nonwhite are attributes in our society that increase the chances of poverty and of lower-class standing.

Reality 7: Racism and sexism significantly compound the effects of class in society.

NOTES

1. See Jay MacLead, *Ain't No Makin' It: Aspirations and Attainment in a Lower-Income Neighborhood* (Boulder, CO: Westview Press, 1995); Benjamin DeMott, *The Imperial Middle* (New York: Morrow, 1990); Ira Katznelson, *City Trenches: Urban Politics and Patterning of Class in the United States* (New York: Pantheon Books, 1981); Charles W. Tucker, "A Comparative Analysis of Subjective Social Class: 1945–1963," *Social Forces*, no. 46, June 1968, pp. 508–514; Robert Nisbet, "The Decline and Fall of Social Class," *Pacific Sociological Review*, vol. 2, Spring 1959, pp. 11–17; and Oscar Glantz, "Class Consciousness and Political Solidarity," *American Sociological Review*, vol. 23, August 1958, pp. 375–382.

2. Susan Ostander, "Upper-Class Women: Class Consciousness as Conduct and Meaning," in G. William Domhoff, *Power Structure Research* (Beverly Hills, CA: Sage Publications, 1980, pp. 78–79). Also see Stephen Birmingham, *America's Secret Aristocracy* (Boston: Little Brown, 1987).

3. Lawrence Mishel, Jared Bernstein, and Heather Boushey, *The State of Working America: 2002–03* (Ithaca, NY: ILR Press, Cornell University Press, 2003, p. 277).

4. The number of individuals filing tax returns showing a gross adjusted income of $1 million or more in 2000 was 241,068 (Tax Stats at a Glance, Internal Revenue Service, U.S. Treasury Department, available at www.irs.ustreas.gov/taxstats/article/0,,id=102886,99. html).

5. Bernadette D. Proctor and Joseph Dalaker, "U.S. Census Bureau, Current Population Reports," *Poverty in the United States: 2001* (Washington, DC: U.S. Government Printing Office, 2002, pp. 1–5).

6. Martha Burt, "A New Look at Homelessness in America" (Washington DC: The Urban Institute, February 2000).

7. Proctor and Dalaker, op. cit., p. 4.

8. Mishel et al., op. cit., p. 53.

9. Mishel et al., ibid., p. 280.

10. Based on a comparison of 19 industrialized states: Mishel et al., ibid., pp. 411–412.

11. See The Center on Budget and Policy Priorities, Economic Policy Institute, "Pulling Apart: State-by-State Analysis of Income Trends," January 2000, fact sheet; "Current Population Reports: Consumer Income" (Washington, DC: U.S. Department of Commerce, 1993); The World Bank, "World Development Report: 1992" (Washington, DC: International Bank for Reconstruction and Development, 1992); The World Bank, "World Development Report 1999/2000," pp. 238–239.

12. Derived from Mishel et al., op. cit., p. 281.

13. Mishel et al., ibid., p. 54.

14. Mishel et al., ibid., p. 70.

15. Mishel et al., ibid., p. 280.

16. Alan Blinder, quoted by Paul Krugman, in "Disparity and Despair," *U.S. News and World Report*, March 23, 1992, p. 54.

17. Paul Samuelson, *Economics*, 10th ed. (New York: McGraw-Hill, 1976, p. 84).

18. Joseph Dalaker, "U.S. Census Bureau, Current Population Reports, series P60–207," *Poverty in the United States: 1998* (Washington, DC: U.S. Government Printing Office, 1999, p. v).

19. Michael Harrington, *The Other America* (New York: Macmillan, 1962, pp. 12–13).

20. Stuart Ewen and Elizabeth Ewen, *Channels of Desire: Mass Images and the Shaping of American Consciousness* (New York: McGraw-Hill, 1982).

21. Andrew Ross, *No-Collar: The Humane Work Place and Its Hidden Costs* (New York: Basic Books, 2002).

22. Based on a poverty threshold for a family of three in 2003 of $15,260.

23. The median income in 2001 was $38,275 for men, $29,214 for women, and $42,228 for households. Carmen DeNavas-Walt and Robert Cleveland, "U.S. Census Bureau, Current Population Reports," *Money Income in the United States: 2001* (Washington, DC: U.S. Government Printing Office, 2002, p. 4).

24. E. Pamuk, D. Makuc, K. Heck, C. Reuben, and K. Lochner, *Socioeconomic Status and Health Chartbook, Health, United States, 1998* (Hyattsville, MD: National Center for Health Statistics, 1998, pp. 145–159); Vincente Navarro "Class, Race, and Health Care in the United States," in Bersh Berberoglu, *Critical Perspectives in Sociology*, 2nd ed. (Dubuque, IA: Kendall/Hunt, 1993, pp. 148–156); Melvin Krasner, *Poverty and Health in New York City* (New York: United Hospital Fund of New York, 1989). See also U.S. Dept. of Health and Human Services, *Health Status of Minorities and Low Income Groups, ?1985*; and Dan Hughes, Kay Johnson, Sara Rosenbaum, Elizabeth Butler, and Janet Simons, *The Health of America's Children* (The Children's Defense Fund, 1988).

25. E. Pamuk et al., op. cit.; Kenneth Neubeck and Davita Glassberg, *Sociology; A Critical Approach* (New York: McGraw-Hill, 1996, pp. 436–438); Aaron Antonovsky, "Social Class, Life Expectancy, and Overall Mortality," in *The Impact of Social Class* (New York: Thomas Crowell, 1972, pp. 467–491). See also Harriet Duleep, "Measuring the Effect of Income on Adult Mortality Using Longitudinal Administrative Record Data," *Journal of Human Resources*, vol. 21, no. 2, Spring 1986.

26. E. Pamuk et al., op. cit., fig. 20; Dennis W. Roncek, "Dangerous Places: Crime and Residential Environment," *Social Forces*, vol. 60, no. 1, September 1981, pp. 74–96.

27. Richard De Lone, *Small Futures* (New York: Harcourt Brace Jovanovich, 1978, pp. 14–19).

28. Derived from The College Entrance Examination Board, "1999, A Profile of College Bound Seniors: SAT Test Takers;" available at www.collegeboard.org/sat/cbsenior/yr1999/NAT/natbk499.html#income.

29. William H. Sewell, "Inequality of Opportunity for Higher Education," *American Sociological Review*, vol. 36, no. 5, 1971, pp. 793–809.

30. The Mortenson Report on Public Policy Analysis of Opportunity for Postsecondary Education, "Postsecondary Education Opportunity" (Iowa City, IA: September 1993, no. 16).

31. De Lone, op. cit., pp. 14–19.

32. Howard Tuchman, *Economics of the Rich* (New York: Random House, 1973, p. 15).

33. Howard Wachtel, *Labor and the Economy* (Orlando, FL: Academic Press, 1984, pp. 161–162).

34. Derived from Proctor and Dalaker, op. cit., p. 3.

Suggestions for Further Reading

Baird, Robert M., and Stuart E. Rosenbaum, eds. *Bigotry, Prejudice, and Hatred.* Buffalo, NY: Prometheus Press, 1992.

Brandt, Eric, ed. *Dangerous Liaisons: Blacks, Gays and the Struggle for Equality.* New York: New Press, 1999.

Cose, Ellis. *The Rage of a Privileged Class.* New York: Collins, 1994.

DeMott, Benjamin. *The Trouble with Friendship: Why Americans Can't Think Straight about Race.* New York: Atlantic Monthly Press, 1995.

Dusky, Lorraine. *Still Unequal: The Shameful Truth about Women and Justice in America.* New York: Crown Books, 1996.

Dyer, Richard. *White.* London and New York: Routledge, 1997.

Essed, Philomena. *Everyday Racism.* Claremont, CA: Hunter House, 1990.

Faludi, Susan. *Backlash: The Undeclared War against American Women.* New York: Crown Publishers, 1991.

Harris, Leonard. *Racism.* New York: Humanities Books, 1999.

Johnson, Allan G. *Privilege, Power and Difference.* New York: McGraw-Hill, 2001.

Kadi, Joanne. *Thinking Class: Sketches from a Cultural Worker.* Boston: South End Press, 1996.

Kimmel, Michael. *The Gendered Society.* New York: Oxford University Press, 2000.

King, Larry L. *Confessions of a White Racist.* New York: Viking Press, 1971.

Kleg, Milton. *Hate, Prejudice and Racism.* Albany: State University of New York Press, 1996.

Lipsitz, George. *The Possessive Investment in Whiteness.* Philadelphia: Temple University Press, 1998.

Pharr, Suzanne. *Homophobia as a Weapon of Sexism.* Inverness, CA: Chardon Press, 1988.

Pincus, F. L., and H. J. Erlich. *Race and Ethnic Conflict: Contending Views on Prejudice, Discrimination and Ethnoviolence.* Boulder, CO: Westview, 1994.

Rhode, Deborah L. *Speaking of Sex: The Denial of Gender Inequality.* Cambridge, MA: Harvard University Press, 1997.

Ronai, Carol R., et al. *Everyday Sexism in the Third Millennium.* New York and London: Routledge, 1997.

Shipler, David K. *A Country of Strangers: Blacks and Whites in America.* New York: Knopf, 1997.

Wellman, David T. *Portraits of White Racism.* Cambridge: Cambridge University Press, 1977.

Williams, Lena. *It's the Little Things, The Everyday Interactions That Get Under the Skin of Blacks and Whites.* New York: Harcourt, 2000.

Discrimination in Everyday Life

THE SYSTEMS OF OPPRESSION WE HAVE BEEN STUDYING—racism, sexism, heterosexism, and class privilege—express themselves in everyday life in a variety of ways. Sometimes they are reflected in the prejudiced attitudes that people carry with them into the workplace or the community; sometimes they erupt in racist, sexist, or homophobic utterances that reach us across the playground or through our car radio. Sometimes they are in evidence in the discriminatory policies and practices of government and business as they carry out their routine operations. In Part III of the text we will have an opportunity to read newspaper stories about incidents where individuals or groups were discriminated against because of their race/ethnicity, gender, sexual orientation, class position, or some combination of these.

Refusing to hire a qualified person because of his or her race/ethnicity, gender, or sexual orientation, or refusing to rent that person an apartment or sell them a home, are fairly straightforward examples of discrimination. Most people would agree that such behavior is unfair or unjust. But once we move beyond these clear-cut cases, it becomes difficult to reach agreement. Is the joke told by a popular radio personality portraying women or gays in a derogatory way sexist, racist, and homophobic, or is it merely a joke? Does the fact that most major U.S. corporations have few if any women in senior management positions in itself indicate discriminatory hiring policies? Is the underrepresentation of women of all colors and men of color in the United States Congress de facto evidence of racism and sexism in society, or does it merely reflect a shortage of qualified individuals? Who determines what it means to be qualified? How do we arrive at the criteria according to which students are admitted to colleges and professional schools, or by which senior management is hired? Is it possible that the very criteria employed already reflect a subtle but pervasive race, class, and gender bias? Can individuals and institutions be racist, sexist, and homophobic in the course of their normal, everyday operation, quite apart from—even without—their conscious or explicit intent? These are just some of the questions that are raised by the newspaper articles that appear in Part III.

The first article in this Part of the text provides an excerpt from a 1981 report issued by the U.S. Commission on Civil Rights. It provides a historical overview of the kinds of discrimination against women and "minorities" that is part of our shared history. In addition, it offers some categories and distinctions that will prove useful as we read about the cases in the news articles that follow. According to this report, discrimination can take many forms. It can exist at the level of individual attitudes and behavior, as when doctors refuse to treat patients because of their sexual orientation; it can be carried out through the routine application of the rules, policies, and practices of organizations when they unfairly prevent members of certain groups from, for example, receiving a promotion or being given highly valued work assignments; and it can be carried out in the day-to-day, unexamined practices of schools, government agencies, and other institutions so that it is so pervasive within the social structure as to constitute structural discrimination. Structural discrimination refers to an interlocking cycle of discrimination where discrimination in one area, for example, education, leads to discrimination in other areas, such as employment and housing, creating a cycle of discrimination and disadvantage from which it is difficult to emerge.

As the articles in this Part make clear, discrimination of every type is a fact of life in every area of contemporary society. Why then do so many people, in particular, so many young people, seem to believe that racism and sexism are largely things of the past? Perhaps because so many people mistakenly believe that whether an act is discriminatory or racist can be determined by examining the motives of the person involved rather than looking at the consequences of the act itself. (If you haven't already looked at Selection 13 in Part II, "On the Nature of Contemporary Prejudice," you might find it interesting to read it now.) In fact, racism and sexism can be unintentional as well as intentional and good people who mean well can inadvertently do and say things that are racist and sexist or homophobic. For example, the recruiters who fail to hire a woman because they believe that women will be uncomfortable functioning within the prevailing company culture, may indeed mean well, but intentions aside, this is a clear example of discrimination because it effectively denies women access to certain jobs. If the company culture is not welcoming to women, the right thing to do is to change that culture, not to deny women employment.

As the members of the U.S. Civil Rights Commission point out, even superficially "color blind" or "gender neutral" organizational practices can end up placing women and men of color or white women at a disadvantage. Seemingly innocuous height requirements for a particular job may discriminate disproportionately against members of certain ethnic groups or women; "standard" ways of posting job openings may exclude those who are not part of the "old boys' network"; and even those of us who mean no harm can reinforce heterosexism, racism, sexism, or class privilege by our unexamined and seemingly innocent choices. As the news clippings in this Part make clear, racism, sexism, heterosexism, and class privilege are part of both our past and our present, part of our history and part of everyday life. Learning to recognize discrimination is an essential prerequisite for acting to end it.

22

The Problem:
Discrimination

U.S. Commission on Civil Rights

Making choices is an essential part of everyday life for individuals and organizations. These choices are shaped in part by social structures that set standards and influence conduct in such areas as education, employment, housing, and government. When these choices limit the opportunities available to people because of their race, sex, or national origin, the problem of discrimination arises.

Historically, discrimination against minorities and women was not only accepted but it was also governmentally required. The doctrine of white supremacy used to support the institution of slavery was so much a part of American custom and policy that the Supreme Court in 1857 approvingly concluded that both the North and the South regarded slaves "as beings of an inferior order, and altogether unfit to associate with the white race, either in social or political relations; and so far inferior, that they had no rights which the white man was bound to respect."[1] White supremacy survived the passage of the Civil War amendments to the Constitution and continued to dominate legal and social institutions in the North as well as the South to disadvantage not only blacks,[2] but other racial and ethnic groups as well—American Indians, Alaskan Natives, Asian and Pacific Islanders and Hispanics.[3]

While minorities were suffering from white supremacy, women were suffering from male supremacy. Mr. Justice Brennan has summed up the legal disabilities imposed on women this way:

> [T]hroughout much of the 19th century the position of women in our society was, in many respects, comparable to that of blacks under the pre–Civil War slave codes. Neither slaves nor women could hold office, serve on juries, or bring suit in their own names, and married women traditionally were denied the legal capacity to hold or convey property or to serve as legal guardians of their own children.[4]

In 1873 a member of the Supreme Court proclaimed, "Man is, or should be, woman's protector and defender. The natural and proper timidity and delicacy

From *Affirmative Action in the 1980s*. U.S. Commission on Civil Rights 65 (January 1981): 9–15.

which belongs to the female sex evidently unfits it for many of the occupations of civil life."[5] Such romantic paternalism has alternated with fixed notions of male superiority to deny women in law and in practice the most fundamental of rights, including the right to vote, which was not granted until 1920;[6] the Equal Rights Amendment has yet to be ratified.[7]

White and male supremacy are no longer popularly accepted American values. The blatant racial and sexual discrimination that originated in our conveniently forgotten past, however, continues to manifest itself today in a complex interaction of attitudes and actions of individuals, organizations, and the network of social structures that make up our society.

Individual Discrimination

The most common understanding of discrimination rests at the level of prejudiced individual attitudes and behavior. Although open and intentional prejudice persists, individual discriminatory conduct is often hidden and sometimes unintentional.[8] Some of the following are examples of deliberately discriminatory actions by consciously prejudiced individuals. Some are examples of unintentionally discriminatory actions taken by persons who may not believe themselves to be prejudiced but whose decisions continue to be guided by deeply ingrained discriminatory customs.

- Personnel officers whose stereotyped beliefs about women and minorities justify hiring them for low level and low paying jobs exclusively, regardless of their potential experience or qualifications for higher level jobs.[9]
- Administrators, historically white males, who rely on "word-of-mouth" recruiting among their friends and colleagues, so that only their friends and protégés of the same race and sex learn of potential job openings.[10]
- Employers who hire women for their sexual attractiveness or potential sexual availability rather than their competence, and employers who engage in sexual harassment of their female employees.[11]
- Teachers who interpret linguistic and cultural differences as indications of low potential or lack of academic interest on the part of minority students.[12]
- Guidance counselors and teachers whose low expectations lead them to steer female and minority students away from "hard" subjects, such as mathematics and science, toward subjects that do not prepare them for higher paying jobs.[13]
- Real estate agents who show fewer homes to minority buyers and steer them to minority or mixed neighborhoods because they believe white residents would oppose the presence of black neighbors.[14]
- Families who assume that property values inevitably decrease when minorities move in and therefore move out of their neighborhoods if minorities do move in.[15]

- Parole boards that assume minority offenders to be more dangerous or more unreliable than white offenders and consequently more frequently deny parole to minorities than to whites convicted of equally serious crimes.[16]

These contemporary examples of discrimination may not be motivated by conscious prejudice. The personnel manager is likely to deny believing that minorities and women can only perform satisfactorily in low level jobs and at the same time allege that other executives and decisionmakers would not consider them for higher level positions. In some cases, the minority or female applicants may not be aware that they have been discriminated against—the personnel manager may inform them that they are deficient in experience while rejecting their applications because of prejudice; the white male administrator who recruits by word-of-mouth from his friends or white male work force excludes minorities and women who never learn of the available positions. The discriminatory results these activities cause may not even be desired. The guidance counselor may honestly believe there are no other realistic alternatives for minority and female students.

Whether conscious or not, open or hidden, desired or undesired, these acts build on and support prejudicial stereotypes, deny their victims opportunities provided to others, and perpetuate discrimination, regardless of intent.

Organizational Discrimination

Discrimination, though practiced by individuals, is often reinforced by the well-established rules, policies, and practices of organizations. These actions are often regarded simply as part of the organization's way of doing business and are carried out by individuals as just part of their day's work.

Discrimination at the organizational level takes forms that are similar to those on the individual level. For example:

- Height and weight requirements that are unnecessarily geared to the physical proportions of white males and, therefore, exclude females and some minorities from certain jobs.[17]
- Seniority rules, when applied to jobs historically held only by white males, make more recently hired minorities and females more subject to layoff—the "last hired, first fired" employee—and less eligible for advancement.[18]
- Nepotistic membership policies of some referral unions that exclude those who are not relatives of members who, because of past employment practices, are usually white.[19]
- Restrictive employment leave policies, coupled with prohibitions on part-time work or denials of fringe benefits to part-time workers, that make it difficult for the heads of single parent families, most of whom are women, to get and keep jobs and meet the needs of their families.[20]

- The use of standardized academic tests or criteria, geared to the cultural and educational norms of the middle-class or white males, that are not relevant indicators of successful job performance.[21]
- Preferences shown by many law and medical schools in the admission of children of wealthy and influential alumni, nearly all of whom are white.[22]
- Credit policies of banks and lending institutions that prevent the granting of mortgage monies and loans in minority neighborhoods, or prevent the granting of credit to married women and others who have previously been denied the opportunity to build good credit histories in their own names.[23]

Superficially "color blind" or "gender neutral," these organizational practices have an adverse effect on minorities and women. As with individual actions, these organizational actions favor white males, even when taken with no conscious intent to affect minorities and women adversely, by protecting and promoting the status quo arising from the racism and sexism of the past. If, for example, the jobs now protected by "last hired, first fired" provisions had always been integrated, seniority would not operate to disadvantage minorities and women. If educational systems from kindergarten through college had not historically favored white males, many more minorities and women would hold advanced degrees and thereby be included among those involved in deciding what academic tests should test for. If minorities had lived in the same neighborhoods as whites, there would be no minority neighborhoods to which mortgage money could be denied on the basis of their being minority neighborhoods.

In addition, these barriers to minorities and women too often do not fulfill legitimate needs of the organization, or these needs can be met through other means that adequately maintain the organization without discriminating. Instead of excluding all women on the assumption that they are too weak or should be protected from strenuous work, the organization can implement a reasonable test that measures the strength actually needed to perform the job or, where possible, develop ways of doing the work that require less physical effort. Admissions to academic and professional schools can be decided not only on the basis of grades, standardized test scores, and the prestige of the high school or college from which the applicant graduated, but also on the basis of community service, work experience, and letters of recommendation. Lending institutions can look at the individual and his or her financial ability rather than the neighborhood or marital status of the prospective borrower.

Some practices that disadvantage minorities and women are readily accepted aspects of everyday behavior. Consider the "old boy" network in business and education built on years of friendship and social contact among white males, or the exchanges of information and corporate strategies by business acquaintances in racially or sexually exclusive country clubs and locker rooms paid for by the employer.[24] These actions, all of which have a discriminatory impact on minorities and women, are not necessarily acts of conscious prejudice. Because such actions are so often considered part of the "normal" way of doing things, people have difficulty recognizing that they are discriminating and therefore resist abandoning these practices despite the clearly discriminatory results. Consequently, many decision-makers have difficulty considering, much less accepting, nondiscriminatory alternatives that may work just as well or better to advance legitimate organizational interests but without systematically disadvantaging minorities and women.

This is not to suggest that all such discriminatory organizational actions are spurious or arbitrary. Many may serve the actual needs of the organization. Physical size or strength at times may be a legitimate job requirement; sick leave and insurance policies must be reasonably restricted; educational qualifications are needed for many jobs; lending institutions cannot lend to people who cannot reasonably demonstrate an ability to repay loans. Unless carefully examined and then modified or eliminated, however, these apparently neutral rules, policies, and practices will continue to perpetuate age-old discriminatory patterns into the structure of today's society.

Whatever the motivation behind such organizational acts, a process is occurring, the common denominator of which is unequal results on a very large scale. When unequal outcomes are repeated over time and in numerous societal and geographical areas, it is a clear signal that a discriminatory process is at work.

Such discrimination is not a static, one-time phenomenon that has a clearly limited effect. Discrimination can feed on discrimination in self-perpetuating cycles.[25]

- The employer who recruits job applicants by word-of-mouth within a predominantly white male work force reduces the chances of receiving applications from minorities and females for open positions. Since they do not apply, they are not hired. Since they are not hired, they are not present when new jobs become available. Since they are not aware of new jobs, they cannot recruit other minority or female applicants. Because there are no minority or female employees to recruit others, the employer is left to recruit on his own from among his predominantly white and male work force.[26]
- The teacher who expects poor academic performance from minority and female students may not become greatly concerned when their grades are low. The acceptance of their low grades removes incentives to improve. Without incentives to improve, their grades remain low. Their low grades reduce their expectations, and the teacher has no basis for expecting more of them.[27]
- The realtor who assumes that white home owners do not want minority neighbors "steers" minorities to minority neighborhoods. Those steered to minority neighborhoods tend to live in minority neighborhoods. White neighborhoods then remain white, and realtors tend to assume that whites do not want minority neighbors.[28]
- Elected officials appoint voting registrars who impose linguistic, geographic, and other barriers to minority voter registration. Lack of minority registration leads to low voting rates. Lower minority voting rates lead to the election of fewer minorities. Fewer elected minorities leads to the appointment of voting registrars who maintain the same barriers.[29]

Structural Discrimination

Such self-sustaining discriminatory processes occur not only within the fields of employment, education, housing, and government but also between these structural areas. There is a classic cycle of structural discrimination that reproduces itself. Discrimination in education denies the credentials to get good jobs. Discrimination in employment denies the economic resources to buy good housing. Discrimination in housing confines minorities to school districts providing inferior education, closing the cycle in a classic form.[30]

With regard to white women, the cycle is not as tightly closed. To the extent they are raised in families headed by white males, and are married to or live with white males, white women will enjoy the advantages in housing and other areas that such relationships to white men can confer. White women lacking the sponsorship of white men, however, will be unable to avoid gender-based discrimination in housing, education, and employment. White women can thus be the victims of discrimination produced by social structures that is comparable in form to that experienced by minorities.

This perspective is not intended to imply that either the dynamics of discrimination or its nature and degree are identical for women and minorities. But when a woman of any background seeks to compete with men of any group, she finds herself the victim of a discriminatory process. Regarding the similarities and differences between the discrimination experienced by women and minorities, one author has aptly stated:

> [W]hen two groups exist in a situation of inequality, it may be self-defeating to become embroiled in a quarrel over which is more unequal or the victim of greater oppression. The more salient question is how a condition of inequality for both is maintained and perpetuated—through what means is it reinforced?[31]

The following are additional examples of the interaction between social structures that affect minorities and women:

- The absence of minorities and women from executive, writing, directing, news reporting, and acting positions in television contributes to unfavorable stereotyping on the screen, which in turn reinforces existing stereotypes among the public and creates psychological roadblocks to progress in employment, education, and housing.[32]
- Living in inner-city high crime areas in disproportionate numbers, minorities, particularly minority youth, are more likely to be arrested and are more likely to go to jail than whites accused of similar offenses, and their arrest and conviction records are then often used as bars to employment.[33]
- Because of past discrimination against minorities and women, female and minority-headed businesses are often small and relatively new. Further disadvantaged by contemporary credit and lending practices, they are more

likely than white male–owned businesses to remain small and be less able to employ full-time specialists in applying for government contracts. Because they cannot monitor the availability of government contracts, they do not receive such contracts. Because they cannot demonstrate success with government contracts, contracting officers tend to favor other firms that have more experience with government contracts.[34]

Discriminatory actions by individuals and organizations are not only pervasive, occurring in every sector of society, but also cumulative with effects limited neither to the time nor the particular structural area in which they occur. This process of discrimination, therefore, extends across generations, across organizations, and across social structures in self-reinforcing cycles, passing the disadvantages incurred by one generation in one area to future generations in many related areas.[35]

These interrelated components of the discriminatory process share one basic result: the persistent gaps seen in the status of women and minorities relative to that of white males. These unequal results themselves have real consequences. The employer who wishes to hire more minorities and women may be bewildered by charges of racism and sexism when confronted by what appears to be a genuine shortage of qualified minority and female applicants. The guidance counselor who sees one promising minority student after another drop out of school or give up in despair may be resentful of allegations of racism when there is little he or she alone can do for the student. The banker who denies a loan to a female single parent may wish to do differently, but believes that prudent fiscal judgment requires taking into account her lack of financial history and inability to prove that she is a good credit risk. These and other decisionmakers see the results of a discriminatory process repeated over and over again, and those results provide a basis for rationalizing their own actions, which then feed into that same process.

When seen outside the context of the interlocking and intertwined effects of discrimination, complaints that many women and minorities are absent from the ranks of qualified job applicants, academically inferior and unmotivated, poor credit risks, and so forth, may appear to be justified. Decisionmakers like those described above are reacting to real social problems stemming from the process of discrimination. But many too easily fall prey to stereotyping and consequently disregard those minorities and women who have the necessary skills or qualifications. And they erroneously "blame the victims" of discrimination,[36] instead of examining the past and present context in which their own actions are taken and the multiple consequences of these actions on the lives of minorities and women.

The Process of Discrimination

Although discrimination is maintained through individual actions, neither individual prejudices nor random chance can fully explain the persistent national patterns of inequality and underrepresentation. Nor can these patterns be blamed on the persons who are at the bottom of our economic, political, and social order. Overt racism and sexism as embodied in popular notions of white and male supremacy have been widely repudiated, but our history of discrimination based on race, sex, and national origin has not been readily put aside. Past discrimination continues to have present effects. The task today is to identify those effects and the forms and dynamics of the discrimination that produced them.

Discrimination against minorities and women must now be viewed as an interlocking process involving the attitudes and actions of individuals and the organizations and social structures that guide individual behavior. That process, started by past events, now routinely bestows privileges, favors, and advantages on white males and imposes disadvantages and penalties on minorities and women. This process is also self-perpetuating. Many normal, seemingly neutral, operations of our society create stereotyped expectations that justify unequal results; unequal results in one area foster inequalities in opportunity and accomplishment in others; the lack of opportunity and accomplishment confirms the original prejudices or engenders new ones that fuel the normal operations generating unequal results.

As we have shown, the process of discrimination involves many aspects of our society. No single factor sufficiently explains it, and no single means will suffice to eliminate it. Such elements of our society as our history of *de jure* discrimination, deeply ingrained prejudices,[37] inequities based on economic and social class,[38] and the structure and function of all our economic, social, and political institutions[39] must be continually examined in order to understand their part in shaping today's decisions that will either maintain or counter the current process of discrimination.

It may be difficult to identify precisely all aspects of the discriminatory process and assign those parts their appropriate importance. But understanding discrimination starts with an awareness that such a process exists and that to avoid perpetuating it, we must carefully assess the context and consequences of our everyday actions. . . .

NOTES

1. Dred Scott v. Sandford, 60 U.S. (19 How.) 393, 408 (1857).

2. For a concise summary of this history, see U.S. Commission on Civil Rights, *Twenty Years After Brown*, pp. 4–29 (1975); *Freedom to the Free: 1863, Century of Emancipation* (1963).

3. The discriminatory conditions experienced by these minority groups have been documented in the following publications by the U.S. Commission on Civil Rights: *The Navajo Nation: An American Colony* (1975); *The Southwest Indian Report* (1973); *The Forgotten Minority: Asian Americans in New York City* (State Advisory Committee Report 1977); *Success of Asian Americans: Fact or Fiction?* (1980); *Stranger in One's Land* (1970); *Toward Quality Education for Mexican Americans* (1974); *Puerto Ricans in the Continental United States: An Uncertain Future* (1976).

4. Frontiero v. Richardson, 411 U.S. 677, 684–86 (1973), citing L. Kanowitz, *Women and the Law: The Unfinished Revolution*, pp. 5–6 (1970), and G. Myrdal, *An American*

Dilemma 1073 (20th Anniversary Ed., 1962). Justice Brennan wrote the opinion of the Court, joined by Justices Douglas, White, and Marshall. Justice Stewart concurred in the judgment. Justice Powell, joined by Chief Justice Burger and Justice Blackmun, wrote a separate concurring opinion. Justice Rehnquist dissented. See also H. M. Hacker, "Women as a Minority Group," *Social Forces*, vol. 30 (1951), pp. 60–69; W. Chafe, *Women and Equality: Changing Patterns in American Culture* (New York: Oxford University Press, 1977).

5. Bradwell v. State, 83 U.S. (16 Wall) 130, 141 (1873) (Bradley, J., concurring), quoted in *Frontiero, supra* note 4.

6. U.S. Const. amend. XIX.

7. See U.S. Commission on Civil Rights, *Statement on the Equal Rights Amendment* (December 1978).

8. See, e.g., R. K. Merton, "Discrimination and the American Creed," in R. K. Merton, *Sociological Ambivalence and Other Essays* (New York: The Free Press, 1976), pp. 189–216. In this essay on racism, published for the first time more than 30 years ago, Merton presented a typology which introduced the notion that discriminatory actions are not always directly related to individual attitudes of prejudice. Merton's typology consisted of the following: Type I—the unprejudiced nondiscriminator; Type II—the unprejudiced discriminator; Type III—the prejudiced nondiscriminator; Type IV—the prejudiced discriminator. In the present context, Type II is crucial in its observation that discrimination is often practiced by persons who are not themselves prejudiced, but who respond to, or do not oppose, the actions of those who discriminate because of prejudiced attitudes (Type IV). See also D. C. Reitzes, "Prejudice and Discrimination: A Study in Contradictions," in *Racial and Ethnic Relations*, ed. H. M. Hughes (Boston: Allyn and Bacon, 1970), pp. 56–65.

9. See R. M. Kanter and B. A. Stein, "Making a Life at the Bottom," in *Life in Organizations, Workplaces as People Experience Them*, ed. Kanter and Stein (New York: Basic Books, 1976), pp. 176–90; also L. K. Howe, "Retail Sales Worker," ibid., pp. 248–51; also R. M. Kanter, *Men and Women of the Corporation* (New York: Basic Books, 1977).

10. See M. S. Granovetter, *Getting a Job: A Study of Contract and Careers* (Cambridge: Harvard University Press, 1974), pp. 6–11; also A. W. Blumrosen, *Black Employment and the Law* (New Brunswick, N.J.: Rutgers University Press, 1971), p. 232.

11. See U.S. Equal Employment Opportunity Commission, "Guidelines on Discrimination Because of Sex," 29 C.F.R. §1604.4 (1979); L. Farley, *Sexual Shakedown: The Sexual Harassment of Women on the Job* (New York: McGraw-Hill, 1978), pp. 92–96, 176–79; C. A. Mackinnon, *Sexual Harassment of Working Women* (New Haven: Yale University Press, 1979), pp. 25–55.

12. See R. Rosenthal and L. F. Jacobson, "Teacher Expectations for the Disadvantaged," *Scientific American*, 1968 (b) 218, 219–23; also D. Bar Tal, "Interactions of Teachers and Pupils," in *New Approaches to Social Problems*, ed. I. H. Frieze, D. Bar Tal, and J. S. Carrol (San Francisco: Jossey Bass, 1979), pp. 337–58; also U.S. Commission on Civil Rights, *Teachers and Students, Report V: Mexican American Education Study. Differences in Teacher Interaction with Mexican American and Anglo Students* (1973), pp. 22–23.

13. Ibid.

14. U.S. Department of Housing and Urban Development, "Measuring Racial Discrimination in American Housing Markets: The Housing Market Practices Survey" (1979); D. M. Pearce, "Gatekeepers and Home Seekers: Institutional Patterns in Racial Steering," *Social Problems*, vol. 26 (1979), pp. 325–42; "Benign Steering and Benign

Quotas: The Validity of Race Conscious Government Policies to Promote Residential Integration," 93 *Harv. L. Rev.* 938, 944 (1980).

15. See M. N. Danielson, *The Politics of Exclusion* (New York: Columbia University Press, 1976), pp. 11–12; U.S. Commission on Civil Rights, *Equal Opportunity in Suburbia* (1974).

16. See L. L. Knowles and K. Prewitt, eds., *Institutional Racism in America* (Englewood Cliffs, N.J.: Prentice Hall, 1969), pp. 58–77, and E. D. Wright, *The Politics of Punishment* (New York: Harper and Row, 1973). Also, S. V. Brown, "Race and Parole Hearing Outcomes," in *Discrimination in Organizations*, ed. R. Alvarez and K. G. Lutterman (San Francisco: Jossey Bass, 1979), pp. 355–74.

17. Height and weight minimums that disproportionately exclude women without a showing of legitimate job requirement constitute unlawful sex discrimination. See Dothard v. Rawlinson, 433 U.S. 321 (1977); Bowe v. Colgate Palmolive Co., 416 F.2d 711 (7th Cir. 1969). Minimum height requirements used in screening applicants for employment have also been held to be unlawful where such a requirement excludes a significantly higher percentage of Hispanics than other national origin groups in the labor market and no job relatedness is shown. See Smith v. City of East Cleveland, 520 F.2d 492 (6th Cir. 1975).

18. U.S. Commission on Civil Rights, *Last Hired, First Fired* (1976); Tangren v. Wackenhut Servs., Inc., 480 F. Supp. 539 (D. Nev. 1979).

19. U.S. Commission on Civil Rights, *The Challenge Ahead, Equal Opportunity in Referral Unions* (1977), pp. 84–89.

20. A. Pifer, "Women Working: Toward a New Society," pp. 13–34, and D. Pearce, "Women, Work and Welfare: The Feminization of Poverty," pp. 103–24, both in K. A. Fernstein, ed., *Working Women and Families* (Beverly Hills: Sage Publications, 1979). Disproportionate numbers of single-parent families are minorities.

21. See Griggs v. Duke Power Company, 401 U.S. 424 (1971); U.S. Commission on Civil Rights, *Toward Equal Educational Opportunity: Affirmative Admissions Programs at Law and Medical Schools* (1978), pp. 10–12; I. Berg, *Education and Jobs: The Great Training Robbery* (Boston: Beacon Press, 1971), pp. 58–60.

22. See U.S. Commission on Civil Rights, *Toward Equal Educational Opportunity: Affirmative Admissions Programs at Law and Medical Schools* (1978), pp. 14–15.

23. See U.S. Commission on Civil Rights, *Mortgage Money: Who Gets It? A Case Study in Mortgage Lending Discrimination in Hartford, Conn.* (1974); J. Feagin and C. B. Feagin, *Discrimination American Style, Institutional Racism and Sexism* (Englewood Cliffs, N.J.: Prentice Hall, 1976), pp. 78–79.

24. See *Club Membership Practices by Financial Institutions: Hearing before the Comm. on Banking, Housing and Urban Affairs, United States Senate*, 96th Cong., 1st Sess. (1979). The Office of Federal Contract Compliance Programs of the Department of Labor has proposed a rule that would make the payment or reimbursement of membership fees in a private club that accepts or rejects persons on the basis of race, color, sex, religion, or national origin a prohibited discriminatory practice. 45 Fed. Reg. 4954 (1980) (to be codified in 41 C.F.R. §60–1.11).

25. See U.S. Commission on Civil Rights, *For All the People . . . By All the People* (1969), pp. 122–23.

26. See note 10.

27. See note 12.

28. See notes 14 and 15.

29. See Statement of Arthur S. Flemming, Chairman, U.S. Commission on Civil Rights, before the Subcommittee on Constitutional Rights of the Committee on the Judiciary of the U.S. Senate on S.407, S.903, and S.1279, Apr. 9, 1975, pp. 15–18, based on U.S. Commission on Civil Rights, *The Voting Rights Act: Ten Years After* (January 1975).

30. See, e.g., U.S. Commission on Civil Rights, *Equal Opportunity in Suburbia* (1974).

31. Chafe, *Women and Equality*, p. 78.

32. U.S. Commission on Civil Rights, *Window Dressing on the Set* (1977).

33. See note 16; Gregory v. Litton Systems, Inc., 472 F.2d 631 (9th Cir. 1972); Green v. Mo.-Pac. R.R., 523 F.2d 1290 (8th Cir. 1975).

34. See U.S. Commission on Civil Rights, *Minorities and Women as Government Contractors*, pp. 20, 27, 125 (1975).

35. See, e.g., A. Downs, *Racism in America and How to Combat It* (U.S. Commission on Civil Rights, 1970); "The Web of Urban Racism," in *Institutional Racism in America*, ed. Knowles and Prewitt (Englewood Cliffs, N.J.: Prentice Hall, 1969), pp. 134–76. Other factors in addition to race, sex, and national origin may contribute to these interlocking institutional patterns. In *Equal Opportunity in Suburbia* (1974), this Commission documented what it termed "the cycle of urban poverty" that confines minorities in central cities with declining tax bases, soaring educational and other public needs, and dwindling employment opportunities, surrounded by largely white, affluent suburbs. This cycle of poverty, however, started with and is fueled by discrimination against minorities. See also W. Taylor, *Hanging Together, Equality in an Urban Nation* (New York: Simon & Schuster, 1971).

36. The "self-fulfilling prophecy" is a well-known phenomenon. "Blaming the victim" occurs when responses to discrimination are treated as though they were the causes rather than the results of discrimination. See Chafe, *Women and Equality*, (pp. 76–78; W. Ryan, *Blaming the Victim* (New York: Pantheon Books, 1971).

37. See, e.g., J. E. Simpson and J. M. Yinger, *Racial and Cultural Minorities* (New York: Harper and Row, 1965), pp. 49–79; J. M. Jones, *Prejudice and Racism* (Reading, Mass.: Addison Wesley, 1972), pp. 60–111; M. M. Tumin, "Who Is Against Desegregation?" in *Racial and Ethnic Relations*, ed. H. Hughes (Boston: Allyn and Bacon, 1970), pp. 76–85; D. M. Wellman, *Portraits of White Racism* (Cambridge: Cambridge University Press, 1977).

38. See, e.g., D. C. Cox, *Caste, Class and Race: A Study in Social Dynamics* (Garden City, N.Y.: Doubleday, 1948); W. J. Wilson, *Power, Racism and Privilege* (New York: Macmillan, 1973).

39. H. Hacker, "Women as a Minority Group," *Social Forces*, vol. 30 (1951), pp. 60–69; J. Feagin and C. B. Feagin, *Discrimination American Style*; Chafe, *Women and Equality*; J. Feagin, "Indirect Institutionalized Discrimination," *American Politics Quarterly*, vol. 5 (1977), pp. 177–200; M. A. Chesler, "Contemporary Sociological Theories of Racism," in *Towards the Elimination of Racism*, ed. P. Katz (New York: Pergamon Press, 1976); P. Van den Berghe, *Race and Racism: A Comparative Perspective* (New York: Wiley, 1967); S. Carmichael and C. Hamilton, *Black Power* (New York: Random House, 1967); Knowles and Prewitt, *Institutional Racism in America*; Downs, *Racism in America and How to Combat It.*

Racial Disparities Seen as Pervasive in Juvenile Justice

Fox Butterfield

Black and Hispanic youths are treated more severely than white teenagers charged with comparable crimes at every step of the juvenile justice system, according to a comprehensive report released yesterday that was sponsored by the Justice Department and six of the nation's leading foundations.

The report found that minority youths are more likely than their white counterparts to be arrested, held in jail, sent to juvenile or adult court for trial, convicted and given longer prison terms, leading to a situation in which the impact is magnified with each additional step into the juvenile justice system.

In some cases, the disparities are stunning. Among young people who have not been sent to a juvenile prison before, blacks are more than six times as likely as whites to be sentenced by juvenile courts to prison. For those young people charged with a violent crime who have not been in juvenile prison previously, black teenagers are nine times more likely than whites to be sentenced to juvenile prison. For those charged with drug offenses, black youths are 48 times more likely than whites to be sentenced to juvenile prison.

Similarly, white youths charged with violent offenses are incarcerated for an average of 193 days after trial, but blacks are incarcerated an average of 254 days and Hispanics are incarcerated an average of 305 days.

"The implications of these disparities are very serious," said Mark Soler, the president of the Youth Law Center, a research and advocacy group in Washington who also is the leader of the coalition of civil rights and youth advocacy organizations that organized the research project.

"These disparities accumulate, and they make it hard for members of the minority community to complete their education, get jobs and be good husbands and fathers," Mr. Soler said.

The report, "And Justice for Some," does not address why such sharp racial imbalances exist. But Mr. Soler suggested that the cause lay not so much in overt discrimination as in "the stereotypes that the decision makers at each point of the system rely on." A judge looking at a young person, Mr. Soler said, may be influenced by the defendant's baggy jeans or the fact that he does not have a father.

In the past, when studies have found racial disparities in the number of adult black or Hispanic prison inmates, critics have asserted that the cause was simply that members of minorities committed a disproportionate number of crimes. That may be true, Mr. Soler said, but it does not account for the extreme disparities found in the report, nor for disparities at each stage of the juvenile justice process.

"When you look at this data, it is undeniable that race is a factor," Mr. Soler said.

The report, the most thorough of its kind, is based on national and state data initially compiled by the Federal Bureau of Investigation; the Office of Juvenile Justice and Delinquency Prevention, a Justice Department agency; the Census Bureau and the National Center for Juvenile Justice, the research arm of the National Council of Juvenile and Family Court Judges. The report was written by Eileen Poe-Yamagata and Michael A. Jones, senior researchers with the National Council on Crime and Delinquency, in San Francisco.

An unusual feature of the report is that its costs were underwritten by the Justice Department and several leading foundations: the Ford Foundation; the MacArthur Foundation; the Rockefeller Foundation; the Walter Johnson Foundation; the Annie E. Casey Foundation, which specializes in issues relating to young people; and the Center on Crime, Communities and Culture of George Soros's Open Society Institute.

Hugh B. Price, the president of the National Urban League, said that "this report leaves no doubt that we are faced with a very serious national civil rights issue, virtually making our system juvenile injustice."

Mr. Soler and the coalition that put the report together want Congress to give the Justice Department at least $100 million to reduce racial disparities and require states to spend a quarter of their federal juvenile justice grants on the issue.

A spokesman for Representative Bill McCollum, the Florida Republican who is the chairman of the House Judiciary Committee's Subcommittee on Crime, said he would have no comment because he had not seen the report. Mr. McCollum sponsored a bill last year that would have increased the number of juveniles tried in adult court.

Nationally, the report found that blacks under the age of 18 make up 15 percent of their age group, but 26 percent of those young people arrested, 31 percent of those sent to juvenile court, 44 percent of those detained in juvenile jails and 32 percent of those found guilty of being a delinquent. Similarly, young blacks account for 46 percent of all juveniles tried in adult criminal courts, 40 percent of those sent to juvenile prisons and 58 percent of all juveniles confined in adult prisons.

"White" Names Give Job Seekers an Edge

CHICAGO   It helps to have a white-sounding first name when looking for work, a new study has found.

Résumés with white-sounding first names elicited 50 percent more responses than ones with black-sounding names, according to a study by professors at the University of Chicago Graduate School of Business and the Massachusetts Institute of Technology.

The professors sent about 5,000 résumés in response to want ads in the Boston Globe and Chicago Tribune. They found that the "white" applicants they created received one response—a call, letter or e-mail—for every 10 résumés mailed, while "black" applicants with equal credentials received one response for every 15 résumés sent.

The study authors, including University of Chicago associate professor of economics Marianne Bertrand, said the results can solely be attributed to name manipulation.

"Our results so far suggest that there is a substantial amount of discrimination in the job recruiting process," they wrote.

The professors analyzed birth certificates in coming up with what names to use. The white names included Neil, Brett, Greg, Emily, Anne and Jill. Some of the black names used were Tamika, Ebony, Aisha, Rasheed, Kareem and Tyrone.

Companies that purported to be equal-opportunity employers were no more likely to respond to black résumés than other businesses were, the study found.

Carolyn Nordstrom, president of Chicago United, a group that seeks to increase corporate diversity, said the study shows the need to educate those that make hiring decisions. "We like to believe that this has changed, but this is evidence that it hasn't," she said.

Equality at Work Remains Elusive

Rachel Smolkin

BRYN MAWR, PA   Lisa Marchisio sat in an empty math classroom, completing her differential equations and grousing to a friend about theorems that haunt her dreams.

Between complaints about "dead mathematicians" on a foggy April morning, the 21-year-old juniors at this elite women's college pondered their futures in a work force where women remain clustered in lower-paying jobs and often find themselves excluded from top executive positions.

Decades after the women's liberation movement of the 1960s spawned widespread demands for gender equality in the work place, even young women with every advantage wonder if it's likely to arrive any time soon.

"Slowly, over time, it seems like it will happen," Marchisio said. "It has to happen eventually. I hope."

Susanna Jones, a 20-year-old English major, also is "hopeful."

"The opportunities I'm having now, my mother certainly didn't have," she said.

Secluded on suburban Philadelphia's affluent Main Line, Bryn Mawr's campus is tranquil and secure. Its Gothic stone buildings and rows of arcing trees on the campus green offer temporary shelter to 1,300 young women who must eventually reenter a male-female world.

Their plans to go to medical and law school, to pursue careers in architecture or doctoral degrees in math, reflect women's surge into the labor force over the past three decades and foretell considerable advancement during the next three.

Their qualms highlight the barriers that remain.

The number of highly placed women at top companies and in leadership positions at universities, unions and the military remains startlingly low, suggesting that a critical mass of qualified women is not enough to ensure professional parity.

Without question, young women today enter a work force radically transformed. Thirty-eight years after author Betty Friedan in "The Feminine Mystique" skewered the suburban home as a "comfortable concentration camp," women have burst into new careers.

More women than men now attend college—a trend fueled by larger numbers of African American and Hispanic women going to college than their male peers and by significant numbers of older women returning to school. More women than men also earn master's degrees.

High-school girls are taking advanced math and science classes in greater numbers than a decade ago, narrowing the gender gap documented in the American Association of University Women's landmark 1992 report, "How Schools Shortchange Girls."

Over the past 30 years, the percentage of physicians who are women has tripled and nearly half of entering medical school students are now women. Women also are expected to make up the majority of entering law students for the first time this fall.

"Women are the emerging majority of the legal profession," said Martha Barnett, president of the American Bar Association. "And in the next 20 years, women could well be the majority of the profession."

JoAnn Heffernan Heisen, chief information officer for Johnson & Johnson, is similarly optimistic about the corporate world. She predicts senior management in major corporations will be evenly balanced between men and women in 15 years.

"I really feel that the women who are in middle and senior management now are making such significant contributions that they will be recognized over the next 15 or 20 years," said Heisen, currently the only woman on Johnson & Johnson's executive committee.

Nevertheless, when the optimistic Heisen began her career at Chase Manhattan Bank in 1972, she assumed women would achieve higher status more quickly than they have.

The Pipeline Leaks

A recent American Bar Association report, "The Unfinished Agenda: Women and the Legal Profession," documents pervasive inequalities. Women account for almost 30 percent of the profession but only about 15 percent of federal judges and law firm partners, 10 percent of law school deans and general counsels, and 5 percent of managing partners of large firms.

"A widespread assumption is that barriers have been coming down, women have been moving up, and it is only a matter of time before full equality becomes an accomplished fact," the report says. "Such perceptions are hard to square with the facts. Time alone and women's relatively recent admission to the profession cannot explain the extent of sex-based disparities in pay or promotion."

Women in legal practice earn an average $20,000 a year less than men. Surveys of law firms and corporate counsel salaries have found a significant pay gap even among men and women with similar positions and experience.

So while there may be many more women in the pipeline heading toward the heights of the legal profession, "the pipeline leaks," said Deborah L. Rhode, the report's author and a professor at Stanford School of Law.

A look at corporate America tells a similar story.

Only four women are CEOs of Fortune 500 companies: Carleton Fiorina at Hewlett-Packard, Andrea Jung at Avon Products, Marion Sandler of Golden West Financial Corp. and Cinda Hallman of Spherion Corp., a temporary staffing company. The figure is double last year's total of two.

Women make up 12.5 percent of Fortune 500 corporate officers and only 4.1 percent of top earners, according to Catalyst, a research group that tracks women executives. Catalyst projects that women corporate officers will be underrepresented far into the future, holding only 27 percent of Fortune 500 corporate officer positions by 2020.

Not one of the top 25 media conglomerates is headed by a woman. Women account for only 9 percent of board members and 13 percent of top executives in major media, telecom and e-companies, according to a recent study by the Annenberg Public Policy Center of the University of Pennsylvania.

"I thought the numbers were sobering," said Federal Communications Commissioner Susan Ness. "Initially we figured with those companies founded during the old boys'-network world that the numbers would be worse. But it's just as bad with the new companies. Instead of the old boys' network, it's the new boys' network."

In other fields, too, women are scattered through the pipeline but seldom reach the top.

Women increasingly serve as elected local and regional union officers. They hold appointed national staff positions, but few are found among the top elected officers.

They have stormed statewide politics and hold a record 72 seats in Congress — out of 535. But only five of the nation's 50 governors are women. Women have yet to break into senior congressional leadership positions and rarely have chaired congressional committees.

In the armed services, the advent of an all-volunteer force in 1973 dramatically increased the number of women. But Department of Defense policies still restrict women's access to combat positions, barring women from central military functions and impeding their advancement.

The wage gap between men and women has narrowed since 1979 but has stagnated in recent years. Full-time working women earn 72 percent as much as full-time working men, on average.

"The wage gap has not been noticeably narrowing over the 1990s, a period of increased employment tenure and work force participation by women," said Vicky Lovell, study director at the Institute for Women's Policy Research. "That does not bode well for a substantial closing of the wage gap over the next 30 years."

The gap persists in part because most women remain concentrated in jobs traditionally considered "women's work" and undervalued by society. More than 70 percent of clerical workers, cashiers, librarians, child-care workers, nurses and elementary school teachers are women. Nearly 99 percent of pre-kindergarten and kindergarten teachers are women.

"I think the perception is still that dealing with children and teaching children is a woman's job, which is unfortunate because certainly both sexes are capable," said Brian McCarthy, a 20-year-old political science major at coeducational Haverford College, which shares some programs with Bryn Mawr.

Men in female-dominated jobs also are paid poorly, but they still earn about 20 percent more per hour than women in the same jobs, according to one of the institute's studies. Only 8.5 percent of working men are in female-dominated jobs, compared with more than 55 percent of working women.

Other professions remain bastions for men. Women make up only 1.3 percent of plumbers, pipefitters and steamfitters and only 1.2 percent of heating, air conditioning and refrigeration mechanics, according to the Bureau of Labor Statistics. These occupations offer men with high school educations well-paying opportunities that remain largely closed to women.

Kid Care vs. Mr. Big Shot

In colleges, male students continue to dominate degrees in computer science, the physical sciences and engineering—majors that lead to lucrative jobs in both traditional and high-tech business sectors.

Women earned only 3 percent of the engineering bachelor's degrees in 1976. By 1998, that number had quintupled, but still was only 17 percent.

"Even more disturbing to me is the trend over the last 10 years: The graphs are fairly flat," said David Daniel, dean of the College of Engineering at the University of Illinois at Urbana-Champaign.

"Engineering is not viewed as a cool profession for young women," Daniel said. "It's easy for a young woman to turn on the television and have a very clear message and signal that the medical profession welcomes them, that the legal profession welcomes them, but there is no such message from the popular media about engineering as a profession for women."

During the past decade, the percentage of women earning computer science degrees actually has dropped, from 37 percent in 1984 to 27 percent in 1998.

"It exacerbates the wage gap if women end up being closed out of high-paying jobs where the country is looking to recruit highly trained workers," said Marcia Greenberger, co-president of the National Women's Law Center, a nonprofit group that tries to advance women's interests. "Engineering and computer science are high on the list of fields that offer jobs with good pay, good benefits and a strong future."

Society's lack of esteem for "women's work" frustrates Bryn Mawr's Susanna Jones, who hopes pay in women-dominated jobs will increase.

"Traditional 'women positions,' in terms of nursing, in terms of teaching and child care, are still severely discriminated against," Jones said.

"People who work at day care spend 40 hours a week raising children who aren't their own, pouring their heart and souls out, and they get paid minimum wage," she said. "meanwhile, Mr. Big Shot on Wall Street is cruising along on his speed boat in the Caribbean. I mean, that makes me sick, but I think there's hope. I'm hopeful that things will change."

26

Wal-Martyrs

Meg Cox

AT 24, KIM MILLER HAD HIGH expectations when she joined Wal-Mart as a cashier in Ocala, Florida. The company's motto, OUR PEOPLE MAKE THE DIFFERENCE, along with regular staff pep rallies, assurances of training and advancement, and an "open-door policy" for airing grievances were all signs of a promising future. But for nine years, Miller's career stagnated while she watched men with less experience advance. Formal announcements about job openings were erratic. And when she complained that a boss called her a "bitch," and that male coworkers watched a porn video during work hours, she was told the problem was a "personality conflict," and no action was taken.

So on June 19 of this year, Miller joined five other current and former female employees of Wal-Mart and took some action of her own. Together, the women filed a lawsuit in San Francisco's federal court, charging that Wal-Mart Stores Inc., the nation's largest private employer, has a pervasive and conscious pattern of discriminating against women. And class-action status is being sought for an estimated seven hundred thousand current and former women workers, requesting back pay and unspecified damages and an end to Wal-Mart's discriminatory practices. It is the biggest employment discrimination lawsuit ever, and though the battle will be long and brutal, a victory could spark major changes in how women everywhere are treated in the workplace.

The suit charges that Wal-Mart has the worst record of advancing women of any major discount retailer. Although 72 percent of its hourly workers are women, they comprise only 37 percent of the company's managers. In contrast, the suit maintains that at Wal-Mart's major competitors, women hold more than half of the management jobs. The importance of the lawsuit extends well beyond Wal-Mart because the company is held up as a model by those hoping to ape its success. From a single store in 1962, Wal-Mart has become a retailing legend, with more than four thousand stores and over one million employees worldwide. The chain is now bigger than Sears, J.C. Penney, and Kmart combined, and its enormous profits have made the descendants of founder Sam Walton one of the richest families in the United States.

Teresa Ghilarducci, an economics professor at Indiana's University of Notre Dame, says this case breaks new ground not just because of the size of its target, but also because it deals with the deeply entrenched discrimination women face in low-paying jobs. "We can talk about the importance of women moving into the boardroom, but the majority of women don't work in white-collar jobs," says Ghilarducci.

While Wal-Mart prides itself on granting full-time status and benefits to people who work as few as 29 hours a week, author Barbara Ehrenreich, who took a low-wage job at Wal-Mart to conduct research for her book *Nickel and Dimed*, reports that the average employee is expected to pay $150 a month for health coverage, but many can't afford it. In addition, says Al Zack of the United Food and Commercial Workers union (UFCW), "Wal-Mart managers are taught to use the open-door grievance policy to identify troublemakers." Micki Earwood, a plaintiff from Urbana, Ohio, knows this all too well. "I was told I couldn't be promoted unless I moved to New York, and there I was a single mother with a four-year-old," she says. "In the next two years, I watched three men get promoted and none of them left the state. There were bike-assembly guys and stock boys making two dollars an hour more than a woman department head who had been there much longer." Within a week of complaining about these disparities to the district manager, Earwood was fired in spite of her 12 years at the company.

The lawyers handling the case, who are from three private law firms and three public interest legal groups, say that more than three hundred women employees have contacted them since the case was filed. For the next year, attorneys will gather these women's stories in an effort to prove that what has happened to them represents the rule, not the exception. If they get the court to grant class-action status, they will proceed to trial, which could take years.

In the past decade, Wal-Mart has been accused of discriminating against the disabled, people of color, and anyone who ever even thought of joining a union. But the company is infamous for vigorously fighting back. It stalls, refuses to settle routine cases, and appeals even small defeats to a higher court, says Lewis Laska, who, as head of the Wal-Mart Litigation Project, assists lawyers who sue the company. Things are so bad that the UFCW started an online support and advocacy group that calls itself WalMartyrs (www.walmartyrs.com) to help former employees who have experienced discrimination.

"I know we're like David taking on Goliath," says Jocelyn Larkin of Impact Fund, a public-interest law firm in Berkeley, California, that is representing the women, "but we're prepared for this. Can we win? I think the chances are great. The evidence is overwhelming. But it may be a long haul."

27

Sex Bias Cited in Vocational Ed

Pervasive sex segregation persists in high school vocational programs around the country—including in Maryland and Virginia—30 years after Congress passed a law barring such discrimination in education, according to a study released today.

The D.C.-based National Women's Law Center plans to file legal petitions today in all 12 regions of the Department of Education's Office of Civil Rights, requesting investigations into whether vocational and technical high schools and classes violate Title IX and demanding that action be taken to remedy all conduct that does not comply with federal law.

"There are just stunning patterns of sex segregation in schools across the country," said Jocelyn Samuels, vice president and director of educational opportunities for the law center. "The primary problems in career ed are inattention and lack of perception that there is a problem."

The center's survey on vocational programs marks the 30th anniversary of the federal law—Title IX of the Education Amendments—that bars sex discrimination in schools and other educational programs receiving federal funds. That includes almost all public elementary and secondary schools and most colleges and universities.

The survey found that girls still are clustered in classes that lead to traditionally female jobs in cosmetology, child care and other low-paying fields, while boys dominate classes that lead to traditionally male—and high-paying—careers in technology and the trades. Young women enrolled in such programs earn a median hourly wage of $8.49 as a hairdresser, for example, compared with $30.06 an hour in the traditionally male career of plumbing and pipe fitting.

The pattern was consistent in all states surveyed, including California and New York. In Maryland, for example, data showed that female students make up 99 percent of the student body in cosmetology courses, 84 percent in child care courses, 93 percent in courses that prepare students to work as assistants in the health-care field, and 89 percent in courses that prepare students for other health-care occupations.

Male students make up 84 percent of those in drafting courses, 84 percent in computer installation and repair courses, 95 percent in carpentry courses and 95 percent in automotive classes.

Maryland education officials said they could not comment because they had not seen the report.

In Fairfax County, one of the richest counties in the country, boys outnumber girls in every technology class in every high school, according to research by the Fairfax County Office for Women.

In 2000–01, girls accounted for only 5 percent of students in design and technology courses, 10 percent in network administration courses and 27 percent in computer science classes, the data showed. Only 5 percent of students in courses given by CISCO Networking Academies at three Fairfax high schools were girls.

Lesley Persily, program analyst for the county's Office for Women, said the Fairfax Board of Education requested information in 1998 on how well schools were complying with Title IX.

"We released the data in 1998 in computer technology, and it showed that every single class had a majority of boys," she said. "Really, the numbers haven't changed since then."

Marty Abbott, director of high school instruction in Fairfax, said: "This is an issue we have always been concerned with. . . . We felt we had made some strides with our middle schools and some of our high school courses, and we know that still at some of the very top-level courses we need to see more girls enrolling in those courses. But we have put a lot of effort into this, and we were hoping those numbers would appear stronger at this point."

One problem discovered by the investigators for the law center was there is no systematic requirement for data collection on vocational schools and programs. Some states keep data haphazardly, and some don't keep any at all. Furthermore, the law center said Virginia and a number of other states, as well as the District of Columbia, do not have Title IX coordinators, a violation of the law.

Girls are still not advised about the possibilities in different trades, and they face harassment once they enter these fields, said Melissa Barbier, director of girls programs for Chicago Women in Trades, a 20-year organization dedicated to promoting women and girls in the trades.

She said it is vital for teachers and counselors to not only help women understand their options but to advocate for them.

"A shop teacher, for example, plays a big role in referring students to certain employers they have relationships with. What we are finding is that even teachers who support students inside the classroom are not helping them make the next link because they are not willing to advocate for their female students."

Supporters of Title IX recently have become alarmed by some Bush administration proposals that they regard as turning the clock back on educational opportunities for women.

The administration announced its intention recently to support single-sex schools and classes. And last week, it declined to comment on the merits of a lawsuit filed by the National Wrestling Coaches Association and other groups challenging Title IX athletic protections. It argued instead that the suit should be dismissed on procedural grounds.

Though Title IX applies to all aspects of education, it is best known for opening the door to athletics for females. The number of college women participating in competitive athletics is now four times the pre-Title IX rate, and the number of high school girls playing competitive sports has risen from 300,000 before Title IX to 2.65 million by 1999.

Still, women in Division I colleges represent more than half of the student body, yet they receive only 41 percent of athletic scholarship dollars, 30 percent of recruiting dollars and 33 percent of overall athletic budgets, according to the law center.

28

EEOC Files Sexual Harassment Suit against Denny's

A Denny's general manager and another co-worker repeatedly sexually harassed a 16-year-old employee, and she was fired after she complained, the U.S. Equal Employment Opportunity Commission alleged Tuesday.

The EEOC sued in U.S. District Court for the Southern District of Illinois on behalf of Becky Hilliard of Murphysboro, claiming civil rights violations and sexual harassment.

"It's making her feel like she's a piece of cattle, literally a piece of meat," said her attorney, Shari Rhode. "It's done wondrous damage to her self esteem." Hilliard started working at the Denny's restaurant in Carbondale in April 2000, when she was a freshman in high school.

For about the next year, the store's general manager—who is in his 40s—allegedly would routinely pat her on the rear, touch her blouse around her breasts and put his hands in the lower pockets of her apron, Rhode said.

Associated Press (September 3, 2002). Copyright © 2002. Reprinted with permission of The Associated Press.

The co-worker allegedly used "very sexually graphic words," comments and different profanities, Rhode said.

That man, who is in his 20s, also made sexual gestures to Hilliard, other workers and customers, Rhode said.

The federal agency is seeking compensatory damages and lost wages for Hilliard, EEOC St. Louis regional attorney Robert Johnson said.

The manager is on unpaid leave, and the co-worker was fired last year, Denny's spokeswoman Debbie Atkins said. Management investigated the claims and found the results inconclusive, Atkins said in a prepared statement.

"We have worked in good faith with the agency to resolve the matter and are baffled by their decision to file a lawsuit," Atkins said. "We will defend ourselves vigorously."

The accused employees were not identified in the lawsuit, and neither the company nor the EEOC would give their names.

Rhode said Hilliard reported the events to other managers but nothing was done.

After she notified the EEOC, her work hours were cut and she eventually was fired for using profanity in the workplace, Rhode said. However, her language was commonly used by co-workers who were not punished, Rhode said.

Rhode said she plans to formally join the EEOC's lawsuit soon and would add charges including willful infliction of emotional distress, battery and negligence. The maximum Hilliard could receive under federal law is $300,000.

"We want to make sure the company provides a remedy for people who complain about sexual harassment, not retaliate against them and ultimately fire them," Johnson said. "That's not what we expect from companies."

Nationwide, Denny's has faced similar lawsuits in the past.

In 2000, the EEOC settled a sexual harassment lawsuit against the company for $60,350 after a general manager at a location in Florida made sexual comments and touched a female employee.

Denny's also settled with the EEOC in January 2000 after eight Seattle women complained their male co-workers sexually harassed them. Under that settlement, Denny's agreed to pay a total of $425,000 to the women and $50,000 to Seattle's YWCA.

29

Anti-Muslim Crimes Jump after Sept. 11 in Jersey and U.S.

Brian Donohue

The September 2001 terrorist attacks sparked a nationwide surge in hate crimes against Muslims and people of Middle Eastern descent, according to an FBI report released yesterday.

Incidents targeting Muslims increased from 28 in 2000 to 481 in 2001.

Overall, hate crimes rose by 17 percent from 2000 to 2001, from 8,063 to 9,730 incidents. FBI officials said part of the overall increase is attributed to better reporting among local law enforcement agencies.

But the report also stated the increases, especially in crimes against Arabs and Muslims, occurred "presumably as a result of the heinous incidents that occurred on Sept. 11."

New Jersey officials reported 767 bias crimes last year, the second-highest state total behind California, which had 2,246.

The New Jersey statistics, released in September, show Arabs and Muslims were victims in five bias crimes in 2000 and 92 bias crimes last year.

The incidents ranged from a person throwing a rock through the window of a Muslim-owned store in Franklin Township to a Pakistani man assaulted by a group of men in Old Bridge on Sept. 11, 2001.

In one of the most serious incidents last year, a former resident of Milltown in Middlesex County was shot and killed while working in his grocery store in Texas. That murder was one of 10 bias-related murders in the country last year.

Mohamed Younes, President of the Totowa-based American Muslim Union, said members of the Muslim community remain concerned over a continued backlash.

The Sept. 11 terrorists, he said, "not only hijacked the planes, they hijacked our religion and gave it a bad name."

"We as Americans see this as very unfair, because it's not the American way," Younes said. "At the same time, we understand, because the media has painted the picture of Muslims in a very bad way."

Brian Donohue, "Anti-Muslim crimes jump after Sept. 11 in Jersey and U.S.", *Star Ledger* (November 26, 2002).

The highest number of bias crimes nationwide continues to be aimed at blacks and Jews.

There were 2,899 bias crimes against black victims nationwide, by far the largest single category of bias crimes.

Among religious groups, Jews remain the most frequent targets of bias-motivated criminals, comprising 56.5 percent of those cases. Anti-Islamic crimes were 26.2 percent of all crimes against religious groups.

"As we continue to fight against terrorism, there has to be a parallel battle against bigotry, and it is crucial to ensure that there be no backlash against Arabs and Muslims," said Charles "Shai" Goldstein, New Jersey regional director of the Anti-Defamation League. "Extremists who commit these crimes must be confronted and convicted."

The number of bias crimes in New Jersey may be returning to pre-Sept. 11, 2001, levels.

According to preliminary statistics compiled by the state Attorney General's Office, the number of bias crimes committed in the first six months of 2002 is down 11 percent compared with the same period last year, before the attacks.

30

Asian American Journalists Association (AAJA) Objects to Syndicated Cartoonist's Use of Racist Stereotypes of Asians

SAN FRANCISCO   The 1,700-member Asian American Journalists Association (AAJA) today demanded that an editorial cartoonist practice responsible journalism by ending the use of racial stereotypes and ethnic caricatures in his work.

Patrick Oliphant published Monday a cartoon on the subject of the American crew detained by China by portraying a confrontation between Uncle Sam and a bucktooth, bespectacled Chinese waiter.

In a letter to John P. McMeel, chairman of the Andrews McMeel Universal, AAJA national president Victor Panichkul said that Oliphant's "editorial cartoon crossed the line from acerbic depiction to racial caricature and is absolutely unacceptable."

Andrews McMeel Universal is the largest independent newspaper syndicate in the world, and the distributor of Oliphant's editorial cartoons.

"Editorial cartoonists often have more editorial leeway in connection with vigorous political expression," said Panichkul, "but this in no way excuses base ethnic insult. Gross racial parodies cannot be explained away as merely tart 'opinion' that is not intended to be offensive."

Panichkul pointed out specific offensive characterizations in the cartoon:

- The "Chinese" character has thick glasses and buckteeth reminiscent of the anti-Japanese propaganda of World War II.
- "Crispy fried cat gizzards" refers to the traditional racist allusion to Asians eating cats and dogs.
- "Apologize lotten Amellican!" is another traditional racist resort to pidgin English.

"AAJA Objects to Syndicated Cartoonist's Use of Racist Stereotypes of Asians," Pr Newswire Association, Inc. (April 13, 2001).

Panichkul also referenced previous concerns expressed to Andrews McMeel Universal about previous Oliphant cartoons on April 30, 1999, asserting that Chinese eat dogs, and May 11, 1999, implying that all Chinese operate laundries.

AAJA suggests new organizations refer to AAJA's stylebook, *All-American: How to Cover Asian America*, for examples on how to better cover Asian Americans and avoid negative stereotypes. The handbook order forms can be obtained online at the AAJA Web site: http://aaja.org/html/news_html/news_stylebook.html.

AAJA is a non-profit educational association based in San Francisco, devoted to training and developing Asian American journalists and ensuring fair and accurate coverage of the Asian American community. It has 1,700 members in 18 chapters across the United States and Asia. AAJA is celebrating its 20th anniversary this year.

31

EEOC Sues Arizona Diner for National Origin Bias against Navajos and Other Native Americans

U.S. Equal Employment Opportunity Commission

PHOENIX   The U.S. Equal Employment Opportunity Commission (EEOC) announced that it filed a national origin discrimination lawsuit under Title VII of the Civil Rights Act of 1964 on behalf of Native American employees who were subjected to an unlawful English-only policy precluding them from speaking Navajo in the workplace and terminating them for refusing to sign an agreement to abide by the restrictive language policy. The lawsuit, the first-ever English-only suit by the Commission on behalf of Native Americans, was filed by the EEOC's Phoenix District Office against RD's Drive-In, a diner located in Page, Arizona—a community adjacent to the Navajo reservation.

Reiterating a message she delivered last June to the 25th Anniversary Conference of the Council for Tribal Employment Rights—whose members represent the employment interest of Indian tribes on reservations in several states— EEOC Chair Cari M. Dominguez said: "The Commission is committed to advancing job opportunities and protecting the employment rights of Native Americans."

The suit, *EEOC v RD's Drive In*, CIV 02 1911 PHX LOA, states that in approximately June 2000, RD's posted a policy stating: *"The owner of this business can speak and understand only English. While the owner is paying you as an employee, you are required to use English at all times. The only exception is when the customer can not understand English. If you feel unable to comply with this requirement, you may find another job."*

This policy, in an early form, prohibited employees from speaking "Navajo" in the workplace. Two employees, Roxanne Cahoon and Freda Douglas, refused to agree to the policy because they believed it to be discriminatory. As a result, they were asked to leave their employment by RD's. In addition, at least two other employees resigned prior to being terminated because they could not agree to the policy. The vast majority of the employees working at the time spoke Navajo.

Charles Burtner, Director of the EEOC's Phoenix District Office, said: "We investigated this case. We found that the policy at issue, by its own terms, extended to breaks and appeared to be directly primarily to the use of the Navajo language. We found that this policy and its implementation is a form of national origin discrimination, which violates Title VII. Further, the employer's decision to terminate employees who questioned the policy is particularly troubling. Again, we found these terminations to be a form of retaliation, which is illegal."

Mary O'Neill, Acting Regional Attorney of the Phoenix District Office, said: "This case represents a rare lawsuit by the EEOC challenging workplace language restrictions directed at native languages. It is amazing that, in a country that cherishes diversity, an employer will prohibit the use of indigenous languages in the workplace and terminate Native American employees who question whether that is lawful. In fact, in 1990, Congress enacted a statute specifically designed to protect and preserve Native languages."

The lawsuit seeks monetary relief, including back pay with prejudgment interest and compensatory and punitive damages. The Commission is also seeking an injunction prohibiting future discrimination and any other curative relief to prevent the company from engaging in any further discriminatory practices. The EEOC filed suit only after investigating the case, finding that discrimination took place, and exhausting its conciliation efforts to reach a voluntary settlement.

In addition to enforcing Title VII of the Civil Rights Act of 1964, which prohibits employment discrimination based on sex, race, color, religion, or national origin, the Commission enforces Title I of the Americans with Disabilities Act, which prohibits discrimination against people with disabilities in the private sector; the Age Discrimination in Employment Act of 1967; the Equal Pay Act of 1963; the Civil Rights Act of 1991; and the provisions of the Rehabilitation Act of 1973 which prohibit discrimination affecting people with disabilities in the federal sector. Further information about the Commission is available on the Agency's web site at www.eeoc.gov.

32

Poll Finds Latinos Are Objects of Negative Perceptions

Michael A. Fletcher

ELGIN, IL Eight months pregnant, Sabrina Roman was watching television with her 2-year-old son when she heard an urgent knock out front. She pushed herself up from the couch, opened the front door and found herself face-to-face with a city inspector and a police officer.

Everyone in the house had to leave immediately or face arrest, she recalls the inspector saying. Roman said they were being thrown out, in part, because there were mattresses on the basement floor, which city officials took as a sure sign that people were living there illegally.

Roman, 21, says she pleaded that no one lived in the basement, that the mattresses were there because her family laid on them to watch television. But the inspector was not hearing it. He slapped a red notice on the door declaring the house uninhabitable and told Roman to gather some belongings and leave.

"I couldn't believe they would just put us out like that," she said. "I was mad. I was really angry."

Many Latinos see bias in law enforcement. But many non-Latino whites see only a struggle to maintain safety standards and beat back creeping blight caused by an influx of hard-working but low-income residents. Those differing perceptions have heightened racial tensions in Elgin and elsewhere.

A national poll by the Washington Post, the Henry J. Kaiser Family Foundation and Harvard University found that racial groups differ sharply over the amount of discrimination they believe is faced by Latinos. More than half of the nation's Latinos—55 percent—say that discrimination against Latinos is a big problem. By contrast, only 27 percent of non-Latino whites and 44 percent of blacks view discrimination against Latinos as a major concern.

The poll also found that two in five Latinos say they, a family member or close friend have experienced discrimination in the past five years because of their race or ethnicity.

The poll and interviews with whites and Latinos suggest there exists a gap in perceptions about just how much discrimination Latinos face. And some of that discrimination, the poll suggests, is fueled by stereotypes that whites—and blacks—have of Latinos.

The battles now roiling Elgin are hardly new. Generations ago municipalities used similar occupancy codes to limit the number of black, Jewish, Irish or Italian residents.

"All of a sudden people were going in the back yards and hearing Spanish spoken or seeing people congregating on stoops or in their yards," said Joan Laser, an assistant U.S. attorney in Chicago. "In some ways people were living a different lifestyle, but they were not doing anything the least bit offensive."

Some of the fear might be rooted in the mistaken perceptions many Americans have of their Latino neighbors. The Post/Kaiser/Harvard survey found, for example, that many whites and blacks overestimate the share of Latinos who live in poverty, are illegal immigrants or receive welfare.

Half of both blacks and whites said that they believe at least half of the nation's Latinos live in poverty. The Latino poverty rate, meanwhile, is nearly 26 percent.

About six in 10 of those polled think that most of the Latinos who came to the United States in the past decade were illegal immigrants. In reality, about one in four Latinos who have immigrated to the United States since 1992 came illegally, according to INS estimates.

Also, more than a third of the poll's respondents said that at least half of the nation's legal Latino residents collect welfare. In fact, about 6.9 percent of the nation's Latinos over age 15 receive either public assistance or federal disability payments. Or just over a quarter receive welfare, if that definition is broadened to include housing assistance or Medicaid.

In Elgin, 35 miles northwest of Chicago, as long as a century ago the city's population was nearly a quarter foreign-born and business boomed. Then, the immigrants were mostly from Germany and Sweden, and they worked in the local foundry or the sprawling watch factory that at its peak employed 4,000 people and made Elgin watches a household name.

After the old economy faded and the city and surrounding towns spent decades in the doldrums, business is once against humming.

Now Elgin's immigrants are largely Latino, mostly from Mexico, and their growing presence is lubricating the economy even as it reveals a fundamental dilemma.

On one hand, Elgin needs low-cost workers to clean the malls, run the hospital laundry and staff the small factories that are creating a bounty of new jobs and giving the area new economic life.

But few of those jobs pay well, and the area has little low-income housing, leaving the heavily Latino work force to share homes and apartments.

From 1995 to 1998, Elgin issued 268 citations for occupancy code violations, and two-thirds of them went to families with Hispanic surnames. Hundreds of other Latinos, many of whom speak little English, say they have been confronted with threats of eviction or arrest after their landlords were cited with code violations.

"These kinds of code issues, even if they were on the books, would not be enforced if this community were all-white," said Bernie J. Kleina, executive director of the HOPE Fair Housing Center, an advocacy group preparing to file a complaint with federal officials alleging that Elgin's housing code enforcement discriminates against Latinos.

"You should not see that kind of extreme enforcement actions unless there is some sort of pressing health or safety concern."

Many homeowners here say this issue has nothing to do with discrimination, but instead reflects their desire to protect their property values and way of life.

"If you are paying one property tax and have two or three families living in a house, that is not fair to the rest of us," said Betsy Couture, an Elgin community leader. "You are demanding more in service than you pay in taxes."

33

Injured Laborers File $66M Suit:
Suing Men Charged in Bias Attacks, 7 Groups

Robert E. Kessler

Two Mexican day laborers have filed a federal civil rights lawsuit seeking $66 million in damages from two men charged with brutally beating them in Shirley last year, as well as seven groups they say created an environment supporting violence against Latino immigrants.

The suit by Israel Perez and Magdaleno Estrada Escamilla, who have since returned to Mexico, is part of a class action on behalf of Latino day laborers across the United States. Besides the monetary damages, the suit seeks a court order barring both men, Ryan Wagner, 20, of Maspeth, and Christopher Slavin, 29, of Hicksville, as well the seven groups that oppose illegal immigration, from harassing or assaulting any Latino day laborers. The suit charges that the defendants deprived the laborers of their right to the same security enjoyed by white people, conspired to create a climate of fear within the Latino communities, and deprived the workers of their rights to free speech, free assembly and free association under the First and 14th Amendments.

Slavin was convicted in August of attempted murder and assault in connection with the attack and faces up to 50 years in prison when he is sentenced. Wagner's trial is scheduled for November.

Frederick Brewington of Hempstead, who filed the suit on behalf of the men in U.S. District Court in Central Islip on Sept. 17, declined to comment yesterday.

Slavin's attorney, Robert Del Col of Huntington, who maintains his client is innocent and is a victim of perjured testimony, said of the suit: "It doesn't surprise me that money was the bottom line. . . . That's a motive to lie . . . fabricate."

Wagner's attorney, Thomas Liotti of Garden City, said his client isn't associated with racist organizations, nor is he a racist.

The organizations named in the suit are the Long Island-based Sachem Quality of Life, American Patrol, headquartered in Sherman Oaks, Calif., the Posse Comitatus and the Sheriff's Posse Comitatus, headquartered in Ulysses, Pa., the National Alliance in Hillsboro, Va., and the Creativity Movement and the World Church of the Creator, in East Peoria, Ill.

Ray Wysolmierski of Farmingville, a spokesman for the Sachem Quality of Life Organization, scoffed at news of the lawsuit.

Wysolmierski said the lawsuit would not stop the group from expressing its views. "They can't stop us from saying what we have to say," he said. "This guy [Brewington] wants to take away somebody else's civil rights."

Wysolmierski also suggested that Brewington is suing the wrong people, and said he should target the U.S. government, whose policies he said have allowed undocumented immigrants to enter the country.

He added that if the two Mexican men "weren't here they wouldn't have had anything happen to them."

Glenn Spencer of American Patrol said his organization opposes illegal immigration and was just exercising its right to free speech at meetings on Long Island. Spencer, in a telephone interview from his California office said, "I deny any connection between [the attack on the day laborers and] our attempt to warn the American people about the threat represented by illegal immigrants as evidenced clearly by the tragic loss of life on Sept. 11 [at the World Trade Center and Pentagon]—7,000 people are dead in Manhattan because our government refuses to enforce our immigration laws."

Spokesmen for other groups could not be reached for comment.

Staff writer Bart Jones contributed to this story.

34

Store Staff Sue Bosses over Abuse

Rudy Larini

They go by names like "99-Cent Dreams," but working at dollar-discount stores was more like a nightmare, according to a group of immigrant employees who filed a federal lawsuit against the chain yesterday.

The group of eight employees, mostly Mexican, assert in their class-action suit that they were forced to work under cruel and unlawful conditions with long hours and no overtime pay. Shifts sometimes lasted 24 hours or more, with little or no break for sleep, and the employees say they sometimes were locked in the stores overnight.

They were subjected to verbal abuse and threatened with retaliation, such as losing their jobs or being reported to immigration authorities, if they complained about their working conditions or lack of adequate compensation, the suit alleges.

"We cannot and will not tolerate exploitative and abusive working conditions in our back yard," said staff attorney Jennifer Ching of the American Civil Liberties Union of New Jersey, which filed the litigation on the workers' behalf.

Named as defendants were three corporations—Universal Distribution Center LLC, Dollar Star Inc. and Dollar Strength LLC—that operate 99-cent discount stores in a half-dozen New Jersey towns and throughout the region under various names. The suit also named three individuals, Kishor Thakkar, Mohammed Arif and Mahommed Yousuf, described as principal officers of the corporations.

Executives at the companies did not respond to requests for comment.

At a news conference yesterday at the International Institute of New Jersey in Jersey City, several of the immigrant employees told of their ordeal in Spanish through a translator.

Fernando Islas, 25, of Jersey City said he and others were forced to work 24-hour shifts at a store in Yonkers, N.Y., with only a two-hour break for sleep. Bosses would promise to return late at night to drive them home to Jersey City, he said, but they would fail to come back. When locked in the store overnight, the employees had no bedding and slept on cardboard boxes with newspaper for blankets, he added.

Islas said he was told when he started working that he would be paid $235 a week, but had to work 70 hours to earn that amount. The federal minimum wage is $5.15 an hour, and federal labor law requires payment of overtime at 1½ times the regular rate for work in excess of 40 hours a week.

Daniel Cirio Perez, 27, of Jersey City said that working the 24-hour shifts, the employees were fed once a day with take-out food and had to resort to opening boxes of snack foods in the stores to supplement their meager meals. The workers also allege they were victims of discrimination based on their nationality.

"With Mexicans, you feed them bread and water and they'll work all day, as long as you want them to," Oscar Roldan, 30, of Jersey City said his bosses would say.

"We hope this case will give strength to other immigrant workers," Roldan said. "We need to remember the important message that we are all human beings and we have feelings."

After the press conference, the employees were joined by other protesters in a demonstration outside the 99-Cent Dreams store on John F. Kennedy Boulevard just off Journal Square.

A sign over the store's entrance read "Largest 99-cent store in New Jersey welcomes you," but the protesters changed, "99 cents, shame on you" and "Hey, hey, ho, ho—99 cents has gotta go." Inside, a store manager would not give his name or comment on the allegations.

He referred inquiries to a Universal Distribution Center office in Union County, which did not return repeated calls for comment. None of the three corporate officers named in the complaint could be reached for comment.

Other 99-cent stores in New Jersey mentioned in the lawsuit are located in Hackensack, Orange, East Orange, Elizabeth, Union City and New Brunswick.

Ching declined to discuss the immigration status of the discount store workers, but said they are entitled to labor law protection whether they are in the country legally or not.

A spokesman for the Immigration and Naturalization Service in Newark confirmed that the INS's own guidelines preclude it from getting involved in labor disputes.

However, the spokesman, Kerry Gill, said it's not clear whether the immigrants' lawsuit constitutes a labor dispute.

"These men are very courageous," said Denis Johnston, director of the Immigrant Rights Program of the American Friends Service Committee in Newark. "They are setting an example for other immigrant workers."

Johnston said each of the workers' claims seeks to recover "multiple thousands" of dollars in back wages, as well as punitive damages from their employers for threatening to retaliate against them.

The Loneliest Athletes

Jennifer Jacobson

At a university in New England, the soccer player lives with three of his female friends, never with the guys on his team. When he hangs out with his buddies, he kisses the girls, as they do—but, should the opportunity arise, he declines to have sex with them. He tells them that because he's Roman Catholic, he's saving himself for marriage.

What he does not tell them is that he is gay.

He would not give his name or talk to *The Chronicle*. A counselor who worked with him related his story and his decision not to go public.

Athletes "who identify themselves as bisexual or gay are so deeply closeted that they will only talk about it with a very intimate group of people," says the counselor, who agreed to talk on the condition of anonymity. "They spend most of their time attempting to hide it from their team and others. Even talking about it anonymously with a person in their own closed room would provoke anxiety."

At most colleges, the athletics department is the most homophobic place on the campus. The culture of sports tends to be conservative, and most people within it equate male heterosexuality with strength—and homosexuality with weakness. Many athletes and coaches alike don't know how to deal with gay teammates. And some coaches try to steer recruits (and parents) away from rival colleges by describing their teams as having too many gay athletes.

Yet gay athletes do make their way through college sports programs, if sometimes uncomfortably.

Not many of them are willing to talk about it. Those who are, however, say that the highly visible men's sports of football, basketball, hockey, and baseball remain the most unaccepting of gay athletes. The climate, though still far from friendly, is not as hostile in other men's sports.

And gay female athletes face a very different, but no less challenging, set of problems, given that in certain women's sports, the presumption—fair or not—is that many athletes are gay.

From *The Chronicle of Higher Education* (November 1, 2002). Reprinted with the permission of the author.

Quiet in the Closet

There are still no openly gay athletes in the professional major leagues in baseball, basketball, football, or hockey. So, with no role models in the most macho and largest-grossing sports, it's no wonder that gay college athletes in those sports have stayed closeted, too.

When rumors swirled this year that the New York Mets' catcher Mike Piazza was gay, he summarily denied it. Last month, Jeremy Shockey, a rookie tight end for the New York Giants, apologized for statements he made on Howard Stern's radio show about the possibility of encountering gay teammates.

Asked if he thought there were any gay athletes in the National Football League, Mr. Shockey said, "I don't know. I don't like to think about that. I hope not." Asked if he had had any gay teammates at the University of Miami, he said no. "I mean, if I knew there was a gay guy on my college football team, I probably wouldn't, you know, stand for it. You know, I think, you know, they're going to be in the shower with us and stuff, so I don't think that's going to work."

More than a few coaches and athletes share Mr. Shockey's sentiments on homosexuality. Among the members of the Fellowship of Christian Athletes, which has a large following, is Rice University's football coach, Ken Hatfield, who says homosexuality clearly conflicts with his religious beliefs. "I believe in the Bible," he declares.

He has been a member of the fellowship since 1965. Its "sexual purity" policy states: "God desires His children to lead pure lives of holiness. The Bible is clear in teaching of sexual sin, including sex outside of marriage and homosexual acts. Neither heterosexual acts outside of marriage nor any homosexual act constitute an alternative lifestyle acceptable to God."

A collegiate coach for 36 years, Mr. Hatfield has never had a player come out to him.

If a player did go public about being homosexual, the coach would be concerned both about the effect on the team and about what the parents of other athletes would think, he says. He would ask the player, "What happened? What changed since we recruited you? When did this come about?"

After all, people make a choice about homosexuality, Mr. Hatfield says, just as they make choices about drinking, about going to church. "I've never seen any scientific study say there's a homosexual gene."

He says that while he would not necessarily kick a player off the team for being gay, he probably would think hard about it.

The predominance of attitudes like that may keep many athletes firmly in the closet, counselors and others say. "I hear from students I work with that there are gay male athletes on the football team and on several other teams," says Benjamin Davidson, who is the director of the Lesbian-Gay-Bisexual-Transgendered Community Resources Center at Stanford University. "The fact that I don't know and don't have contact with these students is probably a testament to how difficult it is" for gay athletes, "not just at Stanford but anywhere."

In his three years at Stanford, Mr. Davidson has met with only two gay male athletes. He has had only informal conversations with Dwight Slater, a football player who quit the team in the 1998-99 academic year after coming out to his coach as a freshman. Mr. Slater did not respond to e-mail requests for an interview, but as a senior he told *The Advocate*, a national newspaper about gay life, that he "was forced out of football." He added: "I will never forget how Coach [Tyrone Willingham] seemed relieved when I told him I was leaving the team. He had my papers prepared for me to sign. Who knows what would have happened had I just been allowed to be myself? Perhaps I'd be preparing for the NFL draft."

36

Attacks on Gays Upset Los Angeles Suburb

Charlie LeDuff

WEST HOLLYWOOD   A heavy worry has settled over the normally carefree streets here after a gay man was attacked earlier this week by two men swinging a baseball bat and a metal pipe. The police say they believe the motivation for the beating was homophobia.

The attack is especially upsetting to residents as it comes on the heels of two other assaults on gay men this month. In one of those cases, a young actor was left in critical condition with a swollen brain and unable to breathe without a machine's help. The authorities believe that the same two men, who remain at large, delivered the beatings.

"We're doing everything we can to find them," said Deputy Sheriff Richard Pena of Los Angeles County. "Let me assure the citizens: these men are going to be caught."

The latest attack came early Sunday morning, when two men jumped out of a car and beat a 55-year-old gay man as his back was turned, the authorities said.

The man, whose name has not been released, was rescued by a cab driver who chased the attackers before speeding the victim away. The injured man checked himself into a local hospital and has since been released.

The beating happened near the busy intersection of Santa Monica Boulevard and Palm Avenue, the site of two attacks on Sept. 2. In one case, Treve Broudy, an actor, was left bloody and unconscious on the sidewalk. A friend of his escaped serious injury.

The police said Mr. Broudy was hugging the friend good-bye when two men pummeled him from behind.

Police patrols have been doubled in West Hollywood, and undercover officers are working the streets of this two-square-mile community, home to sizable gay, lesbian and Jewish populations. Rewards of more than $80,000 have been posted for information leading to an arrest.

Still, some residents don't feel safe. "I can't believe they had that much gall to come back and do it twice," said Stan Delfs, a retired school teacher, as he waited for his food order at a lunch counter near the scene of the attacks. "You stop and think now. I think twice about going out after 10 and certainly not after midnight anymore."

The fact that anyone would come to the heart of a gay community to find people to hurt is part of a wider, more disturbing trend in Los Angeles, where gays and lesbians are increasingly the victims of beatings and harassment, said Rebecca Isaacs, interim executive director of the L. A. Gay and Lesbian Center.

According to statistics kept by the center, 63 gay people reported in 2000 that they were victims of violence simply because of their sexual orientation. The number this year has already reached 95, the center said.

"In these kinds of hate crimes the virulence is very high," Ms. Isaacs said. "The level of brutality has to do with fear and loathing. They go after someone because of their sexuality and they do it with bats and metal pipes."

West Hollywood is a clean and well-kept city that prides itself on its laissez-faire attitude. It is a town of 36,000 tucked between Beverly Hills and Hollywood, and the population swells to 100,000 on weekend evenings because of its nightclubs and other attractions.

"Intolerance is not what we're about," said Assemblyman Paul Koretz, a former mayor of West Hollywood.

Nine days ago, two Jewish men were accosted by a group of Muslims outside a West Hollywood nightclub. The mob beat the two with feet and fists while chanting, "Kill the Jews," the police said. The authorities say they believe that it was a rivalry between two groups of Persians, many of whom live in the area. Men were charged with assault with a deadly weapon.

But the buzz around town today focused on the gay-bashings. There are reminders everywhere—on the streets and in the shop windows. The wanted posters are inescapable: Suspect No. 1, perhaps 5 feet 5 inches tall, wears a nylon cap. Suspect No. 2 is more than 6 feet tall and wears his hair in cornrows. They drive a 1987 or 1988 Nissan with tinted windows, either brown or faded red.

Though some residents are anxious, others are defiant. "I'm from New York, so let them come after me," said Joe Carino, 25, a muscular bartender at The Abbey, a bar and restaurant popular with gay men. "In fact, I walk extra slow now."

37

When Bias Hits Golf, All Eyes on Tiger

Paul Vitello

Here's a quiz, you golf buffs.

The head of a national women's organization protests the fact that the Masters Golf Tournament—a premier event of the season—is held at a private golf course in Augusta, Ga., that denies membership to women.

Either the club opens its doors to women, or the tournament should go elsewhere, she says.

Which of the following people are now put on the spot as a result of this protest?

(a) The 300 male members of the Augusta National Golf Club? Most are CEOs or entrepreneurs, used to influencing people. All pay more for their club memberships (upwards of $200,000) than they have ever paid to any but a select few of their employees. All benefit from the vast American consumer economy—approximately half of which is fueled by women.

(b) The Professional Golf Association? The PGA officially prohibits major tournaments from being held at clubs that bar women. But in the case of the annual Masters Tournament, which has always been held at Augusta, the PGA weasels out of its own rule by calling the Masters an "unofficial" stop on the tour.

(c) The scores of male golfers who have played the Masters Tournament at Augusta since the 1930s—never saying a peep about the discriminatory membership rule that would exclude their mothers, wives and sisters should any of them have ever tried to join? Maybe, like a lot of men, their mothers, wives and sisters would have sought membership at Augusta less for the golf than for the business advantages it might proffer—a chance to take a prospective client out for four hours on one of the best golf courses in the country, a chance to sell an idea. Didn't those golf pros ever think of their mothers, wives and sisters as people with rights?

(d) CBS television executives? CBS broadcasts the Masters Tournament to a worldwide audience of millions. Under normal circumstances, CBS would earn large profits, though since the controversy began, Augusta officials released all advertisers from the event, to protect them from potential bad publicity. At this point, the Masters is scheduled to be broadcast (in April) commercial-free.

(e) Tiger Woods?

The answer, of course, is (e) Tiger Woods. He is the great American golf phenom whose father is African-American, and whose mother is Thai, and who therefore carries what might be called the American black man's burden: to be the first to fall on his sword in the cause of justice.

Since the issue of gender discrimination at Augusta was raised several months ago (in a letter from Martha Burk, head of the National Council of Women's Organizations, to William "Hootie" Johnson, head of Augusta National), Woods' name has become almost synonymous with the controversy.

The women's organization never mentioned him. The PGA never mentioned him. But somehow, because the subject was discrimination, the attention turned to the man of color—the guy whose ancestors were hurt most by the ugly history of white-men-only discrimination in America. Journalists sought his opinion. As the representative of your race, don't you think . . . .

The *New York Times* editorial page called upon him to boycott. It would send "a powerful message that discrimination isn't good for the golfing business," the *Times* said last month.

Jesse Jackson even nudged him to speak out: "He's much too intelligent and too much a beneficiary of our struggles to be neutral," Jackson said.

Woods has spoken out. More than any other man on the professional tour, he has spoken clearly on the issue, saying that women should be invited to join Augusta National. In a poll conducted by the *Atlanta Journal-Constitution* newspaper, more than half of the pros scheduled to play at the Masters either said they did not have an opinion, or said the club should do as it pleases.

Tiger Woods spoke up, but said he would not drop out.

"It's frustrating because I'm the only player they are asking," Woods told the Associated Press two days after the *Times* editorial. "They're asking me to give up an opportunity no one has ever had—winning the Masters three years in a row."

In an interview yesterday, Burk concurred that all the focus on Tiger Woods was unfair.

"We have never contacted him or called on him to boycott the tournament," Burk said. "What we have said is that we would like to see strong statements from all the players. . . . The only entity that should boycott the Masters is the PGA tour." The PGA has said it will not boycott the tournament. CBS is planning to broadcast the tournament.

One member of the Augusta National Golf Club, a retired CBS executive, as it turns out, has resigned from the club to protest its discriminatory policy.

So far that is it.

And how do the Augusta National Golf Clubs of America get away with it?

They get away with it because it is always made to look like the Tiger Woods' of America's problem.

38

America's Impossible Dream: A House

Jennifer Loven

WASHINGTON   The average janitor earns enough to rent a one-bedroom apartment and pay for life's other necessities in just six of the nation's 60 largest cities. A retail salesperson can make ends meet in half that many locations. Both can forget about buying a home.

That conclusion from the National Housing Conference, a non-profit coalition of industry experts, advocates and academics, mirrors the findings of several reports since the summer documenting the struggle of working families to find affordable housing.

The results suggest a worsening of the affordable housing shortage affecting the working poor, even before the recession pushed thousands out of work and squeezed family budgets even tighter.

At a Senate Banking, Housing and Urban Affairs Committee hearing last month, lawmakers said the situation has reached crisis proportions.

"These families live one unexpected medical bill, one car repair, one bout of unemployment away from possible homelessness," said Chairman Paul Sarbanes (D-Md.).

Rising wages from the long economic expansion landed a record number of Americans in bigger, fancier homes and helped more of the very poorest put roofs over their heads. But it also contributed to the shortage of affordable housing.

Escalating land prices made it less profitable to build new low- and moderate-priced housing. As a result, there still are 5 million fewer apartments nationwide than are needed for people with the lowest incomes, according to the Washington-based National Low Income Housing Coalition.

The shortage forces many to choose from a range of unattractive options: Doubling up with other families, sacrificing other needs to pay rent, or living in a shelter or on the street.

In 60 large cities where the National Housing Conference compared housing costs with median earnings in entry-level occupations, only Oklahoma City, St. Louis and Cincinnati were affordable in 1999 for the typical retail clerk. That employee earned a median income nationally of $7.66 an hour—compared with a median paycheck of about $16 an hour for all U.S. workers.

Home is where the money goes.

The National Housing Conference compared housing costs with earnings and found that nearly 14 percent of American households use more than half of their income to put a roof over their heads. The government considers 30 percent reasonable.

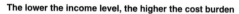

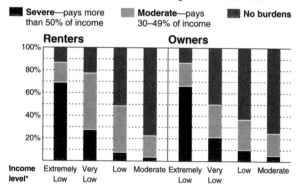

The average janitor—paid a median of $7.90 an hour—could swing rent and other living expenses in only six cities: the previous three plus Pittsburgh; Columbus, Ohio; and Indianapolis.

Salome Torres lives that reality.

He brings home $560 every two weeks as a janitor in Orange County, Calif., and finds extra money working weekend odd jobs.

*Based on area median income, which is the point at which half of the people earn more and half earn less. Extremely low income is defined as earning less than 30 percent of the area median, very low is 30–49 percent, low is 50–70 percent, and moderate is 80–120 percent.

SOURCE: National Low Income Housing Coalition.   Associated Press

Covering the rent on his one-bedroom apartment takes $620 a month, leaving the rest to pay for expenses for his wife, Isabel, and their three young children.

"Sometimes we do fall behind if someone gets sick," Torres, a Mexican immigrant, said through a translator. "Sometimes it's even difficult to get food. It's very difficult."

Like the Torres family, nearly one in seven American households must use more than half its income for shelter, well above the 30 percent level considered reasonable for housing.

Nearly 30 percent of those 13 million households include at least one full-time worker, the conference found in its June report.

NLIHC President Sheila Crowley said lower-income Americans have been shortchanged because federal support for affordable housing has not kept pace with inflation. She noted the number of government vouchers that help low-income families pay for private-sector apartment rents has increased little in recent years, resulting in a five-year wait for housing in some cities.

And the number of rental units considered affordable for working poor and poor families dropped by more than 1 million between 1997 and 1999, according to the Department of Housing and Urban Development.

Congress made small changes this year that could help stem the affordable housing drain. But a long-term solution remains elusive, advocates say.

39

Minority Health Care Found Lacking
Disparity Seen in Testing, Surgery

Tony Pugh

WASHINGTON   Racial and ethnic minorities generally receive lower-quality health care and less intensive diagnostic services than white patients, even when their income, insurance and medical conditions are similar, according to a new government report released yesterday.

The findings are "unacceptable" because they contribute to higher minority death rates for cancer, heart disease and HIV infection. That's the conclusion reached by a special committee of the Institute of Medicine, a unit of the National Academy of Sciences. The report was mandated by Congress in the Minority Health Disparities Act of 2000 and is the third study this month to examine the unequal treatment of minority patients. The Congressional Black Caucus and the National Institutes of Health have both made the issue a top priority.

The Institute of Medicine's 15-member panel found that minorities are less likely than whites to get proper heart medication, heart bypass surgery, kidney dialysis and transplants. The gap is greatest between African-Americans and whites.

The report highlights one of the most glaring and persistent problems facing a medical community that prides itself on quality care for all.

"We were amazed, some of us surprised and shocked, at the evidence of disparities," said report committee chairman Dr. Alan Nelson, a former president of the American Medical Association and current adviser to the Washington-based American College of Physicians–American Society of Internal Medicine.

"The real challenge lies not in debating whether disparities exist, because the evidence is overwhelming, but in implementing strategies to reduce and eliminate them," Nelson added.

Among the more dramatic findings cited by the panel are:

- A study of 11,000 lung cancer patients that found 76 percent of whites and only 64 percent of blacks got surgery for the disease. After five years, whites in the study had a 34 percent survival rate compared with 26 percent for blacks.

From *The San Diego Union-Tribune* (March 21, 2002) p. A-3.

- A report on 13,000 heart patients that found 100 whites had surgery to clear congested arteries for every 74 blacks.
- A study of nearly 16,000 urban emergency room visitors that found blacks 50 percent more likely than whites to be denied coverage by their health plans.

"It's hard to ignore the evidence," said Adolph Falcon, vice president for science and policy for the National Alliance for Hispanic Health, a Washington-based network of Hispanic health professionals. "Any reasonable reading of it will show there's a significant need for services that address the unique needs of different communities."

The panel found that though socioeconomic factors like poverty, lack of insurance and language barriers contribute to the disparity, they do not fully account for differences in care. Though there is no evidence that physician bias plays a role, the study noted that "health care providers' diagnostic and treatment decisions, as well as their feelings about patients, are influenced by race and ethnicity."

The report recommends more research into medical provider bias; better data collection on minority patient care; more cross-cultural training for health care personnel; and wider use of language translators. It also calls for more minority doctors.

40

Study Finds the Nation's Public School Districts Are Resegregating by Race

Jay Lindsay

Almost 50 years after state-sponsored school segregation was outlawed, American public schools are becoming increasingly divided by race, even as minority populations increase nationwide, according to a new report.

The Civil Rights Project at Harvard University found integration between whites and blacks to be decreasing or steady in all but a handful of the nation's largest school districts over the last 14 years.

Associated Press (August 8, 2002). Copyright 2002. Reprinted by permission of The Associated Press.

The report's authors say the "resegregation" trend is a result of recent court rulings that dismantled race-based desegregation laws, and also reflects discouragement over stalled integration efforts.

"I think a lot of people think that nothing can be done, and the efforts have failed," said Chungmei Lee, a co-author of the report.

Lee said integration is crucial to improve education and prepare students to live in a diverse culture.

Attorney Chester Darling, who represents parents fighting a desegregation policy in Lynn, Massachusetts, questioned the study's assumptions about diversity's value. He also said any new push to create school diversity must be driven by parents and not government.

"When you have a government involved in enforcing a particular form of diversity, then you have a government making decisions that are illegal," he said.

Concentration in the South

The report measured the changing "exposure index" between races in school districts with enrollments larger than 25,000. For instance, a black-white exposure index of 23 percent means the average black student attends a school where 23 percent of the students are white.

In a sample of 185 of the districts, black exposure to whites increased in only four of the districts between 1986 and 2000. Latino exposure to whites increased in only three districts. White isolation increased in 53 districts, the report said.

The study found resegregation to be the most rapid in Clayton County, Georgia, where the average black student goes to a school that is 23.1 percent white, down from 68.7 percent white in 1986.

The 20 most rapidly resegregating school districts are concentrated in the South, with eight in Texas and three in Georgia.

But the most stable districts are also in the South, the report noted, in what it said might be a lingering effect of defunct integration plans that were once heavily concentrated in the South.

Lee said successful integration is simply a matter of balancing resources, which are often in short supply in the poor neighborhoods where many minorities live. The report recommends combining city and suburban school districts into one entity, joining various racial groups in the process.

Rich Kahlenberg of The Century Foundation, a New York-based think tank, said communities need to focus on income disparities if they want to legally desegregate.

"People are stuck in the old paradigm of race," he said. "But that's outmoded because we have some new legal realities to deal with."

41

Colleges Out of Reach for Low-Income Students

Albert B. Crenshaw

While the middle class struggles with college costs, an increasing number of lower-income parents are defeated by them, a congressionally appointed panel has found.

Children from families that are primarily immigrants and minorities will be shut out of college by a combination of rising tuition and stagnant aid programs, the panel found.

About 170,000 college-qualified high school graduates won't be able to afford even a two-year college this year, according to the Advisory Committee on Student Financial Assistance.

About 4.4 million qualified students will be unable to attend a four-year college in the next 10 years, the panel said.

The students are willing and able to work, and they are willing and able to borrow, to a point. But soaring costs have made such supplements inadequate.

The report explodes the popular assumption that if low-income students are willing to work hard enough they can make it, said Juliet V. Garcia, who chaired the committee.

"People understand that low-income students are at a disadvantage," but they think there is adequate aid available for these students to get through college "without excessive borrowing or excessive work," Garcia said. That's not true, she said.

The committee's purpose, as the name suggests, is to advise policymakers on students' financial needs and possible ways to meet them. In the past, simple but helpful ideas from the panel, such as providing a free federal form that students can use to apply for financial aid, have made their way into government programs.

But Garcia, president of the University of Texas at Brownsville, said there is no simple solution for the cost problem. Recent improvements in federal aid, notably boosts in the Pell grant program, have not come close to returning government aid to the levels of 20 years ago.

She conceded that the federal government alone cannot be expected to solve the problem. State legislatures are pressing public colleges to raise tuition, and colleges themselves, public and private, are focused on other areas.

Thus, Garcia said, cooperation is needed among the federal government, states and colleges. That may be asking a lot.

Middle-class students and their families are clawing their way toward the most prestigious institutions because they seem to offer the best economic prospects after graduation. And they are demanding that government help pay for them.

Colleges and universities are focused on their own reputations, which they seek to enhance by attracting top scholars—with light teaching loads as part of the bargain—and top students, to whom they often offer generous aid packages regardless of need.

Politicians at the federal level, recognizing that middle-class families vote, have lavished tax benefits on them: tuition credits, tax-free saving and the like. Middle-class families like these benefits, of course, but tax breaks help only those who pay income tax, and nearly half of Americans don't—not because they cheat, but because they don't make enough money.

Politicians at the state level, squeezed by plunging tax revenue, are quick to see higher education as an expense that can be held down, leaving schools to cut costs or raise tuition and fees.

Even though there remain some blue-collar jobs that offer steady employment and good wages—know any skilled carpenters who are out of work?—higher education remains a ticket to a better life. Denying it to poor people who have done what society has asked—stayed in school, studied hard, gotten good grades and scores—will not only stifle their ambition, but it also will undermine the moral authority of the majority.

The committee urged policymakers to strengthen "long-term intervention" programs, meaning improve education at the elementary level, and couple those improvements with a promise that playing by the rules will lead poor students to college.

That means more direct aid, but also a commitment to expand colleges to accommodate the "echo boom" and the rising tide of immigrant children. California will need something like a million new college "seats" in the coming years and Texas 500,000, according to several estimates.

The Higher Education Act of 1965 expires next year, and the coming debate over its renewal could provide a focus for addressing these problems. It's also a chance for families at all economic levels to make their views known to their legislators. It's a debate all families should follow. We all have a stake in it.

The Internal Revenue Service's tax-collection ability continues to plunge, a study by Congress' General Accounting office finds.

"We estimate that at the end of fiscal year 2001, the IRS had deferred collecting taxes from 1.3 million taxpayers who collectively owed about $16.1 billion. IRS officials said that absent significant operational change, they had little expectation of reopening many deferred collection cases," the report said.

The GAO cited overwork and understaffing at the IRS and "increased compliance and collection procedural controls mandated by Congress to better safeguard taxpayer interests."

"Unbanked" consumers—primarily low-income people without bank accounts—spend at least $4 billion on check-cashing and bill-payment services annually, according to a study by the Brookings Institution. Households with annual incomes of less than $25,000 are estimated to have $175 billion in financial assets, the study found. That adds up to a major opportunity for financial institutions to use new technology to lower transaction costs enough to make those consumers attractive customers, the report said.

"Money . . . has gone digital," report author Robert Weissbourd wrote. Technology has resulted in smart cards, debit cards, ATMs, point-of-service and Internet bill paying, delivery channels that are turning lower-income communities into more attractive markets for financial services institutions, he said.

42

Are America's Schools Leaving Latinas Behind?

AAUW

WASHINGTON DC   U.S. schools are not meeting the educational needs of America's fastest-growing female minority population—Latinas—according to a new report released today by the American Association of University Women (AAUW) Education Foundation.

This comprehensive report, *¡Si, Se Puede! Yes, We Can: Latinas in School*, reviews the educational (K-12) status and progress of Latinas. It explores the cultural interaction between America's Hispanic children and the schools they attend. Authored by Angela B. Ginorio and Michelle Huston, the report looks at Latinas and how their futures—or "possible selves"—are influenced by their families, their culture, their peers, their teachers, and the media.

The report found that Latinas bring many personal strengths and cultural resources to the schools they attend. For them to become successful, the report contends, schools need to view bilingualism and other values as assets rather than liabilities. For example, "going away to college" is often a high school counselor's

Reprinted by permission from an American Association of University Women press release.

definition to success, but some Latinas, because of family responsibilities, believe it is important to stay close to home.

"Instead of making all students fit into a single educational box, schools need to move out of the box to meet the needs of its changing student population," said Jacqueline Woods, executive director of AAUW.

In spite of the importance of education to the Latino community, family needs and peer pressure often clash with school expectations for Latinas. For example, the report finds that "many Latinas face pressure about going to college from boyfriends and fiancees who expect their girlfriends or future wives not to be 'too educated' and from peers who accuse them of 'acting White' when they attempt to become better educated or spend time on academics."

"Contrary to popular beliefs about Hispanic communities," said Ginorio, "most parents hope that their children will excel in school, yet Latino families' economic and social position often defer the realization of those dreams. Moreover, school practices such as tracking impose low expectations that create self-fulfilling prophecies."

According to the report, Latinas are lagging behind other racial and ethnic groups of girls in several key measures of educational achievement and have not benefited from gender equity to the extent that other groups of girls have. Analyzing the differences in educational achievement between Latinas and other groups of girls, the report finds that:

- The high school graduation rate for Latinas is lower than for girls in any other racial or ethnic group.
- Latinas are less likely to take the SAT exam than their White or Asian counterparts, and those who do score lower on average than those groups of girls.
- Compared with their female peers, Latinas are under-enrolled in Gifted and Talented Education (GATE) courses and underrepresented in AP courses.
- Latinas are the least likely of any group of women to complete a bachelor's degree.

Although Latinas fare worse than other racial and ethnic groups of girls on most measures of educational performance, they perform better than their male peers on many measures. In reviewing educational data comparing Latinas to Latinos, the report finds that:

- In the fourth grade, Latinas score higher than Latinos in reading and history; by eighth grade, they score higher in mathematics and reading; and by the 12th grade, they score higher in science and reading.
- Latinas outnumber Latinos in taking the SAT exam (58 percent to 42 percent in 1999), yet score lower than Latinos who do take the exam on both the math and verbal section. The gender gap among Hispanics is greater than among any other group.
- Latinas take the same number of or more AP exams than Latinos, but score lower in AP math and science exams.

- Latinas are almost three times less likely to be suspended and less likely to be referred for special education as Latinos.

According to the report, Hispanic girls and boys suffer similar educational challenges in the schools they attend compared to their White and Asian counterparts, and urges schools to pay closer attention to the problems faced by both Latinas and Latinos. The report also notes variations within the Latina community according to culture of origin and region.

"America's public schools must address the psychological, social, cultural, and community factors that affect the education of Hispanic students," said Woods. "Otherwise, Latinas and Latinos will too often continue to be victims of a second-rate education that can change the American dream into a nightmare. We rely on our schools to open the doors for Latinas and Latinos to higher education and better paying jobs."

The report provides clear and compelling evidence that both Latinas and Latinos face stereotyping and other obstacles that discourage success in school. Some obstacles are different for Latinas than for Latinos. Latinas are three times as likely to fear for their personal safety in school as other girls. And Latinos are often assumed to be gang members by teachers and counselors simply because they speak Spanish.

"If we want Latinas to succeed as other groups of girls have," continued Ginorio, "schools need to work with and not against their families and communities and the strengths that Latinas bring to the classroom. We need to recognize cultural values and help Latinas harmonize these values with girls' aspirations to education and learning."

The report offers a number of strong recommendations and new approaches:

- *All adults need to encourage academic success.* Latinas need to hear from all the adults in their lives that college and professional careers are rewarding options and ones that they can achieve. Advisors must curtail tendencies to promote gender- and racially stereotyped careers as well as ensure that Latinas are not under-represented in college-preparatory classes.
- *Recruit and train teachers from the Hispanic community* so that we can have educators who can serve as role models and who can better connect the educational goals of the school to the cultural background of its students.
- *Involve the whole family in the process of college preparation.* College requirements need to be demystified and families need to understand longer-term benefits of attending college even if it means moving away from home.
- *Deal meaningfully with stereotypes and societal issues such as teen pregnancy that impact school performance.* This includes offering childcare and alternative scheduling and therefore recognizing that being a young mother and a student intent on completing her education are not incompatible.

The All-Boy Network:
Public Affairs Shows Reflect Shortage of Women in Power

Howard Kurtz

Most of the officials, lawmakers, experts and pontificators who parade their opinions on Sunday morning television have something in common.

They don't wear pantyhose.

Women represent only 10.7 percent of guests on the five major network shows, according to a study being released today by the White House Project, a New York-based group that promotes women in leadership positions.

"It's a vicious cycle," says Marie Jones, the project's chairman and president of the Ms. Foundation. "It's probably easier to get people who you've known, who you've seen, who've got juice, like John McCain. I think there are women who have juice, but it takes a little time to get on and show you have juice." Male chauvinism can't be the culprit, since four of the five programs are produced by women. Most of them are united in arguing that they face a largely white male power structure in booking guests.

From January 2000 through last June, female guests constituted 13.7 percent of the lineup on CNN's "Late Edition," 11.8 percent on ABC's "This Week," 9.2 percent on "Fox News Sunday," 8.9 percent on CBS's "Face the Nation" and 8.6 percent on NBC's "Meet the Press." (The figures exclude presidential candidates, who were all men during the time period, and journalists affiliated with the network.)

Even these small numbers plunged after Sept. 11, with women comprising just 6.8 percent of the Sunday lineup over the next seven weeks, foreign officials excluded. The number of women on last Sunday's shows, dominated by Secretary of State Colin Powell, Attorney General John Ashcroft and Defense Secretary Donald Rumsfeld: none.

"I don't consider it a problem," says Nancy Nathan, executive producer of "Meet the Press." "Our audience is more than half women. We think they would be insulted if we were not presenting the news makers but were somehow skewing it to present others."

The picture is brighter on the journalistic front. "If you look at our show, not only am I sitting there every Sunday, but there are women correspondents, women on the round table," says Cokie Roberts, co-host of "This Week." Gloria Borger shares the anchoring duties on "Face the Nation."

Roberts says the top policymakers in the Bush administration are men, except for national security adviser Condoleezza Rice, whom every program considers a terrific guest, and White House counselor Karen Hughes, who avoids Sunday interviews. "Women in this administration tend to be in jobs that right now we're not wildly interested in," Robert says.

Beyond their meager numbers, female guests were also invited back far less often. For example, 19 and 21 male senators were repeat guests on "This Week" and "Meet the Press," respectively, but no female senators made a return appearance.

For the cognoscenti, the most frequent male guests during the 18-month period were John McCain (50 times), Joe Lieberman (27), Karl Rove (25), Mitch McConnell (24), Dick Cheney (24), Chuck Hagel (23), Trent Lott (22) and Tom Daschle (21). The most frequent women: Madeleine Albright (12), Karen Hughes (10), Rice (8), Christine Todd Whitman (7), Kay Bailey Hutchison (7), and Barbara Boxer, Mary Matalin and Doris Kearns Goodwin (6 each). Hughes appeared as a campaign spokeswoman before President Bush took office.

"If you look at the high-profile Cabinet secretaries, except for Madeleine Albright and Dr. Rice, they are men," says Carin Pratt, executive producer of "Face the Nation." "This is not something we control. My staff is women. Our bureau chief is a woman. We make a concerted effort. To think this is a bias against women is totally untrue. My job is to put the highest-level people on the broadcast."

Says Marty Ryan, executive producer of "Fox News Sunday": "You tend to want to go to a committee chairman or a leader of one of the parties, and right now they're mostly male. The White House has a number of excellent Cabinet secretaries who are female, and we've booked all of them."

Sue Bunda, CNN's senior vice president, says all the programs face the reality that "there's only one secretary of state," who is obviously a man. "When the opportunity is there, within the mission of the show, we're very committed to booking many voices," Bunda says. "I hesitate to say women, because I see it as a broader, more diverse world."

Considering non-government roles, however, women comprised only 19 percent of the private professionals on the programs and 12 percent of the media commentators.

Roberts says that when outside experts or business people are needed, "I will say to the producers—all of whom are women—is there a woman? Is there a minority? Often there is."

They should probably talk fast. When women got on the air, the study found, they spoke 16 percent fewer words than men. Put another way, of the 474,834 words spoken on "Meet the Press," 34,371 were uttered by women.

Correction (December 8, 2001): An article on public affairs shows in the Dec. 5 *Style* section misidentified the chairman of the White House Project, a women's advocacy group. She is Marie Wilson.

Despite Some Progress, Minorities Remain an Unseen Presence

Matt Zoller Seitz

PASADENA, Calif.   At the Television Critics Association's fall TV preview in Pasadena two years ago, the major networks spent much of their time defending television's complexion.

A number of studies suggested that despite progress made in previous years, television still didn't look very much like America. The casts of most dramas and comedies were still overwhelmingly (sometimes exclusively) Caucasian; ditto the behind-the-scenes line-up of writers, directors, producers and crew members. African-Americans were represented by a handful of UPN and WB sitcoms segregated on particular nights, and Latinos and Asians were all but invisible.

Clearly, something had to be done. The NAACP called for a protest. The heads of major networks commissioned studies, appointed executives to keep an eye on racial diversity, and even signed agreements pledging to interview, hire and promote more people of color. The producers of several network dramas, including "The District" and "The West Wing," shoehorned black performers into casts that were mostly white.

Two fall previews later, diversity is a hot topic again, and the situation does not seem to have improved.

Yes, UPN still has a bloc of sitcoms with predominantly black casts, all grouped on Monday night—including a new series, "Half-and-Half." But the WB's equivalent vanished after veterans Steve Harvey and Jamie Foxx left the network. The WB does have a new comedy, "Greetings from Tucson," about a Mexican/Irish family.

But apart from ABC's returning sitcom "The George Lopez Show," the Big Four networks have no new sitcoms with nonwhite leads.

Another complication: This fall, two returning series with African-American stars, Fox's "The Bernie Mac Show" and ABC's "My Wife and Kids," will be pitted against each other on Wednesdays at 8 p.m.

From the *Star Ledger* (July 16, 2002) p. 28.

"It would be a loss if one show was canceled because we all started watching one particular show," said Mo'Nique, star of UPN's "The Parkers," in a network-sponsored panel about diversity.

Nonwhite performers have prominent roles on many returning series, from NBC's "ER" to ABC's "NYPD Blue" to Fox's "Boston Public" to HBO's "The Wire." Yet with rare exceptions, they tend to be on the sidelines of the action while white performers play out the meatier storylines.

The same dynamic will likely hold true for this year's crop of freshman dramas. CBS' "CSI: Miami" is set in one of the most racially diverse, Latino-heavy cities in the United States, yet it stars David Caruso and Kim Delaney, both white.

Les Moonves, president and CEO of CBS, disputed the charge that "CSI: Miami" overlooked minorities during the casting process. He noted that of six major characters on the crime drama, two were cast with nonwhite actors—George Delco, a Hispanic, and Khandi Alexander, who is African-American.

"There is not a major role that comes up where this is not discussed: 'Can we put an African-American, a Latino or an Asian in this part?' " Moonves said.

He added that when a CBS series role does not require a particular race or nationality, the casting process becomes "a jump ball," with actors of all colors competing for the part, and the best performer winning.

The only new one-hour network programs with black leads are Fox's "Cedric the Entertainer Presents" and "Fastlane" (unless you count UPN's upcoming "The Twilight Zone," in which Forest Whitaker replaces Rod Serling as host).

It's still rare to see a one-hour drama built around nonwhite performers; the most notable exceptions air on PBS ("American Family"), HBO ("Oz," "The Wire") and Showtime ("Resurrection Blvd.," "Soul Food").

While TV shows in general have become more integrated over the years, several studies have demonstrated that on both sitcoms and dramas, black, Latino and Asian performers have a hard time landing recurring roles—and when they do get those roles, they are more likely to be featured as supporting characters than leads.

A report by Children Now, a nonprofit group that studies the impact of pop culture images on children's perception of race, found that many apparent improvements in diversity since 2000 haven't really improved anything.

According to the study, between 2000 and this year, Latino presence on TV doubled from 2 percent to 4 percent, but the roles tended to be secondary or worse, and the actors were often asked to play characters of low social status. Latinas and female Asians saw their representation increase (from 2 to 4 percent, and from 3 to 4 percent, respectively), but were offered very few leading or even secondary roles.

African-Americans are slightly over-represented on TV, with approximately 15 percent of speaking parts, while they make up 12 percent of the real-world U.S. population. Yet they're rarely placed at the center of the drama—especially if the drama features a racially mixed cast.

Television in general seems more segregated now than it was two years ago. According to the Children Now study, the top casts of 51 percent of current TV series were either entirely white or entirely black; two seasons ago, 43 percent of programs fit that description.

The top casts of network sitcoms are also less likely to be racially mixed today than they were two seasons ago. According to the study, 14 percent of sitcoms that aired in the 2000-2001 season had ethnically diverse casts; this past season, that figures was cut in half.

"Living Single" executive producer Yvette Lee Bowser said she agreed to develop UPN's "Half and Half" because there were so few programs featuring nonwhite characters. "I said, 'There are not enough of us, people of color, working in the industry in general, and I think I would be remiss not to provide an opportunity, not only for myself, but for African-American actors,' " she said.

"There is always room for improvement," said Linda Park, Japanese-American co-star of UPN's "Enterprise."

"Personally, from an acting point of view, the biggest ways I can see that are in writing—in the roles that are written for minorities as well as open-mindedness in casting," Park said.

Roughly 80 percent of network television's writing, directing and producing jobs go to white men.

Off the record, executives producers and actors offered numerous theories for why minorities are having problems advancing in an industry that seems genuinely interested in fixing a bad situation.

Some said that minority-heavy programs tend not to get made because they don't do as well in syndication as mostly white shows, and because white viewers are less interested in shows that star non-white performers, and vice versa. ("The Bernie Mac Show" is the number one program among African-American viewers, yet it ranks 94th in white households.)

Others suggested that networks and production companies are unconsciously rather than consciously racist—that people tend to hire and promote people they feel comfortable with, and that the same dynamic would exist if television were run by blacks, Latinos or Asians.

45

Students Defend Icon That Offends

Sam McManis

At the entrance to Vallejo High School's library, glued carefully into a scrapbook and preserved in a glass case, are news clippings from '60s campus uprisings. One headline, faded but still stark in its message, reads: "Negro Students in VHS Boycott." Another story details a student protest over alleged police brutality against blacks on campus.

They make it a point to remember, even celebrate, a previous generation's civil rights activism at this school—the prejudice overcome, the equality hard won. This week, in that same library, nearly 200 Vallejo students chose to spend their lunch break at an old-fashioned teach-in sponsored by the school's ACLU club rather than bolting to the nearby Jack in the Box or hanging in the quad under the 30-foot mural of the stoic Apache mascot.

Subject: whether to replace that Apache mascot, which has drawn the wrath of the Vallejo Inter-Tribal Council as being stereotypical and demeaning toward American Indians.

Not a new issue, of course. Indian mascot controversies crop up every year in the Bay Area. Some schools, such as Tomales High in Sonoma County and Sequoia High in Redwood City, have chosen to "retire" offending mascots after much debate. Others, such as John Swett High in Crockett, have had students' efforts rebuffed by school boards.

Now, Vallejo.

But here was where the mascot-controversy issue veered off its usual politically correct course.

Nearly all the participating Vallejo students showed up to defend their beloved Apache mascot, not to express solidarity with American Indians hoping for a sympathetic audience at a school whose enrollment is made up of 78 percent people of color.

The forum provided a glimpse into how teenagers think—or don't think—about race and whether they are willing to identify with another minority's feelings of oppression and marginality.

Students were polite and respectful, at least at the start, and it seemed common ground might be reached.

They listened as Midge Wagner, secretary of the Vallejo Inter-Tribal Council, told them how the school's Apache fight song makes a "mockery" of her heritage and is "a stereotype of every Western movie ever made." They listened as Dennis Carr, another tribal elder, said it's "humiliating to be reduced to a lower life form like an animal by being represented as a mascot" and how Apaches never even stepped foot in California. (The Patiwin people settled in Vallejo).

And they listened to those who are not Indians, such as Vallejo writer Kenneth Brooks, who tried to reach the largely African American contingent of students with a personal appeal.

"I grew up in a time when stereotypical images of blacks were widely seen, and everybody expected me to sing and dance because all blacks were portrayed that way," Brooks told the students. "Taking another person's culture, like the Apaches, and use it any way you want is not right."

Students listened, all right, but most did not hear. Or, if they heard, they dismissed the arguments out of hand. A generation removed from the civil rights struggle, these teenagers just didn't understand the pleas of American Indians.

The local Indian speakers have done these forums before and know it's hard to reach students, but they held hope for Vallejo High because its dominant ethnic group is African American (31.5 percent).

All but a handful of students chose to show solidarity not with Indians as a fellow ethnic minority group, but instead to unite as part of a more communal group—Apache students. Once the students took the microphone, the debate devolved into tears and arguments between passionate students defending their right to maintain a 60-year tradition and Indians defending their heritage.

Instead of raising consciousness, the event mostly just raised ire.

LaTeresa Boykin, an 11th-grader who is African American, was typical of the pro-Apache speakers.

"Why aren't you honored?" she asked the tribal elders. "You should be that we use an Indian name. Most people would be. Like they name schools after Martin Luther King. Maybe there are some people who don't understand your culture and yell the woo-woo thing at games, but all we are asking here is to be Apaches. We're not trying to drag your name through the dirt. We're just trying to keep the tradition of our school name."

Even a representative of La Raza, the school Latino activist club, defended the Apache mascot. The only two speakers advocating a mascot change were white. But a history teacher at the school, who is white, denounced the anti-mascot faction, saying, "I don't want to see a small group make a decision that will affect all the students."

When lunch ended, the students trudged back to class having safely snuffed out the nascent mascott-change movement. None of which came as a surprise to Charlie Toledo, an American Indian activist from Napa.

"What we just saw," she said, "is a lot of minority students, especially the black students, hurting. They've had a lot of things taken away from them, and they don't want their mascot taken away, too. But I'm a Native American. You think I don't know what it's like to have things taken away?"

Sam McManis can be reached at (925) 974-8346 or at smcmanis@sfchronicle.com.

46

The Baby Boy Payoff

Richard Morin

More evidence that men are squealing little chauvinist piggies: It seems daddies not only shower their sons with more attention but also work harder and earn more money after the birth of a boy than they do after the birth of a girl.

At the same time, the sex of a child has no impact on the hours that women work outside the home or the wages they earn, reported economists Shelly Lundberg and Elaina Rose of the University of Washington.

The good news is that men work harder and earn more after the birth of a baby, regardless of its sex. It's just that this "baby premium" is twice as large if the baby is a boy than if it's a girl, the economists reported in an article published in the latest issue of the Review of Economics and Statistics.

All of this would seem to suggest that many men, in some fundamental sense, don't love their daughters as much or at least in quite the same way as they do their sons.

"I'm really reluctant to put it that way," Lundberg said. "But these results do suggest that, in the United States, fathering daughters is still something different than fathering sons. . . . Men appear to place a higher value on marriage and their family and seem to be more willing to make a bigger investment in their family if they have sons."

The economists examined data collected annually from 2,243 individuals between 1968 and 1992 for the Panel Study of Income Dynamics (PSID). This ongoing study directed by the University of Michigan follows a randomly selected national sample of men, women and children as they age in order to track changes in their family status and economic fortunes.

The first thing that Rose and Lundberg confirmed was what every father already knows: There's something about having a child that either inspires or forces guys to work harder and earn more.

On average, Lundberg and Rose said that the birth of a child increases a man's wage rate by 4.2 percent and his annual time at work by 38 hours compared with a man who doesn't have children, controlling for other relevant factors.

They also found that daddies work hardest after the birth of their first child—an increase of an average of 82 hours a year. But the effect wears off quickly. Extra time spent at work increases by an additional 26 hours after a second baby arrives, and largely vanishes after the births of subsequent children.

Then Rose and Lundberg wondered if the sex of the baby made a difference. It did—and the differences were huge: Men worked, on average, about 118 hours a year more if their first child was a boy but only 54 hours more if their first-born was a girl. They also found that the same pattern held regardless of birth order.

"I was completely astonished," Lundberg said. So much so that she worried that they had made some simple but fundamentally stupid error. "We went over this with a fine-toothed comb." Their findings stood.

Colleagues were skeptical, at least at first. "People said, 'No, this can't be true,'" Lundberg said. "People are very reluctant to believe that they treat their daughters differently than their sons."

Spurred to dig deeper into the data, Lundberg recently discovered that an unmarried mother is about 25 percent more likely to marry the father of her baby if the child is a boy than if it is a girl. Other researchers have found that the likelihood that a marriage will survive increases by about 7 percent if the couple have a boy than if they have a girl. And it's well known that fathers spend more time with their sons than with their daughters.

So why do daddies seem to work harder and earn more if their baby is a boy? "That's still a bit of a mystery," Lundberg said.

Lundberg and her husband, also an economist, have two children—both girls.

And no, she laughs, in response to the obvious question, "He spends a lot of time with his daughters. And he works very, very hard."

Suggestions for Further Reading

See daily papers as well as weekly and monthly national magazines for continuing accounts of discrimination and harassment.

The Economics of Race, Class, and Gender in the United States

ALTHOUGH IT IS FASHIONABLE TO DENY THE EXISTENCE of rich and poor and to proclaim us all "middle class," class divisions are real and the gap between rich and poor in the United States is growing at an alarming rate. In fact, it is wider now than it has ever been since World War II. Being born into a particular class, racial/ethnic group, and sex has repercussions that affect every aspect of a person's life. In Part IV, we attempt to understand something of their impact by turning our attention from lottery winners' windfalls and sports stars' salaries to statistics that reveal the economic realities faced by most ordinary people in their daily lives. Selection 47 by Holly Sklar, "Imagine a Country—2003," provides a dramatic and thought-provoking introduction to Part IV.

The 1990s was an incredible decade for economic growth, but the start of the new century saw workers' pensions, 401K plans, and dot.com millionaires vanish overnight and the proportion of Americans living in poverty rise significantly. The story of the new century continues to be a persistent increase in the gap between rich and poor, which has been increasing slowly but steadily since 1973. Selection 48 charts the most recent rise and reports on related economic developments. According to the director of one research institute quoted in this article, "income inequality either set a record in 2001 or tied for the highest level on record." Selection 49 takes a look at the way out-of-control CEO (chief operating officer) salaries, benefits, and perks have fueled this gap.

In Selection 50, Julianne Malvaux argues that "in recession and recovery, African Americans remain at the periphery of the economy" and offers some suggestions as to why this continues to be the case. In this context, readers will find particularly interesting her discussion of the race and class implications of the public response to the catastrophic events of September 11, 2001. In Selection 51, Dalton Conley addresses some of these issues head-on in his essay entitled "Being Black, Living in the Red: Wealth Matters." Conley, as well as an increasing number of other social scientists, are turning their attention to differences in accumulated wealth to explain the differences in standard of living and quality of life enjoyed by different racial/ethnic groups. Conley points out that in the United States, "at all income, occupational, and education levels, black families on average have drastically lower levels of wealth than similar white families." This, he believes, accounts for the persistence of black–white inequality. Others have pointed to this difference in wealth (or assets) to suggest that what it means to be "middle class" (as defined by income) differs dramatically for members of different racial/ethnic groups. According to this analysis, African American and other "minority" group families are more likely to be called upon to support a large extended family with their middle-class earnings than are whites. But, as Conley and others point out, because of the effects of long-term racism and long-term discrimination, "black middle class families are often less likely to have the financial assets that whites (whose families have been middle class for several generations) can count on."

In sharp contrast to the reality that the articles and statistics in this section describe, namely, that differences in race/ethnicity, class, and sex have enormous impact on economic status, the mythology of the American Dream continues to assure us that hard work and ability, not family background or connections, is the key to success. In Selection 52, "The Sons Also Rise," Princeton professor Paul Krugman reports on a recent study that once again contradicts this myth. Krugman tells us that "the children of today's wealthy" have "a huge advantage over those who chose the wrong parents." And he adds the sobering news that "the spectacular increase in American inequality has made the gap between the rich and the middle class wider, and hence more difficult to cross, than it was in the past."

Selection 53 relies on charts and graphs to present an overview of the way in which differences in race/ethnicity and sex affect occupation and earnings in the United States today. These materials graphically illustrate the persistence of a wage gap between women and men over many years and then go on to provide specific information about pay differentials in a number of occupations. If you have already read some of the newspaper accounts of cases of discrimination included in Part III, this data may not come as much of a surprise. But other data provided by the National Committee on Pay Equity may well surprise you. Current statistics that highlight differences in earning correlated with sex and race/ethnicity tell us that female college graduates in general earn $13,243 a year *less* than male graduates and that similar inequities are to be found when we compare earnings for women and men by race/ethnicity at different levels of educational achievement. Taken together, the materials in this Selection document a persistent wage gap based on race and sex over many years and suggest that racism and sexism, not ability or qualifications, have determined which jobs women and men do and how much worth is attached to their work.

The differences in earnings over time, combined with other variables, mean that many older women face enormous financial problems as they begin retirement. Selection 54 looks at the ways in which the factors unique to women's work life and social role impact their earnings and advancement over their work life and translate into economic insecurity in later years. The choices such women face, between paying rent or buying groceries, between paying for utilities or prescription drugs, are in sharp contrast to those faced by Patricia Duff as she contemplates life as a single parent after her divorce from billionaire Ronald O. Perelman. As Selection 55 reports, Ms. Duff, herself a millionaire, believes that she will require child support in the amount of $4,400 *a day* over the next 14 years to raise her 4-year-old daughter. The budget items specified in this newspaper story provide an interesting look at how "the other half" lives and testify to the dramatic differences in lifestyle that result from the differences in income and wealth that we are examining.

Selection 56, "The Education of Jessica Rivera," tells the story of a 20-year-old college student who, during an earlier time period, might well have provided us with a dramatic example of upward mobility through hard work and determination. Rivera's story is heartbreaking in many respects and underscores the pointless and punitive nature of many recent changes in welfare policy. As conservative politicians carry out a war against the poor, denying those on welfare or in prison the opportunity to acquire a college education and hence the credentials that may lead to a better life, it is no wonder that the gap between rich and poor is growing ever wider, and, as Selection 56 suggests, ever harder to cross.

Katherine Newman suggests that the move to end welfare as we know it has been one of the most dramatic responses to recent changes in the U.S. economy. But according to Newman, "dismantling the welfare system is not the way to solve the problem of persistent poverty." She views the current attack on the poor and their children as an attempt to find a convenient scapegoat for problems that are far more systemic. (Some would argue that this kind of thinking provides yet another illustration of "blaming the victim," a phenomenon that William Ryan describes in his essay of the same title in Part VII.) Both Selections 56 and 57 ask readers to take a long and hard look at poverty in U.S. society and ask us to bring a critical eye to some contemporary proposals that seek to address poverty by making war on its victims.

Imagine a Country—2003

Holly Sklar

Imagine a country where one out of five children is born into poverty, and wealth is being redistributed upward. Since the 1970s, the top 1 percent of households has doubled their share of the nation's wealth. The top 1 percent has close to 40 percent of the wealth—nearly the same amount as the bottom 95 percent of households.

Imagine a country where economic inequality is going back to the future circa the 1930s. The after-tax income of the top 1 percent of tax filers was about half that of the bottom 50 percent of tax filers in 1986. By the late 1990s, the top 1 percent had a larger share of after-tax income than the bottom 50 percent.

Imagine a country with a greed surplus and justice deficit.

Imagine a country where the poor and middle class bear the brunt of severe cutbacks in education, health, environmental programs and other public services to close state and federal budget deficits fueled by ballooning tax giveaways for wealthy households and corporations.

It's not Argentina.

Imagine a country which demands that people work for a living while denying many a living wage.

Imagine a country where health care aides can't afford health insurance. Where people working in the food industry depend on food banks to help feed their children. Where childcare teachers don't make enough to save for their own children's education.

It's not the Philippines.

Imagine a country where productivity went up, but workers' wages went down. In the words of the national labor department, "As the productivity of workers increases, one would expect worker compensation [wages and benefits] to experience similar gains." That's not what happened.

Since 1968, worker productivity has risen 81 percent while the average hourly wage barely budged, adjusting for inflation, and the real value of the minimum wage dropped 38 percent.

Imagine a country where the minimum wage just doesn't add up. Where minimum wage workers earn more than a third less than their counterparts earned a third of a century ago, adjusting for inflation. Where a couple with two children would have to work more than three full-time jobs at the $5.15 minimum wage to make ends meet.

It's not Mexico.

Imagine a country where some of the worst CEOs make millions more in a year than the best CEOs of earlier generations made in their lifetimes. CEOs made 45 times the pay of average production and nonsupervisory workers in 1980. They made 96 times as much in 1990, 160 times as much in 1995 and 369 times as much in 2001. Back in 1960, CEOs made an average 38 times more than schoolteachers. CEOs made 63 times as much in 1990 and 264 times as much as public school teachers in 2001.

Imagine a country that had a record-breaking ten-year economic expansion in 1991–2001, but millions of workers make wages so low they have to choose between eating or heating, health care or childcare.

A leading business magazine observed, "People who worked hard to make their companies competitive are angry at the way the profits are distributed. They think it is unfair, and they are right."

It's not England.

Imagine a country where living standards are falling for younger generations despite increased education. Since 1973, the share of workers without a high school degree has fallen by half. The share of workers with at least a four-year college degree has doubled. But the 2002 average hourly wage for production and nonsupervisory workers (the majority of the workforce) is 7.5 percent below 1973, adjusting for inflation. Median net worth (assets minus debt) dropped between 1995 and 2001 for households headed by persons under age 35 and households that don't own their own home.

About one out of four workers makes $8.70 an hour or less. That's not much more than the real value of the minimum wage of 1968 at $8.27 in inflation-adjusted dollars.

It's not Russia.

Imagine a country where for more and more people a job doesn't keep you out of poverty, it keeps you working poor. Imagine a country much richer than it was 25 years ago, but the percentage of full-time workers living in poverty has jumped 50 percent.

Imagine a country that sets the official poverty line well below the actual cost of minimally adequate housing, health care, food and other necessities. You were not counted as poor in 2001 (latest available final data) unless you had pre-tax incomes below these thresholds: $9,214 for a person under 65, $8,494 for a person 65 and older, $11,569 for a two-person family, $14,128 for a three-person family and $18,104 for a family of four. On average, households need more than double the official poverty threshold to meet basic needs.

Imagine a country where homelessness is on the rise, but federal funding for low-income housing is about 50 percent lower than it was in 1976, adjusting for inflation. The largest federal housing support program is the mortgage interest deduction, which disproportionately benefits higher-income families.

Imagine a country where more workers are going back to the future of sweatshops and day labor. Corporations are replacing full-time jobs with disposable "contingent workers." They include temporary employees, contract workers and "leased" employees—some of them fired and then "rented" back at a large discount by the same company—and involuntary part-time workers, who want permanent full-time work.

It's not Spain.

How do workers increasingly forced to migrate from job to job, at low and variable wage rates, without health insurance or paid vacation, much less a pension, care for themselves and their families, pay for college, save for retirement, plan a future, build strong communities?

Imagine a country where after mass layoffs and union busting, just 13.5 percent of workers are unionized. One out of three workers were union members in 1955. Full-time workers who were union members had median 2001 weekly earnings of $718 compared with just $575 for workers not represented by unions.

Imagine a country where the concerns of working people are dismissed as "special interests" and the profit-making interests of globetrotting corporations substitute for the "national interest."

Imagine a country negotiating "free trade" agreements that help corporations trade freely on cheap labor at home and abroad.

One ad financed by the country's agency for international development showed a Salvadoran woman in front of a sewing machine. It told corporations, "You can hire her for 33 cents an hour. Rosa is more than just colorful. She and her co-workers are known for their industriousness, reliability and quick learning. They make El Salvador one of the best buys." The country that financed the ad intervened militarily to make sure El Salvador would stay a "best buy" for corporations.

It's not Canada.

Imagine a country where nearly two-thirds of women with children under age 6 and more than three-fourths of women with children ages 6–17 are in the labor force, but affordable childcare and after-school programs are scarce. Apparently, kids are expected to have three parents: Two parents with jobs to pay the bills, and another parent to be home in mid-afternoon when school lets out—as well as all summer.

Imagine a country where women working full time earn 76 cents for every dollar men earn. Women don't pay 76 cents on a man's dollar for their education, rent, food or childcare. The gender wage gap has closed just 12 cents since 1955, when women earned 64 cents for every dollar earned by men. There's still another 24 cents to go.

The average woman high school graduate who works full time from ages 25 to 65 will earn about $450,000 less than the average male high school graduate; the gap widens to $900,000 for full-time workers with bachelor's degrees. "Men with professional degrees may expect to earn almost $2 million more than their female counterparts over their work-life," says a government report.

Imagine a country where childcare workers, mostly women, generally make about as much as parking lot attendants and much less than animal trainers. Out of 700 occupations surveyed by the labor department, only 15 have lower average wages than childcare workers.

Imagine a country where most minimum wage workers are women, while 95 percent of the top-earning corporate officers at the largest 500 companies are men, as are 90 percent of the most influential positions, from CEOs to executive vice president. Less than 2 percent of corporate officers at the largest companies are women of color.

Imagine a country where discrimination against women is pervasive from the bottom to the top of the pay scale, and it's not because women are on the "mommy track." In the words of a leading business magazine, "At the same level of management, the typical woman's pay is lower than her male colleague's—even when she has the exact same qualifications, works just as many years, relocates just as often, provides the main financial support for her family, takes no time off for personal reasons, and wins the same number of promotions to comparable jobs."

Imagine a country where instead of rooting out discrimination, many policy makers are busily blaming women for their disproportionate poverty. If women earned as much as similarly qualified men, poverty in single-mother households would be cut in half.

It's not Japan.

Imagine a country where the awful labeling of children as "illegitimate" has again been legitimized. Besides meaning born out of wedlock, illegitimate also means illegal, contrary to rules and logic, misbegotten, not genuine, wrong—to be a bastard. The word illegitimate has consequences. It helps make people more disposable. Single mothers and their children have become prime scapegoats for illegitimate economics.

Imagine a country where violence against women is so epidemic it is their leading cause of injury. So-called "domestic violence" accounts for more visits to hospital emergency departments than car crashes, muggings and rapes combined. Nearly a third of all murdered women are killed by husbands, boyfriends and ex-partners (less than a tenth are killed by strangers). Researchers say, "Men commonly kill their female partners in response to the woman's attempt to leave an abusive relationship."

The country has no equal rights amendment.

It's not Pakistan.

Imagine a country where homicide is the second-largest killer of young people, ages 15–24; "accidents," many of them drunk driving fatalities, are first. It leads major industrialized nations in firearms-related deaths for children under 15. Increasingly lethal weapons designed for hunting people are produced for profit by major manufacturers and proudly defended by a politically powerful national rifle association.

Informational material from a national shooting sports foundation asks, "How old is old enough?" to have a gun, and advises parents:

> Age is not the major yardstick. Some youngsters are ready to start at 10, others at 14. The only real measures are those of maturity and individual responsibility. Does your youngster follow directions well? Would you leave him alone in the house for two or three hours? Is he conscientious and reliable? Would you send him to the grocery store with a list and a $20 bill? If the answer to these questions or similar ones are "yes" then the answer can also be "yes" when your child asks for his first gun.

It's not France.

Imagine a country whose school system is rigged in favor of the already privileged, with lower caste children tracked by race and income into the most deficient and demoralizing schools and classrooms. Public school budgets are heavily determined by private property taxes, allowing higher income districts to spend much more than poor ones. In the state with the largest gap in 1999–2000, state and local spending per pupil in districts with the lowest child poverty rates was more than $2,152 greater than districts with the highest child poverty rates. The difference amounts to about $861,000 for a typical elementary school of 400 students—money that could be used for teachers, books and other resources. Disparities are even wider among states, with spending in districts with enrollments of 15,000 or more ranging from $3,932 per pupil in one district to $14,244 in another.

In rich districts kids take well-stocked libraries, laboratories and state-of-the-art computers for granted. In poor schools they are rationing out-of-date textbooks and toilet paper. Rich schools often look like country clubs—with manicured sports fields and swimming pools. Poor schools often look more like jails—with concrete grounds and grated windows. College prep courses, art, music, physical education, field trips and foreign languages are often considered necessities for the affluent, luxuries for the poor.

Wealthier citizens argue that lack of money isn't the problem in poorer schools—family values are—until proposals are made to make school spending more equitable. Then money matters greatly for those who already have more.

It's not India.

Imagine a country whose constitution once counted black slaves as worth three-fifths of whites. Today, black per capita income is about three-fifths of whites.

Imagine a country where racial disparities take their toll from birth to death. The black infant mortality rate is more than double that of whites. Black life expectancy is nearly six years less. Black unemployment is more than twice that of whites and the black poverty rate is almost triple that of whites.

Imagine a country where the government subsidized decades of segregated suburbanization for whites while the inner cities left to people of color were treated as outsider cities—separate, unequal and disposable. Recent studies have documented continuing discrimination in education, employment, banking, insurance, housing and health care.

It's not South Africa.

Imagine a country where the typical non-Hispanic white household has seven times the net worth (including home equity) as the typical household of color. From 1995 to 2001, the typical white household's net worth rose from $88,500 to $120,900 while the net worth of the typical household of color fell from $18,300 to $17,100.

Imagine a country that doesn't count you as unemployed just because you're unemployed. To be counted in the official unemployment rate you must have searched for work in the past four weeks. The government doesn't count people as "unemployed" if they are so discouraged from long and fruitless job searches they have given up looking. It doesn't count as "unemployed" those who couldn't look for work in the past month because they had no childcare, for example. If you need a full-time job, but you're working part-time—whether 1 hour or 34 hours weekly—because that's all you can find, you're counted as employed.

A leading business magazine observed, "Increasingly the labor market is filled with surplus workers who are not being counted as unemployed."

It's not Germany.

Imagine a country where there is a shortage of jobs, not a shortage of work. Millions of people need work and urgent work needs people—from creating affordable housing, to repairing bridges and building mass transit, to cleaning up pollution and converting to renewable energy, to staffing after-school programs and community centers.

Imagine a country with full prisons instead of full employment. The jail and prison population has nearly quadrupled since 1980. The nation is Number One in the world when it comes to locking up its own people. In 1985, 1 in every 320 residents were incarcerated. By 2001, the figure had increased to 1 in every 146.

Imagine a country where prison labor is a growth industry and so-called "corrections" spending is the fastest growing part of state budgets. Apparently, the government would rather spend $25,000 a year to keep someone in prison than on cost-effective programs of education, community development, addiction treatment and employment to keep them out. In the words of a national center on institutions and alternatives, this nation has "replaced the social safety net with a dragnet."

Imagine a country that has been criticized by human rights organizations for expanding rather than abolishing use of the death penalty—despite documented racial bias and growing evidence of innocents being sentenced to death.

It's not China.

Imagine a country that imprisons black people at a rate much higher than apartheid South Africa. One out of seven black men ages 25–29 are incarcerated. Many more are on probation or on parole. Looking just at prisons and not local jails, 10 percent of black males ages 25–29 were locked up at the end of 2001, compared with 1 percent of white males. Black non-Hispanic women are five times more likely to be imprisoned than white non-Hispanic women.

Meanwhile, nearly one out of three black men and women ages 16–19 are officially unemployed, as are one out of five ages 20–24. Remember, to be counted in the official unemployment rate you must be actively looking for a job and not finding one. "Surplus" workers are increasingly being criminalized.

A 1990 justice department report observed, "The fact that the legal order not only countenanced but sustained slavery, segregation, and discrimination for most of our Nation's history—and the fact that the police were bound to uphold that order— set a pattern for police behavior and attitudes toward minority communities that has persisted until the present day." A 1992 newspaper headline reads, "GUILTY ... of being black: Black men say success doesn't save them from being suspected, harassed and detained." "Driving while black" has become a well-known phrase.

Imagine a country waging a racially biased "War on Drugs." More than three out of four drug users are white, according to government data, but three out of four state prisoners convicted of drug offenses are black and Latino. Racial disparities in drug and other convictions are even wider when non-Hispanic whites are distinguished more accurately from Latinos.

A study in a prominent medical journal found that drug and alcohol rates were slightly higher for pregnant white women than pregnant black women, but black women were about ten times more likely to be reported to authorities by private doctors and public health clinics—under a mandatory reporting law. Poor women were also more likely to be reported.

It is said that truth is the first casualty in war, and the "War on Drugs" is no exception. Contrary to stereotype, "The typical cocaine user is white, male, a high school graduate employed full time and living in a small metropolitan area or suburb," says the nation's former drug czar. A leading newspaper reports that law officers and judges say, "Although it is clear that whites sell most of the nation's cocaine and account for 80% of its consumers, it is blacks and other minorities who continue to fill up [the] courtrooms and jails, largely because, in a political climate that demands that something be done, they are the easiest people to arrest." They are the easiest to scapegoat.

It's not Australia.

Imagine a country where the cycle of unequal opportunity is intensifying. Its beneficiaries often slander those most systematically undervalued, underpaid, underemployed, underfinanced, underinsured, underrated and otherwise underserved and undermined—as undeserving, "underclass," impoverished in moral and social values and lacking the proper "work ethic." The oft-heard stereotype of deadbeat poor people masks the growing reality of dead-end jobs and disposable workers.

Imagine a country that abolished aid to families with dependent children while maintaining aid for dependent corporations.

Imagine a country where state and local governments are rushing to expand lotteries, video poker and other government-promoted gambling to raise revenues, disproportionately from the poor, which they should be raising from a fair tax system.

Imagine a country whose military budget tops average Cold War levels although the break up of the Soviet Union produced friends, not foes. This nation spends almost as much on the military as the rest of the world combined and leads the world in arms exports.

Imagine a country that ranks first in the world in wealth and military power, and 34th in child mortality (under five), tied with Malaysia and well behind countries such as Singapore and South Korea. If the government were a parent it would be guilty of child abuse. Thousands of children die preventable deaths.

Imagine a country where health care is managed for healthy profit. In many countries health care is a right, but in this nation one out of six people under age 65 has no health insurance, public or private.

Health care is literally a matter of life and death. Lack of health insurance typically means lack of preventive health care and delayed or second-rate treatment. The uninsured are at much higher risk for chronic disease and disability, and have a 25 percent greater chance of dying (adjusting for physical, economic and behavioral factors). Uninsured women are 49 percent more likely to die than women with insurance during the four to seven years following an initial diagnosis of breast cancer.

Imagine a country where many descendants of its first inhabitants live on reservations strip-mined of natural resources and have a higher proportion of people in poverty than any other ethnic group.

Imagine a country where 500 years of plunder and lies are masked in expressions like "Indian giver." Where the military still dubs enemy territory, "Indian country."

Imagine a country which has less than 5 percent of the world's population, but uses more than 40 percent of the world's oil resources and about 20 percent of the coal and wood. It is the number one contributor to acid rain and global warming. It has obstructed international action on the environment and climate change.

It's not Brazil.

Imagine a country where half the eligible voters don't vote. The nation's senate and house of representatives are not representative of the nation. They are overwhelmingly white, male and millionaire.

At least 170 senators and congresspeople are millionaires. That's nearly one out of three members of the house and senate. Just 1 percent of the population they represent are millionaires.

Imagine a country where white men who are "falling down" the economic ladder are being encouraged to believe they are falling because women and people of color are climbing over them to the top or dragging them down from the bottom. That way, they will blame women and people of color rather than corporate and government policy. They will buy the myth of "reverse discrimination." Never mind that white males hold most senior management positions and continuing unreversed discrimination is well documented.

Imagine a country with a president who, even more than his father before him, "was born on third base and thought he hit a triple." The president wants to undo affirmative action. Never mind that despite all his advantages he was a mediocre student who relied on legacy affirmative action for the children of rich alumni to get into a top prep school and college. Never mind that he rode his family connections in business and politics.

Imagine a country where on top of discrimination comes insult. It's common for people of color to get none of the credit when they succeed—portrayed as undeserving beneficiaries of affirmative action and "reverse discrimination"—and all of the blame when they fail.

Imagine a country where a then presidential press secretary boasted to reporters: "You can say anything you want in a debate, and 80 million people hear it. If reporters then document that a candidate spoke untruthfully, so what? Maybe 200 people read it, or 2,000 or 20,000."

Imagine a country where politicians and judges whose views were formerly considered far right on the political spectrum now rule both houses of congress and the presidency and increasingly dominate the judiciary.

Imagine a country whose leaders misuse a fight against terrorism as camouflage for undermining democracy. Fundamental civil liberties, including the right not to be thrown into prison indefinitely on the word of government officials, are being tossed aside. The attorney general attacked critics of administration policy with McCarthyite words: "To those who scare peace-loving people with phantoms of lost liberty, my message is this: Your tactics only aid terrorists for they erode our national unity. . . . They give ammunition to [our] enemies and pause to [our] friends." The attorney general would burn democracy in the name of saving it.

It's not Italy.

It's the United States.

Decades ago Martin Luther King Jr. called on us to take the high road in *Where Do We Go From Here: Chaos or Community?* (Harper & Row, 1967). King wrote:

> A true revolution of values will soon cause us to question the fairness and justice of many of our past and present policies. We are called to play the good Samaritan on life's roadside; but . . . one day the whole Jericho road must be transformed so that men and women will not be beaten and robbed as they make their journey through life. . . . A true revolution of values will soon look uneasily on the glaring contrast of poverty and wealth. . . . There is nothing but a lack of social vision to prevent us from paying an adequate wage to every American citizen whether he be a hospital worker, laundry worker, maid or day laborer. There is nothing except shortsightedness to prevent us from guaranteeing an annual minimum—and *livable*—income for every American family.

SELECTED SOURCES

Business Week, annual reports on executive pay.
Catalyst, "2002 Census of Women Corporate Officers and Top Earners," New York.
Center for Defense Information, Washington, DC.

Center on Budget and Policy Priorities, Washington, DC.

Ira J. Chasnoff et al., "The Prevalence of Illicit-Drug or Alcohol Use During Pregnancy and Discrepancies in Mandatory Reporting in Pinellas County, Florida," *New England Journal of Medicine*, April 26, 1990.

Citizens for Tax Justice, Washington, DC.

Cushing N. Dolbeare and Sheila Crowley, *Changing Priorities: The Federal Budget and Housing Assistance, 1976–2007* (Washington, DC: National Low Income Housing Coalition, 2002).

Economic Policy Institute, Washington, DC, *The State of Working America 2002–2003* and other publications.

The Education Trust, *The Funding Gap: Low-Income and Minority Students Receive Fewer Dollars* (Washington, DC: August 2002).

Federal Reserve Board Division of Research and Statistics, Ana M. Aizcorbe et al., "Recent Changes in U.S. Family Finances: Evidence from the 1998 and 2001 Survey of Consumer Finances," *Federal Reserve Bulletin*, January 2003.

Anne B. Fisher, "When Will Women Get To The Top?" *Fortune*, September 21, 1992.

Joint Economic Committee (U.S. House and Senate), Democratic Staff, "The Tale of the Top 1 Percent," January 2003.

The Kaiser Family Foundation Commission on Medicaid and Uninsured, *Sicker and Poorer: The Consequences of Being Uninsured* (Menlo Park, CA: May 2002).

Jonathan Kozol, *Savage Inequalities: Children in America's Schools* (New York: Crown Publishers, 1991).

Leadership Conference on Civil Rights, *Justice on Trial: Racial Disparities in the American Criminal Justice System* (Washington, DC: 2000).

Peter Medoff and Holly Sklar, *Streets of Hope: The Fall and Rise of an Urban Neighborhood* (Boston: South End Press, 1994).

National Academy of Sciences, Institute of Medicine, Washington, DC.

National Center on Institutions and Alternatives, *Masking the Divide: How Officially Reported Prison Statistics Distort the Racial and Ethnic Realities of Prison Growth* (Alexandria, VA: May 2001).

National Labor Committee, New York.

The Sentencing Project, Washington, DC.

Holly Sklar, Laryssa Mykyta, and Susan Wefald, *Raise the Floor: Wages and Policies That Work for All of Us* (Boston: South End Press, 2002).

United Nations Children's Fund, *The State of the World's Children 2003*.

U.S. Bureau of the Census.

U.S. Centers for Disease Control and Prevention, National Center for Health Statistics.

U.S. Department of Health and Human Services, Substance Abuse and Mental Health Services Administration, *National Household Survey on Drug Abuse*.

U.S. Department of Justice, Bureau of Justice Statistics.

U.S. Department of Labor, Bureau of Labor Statistics.

Violence Policy Center, Washington, DC.

Hubert Williams and Patrick V. Murphy, "The Evolving Strategy of Police: A Minority View," *Perspectives on Policing*, U.S. Department of Justice (January 1990).

Number of People Living in Poverty Increases in U.S.

Robert Pear

WASHINGTON, Sept. 24   The proportion of Americans living in poverty rose significantly last year, increasing for the first time in eight years, the Census Bureau reported today. At the same time, the bureau said that the income of middle-class households fell for the first time since the last recession ended, in 1991.

The Census Bureau's annual report on income and poverty provided stark evidence that the weakening economy had begun to affect large segments of the population, regardless of race, region or class. Daniel H. Weinberg, chief of income and poverty statistics at the Census Bureau, said the recession that began in March 2001 had reduced the earnings of millions of Americans.

The report also suggested that the gap between rich and poor continued to grow.

All regions except the Northeast experienced a decline in household income, the bureau reported. For blacks, it was the first significant decline in two decades; non-Hispanic whites saw a slight decline. Even the incomes of Asians and Pacific Islanders, a group that achieved high levels of prosperity in the 1990's, went down significantly last year.

"The decline was widespread," Mr. Weinberg said.

The Census Bureau said the number of poor Americans rose last year to 32.9 million, an increase of 1.3 million, while the proportion living in poverty rose to 11.7 percent, from 11.3 percent in 2000.

Median household income fell to $42,228 in 2001, a decline of $934 or 2.2 percent from the prior year. The number of households with income above the median is the same as the number below it.

A family of four was classified as poor if it had cash income less than $18,104 last year. The official poverty levels, updated each year to reflect changes in the Consumer Price Index, were $14,128 for a family of three, $11,569 for a married couple and $9,039 for an individual.

The bureau's report is likely to provide fodder for the Congressional campaigns. The White House said the increase in poverty resulted, in part, from an economic slowdown that began under President Bill Clinton. But Democrats said the data showed the failure of President Bush's economic policies and his tendency to neglect the economy.

Mr. Bush said today that he remained optimistic. "When you combine the productivity of the American people with low interest rates and low inflation, those are the ingredients for growth," Mr. Bush said.

But Senator Paul S. Sarbanes, Democrat of Maryland, said the administration should "start paying attention to the economic situation." Richard A. Gephardt of Missouri, the House Democratic leader, expressed amazement that Mr. Bush, after being in office for 20 months, was still blaming his predecessor.

Rudolph G. Penner, a former director of the Congressional Budget Office, said: "The increase in poverty is most certainly a result of the recession. The slow recovery, the slow rate of growth, has been very disappointing. Whether that has a political impact this fall depends on whether the election hinges on national conditions or focuses on local issues."

Although the poverty rate, the proportion of the population living in poverty, rose four-tenths of a percentage point last year, it was still lower than in most of the last two decades. The poverty rate exceeded 12 percent every year from 1980 to 1998. As the economy grew from 1993 to 2000, the rate plunged, to 11.3 percent from 15.1 percent, and the poverty rolls were reduced by 7.7 million people, to 31.6 million.

The latest recession showed an unusual pattern, seeming to raise poverty rates among whites more than among minority groups, Mr. Weinberg said.

Increases in poverty last year were concentrated in the suburbs, in the South and among non-Hispanic whites, the Census Bureau said. Indeed, non-Hispanic whites were the only racial group for whom the poverty rate showed a significant increase, to 7.8 percent in 2001, from 7.4 percent in 2000.

Poverty rates for minority groups were once much higher. But last year, the bureau said, they remained "at historic lows" for blacks (22.7 percent), Hispanics (21.4 percent) and Asian Americans (10.2 percent).

With its usual caution, the Census Bureau said the data did not conclusively show a year-to-year increase in income inequality. But the numbers showed a clear trend in that direction over the last 15 years.

The most affluent fifth of the population received half of all household income last year, up from 45 percent in 1985. The poorest fifth received 3.5 percent of total household income, down from 4 percent in 1985. Average income for the top 5 percent of households rose by $1,000 last year, to $260,464, but the average declined or stayed about the same for most other income brackets.

Robert Greenstein, executive director of the Center on Budget and Policy Priorities, a liberal research institute, said, "The census data show that income inequality either set a record in 2001 or tied for the highest level on record."

Median earnings increased 3.5 percent for women last year, but did not change for men, so women gained relative to men.

"The real median earnings of women age 15 and older who worked full time year-round increased for the fifth consecutive year, rising to $29,215—a 3.5 percent increase between 2000 and 2001," Mr. Weinberg said. The comparable figure for men was unchanged at $38,275. So the female-to-male earnings ratio reached a high of 0.76. The previous high was 0.74, first recorded in 1996.

Democrats said the data supported their contention that Congress should increase spending on social welfare programs, resisted by many Republicans. But Wade F. Horn, the administration's welfare director, said the number of poor children was much lower than in 1996, when Congress overhauled the welfare law to impose strict work requirements.

Of the 32.9 million poor people in the United States last year, 11.7 million were under 18, and 3.4 million were 65 or older. Poverty rates for children, 16.3 percent, and the elderly, 10.1 percent, were virtually unchanged from 2000. But the poverty rate for people 18 to 64 rose a half percentage point, to 10.1 percent.

Median household income for blacks fell last year by $1,025, or 3.4 percent, to $29,470. Median income of Hispanics, at $33,565, was virtually unchanged. But household income fell by 1.3 percent for non-Hispanic whites, to $46,305, and by 6.4 percent for Asian Americans, to $53,635.

The Census Bureau report also included these findings:

- There were 6.8 million poor families last year, up from 6.4 million in 2000. The poverty rate for families rose to 9.2 percent, from a 26-year low of 8.7 percent in 2000.
- The rate in the South rose to 13.5 percent, from 12.8 percent in 2000. The South is home to more than 40 percent of all the nation's poor, and it accounted for more than half of the national increase in the number of poor last year.
- The poverty rate for the suburbs rose to 8.2 percent last year, from 7.8 percent in 2000. The number of poor people in suburban areas rose by 700,000, to 12 million. There was virtually no change in the rates in central cities (16.5 percent) and outside metropolitan areas (14.2 percent).

The bureau said the number of "severely poor" rose to 13.4 million last year, from 12.6 million in 2000. People are considered to be severely poor if their family incomes are less than half of the official poverty level.

49

CEOs: New Century, Same Story

Meet William A. Wise, the chief executive of the El Paso Corp., a Houston-based energy powerhouse. Never heard of him? No reason you should have. Wise, unlike his counterparts across town at Enron, doesn't make many headlines. He's just an ordinary, run-of-the-mill big-time CEO.

And that's exactly why William A. Wise deserves a closer look. Last year, in his ordinaryness, Wise personified America's corporate elite.

In 2001, a most distressing recession year, that elite—and William A. Wise— did quite well.

Over the year, the *Wall Street Journal* reports, Wise made $8.2 million in salary and various bonuses, as well as $90,000 more in assorted perks.

El Paso also saw fit to bless Wise with a pile of new stock options potentially worth some $73 million. To make room for all these new options, Wise unloaded some of his old ones. That move brought in an additional $11 million.

Enough already? Not quite. In February 2001, the El Paso Corp. loaned Wise 80 percent of the money he needed to buy $5 million worth of shares in the company's hot new telecom venture.

This new venture in short order went sour. No big deal. In October, El Paso bought back the stock Wise had

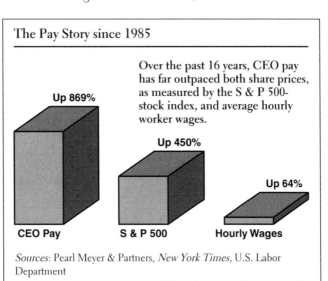

The Pay Story since 1985

Over the past 16 years, CEO pay has far outpaced both share prices, as measured by the S & P 500- stock index, and average hourly worker wages.

Up 869%

Up 450%

Up 64%

CEO Pay S & P 500 Hourly Wages

Sources: Pearl Meyer & Partners, *New York Times*, U.S. Labor Department

From *Too Much*. Reprinted by permission of Apex Press.

purchased, at a price high enough to make him a 26 percent return on his original investment. Wise cleared $257,762 on the deal in all. Small change maybe, but not bad for eight months.

For the El Paso Corp., apparently, nothing was too good for William A. Wise. Funny thing. Most big American corporations last year felt the same way about *their* chief executives—and they showed that appreciation, *USA Today* reported late in March, by hiking overall CEO pay 24 percent. Not a bad pay hike for a year when company share prices sank, on average, 13 percent.

In 2001, by hook or by crook, by loan or by bonus, by any means necessary, corporate America made sure that, despite a dismal economy, few executives felt any pain.

But pain was exactly what top CEOs should have felt last year, at least according to the line defenders of excessive CEO pay advanced back in the 1990s.

At that time, corporate flacks claimed that rising share prices justified soaring executive pay. Executives, went the claim, had "delivered" those higher stock prices. They deserved to be paid for their achievement.

How much did William A. Wise deliver in 2001? Not much. His company's shares sank 38 percent.

Wise, incidentally, ended up giving up—to charity—the quarter million dollars he made on his eight-month loan. Seems news about the little windfall leaked out, to the embarrassment of the El Paso Corp.'s Enron-conscious PR department.

The rest of Wise's $92 million or so of 2001 compensation goodies? He kept them.

50

Still at the Periphery
The Economic Status of African Americans

Julianne Malveaux

Whether you measure income, wealth, home ownership, or employment status, the differences in economic status between African Americans and whites are significant and persistent. To be sure, some gaps are narrowing. African Americans have vastly improved their status since 1940, when more than half of us lived in poverty, and 70 percent of all African American women worked as private household workers. Visible indicators of success include magazine covers touting the presence of African Americans in management (see, for example, *Newsweek*, January 20, 2002). But the status of African Americans in the middle and at the bottom is far less visible, and far more often ignored.

Average data paints a good comparative picture. According to the 2000 census, mean white wage and salary income was $36,249, compared to $25,960 for African Americans. Thus, African Americans earned 71.6 percent of what whites earned. While education and occupational choices are factors, there is an earning gap between whites and people of color even when we control for education. For example, among men over age 25 with a bachelor's degree or more, African Americans earned $40,360, and white men earned $51,469. In percentage terms, college-educated African American men earned 78 percent of what white men earned.[1]

Yet, income data provides an incomplete picture of the economic status of African Americans. The long-term status of African Americans is better reflected by wealth data, and here the gaps are more glaring. The Survey of Consumer Finance,[2] which reports on wealth status every three years, aggregates African Americans and Hispanics in the category "nonwhite." In 1998, the latest year for which data is available,[3] the mean, or average, wealth for white families was $334,400, while the mean wealth for nonwhite families was $101,700. In other words, nonwhite families had just 30 percent of the wealth of white families.

Mean data perhaps present a more optimistic picture than the reality. Median wealth, or the level of wealth at which half of a population falls above and half falls below, in 1998 was $94,900 for white families and $16,400 for nonwhite families. The median wealth for nonwhite families was 17.2 percent of the weatlh of white families. Interestingly, the median wealth of nonwhite families dropped by $400 between 1995 and 1998, while the median wealth of white families rose by more than $13,000, or 16 percent. During a period of economic expansion, then, nonwhite families at the bottom saw their wealth status erode.

One of the most important assets for middle-income people is a home. Indeed, home ownership is often the bridge over which low-income people cross to middle class status. Home ownership provides people with stability, but also with a vehicle to increase their net worth. The glaring racial gap in home ownership speaks to the many ways that economic expansion has had a limited reach. While overall home ownership in our nation reached an all-time high of 66.8 percent in 1999, the racial gap in home ownership narrowed only slightly amidst all this growth. Thus, while the rate of home ownership among whites grew to 73 percent, the rates remained at 46 and 45 percent, respectively, for African Americans and Hispanics. Home ownership among Asian Americans was about 54 percent, and it did not grow as much as the white rate grew during expansion.

Stagnant home ownership rates among people of color illustrate the limits of celebrating macroeconomic growth without looking at its microeconomic reverberations. Lower interest rates made it possible for more whites to own homes; it also increased their wealth basis, because refinancing allowed them to capitalize on the increased value of their homes. People of color who were in the same position had many of the same opportunities, but the large gap in home ownership statistics suggests that a sizable part of the African American and Hispanic population saw a market improve but had no opportunity to take advantage of it. Many were not home owners and could not buy, despite some expansion of access to home ownership. Because they did not own homes, they could not engage in the kind of wealth accumulation that home owners, buoyed by interest rates that were lower than they have been in a generation (as low as six percent), were able to engage in.

The Impact of the "Boom Years"

Much has been made of the economic expansion that began in 1991 and continued for ten full years. During this expansion, gross domestic product grew by about four percent a year, and by as much as seven percent in some quarters. This expansion fueled a phenomenal growth in stock prices, with the Dow Jones Industrial average growing by more than 20 percent each year between 1995 and 1999. It also had a positive effect on the growth and development of small business, on the increased collection of federal, state, and local tax revenue, and on macroeconomic optimism. Unfortunately, though, while there was such macroeconomic ecstasy that Federal Reserve Board Chairman Alan Greenspan described the stock market as "irrationally exuberant," there was a persistent microeconomic angst because good times did not trickle down swiftly enough to people who lived at the periphery of the economy.

For many, then, living in the latter part of the twentieth century was like living in the midst of a party that one hadn't been invited to. It was like putting your nose up against the window of a candy store, watching others buy the brightly colored sweets while understanding that you had not the means to afford them. It was hearing about letting the good times roll, and being made to feel guilty because you weren't rolling with the good times. Indeed, between welfare deform and economic expansion, poverty was demonized. Once we believed that people who were poor were victims of an unjust system. By the late 1990s, the era of "no excuses," we began to believe that people were poor because there was something wrong with them.

So we raised the minimum wage in 1996, during an election year, and with much ado. But the minimum wage has not gone up since then, and more than 10 million Americans, mostly women, disproportionately women of color, and many mothers and household heads, earn just $10,700 a year when they work full-time, full year. The people who hold these jobs are essential to holding our worlds together—they care for our parents and our children, serve our food, and clean our hospitals. Yet they are disregarded, and are perhaps the sole group of people who can say they gained little or nothing from economic expansion. They have become a political pawn, ignored in the 2000 budget deliberations, held hostage to a set of business tax cuts in 2001 discussions. A disproportionate number of these workers are African American women.

They have jobs. The traditional ratio between Black and white unemployment, two to one, did not weaken during economic expansion and is debilitating during economic downturns. When the overall unemployment rate hovered at 4 percent, the white unemployment rate dipped to 3.5 percent and the Black unemployment rate was more than double, at 7.2 percent. In late 2001, with recession and the aftermath of September 11 driving layoffs, the overall unemployment rate in December was 5.8 percent, the white unemployment rate was 5.1 percent, and the Black unemployment rate was 10.2 percent, according to the Census Bureau's Current Population Survey. If a 10.2 percent unemployment rate were observed among the overall population, it would be interpreted as a "depression level" unemployment rate. Nevertheless, President George Bush has announced that he will cut funding for urban (read inner-city residents, mostly African American and Latino) job training programs by 70 percent, from $225 million to $45 million.

Thus, while some African Americans experienced benefits due to economic expansion, those at the bottom—the 25 percent who remain in poverty—did not find their circumstances much improved. Instead, thanks to "welfare deform," the demonization of poverty, and the blind eye that policymakers have turned to the poor their situation has actually gotten worse. Some few policy initiatives have focused on economic development and closing gaps, but the peripheral status of workers on the bottom, a disproportionate number of whom are African American, has been largely ignored.

Recession for Some, Depression for Others

If this was the case during expansion, it has been exacerbated during the economic contraction that began, according to the National Bureau of Economic Research, in March 2001, and is projected to continue through the third quarter of 2002. Those at the bottom are hit hardest, but even those who are not among the working poor can expect economic challenges. Many workers bounce back quickly from layoffs, but it often takes African American workers longer to find comparable jobs. The old saying of "last hired, first fired" for people of color has not been swept away by the new economy.

Beyond that, the economic slowdown means those corporations that briefly used their profits to engage inner-city residents in the new economy are now less likely to spend that money. Though no company has pulled its dollars out of programs to develop computer literacy, to train inner-city workers, or to wire inner-city community centers and churches for the Internet, companies who make contributions out of corporate profits now have much less to give. Those philanthropists who were awash in stock-market profits a year or two ago are now trying to make charitable dollars stretch, and they have less money to use for innovative programs. . . .

The "War on Terrorism"

The economy was already slowing when the tragic events of September 11, 2001, shook both the economy and nation's confidence. Still, the loss of 3,000 lives must be put in perspective—the world has lost as many lives on days like this before. Perhaps a slave ship sank; perhaps a gas chamber worked overtime. Those who behave as if we have never seen loss of life like that on 9-11 ignore the principle of shared status that suggests that a life is a life, and that all life must be valued equally.

Similarly, the 9-11 relief funds exhibit our nation's class bias, and bias against working people. In other words, it has been reported that the family of a broker who once earned $150,000 will get millions of dollars in federal relief, while the family of a dishwasher who earned $20,000 will get just $400,000. While these are estimates that may vary with circumstances, the message is that government will value lives based on earnings. Insurance companies do that, and some workers were better insured than others! The federal government ought to embrace the principle of shared status and compensate families and survivors on some equal basis. Otherwise, their awards embrace the discrimination that people have experienced during their entire lives. It is said that people are all in the same boat, dying equally as the Twin Towers toppled. They may have died equally, but they didn't live equally, and debates around death benefits make this clear.

There are other race and class implications of the ways that the public has responded to September 11. Millions of dollars have been contributed to help victims, but thousands of charities that help people on the bottom are losing funds.

Those who are hungry and homeless are somehow ignored as compassion shifts to 9-11 victims and their families. Further, public policy wants to bail out those industries affected by 9-11, but they don't want to bail out the people affected by industrial dislocation. Thus, airlines have a bailout fund of billions of dollars, but those who clean airports, or who work in hotels, or even who work for airlines, are not covered by bailout funds. Some are worthy of help, others are not. Workers who lost their jobs and livelihoods in the collapse of the Twin Towers will be helped, but peddlers who sold them fruit and coffee as they entered the building may have more difficulty documenting their need for help and receiving it.

Race, Class, and Enron

Class matters, which are clearly intertwined with race matters, will be the focus of discussion for the 107th Congress in the wake of the Enron bankruptcy. It was amazing to watch that company play the "wife card" in January, 2001, when Linda Lay told NBC reporter Lisa Myers that her family had "lost everything" and had little more than their ($7 million) home. Actually, the family owns more than a dozen properties, some of which are for sale. Kenneth Lay also holds more than $10 million in stock in companies other than Enron. There is a certain form of hubris that allows a family to take to the airwaves and plead poverty, even as their actions have impoverished thousands of Enron workers.

The Enron case is important to African Americans and other people of color because it is a textbook case on double standards. It suggests that the wealthy have differential access to politicians than others do, that they gain loans and credit through different lending standards, that they have different requirements for accounting, and even for declaring bankruptcy. It is ironic that as Enron has filed the nation's largest bankruptcy claim, credit card companies have been asking that Congress make it more difficult for the average American to declare bankruptcy. In legislation proposed in the spring of 2001, at a time when individual bankruptcies exceeded 1.2 million, and the average person filing for bankruptcy earned $22,000,[4] credit card companies asked that their repayments be prioritized—even over child support payments.

If African Americans had the access Enron had, we might have reparations by now. Enron is a plea for campaign finance reform, a reminder of the way the power pie is divided, and an illustration of the reasons that the gaps between African Americans and whites, between the haves and have nots, are so great. While senior Enron managers traded their stock, those who participated in the company's retirement plan, putting their own money into a company-administered 401(k) plan, watched their savings evaporate as the stock price plummeted from a high of $70 a year ago to just 38 cents in January, 2002. For a 10-day period, when stock prices dropped by 20 percent, workers could not trade their stock because the pension administrator was being changed and transactions were frozen. Meanwhile, former CEO Kenneth Lay urged employees to buy stock in September 2001, even as he had sold tens of millions of dollars of stock of his own.

Yet according to the National Compensation Survey, which measured benefits available to workers in private companies, most people are not covered by retirement benefits. Just 48 percent of all Americans have either a defined benefit plan or a defined contribution plan, with the remainder relying on Social Security and their own savings for retirement. While 48 percent of all workers had employer contributions to a pension plan, just 32 percent of African Americans and 36 percent of Hispanics worked for companies that contributed to a pension plan. The Enron debacle reminds us of the differential economic status of African Americans and whites. The vast majority of African American workers, because of their occupational and industrial status, were not directly affected by this scandal. But those who had pensions with Enron suffered measurably.

How Long at the Periphery?

In recession and recovery, African Americans remain at the periphery of the economy. We are not full participants because of our differential incomes, differential wealth holding, and differential treatment in the labor market. The gaps persist even as the market fluctuates, and they are highlighted by exogenous shocks, like the events of September 11 and the bankruptcy of Enron. While there has been progress from a generation ago, African Americans are not "players" in the economy, especially when the interests of our community are being brokered. . . .

NOTES

1. All of the data in this section came from the United States Bureau of Census, *Current Population Survey, 2001* (Washington, D.C.).

2. Federal Reserve System of the United States, *Survey of Consumer Finance* (Washington, D.C., 1998).

3. Data for 2001 will be released in 2003.

4. SMR Research Corporation, *The Credit Risk Outlook for 2002* (Hackettstown, NJ: SMR Research Corporation, 2001).

Being Black, Living in the Red: *Wealth Matters*

Dalton Conley

If I could cite one statistic that inspired this study, it would be the following: in 1994, the median white family had assets worth more than seven times those of the median nonwhite family. Even when we compare white and minority families at the same income level, whites enjoy a huge advantage in wealth. For instance, at the lower end of the income spectrum (less than $15,000 per year), the median African American family has no assets, while the equivalent white family holds $10,000 worth of equity. At upper income levels (greater than $75,000 per year), white families have a median net worth of $308,000, almost three times the figure for upper-income African American families ($114,600).[1]

Herein lie the two motivating questions of this study. First, why does this wealth gap exist and persist over and above income differences? Second, does this wealth gap explain racial differences in areas such as education, work, earnings, welfare, and family structure? In short, this study examines where race *per se* really matters in the post–civil rights era and where race simply acts as a stand-in for that dirty word of American society: class. The answers to these questions have important implications for the debate over affirmative action for social policy in general.

An alternative way to conceptualize what this article is about is to contrast the situations of two hypothetical families. Let's say that both households consist of married parents, in their thirties, with two young children.[2] Both families are low-income—that is, the total household income of each family is approximately the amount that the federal government has "declared" to be the poverty line for a family of four (with two children). In 1996, this figure was $15,911.

Brett and Samantha Jones (family 1) earned about $12,000 that year. Brett earned this income from his job at a local fast-food franchise (approximately two thousand hours at a rate of $6 per hour). He found himself employed at this low-wage job after being laid off from his relatively well-paid position as a sheet metal worker at a local manufacturing plant, which closed because of fierce competition from companies in Asia and Latin America. After six months of unemployment, the only work Brett could find was flipping burgers alongside teenagers from the local high school.

Fortunately for the Jones family, however, they owned their own home. Fifteen years earlier, when Brett graduated from high school, married Samantha, and landed his original job as a sheet metal worker, his parents had lent the newlyweds money out of their retirement nest egg that enabled Brett and Samantha to make a 10 percent down payment on a house. With Samantha's parents cosigning—backed by the value of their own home—the newlyweds took out a fifteen-year mortgage for the balance of the cost of their $30,000 home. Although money was tight in the beginning, they were nonetheless thrilled to have a place of their own. During those initial, difficult years, an average of $209 of their $290.14 monthly mortgage payment was tax deductible as a home mortgage interest deduction. In addition, their annual property taxes of $800 were completely deductible, lowering their taxable income by a total of $3,308 per year. This more than offset the payments they were making to Brett's parents for the $3,000 they had borrowed for the down payment.

After four years, Brett and Samantha had paid back the $3,000 loan from his parents. At that point, the total of their combined mortgage payment ($290.14), monthly insurance premium ($50), and monthly property tax payment ($67), minus the tax savings from the deductions for mortgage interest and local property taxes, was less than the $350 that the Smiths (family 2) were paying to rent a unit the same size as the Joneses' house on the other side of town.

That other neighborhood, on the "bad" side of town, where David and Janet Smith lived, had worse schools and a higher crime rate and had just been chosen as a site for a waste disposal center. Most of the residents rented their housing units from absentee landlords who had no personal stake in the community other than profit. A few blocks from the Smiths' apartment was a row of public housing projects. Although they earned the same salaries and paid more or less the same monthly costs for housing as the Joneses did, the Smiths and their children experienced living conditions that were far inferior on every dimension, ranging from the aesthetic to the functional (buses ran less frequently, large supermarkets were nowhere to be found, and class size at the local school was well over thirty).

Like Brett Jones, David Smith had been employed as a sheet metal worker at the now-closed manufacturing plant. Unfortunately, the Smiths had not been able to buy a home when David was first hired at the plant. With little in the way of a down payment, they had looked for an affordable unit at the time, but the real estate agents they saw routinely claimed that there was just nothing available at the moment, although they promised to "be sure to call as soon as something comes up. . . ." The Smiths never heard back from the agents and eventually settled into a rental apartment.

David spent the first three months after the layoffs searching for work, drawing down the family's savings to supplement unemployment insurance—savings that were not significantly greater than those of the Joneses, since both families had more or less the same monthly expenses. After several months of searching, David managed to land a job. Unfortunately, it was of the same variety as the job Brett

Jones found: working as a security guard at the local mall, for about $12,000 a year. Meanwhile, Janet Smith went to work part time, as a nurse's aide for a home health care agency, grossing about $4,000 annually.

After the layoffs, the Joneses experienced a couple of rough months, when they were forced to dip into their small cash savings. But they were able to pay off the last two installments of their mortgage, thus eliminating their single biggest living expense. So, although they had some trouble adjusting to their lower standard of living, they managed to get by, always hoping that another manufacturing job would become available or that another company would buy out the plant and re-open it. If worst came to worst, they felt that they could always sell their home and relocate in a less expensive locale or an area with a more promising labor market.

The Smiths were a different case entirely. As renters, they had no latitude in re-ducing their expenses to meet their new economic reality, and they could not af-ford their rent on David's reduced salary. The financial strain eventually proved too much for the Smiths, who fought over how to structure the family budget. After a particularly bad row when the last of their savings had been spent, they de-cided to take a break; both thought life would be easier and better for the children if Janet moved back in with her mother for a while, just until things turned around economically—that is, until David found a better-paying job. With no house to an-chor them, this seemed to be the best course of action.

Several years later, David and Janet Smith divorced, and the children began to see less and less of their father, who stayed with a friend on a "temporary" basis. Even though together they had earned more than the Jones family (with total in-comes of $16,000 and $12,000, respectively), the Smiths had a rougher financial, emotional, and family situation, which, we may infer, resulted from a lack of prop-erty ownership.

What this comparison of the two families illustrates is the inadequacy of rely-ing on income alone to describe the economic and social circumstances of fami-lies at the lower end of the economic scale. With a $16,000 annual income, the Smiths were just above the poverty threshold. In other words, they were not de-fined as "poor," in contrast to the Joneses, who were.[3] Yet the Smiths were worse off than the Joneses, despite the fact that the U.S. government and most re-searchers would have classified the Jones family as the one who met the threshold of neediness, based on that family's lower income.

These income-based poverty thresholds differ by family size and are adjusted annually for changes in the average cost of living in the United States. In 1998, more than two dozen government programs—including food stamps, Head Start, and Medicaid—based their eligibility standards on the official poverty threshold. Additionally, more than a dozen states currently link their needs standard in some way to this poverty threshold. The example of the Joneses and the Smiths should tell us that something is gravely wrong with the way we are measuring economic hardship—poverty—in the United States. By ignoring assets, we not only give a distorted picture of life at the bottom of the income distribution but may even cre-ate perverse incentives.

Of course, we must be cautious and remember that the Smiths and the Joneses are hypothetically embellished examples that may exaggerate differences. Perhaps the Smiths would have divorced regardless of their economic circumstances. The hard evidence linking modest financial differences to a propensity toward marital dissolution is thin; however, a substantial body of research shows that financial issues are a major source of marital discord and relationship strain.[4] It is also possible that the Smiths, with nothing to lose in the form of assets, might have easily slid into the world of welfare dependency. A wide range of other factors, not included in our examples, affect a family's well-being and its trajectory. For example, the members of one family might have been healthier than those of the other, which would have had important economic consequences and could have affected family stability. Perhaps one family might have been especially savvy about using available resources and would have been able to take in boarders, do under-the-table work, or employ another strategy to better its standard of living. Nor do our examples address educational differences between the two households.

But I have chosen not to address all these confounding factors for the purpose of illustrating the importance of asset ownership *per se*. Of course, homeownership, savings behavior, and employment status all interact with a variety of other measurable and unmeasurable factors. This interaction, however, does not take away from the importance of property ownership itself.

The premise of this study is a relatively simple and straightforward one: in order to understand a family's well-being and the life chances of its children—in short, to understand its class position—we not only must consider income, education, and occupation but also must take into account accumulated wealth (that is, property, assets, or net worth—terms that I will use interchangeably). While the importance of wealth is the starting point of the study, its end point is the impact of the wealth distribution on racial inequality in America. As you might have guessed, an important detail is missing from the preceding description of the two families: the Smiths are black and have fewer assets than the Joneses, who are white.

At all income, occupational, and education levels, black families on average have drastically lower levels of wealth than similar white families. The situation of the Smiths may help us to understand the reason for this disparity of wealth between blacks and whites. For the Smiths, it was not discrimination in hiring or education that led to a family outcome vastly different from that of the Joneses; rather, it was a relative lack of assets from which they could draw. In contemporary America, race and property are intimately linked and form the nexus for the persistence of black–white inequality.

Let us look again at the Smith family, this time through the lens of race. Why did real estate agents tell the Smiths that nothing was available, thereby hindering their chances of finding a home to buy? This well-documented practice is called "steering," in which agents do not disclose properties on the market to qualified African American home seekers, in order to preserve the racial makeup of white communities—with an eye to maintaining the property values in those neighborhoods. Even if the Smiths had managed to locate a home in a predominantly African American neighborhood, they might well have encountered difficulty in obtaining a home mortgage because of "redlining," the procedure by which banks code such neighborhoods "red"—the lowest rating—on their loan evaluations, thereby making it next to impossible to get a mortgage for a home in these districts. Finally, and perhaps most important, the Smiths' parents were more likely to have been poor and without assets themselves (being black and having been born early in the century), meaning that it would have been harder for them to amass enough money to loan their children a down payment or to cosign a loan for them. The result is that while poor whites manage to have, on average, net worths of over $10,000, impoverished blacks have essentially no assets whatsoever.[5]

Since wealth accumulation depends heavily on intergenerational support issues such as gifts, informal loans, and inheritances, net worth has the ability to pick up both the current dynamics of race and the legacy of past inequalities that may be obscured in simple measures of income, occupation, or education. This thesis has been suggested by the work of sociologists Melvin Oliver and Thomas Shapiro in their recent book *Black Wealth/White Wealth*.[6] They claim that wealth is central to the nature of black–white inequality and that wealth—as opposed to income, occupation, or education—represents the "sedimentation" of both a legacy of racial inequality as well as contemporary, continuing inequities. Oliver and Shapiro provide a textured description of the divergence of black–white asset holdings. They touch on some of the causal factors leading to this growing gap, such as differential mortgage interest rates paid by black and white borrowers. . . .

It is the hypothesis of this study that certain tenacious racial differences—such as deficits in education, employment, wages, and even wealth itself among African Americans—will turn out to be indirect effects, mediated by class differences. In other words, it is not race *per se* that matters directly; instead, what matters are the wealth levels and class positions that are associated with race in America. In this manner, racial differences in income and asset levels have come to play a prominent role in the perpetuation of black–white inequality in the United States.

This is not to say that race does not matter; rather, it maps very well onto class inequality, which in turn affects a whole host of other life outcomes. In fact, when class is taken into consideration, African Americans demonstrate significant net *advantages* over whites on a variety of indicators (such as rates of high school graduation, for instance). In this fact lies the paradox of race and class in contemporary America. . . .

Is It All Black and White?

Throughout this introduction, I have spoken only of blacks and whites when addressing the issue of race. America is no longer a biracial society, however. So why examine the impact of wealth and property issues with respect to blacks and whites exclusively? One reason for this strategy is technical. It is very difficult to find useful, longitudinal data on assets for the American population; this is particularly true for minorities who make up a small percentage of the population, even when their numbers are growing rapidly. . . .

That said, there are other reasons why this shortcoming should not be so troubling. Perhaps the most important is that on almost all measures—including property ownership—blacks and whites demonstrate the greatest disparities of all racial groups in the United States.[7] This holds true for indicators ranging from residential segregation to wages to academic achievement. In other words, what is true for Latinos in terms of hindered life chances appears even more true for African Americans. Further, within the Hispanic population, wide variation exists in wealth and other factors. Certain groups such as Cubans and Spaniards tend to fall close to whites for a variety of indicators, whereas other groups such as Mexicans, Puerto Ricans, and Dominicans more resemble the African American population by socioeconomic and family measures. In short, the Hispanic population demonstrates much variation but largely falls between blacks and whites (closer to African Americans on average). Even more interesting, skin color within the Hispanic population is a good predictor of where on the spectrum between blacks and whites an individual is likely to fall. In other words, the "blacker" a Hispanic person looks, the morel likely he or she is to resemble the African American demographic profile; the "whiter" a Hispanic person appears, the more he or she will resemble the demographic profile of European ethnic groups.[8]

What about Asian Americans, the so-called "model minority" (that is, a group that has been socioeconomically successful despite its minority status)? At one time in American history, Jews were considered the "model minority" and were pointed to as an example of how "anyone can make it in America" (the implied question asking why blacks could not do the same thing). Interestingly, Jews today are no longer generally considered a separate race but instead form part of the white community. In fact, sociologist Andrew Hacker claims that there are only two races in America, white and nonwhite; therefore, for instance, Pakistanis with very dark skin can be considered symbolically "white" in his scheme. He argues that today Asian Americans fall under the "white umbrella" as an "in-group"—in other words, they are not systematically excluded from reaping the benefits of American capitalism, as are those under the "black umbrella," the "out-group." Correspondingly, today the role of model minority has been largely taken over by Asian Americans.[9]

The issue of entrepreneurship also comes into play when making comparisons. If many Chinese and Koreans, for example, can come to the United States with nothing and manage to excel in school and start businesses with little formal capital, why cannot African Americans do the same? The answer to this question may lie in a long cultural history of entrepreneurship among these Asian ethnic groups—or perhaps in their very status as immigrants. "Immigrants in the United States, Canada and Australia," write Ivan Light and Carol Rosenstein in *Race, Ethnicity, and Entrepreneurship in Urban America*, "continued to manifest higher rates of self-employment than the native born, a proclivity they have displayed for at least a century."[10] By definition, immigrants are the world's overachievers, so they do not form a valid comparison group for the native black or white communities. The act of migrating itself is an important causal factor to be reckoned with before any judgments are made about the relative proclivities of ethnic groups toward entrepreneurial activity.

Research has supported this immigrant exceptionalism argument, finding in one case, for instance, "that successive generations of white ethnics [in Providence] evidence successively lower rates of self-employment."[11] Another study found that when "human capital" (education) is held constant, Asian American and African American entrepreneurship rates are essentially the same.[12] Other work contradicts this finding, however, finding a net lower rate of self-employment among blacks even after factoring out a variety of other variables.[13]

Theories of entrepreneurship may offer some explanation. One theory holds that a group's rate of self-employment will be high when it faces disadvantage in the rest of the labor market.[14] Thus, the fact that Asian Americans get a "low" return on their educational credentials could help to explain their higher rates of entrepreneurship. But what about African Americans? As we have already seen, black Americans receive lower wages than the majority group (whites) at the same education levels. According to the theory, we should then expect African Americans to have a higher than average rate of self-employment; instead, the rate is lower (3.7 percent in 1993, compared to 9.0 percent for whites). These rates may indicate that this theory of "labor market disadvantage" is missing an important component: group resources (that is, levels of human capital). It is one thing to have high levels of education (as Asian Americans do) and not be adequately rewarded for them. It is quite a different situation to have lower than average education levels (as African Americans do) and receive still lower returns on these years of schooling. In other words, the labor market equilibrium will balance itself in favor of self-employment only when the resources are there to begin with.[15]

Consumer racism has also been shown to have a role in depressing the rate of black entrepreneurship.[16] If nonblack consumers—who obviously form the largest part of the market—automatically prefer a white electrician or barber to a black one, for instance, this discourages African American self-employment. It is also important to realize that the rates of entrepreneurial activity for one group are not independent of the rates for other groups. While there has been no evidence to show that Asian American businesses have "prevented" black ones from forming, we do have evidence that rates of Asian entrepreneurship increase in communities with a high percentage of black residents (net of the size of the Asian population).[17] In other words, Koreans, for example, may not be displacing black businesses, but they are filling a consumer need in black communities that otherwise would have gone untended since African Americans may lack the financial and educational resources to start such enterprises. Entrepreneurship is related to immigration, labor market prospects, and wealth endowments in complex ways. Thus, even if the data were available, comparing Asian immigrants with native-born black Americans is neither simple nor fruitful. The clearer comparison is between blacks and whites, the vast majority of whom are native-born.

NOTES

1. Data from the Panel Study of Income Dynamics (PSID), 1994 Wealth Supplement. The PSID is an ongoing study conducted by the Survey Research Center, Institute for Social Research, at the University of Michigan; see the PSID Web site at *www.isr.umich.edu/src/psid*.

2. These family descriptions were extrapolated from profiles of specific families who were interviewed for this study. The age, racial, income, family size, wealth, housing tenure, and divorce descriptions of these families come directly from cases 4348 and 1586 of the PSID 1984 wave (inflation-adjusted to 1996 dollars). The names and other details are fictitious but are in line with previous research that would suggest such profiles.

3. Neither family received health insurance from an employer. Since the Smiths' income was under 185 percent of the poverty line, their children were eligible for Medicaid. (In most states, the Joneses' children would also have been eligible for Medicaid since that family's wealth was in the form of a home, which is excluded from the asset limits of many states.)

4. See, e.g., G. Levinger and O. Moles, eds., *Divorce and Separation: Contexts, Causes, and Consequences* (New York: Basic Books, 1979); and R. Conger, G.H. Elder, et al., "Linking Economic Hardship to Marital Quality and Instability," *Journal of Marriage and the Family* 52 (1990): 643–56.

5. Throughout this study, the terms "black" and "African American" are used interchangeably, as are the terms "Hispanic" and "Latino." Black people of Caribbean origin make up a negligible portion of the data sample.

6. M. Oliver and T. Shapiro, *Black Wealth/White Wealth: A New Perspective on Racial Inequality* (New York: Routledge, 1995).

7. There are two general exceptions to this statement. First, Native Americans, who make up a very small portion of the population, tend to be more socioeconomically disadvantaged than blacks (although this varies by nation/tribe). Second, educational data show that some Latino groups (particularly those with limited English literacy on average) do more poorly than blacks on some measures.

8. For a discussion of skin tone and stratification, see, e.g., V.M. Keith and C. Herring, "Skin Tone and Stratification in the Black Community," *American Journal of Sociology* 97 (1991): 760–78.

9. A. Hacker, *Two Nations: Black and White, Separate, Hostile, and Unequal* (New York: Ballantine, 1992).

10. I. Light and C. Rosenstein, *Race, Ethnicity, and Entrepreneurship in Urban America* (New York: Aldine de Gruyter, 1995), p.17.

11. Ibid., p.18.

12. R.L. Boyd, "Black and Asian Self-Employment in Large Metropolitan Areas: A Comparative Analysis," *Social Problems* 37 (1990): 258–73.

13. Light and Rosenstein, *Race, Ethnicity, and Entrepreneurship*.

14. H.W. Aurand, "Self Employment: Last Resort of the Unemployed," *International Social Science Review* 58 (1983): 7–11.

15. Light and Rosenstein, *Race, Ethnicity, and Entrepreneurship*.

16. G.J Borjas and S.G. Bronars, "Consumer Discrimination and Self-Employment," *Journal of Political Economy* 97 (1989): 581–605.

17. Ibid.

The Sons Also Rise

Paul Krugman

America, we all know, is the land of opportunity. Your success in life depends on your ability and drive, not on who your father was.

Just ask the Bush brothers. Talk to Elizabeth Cheney, who holds a specially created State Department job, or her husband, chief counsel of the Office of Management and Budget. Interview Eugene Scalia, the top lawyer at the Labor Department, and Janet Rehnquist, inspector general at the Department of Health and Human Services. And don't forget to check in with William Kristol, editor of *The Weekly Standard*, and the conservative commentator John Podhoretz.

What's interesting is how little comment, let alone criticism, this roll call has occasioned. It might be just another case of kid-gloves treatment by the media, but I think it's a symptom of a broader phenomenon: inherited status is making a comeback.

It has always been good to have a rich or powerful father. Last week my Princeton colleague Alan Krueger wrote a column for *The Times* surveying statistical studies that debunk the mythology of American social mobility. "If the United States stands out in comparison with other countries," he wrote, "it is in having a more static distribution of income across generations with fewer opportunities for advancement." And Kevin Phillips, in his book "Wealth and Democracy," shows that robber-baron fortunes have been far more persistent than legend would have it.

But the past is only prologue. According to one study cited by Mr. Krueger, the heritability of status has been increasing in recent decades. And that's just the beginning. Underlying economic, social and political trends will give the children of today's wealthy a huge advantage over those who chose the wrong parents.

For one thing, there's more privilege to pass on. Thirty years ago the C.E.O. of a major company was a bureaucrat—well paid, but not truly wealthy. He couldn't give either his position or a large fortune to his heirs. Today's imperial C.E.O.'s, by contrast, will leave vast estates behind—and they are often able to give their children lucrative jobs, too. More broadly, the spectacular increase in American inequality has made the gap between the rich and the middle class wider, and hence more difficult to cross, than it was in the past.

Meanwhile, one key doorway to upward mobility—a good education system, available to all—has been closing. More and more, ambitious parents feel that a public school education is a dead end. It's telling that Jack Grubman, the former Salomon Smith Barney analyst, apparently sold his soul not for personal wealth but for two places in the right nursery school. Alas, most American souls aren't worth enough to get the kids into the 92nd Street Y.

Also, the heritability of status will be mightily reinforced by the repeal of the estate tax—a prime example of the odd way in which public policy and public opinion have shifted in favor of measures that benefit the wealthy, even as our society becomes increasingly class-ridden.

It wasn't always thus. The influential dynasties of the 20th century, like the Kennedys, the Rockefellers and, yes, the Sulzbergers, faced a public suspicious of inherited position; they overcame that suspicion by demonstrating a strong sense of noblesse oblige, justifying their existence by standing for high principles. Indeed, the Kennedy legend has a whiff of Bonnie Prince Charlie about it; the rightful heirs were also perceived as defenders of the downtrodden against the powerful.

But today's heirs feel no need to demonstrate concern for those less fortunate. On the contrary, they are often avid defenders of the powerful against the downtrodden. Mr. Scalia's principal personal claim to fame is his crusade against regulations that protect workers from ergonomic hazards, while Ms. Rehnquist has attracted controversy because of her efforts to weaken the punishment of health-care companies found to have committed fraud.

The official ideology of America's elite remains one of meritocracy, just as our political leadership pretends to be populist. But that won't last. Soon enough, our society will rediscover the importance of good breeding, and the vulgarity of talented upstarts.

For years, opinion leaders have told us that it's all about family values. And it is—but it will take a while before most people realize that they meant the value of coming from the right family.

The Wage Gap

National Committee on Pay Equity

The Wage Gap: 2000

2000 Median Annual Earnings Year-Round, Full-Time Workers

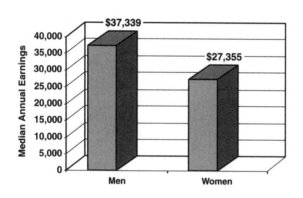

Wage Gap: 73%

2000 Median Annual Earnings by Race and Sex

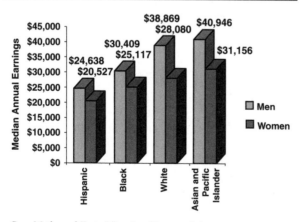

From "The Wage Gap: Myths and Facts." Reprinted by permission.

The Wage Gap: 2000 by Race and Sex

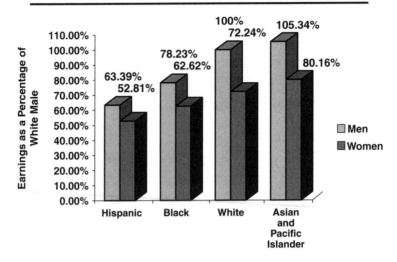

NOTES

- The wage gap is a statistical indicator often used as an index of the status of women's earnings relative to men's. It is also used to compare the earnings of people of color to those of White men.
- The wage gap is expressed as a percentage (for example, in 2000, white women earned 72 percent as much as men) and is calculated by dividing median annual earnings for women by median annual earnings for men.
- To calculate the wage gap for each race/sex group, median annual earnings are divided by those of White males, who are not subject to race- or sex-based wage discrimination.
- Individual earnings data for Asian/Pacific Islanders and Native Americans may not be representative due to the small size of the sample.
- Statistics are from the Census Bureau *Current Population Reports*, Series P-60, U.S. Commerce Department.

Highlights of Women's Earnings in 2001

The report "Highlights of Women's Earnings in 2001," released in May 2002, is based on earnings data from the Current Populations Survey (CPS), a monthly survey of approximately 50,000 households conducted by the U.S. Census Bureau for the Bureau of Labor Statistics. The report contains statistical data on the median weekly earnings of full-time wage and salary workers in 2001 by selected characteristics including: occupation, gender, state, hours usually worked (full and part-time), marital status, presence and age of own children under 18, race,

Hispanic origin, educational attainment and age. Also included in the data are hourly earnings by selected characteristics.

The report shows little change from last year. The earnings data show a wage ratio of women's to men's median weekly earnings of 76 percent in 2001. The earnings ratio in 2001 was unchanged from the earnings ratio of 76 percent in 2000. Median weekly wages for women and men follow:*

	Women	Men	Ratio
Median weekly wages 2001	$511	$672	76%
Median weekly wages 2000	$491	$646	76%

Looking at age, women in the 45 to 54 age group had the highest earnings, with a wage ratio that increased slightly between 2000 and 2001. Women aged 20–24 had a slightly lower earnings ratio in 2001:

	Women 45–54	Men 45–54	Ratio
Median weekly wages 2001	$588	$799	73.6%
Median weekly wages 2000	$565	$777	72.7%

	Women 20–24	Men 20–24	Ratio
Median weekly wages 2001	$375	$410	91.5%
Median weekly wages 2000	$364	$396	92.9%

The earnings difference was widest among whites and the ratios of earnings by race and Hispanic origin showed little change over the past year:

Women/Men Earnings Ratio, Median Weekly Wages

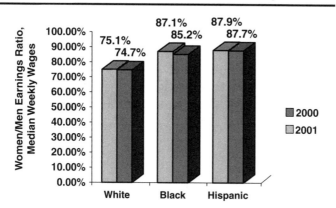

Sources: U.S. Department of Labor, Bureau of Labor Statistics, Highlights of Women's Earnings in 2001, Report 960, May 2002 & Highlights of Women's Earnings in 2000, Report 952, August 2001.

In 2001, the median weekly earnings of full-time wage and salary worker female college graduates was $784 compared to male college graduates' median weekly earnings of $1,082, a ratio of 72.5 percent, a slightly lower ratio than last year. The comparable figures in 2000 were $760 for female college graduates and $1,022 for male college graduates, a ratio of 74.4 percent.

Women's share of professional specialty and executive, administrative, and managerial occupations, typified by high earnings, was unchanged. Women comprised 51.8 percent of those in professional specialty occupations in 2001 and 51.9 percent in 2000. Women's share of full-time wage and salary workers in executive, administrative, and managerial occupations was 47.1 percent in 2001 compared to 47.0 percent in 2000.

Women who worked part-time (less than 35 hours per week) represented 24.6 percent of all female wage and salary workers in 2001, essentially unchanged from 24.5 percent in 2000, while the share of men who worked part-time was 10.6 percent in 2001 compared to 10 percent in 2000.

Women of Color in the Workplace

The wage gap is most severe for women of color. Consider these facts about the paychecks of black and Hispanic women in the workplace:*†

- Of full-time workers, black women's median weekly earnings ($429) were only 64 percent of the earnings of white men ($669) in the year 2000.
- In one year, the average black woman earns approximately $12,000 less than the average white man does. Over a thirty-five year career, this adds up to $420,000!
- Among full-time, year-round workers, black women with Bachelors' degrees make only $1,545 more per year than white males who have only completed high school.
- Black women account for 30 percent of all female-headed families in the U.S. They have a median income of $18,244 annually, while families headed by white males (no wife present) have a median income of $39,240. [Notes: (1) Income is more inclusive than earnings. (2) The term "female-headed families" does not necessarily include the presence of children.]

---

*Sources: U.S. Department of Labor, Bureau of Labor Statistics; U.S. Department of Commerce, Census Bureau.
†Additional notes: (1) Hispanic workers can be of any race. (2) Individual earnings data for Asian/Pacific Islanders and Native Americans are available, yet they are form a very small sample and thus are not as reliable. NCPE encourages advocates interested in additional data on Asian/Pacific Islanders and Native Americans to notify their Congressional representatives and encourage support for research in this area.

- According to the Census Bureau, in 2000, the median full-time earnings for Hispanic women were $20,527, only 52% of the median earnings of white men ($37,339).
- In one year, the average Hispanic woman working full-time earns $17,837 less than the average white man does. Over a 30-year career, that adds up to $510,000!
- The median income of a female Hispanic householder ($20,765) is only 46% of the incomes of single white male householders ($44,988). (*Note:* Income is more inclusive than earnings.)
- Hispanic women with a high school diploma earn $22,469. That is 33% less than white men with the same level of education.

Profile of the Wage Gap by Selected Occupations

According to an analysis of data provided by the U.S. Department of Labor's Bureau of Labor Statistics, women are paid less in almost every occupational classification for which data is available.[*]

Even in job categories where women make up the majority of workers, women are paid less. Only in two categories, miscellaneous food preparation and legal assistant, do women make more money. The women in miscellaneous food preparation average $6 more per week than men in the same occupation. They earn 102 percent of men's earnings. Female legal assistants earn 104 percent of the earnings of comparable men; they earn $20 more per week.

Below are median earnings for women and men in selected occupations. The earnings gap and earnings ratio (as a percentage) are shown, as well as the percentage of workers in each occupation who are women.

Table I
Occupations with Estimated Earnings of under $20,000[†]

Occupation	Percent Women	Men's Wages	Women's Wages	Earnings Gap	Earnings Ratio (%)
Waiter/Waitress	72%	$343	$282	$61	82%
Cleaning & Building Service Occupations	29%	$358	$288	$70	80%
Bartender	55%	$379	$293	$86	77%
Dry Cleaning Machine Operators	55%	$301	$270	$31	90%

[†]Approximate annual earnings categories were estimated by multiplying median weekly wages for men by 52 weeks.

[*]Data was analyzed using 1998 Household Data Annual Averages, Bureau of Labor Statistics.

Table II
Occupations with Estimated Earnings between $20,000 and $33,000

Occupation	Percent Women	Men's Wages	Women's Wages	Earnings Gap	Earnings Ratio (%)
Bus Driver	41%	$476	$352	$124	74%
Sales Worker;					
Retail & Personal	56%	$412	$272	$140	66%
Mechanics & Repairers	4%	$599	$519	$ 80	87%
Admin. Support,					
incl. clerical	76%	$518	$418	$100	81%
Construction Trades	2%	$545	$408	$137	75%

Table III
Occupations with Estimated Earnings above $33,000

Occupation	Percent Women	Men's Wages	Women's Wages	Earnings Gap	Earnings Ratio (%)
Accountants &					
Auditors	60%	$ 821	$618	$203	75%
Securities & Financial					
Services Sales	31%	$ 930	$598	$332	64%
Pharmacists	42%	$1,146	$985	$161	86%
Engineers	10%	$1,011	$831	$180	82%
Physicians	32%	$1,255	$966	$289	77%
Teachers,					
College & Univ.	37%	$ 998	$769	$229	77%
Lawyers	34%	$1,350	$951	$399	70%
Editors and					
Reporters	44%	$ 812	$616	$196	76%

Table IV
Other Occupations in Which the Majority of Workers Are Women

Occupation	Percent Women	Men's Wages	Women's Wages	Earnings Gap	Earnings Ratio (%)
Registered Nurse	91%	$774	$734	$40	95%
Social Worker	65%	$609	$568	$41	93%
Elementary School Teacher	84%	$749	$677	$72	90%
Secretaries, Stenographers, & Typists	98%	$484	$436	$48	90%
Cashiers	75%	$302	$259	$43	86%

The Wage Gap by Education: 2001

Following are wages reflecting the median earnings in 2001 for full-time, year-round workers, 25 years and older.

	Total	H.S. Grad.	Bachelor's	Master's
All Men	$40,706	$33,037	$53,108	$66,934
White	$41,317	$34,792	$55,307	$67,423
Non-Hispanic Whites	$43,525	$35,703	$55,845	$67,818
Black	$32,180	$27,422	$42,999	$51,336
Hispanic	$26,502	$26,944	$44,778	$60,661

	Total	H.S. Grad.	Bachelor's	Master's
All Women	$30,504	$24,253	$39,865	$48,343
White	$30,890	$24,736	$40,192	$48,615
Non-Hispanic Whites	$31,659	$25,171	$40,454	$48,757
Black	$27,351	$22,341	$36,253	$43,884
Hispanic	$22,192	$21,600	$34,060	$46,169

Data Source: U.S. Census Bureau, Current Population Survey, March 2002, Table PINC-03 "Educational Attainment"—People 25 years old and over by total money earnings in 2001 'Work' experience in 2001, age, race, Hispanic origin and sex.
Updated November 2002.

Key Findings

- Female college graduates are behind male college graduates by $13,243.
- A black college-educated female earns $19,054 less annually than the college-educated white male.
- A Hispanic college-educated female makes $21,247 less annually than the college-educated white male.

The Wage Gap over Time

In Real Dollars, Women See a Continuing Gap

Since the Equal Pay Act was signed in 1963, the wage gap has been closing at a very slow rate. In 1963, women who worked full-time, year-round made 59 cents on average for every dollar earned by men. In 2000, women earned 73 cents to the dollar. That means that the wage gap has narrowed by a little over a third of a penny per year!

Over the past 38 years, the real median earnings of women have fallen short by a total of $497,319—nearly half a million dollars. Thus, on an annual basis the average woman earns approximately $13,087 less than the average man does.

The wage gap narrowed from 64% in 1986 to 73% in 2000, but some of this is due to a decrease in men's real wages rather than an increase in women's real wages. In fact, since last year, the wage gap has narrowed slightly by one percentage point due to a decline in men's earnings and a leveling off among those of women.

Year	Women's Earnings	Men's Earnings	Dollar Difference	Percent
2000	$27,355	$37,339	$ 9,984	73.0%
1999	$27,208	$37,701	$10,493	72.2%
1998	$27,290	$37,296	$10,006	73.2%
1997	$26,720	$36,030	$ 9,310	74.2%
1996	$25,919	$35,138	$ 9,219	73.8%
1995	$25,260	$35,365	$10,105	71.4%
1994	$25,558	$35,513	$ 9,955	72.0%
1993	$25,579	$35,765	$10,186	71.5%
1992	$25,791	$36,436	$10,645	70.8%
1991	$25,457	$36,440	$10,983	69.9%
1990	$25,451	$35,538	$10,087	71.6%
1989	$25,310	$36,855	$11,545	66.0%
1988	$24,774	$37,509	$12,735	66.0%
1987	$24,663	$37,389	$12,726	65.2%
1986	$24,479	$38,088	$13,609	64.3%

Year	Women's Earnings	Men's Earnings	Dollar Difference	Percent
1985	$23,978	$37,131	$13,153	64.6%
1984	$23,453	$36,842	$13,389	63.7%
1983	$22,961	$36,106	$13,055	63.6%
1982	$22,367	$36,224	$13,857	61.7%
1981	$21,830	$36,854	$15,024	59.2%
1980	$22,279	$37,033	$14,754	60.2%
1979	$22,446	$37,622	$15,176	59.7%
1978	$22,617	$38,051	$15,005	59.4%
1977	$21,743	$36,901	$15,158	58.9%
1976	$21,738	$36,114	$14,376	60.2%
1975	$21,297	$36,207	$14,910	58.8%
1974	$21,419	$36,456	$15,037	58.8%
1973	$21,397	$37,381	$15,984	56.6%
1972	$21,185	$36,614	$15,429	57.9%
1971	$20,691	$34,771	$14,080	59.5%
1970	$20,567	$34,642	$14,075	59.4%
1969	$20,156	$34,241	$14,085	58.9%
1968	$18,836	$32,389	$13,553	58.2%
1967	$18,241	$31,568	$13,327	57.8%
1966	$17,874	$31,055	$13,181	57.6%
1965	$17,852	$29,791	$11,939	59.9%
1964	$17,368	$29,362	$11,994	59.1%
1963	$16,908	$28,684	$11,776	58.9%
1962	$16,587	$27,972	$11,385	59.3%
1961	$16,272	$27,463	$11,191	59.2%
1960	$16,144	$26,608	$10,464	60.7%

Source: Census Bureau, 2000 Current Population Reports, Median Earning of Workers 15 Years Old and Over by Work Experience and Sex
Note: All figures in 2000 dollars; updated September, 2001.

Her Next Step?
Growing Numbers of American Women Face Retirement Financially Insecure

Albert B. Crenshaw

In many ways, Irene LaMarche has lived a classic American life: college, work, marriage, family, divorce, work, retirement.

But now, at 76, she can't make ends meet.

Some of her early jobs didn't pay into Social Security but instead gave her small lump sums when she left them, and she has no pension coverage from her ex-husband. The Boise, Idaho, resident did get $60,000 from selling her home, and she invested that. All told, she now has a total income of a little over $1,000 a month, and this spring she had to move out of her apartment when the rent jumped to $795. She has found a cheaper place, but even so she needs public assistance to cover the $545 monthly rent.

"I have never lived extravagantly and have scrimped all my life," she told the Senate Committee on Aging recently, and the rent subsidy "is the first help I've ever asked for."

Joan Mackey's story is similar. The Philadelphia woman divorced her abusive husband after 21 years of marriage and, concerned only with her safety and support for her three children, didn't pay much attention to the nuances of the property settlement.

So when her ex-husband became fatally ill a couple of years later, she believed him when he assured her that she would get pension benefits from his employer.

Wrong, said the employer. Because her attorney had not asked for a court order during the divorce proceedings, her husband's former employer said it could not pay.

Mackey now works as a real estate agent and does direct marketing for a dry-cleaning company of which she is part owner, and she is trying to build a

From *The Washington Post* (June 2, 2002) © 2002, the Washington Post. Reprinted with permission.

retirement nest egg. But "I am now 48 years old, and I am very worried about what I will live on when I can't work anymore," she said.

"I know I am not alone in being very frightened about my future financial security," she added.

- In 2000, the median personal income for women 65 and older was $10,899. For men in the same age group, it was $19,168.
- For 1 in 4 women, Social Security is the only source of income.
- Fewer than 1 in 5 women age 65 and older received a private pension in 2000.
- More single young women ages 21-34 (53 percent) said they were living from paycheck to paycheck than did single young men (42 percent).

Indeed she is not alone. LaMarche, a current retiree, and Mackey, a baby boomer, reflect the situations of a growing number of American women.

Divorce, childbearing and family demands. Bad advice, discrimination, longer lifespans. Those and a host of other factors conspire to place women at much greater risk of financial trouble in retirement than men—and may consign millions of them to poverty or near-poverty in their old age.

Compared with men, women on average live longer but:

- Earn less.
- Save less.
- Are less likely to have a pension.

"Women's experience growing old in America is very different from men's," said Laurie Young, executive director of the Older Women's League, a nonprofit women's group in Washington. "The financial problems women often face in old age are an extension of the problems and choices they faced earlier in their lives."

Although more women are now in the workforce than ever before—and they have made considerable progress on pay and other issues—they still earn less than men in most jobs. On average, according to the Women's Institute for Secure Retirement, a Washington-based education and advocacy group, women earn 73 cents for every dollar that men earn. And according to calculations by the Institute for Women's Policy Research, a 25-year-old woman with a college degree would typically earn about $523,000 less than a man over her lifetime.

About two-thirds of women working full time earn less than $30,000 a year, said Cindy Hounsell, executive director of the women's institute. And, despite improvements in opportunity and pay, many younger women aren't getting ahead.

For example, younger women are more likely to carry credit card debt than younger men are, she said.

In addition, women's careers tend to be much more erratic than men's, primarily because of childbearing and other family demands.

This pattern often means first quitting work to stay home with young children, and then perhaps quitting again, or working what amounts to two jobs later in life, to care for a parent or other relative.

On average, women spend 12 years out of the workforce for family caregiving over the course of their lives, according to the Older Women's League. And not just for children. Currently, as many as 52 million Americans, mostly women, are "informal caregivers, providing unpaid care and financial support to people with chronic illnesses or disabilities," the group figures.

"Caregiving can be an economic disaster for women and is one of the largest barriers to their retirement security," said Young. "Caregiving shapes women's workforce participation, as they often take more-flexible, lower-wage jobs with few benefits, or stop working altogether in order to provide unpaid caregiving services."

"As a result of caregiving, women lose an average of $550,000 in lifetime wage wealth and about $2,100 annually in already desperately needed Social Security benefits," she said.

The pattern of women's employment has an even harsher effect on pensions than lower earnings do. Traditional pension plans generally employ a formula in calculating benefits that rewards long-tenured, higher-paid workers. Those who are paid less, and especially those who are on the job fewer years, get much lower benefits or none at all.

Some experts have been optimistic that the shift in company pensions in recent years toward 401(k) and similar plans would benefit women. These pensions are usually "portable," meaning that they can be transferred to a new employer or rolled over into an individual retirement account so that there is less of a penalty for changing jobs.

But a new study by the Institute for Women's Policy Research, funded in part by the Labor Department, found that things may not work out that way. In practice, workers who leave a job are allowed, or sometimes even required, to take the money from their 401(k) or similar retirement plan in a lump sum.

When such distributions are made, it appears that women, in part because of the financial pressure they are under, are more likely to spend the money than to roll it over into an IRA or transfer it to a plan at their new employer.

"Both men and women spend their lump-sum payments at an alarming rate. Women's slightly greater propensity to use pension payments for everyday expenses"—23.3 percent who received a lump-sum distribution vs. 20.9 percent of men—suggests the trend toward 401(k) and similar plans could create special problems for women, the study said.

A further problem in private pensions and benefits arises when women depend on their husbands. Over the years, laws have been changed to prevent men from opting for a pension annuity that is higher but ends at his death, leaving his widow with nothing. Today, the wife has to agree in writing to such a choice.

All of those facts—women as childbearers, women as caregivers, women in and out of the workforce—would be rendered harmless were it not for another fact of modern American life: divorce. If the childbearer and caregiver has a husband who works steadily throughout the years, earning the maximum Social Security benefits, qualifying for a pension, and/or contributing to a 401(k) plan or IRA, she can face retirement at his side, well provided for. But so often that's not the case.

In divorces, as Mackey found, employer-sponsored pensions and insurance are property to be divided up between the spouses. While wives have claims on these assets, they often undervalue them when compared with more visible (and more immediately needed) assets such as the house. As a result, they often don't fight for the pension or insurance rights.

John Hotz of the Pension Rights Center in Washington warned women not to give up their claim to the husband's pension without proper compensation. The pension could be worth thousands and thousands of dollars over their retired lifetimes.

Mackey said her husband's pension would have been worth $150 to $200 a month—not a large sum, but month after month, year after year, a welcome supplement to Social Security and her own savings.

In addition to the male-female gap in private pensions, the Social Security system doesn't always work in women's favor.

LaMarche, for example, held several public-school teaching jobs that were exempt from the Social Security system at the time, so she earned no credits for those years. Instead, she got a lump sum from the schools' plan when she left—which she spent because she needed the money.

And married women who do work and pay their Social Security taxes often find that they are required to choose between their husband's benefits and their own. Because their husband's benefits are typically larger, the women take them—but then they get nothing for all the taxes they have paid into the system. Like many of the "marriage penalties" that now plague working women under the income tax law, these rules were written at a time when most married women did not work outside the home and were intended to protect, not hurt, them.

But today "6 of every 10 women pay a huge amount of Social Security taxes, usually more than they pay in income taxes, and receive no added benefits," said former Social Security commissioner Dorcas R. Hardy.

"A woman who works outside the home and qualifies for half her husband's retirement benefit will pay Social Security payroll taxes week after week, decade after decade, but she will receive benefits no higher than those received by another woman who is not in the workforce and pays no payroll taxes at all," Hardy said.

"She might as well take those tax dollars, including the payroll taxes paid by her employer—a total of roughly one-eighth of her income—and start a bonfire," she said.

The overall picture is beginning to worry policymakers, as Sen. Larry E. Craig (R-Idaho) made clear at the Committee on Aging hearing where most of the women's groups appeared. But there are no easy answers.

Certain fixes would help, experts say.

For example, Hotz of the Pension Rights Center said one helpful thing would be changes in the law to clarify that surviving ex-spouses have the right to their ex-husband's pension benefits unless they specifically forgo them. He said this would be particularly helpful to less sophisticated women who now often lose such benefits because they do not know to ask for them.

But broader changes, such as restructuring Social Security, providing assistance to female caregivers, equalizing women's pay and others that many groups advocate, run afoul of costs, resistance from employers and others, and fears of unintended consequences of the sort that now hit married working women under Social Security and the tax law.

So in the meantime many are urging women to educate themselves, to save and invest, and to take pension benefits into account whenever they take or leave a job.

Savings of even most amounts over a long period can produce a substantial nest egg, one that could be enough to avoid poverty in old age. But women—and men, too—must understand that they have to start early and invest carefully.

Many middle-class families that have trouble saving could in fact squeeze from their budgets enough to participate in their 401(k) or other retirement plan. But lower-wage women may not be able to, even assuming they are eligible.

Said Hounsell of the Women's Institute for a Secure Retirement: "As long as women earn less money than men, work part time and experience more interruptions from paid work, retirement security will remain elusive."

55

Billionaire's Ex-Wife Wants $4,400 a Day to Raise Daughter

David Rohde

Patricia Duff unveiled for the first time yesterday exactly how much child support she says she needs from her billionaire ex-husband, Ronald O. Perelman, to raise their 4-year-old daughter—$4,400 a day for the next 14 years.

Ms. Duff's request, which totals $22.3 million, came as she concluded her phase of a snail-like custody trial in State Supreme Court in Manhattan. Ms. Duff, a prominent Democratic fund-raiser who is worth $23 million, and Mr. Perelman, the majority owner of Revlon Inc. who is worth an estimated $6 billion, have been locked in an ugly custody and child support battle over their daughter, Caleigh, for the last three years.

If Ms. Duff is awarded the amounts that she requested, Mr. Perelman will pay $1.6 million a year in child support, in addition to $1.3 million in alimony, to Ms. Duff until Caleigh turns 18. Ms. Duff's supporters contend that such a settlement is piddling to a multibillionaire like Mr. Perelman.

On the witness stand yesterday, Ms. Duff presented a detailed budget listing Caleigh's monthly living expenses. According to Ms. Duff, she spends $9,953 each month on travel expenses for Caleigh and her nanny. A total of $3,175 a month is spent on clothing for Caleigh, and $3,585 on "recreational" activities, she said. The cost of Caleigh's personal domestic employees—apparently nannies and maids—is $30,098 a month, and the 4-year-old dines out at a cost of $1,450 a month, Ms. Duff said.

As they have throughout the trial, Mr. Perelman's representatives ridiculed the figures and suggested that Ms. Duff was trying to use her daughter to pad her income. "In her testimony, Ms. Duff was only able to estimate actual expenses for Caleigh of $5,000 a month, or $60,000 a year," said Allen Rubenstein, a spokesman for Mr. Perelman. "These numbers speak for themselves."

In a June 1998 affidavit, Ms. Duff estimated her monthly child support needs at $87,000 a month. The figure that she proposed yesterday was $132,000 a month.

She also included a request that Mr. Perelman pay part of Caleigh's housing costs. The cost of the Upper East Side apartment and the Connecticut and East Hampton, N.Y., homes that Ms. Duff is proposing would range from $1 million a year to $750,000 a year, she said. She also estimated $1.3 million to $2 million in initial first-year start-up costs.

Ms. Duff's time on the witness stand was not as contentious as in recent days, when she was repeatedly reprimanded by Justice Franklin R. Weissberg for failing to answer questions. When asked whether Caleigh's nanny also flew first-class on four weekend trips to Florida in 1997, she replied, "Absolutely."

After her testimony, Ms. Duff repeated the argument of her lawyer, Richard D. Emery, that Caleigh should enjoy the same standard of living as Mr. Perelman's children from previous marriages. She said the life style that she was requesting paled in comparison to the type of luxury that Mr. Perelman lived in.

"It's not private jets," she said. "It's not a big yacht. It's rough parity with an Upper East Side family. It's a privileged life, no question about it."

56

The Education of Jessica Rivera

Kim Phillips-Fein

Jessica Rivera (not her real name) is a slight, composed 20-year-old Hunter College student. She grew up in the Bronx, raised by her mother and extended family. No one in her family has completed college, so Rivera was thrilled to get accepted to Hunter College, one of the best schools in the City University of New York. "It was my top choice," she says.

In the legendary heyday of City College in the 1930s and '40s, Rivera's could have been a classic story of upward mobility. Had she enjoyed similar opportunities, she might even have wound up with Irving Howe and Daniel Bell, "arguing the world" in the cafeteria alcoves. But Rivera's mother—who was injured at the Bronx factory that she worked at many years ago—is on public assistance. When Rivera turned 18, welfare caseworkers told her she would have to report for twenty to thirty hours a week to the city's Work Experience Program (WEP) if she wanted to keep collecting the benefits she and her mother depend on. "They offered me jobs working in the park, cleaning toilets, cleaning transportation." The long hours would have made it nearly impossible to continue at Hunter as a full-time student. At 18, Rivera was faced with a choice between quitting school for a dead-end job and losing her family's income.

For middle-class Americans, society offers myriad incentives for higher education: scholarships, interest-free loans and the "Hope" tax credits. But for women on welfare, it's a different story. In September the 1996 welfare reform law was up for Congressional reauthorization. The vote did not happen then, because of divergences between a bill in the Senate, written by moderate Republicans and Democrats, and the Bush Administration's vision of welfare reform, reflected in a House bill. The welfare law expired September 30, and no compromise bill or temporary legislation is yet ready to take its place.

One of the sticking points was that the Senate legislation would have made it easier for welfare recipients to go to college. Bush, however, told the *New York Times* in July that he does not think a college education teaches "the importance of work," nor does he think it can "[help] people achieve the dignity necessary so that they can live a free life, free from government control." Now that all three branches of government are controlled by Republicans, it seems likely that the Bush Administration's vision will soon be reflected in law.

From *The Nation* (November 25, 2002) pp. 20–23.

The Personal Responsibility and Work Opportunity Reconciliation Act of 1996 mandates that recipients of public assistance work in return for their checks. They must either find jobs or, failing this, participate in state-run work programs for a minimum of thirty hours a week (split between twenty hours of paid or unpaid work, and ten hours of participation in other programs like job-search services). Should states fail to meet this work requirement, they face the loss of federal grants. (Many cities, like New York, have raised the number of required work hours above the federal minimum—in the case of New York, to thirty-five per week. It's called a "simulated work week.")

Under the 1996 law, college education cannot be substituted for any part of the primary work requirement. In New York City the result is clear: Before welfare reform, 28,000 CUNY students were on welfare. By spring 2002, 5,000 were—a decline even steeper than the celebrated 60 percent drop in New York City's welfare rolls. Today, although nearly 60 percent of welfare recipients in the city lack a high school diploma or a GED, only 2 percent are enrolled in ESL or GED programs, and fewer than 4 percent are engaged in full-time education or training. "New York City has one of the most sophisticated systems of higher education in the country, but welfare recipients are essentially shut out of it," says Wendy Bach, an attorney at the Urban Justice Center who works with welfare recipients.

The basic presumption behind welfare reform is the harsh moral logic of the workhouse. Welfare recipients, so the theory goes, are poor because they lack the discipline to hold down a job. But women who are struggling to seize hold of a little bit of upward mobility have a different experience: They feel like they work all the time.

Patricia Williams, a 32-year-old Brooklyn native and mother of a gorgeous, energetic 18-month-old girl, graduated from Hunter last year. She plans to go back to school someday for a master's. "I want to run a high-quality daycare center," says Williams, who was orphaned at an early age. When she started working, she did temp jobs—"everything from assembling the folders for the new Macy's event to setting up perfume samples to shelling nuts." After a while she decided to get an associate's degree in computer services. Lacking parents who could help her out, she applied for welfare as a kind of financial aid. "I went on public assistance to get ahead." After completing her degree, she enrolled at Hunter. But then came welfare reform, and she had to enter WEP.

William's first assignment under WEP was housekeeping at a community senior-citizen center in downtown Manhattan. It wasn't a job she would have chosen—she lives in Brooklyn and commutes to Hunter, on the Upper East Side, for school. But she got up at 5:30 every morning to be at work at 7:30, "cleaning bathrooms and gathering garbage." At noon, she went uptown for class, then back downtown in the late afternoon for another stint of maid work. At the community center, "they knew me as Pat the WEP worker," she said. "They didn't know that I had my associate's, or that I was working toward my bachelor's."

The final straw came in her last semester at Hunter. She asked her supervisor for a change in her schedule, so that she could fulfill a student teaching requirement she needed in order to graduate. "I said I would work late, on weekends."

When WEP refused, she quit. Immediately, she lost her food stamps and Medicaid. At a hearing downtown, she says, she asked a city representative, "Is it fair that I am being pulled out of school to do a dead-end WEP job?" The city worker replied, "You need to know what commitment is and what it takes to report to work. . . .

Even as New York moves to the center of the national debate over welfare policy, local politicians are starting to respond to pressure to change the law—much of which is coming from welfare recipients themselves. In 2000 the Welfare Rights Initiative (WRI), a Hunter-based organization of current and former welfare recipients, successfully lobbied the state legislature to enact a bill permitting work-study and internships to substitute for work requirements. In spring 2002 Gifford Miller, the Speaker of the City Council, proposed a bill allowing welfare recipients to substitute college course work for WEP. Meanwhile, in Maine, legislators have used state-level funds to support college students on welfare. The program (called Parents as Scholars) has been very successful. The women it serves earn a median wage of $11.71 upon graduation—compared with $8 for women before entering college; they are also more likely to work in jobs that offer health benefits. Ninety percent of Maine women who earned a degree while on welfare have left the rolls, with every indication that they will stay off.

But while innovative local programs are all to the good, the restrictive federal policies with regard to college for welfare recipients are part of a larger social shift toward a constriction of access to higher education for poor and working-class Americans. . . .

When Bush ran for president in 2000, he described himself as the "education President," because ever since Horatio Alger, education has been touted as the key to upward mobility. But in truth, the question of who has access to college has always been deeply social and political. College enrollments exploded during the great postwar boom, in the heyday of high union density and the welfare state, and today's college gap simultaneously reflects and perpetuates the haughty isolation of the rich.

Young women like Jessica Rivera, though, clearly benefit from whatever changes local organizations can make. Just when she was about to give up on school, Rivera learned about WRI. With legal help provided by the advocacy group, she successfully pleaded her case before a hearing officer to substitute work-study hours for WEP under the state law. The rising junior says she isn't yet sure what she wants to major in, but she knows she wants to get a master's degree—even, someday, a PhD. "Who wants to be on welfare? I'm going to have my own job and be independent—I don't need to depend on anybody," she says cheerfully. But, at the same time, when she thinks about her mother, Rivera's face grows sad and reflective. With a gentleness that seems to contradict her spunk, she softly says, "Some people just have to be on welfare." It is anybody's guess what our President—whose Poppy surely paid for Yale—thinks young women like Rivera will learn about responsibility or commitment picking up trash in Central Park.

57

What Scholars Can Tell Politicians about the Poor

Katherine S. Newman

Welfare reform is a lightning rod for the discontented American middle class, which has been shaken by levels of economic insecurity that were hard to imagine a mere 20 years ago. The years of corporate buyouts, hostile takeovers, mergers, bankruptcies, and downsizing have left the average American with stagnant wages, increasing pressure to work greater hours, and the nagging sense that this scenario is no longer temporary. It is hardly surprising that, in this climate and in the panic over the nation's deficit, the search for scapegoats has taken on a new sense of urgency.

Welfare mothers seem to fill the bill nicely. Conservatives argue that the nation's economy is sagging under the burden of supporting the poor. Cutting off welfare benefits, we are told, is the best medicine: It will eliminate the incentives that reward dependency and replace them with the traditional work ethic. We may lose a few poor people or their children along the way, but ultimately this social-Darwinist strategy is supposed to pay off as the poor straighten up and fly into the labor market.

The recipe is appealing, because it taps into tenets of American culture that date to Benjamin Franklin: belief in the work ethic, hostility toward sloth, and conviction that individuals are the masters of their own fate. And it resonates with voters because conservative welfare reformers have convinced them that there are, in fact, lots of jobs going begging.

For the past two years, my research team has studied a real inner-city labor market, to discover how people go about finding jobs in a depressed area, how much competition exists for employment, and what those who have jobs do with the money they earn. This study of workers in the fast-food industry, in New York City's Harlem, is one-half of a comparative project; the other half is under way in Oakland, Cal., where Carol B. Stack, a professor of education at the University of California at Berkeley, has followed a comparable sample of fast-food workers.

The project was born out of a desire to expand on a much-discussed body of research on the urban underclass. It was spurred largely by the work of the sociologist William Julius Wilson at the University of Chicago. In his landmark 1987 book, *The Truly Disadvantaged: The Inner City, the Underclass, and Public Policy*, Mr. Wilson argues that the decline of manufacturing jobs and the growth of service-industry jobs that demand strong academic credentials have created a massive population of jobless poor in the urban North who are geographically and socially segregated from the mainstream working population. He and other theorists of the underclass maintain that minorities' social isolation removes role models, destroys access to social networks crucial for employment, and undercuts belief in the value of schooling. These negative features of life among the unemployed are said to characterize inner-city ghettos as a whole.

The emphasis on the jobless poor has, however, obscured what I believe is an equally important population: the working poor. These are the people who go to work every day, as Jesse Jackson has said—the people who make beds in hospitals, make change in stores, and serve hamburgers in fast-food restaurants. Academic researchers who study poverty have spent relatively little time examining the lives and struggles of ghetto dwellers who participate in the mainstream economy at its bottom level. So it should not surprise us that policy makers and members of the public think of the poor as distinctly different from working people.

Yet even in some of our most economically depressed inner cities, working for a living remains a key norm. In central Harlem, where my research was conducted, about 40 percent of the population exist on incomes below the poverty line, 29 percent live on public assistance, and 18 percent are officially unemployed. But many people do participate in the mainstream world of work. In fact, 67 percent of the households in this part of New York include at least one full-time worker.

The literature on the underclass emphasizes the social isolation of the poor—the geographic separation of the jobless from the stable working population and their exclusion from vital social networks. Far from being segregated from one another, however, the working and non-working poor in Harlem live together. Because the service-industry employees in our study work for the minimum wage, they are not able to escape from the inner city. They continue to live in some of the city's most depressed neighborhoods, even though they go to work every day and bring their wages home as one contribution (among many) to the support of poverty-level households. They participate in lateral social networks that do, indeed, facilitate job hunting, but since the networks are composed largely of other minimum-wage workers, they do not foster upward mobility.

However, these service workers are also well acquainted with people who live in much better parts of the city and in the suburbs. Their well-off acquaintances constitute a vertical network composed largely of older friends and family members, beneficiaries of the better employment opportunities of the past. These more-fortunate people were able to leave the ghetto when they got a job in manufacturing in the 1960s or later in the public sector (public transit, local utilities, the post office) or in the military.

Because public-sector and military jobs are getting scarcer, and many manufacturing jobs have disappeared, these middle-class friends and relatives cannot do much to help their younger relatives move up in the world. But they do constitute a network of people who present examples of success to nephews, nieces, and grandchildren locked into low-wage jobs. Thus people in the inner city do have role models in these vertical networks, although that's not enough to set them on the path of upward mobility.

In some respects, however, the low-wage earners we have studied are the lucky ones in central Harlem, where jobs are in extremely short supply. In the fast-food industry, where most jobs pay only the minimum wage, and opportunities for significant advancement are modest, the competition for jobs is nonetheless fierce. During the five-month period in 1993 when we tracked this labor market, we found that the ratio of job seekers to job-finders was 14 to 1. That is, 14 people applied for every job opening at $4.25 per hour. When we interviewed the rejected job seekers a year later, we discovered that 73 percent of them were still unemployed, even though they had continued to pound the pavement. There simply were not enough jobs to go around.

We found that people under the age of 20 had a much harder time getting fast-food jobs than did their older counterparts. Restaurant jobs are the stereotypical form of entry-level employment, and in suburban communities boasting many different kinds of jobs, they remain a major mechanism for introducing young people to the world of work. But in the inner city they have become "real" jobs, which adults are taking to try to support their families. This simultaneously removes the opportunity for young people to get a foot in the door and places enormous pressure on households struggling to make ends meet on $4.25 an hour.

African Americans are finding the going particularly rough, even in neighborhoods such as central Harlem, where they constitute a majority of the residents. Although almost 70 percent of the "new hires" in our study were African Americans, black job applicants were more likely than Latinos to be rejected. The applicant pool in Harlem is overwhelmingly composed of blacks, but Latino job seekers enjoy disproportionate success. Only 13.6 percent of African-American applicants for the jobs we studied were hired, while 38 percent of other minority applicants—primarily Latinos—were hired.

We also found that immigrants had an advantage. Employers apparently believe that immigrants from poor countries are better candidates for low-wage jobs because they look upon our minimum wage as a relatively good salary, while native-born job seekers see it as the bottom of the barrel.

Thus competition among members of minority groups struggling for a foothold on the employment ladder is growing, as is the social tension that the competition produces on the street and behind the counter. Although politicians point to the economic success of unschooled immigrants as proof that native-born members of minority groups have retreated to the comforts of the welfare system, our research shows no such thing. Instead, the people we studied are battling for the declining number of opportunities available, with some gaining and most losing.

What we found in Harlem should, at one level, be heartwarming, even to the most conservative policy maker: a strong commitment to the work ethic, a persistent effort to find jobs, and a realistic sense of the rewards of the low-wage world. On the "values" end of this debate, then, much evidence exists to support the notion that the inner-city labor force is eager to join the mainstream. The problem lies in the lack of opportunity—a fact that legislators and other national policy makers ignore or are not aware of.

This is particularly unfortunate for those who need a job to help pay for their education. Fifty-eight percent of the African Americans working in Harlem's fast-food industry have a high-school diploma, and most of the rest are still enrolled in school. More than half of the workers—black and Latino—who have finished high school are taking courses in vocational schools, junior colleges, or regular colleges. Minimum-wage jobs are vital sources of "financial aid" for working poor students. Without this employment, many would find it impossible to continue their schooling.

The country desperately needs more employment opportunities, even at the entry level, to accommodate the demand for work among inner-city residents. This is particularly true if we hope to absorb welfare recipients into the work force—which is going to be much more difficult than most policy makers suggest. Long-term welfare recipients are less qualified for employment in terms of academic credentials and work experience than are today's average job seekers in Harlem. Those forced off the welfare rolls and into the labor market are going to find the competition stiff and their own prospects dim.

Policy makers, as well as scholars, must realize that, in addition to the persistently jobless population described in research literature on the underclass, the United States is blessed with a significant number of responsible poor people who want, above all, to participate in the mainstream economy. Despite their poverty, the working poor continue to believe that education provides the best way out, that getting a job is important, and that people who don't work are not to be admired.

The working poor are, however, faced with the fact that few jobs of any kind are available to them, much less those that can support a family.

Dismantling the welfare system is not the way to solve the problem of persistent poverty. That problem can't be wished away, nor can the inner-city residents who scramble for the few jobs available. Scholars must press policy makers to take into account the persistent efforts of ghetto dwellers to find work, and to reward that diligence with real job opportunities, not mere rhetoric urging them to do exactly what they already are trying to do—find employment.

Suggestions for Further Reading

AFL-CIO and Institute for Women's Policy Research. *Equal Pay for Working Families.* Washington, DC: 1999.

Albelda, Randy. *Economics and Feminism: Disturbances in the Field.* New York: Twayne, 1996.

Anderson, Sarah, et al. *A Decade of Executive Excess: The 1990s.* Boston: United for a Fair Economy, 1999.

Brouwer, Steve. *Sharing the Pie.* New York: Henry Holt, 1998.

Children's Defense Fund. *The State of America's Children.* Washington, DC: Children's Defense Fund, 2001 (published annually).

Collins, Chuck, and Felice Yeskel. *Economic Apartheid in America: A Primer on Economic Inequality and Security.* New York: New Press, 2000.

Domhoff, G. William. *Who Rules America Now?* New York: Simon & Schuster, 1983.

Ehrenreich, Barbara. *Nickel and Dimed.* Owl Books, 2002.

Gans, Herbert J. *The War Against the Poor.* New York: Basic Books, 1995.

Hacker, Andrew. *Two Nations.* New York: Scribner's, 1992.

Hacker, Andrew. *Money: Who Has How Much and Why.* New York: Touchstone Books, 1998.

Hartman, Chester. *Double Exposure: Poverty & Race in America.* Armonk, NY: M. E. Sharpe, 1997.

Keister, Lisa A. *Wealth in America: Trends in Wealth Inequality.* Cambridge: Cambridge University Press, 2000.

Kozol, Jonathan. *Savage Inequalities: Children in America's Schools.* New York: Crown Publishers, 1991.

Mishel, Lawrence, et al. *The State of Working America 2000–2001.* Ithaca, NY: Cornell University Press, 2001.

Newman, Katherine S. *No Shame in My Game: The Working Poor in the Inner City.* New York: Vintage Books, 2000.

Phillips, Kevin. *The Politics of the Rich and the Poor.* New York: Random House, 1990.

Phillips, Kevin. *Wealth in America: A Political History of the American Rich.* Broadway Books, 2002.

Polakrow, Valerie. *Lives on the Edge: Single Women and Their Children in the Other America.* Chicago: University of Chicago Press, 1993.

Sernau, Scott. *Worlds Apart: Social Inequalities in a New Century.* California: Pine Forge Press, 2001.

Sidel, Ruth. *Keeping Women and Children Last.* New York: Penguin Books, 1996.

Sklar, Holly. *Chaos or Community: Seeking Solutions Not Scapegoats for Bad Economics.* Boston: South End Press, 1995.

Sklar, Holly, et al. *Raise the Floor: Wages and Policies That Work for All of Us.* Boston: South End Press, 2002.

Wolff, Edward N. *Top Heavy: The Increasing Inequality of Wealth in America and What Can Be Done About It,* 2nd Ed. New York: New Press, 2002.

In addition to these books, the following organizations are good sources for obtaining current statistics analyzed in terms of race, class, and gender:

The Association for American Indian Affairs, 432 Park Avenue South, New York, NY 10016.

United for a Fair Economy, 37 Temple Place, Boston, MA 02111.

Institute for Women's Policy Research, 1400 20th Street NW, Suite 104, Washington, DC 20036.

Institute for Gay and Lesbian Strategic Studies, P.O. Box 2603, Amherst, MA.

Council on International and Public Affairs, Suite 3C, 777 United Nations Plaza, New York, NY 10017.

The National Urban League, Inc., 500 East 62nd Street, New York, NY 10021.

The National Committee on Pay Equity, 1201 Sixteenth Street NW, Room 422, Washington, DC 20036.

Southern Regional Council, Inc., 60 Walton NW, Atlanta, GA 30303.

PART V

Many Voices, Many Lives: Some Consequences of Racial, Gender, and Class Inequality

STATISTICS CAN TELL US LOT ABOUT LIFE IN ANY given society, yet they paint only part of the picture. They can tell us that more than 110,000 Japanese Americans were herded into relocation camps during World War II, but they can tell us little of the lives lived in those camps or of the repercussions on those lives years later. They can tell us that every day four women die in this country as a result of domestic violence, but they cannot convey what it means to live in an abusive relationship. Statistics can tell us a story with numbers, but they cannot translate those numbers into lived experience. For that, we must turn to stories about people's lives.

Who will tell these stories? For many years, and not so long ago, the voices of the majority of people in our society were missing from the books in libraries and on our course reading lists. The experiences of women from all racial and ethnic groups regardless of their class position were missing, as was the history, culture, and experience of many men. In their place were the writings and teachings of a relatively small group—predominantly privileged, white, and male—who offered their experience and their perspective as if it were universal. Ironically, even books about breast-feeding and childbirth were authored exclusively by male "experts" who defined and described a reality they had never known. White sociologists, psychologists, and anthropologists set themselves up as experts on American Indian, Hispanic, Black, and Asian experience and culture, offering elaborate, critical accounts of the family structure and lifestyle of each group. Novels chronicling the growth to manhood of young white males from the upper or middle class were routinely assigned in high school and college English courses and examined for "universal themes," while novels about the experiences of men of color, working people, and women of all groups were relegated to "special interest" courses and treated as marginal. In short, by definition, serious scholarship, "real" science, and "great" literature was what had been produced by well-to-do white males and often focused exclusively on their experiences; accounts of the lives of other groups, if available at all, were rarely written by members of those groups.

We are fortunate that more accounts of the lives of ordinary people have become available over the past 20 or 30 years, largely as a result of the creation of Women's Studies, Ethnic Studies, and Lesbian and Gay Studies as academic disciplines. These accounts fill in some of the gaps in the limited experience each of us brings to our study of race, class, gender, and sexuality. The selections in Part V are offered as a way of putting flesh and blood around the bare-bones facts provided in Part IV. They provide us with an opportunity to move outside the limits of our particular identity, at least for a few minutes, and find out what the world looks like from someone else's perspective. In Part V we get a glimpse of what it was like to be Japanese American growing up on the West Coast during World War II as Yuri Kochiyama shares his experiences, first in California and then in a relocation camp in Jerome, Arkansas. We listen in as Sonia Shah talks about what it means to be an Asian American in the United States and see how the socially constructed stereotypes and categories embedded in that term look through her eyes. We listen as Evelyn Alsultany, daughter of an Iraqi father and a Cuban mother, talks about her anger and frustration over being asked to choose which part of her identity she will embrace—a choice she refuses to make. We stand on a cardboard box with Dave Grossman, down the street from his junior high, as the seventh-grader proudly announces that he is gay. And we walk the streets of Brooklyn, New York, with June Jordan as she reflects upon her own childhood and the childhood boxer Mike Tyson knew, a 25-minute bus ride from her house. Each of these essays and the others in Part V provide us with unique opportunities to look at everyday life in the United States using the lenses of race, gender, class, and sexuality to see things we may not have noticed before.

In addition, they broaden our range of vision to include some of the other factors that can have significant impact on life choices, among them religion, age, physical condition, and geographical location. Some of these factors are touched upon or highlighted as well in these readings. In some contexts, these factors play a major role in shaping the way others treat us, in determining how much we are paid, what kinds of educational opportunities are available to us, and where and how we live. In other contexts, these variables may well be irrelevant. Reading about them adds another dimension to our understanding of the complex set of additional factors that interact with issues of race, class, gender, and sexuality.

But even as we acknowledge how much there is to learn from looking at the lives and experiences of many different people, there is also danger in this project—the danger of overgeneralizing. It is easy to take the particular experience or the particular beliefs of one member of a group and attribute them to all members of that group. Many students who are members of a religious, racial, or ethnic minority have had the uncomfortable experience of being asked to speak for all members of that minority group at some point in their college years. Failing to see members of minority groups as individuals is typical of a society in which stereotyping flourishes. On the other hand, for the purposes of studying issues of race, class, gender, and sexuality, it is often necessary to look beyond individual differences and generalize about "Native Americans" or "Chicanas" or "men" in order to highlight aspects of their experience that are more typical of that group's experience than of others. As we have already seen, it would be naive to think that the individual exists in a vacuum, untouched by the racism, sexism, heterosexism, and class bias in society. Unless we understand something about the ways different *groups* experience life in the United States, we will never adequately understand the particular experiences of individual people.

The essays in Part V have been selected because they give us a sense of the diversity of life experience in the United States at the same time that they reflect some of the consequences of the inequalities documented in Part IV. For the most part, these articles, poems, and essays need no introduction. They speak for themselves.

58

Census 2000 Shows America's Diversity

Census 2000 results released by the Census Bureau today show a racially diverse America. However, relatively few, about 2.4 percent nationally, took advantage of a first-ever option for respondents to identify themselves as belonging to more than one race.

The first of a series of Census 2000 briefs, titled *Overview of Race and Hispanic Origin*, showed the following for the 274.6 million people who reported only one race:

White	75.1 percent
Black or African American	12.3 percent
American Indian and Alaska Native	0.9 percent
Asian	3.6 percent
Native Hawaiian and Other Pacific Islander	0.1 percent
Some other race	5.5 percent

The Census Bureau also reported that Hispanics, who may be of any race, totaled 35.3 million, or about 13 percent of the total population. This information was obtained from a separate question on Hispanic or Latino origin.

Of the 6.8 million people who reported more than one race, 93 percent reported two races. The most common combinations were:

White and some other race	32 percent
White and American Indian and Alaska Native	16 percent
White and Asian	nearly 13 percent
White and Black or African American	about 11 percent

Of all respondents who reported more than one race, about 7 percent indicated three or more races.

From the U.S. Census Bureau Public Information Office, United States Department of Commerce.

Those who reported only one race are described as "alone," those who selected one or more races as "alone or in combination." The "alone or in combination" percentages are shown below:

White	77.1
Black or African American	12.9
American Indian and Alaska Native	1.5
Asian	4.2
Native Hawaiian and Other Pacific Islander	0.3
Some other race	6.6

Because anyone who reported two or more races is included in the tally for each of those races when using the "alone or in combination" concept, the sum of all these groups exceeds 100 percent of the population.

Nearly 48 percent of Hispanics identified as White alone and about 42 percent reported "Some other race" alone. About 6 percent of all Hispanics reported two or more races compared with less than 2 percent of non-Hispanics. Hispanics accounted for 97 percent of those who reported "Some other race" only.

The race categories for Census 2000 (except for "some other race," which the Census Bureau added) and the "two or more races" category were promulgated in federal race-reporting guidelines by the Office of Management and Budget in 1997. The changes were designed to reflect more accurately the nation's racial diversity.

The question on race for Census 2000 was different from the race question used for the 1990 census, making direct comparisons between the two censuses difficult. The major difference derives from instructing respondents to mark "one or more races" for the first time in a U.S. population census. Other differences include splitting the Asian and Pacific Islander category into two separate race categories in 2000; combining the three separate identifiers Indian (Amer.), Eskimo, Aleut in the category "American Indian or Alaska Native population"; and reversing the order of the questions on race and Hispanic origin, with the one on Hispanic origin placed first in 2000.

To view the Census 2000 brief in its entirety, including 11 national-level tables, go to http://www.census.gov/population/www/cen2000/briefs.html

59

America 2000: A Map of the Mix

As the country becomes more and more diverse, three states and the capital city have seen nonwhites gain majority status.

U.S. Population, in Thousands and Percent Change

	1990	2000	% change '90–'00	2050	% change '00–'50
White, non-Hispanic	188,315	196,659	+4%	207,901	+6%
Black, non-Hispanic	29,304	33,476	+14%	53,555	+60%
Hispanic (of any race)	22,379	32,440	+45%	96,508	+197%
Asian and Pacific Islander*	6,996	10,504	+50%	32,432	+209%
Amer. Ind., Eskimo, Aleut. Isl.*	1,797	2,050	+14%	3,534	+72%

*Non-Hispanic percentages may not total 100 due to rounding. Sources: U.S. Census Bureau, Population Reference Bureau, Immigration and Naturalization Service. Research by Meredith Salisbury. Graphic by Bonnie Scranton—Newsweek.

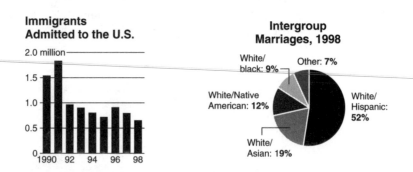

Immigrants Admitted to the U.S.

Intergroup Marriages, 1998

White/black: 9%
Other: 7%
White/Native American: 12%
White/Hispanic: 52%
White/Asian: 19%
White/

Key: Percentage of state population, 1999

Alaska	
72	= White, non-Hispanic
4	= African-American
3	= White Hispanic
5	= Asian, Pacific Islander
16	= Amer. Ind., Eskimo, Aleut. Isl.
Philippines	= Country of origin of greatest number of immigrants in 1998

WHITES: Vermont has the least diversity of the states, with just 2.4% nonwhites.

Maine	
98	
0.5	
0.7	
0.8	
0.5	
Canada	

	Wash.	Mont.	N.D.	Minn.	Mich.	Pa.	N.H.	Mass.
White, non-Hispanic	83	91	93	91	81	86	96	84
African-American	4	0.4	0.6	3	14	10	0.8	7
White Hispanic	6	2	1	2	2	2	1	5
Asian, Pacific Islander	6	0.6	0.8	3	2	2	1	4
Amer. Ind., etc.	2	6	5	1	0.6	0.2	0.2	0.2
Origin	Mexico	China	Canada	Mexico	India	India	India	China

	Idaho	Wyo.	S.D.	Wis.	Ind.	Ohio	Vt.	R.I.
White, non-Hispanic	90	90	89	90	88	86	97.6	86
African-American	0.6	0.9	0.7	6	8	12	0.5	5
White Hispanic	7	6	1	2	2	1	0.8	6
Asian, Pacific Islander	1	0.9	0.7	2	1	1	0.8	2
Amer. Ind., etc.	1	2	8	0.9	0.3	0.2	0.2	0.5
Origin	Mexico	Mexico	Mexico	Mexico	Mexico	India	Canada	Dominican Republic

BLACKS: New York has the highest number of African-Americans with 3.2 million, but is the 10th state by percentage.

	Ore.	Utah	Neb.	Iowa	Ill.	W.Va.	N.Y.	Conn.
White, non-Hispanic	88	89	89	94	71	96	65	80
African-American	2	0.9	4	2	15	3	18	9
White Hispanic	6	7	4	2	10	0.5	11	8
Asian, Pacific Islander	3	3	1	1	3	0.5	6	3
Amer. Ind., etc.	1	1	0.9	0.3	0.2	0.1	0.4	0.2
Origin	Mexico	Mexico	Mexico	Mexico	Mexico	India	Dominican Republic	Jamaica

MINORITIES: White non-Hispanics now make up 49.9% of the population — the first time they have not been a majority.

	Nev.	Colo.	Kans.	Mo.	Tenn.	Ky.	Md.	N.J.	D.C.
White, non-Hispanic	70	78	86	86	81	91	64	68	29
African-American	8	4	6	11	17	7	28	15	61
White Hispanic	15	14	5	1	1	0.8	3	11	6
Asian, Pacific Islander	5	2	2	1	1	0.7	4	6	3
Amer. Ind., etc.	2	0.9	0.9	0.4	0.2	0.1	0.3	0.3	0.3
Origin	Mexico	Mexico	Mexico	Mexico	Mexico	Cuba	El Salvador	India	El Salvador

	Hawaii	Calif.	Ariz.	Okla.	Ark.	Miss.	Ala.	Va.	Dela.	N.C.
White, non-Hispanic	29	49.9	68	80	81	62	72	72	75	73
African-American	3	8	4	8	16	36	26	20	20	22
White Hispanic	4	30	21	3	2	0.7	0.9	3	3	2
Asian, Pacific Islander	64	12	2	1	0.7	0.7	0.7	4	2	1
Amer. Ind., etc.	0.6	0.9	5	8	0.5	0.4	0.3	0.3	0.3	1
Origin	Philippines	Mexico	Mexico	Mexico	Mexico	India	Mexico	El Salvador	India	Mexico

ORIGIN: More immigrants come from Mexico than from any other country— 131,575 in 1998.

	N.M.	La.		Ga.	S.C.
White, non-Hispanic	47	64		66	68
African-American	3	32		29	30
White Hispanic	39	2		3	1
Asian, Pacific Islander	2	1		2	0.9
Amer. Ind., etc.	10	0.4		0.2	0.2
Origin	Mexico	Honduras		Mexico	Mexico

DESTINATION: The most popular states for immigrants are Calif., Fla., Ill., N.J., N.Y., and Texas. They're home to 67% of all immigrants.

	Texas	Fla.
White, non-Hispanic	55	68
African-American	12	15
White Hispanic	29	14
Asian, Pacific Islander	3	2
Amer. Ind., etc.	0.5	0.4
Origin	Mexico	Cuba

Then Came the War

Yuri Kochiyama

I was red, white, and blue when I was growing up. I taught Sunday school, and was very, very American. But I was also very provincial. We were just kids rooting for our high school.

My father owned a fish market. Terminal Island was nearby, and that was where many Japanese families lived. It was a fishing town. My family lived in the city proper. San Pedro was very mixed, predominantly white, but there were blacks also.

I was nineteen at the time of the evacuation. I had just finished junior college. I was looking for a job, and didn't realize how different the school world was from the work world. In the school world, I never felt racism. But when you got into the work world, it was very difficult. This was 1941, just before the war. I finally did get a job at a department store. But for us back then, it was a big thing, because I don't think they had ever hired an Asian in a department store before. I tried, because I saw a Mexican friend who got a job there. Even then they didn't hire me on a regular basis, just on Saturdays, summer vacation, Easter vacation, and Christmas vacation. Other than that, I was working like the others—at a vegetable stand, or doing part-time domestic work. Back then, I only knew of two Japanese American girl friends who got jobs as secretaries—but these were in Japanese companies. But generally you almost never saw a Japanese American working in a white place. It was hard for Asians. Even for Japanese, the best jobs they felt they could get were in Chinatowns, such as in Los Angeles. Most Japanese were either in some aspect of fishing, such as in the canneries, or went right from school to work on the farms. That was what it was like in the town of San Pedro. I loved working in the department store, because it was a small town, and you got to know and see everyone. The town itself was wonderful. People were very friendly. I didn't see my job as work—it was like a community job.

Everything changed for me on the day Pearl Harbor was bombed. On that very day—December 7—the FBI came and they took my father. He had just come home from the hospital the day before. For several days we didn't know where they

From Joann Faung Jean Lee, *Asian American Experiences in the United States: Oral Histories of First to Fourth Generation Americans from China, the Philippines, Japan, India, the Pacific Islands, Vietnam and Cambodia.* © 1991 Joann Faung Jean Lee. Reprinted by permission of McFarland & Company, Inc., Publishers, Jefferson, NC 28640. www.mcfarlandpub.com

had taken him. Then we found out that he was taken to the federal prison at Terminal Island. Overnight, things changed for us. They took all men who lived near the Pacific waters, and had nothing to do with fishing. A month later, they took every fisherman from Terminal Island, sixteen and over, to places—not the regular concentration camps—but to detention centers in places like South Dakota, Montana, and New Mexico. They said that all Japanese who had given money to any kind of Japanese organization would have to be taken away. At that time, many people were giving to the Japanese Red Cross. The first group was thirteen hundred Isseis—my parents' generation. They took those who were leaders of the community, or Japanese school teachers, or were teaching martial arts, or who were Buddhist priests. Those categories which would make them very "Japanesey," were picked up. This really made a tremendous impact on our lives. My twin brother was going to the University at Berkeley. He came rushing back. All of our classmates were joining up, so he volunteered to go into the service. And it seemed strange that here they had my father in prison, and there the draft board okayed my brother. He went right into the army. My other brother, who was two years older, was trying to run my father's fish market. But business was already going down, so he had to close it. He had finished college at the University of California a couple of years before.

They took my father on December 7th. The day before, he had just come home from the hospital. He had surgery for an ulcer. We only saw him once, on December 13. On December 20th they said he could come home. By the time they brought him back, he couldn't talk. He made guttural sounds and we didn't know if he could hear. He was home for twelve hours. He was dying. The next morning, when we got up, they told us that he was gone. He was very sick. And I think the interrogation was very rough. My mother kept begging the authorities to let him go to the hospital until he was well, then put him back in the prison. They did finally put him there, a week or so later. But they put him in a hospital where they were bringing back all these American Merchant Marines who were hit on Wake Island. So he was the only Japanese in that hospital, so they hung a sheet around him that said, Prisoner of War. The feeling where he was was very bad.

You could see the hysteria of war. There was a sense that war could actually come to American shores. Everybody was yelling to get the "Japs" out of California. In Congress, people were speaking out. Organizations such as the Sons and Daughters of the Golden West were screaming "Get the 'Japs' out." So were the real estate people, who wanted to get the land from the Japanese farmers. The war had whipped up such a hysteria that if there was anyone for the Japanese, you didn't hear about it. I'm sure they were afraid to speak out, because they would be considered not only just "Jap" lovers, but unpatriotic.

Just the fact that my father was taken made us suspect to people. But on the whole, the neighbors were quite nice, especially the ones adjacent to us. There was already a six AM to six PM curfew and a five mile limit on where we could go from our homes. So they offered to do our shopping for us, if we needed.

Most Japanese Americans had to give up their jobs, whatever they did, and were told they had to leave. The edict for 9066—President Roosevelt's edict* for evacuation—was in February 1942. We were moved to a detention center that April. By then the Japanese on Terminal Island were just helter skelter, looking for anywhere they could go. They opened up the Japanese school and Buddhist churches, and families just crowded in. Even farmers brought along their chickens and chicken coops. They just opened up the places for people to stay until they could figure out what to do. Some people left for Colorado and Utah. Those who had relatives could do so. The idea was to evacuate all the Japanese from the coast. But all the money was frozen, so even if you knew where you wanted to go, it wasn't that simple. By then, people knew they would be going into camps, so they were selling what they could, even though they got next to nothing for it.

We were fortunate, in that our neighbors, who were white, were kind enough to look after our house, and they said they would find people to rent it, and look after it till we got back. But these neighbors were very, very unusual.

We were sent to an assembly center in Arcadia, California, in April. It was the largest assembly center on the West Coast, having nearly twenty thousand people. There were some smaller centers with about six hundred people. All along the West Coast—Washington, Oregon, California—there were many, many assembly centers, but ours was the largest. Most of the assembly centers were either fairgrounds, or race tracks. So many of us lived in stables, and they said you could take what you could carry. We were there until October.

Even though we stayed in a horse stable, everything was well organized. Every unit would hold four to six people. So in some cases, families had to split up, or join others. We slept on army cots, and for mattresses they gave us muslin bags, and told us to fill them with straw. And for chairs, everybody scrounged around for carton boxes, because they could serve as chairs. You could put two together and it could be a little table. So it was just makeshift. But I was amazed how, in a few months, some of those units really looked nice. Japanese women fixed them up. Some people had the foresight to bring material and needles and thread. But they didn't let us bring anything that could be used as weapons. They let us have spoons, but no knives. For those who had small children or babies, it was rough. They said you could take what you could carry. Well, they could only take their babies in their arms, and maybe the little children could carry something, but it was pretty limited.

I was so red, white, and blue, I couldn't believe this was happening to us. America would never do a thing like this to us. This is the greatest country in the world. So I thought this is only going to be for a short while, maybe a few weeks or something, and they will let us go back. At the beginning no one realized how long this would go on. I didn't feel the anger that much because I thought maybe

---

*Executive Order No. 9066 does not mention detention of Japanese specifically, but was used exclusively against the Japanese. Over 120,000 Japanese were evacuated from the West Coast.

this was the way we could show our love for our country, and we should not make too much fuss or noise, we should abide by what they asked of us. I'm a totally different person now than I was back then. I was naïve about so many things. The more I think about it, the more I realize how little you learn about American history. It's just what they want you to know.

At the beginning, we didn't have any idea how temporary or permanent the situation was. We thought we would be able to leave shortly. But after several months they told us this was just temporary quarters, and they were building more permanent quarters elsewhere in the United States. All this was so unbelievable. A year before we would never have thought anything like this could have happened to us—not in this country. As time went by, the sense of frustration grew. Many families were already divided. The fathers, the heads of the households, were taken to other camps. In the beginning, there was no way for the sons to get in touch with their families. Before our group left for the detention camp, we were saying goodbye almost every day to other groups who were going to places like Arizona and Utah. Here we finally had made so many new friends—people who we met, lived with, shared the time, and got to know. So it was even sad on that note and the goodbyes were difficult. Here we had gotten close to these people, and now we had to separate again. I don't think we even thought about where they were going to take us, or how long we would have to stay there. When we got on the trains to leave for the camps, we didn't know where we were going. None of the groups knew. It was later on that we learned so and so ended up in Arizona, or Colorado, or some other place. We were all at these assembly centers for about seven months. Once they started pushing people out, it was done very quickly. By October, our group headed out for Jerome, Arkansas, which is on the Texarkana corner.

We were on the train for five days. The blinds were down, so we couldn't look out, and other people couldn't look in to see who was in the train. We stopped in Nebraska, and everybody pulled the blinds to see what Nebraska looked like. The interesting thing was, there was a troop train stopped at the station too. These American soldiers looked out, and saw all these Asians, and they wondered what we were doing on the train. So the Japanese raised the windows, and so did the soldiers. It wasn't a bad feeling at all. There was none of that "you Japs" kind of thing. The women were about the same age as the soldiers—eighteen to twenty-five, and we had the same thing on our minds. In camps, there wasn't much to do, so the fun thing was to receive letters, so on our train, all the girls who were my age, were yelling to the guys, "Hey, give us your address where you're going, we'll write you." And they said, "Are you sure you're going to write?" We exchanged addresses and for a long time I wrote to some of those soldiers. On the other side of the train, I'll never forget there was this old guy, about sixty, who came to our window and said, "We have some Japanese living here. This is Omaha, Nebraska." This guy was very nice, and didn't seem to have any ill feelings for Japanese. He had calling cards, and he said "Will any of you people write to me?" We said, "Sure," so he threw in a bunch of calling cards, and I got one, and I wrote to him for years. I wrote to him about what camp was like, because he said, "Let me know what it's like wherever you end up." And he wrote back, and told me what was happening in Omaha, Nebraska. There were many, many interesting experiences too. Our mail was generally not censored, but all the mail from the soldiers was. Letters meant everything.

When we got to Jerome, Arkansas, we were shocked because we had never seen an area like it. There was forest all around us. And they told us to wait till the rains hit. This would not only turn into mud, but Arkansas swamp lands. That's where they put us—in swamp lands, surrounded by forests. It was nothing like California.

I'm speaking as a person of twenty who had good health. Up until then, I had lived a fairly comfortable life. But there were many others who didn't see the whole experience the same way. Especially those who were older and in poor health and had experienced racism. One more thing like this could break them. I was at an age where transitions were not hard—the point where anything new could even be considered exciting. But for people in poor health, it was hell.

There were army-type barracks, with two hundred to two hundred and five people to each block and every block had its own mess hall, facility for washing clothes, showering. It was all surrounded by barbed wire, and armed soldiers. I think they said only seven people were killed in total, though thirty were shot, because they went too close to the fence. Where we were, nobody thought of escaping because you'd be more scared of the swamps—the poisonous snakes, the bayous. Climatic conditions were very harsh. Although Arkansas is in the South, the winters were very, very cold. We had a pot bellied stove in every room and we burned wood. Everything was very organized. We got there in October, and were warned to prepare ourselves. So on our block, for instance, males eighteen and over could go out in the forest to chop down trees for wood for the winter. The men would bring back the trees, and the women sawed the trees. Everybody worked. The children would pile up the wood for each unit.

They told us when it rained, it would be very wet, so we would have to build our own drainage system. One of the barracks was to hold meetings, so block heads would call meetings. There was a block council to represent the people from different areas.

When we first arrived, there were some things that weren't completely fixed. For instance, the roofers would come by, and everyone would hunger for information from the outside world. We wanted to know what was happening with the war. We weren't allowed to bring radios; that was contraband. And there were no televisions then. So we would ask the workers to bring us back some papers, and they would give us papers from Texas or Arkansas, so for the first time we would find out about news from the outside.

Just before we went in to the camps, we saw that being a Japanese wasn't such a good thing, because everybody was turning against the Japanese, thinking we were saboteurs, or linking us with Pearl Harbor. But when I saw the kind of work they did at camp, I felt so proud of the Japanese, and proud to be Japanese, and wondered why I was so white, white when I was outside, because I was always with white folks. Many people had brothers or sons who were in the military and Japanese American servicemen would come into the camp to visit the families, and we felt so proud of them when they came in their uniforms. We knew that it would only be a matter of time before they would be shipped overseas. Also what made us feel proud was the forming of the 442 unit.*

I was one of these real American patriots then. I've changed now. But back then, I was all American. Growing up, my mother would say we're Japanese. But I'd say, "No, I'm American." I think a lot of Japanese grew up that way. People would say to them, "You're Japanese," and they would say, "No, we're Americans." I don't even think they used the hyphenated term "Japanese-American" back then. At the time, I was ashamed of being Japanese. I think many Japanese Americans felt the same way. Pearl Harbor was a shameful act, and being Japanese Americans, even though we had nothing to do with it, we still somehow felt we were blamed for it. I hated Japan at that point. So I saw myself at that part of my history as an American, and not as a Japanese or Japanese American. That sort of changed while I was in the camp.

I hated the war, because it wasn't just between the governments. It went down to the people, and it nurtured hate. What was happening during the war were many things I didn't like. I hoped that one day when the war was over there could be a way that people could come together in their relationships.

Now I can relate to Japan in a more mature way, where I see its faults and its very, very negative history. But I also see its potential. Scientifically and technologically it has really gone far. But I'm disappointed that when it comes to human rights she hasn't grown. The Japan of today—I feel there are still things lacking. For instance, I don't think the students have the opportunity to have more leeway in developing their lives.

We always called the camps "relocation centers" while we were there. Now we feel it is apropos to call them concentration camps. It is not the same as the concentration camps of Europe; those we feel were death camps. Concentration camps were a concentration of people placed in an area, and disempowered and disenfranchised. So it is apropos to call what I was in a concentration camp. After two years in the camp, I was released.

Going home wasn't much of a problem for us because our neighbors had looked after our place. But for most of our Japanese friends, starting over again was very difficult after the war.

I returned in October of 1945. It was very hard to find work, at least for me. I wasn't expecting to find anything good, just something to tide me over until my boyfriend came back from New York. The only thing I was looking for was to work in a restaurant as a waitress. But I couldn't find anything. I would walk from one end of the town to the other, and down every main avenue. But as soon as they found out I was Japanese, they would say no. Or they would ask me if I was in the

---

*American soldiers of Japanese ancestry were assembled in two units: the 442 Regimental Combat Team and the 100th Infantry Battalion. The two groups were sent to battle in Europe. The 100th Battalion had over 900 casualties and was known as the Purple Heart Battalion. Combined, the units received 9,486 purple hearts and 18,143 individual decorations.

union, and of course I couldn't be in the union because I had just gotten there. Anyway, no Japanese could be in the union, so if the answer was no I'm not in the union, they would say no. So finally what I did was go into the rough area of San Pedro—there's a strip near the wharf—and I went down there. I was determined to keep the jobs as long as I could. But for a while, I could last maybe two hours, and somebody would say "Is that a 'Jap'?" And as soon as someone would ask that, the boss would say, "Sorry, you gotta go. We don't want trouble here." The strip wasn't that big, so after I'd go the whole length of it, I'd have to keep coming back to the same restaurants, and say, "Gee, will you give me another chance." I figure, all these servicemen were coming back and the restaurants didn't have enough waitresses to come in and take these jobs. And so, they'd say "Okay. But soon as somebody asks who you are, or if you're a 'Jap,' or any problem about being a 'Jap,' you go." So I said, "Okay, sure. How about keeping me until that happens?" So sometimes I'd last a night, sometimes a couple of nights that no one would say anything. Sometimes people threw cups at me or hot coffee. At first they didn't know what I was. They thought I was Chinese. Then someone would say, "I bet she's a 'Jap'." And I wasn't going to say I wasn't. So as soon as I said "Yeah," then it was like an uproar. Rather than have them say, "Get out," I just walked out. I mean, there was no point in fighting it. If you just walked out, there was less chance of getting hurt. But one place I lasted two weeks. These owners didn't want to have to let me go. But they didn't want to have problems with the people.

And so I did this until I left for New York, which was about three months later. I would work the dinner shift, from six at night to three in the morning. When you are young you tend not to take things as strongly. Everything is like an adventure. Looking back, I felt the people who were the kindest to me were those who went out and fought, those who just got back from Japan or the Far East. I think the worst ones were the ones who stayed here and worked in defense plants, who felt they had to be so patriotic. On the West Coast, there wasn't hysteria anymore, but there were hostile feelings towards the Japanese, because they were coming back. It took a while, but my mother said that things were getting back to normal, and that the Japanese were slowly being accepted again. At the time, I didn't go through the bitterness that many others went through, because it's not just what they went through, but it is also what they experienced before that. I mean, I happened to have a much more comfortable life before, so you sort of see things in a different light. You see that there are all kinds of Americans, and that they're not all people who hate Japs. You know too that it was hysteria that had a lot to do with it.

All Japanese, before they left camp, were told not to congregate among Japanese, and not to speak Japanese. They were told by the authorities. There was even a piece of paper that gave you instructions. But then people went on to places like Chicago where there were churches, so they did congregate in churches. But they did ask people not to. I think psychologically the Japanese, having gone through a period where they were so hated by everyone, didn't even want to admit they were Japanese, or accept the fact that they were Japanese. Of course, they would say they were Japanese Americans. But I think the psychological damage of the wartime period, and of racism itself, has left its mark. There is a stigma to being Japanese. I think that is why such a large number of Japanese, in particular Japanese American women, have married out of the race. On the West Coast I've heard people say that sixty to seventy percent of the Japanese women have married, I guess, mostly whites. Japanese men are doing it too, but not to that degree. I guess Japanese Americans just didn't want to have that Japanese identity, or that Japanese part. There is definitely some self-hate, and part of that has to do with the racism that's so deeply a part of this society.

Historically, Americans have always been putting people behind walls. First there were the American Indians who were put on reservations, Africans in slavery, their lives on the plantations, Chicanos doing migratory work, and the kinds of camps they lived in, and even, too, the Chinese when they worked on the railroad camps where they were almost isolated, dispossessed people—disempowered. And I feel those are the things we should fight against so they won't happen again. It wasn't so long ago—in 1979—that the feeling against the Iranians was so strong because of the takeover of the U.S. embassy in Iran, where they wanted to deport Iranian students. And that is when a group called Concerned Japanese Americans organized, and that was the first issue we took up, and then we connected it with what the Japanese had gone through. This whole period of what the Japanese went through is important. If we can see the connections of how often this happens in history, we can stem the tide of these things happening again by speaking out against them.

Most Japanese Americans who worked years and years for redress never thought it would happen the way it did. The papers have been signed, we will be given reparation, and there was an apology from the government. I think the redress movement itself was very good because it was a learning experience for the Japanese people; we could get out into our communities and speak about what happened to us and link it with experiences of other people. In that sense, though, it wasn't done as much as it should have been. Some Japanese Americans didn't even learn that part. They just started the movement as a reaction to the bad experience they had. They don't even see other ethnic groups who have gone through it. It showed us, too, how vulnerable everybody is. It showed us that even though there is a Constitution, that constitutional rights could be taken away very easily.

Yellow

Frank Wu

Writing Race

I'd like to be as honest as possible in explaining why and how race matters, because it shapes every aspect of my life—and everyone else's. I'd like to do so in a manner that allows my white relatives and my white friends to understand and empathize.

I have learned how naïve I was to have supposed that children grew out of their race and to have expected that adults could not possibly be racist. The lives of people of color are materially different than the lives of whites, but in the abiding American spirit we all prefer to believe that our individualism is most important.

As a member of a minority group everywhere in my country except among family or through the self-conscious effort to find other Asian Americans, I alternate between being conspicuous and vanishing, being stared at or looked through. Although the conditions may seem contradictory, they have in common the loss of control. In most instances, I am who others perceive me to be rather than how I perceive myself to be. Considered by the strong sense of individualism inherent to American society, the inability to define one's self is the greatest loss of liberty possible. We Americans believe in an heroic myth from the nineteenth century, whereby moving to the frontier gives a person a new identity. Even if they do not find gold, silver, or oil, men who migrate to the West can remake their reputations. But moving to California works only for white men. Others cannot invent themselves by sheer will, because no matter how idiosyncratic one's individual identity, one cannot overcome the stereotype of group identity.

Sometimes I have an encounter that demonstrates how easily people can be transfixed by a racial stereotype. In a casual aside, a business colleague, who I thought knew me well enough to know better, may make an earnest remark revealing that his attempt to connect with me can come only through race. Although they rarely mention their personal lives, people always will make it a point to tell me about the hit movie they saw last night or the museum exhibit they toured over the weekend if it had a vaguely Asian theme, whether Chinese, Japanese, Korean,

Vietnamese, or whatever, because, "It reminded me of you." They tell me I resemble the cellist Yo-Yo Ma or their five-year-old son's friend in school. Or in a passing instant, a white boy or a black boy, whom I would credit with childhood innocence, can rekindle my memory of the ordinary intolerance of days past. At an airport or riding on a subway, boys will see me and suddenly strike a karate pose, chop at the air, throw a kick, and utter some sing-song gibberish, before turning around and running away. Martin Luther King Jr. asked to be judged by the content of his character rather than the color of his skin, but in these surreal episodes I am not judged by the content of my character because the dealings have no content except for the racial image. Worse, it is as trivial for others as it is traumatic to me. I may as well be a stage prop. University of California at Berkeley literature professor Elaine Kim has recounted being told by a white friend who'd read Maxine Hong Kingston's *The Woman Warrior,* one of the earliest works of Asian American novels to become a staple of literature courses, that only through the book did she come to understand Kim.[1] The fictional character becomes more believable than a real person, as though it is easier to know Asian Americans through the representation than through the reality.

At other times, I will have another type of encounter in the anonymous rush of contemporary life, one that confirms that people can be oblivious to folks who don't resemble them.[2] To present an analogy, most motorcyclists and bicyclists who ride regularly on city streets are accustomed to the situation in which they will make prolonged eye contact with a driver, who then blithely proceeds to cut off the bike or turn directly in front of it. The person behind the wheel may have seen the rider but responds only to vehicles like her own; anything else doesn't register. Likewise, waiting in line, I am amazed when a white person, sometimes well-dressed and distinguished looking and sometimes not, cuts in front of me or expects to be given VIP treatment. I am galled by not only the action but also the sense of entitlement that this person radiates. I want to say, "Hello? Did you not see the rest of us back here, or did you take it for granted that you were more important?" Of course, sometimes people are momentarily distracted or generally impolite. It happens often enough, however, in cases where it is fair to surmise that race and gender are involved. When whites are disrespected by other whites—for example, when they are ushered to a deserted area of the restaurant near the kitchen—they generally are not plagued by the suspicion that it is for racial reasons. It is easier for them to write off an incident as the consequence of incivility rather than another indication of something worse. Even if people of color are spurned for reasons other than race, the maltreatment harkens back to race because of the uncertainty of the matter. People of color are held to a double standard. Asian Americans are impudent if we presume to behave as others have done without doubting their right; what is assertive and commanding when it comes from a white male is bossy and presumptuous from an Asian American female. . . .

My premise is straightforward. Race is more than black and white, literally and figuratively. Yellow belongs. Gray predominates. I advance these arguments together, and they are mutually reinforcing. Being neither black nor white, Asian

Americans do not automatically side with either blacks or whites. Columbia University professor Gary Okihiro once asked, "is yellow black or white?"[3] Chang-Lin Tien, who was the first Asian American to head a major research university, recalled arriving in the United States in 1956. He says that when he was a graduate student, "I never rode the city buses" in Louisville, Kentucky. He was humiliated when he boarded one and saw that "whites rode in the front and 'coloreds' rode in the rear." He asked, "Just where exactly did an Asian fit in?" He did not wish to be consigned to the back of the bus, but neither did he believe that even if he dared to sit down in the front of the bus, he could stay there in good conscience.[4] Theirs are the best type of question, because they have no answers. . . .

In race matters, words matter, too. Asian Americans have been excluded by the very terms used to conceptualize race. People speak of "American" as if it means "white" and "minority" as if it means "black." In that semantic formula, Asian Americans, neither black nor white, consequently are neither American nor minority. I am offended, both as an academic and as an Asian American. Asian Americans should be included for the sake of truthfulness, not merely to gratify our ego. Without us—and needless to say, without many others—everything about race is incomplete.

It isn't easy to call people on their unconscious errors. If I point out that they said "American" when they meant "white," they will brush it off with, "Well, you know what I mean," or "Why are you bringing up race?" Yet it is worth pondering exactly what they do mean. What they have done through negligence, with barely any awareness, is equate race and citizenship. They may even become embarrassed once the effect is noticed. Asian Americans were upset when the MS-NBC website printed a headline announcing that "American beats out Kwan" after Tara Lipinsky defeated Michelle Kwan in figure skating at the 1998 Winter Olympics.[5] Like gold medalist Lipinsky, Kwan is an American. By implying that Kwan was a foreigner who had been defeated by an "American," the headline in effect announced that an Asian American had been defeated by a white American in a racialized contest. If two white Americans compete against each other in a sporting event—say, rivals Nancy Kerrigan and Tonya Harding—it would be preposterous for the result to be described as one of them defeated by an "American." If Kwan had won, it also would be unlikely for the victory to be described as "American beats out Lipinsky" or "Asian beats out white." Movie producer Christopher Lee recalls that when studio executives were considering making a film version of *Joy Luck Club*, they shied away from it because "there are no Americans in it." He told his colleagues, "There are Americans in it. They just don't look like you."[6]

NOTES

1. Elaine H. Kim, *Asian American Literature: An Introduction to the Writings and Their Social Context* (Philadelphia: Temple University Press, 1982), xix.

2. "Miss Manners," the advice columnist, has addressed this issue, but she prefers to assume that these incidents are not racial. See Judith Martin, "Anger, Fear and Loathing at Airport and at Dinner," *Washington Post*, July 22, 1998, D16.

3. Gary Y. Okihiro, *Margins and Mainstreams: Asians in American History and Culture* (Seattle: University of Washington Press, 1994), 31–63.

4. Chang-Lin Tien, "Affirming Affirmative Action," Perspectives on Affirmative Action . . . and Its Impact on Asian-Pacific Americans (Los Angeles: Leadership Education for Asian Pacifics, 1996), 19.

5. Joann Lee, "Mistaken Headline Underscores Racial Presumptions," *Editor & Publisher*, April 25, 1998, 64.

6. Howard Chua-Eoan, "Profiles in Outrage: America Is Home, But Asian Americans Feel Treated as Outlanders with Unproven Loyalties," *Time*, September 25, 2000, 40.

62

Asian American?

Sonia Shah

I was recently asked to write about Asian American History Month, which, since 1979, has been observed during the month of May.

Despite the fact that I write about Asian American issues on a fairly regular basis, and in many ways consider myself an Asian American, it wasn't easy to figure. The very term, "Asian American History," makes our presence here sound so official, so natural.

Yet the term "Asian America" itself is problematic. Most of the people whom others would characterize as "Asian American" most emphatically don't think of themselves that way. (And many, including most of those in my family, would be almost offended: they are Gujuratis, thank you very much!) Our particular histories, ethnicities, and nationalities are one million times more visceral and meaningful in our lives than pan-Asianness (and what would that be, one wonders: "fusion" cooking?).

The push to unify the disparate peoples and histories of Chinese, Japanese, Vietnamese, Hmong, Pakistanis, Thais, and Indians, among others, comes from both right and left. Of course it would be easier for the U.S. census, but also for the radicals who started the "Yellow Power" movement in the 1960s, among others. But unlike other diverse ethnic/racial groups, such as African Americans and

Reprinted by permission of the author. First appeared in ZNet *Commentary* (April 26, 1999).

Native Americans, Asian Pacific Americans share no common historical trauma like slavery or colonization. We share no "Asian" language or ethnicity or nation or color. What we have in common, most of us would rather forget.

There is an undeniable strategic value in our unity. Americans know so little about Asian cultures, in general, that the stereotypes and fantasies projected upon any one group bleed over onto the next. We have those in common, and it wouldn't do any good to resist some and not the others. As a group, Asians have sometimes been held up as "model minorities" and at other times pilloried as spies and interlopers, but always, it seems, we are held at a distance, no matter how "American" we may become. This is at least partly because our role in American society is largely defined not by our unique contributions per se, but by our assigned roles in the unfolding drama between American labor and capital, and between blacks and whites.

Each wave of Asian immigration to American shores has been triggered by U.S. immigration policy or military interventions in Asia. When American labor has gotten too expensive, due to union organizing victories and the like, immigration laws have strategically shifted to import workers from Asia, whether poor Chinese laborers in the 1800s to build the railroads or professional Asians in the 1960s to service the then-growing welfare state. U.S. military interventions in the Philippines, Korea, Vietnam, and elsewhere likewise resulted in floods of Asian refugees at American gates. Today, the workers, farmers, and small landowners in Asia whose livelihoods have been crushed by the demands of U.S. multinational companies—now freer than ever to do business abroad—are being smuggled illegally into the country.

Predictably, backlashes against these workers have followed in each case. Laws excluding Chinese from becoming citizens, owning property, marrying, or attending public schools with whites were enacted in the mid- to late-1800s. In 1942, the U.S. government stripped 110,000 Japanese Americans of their homes, possessions, and savings and forced them into concentration camps; upon their release— jobless, penniless—the government served as an employment agency, fielding the many requests for servants.

The 1980s economy sparked another wave of anti-Asian violence: in 1982, Chinese American Vincent Chin was beaten to death with a baseball bat by unemployed auto workers who thought he was Japanese (and who served not a single day in jail). In 1987, Navraz Mody was beaten to death by a gang of youths in New Jersey, home of the infamous "dotbusters" (a vicious reference to the Indian bindhi).

Today, many Asian workers serve as a sort of middle-tier wedge between blacks and whites, and between corporate elites and workers—most tragically in Los Angeles during the 1992 riots. Even the much-lauded professional Asians are harrassed and excluded on the basis of their accents, their degrees often devalued and held to higher-than-usual standards. For all the fanfare regarding their success, most of them still make less money than whites with comparable educations. Undocumented Asian workers take the jobs nobody else will tolerate, toiling in sweatshops and factories. In one particularly egregious case, dozens of Thai workers were recently found to have been held against their will in a barbed-wire-enclosed southern California sweatshop between 1990 and 1997.

The model minority myth—consciously encouraged by embattled elites in Asian communities—likewise inserts Asians into the larger drama about blacks and whites. While an education can be had and a living made based on model minority myths (at least for some), it is at the cost of indulging the racist delusion that there can be some "good minorities" in implicit contrast to those other "bad minorities," who have only themselves to blame.

Part of the double-bind of Asian Americans is that retaining our Asian heritages can be almost as difficult as becoming American. The American media continues to be fascinated with Asian misery and senseless oppression. When Americans gain a peek into life in Asia, it is invariably a horror scene: Indonesians eating bark; Chinese women drinking pesticides; Thai prostitutes chained to their beds; dead bodies in rivers, contaminated blood supplies, mudslides, train wrecks, massacres. Non-Asians may be strangely comforted by these tales of distant woe. But what could anyone with ties to those countries feel, beside sorrow, shame, rage, alienation, or: Thank God we're here and not there!

The story of Asian American history, in these ways, is a story of not belonging, of alienation from America and Asia. Yet, despite all this ambivalence and contradiction about our place in U.S. society, Asian Americans have played upon the broader American stage and have made lives and history change as a result.

People such as the human rights advocate Yuri Kochiyama; the feminist activist Anannya Bhattacharjee; the queer activist Urvashi Vaid; the radical poet Janice Mirikitani; the public intellectuals Glenn Omatsu, Peter Kwong; and Mari Matsuda; the filmmakers Richard Fung and Renee Tajima to name just a few, among many others, are building an inspired, radical Asian left to improve all of our lives.

Their legacy—the future of history—are today's vibrant Asian American immigrant worker movements, the growing institution of Asian American Studies in universities, a flourishing Asian American arts community, and more. These people and the institutions they have built, against the odds, are the Asian makers of American history. They have and will continue to force America to reckon with the realities of a diverse, multilingual, yellow and brown, ever-more-vocal Asianized America.

Suicide Note

Janice Mirikitani

. . . An Asian American college student was reported to have jumped to her death from her dormitory window. Her body was found two days later under a deep cover of snow. Her suicide note contained an apology to her parents for having received less than a perfect four point grade average . . .

How many notes written . . .
ink smeared like birdprints in snow.

not good enough   not pretty enough   not smart enough
dear mother and father.
I apologize
for disappointing you.
I've worked very hard,
        not good enough
harder, perhaps to please you.
If only I were a son, shoulders broad
as the sunset threading through pine,
I would see the light in my mother's
eyes, or the golden pride reflected
in my father's dream
of my wide, male hands worthy of work
and comfort.
I would swagger through life
muscled and bold and assured,
drawing praises to me
like currents in the bed of wind, virile
with confidence.
    not good enough   not strong enough   not smart enough

I apologize.
Tasks do not come easily.
Each failure, a glacier.
Each disapproval, a bootprint.
Each disappointment,
ice above my river.
So I have worked hard.
                not good enough
My sacrifice I will drop
bone by bone, perched
on the ledge of my womanhood,
fragile as wings.
                not strong enough
It is snowing steadily
surely not good weather
for flying—this sparrow
sillied and dizzied by the wind
on the edge.
                not smart enough
I make this ledge my altar
to offer penance.
This air will not hold me,
the snow burdens my crippled wings,
my tears drop like bitter cloth
softly into the gutter below.
      not good enough   not strong enough   not smart enough

          Choices thin as shaved
          ice. Notes shredded
          drift like snow

on my broken body,
covers me like whispers
of sorries
sorries.
Perhaps when they find me
they will bury
my bird bones beneath
a sturdy pine
and scatter my feathers like
unspoken song
over this white and cold and silent
breast of earth.

TV Arabs

Jack G. Shaheen

America's bogyman is the Arab. Until the nightly news brought us TV pictures of Palestinian boys being punched and beaten, almost all portraits of Arabs seen in America were dangerously threatening. Arabs were either billionaires or bombers—rarely victims. They were hardly ever seen as ordinary people practicing law, driving taxis, singing lullabies or healing the sick. Though TV news may portray them more sympathetically now, the absence of positive media images nurtures suspicion and stereotype. As an Arab-American, I have found that ugly caricatures have had an enduring impact on my family.

I was sheltered from prejudicial portraits at first. My parents came from Lebanon in the 1920s; they met and married in America. Our home in the steel city of Clairton, Pa., was a center for ethnic sharing—black, white, Jew and gentile. There was only one major source of media images then, at the State movie theater where I was lucky enough to get a part-time job as an usher. But in the late 1940s, Westerns and war movies were popular, not Middle Eastern dramas. Memories of World War II were fresh, and the screen heavies were the Japanese and the Germans. True to the cliché of the times, the only good Indian was a dead Indian. But when I mimicked or mocked the bad guys, my mother cautioned me. She explained that stereotypes blur our vision and corrupt the imagination. "Have compassion for all people, Jackie," she said. "This way, you'll learn to experience the joy of accepting people as they are, and not as they appear in films. Stereotypes hurt."

Mother was right. I can remember the Saturday afternoon when my son, Michael, who was seven, and my daughter, Michele, six, suddenly called out: "Daddy, Daddy, they've got some bad Arabs on TV." They were watching that great American morality play, TV wrestling. Akbar the Great, who liked to hear the cracking of bones, and Abdullah the Butcher, a dirty fighter who liked to inflict pain, were pinning their foes with "camel locks." From that day on, I knew I had to try to neutralize the media caricatures.

It hasn't been easy. With my children, I have watched animated heroes Heckle and Jeckle pull the rug from under "Ali Boo-Boo, the Desert Rat," and Laverne and Shirley stop "Sheik Ha-Mean-Ie" from conquering "the U.S. and the world." I have read comic books like the "Fantastic Four" and "G.I. Combat" whose characters have sketched Arabs as "lowlifes" and "human hyenas." Negative stereotypes were everywhere. A dictionary informed my youngsters that an Arab is a "vagabond, drifter, hobo and vagrant." Whatever happened, my wife wondered, to Aladdin's good genie?

To a child, the world is simple: good versus evil. But my children and others with Arab roots grew up without ever having seen a humane Arab on the silver screen, someone to pattern their lives after. Is it easier for a camel to go through the eye of a needle than for a screen Arab to appear as a genuine human being?

Hollywood producers must have an instant Ali Baba kit that contains scimitars, veils, sunglasses and such Arab clothing as *chadors* and *kufiyahs*. In the mythical "Ay-rabland," oil wells, tents, mosques, goats and shepherds prevail. Between the sand dunes, the camera focuses on a mock-up of a palace from "Arabian Nights"—or a military air base. Recent movies suggest that Americans are at war with Arabs, forgetting the fact that out of 21 Arab nations, America is friendly with 19 of them. And in "Wanted Dead or Alive," a movie that starred Gene Simmons, the leader of the rock group Kiss, the war comes home when an Arab terrorist comes to the United States dressed as a rabbi and, among other things, conspires with Arab-Americans to poison the people of Los Angeles. . . .

The Arab remains American culture's favorite whipping boy. In his memoirs, Terrel Bell, Ronald Reagan's first secretary of education, writes about an "apparent bias among mid-level, right-wing staffers at the White House" who dismissed Arabs as "sand niggers." Sadly, the racial slurs continue. At a recent teacher's conference, I met a woman from Sioux Falls, S.D., who told me about the persistence of discrimination. She was in the process of adopting a baby when an agency staffer warned her that the infant had a problem. When she asked whether the child was mentally ill, or physically handicapped, there was silence. Finally, the worker said: "The baby is Jordanian."

To me, the Arab demon of today is much like the Jewish demon of yesterday. We deplore the false portrait of Jews as a swarthy menace. Yet a similar portrait has been accepted and transferred to another group of Semites—the Arabs. Print and broadcast journalists have started to challenge this stereotype. They are now revealing more humane images of Palestinian Arabs, a people who traditionally suffered from the myth that Palestinian equals terrorist. Others could follow that lead and retire the stereotypical Arab to a media Valhalla.

It would be a step in the right direction if movie and TV producers developed characters modeled after real-life Arab-Americans. We could then see a White House correspondent like Helen Thomas, whose father came from Lebanon, in "The Golden Girls," a heart surgeon patterned after Dr. Michael DeBakey on "St. Elsewhere," or a Syrian-American playing tournament chess like Yasser Seirawan, the Seattle grandmaster.

Politicians, too, should speak out against the cardboard caricatures. They should refer to Arabs as friends, not just as moderates. And religious leaders could state that Islam, like Christianity and Judaism, maintains that all mankind is one family in the care of God. When all image makers rightfully begin to treat Arabs and all other minorities with respect and dignity, we may begin to unlearn our prejudices.

Yes, I Follow Islam, but I'm Not a Terrorist

Nada El Sawy

The tragedy of Sept. 11 gives Americans the chance to learn about a religion they have never understood.

As an Egyptian-American and a Muslim, I've always been dismayed by the way Islam has been generally misrepresented in the media and misunderstood by most Americans. Since the tragic events of Sept. 11, Islam has been in the spotlight, and though leaders such as President George W. Bush and New York Mayor Rudolph Giuliani have made a concerted effort to distinguish it from terrorism, some people still aren't getting the message.

I am a graduate student in journalism, often assigned to write articles about current events. The day after the terrorist attacks I headed out to Brooklyn to cover a story about an Islamic school that had been pelted with rocks and bloody pork chops in the hours after the World Trade Center towers collapsed. Whoever committed this act knew enough about Islam to know that pork is forbidden, but apparently little else about Islamic beliefs. "I wish people would stop calling us terrorists," one sixth grader told me.

When I read about Osama bin Laden or groups like the Egyptian Islamic Jihad, I want to tell them, "You're giving Islam a bad name!" I want to show people that the religion I know is one that calls for patience, harmony and understanding.

Islam may be the world's second largest religion, but in the United States, home to about 6 million of its followers, it remains a mystery. Americans seem to believe that backpacking through Europe or keeping up with the news gives them an understanding of everything about the cultures, religions and traditions that differ from their own. While I'm heartened by the sincere curiosity of some, like the stylist who asked me about my beliefs as he trimmed my hair, most people still have a long way to go.

I have yet to meet anyone—who isn't either especially well read, a religion major or a Muslim—who can accurately describe Islamic beliefs. Many people find it fascinating that I worship Allah without understanding that "Allah" is simply the Arabic word for God. Muslims use the word only because the universal teachings of Islam have been preserved in the Arabic language.

I can recall a Thanksgiving dinner with family friends several years ago when the host offered a small prayer. As we all held hands, he started with the customary thanks for the food, family and friends. Then he proceeded to say, "And thank you to God—or whoever else you choose to worship, may it be Allah . . ." He meant well, but I remember flinching. He and his family had traveled to the Middle East, taken pictures of Muslims praying, read about the cultures they were visiting, but none of it had led to a clear understanding of Islam.

I'm not surprised when classmates confront me with the charge that Muslims around the world are killing in the name of religion. I'm careful not to mention the many Muslims who have been killed in places like Kosovo, Indonesia and Palestine. I don't want to respond with that kind of foolish rebuttal because I abhor the senseless murder of all human beings.

The truth is, fanaticism can spring from misguided excess in any religion, and Muslims who kill in the name of their beliefs are not true Muslims. Aggression is not a tenet of our religion, but rather something that is condemned except in self-defense. The Quran states: "Fight in the cause of Allah those who fight you, but commit no aggression; for Allah loves not transgressors" (al-Baqarah 2:190).

If few people understand that Islam is a peaceful religion, even fewer know how beautiful it can be. When I studied in Cairo during my junior year of college, my grandmother had a religion teacher come to her house every week to teach us the Quran. Hearing him chant the verses was like listening to breathtaking music. There is also an element of poetry in a Muslim's everyday life. One says "Allah" or "ma sha'aAllah" ("as God wills") upon seeing something beautiful, like a sunset or a newborn baby. Whenever family members or friends part, one says, "La illah illaAllah" ("there is only one God") and the other responds, "Muhammad rasoul Allah" ("Muhammad is God's prophet").

To me, informing people about these wonderful aspects of Islam is a pleasure, not a burden. There are signs that Americans may be ready to learn. I was moved recently when I saw a woman on the subway reading a book about Islam to her young daughter. She explained that she was teaching herself, as well as her daughter. If more people take that approach, there will come a day when fanaticism is no longer equated with faith, and Muslims aren't seen as terrorists but as human beings.

66

The Myth of the Latin Woman:
I Just Met a Girl Named María

Judith Ortiz Cofer

On a bus trip to London from Oxford University where I was earning some graduate credits one summer, a young man, obviously fresh from a pub, spotted me and as if struck by inspiration went down on his knees in the aisle. With both hands over his heart he broke into an Irish tenor's rendition of "María" from *West Side Story*. My politely amused fellow passengers gave his lovely voice the round of gentle applause it deserved. Though I was not quite as amused, I managed my version of an English smile: no show of teeth, no extreme contortions of the facial muscles—I was at this time of my life practicing reserve and cool. Oh, that British control, how I coveted it. But María had followed me to London, reminding me of a prime fact of my life: you can leave the Island, master the English language, and travel as far as you can, but if you are a Latina, especially one like me who so obviously belongs to Rita Moreno's gene pool, the Island travels with you.

This is sometimes a very good thing—it may win you that extra minute of someone's attention. But with some people, the same things can make *you* an island—not so much a tropical paradise as an Alcatraz, a place nobody wants to visit. As a Puerto Rican girl growing up in the United States and wanting like most children to "belong," I resented the stereotype that my Hispanic appearance called forth from many people I met.

Our family lived in a large urban center in New Jersey during the sixties, where life was designed as a microcosm of my parents' casas on the island. We spoke in Spanish, we ate Puerto Rican food bought at the bodega, and we practiced strict Catholicism complete with Saturday confession and Sunday mass at a church where our parents were accommodated into a one-hour Spanish mass slot, performed by a Chinese priest trained as a missionary for Latin America.

As a girl I was kept under strict surveillance, since virtue and modesty were, by cultural equation, the same as family honor. As a teenager I was instructed on how to behave as a proper señorita. But it was a conflicting message girls got, since the Puerto Rican mothers also encouraged their daughters to look and act like women and to dress in clothes our Anglo friends and their mothers found too "mature" for our age. It was, and is, cultural, yet I often felt humiliated when I appeared at an American friend's party wearing a dress more suitable to a semiformal than to a playroom birthday celebration. At Puerto Rican festivities, neither the music nor the colors we wore could be too loud. I still experience a vague sense of letdown when I'm invited to a "party" and it turns out to be a marathon conversation in hushed tones rather than a fiesta with salsa, laughter, and dancing—the kind of celebration I remember from my childhood.

I remember Career Day in our high school, when teachers told us to come dressed as if for a job interview. It quickly became obvious that to the barrio girls, "dressing up" sometimes meant wearing ornate jewelry and clothing that would be more appropriate (by mainstream standards) for the company Christmas party than as daily office attire. That morning I had agonized in front of my closet, trying to figure out what a "career girl" would wear because, essentially, except for Marlo Thomas on TV, I had no models on which to base my decision. I knew how to dress for school: at the Catholic school I attended we all wore uniforms; I knew how to dress for Sunday mass, and I knew what dresses to wear for parties at my relatives' homes. Though I do not recall the precise details of my Career Day outfit, it must have been a composite of the above choices. But I remember a comment my friend (an Italian-American) made in later years that coalesced my impressions of that day. She said that at the business school she was attending the Puerto Rican girls always stood out for wearing "everything at once." She meant, of course, too much jewelry, too many accessories. On that day at school, we were simply made the negative models by the nuns who were themselves not credible fashion experts to any of us. But it was painfully obvious to me that to the others, in their tailored skirts and silk blouses, we must have seemed "hopeless" and "vulgar." Though I now know that most adolescents feel out of step much of the time, I also know that for the Puerto Rican girls of my generation that sense was intensified. The way our teachers and classmates looked at us that day in school was just a taste of the culture clash that awaited us in the real world, where prospective employers and men on the street would often misinterpret our tight skirts and jingling bracelets as a come-on.

Mixed cultural signals have perpetuated certain stereotypes—for example, that of the Hispanic woman as the "Hot Tamale" or sexual firebrand. It is a one-dimensional view that the media have found easy to promote. In their special vocabulary, advertisers have designated "sizzling" and "smoldering" as the adjectives of choice for describing not only the foods but also the women of Latin America. From conversations in my house I recall hearing about the harassment that Puerto Rican women endured in factories where the "boss men" talked to them as if sexual innuendo was all they understood and, worse, often gave them the choice of submitting to advances or being fired.

It is custom, however, not chromosomes, that leads us to choose scarlet over pale pink. As young girls, we were influenced in our decisions about clothes and colors by the women—older sisters and mothers who had grown up on a tropical island where the natural environment was a riot of primary colors, where showing your skin was one way to keep cool as well as to look sexy. Most important of all, on the island, women perhaps felt freer to dress and move more provocatively, since, in most cases, they were protected by the traditions, mores, and laws of a Spanish/ Catholic system of morality and machismo whose main rule was: *You may look at my sister, but if you touch her I will kill you.* The extended family and church structure could provide a young woman with a circle of safety in her small pueblo on the island; if a man "wronged" a girl, everyone would close in to save her family honor.

This is what I have gleaned from my discussions as an adult with older Puerto Rican women. They have told me about dressing in their best party clothes on Saturday nights and going to the town's plaza to promenade with their girlfriends in front of the boys they liked. The males were thus given an opportunity to admire the women and to express their admiration in the form of *piropos*: erotically charged street poems they composed on the spot. I have been subjected to a few piropos while visiting the Island, and they can be outrageous, although custom dictates that they must never cross into obscenity. This ritual, as I understand it, also entails a show of studied indifference on the woman's part; if she is "decent," she must not acknowledge the man's impassioned words. So I do understand how things can be lost in translation. When a Puerto Rican girl dressed in her idea of what is attractive meets a man from the mainstream culture who has been trained to react to certain types of clothing as a sexual signal, a clash is likely to take place. The line I first heard based on this aspect of the myth happened when the boy who took me to my first formal dance leaned over to plant a sloppy overeager kiss painfully on my mouth, and when I didn't respond with sufficient passion said in a resentful tone: "I thought you Latin girls were supposed to mature early"—my first instance of being thought of as a fruit or vegetable—I was supposed to *ripen*, not just grow into womanhood like other girls.

It is surprising to some of my professional friends that some people, including those who should know better, still put others "in their place." Though rarer, these incidents are still commonplace in my life. It happened to me most recently during a stay at a very classy metropolitan hotel favored by young professional couples for their weddings. Late one evening after the theater, as I walked toward my room with my new colleague (a woman with whom I was coordinating an arts program), a middle-aged man in a tuxedo, a young girl in satin and lace on his arm, stepped directly into our path. With his champagne glass extended toward me, he exclaimed, "Evita!"

Our way blocked, my companion and I listened as the man half-recited, half-bellowed "Don't Cry for Me, Argentina." When he finished, the young girl said: "How about a round of applause for my daddy?" We complied, hoping this would bring the silly spectacle to a close. I was becoming aware that our little group was attracting the attention of the other guests. "Daddy" must have perceived this too, and he once more barred the way as we tried to walk past him. He began to shout-sing a ditty to the tune of "La Bamba"—except the lyrics were about a girl named María whose exploits all rhymed with her name and gonorrhea. The girl kept saying "Oh, Daddy" and looking at me with pleading eyes. She wanted me to laugh along with the others. My companion and I stood silently waiting for the man to end his offensive song. When he finished, I looked not at him but at his daughter. I advised her calmly never to ask her father what he had done in the army. Then I walked between them and to my room. My friend complimented me on my cool handling of the situation. I confessed to her that I really had wanted to push the jerk into the swimming pool. I knew that this same man—probably a corporate executive, well educated, even worldly by most standards—would not have been likely to regale a white woman with a dirty song in public. He would perhaps have checked his impulse by assuming that she could be somebody's wife or mother, or at least *somebody* who might take offense. But to him, I was just an Evita or a María: merely a character in his cartoon-populated universe.

Because of my education and my proficiency with the English language, I have acquired many mechanisms for dealing with the anger I experience. This was not true for my parents, nor is it true for the many Latin women working at menial jobs who must put up with stereotypes about our ethnic group such as: "They make good domestics." This is another facet of the myth of the Latin woman in the United States. Its origin is simple to deduce. Work as domestics, waitressing, and factory jobs are all that's available to women with little English and few skills. The myth of the Hispanic menial has been sustained by the same media phenomenon that made "Mammy" from *Gone with the Wind* America's idea of the black woman for generations; María, the housemaid or counter girl, is now indelibly etched into the national psyche. The big and the little screens have presented us with the picture of the funny Hispanic maid, mispronouncing words and cooking up a spicy storm in a shiny California kitchen.

This media-engendered image of the Latina in the United States has been documented by feminist Hispanic scholars, who claim that such portrayals are partially responsible for the denial of opportunities for upward mobility among Latinas in the professions. I have a Chicana friend working on a Ph.D. in philosophy at a major university. She says her doctor still shakes his head in puzzled amazement at all the "big words" she uses. Since I do not wear my diplomas around my neck for all to see, I too have on occasion been sent to that "kitchen," where some think I obviously belong.

One such incident that has stayed with me, though I recognize it as a minor offense, happened on the day of my first public poetry reading. It took place in Miami in a boat-restaurant where we were having lunch before the event. I was nervous and excited as I walked in with my notebook in my hand. An older woman motioned me to her table. Thinking (foolish me) that she wanted me to autograph a copy of my brand new slender volume of verse, I went over. She ordered a cup of coffee from me, assuming that I was the waitress. Easy enough to mistake my poems for menus, I suppose. I know that it wasn't an intentional act of cruelty, yet of all the good things that happened that day, I remember that scene most clearly, because it reminded me of what I had to overcome before anyone would take me seriously. In retrospect I understand that my anger gave my reading fire, that I have almost always taken doubts in my abilities as a challenge—and that the result is, most times, a feeling of satisfaction at having won a convert when I see the cold, appraising eyes warm to my words, the body language change, the smile that indicates that I have opened some avenue for communication. That day I read to that woman and her lowered eyes told me that she was embarrassed at her little faux pas, and when I willed her to look up at me, it was my victory, and she graciously allowed me to punish her with my full attention. We shook hands at the end of the reading, and I never saw her again. She has probably forgotten the whole thing but maybe not.

Yet I am one of the lucky ones. My parents made it possible for me to acquire a stronger footing in the mainstream culture by giving me the chance at an education. And books and art have saved me from the harsher forms of ethnic and racial prejudice that many of my Hispanic *compañeras* have had to endure. I travel a lot around the United States, reading from my books of poetry and my novel, and the reception I most often receive is one of positive interest by people who want to know more about my culture. There are, however, thousands of Latinas without the privilege of an education or the entrée into society that I have. For them life is a struggle against the misconceptions perpetuated by the myth of the Latina as whore, domestic, or criminal. We cannot change this by legislating the way people look at us. The transformation, as I see it, has to occur at a much more individual level. My personal goal in my public life is to try to replace the old pervasive stereotypes and myths about Latinas with a much more interesting set of realities. Every time I give a reading, I hope the stories I tell, the dreams and fears I examine in my work, can achieve some universal truth which will get my audience past the particulars of my skin color, my accent, or my clothes.

I once wrote a poem in which I called us Latinas "God's brown daughters." This poem is really a prayer of sorts, offered upward, but also, through the human-to-human channel of art, outward. It is a prayer for communication, and for respect. In it, Latin women pray "in Spanish to an Anglo God/with a Jewish heritage," and they are "fervently hoping/that if not omnipotent,/at least He be bilingual."

67

Los Intersticios:
Recasting Moving Selves

Evelyn Alsultany

> Ethnicity in such a world needs to be recast so that our moving selves can be acknowledged. . . . Who am I? When am I? The questions that are asked in the street, of my identity, mold me. Appearing in the flesh, I am cast afresh, a female of color—skin color, hair texture, clothing, speech, all marking me in ways that I could scarcely have conceived of.
>
> —MEENA ALEXANDER

I'm in a graduate class at the New School in New York City. A white female sits next to me and we begin "friendly" conversation. She asks me where I'm from. I reply that I was born and raised in New York City and return the question. She tells me she is from Ohio and has lived in New York for several years. She continues her inquiry: "Oh . . . well, how about your parents?" (I feel her trying to map me onto her narrow cartography; New York is not a sufficient answer. She analyzes me according to binary axes of sameness and difference. She detects only difference at first glance, and seeks to pigeonhole me. In her framework, my body is marked, excluded, not from this country. A seemingly "friendly" question turns into a claim to land and belonging.) "My father is Iraqi and my mother Cuban," I answer. "How interesting. Are you a U.S. citizen?"

I am waiting for the NYC subway. A man also waiting asks me if I too am Pakistani. I reply that I'm part Iraqi and part Cuban. He asks if I am Muslim, and I reply that I am Muslim. He asks me if I am married, and I tell him I'm not. In cultural camaraderie he leans over and says that he has cousins in Pakistan available for an arranged marriage if my family so desires. (My Cubanness, as well as my own relationship to my cultural identity, evaporates as he assumes that Arab plus Muslim equals arranged marriage. I can identify: he reminds me of my Iraqi relatives and I know he means well.) I tell him that I'm not interested in marriage but thank him for his kindness. (I accept his framework and respond accordingly, avoiding an awkward situation in which he realizes that I am not who he assumes I am, offering him recognition and validation for his [mis]identification.)

From *This Bridge We Call Home*, Gloria E. Anzaldúa and AnaLouise Keating, eds. (Routledge, 2002).

I am in a New York City deli waiting for my bagel to toast. The man behind the counter asks if I'm an Arab Muslim (he too is Arab and Muslim). I reply that yes, I am by part of my father. He asks my name, and I say, "Evelyn." In utter disdain, he tells me that I could not possibly be Muslim; if I were truly Muslim I would have a Muslim name. What was I doing with such a name? I reply (after taking a deep breath and telling myself that it's not worth getting upset over) that my Cuban mother named me and that I honor my mother. He points to the fact that I'm wearing lipstick and have not changed my name, which he finds to be completely inappropriate and despicable, and says that I am a reflection of the decay of the Arab Muslim in America.

I'm on an airplane flying from Miami to New York. I'm sitting next to an Ecuadorian man. He asks me where I'm from. I tell him. He asks me if I'm more Arab, Latina, or American, and I state that I'm all of the above. He says that's impossible. I must be more of one ethnicity than another. He determines that I am not really Arab, that I'm more Latina because of the camaraderie he feels in our speaking Spanish.

I am in Costa Rica. I walk the streets and my brown skin and dark hair blend in with the multiple shades of brown around me. I love this first-time experience of blending in! I walk into a coffee shop for some café con leche, and my fantasy of belonging is shattered when the woman preparing the coffee asks me where I'm from. I tell her that I was born and raised in New York City by a Cuban mother and an Arab father. She replies, "Que eres una gringa."

I am shocked by the contextuality of identity: that my body is marked as gringa in Costa Rica, as Latina in some U.S. contexts, Arab in others, in some times and spaces not adequately Arab, or Latina, or "American," and in other contexts simply as *other*.

My body becomes marked with meaning as I enter public space. My identity fractures as I experience differing dislocations in multiple contexts. Sometimes people otherize me, sometimes they identify with me. Both situations can be equally problematic. Those who otherize me fail to see a shared humanity and those who identify with me fail to see difference; my Arab or Muslim identity negates my Cuban heritage. Identification signifies belonging or home, and I pretend to be that home for the mistaken person. It's my good deed for the day (I know how precious it can be to find a moment of familiarity with a stranger). The bridge becomes my back as I feign belonging, and I become that vehicle for others, which I desire for myself. Although it is illusory, I do identify with the humanity of the situation—the desire to belong in this world, to be understood. But the frameworks used to (mis)read my body, to disconnect me, wear on me. I try to develop a new identity. What should I try to pass for next time? Perhaps I'll just say I'm Cuban to those who appear to be Arab or South Asian. A friend suggests I say I'm an Italian from Brooklyn. I wonder if I could successfully pass for that. Ethnicity needs to be recast so that our moving selves can be acknowledged.

NOTES

I would like to thank Marisol Negrón, Alexandra Lang, María Helena Rueda, Ericka Beckman, Karina Hodoyan, Sara Rondinel, Jessi Aaron, and Cynthia María Paccacerqua for their feedback in our writing seminar at Stanford University with Mary Pratt. I would especially like to thank Mary Pratt for her invaluable feedback, and AnaLouise Keating and Gloria Anzaldúa for their thoughtful editing.

68

The Circuit

Francisco Jiménez

It was that time of year again. Ito, the strawberry sharecropper, did not smile. It was natural. The peak of the strawberry season was over and the last few days the workers, most of them braceros, were not picking as many boxes as they had during the months of June and July.

As the last days of August disappeared, so did the number of braceros. Sunday, only one—the best picker—came to work. I liked him. Sometimes we talked during our half-hour lunch break. That is how I found out he was from Jalisco, the same state in Mexico my family was from. That Sunday was the last time I saw him.

When the sun had tired and sunk behind the mountains, Ito signaled us that it was time to go home. "Ya esora," he yelled in his broken Spanish. Those were the words I waited for twelve hours a day, every day, seven days a week, week after week. And the thought of not hearing them again saddened me.

As we drove home Papá did not say a word. With both hands on the wheel, he stared at the dirt road. My older brother, Roberto, was also silent. He leaned his head back and closed his eyes. Once in a while he cleared from his throat the dust that blew in from outside.

Yes, it was that time of year. When I opened the front door to the shack, I stopped. Everything we owned was neatly packed in cardboard boxes. Suddenly I felt even more the weight of hours, days, weeks, and months of work. I sat down on a box. The thought of having to move to Fresno and knowing what was in store for me there brought tears to my eyes.

From *The Arizona Quarterly*. Copyright © 1973. Reprinted by permission of the author.

That night I could not sleep. I lay in bed thinking about how much I hated this move.

A little before five o'clock in the morning, Papá woke everyone up. A few minutes later, the yelling and screaming of my little brothers and sisters, for whom the move was a great adventure, broke the silence of dawn. Shortly, the barking of the dogs accompanied them.

While we packed the breakfast dishes, Papá went outside to start the "Carcanchita." That was the name Papá gave his old '38 black Plymouth. He bought it in a used-car lot in Santa Rosa in the winter of 1949. Papá was very proud of his little jalopy. He had a right to be proud of it. He spent a lot of time looking at other cars before buying this one. When he finally chose the "Carcanchita," he checked it thoroughly before driving it out of the car lot. He examined every inch of the car. He listened to the motor, tilting his head from side to side like a parrot, trying to detect any noises that spelled car trouble. After being satisfied with the looks and sounds of the car, Papá then insisted on knowing who the original owner was. He never did find out from the car salesman, but he bought the car anyway. Papá figured the original owner must have been an important man because behind the rear seat of the car he found a blue necktie.

Papá parked the car out in front and left the motor running. "Listo," he yelled. Without saying a word, Roberto and I began to carry the boxes out to the car. Roberto carried the two big boxes and I carried the two smaller ones. Papá then threw the mattress on top of the car roof and tied it with ropes to the front and rear bumpers.

Everything was packed except Mamá's pot. It was an old large galvanized pot she had picked up at an army surplus store in Santa Maria the year I was born. The pot had many dents and nicks, and the more dents and nicks it acquired the more Mamá liked it. "Mi olla," she used to say proudly.

I held the front door open as Mamá carefully carried out her pot by both handles, making sure not to spill the cooked beans. When she got to the car, Papá reached out to help her with it. Roberto opened the rear car door and Papá gently placed it on the floor behind the front seat. All of us then climbed in. Papá sighed, wiped the sweat off his forehead with his sleeve, and said wearily: "Es todo."

As we drove away, I felt a lump in my throat. I turned around and looked at our little shack for the last time.

At sunset we drove into a labor camp near Fresno. Since Papá did not speak English, Mamá asked the camp foreman if he needed any more workers. "We don't need no more," said the foreman, scratching his head. "Check with Sullivan down the road. Can't miss him. He lives in a big white house with a fence around it."

When we got there, Mamá walked up to the house. She went through a white gate, past a row of rose bushes, up the stairs to the front door. She rang the doorbell. The porch light went on and a tall husky man came out. They exchanged a few words. After the man went in, Mamá clasped her hands and hurried back to the car. "We have work! Mr. Sullivan said we can stay there the whole season," she said, gasping and pointing to an old garage near the stables.

The garage was worn out by the years. It had no windows. The walls, eaten by termites, strained to support the roof full of holes. The dirt floor, populated by earth worms, looked like a gray road map.

That night, by the light of a kerosene lamp, we unpacked and cleaned our new home. Roberto swept away the loose dirt, leaving the hard ground. Papá plugged the holes in the walls with old newspapers and tin can tops. Mamá fed my little brothers and sisters. Papá and Roberto then brought in the mattress and placed it on the far corner of the garage. "Mamá, you and the little ones sleep on the mattress. Roberto, Panchito, and I will sleep outside under the trees," Papá said.

Early next morning Mr. Sullivan showed us where his crop was, and after breakfast, Papá, Roberto, and I headed for the vineyard to pick.

Around nine o'clock the temperature had risen to almost one hundred degrees. I was completely soaked in sweat and my mouth felt as if I had been chewing on a handkerchief. I walked over to the end of the row, picked up the jug of water we had brought, and began drinking. "Don't drink too much; you'll get sick," Roberto shouted. No sooner had he said that than I felt sick to my stomach. I dropped to my knees and let the jug roll off my hands. I remained motionless with my eyes glued on the hot sandy ground. All I could hear was the drone of insects. Slowly I began to recover. I poured water over my face and neck and watched the dirty water run down my arms to the ground.

I still felt a little dizzy when we took a break to eat lunch. It was past two o'clock and we sat underneath a large walnut tree that was on the side of the road. While we ate, Papá jotted down the number of boxes we had picked. Roberto drew designs on the ground with a stick. Suddenly I noticed Papá's face turn pale as he looked down the road. "Here comes the school bus," he whispered loudly in alarm. Instinctively, Roberto and I ran and hid in the vineyards. We did not want to get in trouble for not going to school. The neatly dressed boys about my age got off. They carried books under their arms. After they crossed the street, the bus drove away. Roberto and I came out from hiding and joined Papá. "Tienen que tener cuidado," he warned us.

After lunch we went back to work. The sun kept beating down. The buzzing insects, the wet sweat, and the hot dry dust made the afternoon seem to last forever. Finally the mountains around the valley reached out and swallowed the sun. Within an hour it was too dark to continue picking. The vines blanketed the grapes, making it difficult to see the bunches. "Vámonos," said Papá, signaling to us that it was time to quit work. Papá then took out a pencil and began to figure out how much we had earned our first day. He wrote down numbers, crossed some out, wrote down some more. "Quince," he murmured.

When we arrived home, we took a cold shower underneath a water-hose. We then sat down to eat dinner around some wooden crates that served as a table. Mamá had cooked a special meal for us. We had rice and tortillas with "carne con chile," my favorite dish.

The next morning I could hardly move. My body ached all over. I felt little control over my arms and legs. This feeling went on every morning for days until my muscles finally got used to the work.

It was Monday, the first week of November. The grape season was over and I could now go to school. I woke up early that morning and lay in bed, looking at the stars and savoring the thought of not going to work and of starting sixth grade for the first time that year. Since I could not sleep, I decided to get up and join Papá and Roberto at breakfast. I sat at the table across from Roberto, but I kept my head down. I did not want to look up and face him. I knew he was sad. He was not going to school today. He was not going tomorrow, or next week, or next month. He would not go until the cotton season was over, and that was sometime in February. I rubbed my hands together and watched the dry, acid stained skin fall to the floor in little rolls.

When Papá and Roberto left for work, I felt relief. I walked to the top of a small grade next to the shack and watched the "Carcanchita" disappear in the distance in a cloud of dust.

Two hours later, around eight o'clock, I stood by the side of the road waiting for school bus number twenty. When it arrived I climbed in. Everyone was busy either talking or yelling. I sat in an empty seat in the back.

When the bus stopped in front of the school, I felt very nervous. I looked out the bus window and saw boys and girls carrying books under their arms. I put my hands in my pant pockets and walked to the principal's office. When I entered I heard a woman's voice say: "May I help you?" I was startled. I had not heard English for months. For a few seconds I remained speechless. I looked at the lady who waited for an answer. My first instinct was to answer her in Spanish, but I held back. Finally, after struggling for English words, I managed to tell her that I wanted to enroll in the sixth grade. After answering many questions, I was led to the classroom.

Mr. Lema, the sixth grade teacher, greeted me and assigned me a desk. He then introduced me to the class. I was so nervous and scared at that moment when everyone's eyes were on me that I wished I were with Papá and Roberto picking cotton. After taking roll, Mr. Lema gave the class the assignment for the first hour. "The first thing we have to do this morning is finish reading the story we began yesterday," he said enthusiastically. He walked up to me, handed me an English book, and asked me to read. "We are on page 125," he said politely. When I heard this, I felt my blood rush to my head; I felt dizzy. "Would you like to read?" he asked hesitantly. I opened the book to page 125. My mouth was dry. My eyes began to water. I could not begin. "You can read later," Mr. Lema said understandingly.

For the rest of the reading period I kept getting angrier and angrier with myself. I should have read, I thought to myself.

During recess I went into the restroom and opened my English book to page 125. I began to read in a low voice, pretending I was in class. There were many words I did not know. I closed the book and headed back to the classroom.

Mr. Lema was sitting at his desk correcting papers. When I entered he looked up at me and smiled. I felt better. I walked up to him and asked if he could help me with the new words. "Gladly," he said.

The rest of the month I spent my lunch hours working on English with Mr. Lema, my best friend at school.

One Friday during lunch hour Mr. Lema asked me to take a walk with him to the music room. "Do you like music?" he asked me as we entered the building.

"Yes, I like corridos," I answered. He then picked up a trumpet, blew on it and handed it to me. The sound gave me goose bumps. I knew that sound. I had heard it in many corridos. "How would you like to learn how to play it?" he asked. He must have read my face because before I could answer, he added: "I'll teach you how to play it during our lunch hours."

That day I could hardly wait to tell Papá and Mamá the great news. As I got off the bus, my little brothers and sisters ran up to meet me. They were yelling and screaming. I thought they were happy to see me, but when I opened the door to our shack, I saw that everything we owned was neatly packed in cardboard boxes.

69

What I Learned about Jews

Joe Wood

The preacher begins his tale, then reads some history: You are black and proud and you will remember that somewhere along the way some of the people in our line were made very low and not tough at all. I recall: We laughed at the whites when their backs were turned, and our mother spit out the lemon seeds under the porch because she said someday a tree with its natty leaves would lick light there long after we moved to the city. We were slaves then and maybe we are still today, slaves, our blackness a badge of terrifying knowledge, a certificate of human accomplishment, its possibility and strength, like a god or a flame inside cupped hands, not something to flee from like a dead body or a bad smell.

While Jews, along with Italians and the Irish, have in most of the century's renderings of American history been assigned the role of "immigrant," and as such are permitted a history before America, Negroes were made in America. That left us with a blank place where a history should be: no place to put our peoplehood and few ways to understand the situation. So we patched our wounds with the pages of the Bible. So in church, our hospital, we tell the tale over and over again; how much we resemble the ancient Jews, how we too are slaves awaiting deliverance. We hold this tale more dear than did the pilgrims who made us slaves—but what of the Jews, who would certainly want their story back?

It was simple and plain. You'd heard that the Jews controlled jazz, the media, the Democratic Party, the civil rights movement and Harlem real estate, and you wondered. You knew this didn't explain why the police beat you up or why the public education system was a mess or why your neighborhood was without cable and regular garbage pickup, but still you wondered.

"Don't let them call you an anti-Semite, sista," he said. "You'll never work again."

"Jewish people run Hollywood, just like they do *The New York Times*," you said.

"Definitely," he said.

"If that's the way it works, why can't I say it?"

"You know why," he said. "The Jews got it sewed up, and refuse to admit it. I'm tired of reading about Israel and the Holocaust. And about how they worked in the civil rights movement. My theory is they produced the civil rights movement and they pumped up King and all them preachers as a public relations diversion so no one would notice them buying mortgages."

"Well . . . ," you said, scratching your nose. You felt guilty whenever someone talked about "the Jews."

He picked up the slack. "I read where the Anti-Defamation League said the whiteboys are the ones writing 'Heil Hitler' and 'Jewboy' and stuff like that on the synagogues. Niggas got better sense than that."

"True," you said.

There was a silence.

"The Jews," he said, pausing. "My theory is the Holocaust messed them up. No matter how comfortable life starts to feel, they always bring back the Nazis. Or use them as an excuse to beat down niggas."

"Six million is a lot of million," you said, in a light voice.

"I'm telling you, Holocaust got them psychotic. But I want to hear them talk about how many million of us died getting here. Six million's only a drop in the ocean compared to what we went through. I want to know how many of us died on their slave ships. They never teach about that Holocaust."

Then he continued. "You don't hate them sometimes?"

Very quickly you said, "No."

"Good. Well I do. I'll be honest. I hate them sometimes. Because they were the minstrels. Al Jolson was a Jew and the Beastie Boys are Jews. Somebody even told me Elvis was a Jew. They bought our stuff for a dime and made a mint off it. Fats Waller to Chuck Berry to all them rappers—it's the Jews making the money. They act like your friend, but they're the No. 1 pimps of niggas. You got to admit that."

"Jewish people definitely don't have a monopoly on that."

"But the Jews were the ones who made Hollywood: Selznick and Goldwyn and Mayer—Jews. It's a fact. Undeniable. Now it's to the point where they don't even have to slander us anymore. They got their Negro minstrels to say what they want in their papers and magazines and they give 'em a dollar and a prize and it's nothing but Negro smiles. You know what I'm saying—they hate niggas because they know we got their number."

You felt the pull of the words. Down. And then you felt guilty inside, because you wanted to say something more, to separate yourself, and you couldn't, so you smiled—even though you knew there was a limit to your solidarity with the brotha. James Baldwin got it right when he wrote about the special disappointment you've reserved for the Jews—also ex-slaves, but that's where your complicity ended. You knew Jewish people didn't cause more black problems than other whites did. You remembered the preacher's story of the mother and her lemon tree, our collective selfhood. This was the real story, and it actually had very little to do with Jews. You remembered, and you comforted yourself by saying your blackness and his blackness was why you smiled, but suddenly you felt the urge to spit something out.

I read a lot as a kid. I was a curious and obedient boy who paid close attention to his parents' exhortations about the improvement of the race. I had a role to play. My parents were determined to see their children become doctors or lawyers or captains of industry or something to help black people to be proud, so I tried hard, very hard—I brought all my books to bed. My mother drove my sister and me to the library, and my father drove us to private school, and when I lay down I would open the books: the Bible, Edith Wharton, Malcolm X, *The New Republic*, James Joyce, Yukio Mishima, Gerard Manley Hopkins, James Baldwin, Spiderman, Tom Wolfe, *Playboy*, Maya Angelou, John le Carré, Kurt Vonnegut.

I also read Norman Mailer's tales and Saul Bellow's stories and Norman Podhoretz's "My Negro Problem—and Ours." Podhoretz's essay described and tried to defend a racist Jew's racism. I still think of that piece whenever I hear talk of black anti-Semitism. But as I bring my own Jewish story to light now, I will refrain from harping on any "Jewish problem"; I will instead try to tell the truth, which is more complicated than words like "problem" allow.

For I grew up feeling a little like a Jew. Most of the children at Riverdale School in the Bronx were Jewish, and I went there for 10 years. I tried to fit in and did. I listened to the same music and wore the same clothes and laughed at Woody Allen movies for the same reasons as my peers. I lived on the other side of town, but I knew the difference between the words "meshugga" and "zaftig"—I spoke the language of my environment. I even adopted my classmates' views of the world.

I shared, for instance, my Jewish schoolmates' dislike of WASP's even though I hadn't met many. The WASP's mainly went to Collegiate and places outside the city like Hotchkiss or Andover, and only the dumbest of their children came to Riverdale. Most of the school's administrators were of Anglo heritage, and this was a problem for many of the Jewish parents. My peers followed their parents' lead. I remember them saying the goyim "ruled the country," then saying "You're a Jew" during a dispute about money; or fawning over Nordic facial features, making fun of the WASP's with Jewish noses. This perspective resembled the distaste for whites expressed around my neighborhood, a blend of vocal contempt and private admiration.

Our parents didn't particularly care for whites, but they weren't hostile in an active way. No one would have acted funny or said anything to any of the block's remaining few, the ones who hadn't moved to Jersey or Westchester. Mostly, you heard talk about Jamaicans or the islanders we derisively called 'Ricans. The whites usually discussed were the Italians, who still had some shops in the area. They were reputedly mafia and were to be avoided if possible, though they were admired for their sense of family and their piety.

But there wasn't much talk of Jews, even in church. I remember a Catholic friend saying they were the ones who betrayed Christ, and it made sense. We had all learned that Jews were the ones who had inhabited the long dark before the coming of the Lord. But no preacher or Sunday school teacher ever said anything directly against Jewish people when I was around, except that we were oppressed, like the blood of Abraham.

When our parents talked about Jews, the topic was usually commerce. You might be able to go to Delancey Street and "Jew down" a shopkeeper, it was said, but you'd probably fail, because they're too smart with money. The Jew doesn't care about anybody but himself. The Jew keeps money and power inside the Jewish community. If you hire a Jewish accountant, he's going to recommend a Jewish lawyer. *Believe me.* Black people, our parents emphasized, need to learn how to stick together the way the Jews do.

This casual collection of attitudes hardened over time at school, where I encountered Jews every day. No matter how Jewish I felt, I could not completely ignore my difference. Lines between black people and Jews were partly hidden, but they were always there. I remember an outraged conversation about the Holocaust among some of the older children on the bus ride back to our side of town. One of the Jewish students had the nerve to argue that the Holocaust was far worse than slavery, and everyone agreed the kid was *arrogant.* From then on I used this word often—I began to record all events that proved it. There was the pity in the voices of otherwise lovely people when the subject of black America came up. There were the patronizing parents who wanted their daughter to date me because, "Why should it matter?" There was the outright racism of certain vicious classmates. In ninth grade, Scott W. told me in the library that I should be glad I'm not still in Africa—if it weren't for Europe I would still be chucking spears. Another classmate said that while black people were gifted at sports and music, Jews had provided the world with intellectual genius. As proof, he ticked off three names: Freud, Einstein, Marx. I got very angry.

For a long time I wondered whether the Jews were really chosen by God, as one of my Jewish classmates suggested. The argument seemed watertight. Wherever Jews were given the chance they have shown themselves to be smarter than anyone else. *Look at how well we've done in America and everywhere else we've gone. Look at the Jews. Look.*

This was reinforced by Riverdale's unofficial story: There exists a WASP-Jewish-black hierarchy, and it is the real ordering structure of the world. It explained our school, the paltry numbers of blacks, the predominance of Jewish students, the continuing dominance of WASP administrators. Everything we saw seemed natural. The blacks were an undiscussed underclass, the Jews were the electorate, the WASP's democracy's vanishing counsel. Each group seemed chosen for its role by nature and God.

But things shifted drastically when I went to college. On entering Yale I studied my Jewish peers, and kept a firm eye on the school's pretensions to Oxford and Cambridge, the way students were asked to call some administrators "Master," as if slavery never happened. Yale was, to say the least, a problematic institution for black students, a cold place that required all sorts of submission, but it was also difficult for Jewish students, and to a degree I hadn't expected.

What I saw challenged any belief I had in Jewish chosenness. For the first time in my life I found myself in a school where Jews were simply one smart group of many. There were also smart people who were blacks and had grown up like me in the rarefied precincts of middle-class whiteness. Black students from cities with high concentrations of Jewish people were familiar with Jewish anxieties about "old" wealth and other WASP virtues, and we also considered anti-Semitism to be a very bad thing. It is fair, however, to say that most of us felt a decidedly grudging admiration for Jewish people. My ideas about Jewish supremacy remained a mix of anger and belief until I witnessed so many of my Jewish classmates folding in the face of Yale's anti-Semitism. I guess I had never had the secret stake my Jewish high-school classmates had in admiring WASP's; seeing Jewish peers genuflect removed any illusions of Jewish chosenness.

Dan and I roomed together during our junior and senior years at Yale. We became close friends even though we competed a lot over grades and once over a woman's affections. We love each other like brothers. Our kinship is not simple. There is the difference in class: Dan is from Wisconsin and his mother is a judge, his father a geneticist; I am from the Bronx and my parents are social workers. While Dan is a serious cyclist and hiker, I am the sort who watches movies and reads. Also, differences lurk within our similarities. In high school, I was one of a very small number of black people at a school of Jews; Dan was a Jew among many Christians. I'm not a nationalist, cultural or otherwise, and Dan is not religious. But alienation has had radically different effects on our lives. While I find more to despise about America each day, Dan's outsider status hasn't affected his love of the country; he believes in this place. There are many divisions between us, and they are real. But so is our bond.

The summer after junior year Dan went to South Africa to monitor what the Government called trials. I remember him working on the application at my desk; I still have a print he gave me of black and white figures tearing down a great house of cards, "Rise and Destruction of Power." Dan took humanism to South Africa and brought me back a distant blackness, as he did when he gave me Miles Davis or Billie Holiday records to check out. There is a passage in John Edgar Wideman's *Brothers and Keepers* in which the author describes wanting to beat down a whiteboy for knowing more about the blues than he did. I understand his rage, but I hardly felt it. Mostly I loved learning about what I didn't know, sometimes covering up how much I was learning, sometimes questioning my friend's authority or authenticity, but always in the main feeling thankful. I believe it is the same mix of sensations Dan felt for me when I talked. I had, after all, grown up among a lot of Jewish people, and he hadn't; his parents had moved from New York to the Midwest. The references I brought from the city contained a curious and appealing atavism: I was a strange native informant reporting on his ancestral home, and he was a native alien of mine.

If Dan was "black" in any way, it was in precisely the same way that I was a "Jew." Our lives were shaped by cross-cultural consumption and the force of political sympathies, neither of which, in the end, necessarily makes you a real group member. Suburban Jewish guys who like black culture—it's a common enough phenomenon, I suppose, as were black kids in the old ghettos who grew up knowing a little Yiddish. Still, our ethnic "guest appearances" counted for something, since they did help make us who we were. Dan and I had chosen each other, after all, because we understood.

Last spring I went to visit Dan in Seattle, where he was clerking for a Federal judge. There was almost no news in that green and fragrant city about blacks and Jews and how we like to fight. It was only Dan and me and my thoughts and the smell of fruit blossoms wafting in through the open window.

I wondered how Dan came to be my brother. Brother. It means something else now. As with the word "immigrant," which in New York no longer means Jews or Italians so much as Dominicans and Haitians and Mexicans and Southeast Asians. Who is a "real" immigrant today, and who is an alien? Who deserves to become a member of the American tribe?

There is a line, a neoconservative "political correctness," on this question. Richard Cohen of *The Washington Post*, for example, had this to say about the boycotts of Asian grocers by blacks: "What a diversion all this picketing and boycotting is. And what a tragedy to boot. In New York, Washington and other cities, certain blacks talk about Asians as if they were involved in a conspiracy against them: Where do they get the money to buy these stores? Certain black leaders curse Asians or, just for good measure, Jews. They are constantly on the lookout for scapegoats. They have so thoroughly accepted the ethic of victimization that they blame others for a situation that they themselves can rectify: open some stores." I think the president of a Korean grocers' group was more to the point when he told a reporter, "We are no different than the Jews, Italians and other Europeans."

Family is made of the people family says are family. Folks like Cohen and the store owner are clearly trying to embrace each other, and leave Negroes outside. They say, *Look at those hard-working Jewish immigrants and sullen, menacing Negroes and remember: the story hasn't changed. Put Dominicans and Haitians and Mexicans here on the problem side, away, and let in the huddled Koreans and*

Eastern Europeans and (white) Cubans — the good ones. They are most like the "model" immigrants who came here early in the century. They deserve to be American. They should be family.

It is as stupid a story as the Rev. Louis Farrakhan's foolishness about Jews, and certainly more dangerous. If family is made of the people family says are family, and if "family" and "immigrant" do not include people who are deemed problematic, collective responsibility for crime, segregated housing, the failure of public education — for all of which blacks are routinely blamed — just disappears. The paradigm is old and familiar.

Dan and I come from better traditions. Today, he is a death penalty defense lawyer. Once in a while, he and I get to talking about pooling our talents to elect him senator from Wisconsin or something. It would make sense: we want more people to get a better deal, especially the most despised, who are so often black. Somehow along the way, Dan and I grew up and examined the stories we'd been told. Thus far, our research has helped usher Dan, the progressive Jew, and me, the progressive black, into the same camp.

But I don't mean to mislead you about my thinking. Politics and the other crossings of our heritages are only part of what Dan and I share. Our brotherhood is made of ethnic sympathies, but it also has nothing to do with our being black or Jewish or any of that, and I love Dan not because he's Jewish or, in some sense, black, and not because I am black or, in some sense, Jewish. While our tribes, and their memories, and their stories, did make us, they also have nothing to do with it. The heart, after all, is raised on a mess of stories, and then it writes its own.

70

Pigskin, Patriarchy, and Pain

Don Sabo

I am sitting down to write as I've done thousands of times over the last decade. But today there's something very different. I'm not in pain.

A half-year ago I underwent back surgery. My physician removed two disks from the lumbar region of my spine and fused three vertebrae using bone scrapings from my right hip. The surgery is called a "spinal fusion." For seventy-two

From *Sex, Violence and Power in Sports: Rethinking Masculinity*, Michael A. Messner and Donald F. Sabo, eds. (Freedom, CA: The Crossing Press). © 1994. Reprinted by permission.

hours I was completely immobilized. On the fifth day, I took a few faltering first steps with one of those aluminum walkers that are usually associated with the elderly in nursing homes. I progressed rapidly and left the hospital after nine days completely free of pain for the first time in years.

How did I, a well-intending and reasonably gentle boy from western Pennsylvania, ever get into so much pain? At a simple level, I ended up in pain because I played a sport that brutalizes men's (and now sometimes women's) bodies. *Why* I played football and bit the bullet of pain, however, is more complicated. Like a young child who learns to dance or sing for a piece of candy, I played for rewards and payoffs. Winning at sport meant winning friends and carving a place for myself within the male pecking order. Success at the "game" would make me less like myself and more like the older boys and my hero, Dick Butkus. Pictures of his hulking and snarling form filled my head and hung over my bed, beckoning me forward like a mythic Siren. If I could be like Butkus, I told myself, people would adore me as much as I adored him. I might even adore myself. As an adolescent I hoped sport would get me attention from the girls. Later, I became more practical-minded and I worried more about my future. What kind of work would I do for a living? Football became my ticket to a college scholarship which, in western Pennsylvania during the early 'sixties, meant a career instead of getting stuck in the steelmills.

The Road to Surgery

My bout with pain and spinal "pathology" began with a decision I made in 1955 when I was 8 years old. I "went out" for football. At the time, I felt uncomfortable inside my body—too fat, too short, too weak. Freckles and glasses, too! I wanted to change my image, and I felt that changing my body was one place to begin. My parents bought me a set of weights, and one of the older boys in the neighborhood was solicited to demonstrate their use. I can still remember the ease with which he lifted the barbell, the veins popping through his bulging biceps in the summer sun, and the sated look of strength and accomplishment on his face. This was to be the image of my future.

That Fall I made a dinner-table announcement that I was going out for football. What followed was a rather inauspicious beginning. First, the initiation rites. Pricking the flesh with thorns until blood was drawn and having hot peppers rubbed in my eyes. Getting punched in the gut again and again. Being forced to wear a jockstrap around my nose and not knowing what was funny. Then came what was to be an endless series of proving myself: calisthenics until my arms ached; hitting hard and fast and knocking the other guy down; getting hit in the groin and not crying. I learned that pain and injury are "part of the game."

I "played" through grade school, co-captained my high school team, and went on to become an inside linebacker and defensive captain at the NCAA Division I level. I learned to be an animal. Coaches took notice of animals. Animals made first team. Being an animal meant being fanatically aggressive and ruthlessly competitive. If I saw an arm in front of me, I trampled it. Whenever blood was spilled, I nodded approval. Broken bones (not mine of course) were secretly seen as little victories within the bigger struggle. The coaches taught me to "punish the other man," but little did I suspect that I was devastating my own body at the same time. There were broken noses, ribs, fingers, toes and teeth, torn muscles and ligaments, bruises, bad knees, and busted lips, and the gradual pulverizing of my spinal column that, by the time my jock career was long over at age 30, had resulted in seven years of near-constant pain. It was a long road to the surgeon's office.

Now surgically freed from its grip, my understanding of pain has changed. Pain had gnawed away at my insides. Pain turned my awareness inward. I blamed myself for my predicament; I thought that I was solely responsible for every twinge and sleepless night. But this view was an illusion. My pain, each individual's pain, is really an expression of a linkage to an outer world of people, events, and forces. The origins of our pain are rooted *outside*, not inside, our skins.

The Pain Principle

Sport is just one of the many areas in our culture where pain is more important than pleasure. Boys are taught that to endure pain is courageous, to survive pain is manly. The principle that pain is "good" and pleasure is "bad" is crudely evident in the "no pain, no gain" philosophy of so many coaches and athletes. The "pain principle" weaves its way into the lives and psyches of male athletes in two fundamental ways. It stifles men's awareness of their bodies and limits our emotional expression. We learn to ignore personal hurts and injuries because they interfere with the "efficiency" and "goals" of the "team." We become adept at taking the feelings that boil up inside us—feelings of insecurity and stress from striving so hard for success—and channeling them in a bundle of rage which is directed at opponents and enemies. This posture toward oneself and the world is not limited to "jocks." It is evident in the lives of many nonathletic men who, as tough guys, deny their authentic physical or emotional needs and develop health problems as a result.

Today, I no longer perceive myself as an *individual* ripped off by athletic injury. Rather, I see myself as just *one more man among many men* who got swallowed up by a social system predicated on male domination. Patriarchy has two structural aspects. First, it is an hierarchical system in which men dominate women in crude and debased, slick and subtle ways. Feminists have made great progress exposing and analyzing this dimension of the edifice of sexism. But it is also a system of *intermale dominance*, in which a minority of men dominates the masses of men. This intermale dominance hierarchy exploits the majority of those it beckons to climb its heights. Patriarchy's mythos of heroism and its morality of power-worship implant visions of ecstasy and masculine excellence in the minds of the boys who ultimately will defend its inequities and ridicule its victims. It is inside this institutional framework that I have begun to explore the essence and scope of "the pain principle."

Taking It

Patriarchy is a form of social hierarchy. Hierarchy breeds inequity and inequity breeds pain. To remain stable, the hierarchy must either justify the pain or explain it away. In a patriarchy, women and the masses of men are fed the cultural message that pain is inevitable and that pain enhances one's character and moral worth. This principle is expressed in Judeo-Christian beliefs. The Judeo-Christian god inflicts or permits pain, yet "the Father" is still revered and loved. Likewise, a chief disciplinarian in the patriarchal family, the father has the right to inflict pain. The "pain principle" also echoes throughout traditional western sexual morality; it is better to experience the pain of *not* having sexual pleasure than it is to have sexual pleasure.

Most men learn to heed these cultural messages and take their "cues for survival" from the patriarchy. The Willie Lomans of the economy pander to the prophets of profit and the American Dream. Soldiers, young and old, salute their neo-Hun generals. Right-wing Christians genuflect before the idols of righteousness, affluence, and conformity. And male athletes adopt the visions and values that coaches are offering: to take orders, to take pain, to "take out" opponents, to take the game seriously, to take women, and to take their place on the team. And if they can't "take it," then the rewards of athletic camaraderie, prestige, scholarship, pro contracts, and community recognition are not forthcoming.

Becoming a football player fosters conformity to male-chauvinistic values and self-abusing lifestyles. It contributes to the legitimacy of a social structure based on patriarchal power. Male competition for prestige and status in sport and elsewhere leads to identification with the relatively few males who control resources and are able to bestow rewards and inflict punishment. Male supremacists are not born, they are made, and traditional athletic socialization is a fundamental contribution to this complex social-psychological and political process. Through sport, many males, indeed, learn to "take it"—that is, to internalize patriarchal values which, in turn, become part of their gender identity and conception of women and society.

My high school coach once evoked the pain principle during a pregame pep talk. For what seemed an eternity, he paced frenetically and silently before us with fists clenched and head bowed. He suddenly stopped and faced us with a smile. It was as though he had approached a podium to begin a long-awaited lecture. "Boys," he began, "people who say that football is a 'contact sport' are dead wrong. Dancing is a contact sport. Football is a game of pain and violence! Now get the hell out of here and kick some ass." We practically ran through the wall of the locker room, surging in unison to fight the coach's war. I see now that the coach was right but for all the wrong reasons. I should have taken him at his word and never played the game!

He Defies You Still:
The Memoirs of a Sissy

Tommi Avicolli

You're just a faggot
No history faces you this morning
A faggot's dreams are scarlet
Bad blood bled from words that scarred[1]

Scene One

A homeroom in a Catholic high school in South Philadelphia. The boy sits quietly in the first aisle, third desk, reading a book. He does not look up, not even for a moment. He is hoping no one will remember he is sitting there. He wishes he were invisible. The teacher is not yet in the classroom so the other boys are talking and laughing loudly.

Suddenly, a voice from beside him:

"Hey, you're a faggot, ain't you?"

The boy does not answer. He goes on reading his book, or rather pretending he is reading his book. It is impossible to actually read the book now.

"Hey, I'm talking to you!"

The boy still does not look up. He is so scared his heart is thumping madly; it feels like it is leaping out of his chest and into his throat. But he can't look up.

"Faggot, I'm talking to you!"

To look up is to meet the eyes of the tormentor.

Suddenly, a sharpened pencil point is thrust into the boy's arm. He jolts, shaking off the pencil, aware that there is blood seeping from the wound.

"What did you do that for?" he asks timidly.

"Cause I hate faggots," the other boy says, laughing. Some other boys begin to laugh, too. A symphony of laughter. The boy feels as if he's going to cry. But he must not cry. Must not cry. So he holds back the tears and tries to read the book again. He must read the book. Read the book.

When the teacher arrives a few minutes later, the class quiets down. The boy does not tell the teacher what has happened. He spits on the wound to clean it, dabbing it with a tissue until the bleeding stops. For weeks he fears some dreadful infection from the lead in the pencil point.

Scene Two

The boy is walking home from school. A group of boys (two, maybe three, he is not certain) grab him from behind, drag him into an alley and beat him up. When he gets home, he races up to his room, refusing dinner ("I don't feel well," he tells his mother through the locked door) and spends the night alone in the dark wishing he would die. . . .

These are not fictitious accounts—I *was* that boy. Having been branded a sissy by neighborhood children because I preferred jump rope to baseball and dolls to playing soldiers, I was often taunted with "hey sissy" or "hey faggot" or "yoo hoo honey" (in a mocking voice) when I left the house.

To avoid harassment, I spent many summers alone in my room. I went out on rainy days when the street was empty.

I came to like being alone. I didn't need anyone, I told myself over and over again. I was an island. Contact with others meant pain. Alone, I was protected. I began writing poems, then short stories. There was no reason to go outside anymore. I had a world of my own.

In the schoolyard today
they'll single you out
Their laughter will leave your ears ringing
like the church bells
which once awed you. . . .[2]

School was one of the more painful experiences of my youth. The neighborhood bullies could be avoided. The taunts of the children living in those endless repetitive row houses could be evaded by staying in my room. But school was something I had to face day after day for some two hundred mornings a year.

I had few friends in school. I was a pariah. Some kids would talk to me, but few wanted to be known as my close friend. Afraid of labels. If I was a sissy, then he had to be a sissy, too. I was condemned to loneliness.

Fortunately, a new boy moved into our neighborhood and befriended me; he wasn't afraid of the labels. He protected me when the other guys threatened to beat me up. He walked me home from school; he broke through the terrible loneliness. We were in third or fourth grade at the time.

We spent a summer or two together. Then his parents sent him to camp and I was once again confined to my room.

Scene Three

High school lunchroom. The boy sits at a table near the back of the room. Without warning, his lunch bag is grabbed and tossed to another table. Someone opens it and confiscates a package of Tastykakes; another boy takes the sandwich. The empty bag is tossed back to the boy who stares at it, dumbfounded. He should be used to this; it has happened before.

Someone screams, "faggot," laughing. There is always laughter. It does not annoy him anymore.

There is no teacher nearby. There is never a teacher around. And what would he say if there were? Could he report the crime? He would be jumped after school if he did. Besides, it would be his word against theirs. Teachers never noticed anything. They never heard the taunts. Never heard the word, "faggot." They were the great deaf mutes, pillars of indifference; a sissy's pain was not relevant to history and geography and god made me to love honor and obey him, amen.

Scene Four

High school Religion class. Someone has a copy of *Playboy*. Father N. is not in the room yet; he's late, as usual. Someone taps the boy roughly on the shoulder. He turns. A finger points to the centerfold model, pink fleshy body, thin and sleek. Almost painted. Not real. The other asks, mocking voice, "Hey, does she turn you on? Look at those tits!"

The boy smiles, nodding meekly; turns away.

The other jabs him harder on the shoulder, "Hey, whatsamatter, don't you like girls?"

Laughter. Thousands of mouths; unbearable din of laughter. In the Arena: thumbs down. Don't spare the queer.

"Wanna suck my dick? Huh? That turn you on, faggot!"

The laughter seems to go on forever. . . .

Behind you, the sound of their laughter
echoes a million times
in a soundless place
They watch how you walk/sit/stand/breathe. . . .[3]

What did being a sissy really mean? It was a way of walking (from the hips rather than the shoulders); it was a way of talking (often with a lisp or in a high-pitched voice); it was a way of relating to others (gently, not wanting to fight, or hurt anyone's feelings). It was being intelligent ("an egghead" they called it sometimes); getting good grades. It meant not being interested in sports, not playing football in the street after school; not discussing teams and scores and playoffs. And it involved not showing fervent interest in girls, not talking about scoring with tits or *Playboy* centerfolds. Not concealing naked women in your history book; or porno books in your locker.

On the other hand, anyone could be a "faggot." It was a catch-all. If you did something that didn't conform to what was the acceptable behavior of the group, then you risked being called a faggot. If you didn't get along with the "in" crowd, you were a faggot. It was the most commonly used put-down. It kept guys in line. They became angry when somebody called them a faggot. More fights started over someone calling someone else a faggot than anything else. The word had power. It toppled the male ego, shattered his delicate facade, violated the image he projected. He was tough. Without feeling. Faggot cut through all this. It made him vulnerable. Feminine. And feminine was the worst thing he could possibly be. Girls were fine for fucking, but no boy in his right mind wanted to be like them. A boy was the opposite of girl. He was not feminine. He was not feeling. He was not weak.

Just look at the gym teacher who growled like a dog; or the priest with the black belt who threw kids against the wall in rage when they didn't know their Latin. They were men, they got respect.

But not the physics teacher who preached pacifism during lectures on the nature of atoms. Everybody knew what he was—and why he believed in the anti-war movement.

My parents only knew that the neighborhood kids called me names. They begged me to act more like the other boys. My brothers were ashamed of me. They never said it, but I knew. Just as I knew that my parents were embarrassed by my behavior.

At times, they tried to get me to act differently. Once my father lectured me on how to walk right. I'm still not clear on what that means. Not from the hips, I guess, don't "swish" like faggots do.

A nun in elementary school told my mother at Open House that there was "something wrong with me." I had draped my sweater over my shoulders like a girl, she said. I was a smart kid, but I should know better than to wear my sweater like a girl!

My mother stood there, mute. I wanted her to say something, to chastise the nun; to defend me. But how could she? This was a nun talking—representative of Jesus, protector of all that was good and decent.

An uncle once told me I should start "acting like a boy" instead of like a girl. Everybody seemed ashamed of me. And I guess I was ashamed of myself, too. It was hard not to be.

Scene Five

Priest: Do you like girls, Mark?
Mark: Uh-huh.

Priest: I mean *really* like them?

Mark: Yeah—they're okay.

Priest: There's a role they play in your salvation. Do you understand it, Mark?

Mark: Yeah.

Priest: You've got to like girls. Even if you should decide to enter the seminary, it's important to keep in mind God's plan for a man and a woman. . . .[4]

Catholicism of course condemned homosexuality. Effeminacy was tolerated as long as the effeminate person did not admit to being gay. Thus, priests could be effeminate because they weren't gay.

As a sissy, I could count on no support from the church. A male's sole purpose in life was to father children—souls for the church to save. The only hope a homosexual had of attaining salvation was by remaining totally celibate. Don't even think of touching another boy. To think of a sin was a sin. And to sin was to put a mark upon the soul. Sin—if it was a serious offense against god—led to hell. There was no way around it. If you sinned, you were doomed.

Realizing I was gay was not an easy task. Although I knew I was attracted to boys by the time I was about eleven, I didn't connect this attraction to homosexuality. I was not queer. Not I. I was merely appreciating a boy's good looks, his fine features, his proportions. It didn't seem to matter that I didn't appreciate a girl's looks in the same way. There was no twitching in my thighs when I gazed upon a beautiful girl. But I wasn't queer.

I resisted that label—queer—for the longest time. Even when everything pointed to it, I refused to see it. I was certainly not queer. Not I.

We sat through endless English classes, and History courses about the wars between men who were not allowed to love each other. No gay history was ever taught. No history faces you this morning. You're just a faggot. Homosexuals had never contributed to the human race. God destroyed the queers in Sodom and Gomorrah.

We learned about Michelangelo, Oscar Wilde, Gertrude Stein—but never that they were queer. They were not queer. Walt Whitman, the "father of American poetry," was not queer. No one was queer. I was alone, totally unique. One of a kind. Were there others like me somewhere? Another planet, perhaps?

In school, they never talked of the queers. They did not exist. The only hint we got of this other species was in religion class. And even then it was clouded in mystery—never spelled out. It was sin. Like masturbation. Like looking at *Playboy* and getting a hard-on. A sin.

Once a progressive priest in senior year religion class actually mentioned homosexuals—he said the word—but was into Erich Fromm, into homosexuals as pathetic and sick. Fixated at some early stage; penis, anal, whatever. Only heterosexuals passed on to the nirvana of sexual development.

No other images from the halls of the Catholic high school except those the other boys knew: swishy faggot sucking cock in an alley somewhere, grabbing asses in the bathroom. Never mentioning how much straight boys craved blowjobs, it was part of the secret.

It was all a secret. You were not supposed to talk about the queers. Whisper maybe. Laugh about them, yes. But don't be open, honest; don't try to understand. Don't cite their accomplishments. No history faces you this morning. You're just a faggot   faggot   no history   just a faggot

Epilogue

The boy marching down the Parkway. Hundreds of queers. Signs proclaiming gay pride. Speakers. Tables with literature from gay groups. A miracle, he is thinking. Tears are coming loose now. Someone hugs him.

> *You could not control*
> *the sissy in me*
> *nor could you exorcise him*
> *nor electrocute him*
> *You declared him illegal illegitimate*
> *insane and immature*
> *But he defies you still.*[5]

NOTES

1. From the poem "Faggot" by Tommi Avicolli, published in *GPU News*, September 1979.
2. Ibid.
3. Ibid.
4. From the play *Judgment of the Roaches* by Tommi Avicolli, produced in Philadelphia at the Gay Community Center, the Painted Bride Arts Center and the University of Pennsylvania; aired over WXPN-FM, in four parts; and presented at the Lesbian/Gay Conference in Norfolk, VA, July 1980.
5. From the poem "Sissy Poem," published in *Magic Doesn't Live Here Anymore* (Philadelphia: Spruce Street Press, 1976).

With No Immediate Cause

Ntozake Shange

every 3 minutes a woman is beaten
every five minutes a
woman is raped/every ten minutes
a lil girl is molested
yet i rode the subway today
i sat next to an old man who
may have beaten his old wife
3 minutes ago or 3 days/30 years ago
he might have sodomized his
daughter but i sat there
cuz the young men on the train
might beat some young women
later in the day or tomorrow
i might not shut my door fast
enuf/push hard enuf
every 3 minutes it happens
some woman's innocence
rushes to her cheeks/pours from her mouth
like the betsy wetsy dolls have been torn
apart/their mouths
menses red & split/every
three minutes a shoulder
is jammed through plaster and the oven door/
chairs push thru the rib cage/hot water or
boiling sperm decorate her body
i rode the subway today
& bought a paper from a
man who might
have held his old lady onto
a hot pressing iron/i dont know
maybe he catches lil girls in the
park & rips open their behinds

with steel rods/i can't decide
what he might have done i only
know every 3 minutes
every 5 minutes every 10 minutes/so
i bought the paper
looking for the announcement
the discovery/of the dismembered
woman's body/the
victims have not all been
identified/today they are
naked and dead/refuse to
testify/one girl out of 10's not
coherent/i took the coffee
& spit it up/i found an
announcement/not the woman's
bloated body in the river/floating
not the child bleeding in the
59th street corridor/not the baby
broken on the floor/

    "there is some concern
    that alleged battered women
    might start to murder their
    husbands & lovers with no
    immediate cause"

i spit up i vomit i am screaming
we all have immediate cause
every 3 minutes
every 5 minutes
every 10 minutes
every day
women's bodies are found
in alleys & bedrooms/at the top of the stairs
before i ride the subway/buy a paper/drink
coffee/i must know/
have you hurt a woman today
did you beat a woman today
throw a child across a room
    are the lil girl's panties
    in yr pocket
did you hurt a woman today

i have to ask these obscene questions
the authorities require me to
establish
immediate cause

73

Requiem for the Champ

June Jordan

Mike Tyson comes from Brooklyn. And so do I. Where he grew up was about a twenty-minute bus ride from my house. I always thought his neighborhood looked like a war zone. It reminded me of Berlin—immediately after World War II. I had never seen Berlin except for black-and-white photos in *Life* magazine, but that was bad enough: Rubble. Barren. Blasted. Everywhere you turned your eyes recoiled from the jagged edges of an office building or a cathedral, shattered, or the tops of apartment houses torn off, and nothing alive even intimated, anywhere. I used to think, "This is what it means to fight and really win or really lose. War means you hurt somebody, or something, until there's nothing soft or sensible left."

For sure I never had a boyfriend who came out of Mike Tyson's territory. Yes, I enjoyed my share of tough guys and/or gang members who walked and talked and fought and loved in quintessential Brooklyn ways: cool, tough, and deadly serious. But there was a code as rigid and as romantic as anything that ever made the pages of traditional English literature. A guy would beat up another guy or, if appropriate, he'd kill him. But a guy talked different to a girl. A guy made other guys clean up their language around "his girl." A guy brought ribbons and candies and earrings and tulips to a girl. He took care of her. He walked her home. And if he got serious about that girl, and even if she was only twelve years old, then she became his "lady." And woe betide any other guy stupid enough to disrespect that particular young Black female.

But none of the boys—none of the young men—none of the young Black male inhabitants of my universe and my heart ever came from Mike Tyson's streets or avenues. We didn't live someplace fancy or middle-class, but at least there were ten-cent gardens, front and back, and coin Laundromats, and grocery stores, and soda parlors, and barber shops, and Holy Roller churchfronts, and chicken shacks, and dry cleaners, and bars-and-grills, and a takeout Chinese restaurant, and all of that usable detail that does not survive a war. That kind of seasonal green turf and daily-life supporting pattern of establishments to meet your needs did not exist inside the gelid urban cemetery where Mike Tyson learned what he thought he needed to know.

From *Technical Difficulties* (New York: Pantheon Books, 1992). Copyright © 1994 by June Jordan. Reprinted with the permission of the author.

I remember when the City of New York decided to construct a senior housing project there, in the childhood world of former heavyweight boxing champion Mike Tyson. I remember wondering, "Where in the hell will those old people have to go in order to find food? And how will they get there?"

I'm talking godforsaken. And much of living in Brooklyn was like that. But then it might rain or it might snow and, for example, I could look at the rain forcing forsythia into bloom or watch how snowflakes can tease bare tree limbs into temporary blossoms of snow dissolving into diadems of sunlight. And what did Mike Tyson ever see besides brick walls and garbage in the gutter and disintegrating concrete steps and boarded-up windows and broken car parts blocking the sidewalk and men, bitter, with their hands in their pockets, and women, bitter, with their heads down and their eyes almost closed?

In his neighborhood, where could you buy ribbons for a girl, or tulips?

Mike Tyson comes from Brooklyn. And so do I. In the big picture of America, I never had much going for me. And he had less. I only learned, last year, that I can stop whatever violence starts with me. I only learned, last year, that love is infinitely more interesting, and more exciting, and more powerful, than really winning or really losing a fight. I only learned, last year, that all war leads to death and that all love leads you away from death. I am more than twice Mike Tyson's age. And I'm not stupid. Or slow. But I'm Black. And I come from Brooklyn. And I grew up fighting. And I grew up and I got out of Brooklyn because I got pretty good at fighting. And winning. Or else, intimidating my would-be adversaries with my fists, my feet, and my mouth. And I never wanted to fight. I never wanted anybody to hit me. And I never wanted to hit anybody. But the bell would ring at the end of another dumb day in school and I'd head out with dread and a nervous sweat because I knew some jackass more or less my age and more or less my height would be waiting for me because she or he had nothing better to do than to wait for me and hope to kick my butt or tear up my books or break my pencils or pull hair out of my head.

This is the meaning of poverty: when you have nothing better to do than to hate somebody who, just exactly like yourself, has nothing better to do than to pick on you instead of trying to figure out how come there's nothing better to do. How come there's no gym/no swimming pool/no dirt track/no soccer field/no ice-skating rink/ no bike/no bike path/no tennis courts/no language arts workshop/no computer science center/no band practice/no choir rehearsal/no music lessons/no basketball or baseball team? How come neither one of you has his or her own room in a house where you can hang out and dance and make out or get on the telephone or eat and drink up everything in the kitchen that can move? How come nobody on your block and nobody in your class has any of these things?

I'm Black. Mike Tyson is Black. And neither one of us was ever supposed to win anything more than a fight between the two of us. And if you check out the mass-media material on "us," and if you check out the emergency-room reports on "us," you might well believe we're losing the fight to be more than our enemies have decreed. Our enemies would deprive us of everything except each other:

hungry and furious and drug-addicted and rejected and ever convinced we can never be beautiful or right or true or different from the beggarly monsters our enemies envision and insist upon, and how should we then stand, Black man and Black woman, face to face?

Way back when I was born, Richard Wright had just published *Native Son* and, thereby, introduced white America to the monstrous produce of its racist hatred.

Poverty does not beautify. Poverty does not teach generosity or allow for sucker attributes of tenderness and restraint. In white America, hatred of Blackfolks has imposed horrible poverty upon us.

And so, back in the thirties, Richard Wright's Native Son, Bigger Thomas, did what he thought he had to do: he hideously murdered a white woman and he viciously murdered his Black girlfriend in what he conceived as self-defense. He did not perceive any options to these psychopathic, horrifying deeds. I do not believe he, Bigger Thomas, had any other choices open to him. Not to him, he who was meant to die like the rat he, Bigger Thomas, cornered and smashed to death in his mother's beggarly clean space.

I never thought Bigger Thomas was okay. I never thought he should skate back into my, or anyone's, community. But I did and I do think he is my brother. The choices available to us dehumanize. And any single one of us, Black in this white country, we may be defeated, we may become dehumanized, by the monstrous hatred arrayed against us and our needy dreams.

And so I write this requiem for Mike Tyson: international celebrity, millionaire, former heavyweight boxing champion of the world, a big-time winner, a big-time loser, an African-American male in his twenties, and, now, a convicted rapist.

Do I believe he is guilty of rape?

Yes I do.

And what would I propose as appropriate punishment?

Whatever will force him to fear the justice of exact retribution, and whatever will force him, for the rest of his damned life, to regret and to detest the fact that he defiled, he subjugated, and he wounded somebody helpless to his power.

And do I therefore rejoice in the jury's finding?

I do not.

Well, would I like to see Mike Tyson a free man again?

He was never free!

And I do not excuse or condone or forget or minimize or forgive the crime of his violation of the young Black woman he raped!

But did anybody ever tell Mike Tyson that you talk different to a girl? Where would he learn that? Would he learn that from U.S. Senator Ted Kennedy? Or from hotshot/scot-free movie director Roman Polanski? Or from rap recording star Ice Cube? Or from Ronald Reagan and the Grenada escapade? Or from George Bush in Panama? Or from George Bush and Colin Powell in the Persian Gulf? Or from the military hero flyboys who returned from bombing the shit out of civilian cities in Iraq and then said, laughing and proud, on international TV: "All I need, now, is a woman"? Or from the hundreds of thousands of American football fans? Or from the millions of Americans who would, if they could, pay surrealistic amounts of money just to witness, up close, somebody like Mike Tyson beat the brains out of somebody?

And what could which university teach Mike Tyson about the difference between violence and love? Is there any citadel of higher education in the country that does not pay its football coach at least three times as much as the chancellor and six times as much as its professors and ten times as much as its social and psychological counselors?

In this America where Mike Tyson and I live together and bitterly, bitterly, apart, I say he became what he felt. He felt the stigma of a priori hatred and intentional poverty. He was given the choice of violence or violence: the violence of defeat or the violence of victory. Who would pay him to rehabilitate innercity housing or to refurbish a bridge? Who would pay him what to study the facts of our collective history? Who would pay him what to plant and nurture the trees of a forest? And who will write and who will play the songs that tell a guy like Mike Tyson how to talk to a girl?

What was America willing to love about Mike Tyson? Or any Black man? Or any man's man?

Tyson's neighborhood and my own have become the same no-win battleground. And he has fallen there. And I do not rejoice. I do not.

School Shootings and White Denial

Tim Wise

I can think of no other way to say this, so here goes: an awful lot of white folks need to pull our heads out of our collective ass. Two more children are dead and thirteen are injured, and another community is scratching its blonde scalp, utterly perplexed as to how a school shooting the likes of the one in Santee, California could happen. After all, as the Mayor of the town said on CNN: "We're a solid town, a good town, with good kids, a good church-going town; an All-American town." Well, maybe that's the problem.

I said this after Columbine and no one listened, so I'll say it again: most whites live in a state of self-delusion. We think danger is black or brown, not to mention poor, and if we can just move far enough away from "those people," we'll be safe. If we can just find an "all-American" town, life will be better, because "things like this don't happen here."

Well excuse me for pointing this out, but in case you hadn't noticed, "here" is about the only place these kinds of things *do* happen.

Oh sure, there's plenty of violence in urban communities and schools. But mass murder, wholesale slaughter, take-a-gun-just-to-see-how-many-you-can-kill kinda' craziness seems made for those "safe" white suburbs or rural communities.

And yet the FBI insists there is no "profile" of a school shooter. Come again? White boy after white boy after white boy decides to use their classmates for target practice, and yet there is no profile? In the past two years, 32 young men have either carried out or planned to carry out (and been foiled at the last minute) mass murder against classmates and teachers, and thirty of these have been white. Yet there is no profile? Imagine if these killers and would-be killers had nearly all been black: would we still hesitate to put a racial face on the perpetrators? Doubtful.

Indeed, if *any* black child—especially in the mostly white suburbs of Littleton or Santee—were to openly discuss plans to murder fellow students, as happened at Columbine and Santana High, you can bet *somebody* would have turned them in

Reprinted by permission of Tim Wise.

and the cops would have beat a path to their door. But when whites discuss murderous intentions, our racial stereotypes of danger too often lead us to ignore it—they're just "talking" and won't really do anything, we tell ourselves. How many kids have to die before we rethink that nonsense? How many dazed parents, Mayors and Sheriffs do we have to listen to, describing how "normal" their community is, and how they can't understand what went wrong?

I'll tell you what went wrong and it's not TV, rap music, video games or a lack of prayer in school. What went wrong is that white Americans decided to ignore dysfunction and violence when it only seemed to affect other communities, and thereby blinded themselves to the chaos that never remains isolated for long. What affects the urban "ghetto" today will be coming to a Wal-Mart near you tomorrow, and was actually there all along. Unless we address the emptiness, pain, isolation and lack of hope felt by too many children of color and the poor, then we ought not be shocked when the support systems aren't there for our kids either.

What went wrong is that we allowed ourselves to be lulled into a false sense of security by media representations of crime and violence that portray both as the province of those who are anything but white like us. We ignore the warning signs, because in our minds, the warning signs don't live in our neighborhood, but across town, in that place where we lock our car doors on the rare occasion we have to drive there. That false sense of security—the result of race and class stereotypes—then gets people killed. And still we act amazed.

But listen up my fellow white Americans: our children are no better, no nicer, no more moral, and no more decent than anyone else. Dysfunction is all around us, whether we choose to recognize it or not. And it's not just the issue of school shootings.

According to the Centers for Disease Control's Youth Risk Behavior Survey, and the "Monitoring the Future" Report from the National Institutes on Drug Abuse, it is our children, and not those of the urban ghetto, who are most likely to use drugs.[1] White high school students are seven times more likely than blacks to have used cocaine; eight times more likely to have smoked crack; ten times more likely to have used LSD; and seven times more likely to have used heroin.

What's more, it is *white* youth, ages 12–17, who are more likely to *sell* drugs: 34% more likely, in fact, than their black counterparts.[2] And it is *white* youth who are twice as likely to binge drink, and nearly twice as likely as blacks to drive drunk.[3] And *white* males are twice as likely as black males to bring a weapon to school.[4]

Yet I would bet a valued body part that there aren't 100 white people in Santee, California, or most anywhere else who have ever heard a single one of the statistics above. Because the media doesn't report on white dysfunction: at least not in a fashion that leads one to recognize the dysfunction as explicitly *white*.

A few years ago, *U.S. News* ran a story entitled: "A Shocking look at blacks and crime." Yet never have they, or any other news outlet, discussed the "shocking" whiteness of these shoot-em-ups. Indeed, every time media commentators discuss the similarities in these crimes, they mention that the shooters were boys who got picked on, but *never* do they seem to notice a certain highly visible melanin defi-ciency. Color-blind, I guess.

White-blind is more like it, as I figure these folks would spot color with a quickness were some of it to stroll into their community. Santee's whiteness is so taken for granted that the Mayor, in that CNN interview, thought nothing of say-ing on the one hand that the town was 82 percent white, but on the other hand that, "this is America." Well that *isn't* America, and it especially isn't California, where whites are only half of the population. This is a town that is *removed* from America, and yet its Mayor thinks *they* are the normal ones—so much so that when asked about racial diversity, he replied that there weren't many of different "ethni-tis-tities." Not a word. Not even close.

I'd like to think that after this one, people would wake up. Take note. Rethink their stereotypes of who the dangerous ones are. But deep down, I know better. The folks hitting the snooze button on this none-too-subtle alarm are my own peo-ple after all, and I know their blindness like the back of my hand.

NOTES

1. The drug usage data comes from Johnston, Lloyd, Patrick O'Malley, and Jerald Bachman, 2000. Monitoring the Future: National Survey Results on Drug Use, 1975–1999, Vol. I: Secondary School Students. The University of Michigan Institute for Social Research, National Institute on Drug Abuse, United States Department of Health and Human Services, National Institutes on Health: 76, 101–102. This can be ordered from the U of Michigan Institute for Social Research. The ordering information is available at http://monitoringthe future.org/pubs.html.

Table 4-9 of the Monitoring the Future Report, page 101, "Racial/Ethnic Comparisons of Lifetime, Annual, Thirty-Day, and Daily Prevalence of Use of Various Drugs: Eighth, Tenth and Twelfth Graders,"

- For pot, 50.3% of white 12th graders have smoked pot, compared to 45.1% of black 12th graders: a difference of 11.5% total.
- For cocaine, 10.3% of white seniors have used, compared to 1.5% of black seniors, for a ratio of roughly 7 to 1.
- For crack, 4.7% of whites have used, compared to 0.6% of blacks, for a ratio of 7.8 to 1 (roughly 8 as I said in the piece)
- For heroin, 2.1% of whites have used, compared to 0.3% of blacks, for a ratio of 7 to 1
- For LSD, 14.2% of whites have used, compared to 1.4% of blacks, for a ratio of 10 to 1
- For Ecstacy, 8% of whites have used, compared to 0.5% of blacks, for a ratio of 16 to 1

2. For sales, the info comes from the Substance Abuse and Mental Health Services Administration, Office of Applied Studies, National Household Survey on Drug Abuse, 1999. Table G.71, at www.samsha.gov/statistics/statistics.html. 3.9% of whites aged 12–17 have sold drugs in the past year, as compared with 2.9% of blacks. Though both numbers are small, this means that whites 12–17 are over a third more likely to have sold than blacks.

3. The info on drinking and drinking and driving comes from Centers for Disease Control and Prevention, 2000. "Morbidity and Mortality Weekly Report, Survey Summary," Volume 49, No. SS-5, Youth Risk Behavior Surveillance System-United States, Wahington, DC: GPO. This can be accessed by going to www.cdc.gov/nccdphp/dash/yrbs/index.htm, and clicking on the fourth link on the page—the one for the 1999 Youth Risk Behavior Survey.

4. The info on white boys bringing weapons to school more often is also from the CDC report . . . table 10 on page 46 of the document, to be precise, where it is noted 11% of white males carried a weapon on school grounds in the last thirty days, while only 5.3% of black males did.

Out of the Closet, but Not Out of Middle School

Libby Copeland

On the last day of seventh grade, Dave Grossman mounted some cardboard boxes down the street from his junior high school and held a one-boy rally.

I'm sick of pretending, he announced into a cheap loudspeaker.

I'm gay.

The affair was a bit botched. Dave's principal, fearing a "disruption," asked him to move his makeshift stage and rainbow flags away from school grounds. The event caused barely an eye-roll from his peers, who scattered from school eager to inaugurate summer.

Still, there was Dave with his loudspeaker and his conviction. Like a soap opera character haunted by a secret past, he had been living two lives. In school, he was a straight kid with straight A's. After classes, he rode the Metro downtown and hung with gay friends past dinner time. He says few people could believe that at 13, he was so certain he was gay.

Two years later, Dave puts it like this: "It was a lot of built-up frustration over everyone saying, 'You're too young, you're too young, you're too young.'"

In the national debate about gay and bisexual identity, age is a volatile fault line along which schools are being forced to pick sides. Gay-youth advocacy groups say the average age of kids who "come out" has decreased substantially in recent years. Whereas once a teenager might have come out in senior year with a burn-your-bridges disinhibition, now that same teenager is making his homosexuality public in middle school or ninth grade.

Puberty is a roulette wheel of biding time and spurting growth. One preteen is sexually active while her classmate is still collecting stickers. American girls are hitting puberty far earlier than they were a century ago, and there's growing awareness of a disconnection between physical and mental maturity. Add the perennial dilemmas of sex education—how much kids should learn, how soon, from whom—and you have a recipe for controversy.

What happens when a middle school student—in braces, in a training bra, inexperienced—announces that she's gay?

It's happening. Ritch Savin-Williams, a developmental psychologist at Cornell University, used data from nine independent studies conducted over the last 20 years to conclude that the average age at which young men label their same-sex attractions as gay dropped from almost 20 in 1979 to just 13 in 1998. They may not, however, definitively call themselves gay until a few years later.

"Every time we sample these kids, the average age is getting younger," says Savin-Williams. "What's different is that now gay kids are becoming like straight kids—they know that they're gay before they have sex."

At Longfellow Middle School in Falls Church, Dave Grossman forced the issue that advocacy groups, educators and mental health providers have been debating for several years: Should the nation's struggle over sex and morality play out inside schools, involving kids in a debate that can be loudspeaker loud? Or should such issues be fought at the ballot box, from church pulpits and at home?

Longfellow's principal, Gail Womble, respected Dave's desire to come out, if not his venue. In the end, she was relieved that Dave said his piece without causing an uproar.

"I did have concerns about how middle school students would meet that kind of disclosure," says Womble, who has since moved to Rachel Carson Middle School in Fairfax. "At this age, we have kids who are old enough to be exploring those feelings and other kids who are still playing with Barbie dolls."

Dave's mother was disgusted by what she felt were "outrageous" banishing dictums imposed on her son, like making Dave move his stage across the street. Donna Brown Grossman says Womble also asked Dave to cover a T-shirt reading "Nobody Knows I'm Gay," and would not let him pass out homemade pamphlets promoting his rally.

"Her reaction was one thing that made me feel that I had to take my child out of the public school system," says Grossman, 48, who subsequently transferred her son to Thornton Friends, a private Quaker school. As school systems debate whether to allow gay support groups, or pass anti-harassment policies on behalf of gays, or show their faculty the controversial documentary "It's Elementary: Talking About Gay Issues in School," proponents on both sides point to the tender age of the youngsters as evidence of the rectitude of their positions.

Gay-rights advocacy groups and much of the mental health community cite 12-year-old gay youngsters as proof that being homosexual is "natural." Christian conservative groups argue that young adolescents bombarded by hormones and pop images of sexuality are especially susceptible to gay "recruiting."

"Those kids are incredibly impressionable, and I think certainly the younger the age, the more they can be swayed," says Peter LaBarbera, editor of the Lambda Report on Homosexuality, which argues that the declining age at which youngsters are coming out is largely the product of gay propaganda inside schools.

"There's different gradations. Love, sexuality: It's a very tangled web."

This is Ellen Sweeney, 18, an assured young woman who was co-leader of the gay discussion group at Sidwell Friends, a private school in Northwest Washington, during this, her senior year. She began to question her own sexuality in seventh grade, joined the discussion group in high school, and recently, has taught workshops to middle school students on gay issues. Incidentally, Sweeney is straight. But, she says, "I question myself up until this day."

This open attitude toward sexuality is a splinter in the skin of many who oppose gay discussion groups. They ask, what if youngsters who would otherwise be straight are encouraged to question, and ultimately, to declare themselves gay?

In the last few years in the Washington area, at least 15 gay discussion groups have cropped up in high schools and one middle school. The majority of the groups are in Montgomery County, where, amid a storm of controversy three years ago, the school board added gay students and teachers to the list of people protected from discrimination. The groups, which range from sanctioned clubs to informal lunch gatherings, serve as sounding boards—to examine homophobia, for example, or the feelings of a member who says she has been "questioning."

The problem with such discussions, opponents say, is that they don't offer an alternative to open-armed acceptance of homosexuality. Janet Folger, national director of the Center for Reclaiming America, an arm of Coral Ridge Ministries, says if gay issues must be part of the school climate, youngsters should at least be exposed to "ex-gays" and told of the health risks of homosexuality.

As things stand, "there is no balance," Folger says. "There is no message of hope . . . that you can walk away from it."

Like many area private schools, Edmund Burke School in the District doesn't see it that way. When a gay-issues discussion group was created there this year, middle school students were included in the weekly lunch meetings. Hugh Taft-Morales, the group's faculty adviser, said the group has "no agenda."

"They are already talking about this," he says. "What we're doing is taking responsibility as adults to raise the level of the discussion."

Although no exhaustive data can be found on discussion groups in schools, the New York-based Gay, Lesbian and Straight Educational Network keeps tabs on clubs that register with it. Its national list has blossomed from roughly 150 high school "Gay/Straight Alliances" last year to about 400 this year, concentrated mainly in Massachusetts, California and the New York City area. In Maryland and Virginia, there are seven registered high school alliances.

"Some people feel it's not our job," says Pamela Latt, principal of Centreville High School, which is on track to become the third high school in Virginia with a registered gay/straight alliance. Centreville has had a gay counseling group for two years, but a few students have been pushing for more.

"Having a counseling group sort of sends the wrong message," says Caroline Zuscheck, 17, a straight student involved in the effort. "It's like if you have an eating disorder or a problem with depression."

But although the principal supports starting an alliance next year, she also has reservations. On one hand, she says, it will contribute to a healthier environment for gay teenagers, a high-risk group. But Latt knows she is treading on important toes in conservative Centreville, where some School Board and community members have already voiced discomfort with a school-sanctioned club. "I don't blame people for being very cautious and careful," she says.

Latt is conflicted for other reasons. She is Catholic and has puzzled over whether homosexuality is wrong (she doesn't think so) and what causes it (she doesn't know). At any rate, she says, the alliance is about "saving lives," not promoting homosexuality. But perhaps in an ideal world, this messy moral stew wouldn't fall into the principal's lap.

"This really shouldn't be a part of my job," Latt says finally. "But I don't think I have a choice."

Amy Levy and her son remember the moment differently. The way Will tells it, his mom was nagging him, Why don't you have a girlfriend? The way Levy tells it, Will's confession came straight out of the clear blue sky.

Never mind why. That moment changed everything. One minute, the mother is dropping her son off in the car. The next, he tells her, "I'm gay," and hops out.

He is 14.

For Levy, 50, that belly-flop into reality challenged a lot of rules. Will was the first openly gay student at his tiny Bethesda private school, which has no specific policies on the issue. In an attempt to carve a comfortable space for himself, Will, now 16, met with teachers. Levy met with teachers. Teachers met with other teachers.

Levy says Will's coming out made them all dissect their feelings about homosexuality. "Do you really believe in what you thought you believed in when it becomes part of your life?" she wonders. (To protect her son, Levy asked that Will's last name, which is different from hers, not be published.)

Gay-rights advocates say this type of discussion is a door slowly creaking open, a departure from past decades when an unofficial "don't ask, don't tell" policy reigned in high schools and middle schools.

At a recent meeting for gay Montgomery County youths, two adults leading the session reminisced about how different it once was: one man, one woman, both in their forties or fifties, both of whom married at 23, both of whom divorced, both of whom realized only in adulthood that they were, in fact, gay.

They listened to the teenagers and then ticked off each belated milestone in their own closeted lives, as if to say, All those years lost.

Dave Grossman is a slight, blue-eyed youth with an energy and intelligence that sometimes gets the better of him. He skipped eighth grade, and, after ninth, went to Simon's Rock, a college in Great Barrington, Mass., designed for kids of high school age. Now he's transferring to American University, entering his second year of college at 15.

While he was growing up, Dave says, instinct told him he liked other boys. He just knew, natural as corn. In fourth grade, he says, "I came to my senses. I was just staring benignly at the boy across from me."

At 11, Dave found online chat rooms and located the gay bulletin board in short order.

At 12, he told his parents, because there was no reason not to, because now he knew for sure, and the knowledge pressed in on him. It was after synagogue on a late summer night. The date sticks in his mind—August 30, 1996. He recalls his mother crying with the shock and the strangeness. "She was like, 'Wow, I didn't even know you had a sexuality.'"

And Dave started his journey, because he saw himself as a young man with a sexuality and an image to build, and he shed his baby fat, his glasses and his gawky hair and hatched a plan to let people know that he had found himself. A stage, a loudspeaker, a grand announcement.

"I was going to do something," he says. "Something that was extravagant."

A showdown of sorts—even if there were few people around to watch. A showdown, at the very least, with the person who mattered.

76

Her Son/Daughter

Kate Bornstein

"Who are you?" asks the third blue-haired lady, peering up at me through the thick lenses of her rhinestone cat glasses. Only it comes out in one word: "Hoowahyoo?" I'm wearing black; we all are. It's my mother's funeral service, after all, and the little old ladies are taking inventory of the mourners. Me, I have to take inventory of my own identities whenever someone asks me who I am, and the answer that tumbles out of my mouth is rarely predictable. But this is my mother's funeral, and I am devastated, and to honor the memory of my mom, I'm telling each of them the who of me I know they can deal with.

"I'm Kate Bornstein," I answer her in this quiet-quiet voice of mine, "Mildred's daughter."

"Daughter?!" She shoots back incredulously the same question each of her predecessors had asked, because everyone knew my mother had two sons.

"Mildred never mentioned she had a daughter." The eyes behind those glasses are dissecting my face, looking for family resemblances. When I was a boy, I looked exactly like my father. Everyone used to say so. Then, when I went through what people would call my sex change, they would say, "You know, you look just like your mother." Except I'm tall. Nearly six feet of me in mourning for the passing of my mother, and I'm confronting this brigade of matrons whose job seems to be to protect my mother from unwanted visitors on this morning of her funeral on the Jersey Shore.

"You're her daughter? So who's your father? It's not Paul, am I right?" Now there would be a piece of gossip these women could gnaw on over their next mah-jongg game. "Mildred had another child," they'd say after calling two bams. "A daughter no less! And Paul, God rest his soul, he never knew."

My mother was raised in a nearly orthodox Jewish household. She lived her life measuring her self-worth by the presence of the men in her life. Her father, a successful merchant, died a year before I was born. Her husband, a successful doctor, died a year before I told her that one of her two sons was about to become a dyke. She preferred the word "lesbian." "My son, the lesbian," she would tell her close friends.

My mother was there the night the rabbi asked me who I was. I was a senior in college, a real hippie: beard, beads and suede knee-high moccasins with fringe hanging down past my calves. I was home for some holiday or other, and my parents wanted to show off their son who was going to Brown. I had always enjoyed Friday night services. To this day, I don't remember what about the rabbi's sermon outraged me, but there I was, jumping to my feet in the middle of the sermon, arguing some point of social justice.

My father was grinning. (He had never been bar mitzvahed, having kicked his rabbi in the shins the first day of Hebrew school.) My mother had her hand over her mouth to keep from laughing. She was never very fond of our rabbi, not since the time he refused to make a house call to console my father the night my grandfather died. So there we were, the rabbi and the hippie, arguing rabbinical law and social responsibility. He finally dismissed me with a nod. I dismissed him with a chuckle, and the service continued. On the way out of the synagogue, we had to file by the rabbi, who was shaking everyone's hand.

"Albert," he said to me, peering up through what would later be known as John Lennon glasses. "Hoowahyoo? You've got the beard, so now you're Jesus Christ?"

I've done my time as an evangelist. Twelve years in the Church of Scientology, and later, when I had escaped Hubbard's minions, four or five years as a reluctant poster child for the world's fledgling transgender movement.

My mother never heard the blue-haired ladies ask "Hoowahyoo?" of the tall-tall woman with mascara running down her cheeks. She never heard a producer from the Ricki Lake show ask me, "Who are you?" when I told her I wasn't a man or a woman. My mother never heard the Philadelphia society matron ask me the same question when I tried to attend her private women-only Alcoholics Anonymous group.

My mother only once asked me, "Who are you?" It was about a week before she died. "Hoowahyoo, Albert?" she asked anxiously, mixing up names and pronouns in the huge dose of morphine. "Who are you?"

I told her the truth: I was her baby, I always would be. I told her I was her little boy, and the daughter she never had. I told her I loved her.

"Ha!" she exclaimed, satisfied with my proffered selection of whos. "That's good. I didn't want to lose any of you, ever."

More and More Young Women Choose Surgical "Perfection"

Ann Gerhart

This is what people see when they look at Lucie Lukesova: A classic Eastern European beauty, ample and soft, with flawless skin, naturally rosy cheeks and sparkling blue eyes.

This is what Lukesova sees when she looks at herself: Fat chin. Big belly. Padded hips.

So a few weeks ago, she had liposuction. She describes it as one of the happiest days of her life. The 3½-hour surgery corrected what she perceived as flaws. Whether it corrected her self-image remains to be seen.

Lukesova is 19.

Teenagers and young women are going under the knife in record numbers, and they're not just getting nose jobs anymore. Last year, cosmetic surgeons performed some 25,000 elective procedures on teens, according to national figures from the American Society of Plastic and Reconstructive Surgeons—a nearly 100 percent increase over 1992. They put breast implants in nearly 2,000 girls. They sucked the fat out of 1,645.

In the Washington area, home to nearly 100 plastic surgeons, a mini tummy tuck and a new chest are just the thing to wear down the graduation aisle under the cap and gown, at least in a certain set. For some cosseted children of perfection-seeking boomers, a Cross pen doesn't pass muster anymore.

Roger Friedman, the head of plastic surgery at Suburban Hospital in Bethesda, did a breast augmentation on an 18-year-old last month.

"She was 5-foot-9 and 125 pounds, and she had breasts like a man," he says. "She was graduating and wanted this done in time for the next step."

And he had done her mother's implants, 10 years ago.

At Suburban Hospital, which has a hefty 46 plastic surgeons on staff, a 19-year-old gets a breast reduction and throws in some abdominal liposuction for good measure; a 14-year-old gets a chin implant; a dozen twentysomethings opt for bigger breasts, all in a week.

In Gaithersburg, Gregory Dick sees about four teenagers each month on the prowl for liposuction or breast augmentation; that's a fourfold increase over eight years ago. He sends nearly half of those away.

"The trouble with adolescent surgery is it's a tricky business," Dick says. "Many times the teenager doesn't know what he or she wants and is responding to peer or media pressure." Several surgeons said they are reluctant to make permanent alterations during the transitional teenage years. "Teenagers' images change as fast as their body," says Mark Mausner, a Chevy Chase surgeon who does about 400 procedures a year. "One day, the dress looks terrific, and the next day, it isn't fitting right."

One 22-year-old Columbia woman says she has been yearning for liposuction for some years. "I have always had a weight problem," she says. Always means ever since she was 13 or 14. "Even when I had lost some weight, there was this one stubborn area where it wouldn't go away," on her stomach and hips, she says. A recent college graduate waiting to hear about her medical school applications, she took $5,000 of her savings and just spent it on a mini tummy tuck and liposuction.

That was her graduation gift to herself. She is five feet tall and weighs about 125 pounds.

Now why wouldn't the nation's capital be a hotbed of plastic, elastic surgical activity? It is a center of image-making. And its affluent, educated, savvy adolescents are keenly aware that their driven, ambitious parents are prodding, shaping, bobbing and tweezing the visuals on themselves.

"In New York, you go to a cocktail party and they'll tell you where they had surgery. In L.A., you go to a party and they'll show you where they had surgery," says Mausner. "In Washington, nobody talks, but everybody has surgery." Add to that all of the following: an obsessive quest for perfection; a fusillade of slender but busty advertising images; a parade of celebrities with cosmetic enhancements in full jiggle, including the 17-year-old pop sensation Britney Spears, now appearing on MTV with her new, improved breasts; cheaper, safer procedures marketed aggressively.

And, in a weird and paradoxical way, feminism itself shares the blame: If a girl can be anything she wants to be—a Citadel rat, a Web millionaire, a professional basketball player—then why can't she carve out a different body for herself? Body Addition and Subtraction At Six Flags America in Largo, a trio of 13-year-olds, taut and already tan in their bathing suits, wait in line for pizza and discuss what offending body lump they will remove first, when they get their liposuction. "I'm fine with my nose. I wouldn't pay the money for the nose. I'm going first for this," says one girl, and she reaches up and grabs the skin where her shoulder meets her back. There is no fat there.

The Big Adult Voice has been sounding the alarm for some years over girls and their poor body image, but eating disorders and depression continue to rise. The increase in elective aesthetic surgery among the young is but the latest manifestation, an extreme and quick fix helped along by a booming economy and overindulgent parents.

Dismay over body image starts for girls even before puberty. Some 40 percent of 9-year-old girls told researchers they feared getting fat; 81 percent of 10-year-olds said the same thing. "All the self-consciousness with body image has filtered down to the very young. I hear a greater preoccupation every year, and most of it is focused on weight," says Rita Freedman, a New York psychologist and author. Young girls and older teens are "convinced that unless they approximate whatever image is touted in the media, they will have no chance of being socially successful."

And the prized female form in fashion ads remains rail-thin, without womanly hips and rump. In the rest of the popular culture, it's skinny while nearly toppling from big breasts. "You are a victim of this crazy ideal body image that is impossible to achieve unless you create it yourself," says L. Kris Gowen, a psychologist and former researcher at the Stanford University Center on Adolescence. "And it's fake. Hey, breasts are fat. To have very large breasts and a skinny body is really counter to the norm." It's the big and glossy norm in the magazine plastic surgery ads, however.

"I don't know anybody who is satisfied with the body," says Lukesova. "I want to add a piece here, cut a piece there." "I find it very hard to find a woman who is happy with her breasts. They are too big, too small, too saggy," says Susan Otero, a reconstructive breast surgeon at Washington Hospital Center. "Everybody has something about them."

The earlier onset of this dissatisfaction, researchers suggest, is because our culture is drenched in visuals.

"We are in a period in time when the myth-making has increased tremendously because of the amount of imagery in our lives," says Freedman, "computers, videos." Children are photographed ceaselessly, almost from the moment of conception. First come the ultrasounds, then the preschool graduations, followed by those pesky professional photographers lurking around the Little League games. At the same time, the marketing to kids is ever more specific. "There is such a commercialization of their bodies—what they should eat, what they should buy, what they should wear," says Freedman. "There is a lot of money to be made by persuading 15-year-olds that their lip color should be blue instead of red."

Sex fogs up this picture most of all. Teenagers and even young women are not old enough to make permanent decisions about changing their bodies through liposuction or breast surgery, the psychologists argue, because their sexual identity is still in flux. The surgeons say they tend to agree, but some among them are wielding the scalpels and pushing up the statistics.

"The breast carries tremendous psychological overlays," says Mausner, whose clients are "everyone, from secretaries to maids to the people you see on television." Sexy is healthy, but "what is considered looking healthy? Being tan and having big breasts. It's ridiculous." Teenagers and women in their early twenties, he says, rarely understand their developing sexuality.

Otero notices that, as a female surgeon who does mostly reconstructive work after mastectomies, "my views of women's breasts are very much different." She's learned with experience that her own aesthetic sense of "what looks natural and pretty" doesn't jibe with her clients who often want the "Playboy breast, with the nipples looking up into the air." She smiles a little, then allows: "It's hard to be a feminist and do breast surgery."

Despite physicians' reluctance to put breast implants in teenagers, the American Society for Aesthetic Plastic Surgery has guidelines on teen surgery that are timidly encouraging. "When one breast significantly differs from the other in terms of either size or shape, surgery can help girls as young as 16," one of the guidelines suggests. And breast reductions are widely accepted as appropriate for girls of 16—and even covered by insurance—even though many times the surgeon must remove and reset the nipples, damaging nerve endings and milk ducts in the process.

The woman from Columbia has a newly minted degree in psychology—and a preliposuction 27-inch waist. She comes from a deeply religious culture that disapproves of too much attention paid to personal appearance. In her studies, she has been thoroughly exposed to the academic research on body-image sickness in girls and young women. So how does she reconcile what she knows to what she feels?

"See, this is the funny thing. I kind of agree with all that," she says, slowly, "but then I succumb to it myself."

Family Dynamics

The parents are often the worst. Dick calls it the "JonBenet Ramsey Syndrome." Overintense, wanting their children to be perfect, baby boomers who refuse to age without a fight, they drag their sons and daughters into the doctor's office and make demands. They wave the checks. Their children sit slumped in the chair, not speaking. Every surgeon has these horror stories.

Gregory Dick: "A mother brought in the daughter because the breasts are deformed, one was one size, and one the other. The daughter didn't seem to mind so much. I said, 'Any pressure from boyfriends?' The parent scoffed. 'What boy would be interested in a girl with breasts like that?' I almost fell out of my chair."

Steven Hopping: "I had a mother; she lost weight and had liposuction, and she had a short, heavy daughter, 15. She had a bad complexion. She was under psychiatric care. The mother pleaded with me and my staff, and reluctantly, I did the lipo. And now, a year later, her weight is up. She's not any happier. That was a mistake I made. You would love to help these people and be the one to save them. I'm a surgeon; I love quick changes myself. But I didn't solve any problems. I just moved it around."

Mark Mausner: "The woman who didn't have perfect breasts as a child wants her daughter to do it. You always have to be aware of the family dynamic and listen carefully to who is talking. Half of the job is psychiatry."

Even mothers who would never dream of sanctioning plastic surgery for their daughters unconsciously hand down a legacy of obsession.

Rita Freedman is treating a 16-year-old girl who has a weight problem. "Her mother is weight-obsessed, and she had lipo. The girl looks at a mother who is much thinner than she used to be, and who is much thinner than herself, and she feels judged. The mother is trying to relax and remove herself from how she feels about her heavy daughter. It's all very difficult." $1,666 PER INCH

"I did this for myself," insists the 22-year-old after her tummy tuck and liposuction. Her parents, who are from the Philippines, never knew until afterward. "I don't think they really understand why I did it."

Plastic surgery is generally accepted now, she says, but she's still a little embarrassed, and doesn't want her name used.

"I know that spending this money on your looks is supposed to be wasteful, but I had saved it up and I didn't really miss it," she says. When the swelling goes down, she says, her surgeon told her the 27-inch waist will be 24 inches. That's the goal: Only $1,666 per inch.

For Lucie Lukesova, having liposuction was "a dream come true."

"I love my body," she says, "but it's a pressure from the friends and acquaintances. They say, 'You should lose some weight.'" She said she has tried, "but I don't have the willpower. I can keep it for two weeks, and then its bye-bye."

She saved some money from her job taking care of her toddler niece, and then she met up with Hopping, a surgeon at Columbia Hospital for Women who is somewhat of a trendsetter in these procedures. He offered to waive his fee if he could use her to demonstrate new liposuction techniques in front of other doctors.

"All the big body is gone," she says excitedly, the week after her procedure. "I'm still swollen, but it looks much smaller." She is thrilled with the way her neck looks, where Hopping removed her flab. Nothing hurts very much. She is doing her normal duties.

Before her fat cells were sucked away, she carefully ticked off her faults in an interview. "I think you are lovely," said the reporter. Lukesova smiled a little, lowered her big, blue eyes and murmured "thank you," but she shook her head. And now? "I am very happy," she says.

"Now, I am looking in the mirror all the time."

Finding My Eye-Dentity

Olivia Chung

I watched the spoken-word group I Was Born With Two Tongues perform and was inspired by their style of reflecting on personal experiences. This piece flowed from my desire for self-expression and hopes of challenging other Asian American girls to question their definition of beauty. I am second-generation Korean American, born and raised in a loving family in Silver Spring, Maryland. Currently, I'm a sophomore at the University of Pennsylvania, pursuing interests in activism, writing, and hip-hop. My ultimate goal is to keep it real and selflessly live for the Lord.

Olivia, you wanna get sang ka pul?

I'm driving my mother to work when she randomly brings up the eyelid question. The question that almost every Korean monoeyelidded girl has had to face in her life. The question that could change the future of my naturally noncreased eyelids, making them crease with the cut of a cosmetic surgeon's knife.

You know your aunt? She used to have beany eyes just like you! She used to put on white and black eyeliner very morning to make them look BIG. Then she went to Korea and got the surgery done. Now look! She looks so much better! Don't you want it done? I would do it. . . .

I think this is about the 346,983,476th time she has brought this topic up. Using the exact same words. You would look so much more prettier with bigger eyes! She says. *You know, because they look kind of squinty and on top of that you have an underbite, so you look really mean . . .* She explains while narrowing her eyes and jutting out her jaw in emphasis of her point.

A couple of years ago, I would have taken her suggestion seriously. I remember reading a section of *Seventeen* magazine, where the once-did-funky-makeup-for-100-anorexic-white-girls-on-runways beauty expert revealed the secret to applying eye makeup. As a desperate preteen girl seeking beauty advice, I remember it perfectly. Put dark shadow right over the eyelashes, light powder all over, medium shadow over the edge of the crease of your eyelid. That's where I always tripped up. Crease? Umm . . . excuse me? These so-called beauty experts never gave me enough expertise to figure out how to put makeup on my face without looking like a character in a kabuki play. I tried to follow the beauty experts' advice. But I decided it wasn't working when people asked me if I had gotten a black eye.

My friends suggested training my eyelids to fold with tape. *My mother did that and now she has a real crease, one of my friends told me.* I, however, never learned the magic behind that, and always felt too embarrassed to ask. Another friend once excitedly showed me how she had bought a bottle of make-your-own-eye-crease glue from Korea. I let her try it on me too. I could barely open my eyes, thanks to the fierce stinging sensation resulting from the glue that got on my eyeball. And when I finally did take a quick glimpse of myself in the mirror, I saw a stranger with uneven eyelids.

The first time I remember being insulted was when I was little. . . .

In kindergarten, I believe. Oh, it was classic: A little blond kid pulled the edges of his eyes out, yelling, *Ching chong chinaman!* I, being new to this game, could only make a weak comeback. *I'm not Chinese. . . . I'm KOREAN.* I remember feeling a confused hurt, realizing that I looked different and not understanding why being different was bad.

Couldn't we all just get along? I had learned that God loves people as they are, as different as they are. I learned that He looks at the heart, and that it really doesn't matter how a person looks. I think my belief in this, combined with my fear of a sharp object cutting the skin above my eye, kept me away form the *sang ka pul* surgery. Yet, I continued to receive comments on my "chinky" eyes, and I always emerged from these situations feeling confused and angry . . . without ever really knowing why. Why couldn't I be accepted with my so-called chinky eyes? Why in the world were they even called "chinky" eyes? If they meant to insult Chinese, all the Chinese people I knew had huge eyes. With the crease.

As I grew older, the childish "ching chong"s came with less frequency. Still, the magazines continue to give me unhelpful directions on how to apply makeup. Still, I witness my own friends getting the surgery done in an effort to be "more beautiful." Still, my mother continuously confronts me with the dreaded eyelid question. *You wanna get* sang ka pul? I always answer her with an *are-you-crazy?* but simple *no.* All the things I wish I could have told her come flowing on this page with my pen. . . .

Umma, my mother, don't you see that my noncreased eyes are beautiful? Asian eyes are beautiful. Your eyes are beautiful. My eyes are beautiful. Asian is beautiful. After all these years of wanting to open up my eyes with tape and glue and surgery, I have opened up my eyes to a different definition of beauty. A broader definition of beauty, one that embraces differences and includes every girl, who can hold her head up, *sang ka pul*-less and chinky-eyed, because being *Asian is beautiful.*

79

The Case of Sharon Kowalski and Karen Thompson:
Ableism, Heterosexism, and Sexism

Joan L. Griscom

In November, 1983, Sharon Kowalski was in a head-on collision with a drunk driver, suffered a severe brain-stem injury, became paralyzed, and lost the ability to speak. Sharon was in a committed partnership with Karen Thompson. Serious conflict soon developed between Karen and Kowalski's parents, erupting in a series of lawsuits that lasted eight years. Karen fought to secure adequate rehabilitation for Sharon as well as access to friends and family of her choice. In 1985, acting under Minnesota guardianship laws, Sharon's father placed her in a nursing home without adequate rehabilitation services and prohibited Karen and others from visiting her. Karen continued to fight through the courts and the media. In 1989, Sharon was finally transferred to an appropriate rehabilitation facility, reunited with lover and friends, and, in 1991, finally allowed her choice to live with Karen.

In this article I tell the story of Sharon Kowalski and Karen Thompson. While the story shows violations of their human rights, it is more than a story of two individuals. The injustices they encountered were modes of oppression that operate at a social-structural level and affect many other people. These oppressions include ableism, discrimination against disabled persons; heterosexism, the structuring of our institutions to legitimate only heterosexual relationships; and sexism, discrimination against women. Their story shows the power of structural discrimination, the intertwining of both our medical and legal systems in ways that denied both of them the fullest quality of life.

A History of the Events

By November 1983, Sharon and Karen had lived in partnership for almost four years. Karen was thirty-six, teaching physical education at St. Cloud State University, devoutly religious, conservative. Sharon was twenty-seven, a fine athlete who had graduated from St. Cloud in physical education and just accepted a staff

Reprinted by permission of the author.

coaching position. She had grown up in the Iron Mine area of Minnesota, a conservative world where women are expected to marry young. Defying such expectations, she became first in her family to attend college, earning tuition working part-time in the mines. After she and Karen fell in love, they exchanged rings, bought a house together, and vowed lifetime commitment.

After the accident Sharon lay in a coma for weeks, and doctors were pessimistic about her recovery. Karen spent hours, daily, talking to her, reading the Bible, massaging and stretching her neck, shoulders, and hands. It is essential to massage and stretch brain-injured persons in comas, for their muscles tend to curl up tightly and incur permanent damage. Early in 1984, Karen saw Sharon moving her right index finger, and found that she could indicate answers to questions by moving it. Later she began to tap her fingers, then slowly learned to write letters and words.

The Kowalski parents became suspicious of the long hours Karen was spending with her, and increasingly Karen feared they would try to exclude her from Sharon's life. After consulting a psychologist, she wrote them a letter explaining their love, in hopes they would understand her importance to Sharon. They reacted with shock, denial, and rage. As the nightmare deepened, Karen consulted a lawyer and learned she had no legal rights, unless she won guardianship. In March, 1984, she therefore filed for guardianship, and Donald Kowalski counterfiled.

Guardianship was awarded to Kowalski, but Karen was granted equal access to medical and financial information and full visitation rights. She continued to participate in both physical and occupational therapy. Sharon improved slowly; Karen made her an alphabet board, and she began to spell out answers to questions. Later she began to communicate by typewriter, and in August spoke a few words. But conflicts continued. The day after the court decision Kowalski incorrectly told Karen she did not have visitation rights, and later tried to cancel her work with Sharon's therapists. When Karen and others took Sharon out on day passes, he objected, subsequently testifying in court that he did not want her out in public. In October, Sharon was moved further away, and Kowalski filed to gain full power as guardian. Karen counterfiled to remove him as guardian.

Months elapsed while the legal battles were fought. Sharon was moved several times, regressed in her skills, and became clinically depressed. The Minnesota Civil Liberties Union (MCLU) entered the case, arguing that under the First Amendment Sharon's rights of free speech and free association were being violated. A tri-county Handicap Services Program submitted testimony of Sharon's capacity to communicate, including a long conversation in which she stated she was gay and Karen was her lover. At Sharon's request, the MCLU asked to represent her and suggested she might testify for herself. The court refused both requests, finding that Sharon lacked understanding to make decisions for herself. In July, 1985, Kowalski was awarded full guardianship. Within a day, he denied visitation to Karen, other friends, the MCLU, and disability rights groups; in two days he transferred her to a nursing home near his home with only minimal rehabilitation facilities. In August, 1985, Karen saw Sharon for what would be the last time for over three years.

As this summary indicates, the medical system failed Sharon in at least three respects. First, it failed to supply rehabilitation in the years when it was vital to her recovery. Stark in the medical record is the fact that this woman who was starting to stand and to feed herself was locked away for over three years with an implanted feeding tube, left insufficiently stretched so that muscles that had been starting to work curled back on themselves again. Second, she was deprived of the bombardment of emotional and physical stimulation needed to regenerate her cognitive faculties. Once in the nursing home, for example, she was forbidden regenerative outside excursions. Third, although medical staff often recognized Sharon's unusual response to Karen, they failed to explain to her parents its importance. Despite an urgent need for counseling to assist the parents, none, except for one court-mandated session, took place.

The failure of the medical system was consistently supported by the legal system. Initially the court ruled that Sharon must have access to a young-adult rehabilitation ward. But once Kowalski won full guardianship, he was able to move her to a nursing home without such a ward. In 1985 the Office of Health Facility Complaints investigated Sharon's right to choose visitors, a right guaranteed by the Minnesota Patient Bill of Rights, and found that indeed her right was being violated. However, the appeals court held that the Patient Bill of Rights was inapplicable, since the healthcare facility was not restricting the right of visitation, the guardian was.

The deficiencies of guardianship law are a central problem in this case. First, a guardian can restrict a person's rights, without legal recourse. As is often said, under present laws a guardian can lock up a person and throw away the key. This is a national problem, affecting the disabled, the elderly, anyone presumed incompetent. Second, guardians are inadequately supervised. Under Minnesota law, a guardian is required to have the ward tested annually for competence. Kowalski never did, and for over three years the courts did not require him to. In 1985, Karen first filed a motion to hold him in contempt for failure to arrange testing and for failure to heed Sharon's wishes for visitation. The courts routinely rejected such motions.

Between 1985 and 1988, Karen and the MCLU pursued repeated appeals to various Minnesota courts, all denied. Karen began to seek help from the media, also disability, gay/lesbian, women's, and church groups. She recognized that the legal precedents could be devastating for others, e.g., gay/lesbian couples or unmarried heterosexual couples. The reserved, closeted, conservative professor was slowly transformed into a passionate public speaker in her quest to secure freedom and rehabilitation for Sharon; and slowly she gained national attention. The alternative press responded; national groups such as the National Organization for Women were supportive; the National Committee to Free Sharon Kowalski formed, with regional chapters. Finally the mainstream media began publishing concerned articles; Karen appeared on national TV programs; state and national politicians, including Jesse Jackson, spoke out. Meanwhile Sharon remained in the nursing home, cut off from friends, physically regressed, psychologically depressed.

The first break in the case came in February, 1988. In response to a new motion from Karen, requesting that Sharon be tested for competence, testing was ordered. In January, 1989, she was moved to the Miller-Dwan Medical Center for a 60-day evaluation. Kowalski unsuccessfully argued in court against both the move and the testing. Sharon immediately expressed her wish to see Karen. On February 2, 1989, Karen visited her for the first time in three and a half years, an event which made banner headlines in the alternative press across the nation. She was, however, highly depressed, with numerous physical problems: for example, her feet had curled up so tightly that she was no longer able to stand. More significant was her cognitive ability; to this day, her short-term memory loss remains considerable.

The competency evaluation nevertheless demonstrated that she could communicate on an adult level and had significant potential for rehabilitation. The report recommended "her return to pre-morbid home environment," and added:

> We believe Sharon has shown areas of potential and ability to make rational choices in many areas of her life. She has consistently indicated a desire to return home . . . to live with Karen Thompson again.

Donald Kowalski subsequently resigned as guardian, for both financial and health reasons, and the parents stopped attending medical conferences. In June, 1989, Sharon was transferred to a long-term rehabilitation center for brain-injured young adults. Here she had extensive occupational, physical, and speech therapy. Again Karen spent hours with her and took her out on trips. She had surgery on her legs, feet, toes, left shoulder and arm to reverse the results of three years of inadequate care. She began to use a speech synthesizer and a motorized wheelchair.

Karen subsequently filed for guardianship. Medical staff testified unanimously that Sharon was capable of deciding for herself what relationships she wanted and where she wished to live. They testified that she was capable of living outside an institution and Karen was best qualified to care for her in a home environment. Witnesses for the Kowalskis opposed the petition. The judge appeared increasingly uncomfortable with the national publicity. While in 1990 he allowed Sharon and Karen to fly out to San Francisco where each received a Woman of Courage Award from the National Organization for Women, he refused Sharon permission to attend the first Disability Pride Day in Boston. He issued a gag order against Karen, which was overturned on appeal. Finally, in April, 1991, he denied Karen guardianship and awarded it to a supposedly "neutral third party," a former classmate of Sharon who lived near the Kowalski parents and had testified against Karen in a 1984 hearing. This decision raised the alarming possibility that Sharon might be returned to the inadequate facility. Karen appealed it.

In December, 1991, the appeals court reversed the judge's ruling and granted guardianship to Karen, on two bases: first, the medical testimony that Sharon was able to make her own choices; and second, the fact that the two women are "a family of affinity" that deserves respect. This is a major decision in U.S. legal history, setting important legal precedents both for disabled people and gay/lesbian families. Sharon and Karen now live together.

The Three Modes of Oppression

Sharon and Karen were denied their rights by three interacting systems of oppression: ableism, heterosexism, and sexism. Originally Karen believed that their difficulties were merely personal problems. All her life she had believed that our social institutions are basically fair, designed to support individual rights. In the book (1) she co-authored with Julie Andrzejewski, she documented her growing awareness that widespread social/political forces were involved in their supposedly personal problems and that the oppression they experienced was systemic.

Ableism was rampant throughout. Sharon's inability to speak was often construed as incompetence, and her particular kinds of communication were not recognized. Quite early Karen noticed some did not speak to Sharon, some talked loudly as if she was deaf, others spoke to her as if she were a child. One doctor discussed her in her presence as if she was not there. When Karen later asked how she felt about this, she typed out "Shitty." Probably one reason she responded to Karen more than anyone was that Karen talked extensively and read to her, played music, asked questions, and constantly consulted her wishes. Although the MCLU and the Handicap Services Program submitted transcripts of long conversations with her, the courts did not accept these as evidence of competence, relying instead on testimony from people who had much less interaction with her. A major article in the St. Paul *Pioneer Press* (1987) described the Kowalskis visiting the room "where their eerily silent daughter lies trapped in her twisted body." Eerily silent? This is the person who typed out "columbine" when asked her favorite flower, answered arithmetical questions correctly, and responded to numerous questions about her life, feelings, and wishes. She also communicates nonverbally in many ways: gestures, smiles, tears, and laughter.

Thanks to ableism, Sharon was often stereotyped as helpless. The presumption of helplessness "traps" her far more severely than her "twisted body." Once a person is labeled helpless, there is no need to consult her wishes, consider her written communications, hear her testimony. When Sharon arrived at Miller-Dwan for competency testing, Karen reported with joy that staff was giving her information and allowing her choices, even if her choice was to do nothing. Most seriously, if a person is seen as helpless, then there is no potential for rehabilitation. As Ellen Bilofsky (2) has written, Sharon was presumed "incompetent until proven competent." If Karen's legal motion for competency testing had not been accepted, Sharon might have remained in the nursing home indefinitely, presumed incompetent.

Finally, ableism can lead to keeping disabled persons hidden, literally out of sight. Kowalski argued against day passes, resisted Karen's efforts to take Sharon out, and testified he would not take her to a church or shopping center because he did not wish to put her "on display . . . in her condition." Although medical staff could see that outside trips provided Sharon with pleasure and stimulation, both important for cognitive rehabilitation, they cooperated with the father in denying them. According to an article in the *Washington Post,* he once said, "What the hell difference does it make if she's gay or lesbian or straight or anything because she's laying there in diapers? . . . let the poor kid rest in peace."

Invisible in the nursing home, cut off from lover and friends, Sharon had little chance to demonstrate competence. The wonder is that after three and a half years of loss, loneliness, and lack of care, she was able to emerge from her depression and respond to her competency examiners. To retain her capacity for response, through such an experience, suggests a strong spirit.

The second mode of oppression infusing this case is heterosexism, the structuring of our institutions so as to legitimate heterosexuality only. Glaringly apparent is the failure to recognize gay/lesbian partnerships. When Karen was first to arrive at the hospital after the accident, she was not allowed access to Sharon or even any information, because she was not "family." Seeing her anguish, a Roman Catholic priest interceded, brought information, and arranged for a doctor to speak with her. Although the two women considered themselves married, in law they were not, and therefore lacked any legal rights as a couple. If heterosexual, there would have been no denial of visitation, no long nightmare of the three-and-a-half year separation. While unmarried heterosexual partners might have trouble securing guardianship, married partners would not.

Because of heterosexism, Sharon's emotional need for her partner and Karen's rehabilitative effect on her were not honored. Because of Sharon's response, Karen was often included in the therapeutic work. Yet, prior to 1989, medical staff often refused to testify to this positive effect. Perhaps they feared condoning the same-sex relationship, perhaps they wished to stay out of the conflict. One neurologist, Dr. Keith Larson, did testify, although stipulating that he spoke as friend of the court, not as witness for Karen.

> The reason I'm here today is . . . to deliver an observation that I have agonized over and thought a great deal about, and prayed a little bit. . . . I cannot help but say that Sharon's friend, Karen, can get out of Sharon physical actions, attempts at vocalization, and longer periods of alertness and attention than can really any of our professional therapists.

Why was it necessary to "agonize" over this testimony? Pray about it? Make such a tremendous effort? Clearly, were one of the partners male, Larson would have had no difficulty. He simply would have reported that the patient responded to her partner. Some medical staff did testify positively, without effort; and after 1989, testimony from medical personnel was strong and unanimous. However, repeatedly, the courts ignored it.

Finally, heterosexism is evident in a consistent tendency to exaggerate the role of sex in same-sex relationships. Many believe that the lives of gay/lesbian people revolve around sex, though evidence from all social-psychological research is that homosexual people are no more sexually active than heterosexual people. Further, gay/lesbian sex is often perceived as sexual exploitation rather than an expression of mutual caring. The final denial of Karen's visitation rights was based on the charge that she might sexually abuse Sharon. A physician hired by the Kowalskis, Dr. William L. Wilson, leveled this charge:

> Karen Thompson has been involved in bathing Sharon Kowalski behind a closed door for a prolonged period of time. . . . Ms. Thompson has [also] alleged a sexual relationship with Sharon Kowalski that existed prior to the accident. Based on this knowledge and my best medical judgment . . . I feel that visits by Karen Thompson at this time would expose Sharon Kowalski to a high risk of sexual abuse.

Accordingly, Wilson directed the nursing home staff not to let Karen visit. Even though under statutes, Karen could have continued to visit while the court decisions were under appeal, the nursing home was obliged to obey the doctor's order.

In this instance, ableism and heterosexism merge. If they were unmarried heterosexual partners, sexual abuse probably would not have been an issue. If married, the issue would not exist. Ableism often denies disabled persons their sexuality, though a person does not lose her sexuality simply because she becomes disabled. Also, a person who loses the capacity to speak has a special need for touching. What were Sharon's sexual rights? When she was starting to emerge from the coma, she once reached out and touched Karen's breast, and later placed Karen's hand on her breast. At the time Karen did not dare ask medical advice for fear of revealing their relationship. Even to raise such questions might have exposed her to more charges of sexual abuse.

While same-sex relationships are often called "anti-family" in our heterosexist society, actually such relationships create family, in that they create stable emotional and economic units. Family, in this sense, may be defined as a kin-like unit of two or more persons related by blood, marriage, adoption, or primary commitment, who usually share the same household. Sharon and Karen considered themselves married. Karen's long pilgrimage over almost nine years testifies to an extraordinary depth of commitment. Sharon consistently said she was gay, Karen was her lover, she wanted to live with her. While marriage has historically occurred between two sexes, history cannot determine its definition. In U.S. history, marriage between black and white persons was forbidden for centuries. In 1967, when the Supreme Court finally declared miscegenation laws unconstitutional, there were still such laws in sixteen states.

Sexism is sufficiently interfused with heterosexism that they are hard to separate. Often sexism enforces a social role on women in which they are subordinated to men. Women in the Minnesota world where Sharon grew up were expected to marry young and submit to their husbands' authority, an intrinsically sexist model. According to this model, her partnership with Karen was illegitimate. Sexism also is apparent in awarding guardianship to the father. Had Sharon been a man rather than a twenty-eight-year-old "girl," such a decision might be less possible; but in a sexist society, it is appropriate to assign an adult woman to her male parent. Finally, our society devalues friendship, especially between women. Once, very early, a doctor advised Karen to forget Sharon. The gist of his remarks was that "Sharon's parents will always be her parents. They have to deal with this, but you don't. Maybe you should go back to leading your own life." Friendship between the two women was unimportant. Ableism as well as sexism is apparent in these remarks.

This case makes clear that the modes of oppression work simultaneously. Like Audre Lorde (3), I argue that "there is no hierarchy of oppression." Disability was not more important than sexuality in curtailing Sharon's freedoms; they worked together seamlessly, in her life as in the legal and medical systems. Admittedly, any individual's perspective on the case may reflect the issue most central to her or his life: e.g., the gay press, reporting the case, emphasized heterosexism, and the disability rights press emphasized ableism. Working in coalition on this case, some women were ill at ease with disability rights activists; and some disability rights groups were anxious about associating with gay/lesbian issues. But there are lesbians and gays in the disabled community, and disabled folks in women's groups. Karen experienced the inseparability of the issues once when invited to speak to a Presbyterian group. They asked her to speak only about ableism since they had already "done" gay/lesbian concerns. She tried, but found it nearly impossible; she had to censor her material, ignore basic facts, leave out crucial connections.

In each mode of oppression, one group of persons takes power over another, and this power is institutionalized. Disabled people, women, gay men and lesbians, and others are all to some degree denied their full personhood by the structures of our society. Their choices can be denied, their sexuality is controlled. On the basis of ableism, heterosexism, and sexism, both Karen Thompson's and Sharon Kowalski's opportunities for the fullest quality of life were taken from them. Sharon lost cognitive ability that might have been saved. As the Minnesota Civil Liberties Union put it, "The convicted criminal loses only his or her liberty; Sharon Kowalski has lost the right to choose whom she may see, who she may like, and who she may love." To change this picture took nearly nine years of struggle by a partner who lived out her vow of lifetime commitment and the work of many committed persons and groups.

Conclusion

Many national groups joined the struggle to provide rehabilitation for Sharon and bring her home, including disability rights activists, gays and lesbians, feminists and male supporters, and civil rights groups. In addition there were thousands of people drawn to this case by simple human rights. After all, any of us could be hit by a drunk driver, become disabled, and in the process lose our legal and medical rights. The Kowalski/Thompson case stands as a warning that in our deeply divided society, freedom is still a privilege and rights are fragile.

People living in nontraditional families need legal protection to secure legal and medical rights. Karen Thompson stresses the importance of making your relationships known to your family of birth, if possible, and informing them of your wishes in case of disability or death. Also, it is essential to execute a durable power of attorney, a document that stipulates a person to make medical and financial decisions for you, in case of need. Copies should be given to your physician. While requirements vary between states and powers of attorney are not always enforceable, they may protect your rights. Information about how to execute them may be found in your public library, in consultation with a competent lawyer, or in Appendix B of the book *Why Can't Sharon Kowalski Come Home?*

NOTES

1. Karen Thompson and Julie Andrzejewski. *Why Can't Sharon Kowalski Come Home?* San Francisco: Spinster/Aunt Lute, 1988. All quotations in text are from this book.
2. Ellen Bilofsky. "The Fragile Rights of Sharon Kowalski." *Health/PAC Bulletin,* 1989, *19,* 4–16.
3. Audre Lorde. "There Is No Hierarchy of Oppressions." *Interracial Books for Children Bulletin,* 1983, *14,* 9.

80

Lame

Joyce Davies

Several words describe the person who cannot walk in an ordinary fashion. My own personal preference is "physically limited" for a rather formal description and plain, old-fashioned "lame" as a short (and somehow *loving*) adjective. "Orthopedically handicapped" is fair enough. But here I conjure up visions of huge rehabilitation clinics or state senators reading amendments in proper medical and legal terms. The two words together are exact but cold. "Handicapped" alone is far too inclusive to apply with much realism to those who cannot walk well, for it has become a grab-bag word that embraces an enormous population of deaf, blind, speech-impaired, and mentally impaired individuals.

"Disabled" goes "handicapped" one better. Here there are legal overtones. To be classified as "disabled" one usually needs a medical stamp to prove inability to earn a living, and this can apply to anyone who is out of commission from a physical or mental illness. Yet both "handicapped" and "disabled" are handy tags to

From *With Wings: An Anthology of Literature by and about Women with Disabilities.* Copyright © 1987 The Feminist Press, by permission of the Feminist Press at the City University of New York, www.feministpress.org.

hang on those who get around with crutches or a walker or a wheelchair. They slip out in ordinary conversation and who am I to mind? I use the words myself.

But "crippled" is an ugly and stumbling word. There is no dignity there at all—only a picture of someone twisted, pitiful, poor, and not very bright. This is a personal prejudice that took hold long ago for reasons sunk deep in the subconscious. But I find when I use "crippled," I am stressing the harshness and purely *physical* fact of paralysis. The word, in its dark intensity, blots out the power and the hope of the spirit.

Of course, "lame" is not an accurate description for a person who cannot walk at all; only paralyzed applies here. But, oh, the hope for improvement embodied in the word "lame"! Perhaps that is one of its appealing connotations, suggesting a mild affliction, though sometimes a stretching of the truth. Once I received a letter from a friend who had a slow recovery from a fall, and she mentioned with beautiful carelessness that we had so much in common with our children and "our lameness." I treasure her conception of me not as disabled or crippled or even handicapped, but simply lame. She is right. To be able to walk with crutches, even though one must resort to a wheelchair in some situations, should classify a person as "lame" if she wishes.

I should like to resurrect the word "lame" because it is gentle and informal. Though there is often more to it than that, we who walk with difficulty are primarily lame and far more fortunate than those thousands of men, women, and children who cannot leave their wheelchairs at all. If "lame" should seem a vague term like "thin" or "fat" or "pretty," so much the better. Most of us would like nothing more than to melt in with the crowd—unlabeled, almost unnoticed.

We had a cat once who appeared, half-starved, at the door to request family membership along with three other cats. One of her paws took a very long time to reach the ground, so she devised an alternate way to walk, scorning the slow limp, and she simply hopped like a rabbit with her three strong legs. Still she had to rest a lot. Fortunately for her, cats have few responsibilities beyond self-preservation and cleanliness and she could accomplish those near the house. The other cats were quite gentle with her, as if they sensed she couldn't handle a hard fight. Yet she was expected to make her own way. No one put a supper dish under her nose or pushed her onto safe high ground in the midst of a dog attack.

And so it was for many of us who went home from a long hospitalization [for polio] thirty years ago. There was no real follow-up care as there is now. We were on our own, especially if we lived far from therapists and the orthopedic specialists who were working full time on new polio cases anyway.

It became a very personal matter between you and your stubborn body. Certain maneuvers failed, and so you tried others. There was a bit of black magic to these first attempts because you didn't plan consciously to get up from a chair in a specific way that came as an inspiration in the middle of the night. Rather you were propelled by a mysterious force—the driving power of muscles unknown to you—to move your body this way or that until something worked. Babies know this.

Their first tentative steps are individual tries at speeding life up a bit. They see people *walking*—a truly fascinating activity. No one lectures them with the scientific approach of a quadracep muscle straining to pull in a forward motion. First one little leg, then another; try and fail; try and fail. If babies stopped to analyze or criticize each attempt, the discouragement level would be too much. Instead their innocent minds shed worry and gather faith that nature has a formula for walking—never mind what it might be.

During my first few weeks at home I discovered from nowhere that I could lock my leg braces, turn around in a chair, stiffen my arms, push with the strong left bicep muscle, and back off to a standing position. This opened up a whole new world. I could grab my crutches and practice walking any old time. Alone. Nature (that old black magic) was on my side. Together we backed into a way of life with the premise that any attempt at motion was better than none at all. Even with an incorrect gait, frightening falls, and the speed of a tortoise, the upright approach beat years in a wheelchair.

My ingenious husband designed stools, ramps, arm slings, and kitchen equipment so that we could remain an independent family. Having been separated too long by war and a wayward virus, we wanted to take care of each other again. There was a strong natural incentive to adjust. But, for my part, I did a most imperfect job. I was asked many times during the first year at home, and am still asked, "How in the world do you manage?" The answer remains, "Not very well. Just average." Sometimes an abundance of love rather than determination makes things possible, if not smooth-running.

81

A Farewell Wish: That Women Will Be Heard

Judy Mann

I am in a profession where many are called and few are chosen. I have been very fortunate for more than 23 years to have had the opportunity to raise my voice over concerns that were frequently unpopular and very often at odds with mainstream orthodoxy. I am one of the few women writing a signed opinion column in a major newspaper that had no barriers in its range of subjects.

That this column has appeared in Washington made it all the more valuable because, face it, New York-Washington is where the political action is. I am retiring with this column, and I do so with the regret that there are so few liberal columnists left in the media and so few women writing serious commentary. I have always felt that the media mirror society and that a society in which women are invisible in the media is one in which they are invisible, period.

Men and women do not see the world through the same lens: Women traditionally are the ones who raise the next generation, and that means we think deeply about the environment our children will grow in, the schools where they will learn, the pesticides on the food they will eat, the safety of the world they will live in, the fairness of the laws they must abide by. We are not the warrior class.

Women are a majority in the United States. By rights, in a democracy, we should occupy 50 percent of the slots on the op-ed pages of America's newspapers. We should occupy 50 percent of the top editorships in newspapers. We should be allowed to bring what interests us—as women and mothers and wives—to the table, and I don't mean token stories about child care.

I mean taking apart the federal budget and seeing if it is benefiting families or the munitions millionaires. I mean looking at the enormous amount of money we've squandered on the "war on drugs" and asking the obvious question: Why are we building more prisons instead of rebuilding broken lives? I mean challenging the miserly foreign-aid budget and raising hell because we are not doing our share to educate women and girls in emerging countries. The Taliban could never have taken root in a society that educated and empowered females. I mean asking difficult questions like why families in these countries continue to have eight and 10 children, who survive thanks to our maternal and child health programs and who then become an increasing burden on already scarce resources. I mean demanding more action about the AIDS situation that is devastating Africa and about the spread of tuberculosis that is resistant to antibiotics. I mean using valuable column space to tell readers about programs that are working and to gain public and political support for them.

The late Nancy Woodhull, a founding editor of *USA Today*, knew the women's movement could bring to account a corporation that tolerated sexual harassment in the workplace. But she also knew that corporations that do good things, like putting women on boards of directors, should be given a pat on the back. She understood as well as anybody the importance of having women's voices in the media, and she probably did more than any other woman in journalism to bring women in various media together so that we could learn from each other and support each other.

There are columns that I am especially proud of because they had impact, but I mention them here because they illustrate the importance of having serious, thoughtful women helping mold public policy.

In the early 1980s, I wrote extensively about automobile safety: getting drunk drivers off the roads and getting laws requiring seat belts and infant seats in cars. In 1986, I was the first columnist in the mainstream press to write about the work of

David and Myra Sadker, who had documented the ways in which girls were treated unfairly in the classroom. In 1990, I wrote a column disclosing that the $750 million in federal funds being spent on AIDS research was 44 times the $17 million being spent on breast cancer research, even though breast cancer had killed 430,000 women since 1980, eight times the 54,000 people who had died because of AIDS. Former congresswoman Mary Rose Oakar (D-Ohio) used the column in a "Dear Colleague" letter and later called me to say it had been instrumental in getting $90 million more for breast cancer research.

I have been one of the few American journalists to campaign against female genital mutilation. On Oct. 4, 1995, I wrote a column decrying a plan by Egypt's minister of health to "medicalize" female genital mutilation by requiring that it be performed only in hospitals. I proposed a ban on sending U.S. aid funds to any hospital in Egypt that allowed this surgery. On Oct. 17, the minister of health, with nudging from the U.S. Agency for International Development, ordered hospitals to stop performing the procedure. In correspondence between the minister and USAID, the minister acknowledged that my column had prompted the reversal of his original decision.

I was among the first to write about the Taliban's horrific treatment of women and girls.

I have been able to introduce books to readers that have changed the way many of us think about gender: Carol Gilligan's "In a Different Voice" and Deborah Tannen's "You Just Don't Understand" are two that I'm particularly proud of having helped shepherd along. I was the first to use the term "gender gap" in the press. I was one of the few columnists who paid attention to the early efforts of women to get into politics and to raise their voices to help achieve a better society for women, children and men.

So I leave with a sense of accomplishment, of enormous gratitude to my readers who have supported the column over these many years, and the fervent hope that more and more women will be given space in our newspapers so that women's voices will be heard. We do have important things to say.

C. P. Ellis

Studs Terkel

We're in his office in Durham, North Carolina. He is the business manager of the International Union of Operating Engineers. On the wall is a plaque: "Certificate of Service, in recognition to C. P. Ellis, for your faithful service to the city in having served as a member of the Durham Human Relations Council. February 1977."

At one time, he had been president (exalted cyclops) of the Durham chapter of the Ku Klux Klan . . .

He is fifty-three years old.

My father worked in a textile mill in Durham. He died at forty-eight years old. It was probably from cotton dust. Back then, we never heard of brown lung. I was about seventeen years old and had a mother and sister depending on somebody to make a livin'. It was just barely enough insurance to cover his burial. I had to quit school and go to work. I was about eighth grade when I quit.

My father worked hard but never had enough money to buy decent clothes. When I went to school, I never seemed to have adequate clothes to wear. I always left school late afternoon with a sense of inferiority. The other kids had nice clothes, and I just had what Daddy could buy. I still got some of those inferiority feelin's now that I have to overcome once in a while.

I loved my father. He would go with me to ball games. We'd go fishin' together. I was really ashamed of the way he'd dress. He would take this money and give it to me instead of putting it on himself. I always had the feeling about somebody looking at him and makin' fun of him and makin' fun of me. I think it had to do somethin' with my life.

My father and I were very close, but we didn't talk about too many intimate things. He did have a drinking problem. During the week, he would work every day, but weekend he was ready to get plastered. I can understand when a guy looks at his paycheck and looks at his bills, and he's worried hard all the week, and his bills are larger than his paycheck. He'd done the best he could the entire week, and there seemed to be no hope. It's an illness thing. Finally you just say: "The heck with it. I'll just get drunk and forget it."

My father was out of work during the depression, and I remember going with him to the finance company uptown, and he was turned down. That's something that's always stuck.

My father never seemed to be happy. It was a constant struggle with him just like it was for me. It's very seldom I'd see him laugh. He was just tryin' to figure out what he could do from one day to the next.

After several years pumping gas at a service station, I got married. We had to have children. Four. One child was born blind and retarded, which was a real additional expense to us. He's never spoken a word. He doesn't know me when I go to see him. But I see him, I hug his neck. I talk to him, tell him I love him. I don't know whether he knows me or not, but I know he's well taken care of. All my life, I had work, never a day without work, worked all the overtime I could get and still could not survive financially. I began to say there's somethin' wrong with this country. I worked my butt off and just never seemed to break even.

I had some real great ideas about this great nation. (Laughs.) They say to abide by the law, go to church, do right and live for the Lord, and everything'll work out. But it didn't work out. It just kept gettin' worse and worse.

I was workin' a bread route. The highest I made one week was seventy-five dollars. The rent on our house was about twelve dollars a week. I will never forget: outside of this house was a 265-gallon oil drum, and I never did get enough money to fill up that oil drum. What I would do every night, I would run up to the store and buy five gallons of oil and climb up the ladder and pour it in that 265-gallon drum. I could hear that five gallons when it hits the bottom of that oil drum, splatters, and it sounds like it's nothin' in there. But it would keep the house warm for the night. Next day you'd have to do the same thing.

I left the bread route with fifty dollars in my pocket. I went to the bank and I borrowed four thousand dollars to buy the service station. I worked seven days a week, open and close, and finally had a heart attack. Just about two months before the last payments of that loan. My wife had done the best she could to keep it runnin'. Tryin' to come out of that hole, I just couldn't do it.

I really began to get bitter. I didn't know who to blame. I tried to find somebody. I began to blame it on black people. I had to hate somebody. Hatin' America is hard to do because you can't see it to hate it. You gotta have somethin' to look at to hate. (Laughs.) The natural person for me to hate would be black people, because my father before me was a member of the Klan. As far as he was concerned, it was the savior of the white people. It was the only organization in the world that would take care of the white people. So I began to admire the Klan.

I got active in the Klan while I was at the service station. Every Monday night, a group of men would come by and buy a Coca-Cola, go back to the car, take a few drinks, and come back and stand around talkin'. I couldn't help but wonder: Why are these dudes comin' out every Monday? They said they were with the Klan and have meetings close-by. Would I be interested? Boy, that was an opportunity I really looked forward to! To be part of somethin'. I joined the Klan, went from member to chaplain, from chaplain to vice-president, from vice-president to president. The title is exalted cyclops.

The first night I went with the fellas, they knocked on the door and gave the signal. They sent some robed Klansmen to talk to me and give me some instructions. I was led into a large meeting room, and this was the time of my life! It was thrilling. Here's a guy who's worked all his life and struggled all his life to be something, and here's the moment to be something. I will never forget it. Four robed Klansmen led me into the hall. The lights were dim, and the only thing you could see was an illuminated cross. I knelt before the cross. I had to make certain vows and promises. We promised to uphold the purity of the white race, fight communism, and protect white womanhood.

After I had taken my oath, there was loud applause goin' throughout the buildin', musta been at least four hundred people. For this one little ol' person. It was a thrilling moment for C. P. Ellis.

It disturbs me when people who do not really know what it's all about are so very critical of individual Klansmen. The majority of 'em are low-income whites, people who really don't have a part in something. They have been shut out as well as the blacks. Some are not very well educated either. Just like myself. We had a lot of support from doctors and lawyers and police officers.

Maybe they've had bitter experiences in this life and they had to hate somebody. So the natural person to hate would be the black person. He's beginnin' to come up, he's beginnin' to learn to read and start votin' and run for political office. Here are white people who are supposed to be superior to them, and we're shut out.

I can understand why people join extreme right-wing or left-wing groups. They're in the same boat I was. Shut out. Deep down inside, we want to be part of this great society. Nobody listens, so we join these groups.

At one time, I was state organizer of the National Rights party. I organized a youth group for the Klan. I felt we were getting old and our generation's gonna die. So I contacted certain kids in schools. They were havin' racial problems. On the first night, we had a hundred high school students. When they came in the door, we had "Dixie" playin'. These kids were just thrilled to death. I begin to hold weekly meetin's with 'em, teachin' the principles of the Klan. At that time, I believed Martin Luther King had Communist connections. I began to teach that Andy Young was affiliated with the Communist party.

I had a call one night from one of our kids. He was about twelve. He said: "I just been robbed downtown by two niggers." I'd had a couple of drinks and that really teed me off. I go downtown and couldn't find the kid. I got worried. I saw two young black people. I had the .32 revolver with me. I said: "Nigger, you seen a little young white boy up here? I just got a call from him and was told that some niggers robbed him of fifteen cents." I pulled my pistol out and put it right at his head. I said: "I've always wanted to kill a nigger and I think I'll make you the first one." I nearly scared the kid to death, and he struck off.

This was the time when the civil rights movement was really beginnin' to peak. The blacks were beginnin' to demonstrate and picket downtown stores. I never will forget some black lady I hated with a purple passion. Ann Atwater. Every time I'd go downtown, she'd be leadin' a boycott. How I hated—pardon the expression, I don't use it much now—how I just hated that black nigger. (Laughs.) Big, fat, heavy woman. She'd pull about eight demonstrations, and first thing you know they had two, three blacks at the checkout counter. Her and I have had some pretty close confrontations.

I felt very big, yeah. (Laughs.) We're more or less a secret organization. We didn't want anybody to know who we were, and I began to do some thinkin'. What am I hidin' for? I've never been convicted of anything in my life. I don't have any court record. What am I, C. P. Ellis, as a citizen and a member of the United Klansmen of America? Why can't I go the city council meeting and say: "This is the way we feel about the matter? We don't want you to purchase mobile units to set in our schoolyards. We don't want niggers in our schools."

We began to come out in the open. We would go to the meetings, and the blacks would be there and we'd be there. It was a confrontation every time. I didn't hold back anything. We began to make some inroads with the city councilmen and county commissioners. They began to call us friend. Call us at night on the telephone: "C. P., glad you came to that meeting last night." They didn't want integration either, but they did it secretively, in order to get elected. They couldn't stand up openly and say it, but they were glad somebody was sayin' it. We visited some of the city leaders in their home and talk to 'em privately. It wasn't long before councilmen would call me up: "The blacks are comin' up tonight and makin' outrageous demands. How about some of you people showin' up and have a little balance?" I'd get on the telephone: "The niggers is comin' to the council meeting tonight. Persons in the city's called me and asked us to be there."

We'd load up our cars and we'd fill up half the council chambers, and the blacks the other half. During these times, I carried weapons to the meetings, outside my belt. We'd go there armed. We would wind up just hollerin' and fussin' at each other. What happened? As a result of our fightin' one another, the city council still had their way. They didn't want to give up control to the blacks nor the Klan. They were usin' us.

I began to realize this later down the road. One day I was walkin' downtown and a certain city council member saw me comin'. I expected him to shake my hand because he was talkin' to me at night on the telephone. I had been in his home and visited with him. He crossed the street. Oh shit, I began to think, somethin's wrong here. Most of 'em are merchants or maybe an attorney, an insurance agent, people like that. As long as they kept low-income whites and low-income blacks fightin', they're gonna maintain control.

I began to get that feeling after I was ignored in public. I thought: Bullshit, you're not gonna use me anymore. That's when I began to do some real serious thinkin'.

The same thing is happening in this country today. People are being used by those in control, those who have all the wealth. I'm not espousing communism. We got the greatest system of government in the world. But those who have it simply don't want those who don't have it to have any part of it. Black and white. When it comes to money, the green, the other colors make no difference. (Laughs.)

I spent a lot of sleepless nights. I still didn't like blacks. I didn't want to associate with 'em. Blacks, Jews, or Catholics. My father said: "Don't have anything to do with 'em." I didn't until I met a black person and talked with him, eyeball to eyeball, and met a Jewish person and talked to him, eyeball to eyeball. I found out they're people just like me. They cried, they cussed, they prayed, they had desires. Just like myself. Thank God, I got to the point where I can look past labels. But at that time, my mind was closed.

I remember one Monday night Klan meeting. I said something was wrong. Our city fathers were using us. And I didn't like to be used. The reactions of the others was not too pleasant: "Let's just keep fightin' them niggers."

I'd go home at night and I'd have to wrestle with myself. I'd look at a black person walkin' down the street, and the guy'd have ragged shoes or his clothes would be worn. That began to do somethin' to me inside. I went through this for about six months. I felt I just had to get out of the Klan. But I wouldn't get out.

Then something happened. The state AFL-CIO received a grant from the Department of HEW, a $78,000 grant: how to solve racial problems in the school system. I got a telephone call from the president of the state AFL-CIO. "We'd like to get some people together from all walks of life." I said: "All walks of life? Who you talkin' about?" He said: "Blacks, whites, liberals, conservatives, Klansmen, NAACP people."

I said: "No way am I comin' with all those niggers. I'm not gonna be associated with those type of people." A White Citizens Council guy said: "Let's go up there and see what's goin' on. It's tax money bein' spent." I walk in the door, and there was a large number of blacks and white liberals. I knew most of 'em by face 'cause I seen 'em demonstratin' around town. Ann Atwater was there. (Laughs.) I just forced myself to go in and sit down.

The meeting was moderated by a great big black guy who was bushy-headed. (Laughs.) That turned me off. He acted very nice. He said: "I want you all to feel free to say anything you want to say." Some of the blacks stand up and say it's white racism. I took all I could take. I asked for the floor and I cut loose. I said: "No, sir, it's black racism. If we didn't have niggers in the schools, we wouldn't have the problems we got today."

I will never forget. Howard Clements, a black guy, stood up. He said: "I'm certainly glad C. P. Ellis come because he's the most honest man here tonight." I said: "What's that nigger tryin' to do?" (Laughs.) At the end of that meeting, some blacks tried to come up shake my hand, but I wouldn't do it. I walked off.

Second night, same group was there. I felt a little more easy because I got some things off my chest. The third night, after they elected all the committees, they want to elect a chairman. Howard Clements stood up and said: "I suggest we elect two co-chairpersons." Joe Beckton, executive director of the Human Relations Commission, just as black as he can be, he nominated me. There was a reaction from some blacks. Nooo. And, of all things, they nominated Ann Atwater, that big old fat black gal that I had just hated with a purple passion, as co-chairman. I thought to myself: Hey, ain't no way I can work with that gal. Finally, I agreed to accept it, 'cause at this point, I was tired of fightin', either for survival or against black people or against Jews or against Catholics.

A Klansman and a militant black woman, co-chairmen of the school commit-tee. It was impossible. How could I work with her? But after about two or three days, it was in our hands. We had to make it a success. This gave me another sense of belongin', a sense of pride. This helped this inferiority feelin' I had. A man who has stood up publicly and said he despised black people, all of a sudden he was willin' to work with 'em. Here's a chance for a low-income white man to be some-thin'. In spite of all my hatred for blacks and Jews and liberals, I accepted the job. Her and I began to reluctantly work together. (Laughs.) She had as many problems workin' with me as I had workin' with her.

One night, I called her: "Ann, you and I should have a lot of differences and we got 'em now. But there's somethin' laid out here before us, and if it's gonna be a success, you and I are gonna have to make it one. Can we lay aside some of these feelin's?" She said: "I'm willing if you are." I said: "Let's do it."

My old friends would call me at night: "C. P., what the hell is wrong with you? You're sellin' out the white race." This begin to make me have guilt feelin's. Am I doin' right? Am I doin' wrong? Here I am all of a sudden makin' an about-face and tryin' to deal with my feelin's, my heart. My mind was beginnin' to open up. I was beginnin' to see what was right and what was wrong. I don't want the kids to fight forever.

We were gonna go ten nights. By this time, I had went to work at Duke University, in maintenance. Makin' very little money. Terry Sanford give me this ten days off with pay. He was president of Duke at the time. He knew I was a Klansman and realized the importance of blacks and whites getting along.

I said: "If we're gonna make this thing a success, I've got to get to my kind of people." The low-income whites. We walked the streets of Durham, and we knocked on doors and invited people. Ann was goin' into the black community. They just wasn't respondin' to us when we made these house calls. Some of 'em were cussin' us out. "You're sellin' us out, Ellis, get out of my door. I don't want to talk to you." Ann was gettin' the same response from blacks: "What are you doin' messin' with that Klansman?"

One day, Ann and I went back to the school and we sat down. We began to talk and just reflect. Ann said: "My daughter came home cryin' every day. She said her teacher was makin' fun of me in front of the other kids." I said: "Boy, the same thing happened to my kid. White liberal teacher was makin' fun of Tim Ellis's fa-ther, the Klansman. In front of other peoples. He came home cryin'." At this point—(he pauses, swallows hard, stifles a sob)—I begin to see, here we are, two people from the far ends of the fence, havin' identical problems, except hers bein' black and me bein' white. From that moment on, I tell ya, that gal and I worked together good. I begin to love the girl, really. (He weeps.)

The amazing thing about it, her and I, up to that point, had cussed each other, bawled each other, we hated each other. Up to that point, we didn't know each other. We didn't know we had things in common.

We worked at it, with the people who came to these meetings. They talked about racism, sex education, about teachers not bein' qualified. After seven, eight nights of real intense discussion, these people, who'd never talked to each other before, all of a sudden came up with resolutions. It was really somethin', you had to be there to get the tone and feelin' of it.

At that point, I didn't like integration, but the law says you do this and I've got to do what the law says, okay? We said: "Let's take these resolutions to the school board." The most disheartening thing I've ever faced was the school system refused to implement any one of these resolutions. These were recommendations from the people who pay taxes and pay their salaries. (Laughs.)

I thought they were good answers. Some of 'em I didn't agree with, but I been in this thing from the beginning, and whatever comes of it, I'm gonna support it. Okay, since the school board refused, I decided I'd just run for the school board.

I spent eighty-five dollars on the campaign. The guy runnin' against me spent several thousand. I really had nobody on my side. The Klan turned against me. The low-income whites turned against me. The liberals didn't particularly like me. The blacks were suspicious of me. The blacks wanted to support me, but they couldn't muster up enough to support a Klansman on the school board. (Laughs.) But I made up my mind that what I was doin' was right, and I was gonna do it regardless what anybody said.

It bothered me when people would call and worry my wife. She's always supported me in anything I wanted to do. She was changing, and my boys were too. I got some of my youth corps kids involved. They still followed me.

I was invited to the Democratic women's social hour as a candidate. Didn't have but one suit to my name. Had it six, seven, eight years. I had it cleaned, put on the best shirt I had and a tie. Here were all this high-class wealthy candidates shakin' hands. I walked up to the mayor and stuck out my hand. He give me that handshake with that rag type of hand. He said: "C. P., I'm glad to see you." But I could tell by his handshake he was lyin' to me. This was botherin' me. I know I'm a low-income person. I know I'm not wealthy. I know they were sayin': "What's this little ol' dude runnin' for school board?" Yet they had to smile and make like they're glad to see me. I begin to spot some black people in that room. I automatically went to 'em and that was a firm handshake. They said: "I'm glad to see you, C. P." I knew they meant it—you can tell about a handshake.

Every place I appeared, I said I will listen to the voice of the people. I will not make a major decision until I first contacted all the organizations in the city. I got 4,640 votes. The guy beat me by two thousand. Not bad for eighty-five bucks and no constituency.

The whole world was openin' up, and I was learnin' new truths that I had never learned before. I was beginnin' to look at a black person, shake hands with him, and see him as a human bein'. I hadn't got rid of all this stuff. I've still got a little bit of it. But somethin' was happenin' to me.

It was almost like bein' born again. It was a new life. I didn't have these sleepless nights I used to have when I was active in the Klan and slippin' around at night. I could sleep at night and feel good about it. I'd rather live now than at any other time in history. It's a challenge.

Back at Duke, doin' maintenance, I'd pick up my tools, fix the commode, unstop the drains. But this got in my blood. Things weren't right in this country, and what we done in Durham needs to be told. I was so miserable at Duke, I could hardly stand it. I'd go to work every mornin' just hatin' to go.

My whole life had changed. I got an eighth-grade education, and I wanted to complete high school. Went to high school in the afternoons on a program called PEP—Past Employment Progress. I was about the only white in class, and the oldest. I begin to read about biology. I'd take my books home at night, 'cause I was determined to get through. Sure enough, I graduated. I got the diploma at home.

I come to work one mornin' and some guy says: "We need a union." At this time I wasn't pro-union. My daddy was anti-labor, too. We're not gettin' paid much, we're havin' to work seven days in a row. We're all starvin' to death. The next day, I meet the international representative of the Operating Engineers. He give me authorization cards. "Get these cards out and we'll have an election." There was eighty-eight for the union and seventeen no's. I was elected chief steward for the union.

Shortly after, a union man come down from Charlotte and says we need a full-time rep. We've got only two hundred people at the two plants here. It's just barely enough money comin' in to pay your salary. You'll have to get out and organize more people. I didn't know nothin' about organizin' unions, but I knew how to organize people, stir people up. (Laughs.) That's how I got to be business agent for the union.

When I began to organize, I began to see far deeper. I began to see people again bein' used. Blacks against whites. I say this without any hesitancy: management is vicious. There's two things they want to keep: all the money and all the say-so. They don't want these poor workin' folks to have none of that. I begin to see management fightin' me with everything they had. Hire anti-union law firms, badmouth unions. The people were makin' a dollar ninety-five an hour, barely able to get through weekends. I worked as a business rep for five years and was seein' all this.

Last year, I ran for business manager of the union. He's elected by the workers. The guy that ran against me was black, and our membership is seventy-five percent black. I thought: Claiborne, there's no way you can beat that black guy. People know your background. Even though you've made tremendous strides, those black people are not gonna vote for you. You know how much I beat him? Four to one. (Laughs.)

The company used my past against me. They put out letters with a picture of a robe and a cap: Would you vote for a Klansman? They wouldn't deal with the issues. I immediately called for a mass meeting. I met with the ladies at an electric component plant. I said: "Okay, this is Claiborne Ellis. This is where I come from.

I want you to know right now, you black ladies here, I was at one time a member of the Klan. I want you to know, because they'll tell you about it."

I invited some of my old black friends. I said: "Brother Joe, Brother Howard, be honest now and tell these people how you feel about me." They done it. (Laughs.) Howard Clements kidded me a little bit. He said: "I don't know what I'm doin' here, supportin' an ex-Klansman." (Laughs.) He said: "I know what C. P. Ellis come from. I knew him when he was. I knew him as he grew, and growed with him. I'm tellin' you now: follow, follow this Klansman." (He pauses, swallows hard.) "Any questions?" "No," the black ladies said. "Let's get on with the meeting, we need Ellis." (He laughs and weeps.) Boy, black people sayin' that about me. I won one thirty-four to forty-one. Four to one.

It makes you feel good to go into a plant and butt heads with professional union busters. You see black people and white people join hands to defeat the racist issues they use against people. They're tryin' the same things with the Klan. It's still happenin' today. Can you imagine a guy who's got an adult high school diploma runnin' into professional college graduates who are union busters? I gotta compete with 'em. I work seven days a week, nights, and on Saturday and Sunday. The salary's not that great, and if I didn't care, I'd quit. But I care and I can't quit. I got a taste of it. (Laughs.)

I tell people there's a tremendous possibility in this country to stop wars, the battles, the struggles, the fights between people. People say: "That's an impossible dream. You sound like Martin Luther King." An ex-Klansman who sounds like Martin Luther King. (Laughs.) I don't think it's an impossible dream. It's happened in my life. It's happened in other people's lives in America.

I don't know what's ahead of me. I have no desire to be a big union official. I want to be right out here in the field with the workers. I want to walk through their factory and shake hands with that man whose hands are dirty. I'm gonna do all that one little ol' man can do. I'm fifty-two years old, and I ain't got many years left, but I want to make the best of 'em.

When the news came over the radio that Martin Luther King was assassinated, I got on the telephone and begin to call other Klansmen. We just had a real party at the service station. Really rejoicin' 'cause that son of a bitch was dead. Our troubles are over with. They say the older you get, the harder it is for you to change. That's not necessarily true. Since I changed, I've set down and listened to tapes of Martin Luther King. I listen to it and tears come to my eyes 'cause I know what he's sayin' now. I know what's happenin'.

POSTSCRIPT: *The phone rings. A conversation. . . .*

"This was a black guy who's director of Operation Breakthrough in Durham. I had called his office. I'm interested in employin' some young black person who's interested in learnin' the labor movement. I want somebody who's never had an opportunity, just like myself. Just so he can read and write, that's all."

Suggestions for Further Reading

Anzaldua, Gloria, ed. *Making Faces, Making Soul: Creative and Critical Perspectives by Women of Color.* San Francisco: Aunt Lute Books, 1990.

Azoulay, Katya Gibel. *Black, Jewish, and Interracial.* Durham: Duke University Press, 1997.

Bean, Joseph. *In the Life: A Black Gay Anthology.* Boston: Alyson Publications, 1986.

Brown, R. M. *RubyFruit Jungle.* New York: Bantam, 1977.

Cisneros, Sandra. *Caramelo.* New York: Knopf, 2002.

Clausen, Jan. *Apples and Oranges: My Journey to Sexual Identity.* Houghton Mifflin, 1999.

Cofer, Judith Ortiz. *The Latin Deli.* Athens: University of Georgia Press, 1993.

Crozier-Hogle, Lois, et al. *Surviving in Two Worlds: Contemporary Native American Voices.* University of Texas Press, 1997.

Danticat, Edwidge. *Breath, Eyes, Memory.* New York: Vintage Books, 1994.

Davis, Lennard. *The Disability Reader.* Routledge, 1997.

Delgado, Richard, and Jean Stefancic. *The Latino/a Condition: A Critical Reader.* New York: NYU Press, 1998.

Findlen, Barbara. *Listen Up: Voices from the Next Feminist Generation.* Seal Press, 1995.

Fong, Timothy, and Larry Shingawa. *Asian American Experiences and Perspectives.* Englewood Cliffs, NJ: Prentice Hall, 2000.

Funderburg, Lise. *Black, White, Other Biracial Americans Talk about Race and Identity.* New York: William Morrow, 1994.

Gwaltney, J. Drylongso. *A Self-Portrait of Black America.* New York: Vintage Books, 1981.

Haley, Alex. *The Autobiography of Malcolm X.* New York: Grove Press, 1964.

Holmes, Sarah, ed. *Testimonies: A Collection of Lesbian Coming Out Stories.* Boston: Alyson Publications, 1988.

Jen, Gish. *Typical American.* New York: Penguin, 1992.

Kim, Elaine H., and Lilia V. Villanueva. *Making More Waves: New Writings by Asian American Women.* Boston: Beacon Press, 1997.

Kimmel, Michael S., and Michael A. Messner, eds. *Men's Lives.* New York: Macmillan, 1997.

Kingston, M. H. *The Woman Warrior.* New York: Vintage Books, 1981.

Latina Feminist Group. *Telling to Live: Latina Feminist Testimonies.* Durham: Duke University Press, 2001.

Moody, A. *Coming of Age in Mississippi.* New York: Dell, 1968.

Nam, Vickie. *Yell-Oh Girls!* New York: HarperCollins, 2001.

Native Americans 500 Years After. Photographs by Joseph C. Farner, text by Michael Dorris. New York: Thomas Crowell, 1975.

Ng, Fae Myenne. *Bone.* New York: Harper Perennial, 1994.

Portas, Alejandros. *Legacies: The Story of the Immigrant Second Generation.* University of California Press, 2001.

Rebollendo, Tey Diana, and Eliana S. Rivero, eds. *Infinite Divisions: An Anthology of Chicana Literature.* Tucson: University of Arizona Press, 1993.

Reid, John. *The Best Little Boy in the World.* New York: G. P. Putnam's Sons, 1973.

Rivera, E. *Family Installments: Memories of Growing Up Hispanic.* New York: Penguin, 1983.

Rubin, L. B. *Worlds of Pain: Life in the Working Class Family*. New York: Basic Books, 1976.

Santiago, Esmeralda. *When I Was Puerto Rican*. New York: Vintage Books, 1993.

Saxon, Marsha, and Florence Howe, eds. *Wings: An Anthology of Literature by and about Women with Disabilities*. New York: The Feminist Press, 1987.

Shah, Sonia. *Dragon Ladies: Asian American Feminists Breathe Fire*. Boston: South End Press, 1997.

Shulman, A. K. *Memoirs of an Ex-Prom Queen*. New York: Knopf, 1972.

Silko, L. M. *Ceremony*. New York: New American Library, 1972.

Smith, B., ed. *Home Girls: A Black Feminist Anthology*. New York: Kitchen Table/Women of Color Press, 1983.

Tan, Amy. *The Joy Luck Club*. New York: Ivy Books, 1990.

Tatum, Charles, ed. *New Chicana/Chicano Writing 2*. Tucson: University of Arizona Press, 1992.

Thompson, Karen, and Julie Andrzejewski. *Why Can't Sharon Kowalski Come Home?* San Francisco: Spinsters/Aunt Lute, 1988.

Turkel, Studs. *Working*. New York: Avon Books, 1972.

Warshaw, Robin. *I Never Called It Rape*. New York: Harper & Row, 1988.

Winged Words: American Indian Writers Speak. Lincoln: University of Nebraska Press, 1990.

Wu, Frank. *Yellow: Race in America Beyond Black and White*. New York: Basic Books, 2003.

Zahava, Irene, ed. *Speaking for Ourselves: Short Stories by Jewish Lesbians*. Freedom, CA: Crossing Press, 1990.

Zhou, Min, and James V. Gatewood, eds. *Contemporary Asian Americans: A Multidisciplinary Reader*. New York: New York University Press, 2000.

Zia, Helen. *Asian American Dreams: The Emergence of an American People*. New York: Farrar, Straus and Giroux, 2000.

PART VI

How It Happened: Race and Gender Issues in U.S. Law

HISTORY HOLDS THE KEY TO BOTH THE PAST AND THE PRESENT. By studying history we can understand how what happened in the past is reflected in the present, and we can distinguish between discriminatory or unjust contemporary policies and practices that represent accidental or aberrant abridgement of rights and those that are part of a pattern of racism and sexism. But whose history shall we study?

History can be written from many different perspectives. The life stories of so-called great men will vary greatly, depending on whether the biographers are their mothers, their wives, their lovers, their peers, their children, or their servants. Each perspective contributes something unique and essential to the portrait. Furthermore, historians now ask why history should be the study of "great men" exclusively, as they increasingly turn their attention to the lives of ordinary people in order to produce a more inclusive and hence more accurate account of the past.

We can even question who decides what counts as history. It was once the case that the war diaries of generals were regarded as important historical documents, whereas the diaries written by women giving an account of their daily lives were ignored or discarded. What made one document invaluable and the other irrelevant? Traditional historians adopted a fairly narrow, Eurocentric perspective on the past and used it as the basis for writing what was then alleged to provide an "objective" and "universal" picture of the past. These texts left out important information and consigned the majority of people in U.S. society to the margins of history. This approach failed to reflect the ways in which women, people of all colors, and working people created the wealth and culture of this country.

It is commonly believed that history involves collecting and studying facts. But what counts as a "fact," and who decides which facts are important? Whose interests are served or furthered by these decisions? For many years, one of the first "facts" that grade-school children learned was that Christopher Columbus discovered America. Yet this "history" is neither clear nor incontrovertible. It is a piece of the past examined from the point of view of white Europeans; it is in their interest to persuade others to believe it, since this "fact" undermines the claims of others. Native Americans might well ask how Columbus could have discovered America in 1492 if they had already been living here for thousands of years. Teaching children that bit of fiction about Columbus served to render Native Americans invisible and thus tacitly excused or denied the genocide carried out by European settlers.

During the contemporary period, many new approaches to history have arisen to remedy the omissions and distortions of the past. Women's history, black history, lesbian and gay history, ethnic history, labor history, and others all propose to transform traditional history so that it more accurately reflects the reality of people's lives, both past and present.

Part VI does not attempt to provide a comprehensive history of the American Republic since its beginning. Rather, it traces the legal status of people of color and women since the first Europeans came to this land. After a preliminary reading (Selection 83) that represents an overview of legal issues as they apply to Native Americans in particular, this Part proceeds by presenting legal documents that highlight developments in legal status. In a few cases, these documents are supplemented with materials that help paint a clearer picture of the issues involved or their implications.

Much is left out by adopting this framework for our study. Most significantly, discussions of the actual political and social movements that brought about the changes in the legal realm are omitted. For this reason, students are urged to supplement their study of the legal documents with the rich accounts of social history from the *Suggestions for Further Reading* at the end of Part VI.

However, the legal documents themselves are fascinating. They make it possible to reduce the record of hundreds of years of history to a manageable size. We can thus form a picture of the rights and status of many so-called minority groups in this country, a picture that contrasts sharply with the one usually offered in high school social studies classes. Most importantly, the documents can help us answer the question raised by material in the first five parts of this text: How did it happen that all women and all people of color came to have such limited access to power and opportunity?

The readings here show that, from the country's inception, the laws and institutions of the United States were designed to create and maintain the privileges of wealthy white males. The discrimination documented in the early parts of this book is no accident. It has a long and deliberate history. Understanding this history is essential if we are to create a more just and democratic society.

On July 4, 1776, the thirteen colonies set forth a declaration of independence from Great Britain. In that famous document, the founders of the Republic explained their reasons for separating from the homeland and expressed their hopes for the new Republic. In lines that are rightly famous and often quoted, the signatories proclaimed that "all Men are created equal, that they are endowed by their Creator with certain unalienable Rights, that among these are Life, Liberty and the Pursuit of Happiness." They went on to assert that "to secure these Rights, Governments are instituted among Men, deriving their just Powers from the Consent of the Governed." When these words were written, however, a large portion of the population of the United States had no legal rights whatsoever. Native Americans, women, indentured servants, poor white men who did not own property, and, of course, Negroes held as slaves could not vote, nor were they free to exercise their liberty or pursue their happiness in the same way that white men with property could. When the authors of the Declaration of Independence proclaimed that all men were created equal and endowed with unalienable rights, they meant "men" quite literally and white men specifically. Negroes held in slavery, as it turned out, were worth "three fifths of all other Persons," a figure stipulated in Article 1, Section 2, of the United States Constitution (see Selection 85). This section of the Constitution, which is often referred to as the "three-fifths compromise," undertook to establish how slaves would be counted for the purposes of determining taxes as well as for calculating representation of the states in Congress.

Faced with the need for an enormous work force to cultivate the land, the European settlers first tried to enslave the American Indian population. Later, the settlers brought over large numbers of "indentured workers" from Europe. These workers were poor white men, women, and children, some serving prison sentences at home, who were expected to work in the colonies for a certain period of time and then receive their freedom. When neither of these populations proved suitable, the settlers began importing African Negroes to serve their purposes.

Records show that the first African Negroes were brought to this country as early as 1526. Initially, the Negroes appear to have had the same status as indentured servants, but the laws reflect a fairly rapid distinction between the two groups. Maryland law made this distinction as early as 1640; Massachusetts legally recognized slavery in 1641; Virginia passed a law making Negroes slaves for life in 1661; and so it went until the number of slaves grew to roughly 600,000 at the time of the signing of the Declaration of Independence.[1] Numerous legal documents, such as An Act for the Better Ordering and Governing of Negroes and Slaves, passed in South Carolina in

1712 and excerpted in Selection 84, prescribed the existence of the slaves, as did the acts modeled on An Act Prohibiting the Teaching of Slaves to Read, a North Carolina statute reprinted here in Selection 86.

When the early European settlers came to this country, there were approximately 2.5 million Native Americans living on the land that was to become the United States. These peoples were divided among numerous separate and autonomous tribes, each with its own highly developed culture and history. The white settlers quickly lumped these diverse peoples into a single and inferior category, "Indians," and set about destroying their culture and seizing their lands. The Indian Removal Act of 1830 was fairly typical of the kinds of laws that were passed to carry out the appropriation of Indian lands. Believing the Indians to be inherently inferior to whites, the U.S. government had no hesitation about legislating the removal of the Indians from valuable ancestral lands to ever more remote and barren reservations. The dissolution of the Indian tribal system was further advanced by the General Allotment Act (Dawes Act) of 1887, which divided tribal landholdings among individual Indians and thereby successfully undermined the tribal system and the culture of which it was a part. In addition, this act opened up lands within the reservation area for purchase by the U.S. government, which then made those lands available to white settlers for homesteading. Many supporters of the allotment policy, who were considered "friends" of the Indians, argued that the benefits of individual ownership would have a "civilizing effect" on them.[2] Instead, it ensured a life of unrelenting poverty for most because it was usually impossible for a family to derive subsistence from the use of a single plot of land, without the support of the tribal community.

While John Adams was involved in writing the Declaration of Independence, his wife, Abigail Adams, took him to task for failing to accord women the same rights and privileges as men: "I cannot say that you are very generous to the ladies; for whilst you are proclaiming peace and good will to men, emancipating all nations, you insist upon retaining an absolute power over wives."[3] Although law and custom consistently treated women as if they were physically and mentally inferior to men, the reality of women's lives was very different. Black female slaves were forced to perform the same inhuman fieldwork as black male slaves and were expected to do so even in the final weeks of pregnancy. They were routinely beaten and abused without regard for the supposed biological fragility of the female sex. White women settlers gave birth to large numbers of children, ten and twelve being quite common and as many as twenty births not being unusual. And they did so in addition to working side by side with men to perform all those duties necessary to ensure survival in a new and unfamiliar environment. When her husband died, a woman often assumed his responsibilities as well. It was not until well into the 1800s, primarily as a result of changes brought about by the Industrial Revolution, that significant class differences began to affect the lives and work of white women.

As women, both black and white, became increasingly active in the anti-slavery movement during the 1800s, many noticed certain similarities be-tween the legal status of women and the legal status of people held as slaves. Participants at the first women's rights convention, held in Seneca Falls, New York, in 1848, listed women's grievances and specified their de-mands. At this time, married women were regarded as property of their hus-bands and had no direct legal control over their own wages, their property, or even their children. The Declaration of Sentiments issued in Seneca Falls was modeled on the Declaration of Independence in the hope that men would extend the declaration's rights to women. It is reprinted in this Part (as Selection 87) along with readings from a variety of sources from the pe-riod that reflect the most typical male responses to women's demand for the vote and other rights (see Selection 88). Similar emotional attacks are still used today to ridicule and then dismiss contemporary feminist demands.

The abysmal legal status of women and people of color in the United States during the nineteenth century is graphically documented in a series of court decisions reproduced in this Part. In *People v. Hall*, 1854 (excerpted in Selection 89), the California Supreme Court decided that a California statute barring Indians and Negroes from testifying in court cases involving whites also applied to Chinese Americans. The judges asserted that the Chinese are "a race of people whom nature has marked as inferior, and who are incapable of progress or intellectual development beyond a certain point." The extent of anti-Chinese feeling in parts of the United States can be further inferred from portions of the California Constitution adopted in 1876 (see Selection 96).

In a more famous case, *Dred Scott v. Sandford*, 1857 (Selection 90), the United States Supreme Court was asked to decide whether Dred Scott, a Negro, was a citizen of the United States with the rights that that implied. Scott, a slave who had been taken from Missouri, a slave state, into the free state of Illinois for a period of time, argued that because he was free and had been born in the United States, he was therefore a citizen. The Court ruled that this was not the case and, using reasoning that strongly parallels *People v. Hall*, offered a survey of U.S. law and custom to show that Negroes were never considered a part of the people of the United States. In *Bradwell v. Illinois*, 1873 (summarized in Selection 94), the Supreme Court ruled that women could not practice law and used the opportunity to carefully distin-guish the rights and prerogatives of women from those of men. The Court maintained that "civil law, as well as nature herself, has always recognized a wide difference in the respective spheres and destinies of man and woman" and went on to argue that women belong in the "domestic sphere."

During the period in which these and other court cases were brought, the United States moved toward and ultimately fought a bloody civil war. It was allegedly fought "to free the slaves," but much more was at stake. The Civil War reflected a struggle to the death between the Southern aristocracy, whose wealth was based on land and whose power rested on a kind of feudal economic-political order, and the Northern capitalists, who came into being by virtue of the Industrial Revolution and who wished to restructure the nation's economic-political institutions to better serve the needs of the new industrial order. Chief among these needs was a large and mobile work force for the factories in the North. Hundreds of thousands of soldiers died in the bloody conflict, while other men purchased army deferments and used the war years to amass tremendous personal wealth. On the Confederate side, men who owned fifty or more slaves were exempted from serving in the army, whereas wealthy Northern men were able to purchase deferments from the Union for the sum of $300. Among those who purchased deferments and went on to become millionaires as a result of war profiteering were John D. Rockefeller, Andrew Carnegie, J. Pierpont Morgan, Philip Armour, James Mellon, and Jay Gould.[4]

In September 1862, President Abraham Lincoln signed the Emancipation Proclamation (Selection 91) as part of his efforts to bring the Civil War to an end by forcing the Southern states to concede. It did not free all slaves; it freed only those in states or parts of states in rebellion against the federal government. Only in September 1865, after the conclusion of the war, were all people held as slaves freed by the Thirteenth Amendment (Selection 92). However, Southern whites did not yield their privileges easily. Immediately after the war, the Southern states began to pass laws known as "The Black Codes," which attempted to reestablish the relations of slavery. Some of these codes are described in this Part in Selection 93, written by the distinguished historian W. E. B. Du Bois.

In the face of such efforts to deny the rights of citizenship to black men, Congress passed the Fourteenth Amendment (Selection 92) in July 1868. This amendment, which continues to play a major role in contemporary legal battles over discrimination, includes a number of important provisions. It explicitly extended citizenship to all those born or naturalized in the United States and guaranteed all citizens "due process" and "equal protection" of the law. In addition, it canceled all debts incurred by the Confederacy in its unsuccessful rebellion while recognizing the validity of the debts incurred by the federal government. This meant that wealthy Southerners who had extended large sums of money or credit to the Confederacy would lose it, whereas wealthy Northern industrialists would be repaid.

Southern resistance to extending the rights and privileges of citizenship to black men persisted, and the Southern states used all their powers, including unbridled terror and violence, to subvert the intent of the Thirteenth and Fourteenth Amendments. The Fifteenth Amendment (Selection 92), which explicitly granted the vote to black men, was passed in 1870 but was received by the Southern states with as little enthusiasm as had greeted the Thirteenth and Fourteenth Amendments.

As the abolitionist movement grew and the Civil War became inevitable, many women's rights activists, also active in the struggle to end slavery, argued that the push for women's rights should temporarily defer to the issue of slavery. In fact, after February 1861, no women's rights conventions were held until the end of the war. Although black and white women had long worked together in both movements, the question of which struggle took precedence created serious splits among women's rights activists, including such strong black allies as Frederick Douglass and Sojourner Truth. Some argued that the evils of slavery were so great that they took precedence over the legal discrimination experienced by middle-class white women. They resented attempts by Elizabeth Cady Stanton and others to equate the condition of white women with that of Negroes held in slavery and argued, moreover, that the women's rights movement had never been concerned with the extraordinary suffering of black women or the special needs of working women. The explicitly racist appeals made by some white women activists as they sought white men's support for women's suffrage did nothing to bridge this schism. While black men received the vote in 1868, at least on paper, women would have to continue their fight until the passage of the Nineteenth Amendment (Selection 99) in 1920. As a result, many women and blacks saw each other as adversaries or obstacles in their struggle for legal equality, deflecting their attention from the privileged white men who provoked the conflict and whose power was reinforced by it.

One special cause for bitterness was the Fourteenth Amendment's reference to "male inhabitants" and the right to vote. This was the first time that voting rights had explicitly been rendered gender-specific. The Fourteenth Amendment was tested in 1875 by *Minor* v. *Happersett* (Selection 95), in which the Court was asked to rule directly on the question of whether women had the vote by virtue of their being citizens of the United States. The Court ruled unanimously that women did not have the vote, arguing that women, like criminals and mental defectives, could legitimately be denied the vote by the states.[5] In a somewhat similar case, *Elk* v. *Wilkins*, 1884 (Selection 97), John Elk, an American Indian who had left his tribe and lived among whites, argued that he was a citizen by virtue of the Fourteenth Amendment and should not be denied the right to vote by the state of Nebraska. The Supreme Court ruled that neither the Fourteenth nor the Fifteenth Amendment applied to Elk. Native Americans became citizens of the United States three years later, under one of the provisions of the Dawes Act of 1887.

Unsuccessful in their attempts to reinstate some form of forced servitude by passage of "The Black Codes," Southern states began to legalize the separation of the races in all aspects of public and private life. In *Plessy* v. *Ferguson,* 1896 (Selection 98), the Supreme Court was asked to rule on whether segregation by race in public facilities violated the Thirteenth and Fourteenth Amendments. In a ruling that was to cruelly affect several generations of black Americans, the Supreme Court decided that restricting Negroes to the use of "separate but equal" public accommodations did not deny them equal protection of the law. This decision remained in effect for almost sixty years until *Brown* v. *Board of Education of Topeka,* 1954 (Selection 101). In the historic *Brown* decision, the Court ruled, in effect, that "separate" could not possibly be "equal." Nonetheless, abolishing segregation on paper was one thing; actually bringing about the integration of public facilities was another. The integration of public schools, housing, and employment in both the North and the South has been a long and often bloody struggle that continues to this day.

The racist attitudes toward Chinese Americans, reflected in the nineteenth-century California statutes and constitution, as we have already seen, extended toward Japanese Americans as well. This racism erupted during the twentieth century after the bombing of Pearl Harbor by Japan on December 7, 1941. Anti-Japanese feelings ran so high that President Franklin Roosevelt issued an executive order allowing the military to designate "military areas" from which it could then exclude any persons it chose. On March 2, 1942, the entire West Coast was designated as such an area, and within a few months everyone of Japanese ancestry (defined as those having as little as one-eighth Japanese blood) was evacuated. More than 110,000 people of Japanese descent, most of them American citizens, were forced to leave their homes and jobs and to spend the war years in so-called relocation camps behind barbed wire.[6] Although the United States was also at war with Germany, no such barbaric treatment was afforded German Americans. The military evacuation of Japanese Americans was challenged in *Korematsu* v. *United States,* 1944. In its decision, excerpted in Selection 100, the Supreme Court upheld the forced evacuation.

The twentieth century has seen the growth of large and diverse movements for race and gender justice. These movements precipitated the creation of a number of commissions and government agencies that were to research and enforce equal treatment for people of color and women, the passage of a number of statutes to this end, and a series of Supreme Court decisions. For women, one of the most significant Court decisions of the recent past was *Roe* v. *Wade,* 1973 (Selection 102), which, for the first time, gave women the right to terminate pregnancy by abortion. Rather than affirming a woman's right to control her body, however, the *Roe* decision is based on the right to privacy. The impact of *Roe* was significantly blunted by *Harris* v. *McRae,* 1980, in which the Court ruled that the right to privacy did not require public funding of medically necessary abortions for women who could not afford them. In practice, this meant that middle-class women who chose abortion could exercise their right but that many poor white women and women of color could not. The single biggest defeat for the women's movement of this period was the failure to pass the much misunderstood Equal Rights Amendment, which is reprinted in Selection 103.

More recently, the Supreme Court was asked to rule on the constitutionality of homosexual intercourse when Michael Hardwick, a practicing homosexual, brought suit challenging the constitutionality of Georgia's sodomy law. In *Bowers* v. *Hardwick,* 1986 (Selection 104), the Court upheld that law. In a broad decision that could have disturbing implications for many different kinds of private sexual conduct between consenting adults, the Supreme Court ruled that it is not unconstitutional to legislate against certain forms of sexual activity. The prohibition against sodomy, as well as other legal issues that have impacted directly on lesbians and gay men, are surveyed in Selection 105,"Lesbian and Gay Rights in Historical Perspective."

NOTES

1. W. Z. Foster, *The Negro People in American History* (New York: International Publishers, 1954), p. 37.

2. U.S. Commission on Civil Rights, *Indian Tribes: A Continuing Quest for Survival,* a report of the United States Commission on Civil Rights, June 1981, p. 34.

3. Letter to John Adams, May 7, 1776.

4. H. Wasserman, *Harvey Wasserman's History of the United States* (New York: Harper & Row, 1975), p. 3.

5. E. Flexner, *Century of Struggle* (Cambridge, MA: Harvard University Press, 1976), p. 172.

6. R. E. Cushman and R. F. Cushman, *Cases in Constitutional Law* (New York: Appleton-Century-Crofts, 1958), p. 127.

Indian Tribes:
A Continuing Quest for Survival

U.S. Commission on Human Rights

Traditional civil rights, as the phrase is used here, include those rights that are secured to individuals and are basic to the United States system of government. They include the right to vote and the right to equal treatment without discrimination on the basis of race, religion, or national origin, among others, in such areas as education, housing, employment, public accommodations, and the administration of justice.

In order to understand where American Indians stand today with respect to these rights, it is important to look at historical developments of the concept of Indian rights along with the civil rights movement in this country. The consideration given to these factors here will not be exhaustive, but rather a brief look at some of the events that are most necessary to a background understanding of this area.

A basic and essential factor concerning American Indians is that the development of civil rights issues for them is in reverse order from other minorities in this country. Politically, other minorities started with nothing and attempted to obtain a voice in the existing economic and political structure. Indians started with everything and have gradually lost much of what they had to an advancing alien civilization. Other minorities have had no separate governmental institutions. Their goal primarily has been and continues to be to make the existing system involve them and work for them. Indian tribes have always been separate political entities interested in maintaining their own institutions and beliefs. Their goal has been to prevent the dismantling of their own systems. So while other minorities have sought integration into the larger society, much of Indian society is motivated to retain its political and cultural separateness.

Although at the beginning of the colonization process Indian nations were more numerous and better adapted to survival on this continent than the European settlers, these advantages were quickly lost. The colonization period saw the rapid expansion of non-Indian communities in numbers and territory covered

Indian Tribes: A Continuing Quest for Survival, a report of the United States Commission on Civil Rights, June 1981, p. 34. Reprinted by permission.

and a shift in the balance of strength from Indian to non-Indian communities and governments. The extent to which Indians intermingled with non-Indian society varied by time period, geographical location, and the ability of natives and newcomers to get along with one another. As a general matter, however, Indians were viewed and treated as members of political entities that were not part of the United States. The Constitution acknowledges this by its separate provision regarding trade with the Indian tribes.[1] Indian tribes today that have not been forcibly assimilated, extinguished, or legally terminated still consider themselves to be, and are viewed in American law, as separate political units.

The Racial Factor

An important element in the development of civil rights for American Indians today goes beyond their legal and political status to include the way they have been viewed racially. Since colonial times Indians have been viewed as an "inferior race"; sometimes this view is condescendingly positive—the romanticized noble savage—at other times this view is hostile—the vicious savage—at all times the view is racist. All things Indian are viewed as inherently inferior to their counterparts in the white European tradition. Strong racist statements have appeared in congressional debates, Presidential policy announcements, court decisions, and other authoritative public utterances. This racism has served to justify a view now repudiated, but which still lingers in the public mind, that Indians are not entitled to the same legal rights as others in this country. In some cases, racism has been coupled with apparently benevolent motives, to "civilize" the "savages," to teach them Christian principles. In other cases, the racism has been coupled with greed; Indians were "removed" to distant locations to prevent them from standing in the way of the development of the new Western civilization. At one extreme the concept of inferior status of Indians was used to justify genocide; at the other, apparently benevolent side, the attempt was to assimilate them into the dominant society. Whatever the rationale or motive, whether rooted in voluntary efforts or coercion, the common denominator has been the belief that Indian society is an inferior lifestyle.

> It sprang from a conviction that native people were a lower grade of humanity for whom the accepted cannons [sic] of respect need not apply; one did not debase oneself by ruining a native person. At times, this conviction was stated explicitly by men in public office, but whether expressed or not, it generated decision and action.[2]

Early assimilationists like Thomas Jefferson proceeded from this assumption with benevolent designs.

> Thus, even as they acknowledged a degree of political autonomy in the tribes, their conviction of the natives' cultural inferiority led them to interfere in their social, religious, and economic practices. Federal agents to the tribes not only negotiated

treaties and tendered payments; they pressured husbands to take up the plow and wives to learn to spin. The more conscientious agents offered gratuitous lectures on the virtues of monogamy, industry, and temperance.

The same underlying assumption provided the basis for Andrew Jackson's attitude. "I have long viewed treaties with the Indians an absurdity not to be reconciled to the principles of our government," he said. As President he refused to enforce the decisions of the U.S. Supreme Court upholding Cherokee tribal autonomy, and he had a prominent role in the forced removal of the Cherokees from Georgia and the appropriation of their land by white settlers. Other eastern tribes met a similar fate under the Indian Removal Act of 1830.[3]

Another Federal Indian land policy, enacted at the end of the 19th century and followed until 1934, that shows the virulent effect of racist assumptions was the allotment of land parcels to individual Indians as a replacement for tribal ownership. Many proponents of the policy were considered "friends of the Indians," and they argued that the attributes of individual land ownership would have a great civilizing and assimilating effect on American Indians. This action, undertaken for the benefit of the Indians, was accomplished without consulting them. Had Congress heeded the views of the purported beneficiaries of this policy, allotment might not have been adopted. Representatives of 19 tribes met in Oklahoma and unanimously opposed the legislation, recognizing the destructive effect it would have upon Indian culture and the land base itself, which was reduced by 90 million acres in 45 years.

An important principle established by the allotment policy was that the Indian form of land ownership was not "civilized," and so it was the right of the Government to invalidate that form. It is curious that the principle of the right to own property in conglomerate form for the benefit of those with a shareholder's undivided interest in the whole was a basis of the American corporate system, then developing in strength. Yet a similar form of ownership when practiced by Indians was viewed as a hallmark of savagery. Whatever the explanation for this double standard, the allotment policy reinforced the notion that Indians were somehow inferior, that non-Indians in power knew what was best for them, and that these suppositions justified the assertion that non-Indians had the power and authority to interfere with the basic right to own property.

Religion is another area in which non-Indians have felt justified in interfering with Indian beliefs. The intent to civilize the natives of this continent included a determined effort to Christianize them. Despite the constitutional prohibition, Congress, beginning in 1819, regularly appropriated funds for Christian missionary efforts. Christian goals were visibly aligned with Federal Indian policy in 1869 when a Board of Indian Commissioners was established by Congress under President Grant's administration. Representative of the spectrum of Christian denominations, the independently wealthy members of the Board were charged by the Commissioner of Indian Affairs to work for the "humanization, civilization and Christianization of the Indians." Officials of the Federal Indian Service were supposed to cooperate with this Board.

The benevolent support of Christian missionary efforts stood in stark contrast to the Federal policy of suppressing tribal religions. Indian ceremonial behavior was misunderstood and suppressed by Indian agents. In 1892 the Commissioner of Indian Affairs established a regulation making it a criminal offense to engage in such ceremonies as the sun dance. The spread of the Ghost Dance religion, which promised salvation from the white man, was so frightening to the Federal Government that troops were called in to prevent it, even though the practice posed no threat to white settlers.

The judiciary of the United States, though it has in many instances forthrightly interpreted the law to support Indian legal claims in the face of strong, sometimes violent opposition, has also lent support to the myth of Indian inferiority. For example, the United States Supreme Court in 1883, in recognizing the right of tribes to govern themselves, held that they had the exclusive authority to try Indians for criminal offenses committed against Indians. In describing its reasons for refusing to find jurisdiction in a non-Indian court in such cases, the Supreme Court said:

> It [the non-Indian court] tries them, not by their peers, nor by the customs of their people, nor the law of their land, but by *superiors* of a different race, according to the law of a social state of which they have an imperfect conception, and which is opposed to the traditions of their history, to the habits of their lives, to the strongest prejudices of their *savage nature*; one which measures the red man's revenge by the maxims of the white man's morality.[4] (emphasis added)

In recognizing the power of the United States Government to determine the right of Indians to occupy their lands, the Supreme Court expressed the good faith of the country in such matters with these words: "the United States will be governed by such considerations of justice as will control a Christian people in their treatment of an ignorant and dependent race."[5]

Another example of racist stereotyping to be found in the courts is this example from the Supreme Court of Washington State:

> The Indian was a child, and a dangerous child, of nature, to be both protected and restrained. . . . True, arrangements took the form of treaty and of terms like "cede," "relinquish," "reserve." But never were these agreements between equals . . . [but rather] that "between a superior and an inferior."[6]

This reasoning, based on racism, has supported the view that Indians are wards of the Government who need the protection and assistance of Federal agencies and it is the Government's obligation to recreate their governments, conforming them to a non-Indian model, to establish their priorities, and to make or approve their decisions for them.

Indian education policies have often been examples of the Federal Government having determined what is "best" for Indians. Having judged that assimilation could be promoted through the indoctrination process of white schools, the Federal Government began investing in Indian education. Following the model established by army officer Richard Pratt in 1879, boarding schools were established where Indian children were separated from the influences of tribal and home life. The boarding schools tried to teach Indians skills and trades that would be useful in white society, utilizing stern disciplinary measures to force assimilation. The tactics used are within memory of today's generation of tribal leaders who recall the policy of deterring communication in native languages. "I remember being punished many times for . . . singing one Navajo song, or a Navajo word slipping out of my tongue just in an unplanned way, but I was punished for it."

Federal education was made compulsory, and the policy was applied to tribes that had sophisticated school systems of their own as well as to tribes that really needed assistance to establish educational systems. The ability of the tribal school to educate was not relevant, given that the overriding goal was assimilation rather than education.

Racism in Indian affairs has not been sanctioned recently by political or religious leaders or other leaders in American society. In fact, public pronouncements over the last several decades have lamented past evils and poor treatment of Indians.[7] The virulent public expressions of other eras characterizing Indians as "children" or "savages" are not now acceptable modes of public expression. Public policy today is a commitment to Indian self-determination. Numerous actions of Congress and the executive branch give evidence of a more positive era for Indian policy.[8] Beneath the surface, however, the effects of centuries of racism still persist. The attitudes of the public, of State and local officials, and of Federal policymakers do not always live up to the positive pronouncements of official policy. Some decisions today are perceived as being made on the basis of precedents mired in the racism and greed of another era. Perhaps more important, the legacy of racism permeates behavior and that behavior creates classic civil rights violations. . . .

NOTES

1. U.S. Const. Art. 1, §8.

2. D'Arcy McNickel, *Native American Tribalism* (New York: Oxford University Press, 1973), p. 56.

3. Act of May 28, 1830, ch. 148, 4 Stat. 411.

4. *Ex Parte Crow Dog*, 109 U.S. 556, 571 (1883).

5. *Missouri, Kansas, and Texas Railway Co. v. Roberts*, 152 U.S. 114, 117 (1894).

6. *State v. Towessnute*, 154 P. 805, 807 (Wash. Sup. Ct. 1916), quoting *Choctaw Nation v. United States*, 119 U.S. 1, 27 (1886).

7. See, e.g., President Nixon's July 8, 1970, Message to the Congress, Recommendations for Indian Policy, H. Doc. No. 91–363, 91st Cong., 2d sess.

8. Ibid; Indian Self-Determination and Education Assistance Act, Pub. L. No. 93–638, 88 Stat. 2203 (1975); Indian Child Welfare Act of 1978, Pub. L. No. 95–608, 92 Stat. 3096; U.S. Department of the Interior, *Report on the Implementation of the Helsinki Final Act* (1979).

An Act for the Better Ordering and Governing of Negroes and Slaves, South Carolina, 1712

Colonial America had a role for the Negro. But the presence of a servile population, presumably of inferior stock, made it necessary to adopt measures of control. As might be expected, the southern colonies had the most highly developed codes governing Negroes. In 1712 South Carolina passed "An Act for the better ordering and governing of Negroes and Slaves." This comprehensive measure served as a model for slave codes in the South during the colonial and national periods. Eight of its thirty-five sections are reproduced below.

Whereas, the plantations and estates of this province cannot be well and sufficiently managed and brought into use, without the labor and service of negroes and other slaves; and forasmuch as the said negroes and other slaves brought unto the people of this Province for that purpose, are of barbarous, wild, savage natures, and such as renders them wholly unqualified to be governed by the laws, customs, and practices of this Province; but that it is absolutely necessary, that such other constitutions, laws and orders, should in this Province be made and enacted, for the good regulating and ordering of them, as may restrain the disorders, rapines and inhumanity, to which they are naturally prone and inclined, and may also tend to the safety and security of the people of this Province and their estates; to which purpose,

I. *Be it therefore enacted*, by his Excellency William, Lord Craven, Palatine, and the rest of the true and absolute Lords and Proprietors of this Province, by and with the advice and consent of the rest of the members of the General Assembly, now met at Charlestown, for the South-west part of this Province, and by the authority of the same, That all negroes, mulatoes, mustizoes or Indians, which at any time heretofore have been sold, or now are held or taken to be, or hereafter shall

From Thomas Cooper and David J. McCord, eds., *Statutes at Large of South Carolina* (10 vols., Columbia, 1836–1841), VII, 352–357.

be bought and sold for slaves, are hereby declared slaves; and they, and their children, are hereby made and declared slaves, to all intents and purposes; excepting all such negroes, mulatoes, mustizoes or Indians, which heretofore have been, or hereafter shall be, for some particular merit, made and declared free, either by the Governor and council of this Province, pursuant to any Act or law of this Province, or by their respective owners or masters; and also, excepting all such negroes, mulatoes, mustizoes or Indians, as can prove they ought not to be sold for slaves. And in case any negro, mulatoe, mustizoe or Indian, doth lay claim to his or her freedom, upon all or any of the said accounts, the same shall be finally heard and determined by the Governor and council of this Province.

II. And for the better ordering and governing of negroes and all other slaves in this Province, *Be it enacted* by the authority aforesaid, That no master, mistress, overseer, or other person whatsoever, that hath the care and charge of any negro or slave, shall give their negroes and other slaves leave, on Sundays, hollidays, or any other time, to go out of their plantations, except such negro or other slave as usually wait upon them at home or abroad, or wearing a livery; and every other negro or slave that shall be taken hereafter out of his master's plantation, without a ticket, or leave in writing, from his master or mistress, or some other person by his or her appointment, or some white person in the company of such slave, to give an account of his business, shall be whipped; and every person who shall not (when in his power) apprehend every negro or other slave which he shall see out of his master's plantation, without leave as aforesaid, and after apprehended, shall neglect to punish him by moderate whipping, shall forfeit twenty shillings, the one half to the poor, to be paid to the church wardens of the Parish where such forfeiture shall become due, and the other half to him that will inform for the same, within one week after such neglect; and that no slave may make further or other use of any one ticket than was intended by him that granted the same, every ticket shall particularly mention the name of every slave employed in the particular business, and to what place they are sent, and what time they return; and if any person shall presume to give any negro or slave a ticket in the name of his master or mistress, without his or her consent, such person so doing shall forfeit the sum of twenty shillings; one half to the poor, to be disposed of as aforesaid, the other half to the person injured, that will complain against the person offending, within one week after the offence committed. And for the better security of all such persons that shall endeavor to take any runaway, or shall examine any slave for his ticket, passing to and from his master's plantation, it is hereby declared lawful for any white person to beat, maim or assult, and if such negro or slave cannot otherwise be taken, to kill him, who shall refuse to shew his ticket, or, by running away or resistance, shall endeavor to avoid being apprehended or taken.

III. *And be it further enacted* by the authority aforesaid, That every master, mistress or overseer of a family in this Province, shall cause all his negro houses to be searched diligently and effectually, once every fourteen days, for fugitive and runaway slaves, guns, swords, clubs, and any other mischievous weapons, and finding any, to take them away, and cause them to be secured; as also, for clothes, goods, and any other things and commodities that are not given them by their master, mistress, commander or overseer, and honestly come by; and in whose custody they find any thing of that kind, and suspect or know to be stolen goods, the same they shall seize and take into their custody, and a full and ample description of the particulars thereof, in writing, within ten days after the discovery thereof, either to the provost marshall, or to the clerk of the parish for the time being, who is hereby required to receive the same, and to enter upon it the day of its receipt, and the particulars to file and keep to himself; and the clerk shall set upon the posts of the church door, and the provost marshall upon the usual public places, or places of notice, a short brief, that such lost goods are found; whereby, any person that hath lost his goods may the better come to the knowledge where they are; and the owner going to the marshall or clerk, and proving, by marks or otherwise, that the goods lost belong to him, and paying twelve pence for the entry and declaration of the same, if the marshall or clerk be convinced that any part of the goods certified by him to be found, appertains to the party inquiring, he is to direct the said party inquiring to the place and party where the goods be, who is hereby required to make restitution of what is in being to the true owner; and every master, mistress or overseer, as also the provost marshall or clerk, neglecting his duty in any the particulars aforesaid, for every neglect shall forfeit twenty shillings.

IV. And for the more effectual detecting and punishing such persons that trade with any slave for stolen goods, *Be it further enacted* by the authority aforesaid, That where any person shall be suspected to trade as aforesaid, any justice of the peace shall have power to take from him suspected, sufficient recognizance, not to trade with any slave contrary to the laws of this Province; and if it shall afterwards appear to any of the justices of the peace, that such person hath, or hath had, or shipped off, any goods, suspected to be unlawfully come by, it shall be lawful for such justice of the peace to oblige the person to appear at the next general sessions, who shall there be obliged to make reasonable proof, of whom he brought, or how he came by, the said goods, and unless he do it, his recognizance shall be forfeited. . . .

VII. And *whereas*, great numbers of slaves which do not dwell in Charlestown, on Sundays and holidays resort thither, to drink, quarrel, fight, curse and swear, and profane the Sabbath, and using and carrying of clubs and other mischievous weapons, resorting in great companies together, which may give them an opportunity of executing any wicked designs and purposes, to the damage and prejudice of the inhabitants of this Province; for the prevention whereof, *Be it enacted* by the authority aforesaid, That all and every the constables of Charlestown, separately on every Sunday, and the holidays at Christmas, Easter and Whitsonside, together with so many men as each constable shall think necessary to accompany him, which he is hereby empowered for that end to press, under the penalty of twenty shillings to the person that shall disobey him, shall, together with such persons, go through all or any the streets, and also, round about Charlestown, and as much further on the neck as they shall be informed or have reason to suspect any meeting or concourse of any such negroes or slaves to be at that time, and to enter into any house, at Charlestown, or elsewhere, to search for such slaves, and as many of them as they can apprehend, shall cause to be publicly whipped in Charlestown, and then to be delivered to the marshall, who for every slave so whipped and delivered to him by the constable, shall pay the constable five shillings, which five shillings shall be repaid the said marshall by the owner or head of that family to which the said negro or slave, doth belong, together with such other charges as shall become due to him for keeping runaway slaves; and the marshall shall in all respects keep and dispose of such slave as if the same was delivered to him as a runaway, under the same penalties and forfeiture as hereafter in that case is provided; and every constable of Charlestown which shall neglect or refuse to make search as aforesaid, for every such neglect shall forfeit the sum of twenty shillings. . . .

IX. *And be it further enacted* by the authority aforesaid, That upon complaint made to any justice of the peace, of any heinous or grievous crime, committed by any slave or slaves, as murder, burglary, robbery, burning of houses, or any lesser crimes, as killing or stealing any meat or other cattle, maiming one the other, stealing of fowls, provisions, or such like trespasses or injuries, the said justice shall issue out his warrant for apprehending the offender or offenders, and for all persons to come before him that can give evidence; and if upon examination, it probably appeareth, that the apprehended person is guilty, he shall commit him or them to prison, or immediately proceed to tryal of the said slave or slaves, according to the form hereafter specified, or take security for his or their forthcoming, as the case shall require, and also to certify to the justice next to him, the said cause, and to require him, by virtue of this Act, to associate himself to him, which said justice is hereby required to do, and they so associated, are to issue their summons to three sufficient freeholders, acquainting them with the matter, and appointing them a day, hour and place, when and where the same shall be heard and determined, at which day, hour and place, the said justices and freeholders shall cause the offenders and evidences to come before them, and if they, on hearing the matter, the said freeholders being by the said justices first sworn to judge uprightly and according to evidence, and diligently weighing and examining all evidences, proofs and testimonies (and in case of murder only, if on violent presumption and circumstances), they shall find such negro or other slave or slaves guilty thereof, they shall give sentence of death, if the crime by law deserve the same, and forthwith by their warrant cause immediate execution to be done, by the common or any other executioner, in such manner as they shall think fit, the kind of death to be inflicted to be left to their judgment and discretion; and if the crime committed shall not deserve death, they shall then condemn and adjudge the criminal or criminals to any other punishment, but not extending to limb or disabling him, without a particular law directing such punishment, and shall forthwith order execution to be done accordingly.

X. And in regard great mischiefs daily happen by petty larcenies committed by negroes and slaves of this Province, *Be it further enacted* by the authority aforesaid, That if any negro or other slave shall hereafter steal or destroy any goods, chattels, or provisions whatsoever, of any other person than his master or mistress, being under the value of twelve pence, every negro or other slave so offending, and being brought before some justice of the peace of this Province, upon complaint of the party injured, and shall be adjudged guilty by confession, proof, or probable circumstances, such negro or slave so offending, excepting children, whose punishment is left wholly to the discretion of the said justice, shall be adjudged by such justice to be publicly and severely whipped, not exceeding forty lashes; and if such negro or other slave punished as aforesaid, be afterwards, by two justices of the peace, found guilty of the like crimes, he or they, for such his or their second offence, shall either have one of his ears cut off, or be branded in the forehead with a hot iron, that the mark thereof may remain; and if after such punishment, such negro or slave for his third offence, shall have his nose slit; and if such negro or other slave, after the third time as aforesaid, be accused of petty larceny, or of any of the offences before mentioned, such negro or other slave shall be tried in such manner as those accused of murder, burglary, *etc.* are before by this Act provided for to be tried, and in case they shall be found guilty a fourth time, of any of the offences before mentioned, then such negro or other slave shall be adjudged to suffer death, or other punishment, as the said justices shall think fitting; and any judgment given for the first offence, shall be a sufficient conviction for the first offence; and any after judgment after the first judgment, shall be a sufficient conviction to bring the offender within the penalty of the second offence, and so for inflicting the rest of the punishments; and in case the said justices and freeholders, and any or either of them, shall neglect or refuse to perform the duties by this Act required of them, they shall severally, for such their defaults, forfeit the sum of twenty-five pounds. . . .

XII. *And it is further enacted* by the authority aforesaid, That if any negroes or other slaves shall make mutiny or insurrection, or rise in rebellion against the authority and government of this Province, or shall make preparation of arms, powder, bullets or offensive weapons, in order to carry on such mutiny or insurrection, or shall hold any counsel or conspiracy for raising such mutiny, insurrection or rebellion, the offenders shall be tried by two justices of the peace and three freeholders, associated together as before expressed in case of murder, burglary, *etc.*, who are hereby empowered and required to try the said slaves so offending, and inflict death, or any other punishment, upon the offenders, and forthwith by their warrant cause execution to be done, by the common or any other executioner, in such manner as they shall think fitting; and if any person shall make away or conceal any negro or negroes, or other slave or slaves, suspected to be guilty of the beforementioned crimes, and not upon demand bring forth the suspected offender or offenders, such person shall forfeit for every negro or slave so concealed or made away, the sum of fifty pounds; *Provided, nevertheless,* that when and as often as any of the beforementioned crimes shall be committed by more than one negro, that shall deserve death, that then and in all such cases, if the Governor and council of this Province shall think fitting, and accordingly shall order, that only one or more of the said criminals should suffer death as exemplary, and the rest to be returned to the owners, that then, the owners of the negroes so offending, shall bear proportionably the loss of the said negro or negroes so put to death, as shall be allotted them by the said justices and freeholders; and if any person shall refuse his part so allotted him, that then, and in all such cases, the said justices and freeholders are hereby required to issue out their warrant of distress upon the goods and chattels of the person so refusing, and shall cause the same to be sold by public outcry, to satisfy the said money so allotted him to pay, and to return the overplus, if any be, to the owner; *Provided, nevertheless,* that the part allotted for any person to pay for his part or proportion of the negro or negroes so put to death, shall not exceed one sixth part of his negro or negroes so excused and pardoned; and in case that shall not be sufficient to satisfy for the negro or negroes that shall be put to death, that the remaining sum shall be paid out of the public treasury of this Province.

85

The "Three-Fifths Compromise":
The U.S. Constitution, Article I, Section 2

One of the major debates in the Constitutional Convention hinged on the use of slaves in computing taxes and fixing representation. Southern delegates held that slaves should be computed in determining representation in the House, but that they should not be counted in determining a state's share of the direct tax burden. The northern delegates' point of view was exactly the opposite. A compromise was reached whereby three-fifths of the slaves were to be counted in apportionment of representation and in direct taxes among the states. Thus the South was victorious in obtaining representation for its slaves, even though delegate Luther Martin might rail that the Constitution was an insult to the Deity "who views with equal eye the poor African slave and his American master." The "three-fifths compromise" appears in Article I, Section 2.

Representatives and direct Taxes shall be apportioned among the several States which may be included within this Union, according to their respective Numbers, which shall be determined by adding to the whole Number of free Persons, including those bound to Service for a Term of Years, and excluding Indians not taxed, three fifths of all other Persons.

86

An Act Prohibiting the Teaching of Slaves to Read

To keep the slaves in hand, it was deemed necessary to keep them innocent of the printed page. Otherwise, they might read abolitionist newspapers that were smuggled in, become dissatisfied, forge passes, or simply know too much. Hence most states passed laws prohibiting anyone from teaching slaves to read or write. The North Carolina statute was typical.

An Act to Prevent All Persons from Teaching Slaves to Read or Write, the Use of Figures Excepted

Whereas the teaching of slaves to read and write, has a tendency to excite dissatisfaction in their minds, and to produce insurrection and rebellion, to the manifest injury of the citizens of this State:

Therefore,

Be it enacted by the General Assembly of the State of North Carolina, and it is hereby enacted by the authority of the same, That any free person, who shall hereafter teach, or attempt to teach, any slave within the State to read or write, the use of figures excepted, or shall give or sell to such slave or slaves any books or pamphlets, shall be liable to indictment in any court of record in this State having jurisdiction thereof, and upon conviction, shall, at the discretion of the court, if a white man or woman, be fined not less than one hundred dollars, nor more than two hundred dollars, or imprisoned; and if a free person of color, shall be fined, imprisoned, or whipped, at the discretion of the court, not exceeding thirty-nine lashes, nor less than twenty lashes.

From *Acts Passed by the General Assembly of the State of North Carolina at the Session of 1830–1831* (Raleigh, 1831), 11.

II. *Be it further enacted,* That if any slave shall hereafter teach, or attempt to teach, any other slave to read or write, the use of figures excepted, he or she may be carried before any justice of the peace, and on conviction thereof, shall be sentenced to receive thirty-nine lashes on his or her bare back.

III. *Be it further enacted,* That the judges of the Superior Courts and the justices of the County Courts shall give this act in charge to the grand juries of their respective counties.

87

Declaration of Sentiments and Resolutions, Seneca Falls Convention, 1848

The Declaration of Sentiments, adopted in July 1848 at Seneca Falls, New York, at the first woman's rights convention, is the most famous document in the history of feminism. Like its model, the Declaration of Independence, it contains a bill of particulars. Some people at the meeting thought the inclusion of disfranchisement in the list of grievances would discredit the entire movement, and when the resolutions accompanying the Declaration were put to a vote, the one calling for the suffrage was the only one that did not pass unanimously. But it did pass and thus inaugurated the woman's suffrage movement in the United States.

Declaration of Sentiments

When, in the course of human events, it becomes necessary for one portion of the family of man to assume among the people of the earth a position different from that which they have hitherto occupied, but one to which the laws of nature and of nature's God entitle them, a decent respect to the opinions of mankind requires that they should declare the causes that impel them to such a course.

We hold these truths to be self-evident: that all men and women are created equal; that they are endowed by their Creator with certain inalienable rights; that among these are life, liberty, and the pursuit of happiness; that to secure these rights governments are instituted, deriving their just powers from the consent of the governed. Whenever any form of government becomes destructive of these ends, it is the right of those who suffer from it to refuse allegiance to it, and to insist upon the institution of a new government, laying its foundation on such principles, and organizing its powers in such form, as to them shall seem most likely to effect their safety and happiness. Prudence, indeed, will dictate that governments long established should not be changed for light and transient causes; and accordingly all experience hath shown that mankind are more disposed to suffer, while evils are sufferable, than to right themselves by abolishing the forms to which they were accustomed. But when a long train of abuses and usurpations, pursuing invariably the same object, evinces a design to reduce them under absolute despotism, it is their duty to throw off such government, and to provide new guards for their future security. Such has been the patient sufferance of the women under this government, and such is now the necessity which constrains them to demand the equal station to which they are entitled.

The history of mankind is a history of repeated injuries and usurpations on the part of man toward woman, having in direct object the establishment of an absolute tyranny over her. To prove this, let facts be submitted to a candid world.

He has never permitted her to exercise her inalienable right to the elective franchise.

He has compelled her to submit to laws, in the formation of which she had no voice.

He has withheld from her rights which are given to the most ignorant and degraded men—both natives and foreigners.

Having deprived her of this first right of a citizen, the elective franchise, thereby leaving her without representation in the halls of legislation, he has oppressed her on all sides.

He has made her, if married, in the eye of the law, civilly dead.

He has taken from her all right in property, even to the wages she earns.

He has made her, morally, an irresponsible being, as she can commit many crimes with impunity, provided they be done in the presence of her husband. In the covenant of marriage, she is compelled to promise obedience to her husband, he becoming, to all intents and purposes, her master—the law giving him power to deprive her of her liberty, and to administer chastisement.

He has so framed the laws of divorce, as to what shall be the proper causes, and in case of separation, to whom the guardianship of the children shall be given, as to be wholly regardless of the happiness of women—the law, in all cases, going upon the false supposition of the supremacy of man, and giving all power into his hands.

After depriving her of all rights as a married woman, if single, and the owner of property, he has taxed her to support a government which recognizes her only when her property can be made profitable to it.

He has monopolized nearly all the profitable employments, and from those she is permitted to follow, she receives but a scanty remuneration. He closes against her all the avenues to wealth and distinction which he considers most honorable to himself. As a teacher of theology, medicine, or law, she is not known.

He has denied her the facilities for obtaining a thorough education, all colleges being closed against her.

He allows her in Church, as well as State, but a subordinate position, claiming Apostolic authority for her exclusion from the ministry, and, with some exceptions, from any public participation in the affairs of the Church.

He has created a false public sentiment by giving to the world a different code of morals for men and women, by which moral delinquencies which exclude women from society, are not only tolerated, but deemed of little account in man.

He has usurped the prerogative of Jehovah himself, claiming it as his right to assign for her a sphere of action, when that belongs to her conscience and to her God.

He has endeavored, in every way that he could, to destroy her confidence in her own powers, to lessen her self-respect, and to make her willing to lead a dependent and abject life.

Now, in view of this entire disfranchisement of one-half the people of this country, their social and religious degradation—in view of the unjust laws above mentioned, and because women do feel themselves aggrieved, oppressed, and fraudulently deprived of their most sacred rights, we insist that they have immediate admission to all the rights and privileges which belong to them as citizens of the United States.

In entering upon the great work before us, we anticipate no small amount of misconception, misrepresentation, and ridicule; but we shall use every instrumentality within our power to effect our object. We shall employ agents, circulate tracts, petition the State and National legislatures, and endeavor to enlist the pulpit and the press in our behalf. We hope this Convention will be followed by a series of Conventions embracing every part of the country.

Resolutions

Whereas, The great precept of nature is conceded to be, that "man shall pursue his own true and substantial happiness." Blackstone in his Commentaries remarks, that this law of Nature being coeval with mankind, and dictated by God himself, is of course superior in obligation to any other. It is binding over all the globe, in all countries and at all times; no human laws are of any validity if contrary to this, and such of them as are valid, derive all their force, and all their validity, and all their authority, mediately and immediately, from this original; therefore,

Resolved, That such laws as conflict, in any way, with the true and substantial happiness of woman, are contrary to the great precept of nature and of no validity, for this is "superior in obligation to any other."

Resolved, That all laws which prevent woman from occupying such a station in society as her conscience shall dictate, or which place her in a position inferior to that of man, are contrary to the great precept of nature, and therefore of no force or authority.

Resolved, That woman is man's equal—was intended to be so by the Creator, and the highest good of the race demands that she should be recognized as such.

Resolved, That the women of this country ought to be enlightened in regard to the laws under which they live, that they may no longer publish their degradation by declaring themselves satisfied with their present position, nor their ignorance, by asserting that they have all the rights they want.

Resolved, That inasmuch as man, while claiming for himself intellectual superiority, does accord to woman moral superiority, it is pre-eminently his duty to encourage her to speak and teach, as she has an opportunity, in all religious assemblies.

Resolved, That the same amount of virtue, delicacy, and refinement of behavior that is required of woman in the social state, should also be required of man, and the same transgressions should be visited with equal severity on both man and woman.

Resolved, That the objection of indelicacy and impropriety, which is so often brought against woman when she addresses a public audience, comes with a very ill-grace from those who encourage, by their attendance, her appearance on the stage, in the concert, or in feats of the circus.

Resolved, That woman has too long rested satisfied in the circumscribed limits which corrupt customs and a perverted application of the Scriptures have marked out for her, and that it is time she should move in the enlarged sphere which her great Creator has assigned her.

Resolved, That it is the duty of the women of this country to secure to themselves their sacred right to the elective franchise.

Resolved, That the equality of human rights results necessarily from the fact of the identity of the race in capabilities and responsibilities.

Resolved, therefore, That, being invested by the Creator with the same capabilities, and the same consciousness of responsibility for their exercise, it is demonstrably the right and duty of woman, equally with man, to promote every righteous cause by every righteous means; and especially in regard to the great subjects of morals and religion, it is self-evidently her right to participate with her brother in teaching them, both in private and in public, by writing and by speaking, by any instrumentalities proper to be used, and in any assemblies proper to be held; and this being a self-evident truth growing out of the divinely implanted principles of human nature, any custom or authority adverse to it, whether modern or wearing the hoary sanction of antiquity, is to be regarded as a self-evident falsehood, and at war with mankind.

[All the preceding resolutions had been drafted by Elizabeth Cady Stanton. At the last session of the convention Lucretia Mott offered the following, which, along with all the other resolutions except the ninth, was adopted unanimously.—*Ed.*]

Resolved, That the speedy success of our cause depends upon the zealous and untiring efforts of both men and women, for the overthrow of the monopoly of the pulpit, and for the securing to woman an equal participation with men in the various trades, professions, and commerce.

The Antisuffragists:
Selected Papers, 1852–1887

Editorial, New York *Herald* (1852)

The farce at Syracuse has been played out. . . .

Who are these women? What do they want? What are the motives that impel them to this course of action? The *dramatis personae* of the farce enacted at Syracuse present a curious conglomeration of both sexes. Some of them are old maids, whose personal charms were never very attractive, and who have been sadly slighted by the masculine gender in general; some of them women who have been badly mated, whose own temper, or their husbands', has made life anything but agreeable to them, and they are therefore down upon the whole of the opposite sex; some, having so much of the virago in their disposition, that nature appears to have made a mistake in their gender—mannish women, like hens that crow; some of boundless vanity and egotism, who believe that they are superior in intellectual ability to "all the world and the rest of mankind," and delight to see their speeches and addresses in print; and man shall be consigned to his proper sphere—nursing the babies, washing the dishes, mending stockings, and sweeping the house. This is "the good time coming." Besides the classes we have enumerated, there is a class of wild enthusiasts and visionaries—very sincere, but very mad—having the same vein as the fanatical Abolitionists, and the majority, if not all of them, being, in point of fact, deeply imbued with the anti-slavery sentiment. Of the male sex who attend these Conventions for the purpose of taking part in them, the majority are henpecked husbands, and all of them ought to wear petticoats. . . .

How did woman first become subject to man as she now is all over the world? By her nature, her sex, just as the negro is and always will be, to the end of time, inferior to the white race, and, therefore, doomed to subjection; but happier than

From "The Woman's Rights Convention—The Last Act of the Drama," editorial, New York *Herald*, September 12, 1852.

she would be in any other condition, just because it is the law of her nature. The women themselves would not have this law reversed. . . .

What do the leaders of the Woman's Rights Convention want? They want to vote, and to hustle with the rowdies at the polls. They want to be members of Congress, and in the heat of debate to subject themselves to coarse jests and indecent language. . . . They want to fill all other posts which men are ambitious to occupy—to be lawyers, doctors, captains of vessels, and generals in the field. How funny it would sound in the newspapers, that Lucy Stone, pleading a cause, took suddenly ill in the pains of parturition, and perhaps gave birth to a fine bouncing boy in court! Or that Rev. Antoinette Brown was arrested in the middle of her sermon in the pulpit from the same cause, and presented a "pledge" to her husband and the congregation; or, that Dr. Harriot K. Hunt, while attending a gentleman patient for a fit of the gout or *fistula in ano*, found it necessary to send for a doctor, there and then, and to be delivered of a man or woman child—perhaps twins. A similar event might happen on the floor of Congress, in a storm at sea, or in the raging tempest of battle, and then what is to become of the woman legislator?

New York State Legislative Report (1856)*

Mr. Foote, from the Judiciary Committee, made a report on Women's rights that set the whole House in roars of laughter:

"The Committee is composed of married and single gentlemen. The bachelors on the Committee, with becoming diffidence, having left the subject pretty much to the married gentlemen, they have considered it with the aid of the light they have before them and the experience married life has given them. Thus aided, they are enabled to state that the ladies always have the best place and choicest titbit at the table. They have the best seat in the cars, carriages, and sleighs; the warmest place in the winter, and the coolest place in the summer. They have their choice on which side of the bed they will lie, front or back. A lady's dress costs three times as much as that of a gentleman; and, at the present time, with the prevailing fashion, one lady occupies three times as much space in the world as a gentleman.

"It has thus appeared to the married gentlemen of your Committee, being a majority (the bachelors being silent for the reason mentioned, and also probably for the further reason that they are still suitors for the favors of the gentler sex), that, if there is any inequality or oppression in the case, the gentlemen are the sufferers. They, however, have presented no petitions for redress; having, doubtless, made up their minds to yield to an inevitable destiny. . . ."

---

*This Report on Woman's Rights, made to the New York State Legislature and concerning a petition for political equality for women, was printed in an Albany paper in March 1856.

Orestes A. Brownson, The Woman Question (1869 and 1873)*

The conclusive objection to the political enfranchisement of women is, that it would weaken and finally break up and destroy the Christian family. The social unit is the family, not the individual; and the greatest danger to American society is, that we are rapidly becoming a nation of isolated individuals, without family ties or affections. The family has already been much weakened, and is fast disappearing. We have broken away from the old homestead, have lost the restraining and purifying associations that gathered around it, and live away from home in hotels and boarding-houses. We are daily losing the faith, the virtues, the habits, and the manners without which the family cannot be sustained; and when the family goes, the nation goes too, or ceases to be worth preserving. . . .

Extend now to women suffrage and eligibility; give them the political right to vote and to be voted for; render it feasible for them to enter the arena of political strife, to become canvassers in elections and candidates for office, and what remains of family union will soon be dissolved. The wife may espouse one political party, and the husband another, and it may well happen that the husband and wife may be rival candidates for the same office, and one or the other doomed to the mortification of defeat. Will the husband like to see his wife enter the lists against him, and triumph over him? Will the wife, fired with political ambition for place or power, be pleased to see her own husband enter the lists against her, and succeed at her expense? Will political rivalry and the passions it never fails to engender increase the mutual affection of husband and wife for each other, and promote domestic union and peace, or will it not carry into the bosom of the family all the strife, discord, anger, and division of the political canvass? . . .

Woman was created to be a wife and a mother; that is her destiny. To that destiny all her instincts point, and for it nature has specially qualified her. Her proper sphere is home, and her proper function is the care of the household, to manage a family, to take care of children, and attend to their early training. For this she is endowed with patience, endurance, passive courage, quick sensibilities, a sympathetic nature, and great executive and administrative ability. She was born to be a queen in her own household, and to make home cheerful, bright, and happy.

We do not believe women, unless we acknowledge individual exceptions, are fit to have their own head. The most degraded of the savage tribes are those in

---

*This document consists of two articles by Orestes A. Brownson: "The Woman Question. Article I [from the *Catholic World*, May 1869]," in Henry F. Brownson, ed., *The Works of Orestes A. Brownson*, XVIII (Detroit, 1885), 388–89; and "The Woman Question. Article II [a review of Horace Bushnell, *Women's Suffrage: The Reform against Nature* (New York, 1869), from *Brownson's Quarterly Review* for October 1873]," in Henry F. Brownson, *op. cit.*, p. 403.

which women rule, and descent is reckoned from the mother instead of the father. Revelation asserts, and universal experience proves that the man is the head of the woman, and that the woman is for the man, not the man for the woman; and his greatest error, as well as the primal curse of society is that he abdicates his head-ship, and allows himself to be governed, we might almost say, deprived of his rea-son, by woman. It was through the seductions of the woman, herself seduced by the serpent, that man fell, and brought sin and all our woe into the world. She has all the qualities that fit her to be a help-meet of man, to be the mother of his chil-dren, to be their nurse, their early instructress, their guardian, their life-long friend; to be his companion, his comforter, his consoler in sorrow, his friend in trouble, his ministering angel in sickness; but as an independent existence, free to follow her own fancies and vague longings, her own ambition and natural love of power, without masculine direction or control, she is out of her element, and a social anomaly, sometimes a hideous monster, which men seldom are, excepting through a woman's influence. This is no excuse for men, but it proves that women need a head, and the restraint of father, husband, or the priest of God.

Remarks of Senator George G. Vest in Congress (1887)*

MR. VEST. . . . If this Government, which is based on the intelligence of the peo-ple, shall ever be destroyed it will be by injudicious, immature, or corrupt suffrage. If the ship of state launched by our fathers shall ever be destroyed, it will be by striking the rock of universal, unprepared suffrage. . . .

The Senator who last spoke on this question refers to the successful experiment in regard to woman suffrage in the Territories of Wyoming and Washington. Mr. President, it is not upon the plains of the sparsely settled Territories of the West that woman suffrage can be tested. Suffrage in the rural districts and sparsely set-tled regions of this country must from the very nature of things remain pure when corrupt everywhere else. The danger of corrupt suffrage is in the cities, and those masses of population to which civilization tends everywhere in all history. Whilst the country has been pure and patriotic, cities have been the first cancers to appear upon the body-politic in all ages of the world.

Wyoming Territory! Washington Territory! Where are their large cities? Where are the localities in those Territories where the strain upon popular government must come? The Senator from New Hampshire [Henry W. Blair—*Ed.*], who is so conspicuous in this movement, appalled the country some months since by his ghastly array of illiteracy in the Southern States. . . . That Senator proposes now to

*The remarks of Senator George G. Vest (Democrat, Missouri) may be found in the *Congressional Record*, 49th Cong., 2d sess., January 25, 1887, p. 986.

double, and more than double, that illiteracy. He proposes now to give the negro women of the South this right of suffrage, utterly unprepared as they are for it.

In a convention some two years and a half ago in the city of Louisville an intelligent negro from the South said the negro men could not vote the Democratic ticket because the women would not live with them if they did. The negro men go out in the hotels and upon the railroad cars. They go to the cities and by attrition they wear away the prejudice of race; but the women remain at home, and their emotional natures aggregate and compound the race-prejudice, and when suffrage is given them what must be the result? . . .

I pity the man who can consider any question affecting the influence of woman with the cold, dry logic of business. What man can, without aversion, turn from the blessed memory of that dear old grandmother, or the gentle words and caressing hand of that dear blessed mother gone to the unknown world, to face in its stead the idea of a female justice of the peace or township constable? For my part I want when I go to my home—when I turn from the arena where man contends with man for what we call the prizes of this paltry world—I want to go back, not to be received in the masculine embrace of some female ward politician, but to the earnest, loving look and touch of a true woman. I want to go back to the jurisdiction of the wife, the mother; and instead of a lecture upon finance or the tariff, or upon the construction of the Constitution, I want those blessed, loving details of domestic life and domestic love.

. . . I speak now respecting women as a sex. I believe that they are better than men, but I do not believe they are adapted to the political work of this world. I do not believe that the Great Intelligence ever intended them to invade the sphere of work given to men, tearing down and destroying all the best influences for which God has intended them.

The great evil in this country to-day is in emotional suffrage. The great danger to-day is in excitable suffrage. If the voters of this country could think always coolly, and if they could deliberate, if they could go by judgment and not by passion, our institutions would survive forever, eternal as the foundations of the continent itself; but massed together, subject to the excitements of mobs and of these terrible political contests that come upon us from year to year under the autonomy of our Government, what would be the result if suffrage were given to the women of the United States?

Women are essentially emotional. It is no disparagement to them they are so. It is no more insulting to say that women are emotional than to say that they are delicately constructed physically and unfitted to become soldiers or workmen under the sterner, harder pursuits of life.

What we want in this country is to avoid emotional suffrage, and what we need is to put more logic into public affairs and less feeling. There are spheres in which feeling should be paramount. There are kingdoms in which the heart should reign supreme. That kingdom belongs to woman. The realm of sentiment, the realm of love, the realm of the gentler and the holier and kindlier attributes that make the name of wife, mother, and sister next to that of God himself.

I would not, and I say it deliberately, degrade woman by giving her the right of suffrage. I mean the word in its full signification, because I believe that woman as she is to-day, the queen of the home and of hearts, is above the political collisions of this world, and should always be kept above them. . . .

It is said that the suffrage is to be given to enlarge the sphere of woman's influence. Mr. President, it would destroy her influence. It would take her down from that pedestal where she is to-day, influencing as a mother the minds of her offspring, influencing by her gentle and kindly caress the action of her husband toward the good and pure.

89

People v. *Hall,* 1854

Bias against Chinese and other colored "races" was endemic in nineteenth-century California, but perhaps no single document so well demonstrates that bias as this majority opinion handed down by the Chief Justice of the California Supreme Court. Since Chinese miners lived in small, segregated groups, the practical effect of this decision was to declare "open season" on Chinese, since crimes against them were likely to be witnessed only by other Chinese.

The People, Respondent, v. George W. Hall, Appellant

The appellant, a free white citizen of this State, was convicted of murder upon the testimony of Chinese witnesses.

The point involved in this case, is the admissibility of such evidence.

The 394th section of the Act Concerning Civil Cases, provides that no Indian or Negro shall be allowed to testify as a witness in any action or proceeding in which a White person is a party.

The 14th section of the Act of April 16th, 1850, regulating Criminal Proceedings, provides that "No Black, or Mulatto person, or Indian, shall be allowed to give evidence in favor of, or against a white man."

The true point at which we are anxious to arrive, is the legal signification of the words, "Black, Mulatto, Indian and White person," and whether the Legislature adopted them as generic terms, or intended to limit their application to specific types of the human species.

Before considering this question, it is proper to remark the difference between the two sections of our Statute, already quoted, the latter being more broad and comprehensive in its exclusion, by use of the word "Black," instead of Negro.

Conceding, however, for the present, that the word "Black," as used in the 14th section, and "Negro," in 394th, are convertible terms, and that the former was intended to include the latter, let us proceed to inquire who are excluded from testifying as witnesses under the term "Indian."

When Columbus first landed upon the shores of this continent, in his attempt to discover a western passage to the Indies, he imagined that he had accomplished the object of his expedition, and that the Island of San Salvador was one of those Islands of the Chinese sea, lying near the extremity of India, which had been described by navigators.

Acting upon this hypothesis, and also perhaps from the similarity of features and physical conformation, he gave to the Islanders the name of Indians, which appellation was universally adopted, and extended to the aboriginals of the New World, as well as of Asia.

From that time, down to a very recent period, the American Indians and the Mongolian, or Asiatic, were regarded as the same type of human species. . . .

. . . That this was the common opinion in the early history of American legislation, cannot be disputed, and, therefore, all legislation upon the subject must have borne relation to that opinion. . . .

. . . In using the words, "No Black, or Mulatto person, or Indian shall be allowed to give evidence for or against a White person," the Legislature, if any intention can be ascribed to it, adopted the most comprehensive terms to embrace every known class or shade of color, as the apparent design was to protect the White person from the influence of all testimony other than that of persons of the same caste. The use of these terms must, by every sound rule of construction, exclude every one who is not of white blood. . . .

. . . We have carefully considered all the consequences resulting from a different rule of construction, and are satisfied that even in a doubtful case we would be impelled to this decision on grounds of public policy.

The same rule which would admit them to testify, would admit them to all the equal rights of citizenship, and we might soon see them at the polls, in the jury box, upon the bench, and in our legislative halls.

This is not a speculation which exists in the excited and overheated imagination of the patriot and statesman, but it is an actual and present danger.

The anomalous spectacle of a distinct people, living in our community, recognizing no laws of this State except through necessity, bringing with them their prejudices and national feuds, in which they indulge in open violation of law; whose mendacity is proverbial; a race of people whom nature has marked as inferior, and who are incapable of progress or intellectual development beyond a certain point, as their history has shown; differing in language, opinions, color, and physical conformation; between whom and ourselves nature has placed an impassible difference, is now presented, and for them is claimed, not only the right to swear away the life of a citizen, but the further privilege of participating with us in administering the affairs of our Government. . . .

. . . For these reasons, we are of opinion that the testimony was inadmissible. . . .

90

Dred Scott v. *Sandford*, 1857

The question is simply this: Can a negro, whose ancestors were imported into this country, and sold as slaves, become a member of the political community formed and brought into existence by the Constitution of the United States, and as such become entitled to all the rights, and privileges, and immunities, guarantied by that instrument to the citizen? One of which rights is the privilege of suing in a court of the United States in the cases specified in the Constitution.

It will be observed, that the plea applies to that class of persons only whose ancestors were negroes of the African race, and imported into this country, and sold and held as slaves. The only matter in issue before this court, therefore, is whether the descendants of such slaves, when they shall be emancipated, or who are born of parents who had become free before their birth, are citizens of a State, in the sense in which the word citizen is used in the Constitution of the United States. And this being the only matter in dispute on the pleadings, the court must be understood as speaking in his opinion of that class only, that is, of those persons who are the descendants of Africans who were imported into this country, and sold as slaves.

It becomes necessary, therefore, to determine who were citizens of the several States when the Constitution was adopted. And in order to do this, we must recur to the Governments and institutions of the thirteen colonies, when they separated from Great Britain and formed new sovereignties, and took their places in the family of independent nations. We must inquire who, at that time, were recognised as the people or citizens of a State, whose rights and liberties had been outraged by

From Benjamin C. Howard, *Report of the Decision of the Supreme Court of the United States in the Case Dred Scott* . . . (Washington, 1857), 9, 13–14, 15–17, 60.

the English Government; and who declared their independence, and assumed the powers of Government to defend their rights by force of arms.

In the opinion of the court, the legislation and histories of the times, and the language used in the Declaration of Independence, show, that neither the class of persons who had been imported as slaves, nor their descendants, whether they had become free or not, were then acknowledged as a part of the people, nor intended to be included in the general words used in that memorable instrument.

It is difficult at this day to realize the state of public opinion in relation to that unfortunate race, which prevailed in the civilized and enlightened portions of the world at the time of the Declaration of Independence, and when the Constitution of the United States was formed and adopted. But the public history of every European nation displays it in a manner too plain to be mistaken.

They had for more than a century before been regarded as beings of an inferior order, and altogether unfit to associate with the white race, either in social or political relations; and so far inferior, that they had no rights which the white man was bound to respect; and that the negro might justly and lawfully be reduced to slavery for his benefit. He was bought and sold, and treated as an ordinary article of merchandise and traffic, whenever a profit could be made by it. This opinion was at that time fixed and universal in the civilized portion of the white race. It was regarded as an axiom in morals as well as in politics, which no one thought of disputing, or supposed to be open to dispute; and men in every grade and position in society daily and habitually acted upon it in their private pursuits, as well as in matters of public concern, without doubting for a moment the correctness of this opinion.

And in no nation was this opinion more firmly fixed or more uniformly acted upon than by the English Government and English people. They not only seized them on the coast of Africa, and sold them or held them in slavery for their own use, but they took them as ordinary articles of merchandise to every country where they could make a profit on them, and were far more extensively engaged in this commerce than any other nation in the world.

The opinion thus entertained and acted upon in England was naturally impressed upon the colonies they founded on this side of the Atlantic. And, accordingly, a negro of the African race was regarded by them as an article of property, and held, and bought and sold as such, in every one of the thirteen colonies which united in the Declaration of Independence, and afterwards formed the Constitution of the United States. The slaves were more or less numerous in the different colonies, as slave labor was found more or less profitable. But no one seems to have doubted the correctness of the prevailing opinion of the time.

The legislation of the different colonies furnishes positive and indisputable proof of this fact.

The language of the Declaration of Independence is equally conclusive:

It begins by declaring that; "when in the course of human events it becomes necessary for one people to dissolve the political bands which have connected them with another, and to assume among the powers of the earth the separate and equal station to which the laws of nature and nature's God entitle them, a decent respect for the opinions of mankind requires that they should declare the causes which impel them to the separation."

It then proceeds to say: "We hold these truths to be self-evident: that all men are created equal; that they are endowed by their Creator with certain unalienable rights; that among them is life, liberty, and the pursuit of happiness; that to secure these rights, Governments are instituted, deriving their just powers from the consent of the governed."

The general words above quoted would seem to embrace the whole human family, and if they were used in a similar instrument at this day would be so understood. But it is too clear for dispute, that the enslaved African race were not intended to be included, and formed no part of the people who framed and adopted this declaration; for if the language, as understood in that day, would embrace them, the conduct of the distinguished men who framed the Declaration of Independence would have been utterly and flagrantly inconsistent with the principles they asserted; and instead of the sympathy of mankind, to which they so confidently appealed, they would have deserved and received universal rebuke and reprobation.

Yet the men who framed this declaration were great men—high in literary acquirements—high in their sense of honor, and incapable of asserting principles inconsistent with those on which they were acting. They perfectly understood the meaning of the language they used, and how it would be understood by others; and they knew that it would not in any part of the civilized world be supposed to embrace the negro race, which, by common consent, had been excluded from civilized Governments and the family of nations, and doomed to slavery. They spoke and acted according to the then established doctrines and principles, and in the ordinary language of the day, and no one misunderstood them. The unhappy black race were separated from the white by indelible marks, and laws long before established, and were never thought of or spoken of except as property, and when the claims of the owner or the profit of the trader were supposed to need protection.

The state of public opinion had undergone no change when the Constitution was adopted, as is equally evident from its provisions and language.

This brief preamble sets forth by whom it was formed, for what purposes, and for whose benefit and protection. It declares that it is formed by the *people* of the United States; that is to say, by those who were members of the different political communities in the several States; and its great object is declared to be to secure the blessings of liberty to themselves and their posterity. It speaks in general terms of the *people* of the United States, and of *citizens* of the several States, when it is providing for the exercise of the powers granted or the privileges secured to the citizen. It does not define what description of persons are intended to be included under these terms, or who shall be regarded as a citizen and one of the people. It uses them as terms so well understood, that no further description or definition was necessary.

But there are two clauses in the Constitution which point directly and specifically to the negro race as a separate class of persons, and show clearly that they were not regarded as a portion of the people or citizens of the Government then formed.

One of these clauses reserves to each of the thirteen States the right to import slaves until the year 1808, if it thinks proper. And the importation which it thus sanctions was unquestionably of persons of the race of which we are speaking, as the traffic in slaves in the United States had always been confined to them. And by the other provision the States pledge themselves to each other to maintain the right of property of the master, by delivering up to him any slave who may have escaped from his service, and be found within their respective territories. By the first above-mentioned clause, therefore, the right to purchase and hold this property is directly sanctioned and authorized for twenty years by the people who framed the Constitution. And by the second, they pledge themselves to maintain and uphold the right of the master in the manner specified, as long as the Government they then formed should endure. And these two provisions show, conclusively, that neither the description of persons therein referred to, nor their descendants, were embraced in any of the other provisions of the Constitution, for certainly these two clauses were not intended to confer on them or their posterity the blessings of liberty, or any of the personal rights so carefully provided for the citizen

Upon the whole, therefore, it is the judgment of this court, that it appears by the record before us that the plaintiff in error is not a citizen of Missouri, in the sense in which that word is used in the Constitution; and that the Circuit Court of the United States, for that reason, had no jurisdiction in the case, and could give no judgment in it. Its judgment for the defendant must, consequently, be reversed, and a mandate issued, directing the suit to be dismissed for want of jurisdiction.

91

The Emancipation Proclamation

Abraham Lincoln

Emancipation Proclamation by the President of the United States of America: A Proclamation

January 1, 1863

Whereas, on the twenty-second day of September, in the year of our Lord one thousand eight hundred and sixty two, a proclamation was issued by the President of the United States, containing, among other things, the following, to wit:

"That on the first day of January, in the year of our Lord one thousand eight hundred and sixty-three, all persons held as slaves within any State or designated part of a State, the people whereof shall then be in rebellion against the United States, shall be then, thenceforward, and forever free; and the Executive Government of the United States, including the military and naval authority thereof, will recognize and maintain the freedom of such persons, and will do no act or acts to repress such persons, or any of them, in any efforts they may make for their actual freedom.

"That the Executive will, on the first day of January aforesaid, by proclamation, designate the States and parts of States, if any, in which the people thereof, respectively, shall then be in rebellion against the United States; and the fact that any State, or the people thereof, shall on that day be, in good faith, represented in the Congress of the United States by members chosen thereto at elections wherein a majority of the qualified voters of such State shall have participated, shall, in the absence of strong countervailing testimony, be deemed conclusive evidence that such State, and the people thereof, are not then in rebellion against the United States."

Now, therefore I, Abraham Lincoln, President of the United States, by virtue of the power in me vested as Commander-in-Chief, of the Army and Navy of the United States in time of actual armed rebellion against authority and government of the United States, and as a fit and necessary war measure for suppressing said rebellion, do, on this first day of January, in the year of our Lord one thousand eight hundred and sixty-three, and in accordance with my purpose so to do publicly proclaimed for the full period of one hundred days, from the day first above mentioned, order and designate as the States and parts of States wherein the people thereof respectively, are this day in rebellion against the United States, the following, to wit:

Arkansas, Texas, Louisiana (except the Parishes of St. Bernard, Plaquemines, Jefferson, St. Johns, St. Charles, St. James[,] Ascension, Assumption, Terrebonne, Lafourche, St. Mary, St. Martin, and Orleans, including the City of New-Orleans), Mississippi, Alabama, Florida, Georgia, South-Carolina, North-Carolina, and Virginia (except the forty-eight counties designated as West Virginia, and also the counties of Berkley, Accomac, Northampton, Elizabeth-City, York, Princess Ann, and Norfolk, including the cities of Norfolk & Portsmouth [)]; and which excepted parts are, for the present, left precisely as if this proclamation were not issued.

And by virtue of the power, and for the purpose aforesaid, I do order and declare that all persons held as slaves within said designated States, and parts of States, are, and henceforward shall be free; and that the Executive Government of the United States, including the military and naval authorities thereof, will recognize and maintain the freedom of said persons.

And I hereby enjoin upon the people so declared to be free to abstain from all violence, unless in necessary self-defence; and I recommend to them that, in all cases when allowed, they labor faithfully for reasonable wages.

And I further declare and make known, that such persons of suitable condition, will be received into the armed service of the United States to garrison forts, positions, stations, and other places, and to man vessels of all sorts in said service.

And upon this act, sincerely believed to be an act of justice, warranted by the Constitution, upon military necessity, I invoke the considerate judgment of mankind, and the gracious favor of Almighty God.

In witness whereof, I have hereunto set my hand and caused the seal of the United States to be affixed.

Done at the City of Washington, this first day of January, in the year of our Lord one thousand eight hundred and sixty-three, and of the Independence of the United States of America the eighty-seventh.

By the President:
Abraham Lincoln

William H. Steward,
Secretary of State

92

United States Constitution:
Thirteenth (1865), Fourteenth (1868), and Fifteenth (1870) Amendments

Amendment XIII (Ratified December 6, 1865). *Section 1.* Neither slavery nor involuntary servitude, except as a punishment for crime whereof the party shall have been duly convicted, shall exist within the United States, or any place subject to their jurisdiction.

Section 2. Congress shall have power to enforce this article by appropriate legislation.

Amendment XIV (Ratified July 9, 1868). *Section 1.* All persons born or naturalized in the United States, and subject to the jurisdiction thereof, are citizens of the United States and of the state wherein they reside. No State shall make or enforce any law which shall abridge the privileges or immunities of citizens of the United States; nor shall any State deprive any person of life, liberty, or property, without due process of law; nor deny to any person within its jurisdiction the equal protection of the laws.

Section 2. Representatives shall be apportioned among the several states according to their respective numbers, counting the whole number of persons in each state, excluding Indians not taxed. But when the right to vote at any election for the choice of Electors for President and Vice-President of the United States, Representatives in Congress, the executive and judicial officers of a State, or the members of the Legislature thereof, is denied to any of the male inhabitants of such State, being twenty-one years of age, and, citizens of the United States, or in any way abridged, except for participation in rebellion, or other crime, the basis of representation therein shall be reduced in the proportion which the number of such male citizens shall bear to the whole number of male citizens twenty-one years of age in such State.

Section 3. No person shall be a Senator or Representative in Congress, or elector of President and Vice-President, or hold any office, civil or military, under the United States, or under any State, who, having previously taken an oath, as a member of Congress, or as an officer of the United States, or as an executive or judicial officer of any State, to support the Constitution of the United States, shall have engaged in insurrection or rebellion against the same, or given aid or comfort to the enemies thereof. But Congress may by a vote of two-thirds of each House, remove such disability.

Section 4. The validity of the public debt of the United States, authorized by law, including debts incurred for payment of pensions and bounties for services in suppressing insurrection or rebellion, shall not be questioned. But neither the United States nor any State shall assume or pay any debt or obligation incurred in aid of insurrection or rebellion against the United States, or any claim for the loss or emancipation of any slave; but all such debts, obligations, and claims, shall be held illegal and void.

Section 5. The Congress shall have power to enforce, by appropriate legislation, the provisions of this article.

Amendment XV (Ratified February 3, 1870). *Section 1.* The right of citizens of the United States to vote shall not be denied or abridged by the United States or by any State on account of race, color, or previous condition of servitude.

Section 2. The Congress shall have power to enforce this article by appropriate legislation.

93

The Black Codes

W. E. B. Du Bois

The whole proof of what the South proposed to do to the emancipated Negro, unless restrained by the nation, was shown in the Black Codes passed after [President Andrew] Johnson's accession, but representing the logical result of attitudes of mind existing when Lincoln still lived. Some of these were passed and enforced. Some were passed and afterward repealed or modified when the reaction of the North was realized. In other cases, as for instance, in Louisiana, it is not clear just which laws were retained and which were repealed. In Alabama, the Governor induced the legislature not to enact some parts of the proposed code which they overwhelmingly favored.

From W.E.B. Du Bois, *Black Reconstruction* (New York: Harcourt Brace, 1935). Reprinted by permission of David G. Du Bois.

The original codes favored by the Southern legislatures were an astonishing affront to emancipation and dealt with vagrancy, apprenticeship, labor contracts, migration, civil and legal rights. In all cases, there was plain and indisputable attempt on the part of the Southern states to make Negroes slaves in everything but name. They were given certain civil rights: the right to hold property, to sue and be sued. The family relations for the first time were legally recognized. Negroes were no longer real estate.

Yet, in the face of this, the Black Codes were deliberately designed to take advantage of every misfortune of the Negro. Negroes were liable to a slave trade under the guise of vagrancy and apprenticeship laws; to make the best labor contracts, Negroes must leave the old plantations and seek better terms; but if caught wandering in search of work, and thus unemployed and without a home, this was vagrancy, and the victim could be whipped and sold into slavery. In the turmoil of war, children were separated from parents, or parents unable to support them properly. These children could be sold into slavery, and "the former owner of said minors shall have the preference." Negroes could come into court as witnesses only in cases in which Negroes were involved. And even then, they must make their appeal to a jury and judge who would believe the word of any white man in preference to that of any Negro on pain of losing office and caste.

The Negro's access to the land was hindered and limited; his right to work was curtailed; his right of self-defense was taken away, when his right to bear arms was stopped; and his employment was virtually reduced to contract labor with penal servitude as a punishment for leaving his job. And in all cases, the judges of the Negro's guilt or innocence, rights and obligations were men who believed firmly, for the most part, that he had "no rights which a white man was bound to respect."

Making every allowance for the excitement and turmoil of war, and the mentality of a defeated people, the Black Codes were infamous pieces of legislation.

Let us examine these codes in detail.[1] They covered, naturally, a wide range of subjects. First, there was the question of allowing Negroes to come into the state. In South Carolina the constitution of 1865 permitted the Legislature to regulate immigration, and the consequent law declared "that no person of color shall migrate into and reside in this State, unless, within twenty days after his arrival within the same, he shall enter into a bond, with two freeholders as sureties . . . in a penalty of one thousand dollars, conditioned for his good behavior, and for his support."

Especially in the matter of work was the Negro narrowly restricted. In South Carolina, he must be especially licensed if he was to follow on his own account any employment, except that of farmer or servant. Those licensed must not only prove their fitness, but pay an annual tax ranging from $10–$100. Under no circumstances could they manufacture or sell liquor. Licenses for work were to be granted by a judge and were revokable on complaint. The penalty was a fine double the amount of the license, one-half of which went to the informer.

Mississippi provided that "every freedman, free Negro, and mulatto shall on the second Monday of January, one thousand eight hundred and sixty-six, and annually thereafter, have a lawful home or employment, and shall have written evidence thereof . . . from the Mayor . . . or from a member of the board of police . . . which licenses may be revoked for cause at any time by the authority granting the same."

Detailed regulation of labor was provided for in nearly all these states.

Louisiana passed an elaborate law in 1865, to "regulate labor contracts for agricultural pursuits." Later, it was denied that this legislation was actually enacted but the law was published at the time and the constitutional convention of 1868 certainly regarded this statute as law, for they formally repealed it. The law required all agricultural laborers to make labor contracts for the next year within the first ten days of January, the contracts to be in writing, to be with heads of families, to embrace the labor of all the members, and to be "binding on all minors thereof." Each laborer, after choosing his employer, "shall not be allowed to leave his place of employment, until the fulfillment of his contract, unless by consent of his employer, or on account of harsh treatment, or breach of contract on the part of the employer; and if they do so leave, without cause or permission, they shall forfeit all wages earned to the time of abandonment. . . .

"In case of sickness of the laborer, wages for the time lost shall be deducted, and where the sickness is feigned for purposes of idleness, . . . and also should refusal to work be continued beyond three days, the offender shall be reported to a justice of the peace, and shall be forced to labor on roads, levees, and other public works, without pay, until the offender consents to return to his labor. . . .

"When in health, the laborer shall work ten hours during the day in summer, and nine hours during the day in winter, unless otherwise stipulated in the labor contract; he shall obey all proper orders of his employer or his agent; take proper care of his work mules, horses, oxen, stock; also of all agricultural implements; and employers shall have the right to make a reasonable deduction from the laborer's wages for injuries done to animals or agricultural implements committed to his care, or for bad or negligent work. Bad work shall not be allowed. Failing to obey reasonable orders, neglect of duty and leaving home without permission, will be deemed disobedience. . . . For any disobedience a fine of one dollar shall be imposed on the offender. For all lost time from work hours, unless in case of sickness, the laborer shall be fined twenty-five cents per hour. For all absence from home without leave, the laborer will be fined at the rate of two dollars per day. Laborers will not be required to labor on the Sabbath except to take the necessary care of stock and other property on plantations and do the necessary cooking and household duties, unless by special contract. For all thefts of the laborers from the employer of agricultural products, hogs, sheep, poultry or any other property of the employer, or willful destruction of property or injury, the laborer shall pay the employer double the amount of the value of the property stolen, destroyed or injured, one half to be paid to the employer, and the other half to be placed in the general fund provided for in this section. No live stock shall be allowed to laborers without the permission of the employer. Laborers shall not receive visitors during work hours. All difficulties arising between the employers and laborers, under this section, shall be settled, and all fines be imposed, by the former; if not satisfactory to the laborers, an appeal may be had to the nearest justice of the peace and two freeholders, citizens, one of said citizens to be selected by the employer and the other by the laborer; and all fines imposed and collected under this section shall be deducted from the wages due, and shall be placed in a common fund, to be divided among the other laborers employed on the plantation at the time when their full wages fall due, except as provided for above."

Similar detailed regulations of work were in the South Carolina law. Elaborate provision was made for contracting colored "servants" to white "masters." Their masters were given the right to whip "moderately" servants under eighteen. Others were to be whipped on authority of judicial officers. These officers were given authority to return runaway servants to their masters. The servants, on the other hand, were given certain rights. Their wages and period of service must be specified in writing, and they were protected against "unreasonable" tasks, Sunday and night work, unauthorized attacks on their persons, and inadequate food.

Contracting Negroes were to be known as "servants" and contractors as "masters." Wages were to be fixed by the judge, unless stipulated. Negroes of ten years of age or more without a parent living in the district might make a valid contract for a year or less. Failure to make written contracts was a misdemeanor, punishable by a fine of $5 to $50; farm labor to be from sunrise to sunset, with intervals for meals; servants to rise at dawn, to be careful of master's property and answerable for property lost or injured. Lost time was to be deducted from wages. Food and clothes might be deducted. Servants were to be quiet and orderly and to go to bed at reasonable hours. No night work or outdoor work in bad weather was to be asked, except in cases of necessity, visitors not allowed without the master's consent. Servants leaving employment without good reason must forfeit wages. Masters might discharge servants for disobedience, drunkenness, disease, absence, etc. Enticing away the services of a servant was punishable by a fine of $20 to $100. A master could command a servant to aid him in defense of his own person, family or property. House servants at all hours of the day and night, and at all days of the weeks, "must answer promptly all calls and execute all lawful orders. . . ."

Mississippi provided "that every civil officer shall, and every person may, arrest and carry back to his or her legal employer any freedman, free Negro, or mulatto who shall have quit the service of his or her employer before the expiration of his or her term of service without good cause; and said officer and person shall be entitled to receive for arresting and carrying back every deserting employee aforesaid the sum of five dollars, and ten cents per mile from the place of arrest to the place of delivery, and the same shall be paid by the employer and held as a set-off for so much against the wages of said deserting employee."

It was provided in some states, like South Carolina, that any white man, whether an officer or not, could arrest a Negro. "Upon view of a misdemeanor committed by a person of color, any person present may arrest the offender and take him before a magistrate, to be dealt with as the case may require. In case of a misdemeanor committed by a white person toward a person of color, any person may complain to a magistrate, who shall cause the offender to be arrested, and according to the nature of the case, to be brought before himself, or be taken for trial in the district court."

On the other hand, in Mississippi, it was dangerous for a Negro to try to bring a white person to court on any charge. "In every case where any white person has been arrested and brought to trial, by virtue of the provisions of the tenth section of the above recited act, in any court in this State, upon sufficient proof being made to the court or jury, upon the trial before said court, that any freedman, free Negro or mulatto has falsely and maliciously caused the arrest and trial of said white person or persons, the court shall render up a judgment against said freedman, free Negro or mulatto for all costs of the case, and impose a fine not to exceed fifty dollars, and imprisonment in the county jail not to exceed twenty days; and for a failure of said freedman, free Negro or mulatto to pay, or cause to be paid, all costs, fines and jail fees, the sheriff of the county is hereby authorized and required, after giving ten days' public notice, to proceed to hire out at public outcry, at the courthouse of the county, said freedman, free Negro or mulatto, for the shortest time to raise the amount necessary to discharge said freedman, free Negro or mulatto from all costs, fines, and jail fees aforesaid."

Mississippi declared that: "Any freedman, free Negro, or mulatto, committing riots, routs, affrays, trespasses, malicious mischief and cruel treatment to animals, seditious speeches, insulting gestures, language or acts, or assaults on any person, disturbance of the peace, exercising the functions of a minister of the gospel without a license from some regularly organized church, vending spirituous or intoxicating liquors, or committing any other misdemeanor, the punishment of which is not specifically provided for by law, shall, upon conviction thereof, in the county court, be fined not less than ten dollars, and not more than one hundred dollars, and may be imprisoned, at the discretion of the court, not exceeding thirty days. . . ."

The most important and oppressive laws were those with regard to vagrancy and apprenticeship. Sometimes they especially applied to Negroes; in other cases, they were drawn in general terms but evidently designed to fit the Negro's condition and to be enforced particularly with regard to Negroes.

The Virginia Vagrant Act enacted that "any justice of the peace, upon the complaint of any one of certain officers therein named, may issue his warrant for the apprehension of any person alleged to be a vagrant and cause such person to be apprehended and brought before him; and that if upon due examination said justice of the peace shall find that such person is a vagrant within the definition of vagrancy contained in said statute, he shall issue his warrant, directing such person to be employed for a term not exceeding three months, and by any constable of the county wherein the proceedings are had, be hired out for the best wages which can be procured, his wages to be applied to the support of himself and his family. The said statute further provides, that in case any vagrant so hired shall, during his term of service, run away from his employer without sufficient cause, he shall be apprehended on the warrant of a justice of the peace and returned to the custody of his employer, who shall then have, free from any other hire, the services of such vagrant for one month in addition to the original term of hiring, and that the employer shall then have power, if authorized by a justice of the peace, to work such vagrant with ball and chain. The said statute specified the persons who shall be considered vagrants and liable to the penalties imposed by it. Among those declared to be vagrants are all persons who, not having the wherewith to support their families, live idly and without employment, and refuse to work for the usual and common wages given to other laborers in the like work in the place where they are."

In Florida, January 12, 1866: "It is provided that when any person of color shall enter into a contract as aforesaid, to serve as a laborer for a year, or any other specified term, on any farm or plantation in this State, if he shall refuse or neglect to perform the stipulations of his contract by willful disobedience of orders, wanton impudence or disrespect to his employer, or his authorized agent, failure or refusal to perform the work assigned to him, idleness, or abandonment of the premises or the employment of the party with whom the contract was made, he or she shall be liable, upon the complaint of his employer or his agent, made under oath before any justice of the peace of the county, to be arrested and tried before the criminal court of the county, and upon conviction shall be subject to all the pains and penalties prescribed for the punishment of vagrancy."

In Georgia, it was ruled that "All persons wandering or strolling about in idleness, who are able to work, and who have no property to support them; all persons leading an idle, immoral, or profligate life, who have no property to support them and are able to work and do not work; all persons able to work having no visible and known means of a fair, honest, and respectable livelihood; all persons having a fixed abode, who have no visible property to support them, and who live by stealing or by trading in, bartering for, or buying stolen property; and all professional gamblers living in idleness, shall be deemed and considered vagrants, and shall be indicated as such, and it shall be lawful for any person to arrest said vagrants and have them bound over for trial to the next term of the county court, and upon conviction, they shall be fined and imprisoned or sentenced to work on the public works, for not longer than a year, or shall, in the discretion of the court, be bound over for trial to the next term of the county court, and upon conviction, they shall be fined and imprisoned or sentenced to work on the public works, for not longer than a year, or shall, in the discretion of the court, be bound out to some person for a time not longer than one year, upon such valuable consideration as the court may prescribe."

Mississippi provided "That all freedmen, free Negroes, and mulattoes in this state over the age of eighteen years, found on the second Monday in January, 1866, or thereafter, with no lawful employment or business, or found unlawfully assembling themselves together, either in the day or night time, and all white persons so assembling with freedmen, free Negroes or mulattoes, or usually associating with freedmen, free Negroes or mulattoes on terms of equality, or living in adultery or fornication with a freedwoman, free Negro or mulatto, shall be deemed vagrants, and on conviction thereof shall be fined in the sum of not exceeding, in the case of a freedman, free Negro or mulatto, fifty dollars, and a white man two hundred dollars and imprisoned, at the discretion of the court, the free Negro not exceeding ten days, and the white men not exceeding six months."

Sec. 5 provides that "all fines and forfeitures collected under the provisions of this act shall be paid into the county treasury for general county purposes, and in case any freedman, free Negro or mulatto, shall fail for five days after the imposition of any fine or forfeiture upon him or her, for violation of any of the provisions of this act to pay the same, that it shall be, and is hereby made, the duty of the Sheriff of the proper county to hire out said freedman, free Negro or mulatto, to any person who will, for the shortest period of service, pay said fine or forfeiture and all costs; *Provided*, a preference shall be given to the employer, if there be one, in which case the employer shall be entitled to deduct and retain the amount so paid from the wages of such freedman, free Negro or mulatto, then due or to become due; and in case such freedman, free Negro or mulatto cannot be hired out, he or she may be dealt with as a pauper. . . ."

In Alabama, the "former owner" was to have preference in the apprenticing of a child. This was true in Kentucky and Mississippi.

Mississippi "provides that it shall be the duty of all sheriffs, justices of the peace, and other civil officers of the several counties in this state to report to the probate courts of their respective counties semi-annually, at the January and July terms of said courts, all freedmen, free Negroes and mulattoes, under the age of eighteen, within their respective counties, beats, or districts, who are orphans, or whose parent or parents have not the means, or who refuse to provide for and support said minors, and thereupon it shall be the duty of said probate court to order the clerk of said court to apprentice said minors to some competent and suitable person, on such terms as the court may direct, having a particular care to the interest of said minors; *Provided*, that the former owner of said minors shall have the preference when, in the opinion of the court, he or she shall be a suitable person for that purpose. . . ."

"Capital punishment was provided for colored persons guilty of willful homicide, assault upon a white woman, impersonating her husband for carnal purposes, raising an insurrection, stealing a horse, a mule, or baled cotton, and housebreaking. For crimes not demanding death Negroes might be confined at hard labor, whipped, or transported; 'but punishments more degrading than imprisonment shall not be imposed upon a white person for a crime not infamous.'"[2]

In most states Negroes were allowed to testify in courts but the testimony was usually confined to cases where colored persons were involved, although in some states, by consent of the parties, they could testify in cases where only white people were involved. . . .

Mississippi simply reenacted her slave code and made it operative so far as punishments were concerned. "That all the penal and criminal laws now in force in this State, defining offenses, and prescribing the mode of punishment for crimes and misdemeanors committed by slaves, free Negroes or mulattoes, be and the same are hereby reenacted, and declared to be in full force and effect, against freedmen, free Negroes, and mulattoes, except so far as the mode and manner of trial and punishment have been changed or altered by law."

North Carolina, on the other hand, abolished her slave code, making difference of punishment only in the case of Negroes convicted of rape. Georgia placed the fines and costs of a servant upon the master. "Where such cases shall go against the servant, the judgment for costs upon written notice to the master shall operate as a garnishment against him, and he shall retain a sufficient amount for the payment thereof, out of any wages due to said servant, or to become due during the period of service, and may be cited at any time by the collecting officer to make answer thereto."

The celebrated ordinance of Opelousas, Louisiana, shows the local ordinances regulating Negroes. "No Negro or freedman shall be allowed to come within the limits of the town of Opelousas without special permission from his employer, specifying the object of his visit and the time necessary for the accomplishment of the same.

"Every Negro freedman who shall be found on the streets of Opelousas after ten o'clock at night without a written pass or permit from his employer, shall be imprisoned and compelled to work five days on the public streets, or pay a fine of five dollars.

"No Negro or freedman shall be permitted to rent or keep a house within the limits of the town under any circumstances, and anyone thus offending shall be ejected, and compelled to find an employer or leave the town within twenty-four hours.

"No Negro or freedman shall reside within the limits of the town of Opelousas who is not in the regular service of some white person or former owner, who shall be held responsible for the conduct of said freedman.

"No Negro or freedman shall be permitted to preach, exhort, or otherwise declaim to congregations of colored people without a special permission from the Mayor or President of the Board of Police, under the penalty of a fine of ten dollars or twenty days' work on the public streets.

"No freedman who is not in the military service shall be allowed to carry firearms, or any kind of weapons within the limits of the town of Opelousas without the special permission of his employer, in writing, and approved by the Mayor or President of the Board.

"Any freedman not residing in Opelousas, who shall be found within its corporate limits after the hour of 3 o'clock, on Sunday, without a special permission from his employer or the Mayor, shall be arrested and imprisoned and made to work two days on the public streets, or pay two dollars in lieu of said work."[3]

Of Louisiana, Thomas Conway testified February 22, 1866: "Some of the leading officers of the state down there—men who do much to form and control the opinions of the masses—instead of doing as they promised, and quietly submitting to the authority of the government, engaged in issuing slave codes and in promulgating them to their subordinates, ordering them to carry them into execution, and this to the knowledge of state officials of a higher character, the governor and others. And the men who issued them were not punished except as the military authorities punished them. The governor inflicted no punishment on them while I was there, and I don't know that, up to this day, he has ever punished one of them. These codes were simply the old black code of the state, with the word 'slave' expunged, and 'Negro' substituted. The most odious features of slavery were preserved in them. . . ."[4]

NOTES

1. Quotations from McPherson, *History of United States during Reconstruction*, pp. 29–44.
2. Simkins and Woody, *South Carolina during Reconstruction*, pp. 49, 50.
3. Warmoth, *War, Politics and Reconstruction*, p. 274.
4. *Report on the Joint Committee on Reconstruction*, 1866, Part IV, pp. 78–79.

94

Bradwell v. *Illinois*, 1873

Mid-nineteenth century feminists, many of them diligent workers in the cause of abolition, looked to Congress after the Civil War for an express guarantee of equal rights for men and women. Viewed in historical perspective, their expectations appear unrealistic. A problem of far greater immediacy faced the nation. Moreover, the common law heritage, ranking the married woman in relationship to her husband as "something better than his dog, a little dearer than his horse,"[1] was just beginning to erode. Nonetheless, the text of the fourteenth amendment appalled the proponents of a sex equality guarantee. Their concern centered on the abortive second section of the amendment, which placed in the Constitution for the first time the word "male." Threefold use of the word "male," always in conjunction with the term "citizens," caused concern that the grand phrases of the first section of the fourteenth amendment would have, at best, qualified application to women.[2]

From Herma Hill Kay, ed., *Kay's Text Cases and Materials on Sex-Based Discrimination*, 2nd ed. *American Casebook Series.* Copyright © 1993 by Herma Hill Kay. Reprinted with the permission of the West Publishing Company.

For more than a century after the adoption of the fourteenth amendment, the judiciary, with rare exceptions, demonstrated utmost deference to sex lines drawn by the legislature. . . .

The Court's initial examination of a woman's claim to full participation in society through entry into a profession traditionally reserved to men came in 1873 in Bradwell v. Illinois.[3] Myra Bradwell's application for a license to practice law had been denied by the Illinois Supreme Court solely because she was a female. The Supreme Court affirmed this judgment with only one dissent, recorded but not explained, by Chief Justice Chase. Justice Miller's opinion for the majority was placed on two grounds: (1) since petitioner was a citizen of Illinois, the privileges and immunities clause of article IV, section 2 of the Federal Constitution[4] was inapplicable to her claim; and (2) since admission to the bar of a state is not one of the privileges and immunities of United States citizenship, the fourteenth amendment did not secure the asserted right. Justice Bradley, speaking for himself and Justices Swayne and Field, chose to place his concurrence in the judgment on broader grounds. He wrote[5]:

[T]he civil law, as well as nature herself, has always recognized a wide difference in the respective spheres and destinies of man and woman. Man is, or should be, woman's protector and defender. The natural and proper timidity and delicacy which belongs to the female sex evidently unfits it for many of the occupations of civil life. The constitution of the family organization, which is founded in the divine ordinance, as well as in the nature of things, indicates the domestic sphere as that which properly belongs to the domain and functions of womanhood. The harmony, not to say identity, of interests and views which belong, or should belong, to the family institution is repugnant to the idea of a woman adopting a distinct and independent career from that of her husband. So firmly fixed was this sentiment in the founders of the common law that it became a maxim of that system of jurisprudence that a woman had no legal existence separate from her husband, who was regarded as her head and representative in the social state and, notwithstanding some recent modifications of this civil status, many of the special rules of law flowing from and dependent upon this cardinal principle still exist in full force in most States. One of these is, that a married woman is incapable, without her husband's consent, of making contracts which shall be binding on her or him. This very incapacity was one circumstance which the Supreme Court of Illinois deemed important in rendering a married woman incompetent fully to perform the duties and trusts that belong to the office of an attorney and counsellor.

It is true that many women are unmarried and not affected by any of the duties, complications, and incapacities arising out of the married state, but these are exceptions to the general rule. The paramount destiny and mission of woman are to fulfil the noble and benign offices of wife and mother. This is the law of the Creator. And the rules of civil society must be adapted to the general constitution of things, and cannot be based upon exceptional cases.

The humane movements of modern society, which have for their object the multiplication of avenues for woman's advancement, and of occupations adapted to her condition and sex, have my heartiest concurrence. But I am not prepared to say that it is one of her fundamental rights and privileges to be admitted into every office and position, including those which require highly special qualifications and demanding special responsibilities. In the nature of things it is not every citizen of every age, sex, and condition that is qualified for every calling and position. It is the prerogative of the legislator to prescribe regulations founded on nature, reason, and experience for the due admission of qualified persons to professions and callings demanding special skill and confidence. This fairly belongs to the police power of the State; and, in my opinion, in view of the peculiar characteristics, destiny, and mission of woman, it is within the province of the legislature to ordain what offices, positions, and callings shall be filled and discharged by men, and shall receive the benefit of those energies and responsibilities, and that decision and firmness which are presumed to predominate in the sterner sex.

Although the method of communication between the Creator and the judge is never disclosed, "divine ordinance" has been a dominant theme in decisions justifying laws establishing sex-based classifications.[6] Well past the middle of the twentieth century laws delineating "a sharp line between the sexes"[7] were sanctioned by the judiciary on the basis of lofty inspiration as well as restrained constitutional interpretation. . . .

NOTES

1. Alfred, Lord Tennyson, *Locksley Hall* (1842); see Johnston, Sex and Property: The Common Law Tradition, The Law School Curriculum, and Developments Toward Equality, 47 N.Y.U.L. Rev. 1033, 1044–1070 (1972).

2. E. Flexner, *Century of Struggle* 142–55 (1959).

3. 83 U.S. (16 Wall.) 130, 21 L. Ed. 442 (1873).

4. Article IV, section 2 reads: "The Citizens of each State shall be entitled to all Privileges and Immunities of Citizens in the several States."

5. 83 U.S. (16 Wall.) at 141–42.

6. E.g., *State v. Heitman*, 105 Kan. 139, 146–47, 181 P. 630. 633–34 (1919); *State v. Bearcub*, 1 Or. App. 579, 580, 465 P. 2d 252, 253 (1970).

7. *Goesaert v. Cleary*, 335 U.S. 464, 466, 69 S. Ct. 198, 199, 93 L. Ed. 163, 165 (1948). *Goesaert* was disapproved in *Craig v. Boren*, 429 U.S. 190, 210 n. 23, 97 S. Ct. 451, 463, 50 L. Ed. 2d 397, 414 (1976).

95

Minor v. Happersett, 1875

In this case the court held that although women were citizens, the right to vote was not a privilege or immunity of national citizenship before adoption of the 14th Amendment, nor did the amendment add suffrage to the privileges and immunities of national citizenship. Therefore, the national government could not require states to permit women to vote.

96

California Constitution, 1876

In 1876, at the height of the anti-Chinese movement, California adopted a new constitution. Its anti-Chinese provisions, largely unenforceable, represent an accurate measure of public feeling.

Article XIX

Section 1. The Legislature shall prescribe all necessary regulations for the protection of the State, and the counties, cities, and towns thereof, from the burdens and evils arising from the presence of aliens, who are or may become vagrants, paupers, mendicants, criminals, or invalids afflicted with contagious or infectious diseases, and from aliens otherwise dangerous or detrimental to the well-being or

Selection 95 from *Congressional Quarterly's Guide to the U.S. Supreme Court*, 1979, p. 631.

peace of the State, and to impose conditions upon which such persons may reside in the State, and to provide means and mode of their removal from the State upon failure or refusal to comply with such conditions; provided, that nothing contained in this section shall be construed to impair or limit the power of the Legislature to pass such police laws or other regulations as it may deem necessary.

Section 2. No corporation now existing or hereafter formed under the laws of this State, shall, after the adoption of this Constitution, employ, directly or indirectly, in any capacity, any Chinese or Mongolian. The Legislature shall pass such laws as may be necessary to enforce this provision.

Section 3. No Chinese shall be employed on any State, county, municipal, or other public work, except in punishment for crime.

Section 4. The presence of foreigners ineligible to become citizens of the United States is declared to be dangerous to the well-being of the State, and the Legislature shall discourage their immigration by all the means within its power. Asiatic coolieism is a form of human slavery, and is forever prohibited in this State; and all contracts for coolie labor shall be void. All companies or corporations, whether formed in this country or any foreign country, for the importation of such labor, shall be subject to such penalties as the Legislature may prescribe. The Legislature shall delegate all necessary power to the incorporated cities and towns of this State for the removal of Chinese without the limits of such cities and towns, or for their location within prescribed portions of those limits; and it shall also provide the necessary legislation to prohibit the introduction into this State of Chinese after the adoption of this Constitution. This section shall be enforced by appropriate legislation.

97

Elk v. *Wilkins,*
November 3, 1884

John Elk, an Indian who had voluntarily separated himself from his tribe and taken up residence among the whites, was denied the right to vote in Omaha, Nebraska, on the grounds that he was not a citizen. The Supreme Court considered the question of whether Elk had been made a citizen by the Fourteenth Amendment and decided against him.

From *Elk* v. *Wilkins,* 112 *United States Reports: Cases Adjudged in the Supreme Court* (New York: Banks & Brothers).

. . . The plaintiff, in support of his action, relies on the first clause of the first section of the Fourteenth Article of Amendment of the Constitution of the United States, by which "all persons born or naturalized in the United States, and subject to the jurisdiction thereof, are citizens of the United States and of the State wherein they reside"; and on the Fifteenth Article of Amendment, which provides that "the right of citizens of the United States to vote shall not be denied or abridged by the United States or by any State on account of race, color, or previous condition of servitude." . . .

The petition, while it does not show of what Indian tribe the plaintiff was a member, yet, by the allegations that he "is an Indian, and was born within the United States," and that "he had severed his tribal relation to the Indian tribes," clearly implies that he was born a member of one of the Indian tribes within the limits of the United States, which still exists and is recognized as a tribe by the government of the United States. Though the plaintiff alleges that he "had fully and completely surrendered himself to the jurisdiction of the United States," he does not allege that the United States accepted his surrender, or that he has ever been naturalized, or taxed, or in any way recognized or treated as a citizen, by the State or by the United States. Nor is it contended by his counsel that there is any statute or treaty that makes him a citizen.

The question then is, whether an Indian, born a member of one of the Indian tribes within the United States, is, merely by reason of his birth within the United States, and of his afterwards voluntarily separating himself from his tribe and taking up his residence among white citizens, a citizen of the United States, within the meaning of the first section of the Fourteenth Amendment of the Constitution. . . .

Indians born within the territorial limits of the United States, members of, and owing immediate allegiance to, one of the Indian tribes (an alien, though dependent, power), although in a geographical sense born in the United States, are no more "born in the United States and subject to the jurisdiction thereof," within the meaning of the first section of the Fourteenth Amendment, than the children of subjects of any foreign government born within the domain of that government, or the children born within the United States, of ambassadors or other public ministers of foreign nations.

This view is confirmed by the second section of the Fourteenth Amendment, which provides that "representatives shall be apportioned among the several States according to their respective numbers, counting the whole number of persons in each State, excluding Indians not taxed." Slavery having been abolished, and the persons formerly held as slaves made citizens, this clause fixing the apportionment of representatives has abrogated so much of the corresponding clause of the original Constitution as counted only three-fifths of such persons. But Indians not taxed are still excluded from the count, for the reason that they are not citizens. Their absolute exclusion from the basis of representation, in which all other persons are now included, is wholly inconsistent with their being considered citizens. . . .

The plaintiff, not being a citizen of the United States under the Fourteenth Amendment of the Constitution, has been deprived of no right secured by the Fifteenth Amendment, and cannot maintain this action.

98

Plessy v. Ferguson, 1896

After the collapse of Reconstruction governments, Southern whites began gradually to legalize the informal practices of segregation which obtained in the South. One such law was passed by the Louisiana legislature in 1890 and provided that "all railway companies carrying passengers . . . in this State shall provide separate but equal accommodations for the white and colored races."

Plessy v. Ferguson tested the constitutionality of this recent trend in Southern legislation. Plessy was a mulatto who, on June 7, 1892, bought a first-class ticket on the East Louisiana Railway for a trip from New Orleans to Covington, Louisiana, and sought to be seated in the "white" coach. Upon conviction of a violation of the 1890 statute, he appealed to the Supreme Court of Louisiana, which upheld his conviction, and finally to the U.S. Supreme Court, which pronounced the Louisiana law constitutional, on May 18, 1896. The defense of Plessy and attack on the Louisiana statute was in the hands of four men, the most famous of whom was Albion W. Tourgée. M. J. Cunningham, attorney general of Louisiana, was assisted by two other lawyers in defending the statute. The majority opinion of the Court was delivered by Justice Henry B. Brown. John Marshall Harlan dissented and Justice David J. Brewer did not participate, making it a 7–1 decision.

In his dissent to this decision Harlan asserted that "Our Constitution is color-blind, and neither knows nor tolerates classes among citizens. In respect of civil rights, all citizens are equal before the law." He offered the prophecy that "the judgment rendered this day will, in time, prove to be quite as pernicious as the decision made by this tribunal in the Dred Scott *case."*

The constitutionality of this act is attacked upon the ground that it conflicts both with the Thirteenth Amendment of the Constitution, abolishing slavery, and the Fourteenth Amendment, which prohibits certain restrictive legislation on the part of the States.

From *Plessy v. Ferguson,* 163 U.S. 537 *United States Reports: Cases Adjudged in the Supreme Court* (New York, Banks & Brothers, 1896).

1. That it does not conflict with the Thirteenth Amendment, which abolished slavery and involuntary servitude, except as a punishment for crime, is too clear for argument. Slavery implies involuntary servitude—a state of bondage: the ownership of mankind as a chattel, or at least the control of the labor and services of one man for the benefit of another, and the absence of a legal right to the disposal of his own person, property and services. . . .

A statute which implies merely a legal distinction between the white and colored races—a distinction which is founded in the color of the two races, and which must always exist so long as white men are distinguished from the other race by color—has no tendency to destroy the legal equality of the two races, or reestablish a state of involuntary servitude. Indeed, we do not understand that the Thirteenth Amendment is strenuously relied upon by the plaintiff in error in this connection.

2. By the Fourteenth Amendment, all persons born or naturalized in the United States, and subject to the jurisdiction thereof, are made citizens of the United States and of the State wherein they reside; and the States are forbidden from making or enforcing any law which shall abridge the privileges or immunities of citizens of the United States, or shall deprive any person of life, liberty or property without due process of law, or deny to any person within their jurisdiction the equal protection of the laws. . . .

The object of the amendment was undoubtedly to enforce the absolute equality of the two races before the law, but in the nature of things it could not have been intended to abolish distinctions based upon color, or to enforce social, as distinguished from political equality, or a commingling of the two races upon terms unsatisfactory to either. Laws permitting, and even requiring, their separation in places where they are liable to be brought into contact do not necessarily imply the inferiority of either race to the other, and have been generally, if not universally, recognized as within the competency of the state legislatures in the exercise of their police power. The most common instance of this is connected with the establishment of separate schools for white and colored children, which has been held to be a valid exercise of the legislative power even by courts of States where the political rights of the colored race have been longest and most earnestly enforced. . . .

While we think the enforced separation of the races, as applied to the internal commerce of the State, neither abridges the privileges or immunities of the colored man, deprives him of his property without due process of law, nor denies him the equal protection of the laws, within the meaning of the Fourteenth Amendment, we are not prepared to say that the conductor, in assigning passengers to the coaches according to their race, does not act at his peril, or that the provision of the second section of the act, that denies to the passenger compensation in damages for a refusal to receive him into the coach in which he properly belongs, is a valid exercise of the legislative power. Indeed, we understand it to be conceded by the State's attorney, that such part of the act as exempts from liability the railway company and its officers is unconstitutional. The power to assign to a particular coach obviously implies the power to determine to which race the passenger belongs, as well as the power to determine who, under the laws of the particular State, is to be deemed a white, and who a colored person. . . .

It is claimed by the plaintiff in error that, in any mixed community, the reputation of belonging to the dominant race, in this instance the white race, is *property*, in the same sense that a right of action, or of inheritance, is property. Conceding this to be so, for the purposes of this case, we are unable to see how this statute deprives him of, or in any way affects his right to, such property. If he be a white man and assigned to a colored coach, he may have his action for damages against the company for being deprived of his so called property. Upon the other hand, if he be a colored man and be so assigned, he has been deprived of no property, since he is not lawfully entitled to the reputation of being a white man.

In this connection, it is also suggested by the learned counsel for the plaintiff in error that the same argument that will justify the state legislature in requiring railways to provide separate accommodations for the two races will also authorize them to require separate cars to be provided for the people whose hair is of a certain color, or who are aliens, or who belong to certain nationalities, or to enact laws requiring colored people to walk upon one side of the street, and white people upon the other, or requiring white men's houses to be painted white, and colored men's black, or their vehicles or business signs to be of different colors, upon the theory that one side of the street is as good as the other, or that a house or vehicle of one color is as good as one of another color. The reply to all this is that every exercise of the police power must be reasonable, and extend only to such laws as are enacted in good faith for the promotion for the public good, and not for the annoyance or oppression of a particular class. . . .

We consider the underlying fallacy of the plaintiff's argument to consist in the assumption that the enforced separation of the two races stamps the colored race with a badge of inferiority. If this be so, it is not by reason of anything found in the act, but solely because the colored race chooses to put that construction upon it. The argument necessarily assumes that if, as has been more than once the case, and is not unlikely to be so again, the colored race should become the dominant power in the state legislature, and should enact a law in precisely similar terms, it would thereby relegate the white race to an inferior position. We imagine that the white race, at least, would not acquiesce in this assumption. The argument also assumes that social prejudices may be overcome by legislation, and that equal rights cannot be secured to the negro except by an enforced commingling of the two races. We cannot accept this proposition. If the two races are to meet upon terms of social equality, it must be the result of natural affinities, a mutual appreciation of each other's merits and a voluntary consent of individuals.

United States Constitution:
Nineteenth Amendment (1920)

Amendment XIX (ratified August 18, 1920). *Section 1.* The right of citizens of the United States to vote shall not be denied or abridged by the United States or by any State on account of sex.

Section 2. Congress shall have power to enforce this Article by appropriate legislation.

Korematsu v.
United States, 1944

The present case involved perhaps the most alarming use of executive military authority in our nation's history. Following the bombing of Pearl Harbor in December 1941, the anti-Japanese sentiment on the West Coast brought the residents of the area to a state of near hysteria; and in February 1942, President Roosevelt issued an executive order authorizing the creation of military areas from which any or all persons might be excluded as the military authorities might decide. On March 2, the entire West Coast to a depth of about forty miles was designated by the commanding general as Military Area No. 1, and he thereupon proclaimed a curfew in that area for all persons of Japanese ancestry. Later he ordered the compulsory evacuation from the area of all persons of Japanese ancestry, and by the middle of the summer most of these people had been moved inland to "War Relocation Centers," the American equivalent of concentration camps. Congress subsequently made it a crime to violate these military orders. Of the 112,000 persons of Japanese ancestry involved, about 70,000 were native-born American citizens, none of whom had been specifically accused of disloyalty. Three cases were brought to the Supreme Court as challenging the right of the government to override in this manner the customary civil rights of these citizens. In Hirabayashi v. United States, *320 U.S. 81 (1943), the Court upheld the curfew regulations as a valid military measure to prevent espionage and sabotage. "Whatever views we may entertain regarding the loyalty to this country of the citizens of Japanese ancestry, we cannot reject as unfounded the judgment of the military authorities and of Congress that there were disloyal members of that population, whose number and strength could not be precisely and quickly ascertained. We cannot say that the war-making branches of the Government did not have grounds for believing that in a critical hour such persons could not readily be isolated and separately dealt with, and constituted a menace to the national defense and safety. . . ." While emphasizing that distinctions based on ancestry were "by their very nature odious to a free people," the Court nonetheless felt "that in time of war residents having ethnic affiliations with an invading enemy may be a greater source of danger than those of a different ancestry."*

While the Court, in the present case, held valid the discriminatory mass evacuation of all persons of Japanese descent, it also held in Ex parte Endo, *323 U.S. 283 (1944), that an American citizen of Japanese ancestry whose loyalty to this country had been established could not constitutionally be held in a War Relocation Center but must be unconditionally released. The government had allowed persons to leave the Relocation Centers under conditions and restrictions that aimed to guarantee that there should not be "a dangerously disorderly migration of unwanted people to unprepared communities." Permission to leave was granted only if the applicant had the assurance of a job and a place to live, and wanted to go to a place "approved" by the War Relocation Authority. The Court held that the sole purpose of the evacuation and detention program was to protect the war effort against sabotage and espionage. "A person who is concededly loyal presents no problem of espionage or sabotage. . . . He who is loyal is by definition not a spy or a saboteur." It therefore follows that the authority to detain a citizen of Japanese ancestry ends when his loyalty is established. To hold otherwise would be to justify his detention not on grounds of military necessity but purely on grounds of race.*

Although no case reached the Court squarely challenging the right of the government to incarcerate citizens of Japanese ancestry pending a determination of their loyalty, the tenor of the opinions leaves little doubt that such action would have been sustained. The present case involved only the right of the military to evacuate such persons from the West Coast. Justice Murphy, one of the three dissenters, attacked the qualifications of the military to make sociological judgments about the effects of ancestry, and pointed out that the time consumed in evacuating these persons (eleven months) was ample for making an orderly inquiry into their individual loyalty.

Mr. Justice Black delivered the opinion of the Court, saying in part:

The petitioner, an American citizen of Japanese descent, was convicted in a federal district court for remaining in San Leandro, California, a "Military Area," contrary to Civilian Exclusion Order No. 34 of the Commanding General of the Western Command, U.S. Army, which directed that after May 9, 1942, all persons of Japanese ancestry should be excluded from that area. No question was raised as to petitioner's loyalty to the United States. The Circuit Court of Appeals affirmed, and the importance of the constitutional question involved caused us to grant certiorari.

It should be noted, to begin with, that all legal restrictions which curtail the civil rights of a single racial group are immediately suspect. That is not to say that all such restrictions are unconstitutional. It is to say that courts must subject them to the most rigid scrutiny. Pressing public necessity may sometimes justify the existence of such restrictions; racial antagonism never can.

In the instant case prosecution of the petitioner was begun by information charging violation of an Act of Congress, of March 21, 1942, 56 Stat. 173, which provides that ". . . whoever shall enter, remain in, leave, or commit any act in any military area or military zone prescribed, under the authority of an Executive order of the President, by the Secretary of War, or by any military commander designated by the Secretary of War, contrary to the restrictions applicable to any such area or zone or contrary to the order of the Secretary of War or any such military commander, shall, if it appears that he knew or should have known of the existence and extent of the restrictions or order and that his act was in violation thereof, be guilty of a misdemeanor and upon conviction shall be liable to a fine of not to exceed $5,000 or to imprisonment for not more than one year, or both, for each offense."

Exclusion Order No. 34, which the petitioner knowingly and admittedly violated, was one of a number of military orders and proclamations, all of which were substantially based upon Executive Order No. 9066, 7 Fed. Reg. 1407. That order, issued after we were at war with Japan, declared that "the successful prosecution of the war requires every possible protection against espionage and against sabotage to national-defense material, national-defense premises, and national-defense utilities. . . ."

One of the series of orders and proclamations, a curfew order, which like the exclusion order here was promulgated pursuant to Executive Order 9066, subjected all persons of Japanese ancestry in prescribed West Coast military areas to remain in their residences from 8 P.M. to 6 A.M. As is the case with the exclusion order here, that prior curfew order was designed as a "protection against espionage and against sabotage." In Kiyoshi Hirabayashi v. United States, 320 U.S. 81, we sustained a conviction obtained for violation of the curfew order. The Hirabayashi conviction and this one thus rest on the same 1942 Congressional Act and the same basic executive and military orders, all of which orders were aimed at the twin dangers of espionage and sabotage.

The 1942 Act was attacked in the Hirabayashi case as an unconstitutional delegation of power; it was contended that the curfew order and other orders on which it rested were beyond the war powers of the Congress, the military authorities and of the President, as Commander in Chief of the Army; and finally that to apply the curfew order against none but citizens of Japanese ancestry amounted to a constitutionally prohibited discrimination solely on account of race. To these questions, we gave the serious consideration which their importance justified. We upheld the curfew order as an exercise of the power of the government to take steps necessary to prevent espionage and sabotage in an area threatened by Japanese attack.

In the light of the principles we announced in the Hirabayashi case, we are unable to conclude that it was beyond the war power of Congress and the Executive to exclude those of Japanese ancestry from the West Coast war area at the time they did. True, exclusion from the area in which one's home is located is a far greater deprivation than constant confinement to the home from 8 P.M. to 6 A.M. Nothing short of apprehension by the proper military authorities of the gravest imminent danger to the public safety can constitutionally justify either. But exclusion from a threatened area, no less than curfew, has a definite and close relationship to the prevention of espionage and sabotage. The military authorities, charged with the primary responsibility of defending our shores, concluded that curfew provided inadequate protection and ordered exclusion. They did so, as pointed out in our Hirabayashi opinion, in accordance with Congressional authority to the military to say who should, and who should not, remain in the threatened areas.

In this case the petitioner challenges the assumptions upon which we rested our conclusions in the Hirabayashi case. He also urges that by May 1942, when Order No. 34 was promulgated, all danger of Japanese invasion of the West Coast had disappeared. After careful consideration of these contentions we are compelled to reject them.

Here, as in the Hirabayashi case, ". . . we cannot reject as unfounded the judgment of the military authorities and of Congress that there were disloyal members of that population, whose number and strength could not be precisely and quickly ascertained. We cannot say that the warmaking branches of the Government did not have ground for believing that in a critical hour such persons could not readily be isolated and separately dealt with, and constituted a menace to the national defense and safety, which demanded that prompt and adequate measures be taken to guard against it."

Like curfew, exclusion of those of Japanese origin was deemed necessary because of the presence of an unascertained number of disloyal members of the group, most of whom we have no doubt were loyal to this country. It was because we could not reject the finding of the military authorities that it was impossible to bring about an immediate segregation of the disloyal from the loyal that we sustained the validity of the curfew order as applying to the whole group. In the instant case, temporary exclusion of the entire group was rested by the military on the same ground. The judgment that exclusion of the whole group was for the same reason a military imperative answers the contention that the exclusion was in the nature of group punishment based on antagonism to those of Japanese origin.

That there were members of the group who retained loyalties to Japan has been confirmed by investigations made subsequent to the exclusion. Approximately five thousand American citizens of Japanese ancestry refused to swear unqualified allegiance to the United States and to renounce allegiance to the Japanese Emperor, and several thousand evacuees requested repatriation to Japan.

We uphold the exclusion order as of the time it was made and when the petitioner violated it. . . . In doing so, we are not unmindful of the hardships imposed by it upon a large group of American citizens. . . . But hardships are part of war, and war is an aggregation of hardships. All citizens alike, both in and out of uniform, feel the impact of war in greater or lesser measure. Citizenship has its responsibilities as well as its privileges, and in time of war the burden is always heavier. Compulsory exclusion of large groups of citizens from their homes, except under circumstances of direst emergency and peril, is inconsistent with our basic governmental institution. But when under conditions of modern warfare our shores are threatened by hostile forces, the power to protect must be commensurate with the threatened danger. . . .

[The Court dealt at some length with a technical complication that arose in the case. On May 30, the date on which Korematsu was charged with remaining unlawfully in the prohibited area, there were two conflicting military orders outstanding, one forbidding him to remain in the area, the other forbidding him to leave but ordering him to report to an assembly center. Thus, he alleged, he was punished for doing what it was made a crime to fail to do. The Court held the orders not to be contradictory, since the requirement to report to the assembly center was merely a step in an orderly program of compulsory evacuation from the area.]

It is said that we are dealing here with the case of imprisonment of a citizen in a concentration camp solely because of his ancestry, without evidence or inquiry concerning his loyalty and good disposition towards the United States. Our task would be simple, our duty clear, were this a case involving the imprisonment of a loyal citizen in a concentration camp because of racial prejudice. Regardless of the true nature of the assembly and relocation centers—and we deem it unjustifiable to call them concentration camps with all the ugly connotations that term implies—we are dealing specifically with nothing but an exclusion order. To cast this case into outlines of racial prejudice, without reference to the real military dangers which were presented, merely confuses the issue. Korematsu was not excluded from the Military Area because of hostility to him or his race. He was excluded because we are at war with the Japanese Empire, because the properly constituted military authorities feared an invasion of our West Coast and felt constrained to take proper security measures, because they decided that the military urgency of the situation demanded that all citizens of Japanese ancestry be segregated from the West Coast temporarily, and finally, because Congress reposing its confidence in this time of war in our military leaders—as inevitably it must—determined that they should have the power to do just this. There was evidence of disloyalty on the part of some, the military authorities considered that the need for action was great, and time was short. We cannot—by availing ourselves of the calm perspective of hindsight—now say that at that time these actions were unjustified.

Affirmed.

Mr. Justice Frankfurter wrote a concurring opinion. Justices Roberts, Murphy, and Jackson each wrote a dissenting opinion.

101

Brown v. Board of Education of Topeka, 1954

Mr. Chief Justice Warren delivered the opinion of the Court.

These cases come to us from the States of Kansas, South Carolina, Virginia, and Delaware. They are premised on different facts and different local conditions, but a common legal question justifies their consideration together in this consolidated opinion.[1]

In each of the cases, minors of the Negro race, through their legal representatives, seek the aid of the courts in obtaining admission to the public schools of their community on a nonsegregated basis. In each instance, they had been denied admission to schools attended by white children under laws requiring or permitting segregation according to race. This segregation was alleged to deprive the plaintiffs of the equal protection of the laws under the Fourteenth Amendment. In each of the cases other than the Delaware case, a three-judge federal district court denied relief to the plaintiffs on the so-called "separate but equal" doctrine announced by this Court in Plessy v. Ferguson, 163 U.S. 537. Under that doctrine, equality of treatment is accorded when the races are provided substantially equal facilities, even though these facilities be separate. In the Delaware case, the Supreme Court of Delaware adhered to that doctrine, but ordered that the plaintiffs be admitted to the white schools because of their superiority to the Negro schools.

The plaintiffs contend that segregated public schools are not "equal" and cannot be made "equal," and that hence they are deprived of the equal protection of the laws. Because of the obvious importance of the question presented, the Court took jurisdiction.[2] Argument was heard in the 1952 Term, and reargument was heard this Term on certain questions propounded by the Court. . . .[3]

In approaching this problem, we cannot turn the clock back to 1868 when the Amendment was adopted, or even to 1896 when Plessy v. Ferguson was written. We must consider public education in the light of its full development and its present place in American life throughout the Nation. Only in this way can it be determined if segregation in public schools deprives these plaintiffs of the equal protection of the laws.

Today, education is perhaps the most important function of state and local governments. Compulsory school attendance laws and the great expenditures for education both demonstrate our recognition of the importance of education to our democratic society. It is required in the performance of our most basic public responsibilities, even service in the armed forces. It is the very foundation of good citizenship. Today it is a principal instrument in awakening the child to cultural values, in preparing him for later professional training, and in helping him to adjust normally to his environment. In these days, it is doubtful that any child may reasonably be expected to succeed in life if he is denied the opportunity of an education. Such an opportunity, where the state has undertaken to provide it, is a right which must be made available to all on equal terms.

We come then to the question presented: Does segregation of children in public schools solely on the basis of race, even though the physical facilities and other "tangible" factors may be equal, deprive the children of the minority group of equal educational opportunities? We believe that it does.

In Sweatt v. Painter, in finding that a segregated law school for Negroes could not provide them equal educational opportunities, this Court relied in large part on "those qualities which are incapable of objective measurement but which make for greatness in a law school." In McLaurin v. Oklahoma State Regents, the Court, in requiring that a Negro admitted to a white graduate school be treated like all other students, again resorted to intangible considerations: ". . . his ability to study, to engage in discussions and exchange views with other students, and in general, to learn his profession." Such considerations apply with added force to children in grade and high schools. To separate them from others of similar age and qualifications solely because of their race generates a feeling of inferiority as to their status in the community that may affect their hearts and minds in a way unlikely ever to be undone. The effect of this separation on their educational opportunities was well stated by a finding in the Kansas case by a court which nevertheless felt compelled to rule against the Negro plaintiffs:

> Segregation of white and colored children in public schools has a detrimental effect upon the colored children. The impact is greater when it has the sanction of the law; for the policy of separating the races is usually interpreted as denoting the inferiority of the negro group. A sense of inferiority affects the motivation of a child to learn. Segregation with the sanction of law, therefore, has a tendency to [retard] the educational and mental development of negro children and to deprive them of some of the benefits they receive in a racial[ly] integrated school system.[4]

Whatever may have been the extent of psychological knowledge at the time of Plessy v. Ferguson, this finding is amply supported by modern authority.[5] Any language in Plessy v. Ferguson contrary to this finding is rejected.

We conclude that in the field of public education the doctrine of "separate but equal" has no place. Separate educational facilities are inherently unequal. Therefore, we hold that the plaintiffs and others similarly situated for whom the actions have been brought are, by reason of the segregation complained of, deprived of the equal protection of the laws guaranteed by the Fourteenth Amendment. This disposition makes unnecessary any discussion whether such segregation also violates the Due Process Clause of the Fourteenth Amendment.

Because these are class actions, because of the wide applicability of this decision, and because of the great variety of local conditions, the formulation of decrees in these cases presents problems of considerable complexity. On reargument, the consideration of appropriate relief was necessarily subordinated to the primary question—the constitutionality of segregation in public education. We have now announced that such segregation is a denial of the equal protection of the laws. In order that we may have the full assistance of the parties in formulating decrees, the cases will be restored to the docket, and the parties are requested to present further argument on Questions 4 and 5 previously propounded by the Court for the reargument this Term.[6] The Attorney General of the United States is again invited to participate. The Attorneys General of the states requiring or permitting segregation in public education will also be permitted to appear as amici curiae upon request to do so by September 15, 1954, and submission of the briefs by October 1, 1954.

It is so ordered.

NOTES

1. In the Kansas case, Brown v. Board of Education, the plaintiffs are Negro children of elementary school age residing in Topeka. They brought this action in the United States District Court for the District of Kansas to enjoin enforcement of a Kansas statute which permits, but does not require, cities of more than 15,000 population to maintain separate school facilities for Negro and white students. Kan. Gen. Stat. §72-1724 (1949). Pursuant to that authority, the Topeka Board of Education elected to establish segregated elementary schools. Other public schools in the community, however, are operated on a nonsegregated basis. The three-judge District Court, convened under 28 U.S.C. §§2281 and 2284, found that segregation in public education has a detrimental effect upon Negro children, but denied relief on the ground that the Negro and white schools were substantially equal with respect to buildings, transportation, curricula, and educational qualifications of teachers. 98 F. Supp. 797. The case is here on direct appeal under 28 U.S.C. §1253. [The Topeka, Kansas, case would be analogous to a northern school case inasmuch as the school segregation that existed in Topeka was not mandated by state law, and some of the system was integrated. It would be eighteen years before the Court would accept another such case for review. Keyes v. School District No. 1, Denver, 445 F.2d 990 (10th Cir. 1971), *cert. granted,* 404 U.S. 1036 (1972)].

In the South Carolina case, Briggs v. Elliot, the plaintiffs are Negro children of both elementary and high school age residing in Clarendon County. They brought this action in the United States District Court for the Eastern District of South Carolina to enjoin enforcement of provisions in the state constitution and statutory code which require the segregation of Negroes and whites in public schools. S.C. Const., Art. XI, §7; S.C. Code §5377 (1942). The three-judge District Court, convened under 28 U.S.C. §§2281 and 2284, denied the requested relief. The court found that the Negro schools were inferior to the white schools and ordered the defendants to begin immediately to equalize the facilities. But the court sustained the validity of the contested provisions and denied the plaintiffs admission to the white schools during the equalization program. 98 F. Supp. 529. This Court vacated the District Court's judgment and remanded the case for the purpose of obtaining the court's views on a report filed by the defendants concerning the progress made in the equalization program. 342 U.S. 350. On remand, the District Court found that substantial equality had been achieved except for buildings and that the defendants were proceeding to rectify this inequality as well. 103 F. Supp. 920. The case is again here on direct appeal under 28 U.S.C. §1253.

In the Virginia case, Davis v. County School Board, the plaintiffs are Negro children of high school age residing in Prince Edward County. They brought this action in the United States District Court for the Eastern District of Virginia to enjoin enforcement of provisions in the state constitution and statutory code which require the segregation of Negroes and whites in public schools. Va. Const., §140; Va. Code §22-221 (1950). The three-judge District Court, convened under 28 U.S.C. §§2281 and 2284, denied the requested relief. The court found the Negro school inferior in physical plant, curricula, and transportation, and ordered the defendants forthwith to provide substantially equal curricula and transportation and to "proceed with all reasonable diligence and dispatch to remove" the inequality in physical plant. But, as in the South Carolina case, the court sustained the validity of the contested provisions and denied the plaintiffs admission to the white schools during the equalization program. 103 F. Supp. 337. The case is here on direct appeal under 28 U.S.C. §1253.

In the Delaware case, Gebhart v. Belton, the plaintiffs are Negro children of both elementary and high school age residing in New Castle County. They brought this action in the Delaware Court of Chancery to enjoin enforcement of provisions in the state constitution and statutory code which require the segregation of Negroes and whites in public schools. Del. Const., Art. X, §2; Del. Rev. Code §2631 (1935). The Chancellor gave judgment for the plaintiffs and ordered their immediate admission to schools previously attended only by white children, on the ground that the Negro schools were inferior with respect to teacher training, pupil-teacher ratio, extracurricular activities, physical plant, and time and distance involved in travel. 87 A.2d 862. The Chancellor also found that segregation itself results in an inferior education for Negro children (see note 4, infra), but did not rest his decision on that ground. Id., at 865. The Chancellor's decree was affirmed by the Supreme Court of Delaware, which intimated, however, that the defendants might be able to obtain a modification of the decree after equalization of the Negro and white schools had been accomplished. 91 A.2d 137, 152. The defendants, contending only that the Delaware courts had erred in ordering the immediate admission of the Negro plaintiffs to the white schools, applied to this Court for certiorari. The writ was granted, 344 U.S. 891. The plaintiffs, who were successful below, did not submit a cross-petition.

2. 344 U.S. 1, 141, 891.

3. 345 U.S. 972. The Attorney General of the United States participated both Terms as amicus curiae.

4. A similar finding was made in the Delaware case: "I conclude from the testimony that in our Delaware Society, State-imposed segregation in education itself results in the Negro children, as a class, receiving educational opportunities which are substantially inferior to those available to white children otherwise similarly situated." 87 A.2d 862, 865.

5. K. B. Clark, Effect of Prejudice and Discrimination on Personality Development (Midcentury White House Conference on Children and Youth, 1950); Witmer and Kotinsky, Personality in the Making (1952), c. VI; Deutscher and Chein, The Psychological Effects of Enforced Segregation: A Survey of Social Science Opinion, 26 J. Psychol. 259 (1948); Chein, What Are the Psychological Effects of Segregation Under Conditions of Equal Facilities?, 3 Int. J. Opinion and Attitude Res. 229 (1949); Brameld, Educational Costs, in Discrimination and National Welfare (MacIver, ed., 1949), 44–48; Frazier, The Negro in the United States (1949), 674–681. And see generally Myrdal, An American Dilemma (1944).

6. "4. Assuming it is decided that segregation in public schools violates the Fourteenth Amendment

"(a) would a decree necessarily follow providing that, within the limits set by normal geographic school districting, Negro children should forthwith be admitted to schools of their choice, or

"(b) may this Court, in the exercise of its equity powers, permit an effective gradual adjustment to be brought about from existing segregated systems to a system not based on color distinctions?

"5. On the assumption on which questions 4(a) and (b) are based, and assuming further that this Court will exercise its equity powers to the end described in question 4(b),

"(a) should this Court formulate detailed decrees in these cases;

"(b) if so, what specific issues should the decrees reach;

"(c) should this Court appoint a special master to hear evidence with a view to recommending specific terms for such decrees;

"(d) should this Court remand to the courts of first instance with directions to frame decrees in these cases, and if so what general directions should the decrees of this Court include and what procedures should the courts of first instance follow in arriving at the specific terms of more detailed decrees?"

102

Roe v. *Wade,* 1973

This historic decision legalized a woman's right to terminate her pregnancy by abortion. The ruling was based upon the right of privacy founded on both the Fourteenth and Ninth Amendments to the Constitution. The Court ruled that this right of privacy protected the individual from interference by the state in the decision to terminate a pregnancy by abortion during the early portion of the pregnancy. At the same time, it recognized the interest of the state in regulating decisions concerning the pregnancy during the latter period as the fetus developed the capacity to survive outside the woman's body.

103

The Equal Rights Amendment (Defeated)

Section 1. Equality of Rights under the law shall not be denied or abridged by the United States or any state on account of sex.

Section 2. The Congress shall have the power to enforce, by appropriate legislation, the provisions of this article.

Section 3. This amendment shall take effect two years after the date of ratification.

First introduced in Congress in 1923, the ERA was finally passed in 1972. However, because it failed to be ratified by the requisite number of states by its July 1982 deadline, the ERA never became part of the Constitution.

104

Bowers v. Hardwick, 1986

Justice White delivered the opinion of the Court.

In August 1982, respondent Hardwick (hereafter respondent) was charged with violating the Georgia statute criminalizing sodomy by committing that act with another adult male in the bedroom of respondent's home. After a preliminary hearing, the District Attorney decided not to present the matter to the grand jury unless further evidence developed.

Respondent then brought suit in the Federal District Court, challenging the constitutionality of the statute insofar as it criminalized consensual sodomy. He asserted that he was a practicing homosexual, that the Georgia sodomy statute, as administered by the defendants, placed him in imminent danger of arrest, and that the statute for several reasons violates the Federal Constitution. . . .

[2] This case does not require a judgment on whether laws against sodomy between consenting adults in general, or between homosexuals in particular, are wise or desirable. It raises no question about the right or propriety of state legislative decisions to repeal their laws that criminalize homosexual sodomy, or of state-court decisions invalidating those laws on state constitutional grounds. The issue presented is whether the Federal Constitution confers a fundamental right upon homosexuals to engage in sodomy and hence invalidates the laws of the many States that still make such conduct illegal and have done so for a very long time. The case also calls for some judgment about the limits of the Court's role in carrying out its constitutional mandate.

We first register our disagreement with the Court of Appeals and with respondent that the Court's prior cases have construed the Constitution to confer a right of privacy that extends to homosexual sodomy and for all intents and purposes have decided this case. . . .

Accepting the decisions in these cases . . . we think it evident that none of the rights announced in those cases bears any resemblance to the claimed constitutional right of homosexuals to engage in acts of sodomy that is asserted in this case. No connection between family, marriage, or procreation on the one hand and homosexual activity on the other has been demonstrated, either by the Court of Appeals or by respondent. Moreover, any claim that these cases nevertheless stand for the proposition that any kind of private sexual conduct between consenting adults is constitutionally insulated from state proscription is unsupportable. Indeed, the Court's opinion in Carey twice asserted that the privacy right, which the Griswold line of cases found to be one of the protections provided by the Due Process Clause, did not reach so far. . . .

Precedent aside, however, respondent would have us announce, as the Court of Appeals did, a fundamental right to engage in homosexual sodomy. This we are quite unwilling to do. It is true that despite the language of the Due Process Clauses of the Fifth and Fourteenth Amendments, which appears to focus only on the processes by which life, liberty, or property is taken, the cases are legion in which those Clauses have been interpreted to have substantive content, subsuming rights that to a great extent are immune from federal or state regulation or proscription. Among such cases are those recognizing rights that have little or no textual support in the constitutional language. Meyer, Prince, and Pierce fall in this category, as do the privacy cases from Griswold to Carey.

Striving to assure itself and the public that announcing rights not readily identifiable in the Constitution's text involves much more than the imposition of the Justices' own choice of values on the States and the Federal Government, the Court has sought to identify the nature of the rights qualifying for heightened judicial protection. In Palko v. Connecticut . . . (1937), it was said that this category includes those fundamental liberties that are "implicit in the concept of ordered liberty," such that "neither liberty nor justice would exist if [they] were sacrificed." A different description of fundamental liberties appeared in Moore v. East Cleveland . . . (1977) (opinion of POWELL, J.), where they are characterized as those liberties that are "deeply rooted in this Nation's history and tradition.". . .

It is obvious to us that neither of these formulations would extend a fundamental right to homosexuals to engage in acts of consensual sodomy. Proscriptions against that conduct have ancient roots. . . . Sodomy was a criminal offense at common law and was forbidden by the laws of the original thirteen States when they ratified the Bill of Rights. In 1868, . . . the 24 States and the District of Columbia continued to provide criminal penalties for sodomy performed in private and between consenting adults. . . . Against this background, to claim that a right to engage in such conduct is "deeply rooted in this Nation's history and tradition" or "implicit in the concept of ordered liberty" is, at best, facetious.

[3] Nor are we inclined to take a more expansive view of our authority to discover new fundamental rights imbedded in the Due Process Clause. The Court is most vulnerable and comes nearest to illegitimacy when it deals with judge-made constitutional law having little or no cognizable roots in the language or design of the Constitution. . . .

Respondent, however, asserts that the result should be different where the homosexual conduct occurs in the privacy of the home. He relies on Stanley v. Georgia, . . . (1969), where the Court held that the First Amendment prevents conviction for possessing and reading obscene material in the privacy of one's home: "If the First Amendment means anything, it means that a State has no business telling a man, sitting alone in his house, what books he may read or what films he may watch." . . .

Stanley did protect conduct that would not have been protected outside the home, and it partially prevented the enforcement of state obscenity laws; but the decision was firmly grounded in the First Amendment. The right pressed upon us here has no similar support in the text of the Constitution, and it does not qualify for recognition under the prevailing principles for construing the Fourteenth Amendment. Its limits are also difficult to discern. Plainly enough, otherwise illegal conduct is not always immunized whenever it occurs in the home. Victimless crimes, such as the possession and use of illegal drugs, do not escape the law where they are committed at home. Stanley itself recognized that its holding offered no protection for the possession in the home of drugs, firearms, or stolen goods. . . . And if respondent's submission is limited to the voluntary sexual conduct between consenting adults, it would be difficult, except by fiat, to limit the claimed right to homosexual conduct while leaving exposed to prosecution adultery, incest, and other sexual crimes even though they are committed in the home. We are unwilling to start down that road.

[4] Even if the conduct at issue here is not a fundamental right, respondent asserts that there must be a rational basis for the law and that there is none in this case other than the presumed belief of a majority of the electorate in Georgia that homosexual sodomy is immoral and unacceptable. This is said to be an inadequate rationale to support the law. The law, however, is constantly based on notions of morality, and if all laws representing essentially moral choices are to be invalidated under the Due Process Clause, the courts will be very busy indeed. Even respondent makes no such claim, but insists that majority sentiments about the morality of homosexuality should be declared inadequate. We do not agree, and are unpersuaded that the sodomy laws of some 25 States should be invalidated on this basis.

Accordingly, the judgment of the Court of Appeals is

Reversed.

105

Lesbian and Gay Rights in Historical Perspective

Paula L. Ettelbrick

Until June 1969, when the New York City police raided the Stonewall Inn and arrested the bar's lesbian, gay, and transgender patrons, most gay people were forced by laws and social attitudes to live in the shadows of public life. The legal and cultural landscape held no place for gay people except in prisons, mental health institutions, and the closet. The laws and practices that justified the police raid on the Stonewall Inn were themselves reflective of this attitude. At the time, raids on gay-frequented bars were commonplace. Local laws across the country made it illegal for homosexuals to congregate in public places or for men and women to "cross-dress." State liquor authorities regularly closed down bars suspected of having a gay clientele.

In addition, the majority of states criminalized sexual contact between two men or two women, even when it occurred in the privacy of their homes. Federal law allowed the Immigration and Naturalization Service to interrogate foreign travelers to the United States about their sexual orientation and to bar them from entering the country if they were suspected of being gay or bisexual. From the Communist-phobic 1950s through the AIDS-phobic1980s, gay people were considered a security risk. Many were denied or fired from federal jobs in agencies that required employees to obtain security clearances. The security-risk rationale was also one of the rationales for barring gay people from serving in the military. The government regularly removed children from the homes of their gay parents, denied gay people professional licenses necessary to practicing law or medicine, confiscated gay-related magazines, newsletters, and books, and refused to allow gay student groups to exist visibly on campus. Certainly, within this regime of repression, there were no laws that prohibited discrimination, criminalized hate crimes, or recognized family relationships. Gay people were nonentities. When they did dare to make themselves known publicly, the consequences were often devastating.

While gay and lesbian groups such as the Mattachine Society and the Daughters of Bilitis began to form in the 1950s, they, for the most part, offered an underground social venue for gay men and lesbians to find each other outside of the bars or known public sex locations. Though many within these groups advocated for a more public role in changing the laws and attitudes that made their lives so difficult, the raid on Stonewall is credited with irretrievably unleashing the fury and frustration of gay, lesbian, and transgender people. In contrast to prior police raids, when gay bar patrons would try to flee the police or succumb to arrest and often public humiliation when their names were reported in the paper, the Stonewall patrons that night spontaneously fought back, lighting the fire of the nascent gay liberation movement.[1]

Fast forward a mere 34 years to a world in which lesbians and gay men are able to live openly in most parts of the country and the law is in the process of changing to accommodate growing social acceptance. Early university resistance to gay student groups on the grounds that the groups would promote engagement in illegal sexual activity resulted in universal support by appellate courts across the country for the right of gay people under the First Amendment to organize and receive official status as a student group. Now, gay/straight alliances are a growing phenomenon in high schools and some junior high schools across the country.

The United States Supreme Court is on the brink of upending decades of laws that allow states to convict and imprison lesbian and gay couples who dare to have sex with each other in the privacy of their own home, a ruling that would constitute a major landmark in the history of the gay community in the United States. Sodomy laws, after all, have hovered over lesbians and gay men like the sword of Damocles. The dual threat of criminal prosecution and social persecution as a result of being labeled "criminal" has forced generations of lesbians and gay men into hiding. And now, the possibility of ridding the community of the laws that were so central to their oppression and denial of dignity seems within reach. In many ways, sodomy laws are to the gay community what segregation is to the African American community and denial of reproductive freedom is to women—a deliberate reminder by the state that a person is not fully free to chart his or her own course in life.

The United States Census Bureau now allows unmarried partners to be counted in the census, opening the way to identifying same-sex unmarried couples. In 2000, the census data confirmed the "we are everywhere" slogan of the gay community in its finding that same-sex coupled households were counted officially in 99.3% of the counties in the United States. Given that so much public policy is drawn from census data findings and that successful civil rights advocacy is often dependent upon "proving" certain facts about the constituency, the ability to actually be counted carries with it tremendous significance for future lawmaking and policy making. Even without the census data, however, it was widely acknowledged that a growing number of lesbian and gay couples are having and raising children together—a phenomenon virtually unheard of 20 years ago. Increasingly, they are raising their children with the legal sanction of the state. Most states implicitly or explicitly allow gay people to adopt children, and many have come a long way in considering the claims of a gay parent as being equal to those of the straight parent in postdivorce child custody proceedings.

In contrast to 34 years ago, lesbians and gay men serve openly throughout all levels of government (except within the United States military, where federal law mandates discharge for anyone who comes out) and the private sector. Thousands of employers, both public and private, bar discrimination against their lesbian and gay employees and now recognize their relationships by extending employment benefits such as health insurance and bereavement to unmarried domestic partners. The states of Hawaii, Vermont, and California have led the way in passing state laws recognizing lesbian and gay coupled relationships. While the right to marry remains elusive for the moment, serious challenges to discriminatory marriage laws are under way in New Jersey and Massachusetts, and the Connecticut legislature has been moving steadily toward changing its laws to allow same-sex marriage. And, in a long overdue development, a small, but growing, number of city councils have passed laws banning discrimination based upon gender identity, thus recognizing the civil rights of transgender people.

As with all social change movements, we evolve from each other. The ability of the lesbian/gay/bisexual/transgendered (LGBT) movement to evolve and articulate its place in society owes a debt to those who came before and who worked alongside. Among them are the labor movement of the 1930s, for directing our national focus on workplace conditions; the civil rights movement of the 1950s and 1960s, for creating a framework for civil rights that all have benefited from; the anarchist movement of the 1930s and the antiwar movement of the 1960s, for establishing basic freedoms to demonstrate against and dissent from the norms and policies governing society at any time; the reproductive rights movements of the 1960s and 1970s, for drawing the line at state interference in decisions as intimate as whether to have a child; and the women's rights movement of the 1960s, 1970s, 1980s, and 1990s, for continuing to challenge gender stereotypes and patriarchal structures that keep most women, gay men, lesbians, transgender people, and all gender nonconformists in the marginalized reaches of society.

Of course, there is still a very long way to go. The successes, while many in a relatively short time, still seem limited to removing legal and social obstacles rather than affirmatively furthering the dignity and sense of equality with which LGBT people should be able to live. In the immediate aftermath of Stonewall, for example, the gay community approached the American Psychiatric Association (APA) about reconsidering its official and professional view that homosexuality is a mental illness. The mental illness framework rested on shaky ground. Much of what stood as research in the area was conducted among prisoners and institutionalized patients, many of whom faced a multitude of social adjustment and mental health issues. In addition, as interest in sexuality as a field of research grew, the mental illness framework for homosexuality quickly became discredited by researchers like Dr. Evelyn Hooker, who famously challenged her professional colleagues to review the psychological profiles of anonymous men and identify those who were gay. They, of course, failed miserably. Dr. Hooker's study seriously undermined the idea that gay men have a common psychological profile and that it is uniformly one of mental instability. Others like Dr. Alfred Kinsey found human sexuality to be much more varied than was previously thought. In his famous Kinsey scale, he charted his subjects along a zero to six-point continuum between exclusively heterosexual (0) and exclusively homosexual (6). His findings helped substantiate the notion that sexuality is not about identity but about desire.

Despite the decision in 1974 by the APA to remove homosexuality from its list of diagnosable illnesses, the power of its prior policy still reverberates. Courts continue to rely on the cultural view of psychological instability to deny gay parents their children, to keep gay teachers out of the schools, and to send the message that teaching about homosexuality in schools should be disapproved. Further, no federal law bans employers, landlords, and others from discriminating against LGBT people, and more than 75% of the states have failed to ban sexual orientation-based discrimination. No state allows gay couples to marry. The United States Congress passed the Defense of Marriage Act barring the federal government from recognizing any future state law allowing same-sex marriage and reassuring each state that it need not recognize any same-sex marriage performed in another state.[2] In fact, nearly 75% of the states have passed laws officially barring the state from ever recognizing gay marriages. Nebraska has gone so far as to amend its state constitution to bar any form of recognition of gay relationships, including domestic partnership. LGBT students who are harassed or abused in high school and middle school by their peers, and even sometimes by their teachers, have very little legal recourse to stop it.

By global standards, the United States is quickly losing ground as a symbol of full citizenship. A growing number of countries have recognized lesbian and gay relationships by extending most or all of the benefits of marriage. In fact, two countries allow same-sex marriage: Holland and Belgium. The supreme courts of South Africa and Canada have incorporated more contemporaneous perspectives on human rights in their decisions in gay-related cases than seems ever possible in the United States. The European Court of Human Rights has struck down sodomy laws and interpreted sex discrimination law to allow for domestic partner benefits. A number of Latin American countries and municipalities have extended nondiscrimination protections to lesbians and gay men. In international and domestic human rights law, sexual freedom is increasingly viewed as a right as basic as other social and political rights.

By historical standards, the gay rights movement is still quite young and very much still evolving. It has benefited greatly from movements and ideas that have come before. The civil rights, sexual freedom, and economic justice frameworks that lie at the core of advocacy for women and people of color have lent a helping hand to every movement that has succeeded them. At the same time, each constituency is unique and faces distinct challenges in its quest for equality and freedom. Although the morality of women deciding to terminate a pregnancy or of interracial couples marrying has played a significant role in the struggles to change laws and practices affecting women and people of color, the core of the opposition to the LGBT community has been and continues to be premised on the idea that being gay is itself immoral, whereas being a woman, black, or Asian is not, ipso facto, immoral. As a result, the ongoing work of the gay rights movement is that of challenging systems of morality instituted for no reason other than preserving certain social norms. To this end, perhaps the Texas sodomy law case now pending before the Supreme Court will usher in a new stage for the gay rights movement—a stage in which the idea of sexual freedom is considered as much a core of constitutional rights and social justice as political and civil rights have been assumed to be; a stage in which lesbian, gay, bisexual, and transgender people can concentrate fully on building a future rather than tearing down the vestiges of the past.

NOTES

1. Contemporaneous accounts of those responsible for what became known as the "Stonewall Rebellion" indicate that Puerto Rican drag queens and lesbians played prominent roles in the spontaneous initial resistance, in contrast to the mostly white, male, and middle-class image of the gay rights movement since then. The Stonewall was the only gay nightspot that allowed dancing and thus drew a mixed crowd. The *Village Voice* reported at the time that as the bartender, bouncer, and several patrons peacefully succumbed to arrest, it was when a lesbian angrily resisted arrest and put up as struggle that "the scene became explosive. . . . Almost by signal the crowd erupted in cobblestone and bottle heaving." See J. Murdoch and D. Price, *Courting Justice: Gay Men and Lesbians v. The Supreme Court* 150 (Basic Books, 2001).

2. States traditionally recognize marriages performed in other states. For instance, a couple married in Illinois who wish to vacation in Massachusetts do not need to remarry in Massachusetts in order to be acknowledged as a married couple. By the same token, the federal government generally respects the authority of each state to decide who is allowed to marry and will grant federal benefits and privileges as long as the couple has a legal marriage in their state. However, Congress and many state legislatures have enacted schemes that would prohibit couples in same-sex marriages, should that ever come to pass, from having equal respect across state lines or from the federal government.

Suggestions for Further Reading

Acuna, Rudolpho. *Occupied America: A History of Chicanos.* New York: Harper & Row, 1987.

Anderson, Karen. *Changing Women: A History of Racial Ethnic Women in Modern America.* Oxford University Press, 1996.

Aptheker, B. *Woman's Legacy: Essays on Race, Sex, and Class in American History.* Amherst: University of Massachusetts Press, 1982.

Baxendall, R., L. Gordon, and S. Reverby. *America's Working Women: A Documentary History—1600 to the Present.* New York: Random House, 1976.

Berlin, Ira. *Free at Last?* Boston: Little, Brown, 1991.

Berry, M. F., and J. W. Blassingame. *Long Memory: The Black Experience in America.* New York: Oxford University Press, 1982.

Boyer, R. O., and H. Morais. *Labor's Untold Story.* New York: United Electrical, Radio and Machine Workers of America, 1972.

Cluster, D., ed. *They Should Have Served That Cup of Coffee.* Boston: South End Press, 1979.

Cott, Nancy F. *Root of Bitterness: Documents of the Social History of American Women.* Boston: Northeastern Press, 1986.

Davis, Mike. *Prisoners of the American Dream: Politics and Economics in the History of the U.S. Working Class.* Verso, 2000.

Deitz, James L. *Economic History of Puerto Rico: Institutional Change and Capitalist Development.* Princeton, NJ: Princeton University Press, 1986.

Duberman, Martin Baum, Martha Vicinus, and George Chauncey, Jr. *Hidden from History: Reclaiming the Gay and Lesbian Past.* New York: New American Library, 1989.

DuBois, Ellen, and Vicki Ruis. *Unequal Sisters.* New York: Routledge and Kegan Paul, 1990.

Fleischer, Doris Zames, and Frieda Zames. *The Disability Rights Movement From Charity to Confrontation.* Philadelphia: Temple University Press, 2001.

Flexner, Eleanor. *Century of Struggle.* Cambridge, MA: Harvard University Press, 1976.

Gee, E., ed. *Counterpoint: Perspectives on Asian Americans.* Los Angeles: Asian American Studies Center, University of California, Los Angeles, 1976.

Giddings, P. *When and Where I Enter: The Impact of Black Women on Race and Sex in America.* New York: Bantam Books, 1976.

Jacobs, P., and S. Landau, eds. *To Serve the Devil. Vol.1, Natives and Slaves; Vol.2, Colonials and Sojourners: A Documentary Analysis of America's Racial History and Why It Has Been Kept Hidden.* New York: Vintage Books, 1971.

Katz, Jonathan. *Gay American History: Lesbians and Gay Men in the U.S.: A Documentary History.* New York: Avon Books, 1984.

Kessler-Harris, Alice. *In Pursuit of Equity: Women, Men, and the Quest for Economic Citizenship in Twentieth-Century America.* New York: Oxford University Press, 2001.

Konig, Hans. *The Conquest of America: How the Indian Nations Lost Their Continent.* New York: Monthly Review Press, 1993.

Mintz, Sidney. *Caribbean Transformations.* Baltimore, MD: Johns Hopkins Press, 1974.

Perez, Emma. *The Decolonial Imaginary: Writing Chicanas into History.* Bloomington: Indiana University Press, 1999.

Robson, Ruthann. *Lesbian (Out)Law: Survival under the Rule of Law.* Ithaca, NY: Firebrand Books, 1992.

Stampp, K. M. *The Peculiar Institution: Slavery in the Ante-Bellum South.* New York: Vintage Books, 1956.

Takaki, Ronald. *A Different Mirror: Multicultural American History.* Boston: Little, Brown, 1993.

Takaki, Ronald. *From Different Shores: Perspectives on Race and Culture in America.* New York: Oxford University Press, 1987.

United States Commission on Human Rights. *Indian Tribes: A Continuing Quest for Survival.* Washington, DC: United States Commission on Human Rights, 1981.

Wagenheim, K., and O. J. Wagenheim, eds. *The Puerto Ricans: A Documentary History.* New York: Praeger, 1973.

PART VII

Maintaining Race, Class, and Gender Hierarchies: Social Control

THE MOST EFFECTIVE FORMS OF SOCIAL CONTROL are always invisible. Tanks in the streets and armed militia serve as constant reminders that people are not free; furthermore, they provide a focus for anger and an impetus for rebellion. More effective by far are the beliefs and attitudes a society fosters to rationalize and reinforce prevailing distributions of power and opportunity. It is here that stereotypes and ideology have an important role to play. They shape how we see ourselves and others; they affect how we define social issues; and they determine who we hold responsible for society's ills. Each plays a part in persuading people that differences in wealth, power, and opportunity are reflections of natural differences among people, not the results of the economic and political organization of society. If stereotypes, ideology, and language are truly effective, they go beyond rationalizing inequality to rendering it invisible. Once again we find that the social construction of gender, race, and class as hierarchy, which has been examined throughout this book, is at the heart of the belief system that makes the prevailing distribution of wealth and opportunity appear natural and inevitable rather than arbitrary and alterable. In U.S. society the stereotypes and values transmitted through education and the media have played a critical role in perpetuating racism, sexism, and class privilege, even at those times when the law has been used as a vehicle to fight discrimination rather than maintain it.

The selections in Part VII examine some of the ways in which our unconscious beliefs about ourselves and others reinforce existing social roles and class positions and blunt social criticism. Stereotypes and beliefs are perpetuated by the institutions within which we live and grow. In addition to providing us with information and values, education, religion, and the family, along with the media, encourage us to adopt a particular picture of the world and our place in it. These institutions shape our perceptions of others and give us a sense of our own future. The curriculum from elementary school through college and beyond presents a world view that is firmly anchored in white, male, European traditions and knowledge. Rather than identifying and contextualizing its perspective, the core of the traditional curriculum offers this narrow view of the past and present as if it were reality. In addition to severely limiting our understanding of the past and present in this way, the curriculum defines what counts as knowledge and culture in ways that are capable of obliterating the contributions of all but a few.

The mass media selectively provide information, promote certain values, and teach us who and what we should regard as important. Along with other institutions, they shape our definition of community, painting a picture of society divided between "us" and "them." By making inequities and suffering appear to be the result of personal or group deficiency rather than the consequences of injustice, stereotypes and ideology reconcile people to the status quo and prevent them from seeking change. Violence and the threat of violence reinforce ideology and threaten with pain or death those who challenge the prevailing system or its conventions and prescriptions.

In addition to creating and maintaining mistaken beliefs about the causes of unequal distribution of privilege, stereotypes can play an important role in reconciling individuals to discriminatory treatment. If stereotypes are truly effective, they can prevent the individual not only from recognizing discrimination, but even from encountering it by ensuring that he or she does not seek opportunities that are unavailable to members of his or her group.

Selection 106, "Where Bias Begins: The Truth About Stereotypes," suggests that unconscious stereotyping is pervasive in contemporary society and that it may be unavoidable. The research presented in this article supports the claims made by Dovidio and Gaertner (Selection 13) that even people who believe themselves to be unprejudiced are often acting out unconscious prejudices. As Dovidio points out here, this means that good intentions are not enough. They cannot and do not prevent us from acting in ways that perpetuate racism, sexism, and homophobia and they reinforce class privilege. Taken together, the Paul article, the piece by Dovidio and Gaertner, and Selection 107 by Richard Mohr on anti-gay stereotypes make it clear that the unconscious beliefs that people harbor can have powerful consequences for the life chances and well-being of others.

While some stereotyping is so crude that it can be easily dismissed, advertising has become extremely sophisticated in its ability to shape and manipulate unconscious attitudes and values. In "White Lies," Maurice Berger examines the portrayal of a "prototypical" black man in an ad campaign by one of America's more successful designers. After offering a subtle and thought-provoking analysis of the way in which Black masculinity is constructed in the ad, Berger goes on to generalize about the relationship between such portrayals and the maintenance of prevailing relations of dominance and subordination in society. He argues that the cultural and social institutions that are controlled by white people continue to operate to protect white privilege.

Although men in our society continue to be judged by the jobs they hold and the amount of money they earn, women continue to be judged according to a narrow and rigid standard of beauty. The messages that bombard young women from an early age continue to foster the belief that having a tiny waist is infinitely more important than earning an advanced degree or learning a technical skill. Although many women have made considerable strides in the world of work, the prevailing ideology continues to assert that being attractive (read "thin") enough to capture the right man is the real way to success. Aside from its heterosexist bias, this emphasis on physical appearance (and consequently, on unhealthy standards for body weight) is simply one more way in which society keeps women in their place. In Selection 109, "Am I Thin Enough Yet?" Sharlene Hesse-Biber explores some of the consequences of the ways in which women have been encouraged to internalize an artificial and unattainable standard of beauty.

In Selection 111, William Chafe examines the impact of both race and gender stereotypes and ideology by drawing an analogy between sex and race. He argues persuasively that both racism and sexism function analogously as forms of social control. Although Chafe suggests he is comparing the experiences of white women with those of African Americans, a careful reading of his essay suggests that he is really comparing the experiences of white women with those of black men. The reader might be interested in exploring whether Chafe's claim about racism, sexism, and social control holds up equally well when we construct similar accounts of the experiences of African American women, as well as members of other racial/ethnic groups discussed in this book. Chafe begins by analyzing how stereotypes, ideology, and language can distort expectations, perceptions, and experience and then proceeds to ask whose interests are served by this distortion.

While prevailing definitions of femininity suggest that women are most desirable when they are neither powerful, successful, nor independent, men are pressured to be economically successful and physically powerful. In Selection 110, "Pulling Train," Peggy Sanday discusses the role of gang rape in the social construction of masculinity, thereby providing another insight into the process of gender socialization. Reading Sanday's essay in conjunction with

Selection 108 in this Part, Selections 70, 71, and 73 in Part V, as well as Selection 8 in Part I can provide the opportunity for an extended discussion of how masculinity is constructed in contemporary society.

In addition to playing a major role in fostering racial, ethnic, and gender stereotypes, the media's programming and perspective impact on our ability to "see" class at all. This is the point that Gregory Mantsios makes in Selection 112, "Media Magic: Making Class Invisible." "By ignoring the poor and blurring the lines between working people and the upper class," he writes, "the news media creates a universal middle class." By adopting the perspective of those most privileged, it distorts the realities of daily life and encourages most of us to identify with the needs and interests of a privileged few.

According to Angela Davis, prisons in the United States perform a similarly magical feat by making social problems disappear. In her essay, "Masked Racism: Reflections on the Prison Industrial Complex," Davis examines the recent trend toward privatizing the prison system and argues that imprisonment has become the government's response to social problems. She writes, "Homelessness, unemployment, drug addiction, mental illness, and illiteracy are only a few of the problems that disappear from public view when the human beings contending with them are relegated to cages."

In Selection 114, William Ryan considers how stereotyping and ideology reinforce the status quo by directing people's attention away from the economic and social arrangements that perpetuate unequal treatment and by encouraging people to blame the victims of these institutions for their own misery. Ryan's essay introduces a technique he calls "blaming the victim," which effectively allows people to recognize injustice without either assuming responsibility for it or acknowledging the need to make fundamental changes in social and economic institutions.

Part VII ends with an essay by Donaldo Macedo and Lillia Bartolome that takes a closer look at the way in which language and education participate in the ideological construction of the racial/ethnic "other." They contend that this construction of the racial/ethnic "other" plays an important role in the reproduction of undemocratic structures and power relations in contemporary U.S. society. Their analysis of the ways meanings are rigidly constructed so that they privilege certain political positions and make it impossible to express alternative points of view can help explain the persistence of unconscious racist/sexist stereotyping and its consequences as described earlier in this section.

Often, people become overwhelmed and discouraged when they realize how much their unconscious images and beliefs affect their ways of seeing each other and the world; as a result, they fail to go on to analyze the consequences of ideology. Believing that people are naturally prejudiced and can't change is one more bit of ideology that prevents us from questioning prevailing social and economic arrangements and asking whether they serve the best interests of all. By dividing us from each other and confusing us about who profits from these arrangements, ideology and stereotypes imprison us in a false world. In Part VIII of this book, a number of thinkers offer their suggestions about how to move beyond race, class, and gender divisions and bring about social change.

Where Bias Begins:
The Truth about Stereotypes

Annie Murphy Paul

Psychologists once believed that only bigoted people used stereotypes. Now the study of unconscious bias is revealing the unsettling truth: We all use stereotypes, all the time, without knowing it. We have met the enemy of equality, and the enemy is us.

Mahzarin Banaji doesn't fit anybody's idea of a racist. A psychology professor at Yale University, she studies stereotypes for a living. And as a woman and a member of a minority ethnic group, she has felt firsthand the sting of discrimination. Yet when she took one of her own tests of unconscious bias, "I showed very strong prejudices," she says. "It was truly a disconcerting experience." And an illuminating one. When Banaji was in graduate school in the early 1980s, theories about stereotypes were concerned only with their explicit expression: outright and unabashed racism, sexism, anti-Semitism. But in the years since, a new approach to stereotypes has shattered that simple notion. The bias Banaji and her colleagues are studying is something far more subtle, and more insidious: what's known as automatic or implicit stereotyping, which, they find, we do all the time without knowing it. Though out-and-out bigotry may be on the decline, says Banaji, "if anything, stereotyping is a bigger problem than we ever imagined."

Previously, researchers who studied stereotyping had simply asked people to record their feelings about minority groups and had used their answers as an index of their attitudes. Psychologists now understand that these conscious replies are only half the story. How progressive a person seems to be on the surface bears little or no relation to how prejudiced he or she is on an unconscious level—so that a bleeding-heart liberal might harbor just as many biases as a neo-Nazi skinhead.

As surprising as these findings are, they confirmed the hunches of many students of human behavior. "Twenty year ago, we hypothesized that there were people who said they were not prejudiced but who really did have unconscious negative stereotypes and beliefs," says psychologist Jack Dovidio, Ph.D., of Colgate University. "It was like theorizing about the existence of a virus, and then one day seeing it under a microscope."

The test that exposed Banaji's hidden biases—and that this writer took as well, with equally dismaying results—is typical of the ones used by automatic stereotype researchers. It presents the subject with a series of positive or negative adjectives, each paired with a characteristically "white" or "black" name. As the name and word appear together on a computer screen, the person taking the test presses a key, indicating whether the word is good or bad. Meanwhile, the computer records the speed of each response.

A glance at subjects' response times reveals a startling phenomenon: Most people who participate in the experiment—even some African-Americans—respond more quickly when a positive word is paired with a white name or a negative word with a black name. Because our minds are more accustomed to making these associations, says Banaji, they process them more rapidly. Though the words and names aren't subliminal, they are presented so quickly that a subject's ability to make deliberate choices is diminished—allowing his or her underlying assumptions to show through. The same technique can be used to measure stereotypes about many different social groups, such as homosexuals, women, and the elderly.

The Unconscious Comes into Focus

From these tiny differences in reaction speed—a matter of a few hundred milliseconds—the study of automatic stereotyping was born. Its immediate ancestor was the cognitive revolution of the1970s, an explosion of psychological research into the way people think. After decades dominated by the study of observable behavior, scientists wanted a closer look at the more mysterious operation of the human brain. And the development of computers—which enabled scientists to display information very quickly and to measure minute discrepancies in reaction time—permitted a peek into the unconscious.

At the same time, the study of cognition was also illuminating the nature of stereotypes themselves. Research done after World War II—mostly by European emigres struggling to understand how the Holocaust had happened—concluded that stereotypes were used only by a particular type of person: rigid, repressed, authoritarian. Borrowing from the psychoanalytic perspective then in vogue, these theorists suggested that biased behavior emerged out of internal conflicts caused by inadequate parenting.

The cognitive approach refused to let the rest of us off the hook. It made the simple but profound point that we all use categories—of people, places, things—to make sense of the world around us. "Our ability to categorize and evaluate is an important part of human intelligence," says Banaji. "Without it, we couldn't survive." But stereotypes are too much of a good thing. In the course of stereotyping, a useful category—say, woman—becomes freighted with additional associations, usually negative. "Stereotypes are categories that have gone too far," says John Bargh, Ph.D., of New York University. "When we use stereotypes, we take in the gender, the age, the color of the skin of the person before us, and our minds respond with messages that say hostile, stupid, slow, weak. Those qualities aren't out there in the environment. They don't reflect reality."

Bargh thinks that stereotypes may emerge from what social psychologists call in-group/out-group dynamics. Humans, like other species, need to feel that they are part of a group, and as villages, clans, and other traditional groupings have broken down, our identities have attached themselves to more ambiguous classifications, such as race and class. We want to feel good about the group we belong to—and one way of doing so is to denigrate all those who aren't in it. And while we tend to see members of our own group as individuals, we view those in out-groups as an undifferentiated—stereotyped—mass. The categories we use have changed, but it seems that stereotyping itself is bred in the bone.

Though a small minority of scientists argues that stereotypes are usually accurate and can be relied upon without reservations, most disagree—and vehemently. "Even if there is a kernel of truth in the stereotype, you're still applying a generalization about a group to an individual, which is always incorrect," says Bargh. Accuracy aside, some believe that the use of stereotypes is simply unjust. "In a democratic society, people should be judged as individuals and not as members of a group," Banaji argues. "Stereotyping flies in the face of that ideal."

Predisposed to Prejudice

The problem, as Banaji's own research shows, is that people can't seem to help it. A recent experiment provides a good illustration. Banaji and her colleague, Anthony Greenwald, Ph.D., showed people a list of names—some famous, some not. The next day, the subjects returned to the lab and were shown a second list, which mixed names from the first list with new ones. Asked to identify which were famous, they picked out the Margaret Meads and the Miles Davises—but they also chose some of the names on the first list, which retained a lingering familiarity that they mistook for fame. (Psychologists call this the "famous overnight-effect.") By a margin of two-to-one, these suddenly "famous" people were male.

Participants weren't aware that they were preferring male names to female names, Banaji stresses. They were simply drawing on an unconscious stereotype of men as more important and influential than women. Something similar happened when she showed subjects a list of people who might be criminals: without knowing they were doing so, participants picked out an overwhelming number of African-American names. Banaji calls this kind of stereotyping implicit, because people know they are making a judgment—but just aren't aware of the basis upon which they are making it.

Even further below awareness is something that psychologists call automatic processing, in which stereotypes are triggered by the slightest interaction or encounter. An experiment conducted by Bargh required a group of white participants to perform a tedious computer task. While performing the task, some of the participants were subliminally exposed to pictures of African-Americans with neutral expressions. When the subjects were then asked to do the task over again, the ones who had been exposed to the faces reacted with more hostility to the request—because, Bargh believes, they were responding in kind to the hostility which is part of the African-American stereotype. Bargh calls this the "immediate hostile reaction," which he believes can have a real effect on race relations. When African-Americans accurately perceive the hostile expressions that their white counterparts are unaware of, they may respond with hostility of their own—thereby perpetuating the stereotype.

Of course, we aren't completely under the sway of our unconscious. Scientists think that the automatic activation of a stereotype is immediately followed by a conscious check on unacceptable thoughts—at least in people who think that they are not prejudiced. This internal censor successfully restrains overtly biased responses. But there's still the danger of leakage, which often shows up in non-verbal behavior: our expressions, our stance, how far away we stand, how much eye contact we make.

The gap between what we say and what we do can lead African-Americans and whites to come away with very different impressions of the same encounter, says Jack Dovidio. "If I'm a white person talking to an African-American, I'm probably monitoring my conscious beliefs very carefully and making sure everything I say agrees with all the positive things I want to express," he says. "And I usually believe I'm pretty successful because I hear the right words coming out of my mouth." The listener who is paying attention to non-verbal behavior, however, may be getting quite the opposite message. An African-American student of Dovidio's recently told him that when she was growing up, her mother had taught her to observe how white people moved to gauge their true feelings toward blacks. "Her mother was a very astute amateur psychologist—and about 20 years ahead of me," he remarks.

Where Does Bias Begin?

So where exactly do these stealth stereotypes come from? Though automatic-stereotype researchers often refer to the unconscious they don't mean the Freudian notion of a seething mass of thoughts and desires, only some of which are deemed presentable enough to be admitted to the conscious mind. In fact, the cognitive model holds that information flows in exactly the opposite direction: Connections made often enough in the conscious mind eventually become unconscious. Says Bargh: "If conscious choice and decision making are not needed, they go away. Ideas recede from consciousness into the unconscious over time."

Much of what enters our consciousness, of course, comes from the culture around us. And like the culture, it seems that our minds are split on the subjects of race, gender, class, sexual orientation. "We not only mirror the ambivalence we see in society, but also mirror it in precisely the same way," says Dovidio. Our society talks out loud about justice, equality, and egalitarianism, and most Americans accept these values as their own. At the same time, such equality exists only as an ideal, and that fact is not lost on our unconscious. Images of women as sex objects, footage of African-American criminals on the six o'clock news—"this is knowledge we cannot escape," explains Banaji. "We didn't choose to know it, but it still affects our behavior."

We learn the subtext of our culture's messages early. By five years of age, says Margo Monteith, Ph.D., many children have definite and entrenched stereotypes about blacks, women, and other social groups. Adds Monteith, professor of psychology at the University of Kentucky: "Children don't have a choice about accepting or rejecting these conceptions, since they're acquired well before they have the cognitive abilities or experiences to form their own beliefs." And no matter how progressive the parents, they must compete with all the forces that would promote and perpetuate these stereotypes: peer pressure, mass media, the actual balance of power in society. In fact, prejudice may be as much a result as a cause of this imbalance. We create stereotypes—African-American are lazy, women are emotional—to explain why things are the way they are. As Dovidio notes, "Stereotypes don't have to be true to serve a purpose."

Why Can't We All Get Along?

The idea of unconscious bias does clear up some nettlesome contradictions. "It accounts for a lot of people's ambivalence toward others who are different, a lot of their inconsistencies in behavior," says Dovidio. "It helps explain how good people can do bad things." But it also prompts some uncomfortable realizations. Because our conscious and unconscious beliefs may be very different—and because behavior often follows the lead of the latter—"good intentions aren't enough," as John Bargh puts it. In fact, he believes that they count for very little. "I don't think free will exists," he says, bluntly—because what feels like the exercise of free will may be only the application of unconscious assumptions.

Not only may we be unable to control our biased responses, we may not even be aware that we have them. "We have to rely on our memories and our awareness of what we're doing to have a connection to reality," says Bargh. "But when it comes to automatic processing, those cues can be deceptive." Likewise, we can't always be sure how biased others are. "We all have this belief that the important thing about prejudice is the external expression of it," says Banaji. "That's going to be hard to give up."

One thing is certain: We can't claim that we've eradicated prejudice just because its outright expression has waned. What's more, the strategies that were so effective in reducing that sort of bias won't work on unconscious beliefs. "What this research is saying is that we are going to have to change dramatically the way we think we can influence people's behaviors," says Banaji. "It would be naive to think that exhortation is enough." Exhortation, education, political protest—all of these hammer away at our conscious beliefs while leaving the bedrock below untouched. Banaji notes, however, that one traditional remedy for discrimination—affirmative action—may still be effective since it bypasses our unconsciously compromised judgment.

But some stereotype researchers think that the solution to automatic stereotyping lies in the process itself. Through practice, they say, people can weaken the mental links that connect minorities to negative stereotypes and strengthen the ones that connect them to positive conscious beliefs. Margo Monteith explains how it might work. "Suppose you're at a party and someone tells a racist joke—and you laugh," she says. "Then you realize that you shouldn't have laughed at the joke. You feel guilty and become focused on your thought processes. Also, all sorts of cues become associated with laughing at the racist joke: the person who told the joke, the act of telling jokes, being at a party, drinking." The next time you encounter these cues, "a warning signal of sorts should go off—'wait, didn't you mess up in this situation before?'—and your responses will be slowed and executed with greater restraint."

That slight pause in the processing of a stereotype gives conscious, unprejudiced beliefs a chance to take over. With time, the tendency to prevent automatic stereotyping may itself become automatic. Monteith's research suggests that, given enough motivation, people may be able to teach themselves to inhibit prejudice so well that even their tests of implicit bias come clean.

The success of this process of "de-automatization" comes with a few caveats, however. First, even its proponents concede that it works only for people disturbed by the discrepancy between their conscious and unconscious beliefs, since unapologetic racists or sexists have no motivation to change. Second, some studies have shown that attempts to suppress stereotypes may actually cause them to return later, stronger than ever. And finally, the results that Monteith and other researchers have achieved in the laboratory may not stick in the real world, where people must struggle to maintain their commitment to equality under less-than-ideal conditions.

Challenging though that task might be, it is not as daunting as the alternative researchers suggest: changing society itself. Bargh, who likens de-automatization to closing the barn door once the horses have escaped, says that "it's clear that the way to get rid of stereotypes is by the roots, by where they come from in the first place." The study of culture may someday tell us where the seeds of prejudice originated; for now, the study of the unconscious shows us just how deeply they're planted.

Anti-Gay Stereotypes

Richard D. Mohr

A . . . Gallup poll found that only one in five Americans reports having a gay acquaintance.[1] This finding is extraordinary given the number of practicing homosexuals in America. Alfred Kinsey's 1948 study of the sex lives of 5000 white males shocked the nation: 37 percent had at least one homosexual experience to orgasm in their adult lives; an additional 13 percent had homosexual fantasies to orgasm; 4 percent were exclusively homosexual in their practices; another 5 percent had virtually no heterosexual experience; and nearly 20 percent had at least as many homosexual as heterosexual experiences.[2] With only slight variations, these figures held across all social categories: region, religion, political belief, class, income, occupation, and education.

Two out of five men one passes on the street have had orgasmic sex with men. Every second family in the country has a member who is essentially homosexual, and many more people regularly have homosexual experiences. Who are homosexuals? They are your friends, your minister, your teacher, your bankteller, your doctor, your mailcarrier, your secretary, your congressional representative, your sibling, parent, and spouse. They are everywhere, virtually all ordinary, virtually all unknown.

What follows? First, the country is profoundly ignorant of the actual experience of gay people. Second, social attitudes and practices that are harmful to gays have a much greater overall negative impact on society than is usually realized. Third, most gay people live in hiding—in the closet—making the "coming out" experience the central fixture of gay consciousness and invisibility the chief social characteristic of gays.

Society's ignorance of gay people is, however, not limited to individuals' lack of personal acquaintance with gays. Stigma against gay people is so strong that even discussions of homosexuality are taboo. This taboo is particularly strong in academe, where it is reinforced by the added fear of the teacher as molester. So even within the hearth of reason irrational forces have held virtually unchallenged and largely unchallengeable sway. The usual sort of clarifying research that might be done on a stigmatized minority has with gays only just begun—haltingly—in history, literature, sociology, and the sciences.

Yet ignorance about gays has not stopped people from having strong opinions about them. The void which ignorance leaves has been filled with stereotypes. Society holds chiefly two groups of anti-gay stereotypes; the two are an oddly contradictory lot. One set of stereotypes revolves around alleged mistakes in an individual's gender identity: lesbians are women that want to be, or at least look and act like, men—bulldykes, diesel dykes; while gay men are those who want to be, or at least look and act like, women—queens, fairies, limp-wrists, nellies. Gays are "queer," which, remember, means at root not merely weird but chiefly counterfeit—"he's as queer as a three dollar bill." These stereotypes of mismatched or fraudulent genders provide the materials through which gays and lesbians become the butts of ethnic-like jokes. These stereotypes and jokes, though derisive, basically view gays and lesbians as ridiculous.

Another set of stereotypes revolves around gays as a pervasive, sinister, conspiratorial, and corruptive threat. The core stereotype here is the gay person as child molester and, more generally, as sex-crazed maniac. These stereotypes carry with them fears of the very destruction of family and civilization itself. Now, that which is essentially ridiculous can hardly have such a staggering effect. Something must be afoot in this incoherent amalgam.

Sense can be made of this incoherence if the nature of stereotypes is clarified. Stereotypes are not *simply* false generalizations from a skewed sample of cases examined. Admittedly, false generalizing plays a part in most stereotypes a society holds. If, for instance, one takes as one's sample homosexuals who are in psychiatric hospitals or prisons, as was done in nearly all early investigations, not surprisingly one will probably find homosexuals to be of a crazed and criminal cast. Such false generalizations, though, simply confirm beliefs already held on independent grounds, ones that likely led the investigator to the prison and psychiatric ward to begin with. Evelyn Hooker, who in the mid-fifties carried out the first rigorous studies to use nonclinical gays, found that psychiatrists, when presented with results of standard psychological diagnostic tests—but with indications of sexual orientation omitted—were able to do no better than if they had guessed randomly in their attempts to distinguish gay files from nongay ones, even though the psychiatrists believed gays to be crazy and supposed themselves to be experts in detecting craziness.[3] These studies proved a profound embarrassment to the psychiatric establishment, the financial well-being of which was substantially enhanced by "curing" allegedly insane gays. Eventually the studies contributed to the American Psychiatric Association's dropping homosexuality from its registry of mental illnesses in 1973.[4] Nevertheless, the stereotype of gays as sick continues apace in the mind of America.

False generalizations *help maintain* stereotypes; they do not *form* them. As the history of Hooker's discoveries shows, stereotypes have a life beyond facts. Their origin lies in a culture's ideology—the general system of beliefs by which it lives—and they are sustained across generations by diverse cultural transmissions, hardly any of which, including slang and jokes, even purport to have a scientific basis. Stereotypes, then, are not the products of bad science, but are social constructions that perform central functions in maintaining society's conception of itself.

On this understanding, it is easy to see that the anti-gay stereotypes surrounding gender identification are chiefly means of reinforcing still powerful gender roles in society. If, as this stereotype presumes (and condemns), one is free to choose one's social roles independently of gender, many guiding social divisions, both domestic and commercial, might be threatened. The socially gender-linked distinctions would blur between breadwinner and homemaker, protector and protected, boss and secretary, doctor and nurse, priest and nun, hero and whore, saint and siren, lord and helpmate, and God and his world. The accusations "fag" and "dyke" (which recent philology has indeed shown to be rooted in slang referring to gender-bending, especially cross-dressing)[5] exist in significant part to keep women in their place and to prevent men from breaking ranks and ceding away theirs.

The stereotypes of gays as child molesters, sex-crazed maniacs, and civilization destroyers function to displace (socially irresolvable) problems from their actual source to a foreign (and so, it is thought, manageable) one. Thus, the stereotype of child molester functions to give the family unit a false sheen of absolute innocence. It keeps the unit from being examined too closely for incest, child abuse, wife-battering, and the terrorism of constant threats. The stereotype teaches that the problems of the family are not internal to it, but external.

Because this stereotype has this central social function, it could not be dislodged even by empirical studies, paralleling Hooker's efforts, that showed heterosexuals to be child molesters to a far greater extent than the actual occurrence of heterosexuals in the general population.[6] But one need not even be aware of such debunking empirical studies in order to see the same cultural forces at work in the social belief that gays are molesters as in its belief that they are crazy. For one can see them now in society's and the media's treatment of current reports of violence, especially domestic violence. When a mother kills her child or a father rapes his daughter—regular Section B fare even in major urban papers—this is never taken by reporters, columnists, or pundits as evidence that there is something wrong with heterosexuality or with traditional families. These issues are not even raised.

But when a homosexual child molestation is reported it is taken as confirming evidence of the way homosexuals are. One never hears of heterosexual murders, but one regularly reads of "homosexual" ones. Compare the social treatment of Richard Speck's sexually motivated mass murder in 1966 of Chicago nurses with that of John Wayne Gacy's serial murders of Chicago youths. Gacy was in the culture's mind taken as symbolic of gay men in general. To prevent the possibility that The Family was viewed as anything but an innocent victim in this affair, the mainstream press knowingly failed to mention that most of Gacy's adolescent victims were homeless hustlers, even though this was made obvious at his trial.[7] That knowledge would be too much for the six o'clock news and for cherished beliefs.

The stereotype of gays as sex-crazed maniacs functions socially to keep individuals' sexuality contained. For this stereotype makes it look as though the problem of how to address one's considerable sexual drives can and should be answered with repression, for it gives the impression that the cyclone of dangerous psychic forces is *out there* where the fags are, not within one's own breast. With the decline of the stereotype of the black man as raping pillaging marauder (found in such works as *Birth of a Nation, Gone with the Wind,* and *Soul on Ice*), the stereotype of gay men as sex-crazed maniacs has become more aggravated. The stereotype of the sex-crazed threat seems one that society desperately needs to have somewhere in its sexual cosmology.

For the repressed homosexual, this stereotype has an especially powerful allure—by hating it consciously, he subconsciously appears to save himself from himself, at least as long as the ruse does not exhaust the considerable psychic energies required to maintain it, or until, like ultraconservative Congressmen Robert E. Bauman (R-Md.) and Jon C. Hinson (R-Miss.), he is caught importuning hustlers or gentlemen in washrooms.[8] If, as Freud and some of his followers thought, everyone feels an urge for sex partners of both genders, then the fear of gays works to show us that we have not "met the enemy and he is us."[9]

By directly invoking sex acts, this second set of stereotypes is the more severe and serious of the two—one never hears child-molester jokes. These stereotypes are aimed chiefly against men, as in turn stereotypically the more sexed of the genders. They are particularly divisive for they create a very strong division between those conceived as "us" and those conceived as "them." This divide is not so strong in the case of the stereotype of gay men as effeminate. For women (and so the woman-like) after all do have their place. Nonstrident, nonuppity useful ones can even be part of "us," indeed, belong, like "our children," to "us." Thus, in many cultures with overweening gender-identified social roles (like prisons, truckstops, the armed forces, Latin America, and the Islamic world) only passive partners in male couplings are derided as homosexual.[10]

Because "the facts" largely do not matter when it comes to the generation and maintenance of stereotypes, the effects of scientific and academic research and of enlightenment generally will be, at best, slight and gradual in the changing fortunes of gays. If this account of stereotypes holds, society has been profoundly immoral. For its treatment of gays is a grand scale rationalization and moral sleight-of-hand. The problem is not that society's usual standards of evidence and procedure in coming to judgments of social policy have been misapplied to gays, rather when it comes to gays, the standards themselves have simply been ruled out of court and disregarded in favor of mechanisms that encourage unexamined fear and hatred.

Partly because lots of people suppose they do not know a gay person and partly through their willful ignorance of society's workings, people are largely unaware of the many ways in which gays are subject to discrimination in consequence of widespread fear and hatred. Contributing to this social ignorance of discrimination is the difficulty for gay people, as an invisible minority, even to complain of discrimination. For if one is gay, to register a complaint would suddenly target one as a stigmatized person, and so, in the absence of any protections against discrimination, would in turn invite additional discrimination.

Further, many people, especially those who are persistently downtrodden and so lack a firm sense of self to begin with, tend either to blame themselves for their troubles or to view their troubles as a matter of bad luck or as the result of an innocent mistake by others—as anything but an injustice indicating something wrong with society. Alfred Dreyfus went to his grave believing his imprisonment for treason and his degradation from the French military, in which he was the highest ranking Jewish officer, had all just been a sort of clerical error, merely requiring recomputation, rather than what it was—lightning striking a promontory from out of a storm of national bigotry.[11] The recognition of injustice requires doing something to rectify wrong; the recognition of systematic injustices requires doing something about the system, and most people, especially the already beleaguered, simply are not up to the former, let alone the latter.

For a number of reasons, then, discrimination against gays, like rape, goes seriously underreported. What do they experience? First, gays are subject to violence and harassment based simply on their perceived status rather than because of any actions they have performed. A[n] . . . extensive study by the National Gay and Lesbian Task Force found that over 90 percent of gays and lesbians had been victimized in some form on the basis of their sexual orientation.[12] More than one in five gay men and nearly one in ten lesbians had been punched, hit, or kicked; a quarter of all gays had had objects thrown at them; a third had been chased; a third had been sexually harassed and 14 percent had been spit on—all just for being perceived to be gay.

The most extreme form of anti-gay violence is queerbashing—where groups of young men target another man who they suppose is gay and beat and kick him unconscious and sometimes to death amid a torrent of taunts and slurs. Such seemingly random but in reality socially encouraged violence has the same social origin and function as lynchings of blacks—to keep a whole stigmatized group in line. As with lynchings . . . the police and courts have routinely averted their eyes, giving their implicit approval to the practice.

Few such cases with gay victims reach the courts. Those that do are marked by inequitable procedures and results. Frequently judges will describe queerbashers as "just All-American Boys." In 1984, a District of Columbia judge handed suspended sentences to queerbashers whose victim had been stalked, beaten, stripped at knife point, slashed, kicked, threatened with castration, and pissed on, because the judge thought the bashers were good boys at heart—after all they went to a religious prep school.[13]

In the summer of 1984, three teenagers hurled a gay man to his death from a bridge in Bangor, Maine. Though the youths could have been tried as adults and normally would have been, given the extreme violence of their crime, they were tried rather as children and . . . [were to] be back on the streets again automatically when they turn[ed] twenty-one.[14]

Further, police and juries simply discount testimony from gays.[15] They typically construe assaults on and murders of gays as "justified" self-defense—the killer need only claim his act was a panicked response to a sexual overture.[16] Alternatively, when guilt seems patent, juries will accept highly implausible insanity or other "diminished capacity" defenses. In 1981 a former New York City Transit Authority policeman, later claiming he was just doing the work of God, machine-gunned down nine people, killing two, in two Greenwich Village gay bars. His jury found him innocent due to mental illness.[17] The best known example of a successful "diminished capacity" defense is Dan White's voluntary manslaughter conviction for the 1978 assassination of openly gay San Francisco city councilman Harvey Milk—Hostess Twinkies, his lawyer successfully argued, made him do it.[18]

These inequitable procedures and results collectively show that the life and liberty of gays, like those of blacks, simply count for less than the life and liberty of members of the dominant culture. . . .

NOTES

1. "Public Fears—And Sympathies," *Newsweek*, August 12, 1985, p. 23.

2. Alfred C. Kinsey, et al., *Sexual Behavior in the Human Male* (Philadelphia: Saunders, 1948), pp. 650–51. On the somewhat lower incidences of lesbianism, see Alfred C. Kinsey, et al., *Sexual Behavior in the Human Female* (Philadelphia: Saunders, 1953), pp. 472–75.

3. Evelyn Hooker, "The Adjustment of the Male Overt Homosexual," *Journal of Projective Techniques* (1957) 21:18–31, reprinted in Hendrik M. Ruitenbeck, ed., *The Problem of Homosexuality*, pp. 141–61, epigram quote from p. 149 (New York: Dutton, 1963).

4. See Ronald Bayer, *Homosexuality and American Psychiatry* (New York: Basic Books, 1981).

5. See Wayne Dynes, *Homolexis: A Historical and Cultural Lexicon of Homosexuality* (New York: Gay Academic Union, Gai Saber Monograph No. 4, 1985), s.v. dyke, faggot.

6. For studies showing that gay men are no more likely—indeed, are less likely—than heterosexuals to be child molesters and that the most widespread and persistent sexual abusers of children are the children's fathers, stepfathers or mother's boyfriends, see Vincent De Francis, *Protecting the Child Victim of Sex Crimes Committed by Adults* (Denver: The American Humane Association, 1969), pp. vii, 38, 69–70; A. Nicholas Groth, "Adult Sexual Orientation and Attraction to Underage Persons," *Archives of Sexual Behavior* (1978) 7:175–81; Mary J. Spencer, "Sexual Abuse of Boys," *Pediatrics* (July 1986) 78(1):133–38.

7. See Lawrence Mass, "Sanity in Chicago: The Trial of John Wayne Gacy and American Psychiatry," *Christopher Street* [New York] (June 1980) 4(7):26. See also Terry Sullivan, *Killer Clown* (New York: Grosset & Dunlap), 1983, pp. 219–25, 315–16; Tim Cahill, *Buried Dreams* (Toronto: Bantam Books, 1986), pp. 318, 352–53, 368–69.

8. For Robert Bauman's account of his undoing, see his autobiography, *The Gentleman from Maryland* (New York: Arbor House, 1986).

9. On Freud, see Timothy F. Murphy, "Freud Reconsidered: Bisexuality, Homosexuality, and Moral Judgment," *Journal of Homosexuality* (1984) 9(2–3):65–77.

10. On prisons, see Wayne Wooden and Jay Parker, *Men Behind Bars: Sexual Exploitation in Prison* (New York: Plenum, 1982). On the armed forces, see George Chauncey Jr., "Christian Brotherhood or Sexual Perversion? Homosexual Identities and the Construction of Sexual Boundaries in the World War One Era," *Journal of Social History* (1985) 19: 189–211.

11. See Jean-Denis Bredin, *The Affair: The Case of Alfred Dreyfus*, trans. Jeffrey Mehlman (1983; New York: George Braziller, 1986), pp. 486–96.

12. National Gay and Lesbian Task Force, *Anti-Gay/Lesbian Victimization* (New York: National Gay and Lesbian Task Force, 1984). See also "Anti-Gay Violence," Subcommittee on Criminal Justice, Committee on the Judiciary, House of Representatives, 99th Congress, 2nd Session, October 9, 1986, serial no. 132.

13. "Two St. John's Students Given Probation in Assault on Gay," *The Washington Post*, May 15, 1984, p. I.

The 1980 Mariel boatlift, which included thousands of gays escaping Cuban internment camps, inspired U.S. Federal District Judge A. Andrew Hauk in open court to comment of a Mexican illegal alien caught while visiting his resident alien daughter: "And he isn't even a fag like all these faggots we're letting in." *The Advocate* [Los Angeles], November 27, 1980, no. 306, p. 15. Cf. "Gay Refugees Tell of Torture, Oppression in Cuba," *The Advocate*, August 21, 1980, no. 299, pp. 15–16.

14. See *The New York Times*, September 17, 1984, p. D17, and October 6, 1984, p. 6.

15. John D'Emilio writes of the trial of seven police officers caught in a gay bar shakedown racket: "The defense lawyer cast aspersions on the credibility of the prosecution witnesses . . . and deplored a legal system in which 'the most notorious homosexual may testify against a policeman.' Persuaded by this line of argument, the jury acquitted all of the defendants." *Sexual Politics, Sexual Communities: The Making of a Homosexual Minority in the United States, 1940–1970* (Chicago: University of Chicago Press, 1983), p. 183.

16. See for discussion and examples, Pat Califia, "'Justifiable' Homicide?" *The Advocate*, May 12, 1983, no. 367, p. 12; and Robert G. Bagnall, et al., "Burdens on Gay Litigants and Bias in the Court System: Homosexual Panic, Child Custody, and Anonymous Parties," *Harvard Civil Rights–Civil Liberties Law Review* (1984) 19:498–515.

17. *The New York Times*, July 25, 1981, p. 27, and July 26, 1981, p. 25.

18. See Randy Shilts, *The Mayor of Castro Street: The Life and Times of Harvey Milk* (New York: St. Martin's, 1982), pp. 308–25.

White Lies

Maurice Berger

On the left-hand side of the two-page advertisement in *The New York Times Magazine* is a regal head shot of a polo pony framed against a bright-blue background. His neck is long and muscular. Bound in the leather straps of the bridle, his head is a deep mahogany, with a strip of white running down the snout. His mane is closely cropped. His ears are small and rigid. His eyes glisten like black marbles. His nostrils flare. His closed mouth appears almost to be grinning.

On the right-hand side of this advertisement (for Ralph Lauren Polo shirts) is a human counterpart to the majestic horse. The man is strikingly beautiful. His head looks to the left, a perfect pendant to the right-facing horse. His skin is a deep mahogany. His elegant, shaved pate has just a hint of black stubble. His small ears curve upward and slightly away from his head. His eyes are dark and dramatic. His nostrils appear to be slightly flared; white light bounces off the bridge of his nose. His full, luscious lips seem almost to be breaking into a smile. His bright-blue shirt nearly blends into the background, giving the effect of a head and neck that graphically float, naked and powerful, against a sea of blue.

It is strange to see a black man representing a company that made its mark appealing to the American middle-class fascination with WASP wealth and taste—even if the man is Tyson Beckford, the first African American male supermodel. Beckford has been the designer's "Polo man" since March 1995, which suggests, in part, that Lauren is reaching out to prospective black customers. But juxtaposing a picture of a black man to one of an animal—the model is not wearing polo gear and is not even in the same space as the horse, suggesting that the two, rather than interacting, are being compared to each other—is an unfortunate ploy. Intentionally or otherwise, the ad replays a long-standing racist fantasy about black people: no matter how beautiful, smart, or talented, they are in some ways always exotic and animal-like.

This fantasy allows white people to feel superior to black people who they suspect may be more beautiful, more talented, or better endowed than they are. It may explain why black models are rarely seen on the cover of fashion and women's and men's magazines and why images of violent black men and irresponsible black mothers abound in the media. Positive images of black men often center on their physicality or athleticism: "Athletes, more than rappers, are more like national heroes," says Beckford's agent, Bethann Hardison. "But also, when it comes down to black men's bodies, historically it's been about how strong and well defined they are—that's what's had value. It's the same old story." The press release for a recent show of menswear by the designer John Bartlett, unusual in that it featured six black models, celebrated the special prowess of black men: "They just have a certain natural masculinity to them," Bartlett observes.

The association between blackness and innate physicality, masculinity, or naturalness often relegates black men to a less-than-human status in the media. In 1988, for example, TV sportscaster Jimmy "the Greek" Snyder offered this on-air explanation of black athletic gifts: "[T]he slave owner would breed his big black with his big black woman so that he could have a big black kid. . . . The black is a better athlete to begin with because he's been bred to be that way because of his thigh size and his big size. [Blacks can] jump higher and run faster." (Snyder was later fired by CBS Sports.)

Like Lauren's vision of the black man as polo pony, such stereotypes deny the intellectual and human dimension of blackness just as surely as they systematically ascribe to black people bestial traits that are rarely applied to whites (the Marlboro Man, after all, is riding *on* his majestic horse). Sometimes this belittling of blackness is more subtle, though by no means free of the prejudices of racial biology. In 1994, for example, golfer Jack Nicklaus told an interviewer that black men have "different muscles that react in different ways" and thus were anatomically unsuited to play golf. (A few years later, of course, Tiger Woods won the U.S. Open, dispelling Nicklaus's racist assumption forever.) Nicklaus's and Snyder's views of black athleticism both see athletic aptitude as inborn, physical, and even genetic; such traits as intelligence, skill, perseverance, and dedication do not come into play.

Black male models present a problem for the fashion industry, argues Hilton Als, where they "still tend to generate lurid fantasies of subway 'gangstas,' and many American designers aren't sure that black men can *sell*." Lauren has found a way out of this problem: transformed into a metaphorical satyr—half man, half horse—Beckford is freed from the specificity of contemporary black masculinity, thus making him more accessible to the white reader. This effect is also achieved, as John Hoberman points out in *Darwin's Athletes: How Sport Has Damaged Black America and Preserved the Myth of Race*, by dissolving ethnic blackness into a genteel and nonviolent "sporting world that is exclusively and impeccably white: golfing, fishing, tennis, rowing, sailing, and polo—the sports of dynamic imperial males unwinding from the rigors of colonial administration."

Yet Lauren's "Polo man" is only allowed to join this world as the counterpart to one of its beautiful, imperial animals. A handsome model, black or white, can help lure the consumer into the fantasy that buying a particular garment will grant him access to the garment's aura of beauty. The risk, however, is that the consumer may also feel competitive with or even threatened by another man's attractiveness. The very presence of black models, then, challenges the often unconscious desires of white men to see themselves as superior to black men. To some extent, Lauren neutralizes these competitive feelings by inviting us to see mirrored in the face of his mahogany "Polo man" the features of an animal prized for its physical endowments.

Too often, white people acknowledge a particular strength in a black colleague, sports figure, politician, or entertainer but dilute their recognition with the same kind of ambivalence implicit in the Lauren ad. In a study of the racial attitudes of sports reporters, for example, *Boston Globe* writer Derek Jackson analyzed the coverage of five National Collegiate Athletic Association basketball games and seven National Football League play-off games during a single season. More than three-quarters of the adjectives used to describe white football players referred to their brains, while just under two-thirds of the adjectives used for black players referred to their brawn. In basketball, the ratio was 63 percent brains for white players, 77 percent brawn for black players.

Cultural and social institutions controlled by white people have been slow to reward black accomplishment not because African Americans don't excel but because such rewards declare that a black person may, in fact, be more talented, more intelligent, or more beautiful than his white peers. One need look no further than the film industry to see white people's indifference to black people's excellence. Although African Americans buy movie tickets in the disproportionate numbers (they make up 12 percent of the population but 25 percent of movie patrons), black people in Hollywood rarely achieve crossover superstar status, or are thought capable of carrying a movie, or receive such markers of success as Academy Award nominations. The 1997 Oscars were a case in point: all twenty acting nominees were white and a number of their performances were less than outstanding; overlooked were the extraordinary and critically acclaimed work of black actors Djimon Hounsou in *Amistad*; Samuel L. Jackson, Debbi Morgan, and Lynn Whitfield in *Eve's Bayou*; and Pam Grier in *Jackie Brown*. The argument, advanced by several white critics, that these films were weak and thus placed their actors at a disadvantage for Oscar nominations is specious: *Eve's Bayou* was widely praised by critics (though the film apparently did not reach white audiences) and Grier's and Hounsou's white co-stars, Robert Forster and Anthony Hopkins, were nominated. In the end, most black men in Hollywood—from Denzel Washington to James Earl Jones—remain character actors: "In other words, they are *safe*," observes actress Ellen Holly in an op-ed piece in *The New York Times* on the obstacles faced by black actors in the film industry. "They may be doing some of the most riveting work in film . . . but none is breaking the sexual taboos that keep a black man from becoming a high-wattage star."

Mainstream American culture's avoidance of black talent and excellence suggests one of the greatest deficiencies of whiteness: its inability to celebrate and learn from the strengths and accomplishments of black people. Too often, white people live by the rules of self-protection, competitiveness, and self-aggrandizement—rules which tell us that black men may be no more handsome or intelligent than the polo ponies on which their rich white brothers ride.

Am I Thin Enough Yet?

Sharlene Hesse-Biber

"Ever since I was ten years old, I was just a very vain person. I always wanted to be the thinnest, the prettiest. 'Cause I thought, if I look like this, then I'm going to have so many boyfriends, and guys are going to be so in love with me, and I'll be taken care of for the rest of my life. I'll never have to work, you know?"—Delia, college senior

What's Wrong with This Picture?

Pretty, vivacious, and petite, Delia was a picture of fashionable perfection when she first walked into my office. Her tight blue jeans and fringed Western shirt showed off her thin, 5-ft frame; her black cowboy boots and silver earrings completed a presentation that said, "Look at me!"

The perfect picture had a serious price. Delia had come to talk about her "problem." She is bulimic. In secret, she regularly binges on large amounts of food, then forces herself to vomit. It has become a powerful habit, one that she is afraid to break because it so efficiently maintains her thin body. For Delia, as for so many others, being thin is everything.

"I mean, how many bumper stickers have you seen that say 'No Fat Chicks,' you know? Guys don't like fat girls. Guys like little girls. I guess because it makes them feel bigger and, you know, they want somebody who looks pretty. Pretty to me is you have to be thin and you have to have like good facial features. It's both. My final affirmation of myself is how many guys look at me when I go into a bar. How many guys pick up on me. What my boyfriend thinks about me."

Delia's Story

Delia is the eldest child, and only girl, in a wealthy Southern family. Her father is a successful dentist and her mother has never worked outside the home. They fought a lot when she was young—her father was an alcoholic—and they eventually divorced. According to Delia, both parents doted on her.

"I've never been deprived of anything in my entire life. I was spoiled, I guess, because I've never felt any pressure from my parents to do anything. My Dad would say, 'Whatever you want to do, if you want to go to Europe, if you want to go to law school, if you don't want to do anything . . . whatever you want to do, just be happy.' No pressure."

He was unconcerned about her weight, she said, but emphasized how important it was to be pretty. Delia quickly noticed this message everywhere, especially in the media.

"I am so affected by *Glamour* magazine and *Vogue* and all that, because that's a line of work I want to get into. I'm looking at all these beautiful women. They're thin. I want to be just as beautiful. I want to be just as thin. Because that is what guys like."

When I asked what her mother wanted for her, she recited, "To be nice and pretty and sweet and thin and popular and smart and successful and have everything that I could ever want and just to be happy." "Sweet and pretty and thin" meant that from the age of ten she was enrolled in a health club, and learned to count calories. Her mom, who at 45 is "beautiful, gorgeous, thin," gave her instructions on how to eat.

"'Only eat small amounts. Eat a thousand calories a day; don't overeat.' My mom was never critical like, 'You're fat.' But one time, I went on a camping trip and I gained four pounds and she said, 'You've got to lose weight.' I mean, she watched what I ate. Like if I was going to get a piece of cake she would be, 'Don't eat that.'"

At age 13 she started her secret bingeing and vomiting. "When I first threw up I thought, well, it's so easy," she told me. "I can eat and not get the calories and not gain weight. And I was modeling at the time, and I wanted to look like the girls in the magazines."

Delia's preoccupation with thinness intensified when she entered high school. She wanted to be a cheerleader, and she was tiny enough to make it. "When I was sixteen I just got into this image thing, like tiny, thin . . . I started working out more. I was Joe Healthy Thin Exercise Queen and I'd just fight eating because I was working out all the time, you know? And so I'm going to aerobics two or three times a day sometimes, eating only salad and a bagel, and like, no fat. I just got caught up in this circle."

College in New England brought a new set of social pressures. She couldn't go running every day because of the cold. She hated the school gym, stopped working out, and gained four pounds her freshman year. Her greatest stress at college had nothing to do with academics. "The most stressful thing for me is whether I'm going to eat that day, and what am I going to eat," she told me, "more than getting good grades."

After freshman year Delia became a cheerleader again. "Going in, I know I weighed like 93 or 94 pounds, which to me was this enormous hang-up, because I'd never weighed more than 90 pounds in my entire life. And I was really freaked out. I knew people were going to be looking at me in the crowd and I'm like, I've got to lose this weight. So I would just not eat, work out all the time. I loved being on the squad, but my partner was a real jerk. He would never work out, and when we would do lifts he'd always be, 'Delia, go run. Go run, you're too heavy.' I hadn't been eating that day. I had already run seven or eight miles and he told me to run again. And I was surrounded by girls who were all so concerned about their weight, and it was just really this horrible situation."

College life also confirmed another issue for Delia, a cultural message from her earliest childhood. She did *not* want to be a breadwinner. She put it this way, "When I was eight I wanted to be President of the United States. As I grew older and got to college I was like, wow, it's hard for women. I mean, I don't care what people say. If they say the society's liberated, they're wrong. It's still really hard for women. It's like they look through a glass window [*sic*]. They're vice presidents, but they aren't the president. And I just figured, God, how much easier would it be for me to get married to somebody I know is going to make a lot of money and just be taken care of . . . I want somebody else to be the millionaire." . . .

Economic and career achievement is a primary definition of success for men. (Of course, men can also exhibit some self-destructive behaviors in pursuit of this success, such as workaholism or substance abuse.) Delia's upbringing and environment defined success for her in a different way. She was not interested in having a job that earned $150,000 a year, but in marrying the guy who did. She learned to use any tool she could to stay thin, to look good, and to have a shot at her goal.

No wonder she was reluctant to give up her behavior. She was terrified of losing the important benefits of her membership in the Cult of Thinness. She knew she was hurting psychologically and physically, but, in the final analysis, being counted among "the chosen" justified the pain.

"God forbid anybody else gets stuck in this trap. But I'm already there, and I don't really see myself getting out, because I'm just so obsessed with how I look. I get personal satisfaction from looking thin, and receiving attention from guys."

I told Delia about women who have suggested other ways of coping with weight issues. There are even those who advocate fat liberation, or who suggest that fat is beautiful. She was emphatic about these solutions.

"Bullshit. They live in la-la land . . . I can hold onto my boyfriend because he doesn't need to look anywhere else. The bottom line is that appearance counts. And you can sit here and go, 'I feel good about myself twenty pounds heavier,' but who is the guy going to date?"

A Woman's Sense of Worth

Delia's devotion to the rituals of beauty work involved a great deal of time and energy. She weighed herself three times a day. She paid attention to what she put in her mouth; when she had too much, she knew she must get rid of it. She had to act and look a certain way, buy the right clothes, the right makeup. She also watched out for other women who might jeopardize her chances as they vied for the rewards of the system.

A woman's sense of worth in our culture is still greatly determined by her ability to attract a man. Social status is largely a function of income and occupation. Women's access to these resources is generally indirect, through marriage.[1] Even a woman with a successful and lucrative career may fear that her success comes at the expense of her femininity. . . .

Cultural messages on the rewards of thinness and the punishments of obesity are everywhere. Most women accept society's standards of beauty as "the way things are," even though these standards may undermine self-image, self-esteem, or physical well-being. Weight concerns or even obsessions are so common among women and girls that they escape notice. Dieting is not considered abnormal behavior, even among women who are not overweight. But only a thin line separates "normal" dieting from an eating disorder.[2] . . .

Profiting from Women's Bodies

Because women feel their bodies fail the beauty test, American industry benefits enormously, continually nurturing feminine insecurities. Ruling patriarchal interests, like corporate culture, the traditional family, the government, and the media also benefit. If women are so busy trying to control their bodies through dieting, excessive exercise, and self-improvement activities, they lose control over other important aspects of selfhood that might challenge the status quo.[3] In the words of one critic, "A secretary who bench-presses 150 pounds is still stuck in a dead-end job; a housewife who runs the marathon is still financially dependent on her husband."[4]

In creating women's concept of the ideal body image, the cultural mirror is more influential than the mirror reflecting peer group attitudes. Research has shown that women overestimate how thin a body their male and female peers desire. In a recent study using body silhouettes, college students of both sexes were asked to indicate an ideal female figure, the one that they believed most attractive to the same-sex peer and other-sex peer. Not only did the women select a thinner silhouette than the men,[5] but when asked to choose a *personal* ideal, rather than a peer ideal, the women selected an even skinnier model.

Advertisements and Beauty Advice: Buy, Try, Comply

Capitalism and patriarchy most often use the media to project the culturally desirable body to women. These images are everywhere—on TV, in the movies, on billboards, in print. Women's magazines, with their glossy pages of advertising, advertorials, and beauty advice, hold up an especially devious mirror. They offer "help" to women, while presenting a standard nearly impossible to attain. As one college student named Nancy noted in our interviews,

The advertisement showed me exactly what I should be, not what I was. I wasn't tall, I wasn't blonde, I wasn't skinny. I didn't have thin thighs, I didn't have a flat stomach. I am short, have brown curly hair, short legs. They did offer me solutions like dying my hair or a workout or the use of this cream to take away cellulite. . . .

Not everyone is taken in, of course. One student I interviewed dismissed the images she saw in the advertising pages of magazines as "constructed people."

I just stopped buying women's magazines. They are all telling you how to dress, how to look, what to wear, the type of clothes. And I think they are just ridiculous. . . . You can take the most gorgeous model and make her look terrible. Just like you can take a person who is not that way and make them look beautiful. You can use airbrushing and many other techniques. These are not really people. They are constructed people.

Computer-enhanced photography has advanced far beyond the techniques that merely airbrushed blemishes, added highlights to hair, and lengthened the legs with a camera angle. The September 1994 issue of *Mirabella* featured as a cover model "an extraordinary image of great American beauty." According to the magazine, the photographer "hints that she's something of a split personality . . . it wasn't easy getting her together. Maybe her identity has something to do with the microchip floating through space, next to that gorgeous face . . . true American beauty is a combination of elements from all over the world." In other words, the photo is a computerized composite. It is interesting that *Mirabella's* "melting pot" American beauty has white skin and predominantly Caucasian features, with just a hint of other ethnicities.

There are a number of industries that help to promote image, weight, and body obsession, especially among women. If we examine the American food and weight loss industries, we'll understand how their corporate practices and advertising campaigns perpetuate the American woman's dissatisfaction with her looks.

The American Food Industry: Fatten Up and Slim Down

. . . It is not uncommon for the average American to have a diet cola in one hand and high-fat fries and a burger in the other. Food and weight loss are inescapably a key part of the culture of the 1990's. The media bombard us with images of every imaginable type of food—snack foods, fast foods, gourmet foods, health foods, and junk foods. Most of these messages target children, who are very impressionable, and women, who make the purchasing decisions for themselves and their families. At the same time women are subjected to an onslaught of articles, books, videos, tapes, and TV talk shows devoted to dieting and the maintenance of sleek and supple figures. The conflicting images of pleasurable consumption and an ever leaner body type give us a food consciousness loaded with tension and ambivalence.

Social psychologist Brett Silverstein explains that the food industry, like all industries under capitalism, is always striving to maximize profit, growth, concentration, and control. It does so at the expense of the food consumer. "[It] promotes snacking so that consumers will have more than three opportunities a day to consume food, replaces free water with purchased soft drinks, presents desserts as the ultimate reward, and bombards women and children with artificially glamorized images of highly processed foods."[6]

Diet foods are an especially profitable segment of the business. . . .

In 1983, the food industry came up with a brilliant marketing concept, and introduced 91 new "lite" fat-reduced or calorie-reduced foods.[7] The success of lite products has been phenomenal. The consumer equated "lightness" with health. The food industry seemed to equate it with their own expenses—lite foods have lower production costs than "regular" lines, but they are often priced higher. . . .

The Diet and Weight-Loss Industry: We'll Show You the Way

. . . Increasingly, American women are told that they can have the right body if only they consume more and more products. They can change the color of their eyes with tinted contacts, they can have a tanned skin by using self-tanning lotion. They can buy cellulite control cream, spot firming cream, even contouring shower and bath firming gel to get rid of the "dimpled" look. One diet capsule on the market is supposed to be the "fat cure." It is called Anorex-eck, evoking the sometimes fatal eating disorder known as anorexia. It promises to "eliminate the cause of fat formation . . . so quickly and so effectively you will know from the very start why it has taken more than 15 years of research . . . to finally bring you . . . an ultimate cure for fat!"[8] . . .

There are currently more than 17,000 different diet plans, products, and programs from which to choose.[9] Typically, these plans are geared to the female market. They are loaded with promises of quick weight loss and delicious low-calorie meals. . . .

Many of these programs produce food products that they encourage the dieter to buy. The Jenny Craig member receives a set of pre-packaged meals that cost about $10 per day. (It allows for some outside food as well.) Some diet companies are concerned with the problem of gaining weight back and have developed "maintenance" products. Maintenance programs are often expensive and their long-term outcomes are unproven. What *can* be proven are bigger profits and longer dependence on their programs.

The Dis-eased Body: Medicalizing Women's Body Issues

The therapeutic and medical communities tend to categorize women's eating and weight problems as a disease.[10] In this view, behavior like self-starvation or compulsive eating is often called an addiction. An addiction model of behavior assumes that the cause and the cure of the problem lies within the individual. Such an emphasis fails to examine the larger mirrors that society holds up to the individual.[11]

. . . While a disease model lessens the burden of guilt and shame and may free people to work on change, it also has political significance. According to feminist theorist Bette S. Tallen, "The reality of oppression is replaced with the metaphor of addiction." It places the problem's cause within a biological realm, away from outside social forces.[12] Issues such as poverty, lack of education and opportunity, racial and gender inequality remain unexamined. More important, a disease-oriented model of addiction, involving treatment by the health care system, results in profits for the medical-industrial complex. Addiction, Tallen notes, suggests a solution that is personal—"Get treatment!"—rather than political—"Smash patriarchy!" It replaces the feminist view, that the personal is political, with the attitude of "therapism," that the "political is personal."[13] One of Bette Tallen's students told her that she had learned a lot from reading *Women Who Love Too Much* after her divorce from a man who had beaten her. Tallen suggested that "perhaps the best book to read would not be about women who love too much but about men who hit too much."[14]

The idea that overweight is a disease, and overeating represents an addiction, reinforces the dis-ease that American women feel about their bodies. The capitalist and patriarchal mirror held before them supports and maintains their obsession and insecurity. . . .

Women continue to follow the standards of the ideal thin body because of how they are rewarded by being in the right body. Thinness gives women access to a number of important resources: feelings of power, self-confidence, even femininity; male attention or protection; and the social and economic benefits that can follow. . . .

NOTES

1. Pauline B. Bart, "Emotional and Social Status of the Older Woman," in *No Longer Young: The Older Woman in America. Proceedings of the 26th Annual Conference on Aging*, ed. Pauline Bart et al. (Ann Arbor: University of Michigan Institute of Gerontology, 1975), pp. 3–21; Daniel Bar-Tal and Leonard Saxe, "Physical Attractiveness and Its Relationship to Sex-Role Stereotyping," *Sex Roles* 2 (1976): 123–133; Peter Blumstein and Pepper W. Schwartz, *American Couples: Money, Work and Sex* (New York: Willian Morrow, 1983); Glen H. Elder, "Appearance and Education in Marriage Mobility," *American Sociological Review* 34 (1969): 519–533; Susan Sontag, "The Double Standard of Aging," *Saturday Review* (September, 1972), pp. 29–38.

2. J. Polivy and C. P. Herman, "Dieting and Binging: A Causal Analysis," *American Psychologist* 40 (1985):193–201.

3. Ilana Attie and J. Brooks-Gunn, "Weight Concerns as Chronic Stressors in Women," in *Gender and Stress*, eds. Rosalind K. Barnett, Lois Biener, and Grace Baruch (New York: Free Press, 1987), pp. 218–252.

4. Katha Pollitt, "The Politically Correct Body," *Mother Jones* (May 1982): 67. I don't want to disparage the positive benefits of exercising and the positive self-image that can come from feeling good about one's body. This positive image can spill over into other areas of one's life, enhancing, for example, one's self-esteem, or job prospects.

5. See Lawrence D. Cohn and Nancy E. Adler, "Female and Male Perceptions of Ideal Body Shapes: Distorted Views Among Caucasian College Students," *Psychology of Women Quarterly* 16 (1992): 69–79; A. Fallon and P. Rozin, "Sex Differences in Perceptions of Desirable Body Shape," *Journal of Abnormal Psychology* 94 (1985): 102–105.

6. Brett Silverstein, *Fed Up!* (Boston: South End Press, 1984), pp. 4, 47, 110. Individuals may be affected in many different ways, from paying too much (in 1978, concentration within the industry led to the overcharging of consumers by $12 to $14 billion [p. 47]) to the ingestion of unhealthy substances.

7. Warren J. Belasco, "'Lite' Economics: Less Food, More Profit," *Radical History Review* 28–30 (1984): 254–278; Hillel Schwartz, *Never Satisfied* (New York: Free Press, 1986), p. 241.

8. Advertised in *Parade* magazine (December 30, 1984).

9. Deralee Scanlon, *Diets That Work* (Chicago: Contemporary Books, 1991), p. 1.

10. See Stanton Peele, *Diseasing of America: Addiction Treatment Out of Control* (Lexington, MA: D.C. Heath and Co., 1989).

11. There are a few recovery books that point to the larger issues of the addiction model. Anne Wilson Schaef's book, *When Society Becomes an Addict*, looks at the wider institutions of society that perpetuate addiction. She notes that society operates on a scarcity model. This is the "Addictive System." This model assumes that there is never enough of anything to go around and we need to get what we can. Schaef sees society as made up of three systems: A White Male System (the Addictive System), A Reactive Female System (one where women respond passively to men by being subject to their will), and the Emerging Female System (a system where women lead with caring and sensitivity). Society needs to move in the direction of the Emerging Female System in order to end addiction. Another important book is Stanton Peele's *Love and Addiction*. Another book by Stanton Peele, *The Diseasing of America: How the Addiction Industry Captured Our Soul* (Lexington, MA: Lexington Books, 1989), stresses the importance of social change in societal institutions and advocates changing the given distribution of resources and power within the society as a way to overcome the problem of addiction. See Anne Wilson Schaef, *When Society Becomes an Addict* (New York: Harper & Row, 1987), and Stanton Peele, *Love and Addiction* (New York: New American Library, 1975).

12. Bette S. Tallen, "Twelve Step Programs: A Lesbian Feminist Critique," *NWSA Journal* 2 (1990): 396.

13. Tallen, "Twelve Step Programs: A Lesbian Feminist Critique," 404–405.

14. Tallen, "Twelve Step Programs: A Lesbian Feminist Critique," 405.

Pulling Train

Peggy R. Sanday

This article discusses certain group rituals of male bonding on a college campus, in particular, a phenomenon called "pulling train." According to a report issued by the Association of American Colleges in 1985, "pulling train," or "gang banging" as it is also called, refers to a group of men lining up like train cars to take turns having sex with the same woman (Ehrhart and Sandler 1985, 2). This report labels "pulling train" as gang rape. Bernice Sandler, one of its authors, recently reported that she had found more than seventy-five documented cases of gang rape on college campuses in recent years (*Atlanta Constitution*, 7 June 1988). Sandler labeled these incidents gang rape because of the coercive nature of the sexual behavior. The incidents she and Julie K. Ehrhart described in their 1985 report display a common pattern. A vulnerable young woman, one who is seeking acceptance or who is high on drugs or alcohol, is taken to a room. She may or may not agree to have sex with one man. She then passes out, or is too weak or scared to protest, and a train of men have sex with her. Sometimes the young woman's drinks are spiked without her knowledge, and when she is approached by several men in a locked room, she reacts with confusion and panic. Whether too weak to protest, frightened, or unconscious, as has been the case in quite a number of instances, anywhere from two to eleven or more men have sex with her. In some party invitations the possibility of such an occurrence is mentioned with playful allusions to "gang bang" or "pulling train" (Ehrhart and Sandler 1985, 1–2).

The reported incidents occurred at all kinds of institutions: "public, private, religiously affiliated, Ivy League, large and small" (ibid.). Most of the incidents occurred at fraternity parties, but some occurred in residence halls or in connection with college athletics. Incidents have also been reported in high schools. . . .

Just a few examples taken from the Ehrhart and Sandler report (1985, 1–2) are sufficient to demonstrate the coercive nature of the sexual behavior.

> The 17-year-old freshman woman went to the fraternity "little sister" rush party with two of her roommates. The roommates left early without her. She was trying to get a ride home when a fraternity brother told her he would take her home after the party ended. While she waited, two other fraternity members took her into a bedroom to

From Peggy R. Sanday, *Fraternity Gang Rape: Sex, Brotherhood, and Privilege on Campus.* Copyright © 1990. Reprinted by permission of New York University Press.

"discuss little sister matters." The door was closed and one of the brothers stood blocking the exit. They told her that in order to become a little sister (honorary member) she would have to have sex with a fraternity member. She was frightened, fearing they would physically harm her if she refused. She could see no escape. Each of the brothers had sex with her, as did a third who had been hiding in the room. During the next two hours a succession of men went into the room. There were never less than three men with her, sometimes more. After they let her go, a fraternity brother drove her home. He told her not to feel bad about the incident because another woman had also been "upstairs" earlier that night. (Large southern university)

It was her first fraternity party. The beer flowed freely and she had much more to drink than she had planned. It was hot and crowded and the party spread out all over the house, so that when three men asked her to go upstairs, she went with them. They took her into a bedroom, locked the door and began to undress her. Groggy with alcohol, her feeble protests were ignored as the three men raped her. When they finished, they put her in the hallway, naked, locking her clothes in the bedroom. (Small eastern liberal arts college)

A 19-year-old woman student was out on a date with her boyfriend and another couple. They were all drinking beer and after going back to the boyfriend's dorm room, they smoked two marijuana cigarettes. The other couple left and the woman and her boyfriend had sex. The woman fell asleep and the next thing she knew she awoke with a man she didn't know on top of her trying to force her into having sex. A witness said the man was in the hall with two other men when the woman's boyfriend came out of his room and invited them to have sex with his unconscious girlfriend. (Small midwestern college)

Although Ehrhart and Sandler boldly labeled the incidents they described as rape, few of the perpetrators were prosecuted. Generally speaking, the male participants are protected and the victim is blamed for having placed herself in a compromising social situation where male adolescent hormones are known, as the saying goes, "to get out of hand." For a number of reasons, people say, "She asked for it." As the above examples from the Ehrhart and Sandler report suggest, the victim may be a vulnerable young woman who is seeking acceptance or who is weakened by the ingestion of drugs or alcohol. She may or may not agree to having sex with one man. If she has agreed to some sexual activity, the men assume that she has agreed to all sexual activity regardless of whether she is conscious or not. In the minds of the boys involved the sexual behavior is not rape. On many campuses this opinion is shared by a significant portion of the campus community. . . .

The XYZ Express

I first learned about "pulling train" in 1983 from a student who was then enrolled in one of my classes. Laurel had been out of class for about two weeks. I noticed her absence and worried that she was getting behind on her work. When she came back to class she told me that she had been raped by five or six male students at a fraternity house after one of the fraternity's weekly Thursday night parties. Later, I learned from others that Laurel was drunk on beer and had taken four hits of LSD before going to the party. According to the story Laurel told to a campus administrator, after the party she fell asleep in a first-floor room and when she awoke was undressed. One of the brothers dressed her and carried her upstairs, where she was raped by "guys" she did not know but said she could identify if photographs were available. She asked a few times for the men to get off her, but to no avail. According to her account, she was barely conscious and lacked the strength to push them off her.

There is no dispute that Laurel had a serious drinking and drug problem at the time of the party. People at the party told me that during the course of the evening she acted like someone who was "high," and her behavior attracted quite a bit of attention. They described her as dancing provocatively to the beat of music only she could hear. She appeared disoriented and out of touch with what was happening. Various fraternity brothers occasionally danced with her, but she seemed oblivious to the person she was dancing with. Some of the brothers teased her by spinning her around in a room until she was so dizzy she couldn't find her way out. At one point during the evening she fell down a flight of stairs. Later she was pulled by the brothers out of a circle dance, a customary fraternity ritual in which only brothers usually took part.

After the other partyers had gone home, the accounts of what happened next vary according to who tells the story. The differences of opinion do not betray a Rashomon effect as much as they reflect different definitions of a common sexual event. No one disputes that Laurel had sex with at least five or six male students, maybe more. When Anna, a friend of the XYZ brothers, saw Laurel the next day and heard the story from the brothers, her immediate conclusion was that they had raped Laurel. Anna based her conclusion on seeing Laurel's behavior at the party and observing her the following day. It seemed to Anna that Laurel was incapable of consenting to sex, which is key for determining a charge of rape. Anna's opinion was later confirmed by the Assistant District Attorney for Sex Crimes, who investigated but did not prosecute the case.

The brothers claimed that Laurel had lured them into a "gang bang" or "train," which they preferred to call an "express." Their statements and actions during the days after the event seemed to indicate that they considered the event a routine part of their "little sisters program," something to be proud of. Reporting the party activities on a sheet posed on their bulletin board in the spot where the house minutes are usually posted, Anna found the following statement, which she later showed me:

> Things are looking up for the [XYZ] sisters program. A prospective leader for the group spent some time interviewing several [brothers] this past thursday and friday. Possible names for the little sisters include [XYZ] "little wenches" and "The [XYZ] express."

. . . The ideology that promotes "pulling train" is seen in the discourse and practices associated with some parties on campus. Party invitations expressing this ideology depict a woman lying on a pool table, or in some other position suggestive of sexual submission. The hosts of the party promote behavior aimed at seduction. *Seduction* means plying women with alcohol or giving them drugs in order to "break down resistance." A drunken woman is not defined as being in need of protection and help, but as "asking for it." If the situation escalates into sexual activity, the brothers watch each other perform sexual acts and then brag about "getting laid." The event is referred to as "drunken stupidity, women chasing, and all around silliness." The drama enacted parodies the image of the gentleman. Its male participants brag about their masculinity and its female participants are degraded to the status of what the boys call "red meat" or "fish." The whole scenario joins men in a no-holds-barred orgy of togetherness. The woman whose body facilitates all of this is sloughed off at the end like a used condom. She may be called a "nympho" or the men may believe that they seduced her—a practice known as "working a yes out"— through promises of becoming a little sister, by getting her drunk, by promising her love, or by some other means. Those men who object to this kind of behavior run the risk of being labeled "wimps" or, even worse in their eyes, "gays" or "faggots."

The rationalization for this behavior illustrates a broader social ideology of male dominance. Both the brothers and many members of the broader community excuse the behavior by saying that "boys will be boys" and that if a woman gets into trouble it is because "she asked for it," "she wanted it," or "she deserved it." The ideology inscribed in this discourse represents male sexuality as more natural and more explosive than female sexuality. This active, "naturally" explosive nature of male sexuality is expected to find an outlet either in the company of male friends or in the arms of prostitutes. In these contexts men are supposed to use women to satisfy explosive urges. The women who satisfy these urges are included as passive actors in the enactment of a sexual discourse where the male, but not the female, sexual instinct is characterized as an insatiable biological instinct and psychological need.

Men entice one another into the act of "pulling train" by implying that those who do not participate are unmanly or homosexual. This behavior is full of contradictions because the homoeroticism of "pulling train" seems obvious. A group of men watch each other having sex with a woman who may be unconscious. One might well ask why the woman is even necessary for the sexual acts these men stage for one another. As fraternity practices described in this book suggest, the answer seems to lie in homophobia. One can suggest that in the act of "pulling train" the polymorphous sexuality of homophobic men is given a strictly heterosexual form.

Polymorphous sexuality, a term used by Freud to refer to diffuse sexual interests with multiple objects, means that men will experience desire for one another. However, homophobia creates a tension between polymorphous sexual desire and compulsory heterosexuality. This tension is resolved by "pulling train": the brothers vent their interest in one another through the body of a woman. In the sociodrama that is enacted, the idea that heterosexual males are superior to women and to homosexuals is publicly expressed and probably subjectively absorbed. Thus, both homophobia and compulsory heterosexuality can be understood as strategies of knowledge and power centering on sex that support the social stratification of men according to sexual preference.

In group sex, homoerotic desire is simultaneously indulged, degraded, and extruded from the group. The fact that the woman involved is often unconscious highlights her status as a surrogate victim in a drama where the main agents are males interacting with one another. The victim embodies the sexual urges of the brothers; she is defined as "wanting it"—even though she may be unconscious during the event—so that the men can satisfy their urges for one another at her expense. By defining the victim as "wanting it," the men convince themselves of their heterosexual prowess and delude themselves as to the real object of their lust. If they were to admit to the real object, they would give up their position in the male status hierarchy as superior, heterosexual males. The expulsion and degradation of the victim both brings a momentary end to urges that would divide the men and presents a social statement of phallic heterosexual dominance.

By blaming the victim for provoking their own sexual aggression, men control and define acceptable and unacceptable female sexual behavior through the agency of fear. The fear is that a woman who does not guard her behavior runs the risk of becoming the target of uncontrollable male sexual aggression. Thus, although women are ostensibly the controlling agent, it is fear of the imagined explosive nature of male sexuality that ultimately reigns for both sexes. This fear instills in some men and women consciousness of their sexual and social identities.

In sum, the phenomenon of "pulling train" has many meanings. In addition to those meanings that have been mentioned, it is a bonding device that can permanently change a young man's understanding of masculinity. The bonding is accomplished by virtue of coparticipation in a "forbidden" act. As Ward Goodenough (1963) points out, sharing in the forbidden as part of initiation to a group is a powerful bonding device. For example, criminal gangs may require the initiate to perform a criminal act in order to be accepted as a member, an act that once performed is irrevocable. Participation in a "train" performs the same function of bonding the individual to the group and changing his subjectivity. Such bridge-burning acts of one kind or another are standard parts of ritualized identity-change procedures.

The Conditions Promoting "Pulling Train"

We cannot assume that all entering college students have well-established sexual and social identities or ethical positions regarding sexual harassment and abuse. Recent research by psychologists on human subjectivity argues that subjectivity is dynamic and changes as individuals move through the life cycle. The evidence presented here suggests that the masculine subjectivity of insecure males may be shaped, or at least reinforced, by experiences associated with male bonding at college.

[One] example is fraternity initiation rituals in which young men who admit to feelings of low self-esteem upon entering the college setting are forced to cleanse and purify themselves of the despised and dirty feminine, "nerdy," "faggot" self bonded to their mothers. The ritual process in these cases humiliates the pledges in order to break social and psychological bonds to parental authority and to establish new bonds to the brotherhood. The traumatic means employed to achieve these goals induces a state of consciousness that makes abuse of women a means to renew fraternal bonds and assert power as a brotherhood. . . .

. . . Cross-cultural research demonstrates that whenever men build and give allegiance to a mystical, enduring, all-male social group, the disparagement of women is, invariably, an important ingredient of the mystical bond, and sexual aggression the means by which the bond is renewed (Sanday 1981, 1986). As long as exclusive male clubs exist in a society that privileges men as a social category, we must recognize that collective sexual aggression provides a ready stage on which some men represent their social privilege and introduce adolescent boys to their future place in the status hierarchy.

Why has the sexual abuse of women and the humiliation of generations of pledges been tolerated for so long? The answer lies in a historical tendency to privilege male college students by failing to hold them accountable. Administrators protect young men by dissociating asocial behavior from the perpetrator and attributing it to something else. For example, one hears adult officials complaining about violence committed by fraternity brothers at the same time they condone the violence by saying that "things got out of hand" because of alcohol, adolescence, or some other version of "boys will be boys." Refusing to take serious action against young offenders promotes the male privilege that led to the behavior in the first place. At some level, perhaps, administrators believe that by taking effective action to end all forms of abuse they deny young men a forum for training for masculinity. Where this is the case women students cannot possibly experience the same social opportunities or sense of belonging at college as their male peers, even though they spend the same amount of money for the privilege of attending. As colleges and universities face an increasing number of legal suits deriving from rape, murder, and the other forms of abuse reported in fraternities, athletic settings, and dorms, change is clearly imminent. . . .

REFERENCES

Ehrhart, Julie K., and Bernice R. Sandler. 1985. "Campus Gang Rape: Party Games?" Washington, D.C.: Project on the Status of Women, Association of American Colleges.

Goodenough, Ward Hunt. 1963. *Cooperation in Change.* New York: Russell Sage Foundation.

Sanday, Peggy Reeves. 1981. "The Socio-Cultural Context of Rape." *Journal of Social Issues* 37: 5–27.

_____. 1986. "Rape and the Silencing of the Feminine." In *Rape: A Collection of Essays*, edited by Roy Porter and Sylvana Tomaselli. London: Basil Blackwell.

Sex and Race:
The Analogy of Social Control

William Chafe

. . . Analogies should not be limited to issues of substance alone, nor is their purpose to prove that two categories or objects are exactly identical. According to the dictionary, an analogy is "a relation of likeness . . . consisting in the resemblance not of the things themselves but of two or more attributes, circumstances or effects." Within this context, the purpose of an analogy is to illuminate a process or relationship which might be less discernible if only one or the other side of the comparison were viewed in isolation. What, then, if we look at sex and race as examples of how social control is exercised in America, with the primary emphasis on what the analogy tells us about the modes of control emanating from the dominant culture? . . . What if the nature of the analogy is not in the *substance* of the material existence which women and blacks have experienced but in the *forms* by which others have kept them in "their place" and prevented them from challenging the status quo?

The virtues of such an approach are many. First, it provides greater flexibility in exploring how the experience of one group can inform the study of another. Second, it has the potential of developing insights into the larger processes by which the status quo is perpetuated from generation to generation. In this sense, it can teach us about the operation of society as a whole and the way in which variables like sex and race have been made central to the division of responsibilities and power within the society. If the forms of social control used with blacks and women resemble each other in "two or more attributes, circumstances, or effects," then it may be possible to learn something both about the two groups and how the status quo has been maintained over time. The best way to pursue this, in turn, is through looking closely at the process of social control as it has operated on one group, and then comparing it with the process and experience of the second group.

In his brilliant autobiographical novel *Black Boy*, Richard Wright describes what it was like to grow up black in the Jim Crow South. Using his family, the church, his classmates, his jobs, and his fantasies as stage-pieces for his story,

From William H. Chafe, *Women and Equality: Changing Patterns in American Culture*. Copyright © 1977 by Oxford University Press. Used by permission of Oxford University Press, Inc.

Wright plays out the themes of hunger, fear, and determination which permeated his young life. Above all, he provides a searing account of how white Southerners successfully controlled the lives and aspirations of blacks. A series of concentric circles of social control operated in devastating fashion to limit young blacks to two life options—conformity to the white system, or exile.[*]

The outermost circle of control, of course, consisted of physical intimidation. When Richard asked his mother why black men did not fight white men, she responded, "The white men have guns and the black men don't." Physical force, and ultimately the threat of death, served as a constant reminder that whites held complete power over black lives. Richard saw that power manifested repeatedly. When his Uncle Hoskins dared to start his own saloon and act independently of the white power structure, he was lynched. The brother of one of Richard's schoolmates suffered a similar fate, allegedly for fooling with a white prostitute. When Richard worked for a clothing store, he frequently saw the white manager browbeat or physically attack black customers who had not paid their bills on time. When one woman came out of the store in a torn dress and bleeding, the manager said, "That's what we do to niggers when they don't pay their bills."[1]

The result was pervasive fear, anchored in the knowledge that whites could unleash vicious and irrational attacks without warning. Race consciousness could be traced, at least in part, to the tension which existed between anger at whites for attacking blacks without reason, and fear that wanton violence could strike again at any time, unannounced and unrestrained. "The things that influenced my conduct as a Negro," Richard wrote, "did not have to happen to me directly; I needed but to hear of them to feel their full effects in the deepest layers of my consciousness. Indeed the white brutality that I had not seen was a more effective control of my behavior than that which I knew . . . as long as it remained something terrible and yet remote, something whose horror and blood might descend upon me at any moment, I was compelled to give my entire imagination over to it, an act which blocked the springs of thought and feelings in me."[2]

The second circle of control rested in white domination of the economic status of black people. If a young black did not act the part of "happy nigger" convincingly, the employer would fire him. Repeatedly, Richard was threatened with the loss of work because he did not keep his anger and independence from being communicated to his white superiors. "Why don't you laugh and talk like the other niggers?" one employer asked. "Well, sir, there is nothing much to say or smile about," Richard said. "I don't like your looks nigger. Now git!" the boss ordered.

---

[*]Despite the problems created by using a novel for purposes of historical analysis, the interior perspective that is offered outweighs the limitation of "subjectiveness." Wright has been criticized for being overly harsh and elitist in his judgment of his black peers. His depiction of the conditions blacks had to cope with, on the other hand, corresponds well with the historical record. In the cases of both women and blacks, novels provide a vividness of detail and personal experience necessary to understand the larger processes at work in the society, but for the most part unavailable in conventional historical sources. (For amplification of Wright's experience with Jim Crow, see Selection 2, in Part I of this book.)

Only a limited number of economic roles were open to blacks, and if they were not played according to the rules, the job would be lost. A scarce supply of work, together with the demand that it be carried out in a deferential manner, provided a powerful guarantee that blacks would not get out of line.[3]

Significantly, the highest status jobs in the black community—teachers, ministers, civil servants—all depended ultimately upon acting in ways that pleased the white power structure.[*] One did not get the position at the post office or in the school system without being "safe"—the kind of person who would not make trouble. The fundamental precondition for success in the black community, therefore, was acting in ways that would not upset the status quo. When Richard tried to improve his own occupational chances and learn the optical trade, the white men who were supposed to teach him asked: "What are you trying to do, get smart, nigger?"[4]

The third circle of control consisted of the psychological power of whites to define and limit the reach of black aspirations. The sense people have of who they are and what they might become is tied intimately to the expectations communicated to them by others. The verbal cues, the discouragement or encouragement of authority figures, the picture of reality transmitted by friends or teachers—all of these help to shape how people think of themselves and their life chances. Stated in another way, human beings can envision careers as doctors and lawyers or a life of equality with others only to the extent that someone holds forth these ideals as viable possibilities.

Within this realm of social psychology, white Southerners exerted a pervasive and insidious control upon blacks. When Richard took his first job in a white household, he was given a bowl of molasses with mold on it for breakfast, even as his employers ate bacon and eggs. The woman he worked for asked what grade he was in, and when he replied the seventh, she asked, "Then why are you going to school?" When he further answered, "Well, I want to be a writer," she responded: "You'll never be a writer . . . who on earth put such ideas into your nigger head?" By her response, the woman attempted to undercut whatever sense of possibility Richard or other young blacks might have entertained for such a career. In effect, the woman had defined from a white perspective the outer boundaries of a black person's reality. As Richard noted, "She had assumed that she knew my place in life, what I felt, what I ought to be, and I resented it with all my heart . . . perhaps I would never be a writer; but I did not want her to say so." In his own time Richard Wright was able to defy the limits set upon his life by white people. But for the overwhelming majority of his fellow blacks, the ability of whites to intimidate them

---

[*]There is an important distinction, of course, between jobs which were tied to white support and those with an indigenous base in the black community. Black doctors, morticians, and barbers, for example, looked to the black community itself for their financial survival; hence they could be relatively free of white domination. On the other hand, the number of such independent positions was small. Although many people would include ministers in such a category, the visibility of the ministerial role created pressure from blacks concerned with the stability and safety of their churches for ministers to avoid a radical protest position. That started to change during the civil rights movement.

psychologically diminished the chance that they would be able to aspire realistically to a life other than that assigned them within a white racist social structure.[5]

The most devastating control of all, however, was that exercised by the black community itself out of self-defense. In the face of a world managed at every level by white power, it became an urgent necessity that black people train each other to adapt in order to survive. Thus the most profound and effective socialization toward accepting the racial status quo came from Richard's own family and peer group. It was Richard's mother who slapped him into silence "out of her own fear" when he asked why they had not fought back after Uncle Hoskins's lynching. To even ask the question posed a threat to safety. Similarly, it was Richard's Uncle Tom who insisted that Richard learn, almost by instinct, how to be accommodating. If Richard did not learn, the uncle said, he would never amount to anything and would end up on the gallows. Indeed, Richard would survive only if somebody broke his spirit and set the "proper" example.[6]

The instances of social control from within the black community abound in Wright's *Black Boy*. It was not only the white employer, but almost every black he knew, who opposed Richard's writing aspirations. "From no quarter," he recalled, "with the exception of the Negro newspaper editor, had there come a single encouraging word . . . I felt that I had committed a crime. Had I been aware of the full extent to which I was pushing against the current of my environment, I would have been frightened altogether out of my attempts at writing." The principal of his school urged vehemently that Richard give a graduation speech written by the principal rather than by Richard himself so that the proper tone of accommodation could be struck; the reward for going along was a possible teaching job. Griggs, Richard's best friend, was perhaps the most articulate in demanding that Richard control his instincts. "You're black and you don't act a damn bit like it." When Richard replied, "Oh Christ, I can't be a slave," Griggs responded with the ultimate lesson of reality: "But you've got to eat . . . when you are in front of white people, think before you act, think before you speak . . . you may think I'm an Uncle Tom, but I'm not. I hate these white people, hate them with all my heart. But I can't show it; if I did, they'd kill me." No matter where he went or whom he talked to in his own community, Richard found, not support for his protest, but the warning that he must behave externally in the manner white people expected. Whatever the hope of ultimate freedom, survival was the immediate necessity. One could not fight another day if one was not alive.[7]

Paradoxically, even the outlets for resistance within the system provided a means of reinforcing it. There were many ways of expressing unhappiness with one's lot, and all were essential to let off steam. The gang on the corner constantly verbalized resentment and anger against the white oppressor. Yet the very fact that the anger had to be limited to words and out of the earshot of whites meant that in practical terms it was ineffectual. Humor was another form of resistance. Richard and his friends joked that, if they ate enough black-eyed peas and buttermilk, they would defeat their white enemies in a race riot with "poison gas." But the end of the joke was an acknowledgment that the only way in reality to cope with the "mean" white folks was to leave.[8]

Indeed, the most practical form of resistance—petty theft—almost seemed a ploy by white people to perpetuate the system. Just as modern-day department store owners tolerate a certain degree of employee theft as a means of making the workers think they are getting away with something so they will not demand higher wages, so white employers of black people appear to have intentionally closed their eyes to a great deal of minor stealing. By giving blacks a small sense of triumph, white employers were able to tie them even more closely into the system, and prevent them from contemplating outright defiance. As Wright observed:[9]

> No Negroes in my environment had ever thought of organizing . . . and petitioning their white employers for higher wages. . . . They knew that the whites would have retaliated with swift brutality. So, pretending to conform to the laws of the whites, grinning, bowing, they let their fingers stick to what they could touch. And the whites seemed to like it.
>
> But I, who stole nothing, who wanted to look them straight in the face, who wanted to talk and act like a man, inspired fear in them. The southern whites would rather have had Negroes who stole work for them than Negroes who knew, however dimly, the worth of their own humanity. Hence, whites placed a premium upon black deceit; they encouraged irresponsibility, and their rewards were bestowed upon us blacks in the degree that we could make them feel safe and superior.

From a white point of view, a minor exercise of indirect and devious power by blacks was a small price to pay for maintaining control over the entire system. Thus, whites held the power to define black people's options, even to the point of controlling their modes of resistance.*

The result of all this was a system that functioned smoothly, with barely a trace of overt protest or dissension. Everyone seemed outwardly content with their place. At a very early age, Wright observed, "the white boys and the black boys began to play our traditional racial roles as though we had been born to them, as though it was in our blood, as though we were guided by instinct." For most people, the impact of a pervasive system of social control was total: resignation, a lowering of aspirations, a recognition of the bleakness of the future and the hopelessness of trying to achieve major change. In Wright's images life was like a train on a track; once headed in a given direction, there was little possibility of changing one's course.[10]

Wright himself, of course, was the exception. "Somewhere in the dead of the southern night," he observed, "my life had switched onto the wrong track, and without my knowing it, the locomotive of my heart was rushing down a dangerously

---

*It is important to remember that there existed a life in the black community less susceptible to white interference on a daily basis. Black churches, lodges, and family networks provided room for individual self-expression and supplied emotional reinforcement and sustenance. In this connection it is no accident that black institutions are strongest in the South where, until recently, the vast majority of blacks resided. On the other hand, the freedom which did exist came to a quick end wherever blacks attempted to enter activities, occupations, or areas of aspiration involving whites; or defined as white-controlled. Thus even the realm where freedom existed was partially a reflection of white control.

steep slope, heading for a collision, heedless of the warning red lights that blinked all about me, the sirens and the bells and the screams that filled the air." Wright had chosen the road of exile, of acute self-consciousness and alienation. For most blacks of his era, though, the warning red lights, the sirens, the bells, and the screams produced at least outward conformity to the status quo. In the face of forms of social control which effectively circumscribed one's entire life, there seemed no other choice.[11]

Obviously, women have not experienced overtly and directly the same kind of consistent physical intimidation that served so effectively to deter the black people of Richard Wright's childhood from resisting their condition. On the other hand, it seems clear that the physical strength and alleged dominance of men have been an important instrument of controlling women's freedom of action. The traditional image of the male as "protector" owes a great deal to the notion that women cannot defend themselves and that men must therefore take charge of their lives physically. The same notion of male strength has historically been responsible for restricting jobs involving heavy labor to men. Nor is the fear with which women view the potential of being struck or raped by a male lover, husband, or attacker an insignificant reality in determining the extent to which women historically have accepted the dominance of the men in their lives. Richard Wright observed that "the things that influenced my conduct . . . did not have to happen to me directly; I needed but to hear of them to feel their full effects. . . ." Similarly, women who have grown up with the image of powerful and potentially violent men need not have experienced a direct attack to share a sense of fear and intimidation. "Strength," the psychologist Jerome Kagan has observed, "is a metaphor for power." Thus, despite the substantive difference in the way women and blacks have been treated, the form of social control represented by physical strength has operated similarly for both groups.[12]

An even stronger case can be made for the way in which economic controls have succeeded in keeping blacks and women in their place. In 1898 Charlotte Perkins Gilman argued in *Women and Economics* that the root of women's subjection was their economic dependency on men. As long as women were denied the opportunity to earn their own living, she argued, there could never be equality between the sexes. The fact that women had to please their mates, both sexually and through other services, to ensure their survival made honest communication and mutual respect impossible. The prospect of a "present" from a generous husband, or a new car or clothes, frequently served to smooth over conflict, while the implicit threat of withholding such favors could be used to discourage carrying conflict too far.[13]

In fact, the issue of women not controlling their own money has long been one of the most painful and humiliating indexes of inequality between the sexes, especially in the middle class. Since money symbolizes power, having to ask others for it signifies subservience and an inferior status. Carol Kennicott, the heroine of Sinclair Lewis's *Main Street*, recognized the problem. After begging prettily for her household expenses early in her marriage, she started to demand her own separate funds. "What was a magnificent spectacle of generosity to you," she told her husband, "was a humiliation to me. You *gave* me money—gave it to your mistress if she was complaisant." Beth Phail, a character in Marge Piercy's novel *Small Changes*, experienced the same conflict with her husband, who was immediately threatened by the idea of her economic autonomy. Indeed, few examples of psychological control seem more pointed than those represented in husbands' treating their wives as not mature enough to handle their own money.[14]

Even the women who held jobs reflected the pattern by which economic power was used to control women's freedom of action. Almost all women workers were concentrated in a few occupations delineated as "woman's" work. As secretaries, waitresses, cooks, and domestic workers, women on the job conformed to the "service" image of their sex. Significantly, the highest status jobs available— nurses and teachers—tended to reinforce a traditional image of women and the status quo between the sexes, just as the highest jobs available within the black community—teachers and civil servants—reinforced a pattern of accommodation with the existing white power structure. Any woman who chose a "man's job" automatically risked a loss of approval, if not total hostility. For most, the option simply did not exist.

Even those in the most prestigious positions illustrated how money could be used as an instrument of social control. If they were to succeed in raising funds, college administrators in black and women's schools frequently found that they had to shape their programs in conformity to social values that buttressed the status quo. Booker T. Washington represented the most outstanding example of this phenomenon. Repeatedly he was forced to appease white racist presumptions in order to get another donation for Tuskegee. As the funnel through which all white philanthropic aid to blacks was channeled, Washington had to ensure that no money would be spent in a way which might challenge the political values of his contributors, even though privately he fought those political values. But Washington was not alone. During the 1830's Mary Lyons, head of Mt. Holyoke Seminary, agreed not to attend trustee meetings lest she offend male sensibilities, and Mary Alice Baldwin, the very effective leader of the Women's College of Duke University, felt it necessary to pay homage to the conservative tradition of "the Southern lady" as the price for sustaining support of women's education at Duke.[15]

In all of these instances, economic controls functioned in parallel ways to limit the freedom of women and blacks. If a group is assigned a "place," there are few more effective ways of keeping it there than economic dependency. Not only must the group in question conform to the expectations of the dominant class in order to get money to live; those who would do otherwise are discouraged by the fact that no economic incentives exist to reward those who challenge the status quo. The absence of financial support for those who dare to deviate from prescribed norms has served well to perpetuate the status quo in the condition of both women and blacks. "I don't want to be a slave," Richard Wright observed. "But you have to eat," Griggs replied.

The strongest parallel, however, consists of the way in which blacks and women have been given the psychological message that they should be happy with their "place." In both instances, this form of control has effectively limited aspiration to non-conventional roles. Although Beth Phail of *Small Changes* wanted to go to college and law school, her family insisted that her highest aspiration should be marriage and homemaking. A woman should not expect a career. Similarly, when Carol Kennicott told her college boyfriend, "I want to do something with my life," he responded eagerly: "What's better than making a comfy home and bringing up some cute kids . . . ?" The small town atmosphere of Gopher Prairie simply reinforced the pressure to conform. Carol was expected to be a charming hostess, a dutiful wife, and a good homemaker, but not a career woman. Thus, as Sinclair Lewis observed, she was a "woman with a working brain and no work." The messages Carol received from her surroundings were not designed to give her high self-esteem. Her husband called her "an extravagant little rabbit," and his poker partners, she noted, simply expected her "to wait on them like a servant."[16]

Although Carol's personality was atypical, her social experience was not. When high school girls entertained the possibility of a career, they were encouraged to be nurses, not doctors. The qualities that received the most praise were those traditionally associated with being a "lady," not an assertive individual ready to face the world. Significantly, both women and blacks were the victims of two devices designed to discourage non-conformity. Those who sought to protest their status, for example, were subjected to ridicule and caricature. The black protestor was almost certain to be identified with subversive activity, just as the women's rights advocate was viewed as unsexed and a saboteur of the family. (Ordinary blacks and females were subject to a gentler form of humor, no less insidious, as in the characters of Amos 'n Andy's "King Fish" or Lucille Ball's "Lucy.") In addition, it was not uncommon for blacks to be set against blacks and women against women in a competition which served primarily the interests of the dominant group. According to Judith Bardwick and Elizabeth Donavan, girls are socialized to use oblique forms of aggression largely directed at other females, while men's aggression is overt. The stereotype of women doing devious battle over an attractive man is an ingrained part of our folk tradition. Nor is the "divide and conquer" strategy a stranger to the history of black people, as when white workers sowed seeds of suspicion between Richard Wright and another black worker in order to make them fight each other for the entertainment of whites.[17]

In both cases the psychological form of social control has operated in a similar fashion. The aspirations, horizons, and self-images of blacks and women have been defined by others in a limiting and constrictive way. More often than not, the result historically has been an acceptance of society's perception of one's role. The prospect of becoming an architect, an engineer, or a carpenter is not easy to sustain in an environment where the very idea is dismissed as foolish or unnatural. Instead of encouragement to aspire to new horizons of achievement, the message transmitted to blacks and women has been the importance of finding satisfaction with the status quo.

But in the case of women, as with blacks, the most effective instrument of continued control has been internal pressure from the group itself. From generation to generation, mothers teach daughters to please men, providing the instruction that prepares the new generation to assume the roles of mothers and housewives. Just as blacks teach each other how to cope with "whitey" and survive within the system, women school each other in how to win a man, how to appear charming, where to "play a role" in order to avoid alienating a potential husband. When Beth in *Small Changes* rebelled against her husband and fought the idea of tying herself down with a child, it was the other women in her family who urged her to submit and at least give the *appearance* of accepting the role expected of her.[18]

In fact, dissembling in order to conform to social preconceptions has been a frequent theme of women's socialization. As Mirra Komarovsky has demonstrated, college women in the 1940's were taught to hide their real ability in order to make their male friends feel superior. "My mother thinks that it is very nice to be smart in college," one of Komarovsky's students noted, "but only if it doesn't take too much effort. She always tells me not to be too intellectual on dates, to be clever in a light sort of way." It is not difficult to imagine one woman saying to another as Griggs said to Richard Wright, "When you are around white people [men] you have to act the part that they expect you to act." Even if deception was the goal, however, the underlying fact was that members of the "oppressed" group acted as accomplices in perpetuating the status quo.[19]

The most effective device for maintaining internal group discipline was to ostracize those who did not conform. Richard Wright found himself singled out for negative treatment because he refused to accept authority and to smile and shuffle before either his teachers or white people. Beth Phail was roundly condemned by her sisters and mother for not pleasing her husband, and above all for not agreeing to have a child. And Carol Kennicott received hostile glances when she violated her "place" by talking politics with men or seeking to assume a position of independent leadership in the community of Gopher Prairie. The disapproval of her female peers was the most effective weapon used to keep her in line, and, when it appeared that she finally was going to have a child, her women friends applauded the fact that in becoming a mother she would finally get over all her strange ideas and settle down. As Sinclair Lewis observed, "She felt that willy-nilly she was being initiated into the assembly of housekeepers; with the baby for hostage, she would never escape."[20]

The pressure of one's own group represented a double burden. In an environment where success was defined as marriage, and fulfillment as being a happy homemaker, it was hard enough to fight the tide in the first place. If one did, however, there was the additional problem of being seen as a threat to all the other members of the group who had conformed. The resistance of blacks toward Richard Wright and of women toward Carol Kennicott becomes more understandable in light of the fact that in both cases the individual protestors, through their refusal to play the game according to the rules, were also passing judgment on those who accepted the status quo. Thus, historically, women and blacks have kept each other in line not only as a means of group self-defense—protecting the new generation from harm and humiliation—but also as a means of maintaining self-respect by defending the course they themselves have chosen.

Indeed, for women as well as for blacks, even the vehicles for expressing resentment became reinforcements of the status quo. For both groups, the church provided a central emotional outlet—a place where solidarity with one's own kind could be found, and where some protest was possible. Women's church groups provided not only a means of seeking reform in the larger society but also for talking in confidence to other women about the frustrations of being a woman in a male-dominated society. What social humorists have called "hen-sessions" were in fact group therapy encounters where women had a chance to voice their gripes. Humor was frequently a vehicle for expressing a bittersweet response to one's situation, bemoaning, even as one laughed, the pain of being powerless. But as in the case with blacks, venting one's emotions about a life situation—although necessary for survival—was most often an instrument for coping with the situation, rather than for changing it.

Perhaps the most subversive and destructive consequence of a pervasive system of social control is how it permeates every action, so that even those who are seeking to take advantage of the "enemy" end up supporting the system. When Shorty, the elevator man in *Black Boy* known for his wit and hostility to whites, needed some money for lunch one day, he told a white man he would not move the elevator until he got a quarter. "I'm hungry, Mr. White Man. I'm dying for a quarter," Shorty said. The white man responded by asking what Shorty would do for a quarter. "You can kick me for a quarter," Shorty said, bending over. At the end of the elevator ride, Shorty had his quarter. "This monkey's got the peanuts," he said. Shorty was right. He had successfully used racial stereotypes and his own role as a buffoon to get himself some lunch money. But in the process, the entire system of racial imbalance had been strengthened.[21]

Similar patterns run through the history of women's relationships to men. The coquette role is only the most extreme example of a type of manipulative behavior by women that seems to confirm invidious stereotypes. In the classic case of a wife trying to persuade her husband to go along with a desired course of action, the woman may play up to a man's vanity and reinforce his stereotyped notions about being a tower of strength and in control. Similarly, a female employee wishing advancement may adopt a flirtatious attitude toward a male superior. By playing a semi-seductive role and implying a form of sexual payoff for services rendered, she may achieve her immediate goal. But in each of these cases, the price is to become more entrapped in a set of distorted and unequal sex role stereotypes. The fact that overt power is not available and that the ability to express oneself honestly and openly has been denied leads to the use of covert and manipulative power. Thus, a woman may play dumb or a black may act deferential—conforming in each case to a stereotype—as a means of getting his or her way. But the result is pathological power that simply perpetuates the disease. The irony is that, even in trying to outwit the system of social control, the system prevails.

Basic to the entire system, of course, has been the extent to which a clearly defined role was "woven into the texture of things." For blacks the crucial moment
might come as soon as they developed an awareness of whites. In the case of
women, it more likely took place at puberty when the need to begin pleasing potential husbands was emphasized. In either case, what Richard Wright said about
the process of socialization could be said of both groups. "I marveled," he wrote:[22]

> at how smoothly the black boys [women] acted out the role . . . mapped out for
> them. Most of them were not conscious of living a special, separate, stunted way of
> life. Yet I knew that in some period of their growing up—a period that they had no
> doubt forgotten—there had been developed in them a delicate, sensitive control-
> ling mechanism that shut off their minds and emotions from all that the white race
> [society] had said was taboo. Although they lived in America where in theory there
> existed equality of opportunity, they knew unerringly what to aspire to and what not
> to aspire to.

The corollary for both women and blacks, at least metaphorically, has been
that those unable or unwilling to accept the role prescribed for them have been
forced into a form of physical or spiritual exile. Richard Wright understood that
continued accommodation with the white Southern system of racial oppression
would mean the destruction of his integrity and individuality. "Ought one to surrender to authority even if one believed that the authority was wrong?" Wright
asked. "If the answer was yes, then I knew that I would always be wrong, because I
could never do it. . . . How could one live in a world in which one's mind and perceptions meant nothing and authority and tradition meant everything?" The only
alternative to psychological death was exile, and Wright pursued that course, initially in Chicago, later in Paris. In her own way Carol Kennicott attempted the
same journey. "I've got to find out what my work is," she told her husband. "I've
been ruled too long by fear of being called things. I'm going away to be quiet and
think. I'm—I'm going. I have a right to my own life." And Beth Phail finally fled
her home and family because it was the only way to grow up, to find out what "she
wanted," to learn how to be a person in her own right in the world.[23]

Although in reality only a few blacks and women took the exact course adopted
by Richard Wright, Carol Kennicott, and Beth Phail, all those who chose to resist
the status quo shared to some extent in the metaphor of exile. Whether the person
was a feminist like Charlotte Perkins Gilman, a pioneer career woman such as
Elizabeth Blackwell, a runaway slave like Frederick Douglass, or a bold race
leader like W. E. B. Du Bois, the act of challenging prevailing norms meant living
on the edge of alienation and apart from the security of those who accepted the
status quo. Until and unless protest generated its own community of support which
could provide a substitute form of security and reinforcement, the act of deviance
promised to be painful and solitary.

This condition, in turn, reflected an experience of marginality which many
blacks and women shared. In sociological terms, the "marginal" personality is someone who moves in and out of different groups and is faced with the difficulty of

adjusting behavior to the norms of the different groups. By definition, most blacks and most women have participated in that experience, especially as they have been required to accommodate the expectations of the dominant group of white males. The very fact of having to adopt different modes of behavior for different audiences introduces an element of complexity and potential conflict to the lives of those who are most caught up in a marginal existence. House slaves, for example, faced the inordinately difficult dilemma of being part of an oppressed group of slaves even as they lived in intimacy with and under the constant surveillance of the white master-class, thereby experiencing in its most extreme form the conflict of living in two worlds.[24]

Ordinarily, the tension implicit in such a situation is deflected, or as Richard Wright observed, "contained and controlled by reflex." Most house slaves seemed to learn how to live with the conflict by repressing their anger and uneasiness. Coping with the situation became a matter of instinct. But it is not surprising that many slave revolts were led by those house slaves who could not resolve the conflict by reflex, and instead were driven to alienation and protest. For the minority of people who misinterpreted the cues given them or learned too late how to cope, consciousness of the conflict made instinctive conformity impossible. As Richard Wright observed, "I could not make subservience an automatic part of my behavior. . . . while standing before a white man . . . I had to figure out how to say each word . . . I could not grin . . . I could not react as the world in which I lived expected me to." The pain of self-consciousness made the burden almost unbearable. As Maya Angelou has written, awareness of displacement "is the rust on the razor that threatens the throat." In an endless string of injuries, it was the final insult.[25]

Dissenting blacks and women have shared this experience of being "the outsider." Unable to accept the stereotyped behavior prescribed for their group, they have, in Vivian Gornick's words, "stood beyond the embrace of their fellows." With acute vision, Gornick writes, the outsider is able to "see deeply into the circle, penetrating to its very center, his vision a needle piercing the heart of life. Invariably, what he sees is intolerable." On the basis of such a vision, exile is the only alternative available. Yet, ironically, it too serves to reinforce the status quo by removing from the situation those most likely to fight it. Until the members willing to resist become great enough, the system of social control remains unaltered.[26]

It seems fair to conclude, therefore, that a significant resemblance has existed in the forms of social control used to keep women and blacks in their "place." Despite profound substantive differences between women and blacks, and white women and black women, all have been victims of a process, the end product of which has been to take away the power to define one's own aspirations, destiny, and sense of self. In each case a relationship of subservience to the dominant group has been perpetuated by physical, economic, psychological, and internal controls that have functioned in a remarkably similar way to discourage deviancy and place a premium on conformity. "It was brutal to be Negro and have no control over my life," Maya Angelou observes in her autobiography. "It was brutal to be young and already trained to sit quietly." From a feminist perspective, the same words describe the process of control experienced by most women.[27]

The core of this process has been the use of a visible, physical characteristic as the basis for assigning to each group a network of duties, responsibilities, and attributes. It is the physical foundation for discriminatory treatment which makes the process of social control on sex and race distinctive from that which has applied to other oppressed groups. Class, for example, comes closest to sex and race as a source of massive social inequity and injustice. Yet in an American context, class has been difficult to isolate as an organizing principle. Because class is not associated with a visible physical characteristic and many working class people persist in identifying with a middle-class life-style, class is not a category easy to identify in terms of physical or psychological control. (The very tendency to abjure class consciousness in favor of a social mobility ethic, of course, is its own form of psychological control.) Ethnicity too has frequently served as a basis for oppression, but the ease with which members of most ethnic minorities have been able to "pass" into the dominant culture has made the structure of social control in those cases both porous and complicated. Thus although in almost every instance invidious treatment has involved the use of some form of physical, economic, psychological, or internal controls, the combinations have been different and the exceptions frequent.

The analogy of sex and race is distinctive, therefore, precisely to the extent that it highlights in pure form the process of social control which has operated to maintain the existing structure of American society. While many have been victimized by the same types of control, only in the case of sex and race—where physical attributes are ineradicable—have these controls functioned systematically and clearly to define from birth the possibilities to which members of a group might aspire. Perhaps for that reason sex and race have been cornerstones of the social system, and the source of values and attitudes which have both reinforced the power of the dominant class and provided a weapon for dividing potential opposition.

Finally, the analogy provides a potential insight into the strategies and possibilities of social change. If women and blacks have been kept in their "place" by similar forms of social control, the prerequisites for liberation may consist of overcoming those forms of social control through a similar process. In the case of both women and blacks, the fundamental problem has been that others have controlled the power to define one's existence. Thus, to whatever extent women and blacks act or think in a given way solely because of the expectation of the dominant group rather than from their own choice, they remain captive to the prevailing system of social control. The prototypical American woman, writes Vivian Gornick, is perceived as "never taking, always being taken, never absorbed by her own desire, preoccupied only with whether or not she is desired." Within such a context, the "other" is always more important than the "self" in determining one's sense of individual identity. It is for this reason that efforts by blacks and women toward group solidarity, control over one's own institutions, and development of an autonomous and positive self-image may be crucial in breaking the bonds of external dominance.[28]

Yet such a change itself depends on development of a collective consciousness of oppression and a collective commitment to protest. As long as social and political conditions, or the reluctance of group members to participate, preclude the emergence of group action, the individual rebel has little chance of effecting change. Thus the issue of social control leads inevitably to the question of how the existing cycle is broken. What are the preconditions for the evolution of group protest? How do external influences stimulate, or forestall, the will to resist? And through what modes of organization and action does the struggle for autonomy proceed? For these questions too, the analogy of sex and race may provide a useful frame of reference.

Whatever the case, it seems more productive to focus on forms of control or processes of change than to dwell on the substantive question of whether blacks and women have suffered comparable physical and material injury. Clearly, they have not. On the other hand when two groups exist in a situation of inequality, it may be self-defeating to become embroiled in a quarrel over which is more unequal or the victim of greater oppression. The more salient question is how a condition of inequality for both is maintained and perpetuated—through what modes is it reinforced? By that criterion, continued exploration of the analogy of sex and race promises to bring added insight to the study of how American society operates.

NOTES

1. Richard Wright, *Black Boy* (New York, 1937), pp. 48, 52, 150, 157. Quotations used by permission of the publishers Harper and Row, New York.

2. Wright, pp. 65, 150–51.

3. Wright, p. 159.

4. Wright, p. 164.

5. Wright, pp. 127–29.

6. Wright, pp. 139–40.

7. Wright, pp. 147, 153–55, 160–61.

8. Wright, pp. 68–71, 200.

9. Wright, p. 175.

10. Wright, p. 72.

11. Wright, p. 148.

12. Wright, pp. 150–51; Susan Brownmiller, *Against Our Will* (New York, 1975); Jerome Kagan and H. A. Moss, *Birth to Maturity* (New York, 1962).

13. Carl Degler, "Introduction," *The History of Women* (Oxford, 1975).

14. Sinclair Lewis, *Main Street* (New York, 1920), pp. 74, 167; Marge Piercy, *Small Changes* (Greenwich, Conn., 1972), p. 33.

15. Louis P. Harlan, *Booker T. Washington 1856–1901* (New York, 1972); Ralph Ellison, *Invisible Man* (New York, 1952); Eleanor Flexner, *Century of Struggle* (Cambridge, Mass., 1959), p. 33; and Dara DeHaven, "On Educating Women—The Co-ordinate Ideal at Trinity and Duke University," Master's thesis, Duke University, 1974.

16. Piercy, *Small Changes*, pp. 19–20, 29, 40–41; Lewis, *Main Street*, pp. 14–15, 86, 283.

17. Judith Bardwick and Elizabeth Donovan, "Ambivalence: The Socialization of Women" in *Women in Sexist Society: Studies in Power and Powerlessness*, eds. Barbara Moran and Vivian Gornick (New York, 1971); Wright, *Black Boy*, pp. 207–13.

18. Piercy, *Small Changes*, pp. 31, 34, 316–17.

19. Piercy, pp. 30–31, 34, 39; Mirra Komarovsky, "Cultural Contradictions and Sex Roles," *American Journal of Sociology* 52 (November 1946).

20. Lewis, *Main Street*, p. 234.

21. Wright, *Black Boy*, p. 199.

22. Wright, p. 172.

23. Wright, p. 144; Lewis, *Main Street*, pp. 404–5; Piercy, *Small Changes*, p. 41.

24. See Everett Hughes, "Social Change and Status Protest: An Essay on the Marginal Man," *Phylon* 10 (December 1949); and Robert K. Merton, *Social Theory and Social Structure* (New York, 1965), pp. 225–50.

25. Wright, *Black Boy*, p. 130; Maya Angelou, *I Know Why the Caged Bird Sings* (New York, 1970), p. 3.

26. Vivian Gornick, "Woman as Outsider," in Moran and Gornick, pp. 126–44.

27. Angelou, p. 153.

28. Gornick, p. 140.

112

Media Magic:
Making Class Invisible

Gregory Mantsios

Of the various social and cultural forces in our society, the mass media is arguably the most influential in molding public consciousness. Americans spend an average twenty-eight hours per week watching television. They also spend an undetermined number of hours reading periodicals, listening to the radio, and going to the movies. Unlike other cultural and socializing institutions, ownership and control of the mass media is highly concentrated. Twenty-three corporations own more than one-half of all the daily newspapers, magazines, movie studios, and radio and television outlets in the United States.[1] The number of media companies is shrinking and their control of the industry is expanding. And a relatively small number of media outlets is producing and packaging the majority of news and entertainment programs. For the most part, our media is national in nature and single-minded (profit-oriented) in purpose. This media plays a key role in defining our cultural tastes, helping us locate ourselves in history, establishing our national identity, and ascertaining the range of national and social possibilities. In this essay, we will examine the way the mass media shapes how people think about each other and about the nature of our society.

The United States is the most highly stratified society in the industrialized world. Class distinctions operate in virtually every aspect of our lives, determining the nature of our work, the quality of our schooling, and the health and safety of our loved ones. Yet remarkably, we, as a nation, retain illusions about living in an egalitarian society. We maintain these illusions, in large part, because the media hides gross inequities from public view. In those instances when inequities are revealed, we are provided with messages that obscure the nature of class realities and blame the victims of class-dominated society for their own plight. Let's briefly examine what the news media, in particular, tells us about class.

About the Poor

The news media provides meager coverage of poor people and poverty. The coverage it does provide is often distorted and misleading.

The Poor Do Not Exist

For the most part, the news media ignores the poor. Unnoticed are forty million poor people in the nation—a number that equals the entire population of Maine, Vermont, New Hampshire, Connecticut, Rhode Island, New Jersey, and New York combined. Perhaps even more alarming is that the rate of poverty is increasing twice as fast as the population growth in the United States. Ordinarily, even a calamity of much smaller proportion (e.g., flooding in the Midwest) would garner a great deal of coverage and hype from a media usually eager to declare a crisis, yet less than one in five hundred articles in the *New York Times* and one in one thousand articles listed in the *Readers Guide to Periodic Literature* are on poverty. With remarkably little attention to them, the poor and their problems are hidden from most Americans.

When the media does turn its attention to the poor, it offers a series of contradictory messages and portrayals.

The Poor Are Faceless

Each year the Census Bureau releases a new report on poverty in our society and its results are duly reported in the media. At best, however, this coverage emphasizes annual fluctuations (showing how the numbers differ from previous years) and ongoing debates over the validity of the numbers (some argue the number should be lower, most that the number should be higher). Coverage like this desensitizes us to the poor by reducing poverty to a number. It ignores the human tragedy of poverty—the suffering, indignities, and misery endured by millions of children and adults. Instead, the poor become statistics rather than people.

The Poor Are Undeserving

When the media does put a face on the poor, it is not likely to be a pretty one. The media will provide us with sensational stories about welfare cheats, drug addicts, and greedy panhandlers (almost always urban and Black). Compare these images and the emotions evoked by them with the media's treatment of middle-class (usually white) "tax evaders," celebrities who have a "chemical dependency," or wealthy businesspeople who use unscrupulous means to "make a profit." While the behavior of the more affluent offenders is considered an "impropriety" and a deviation from the norm, the behavior of the poor is considered repugnant, indicative of the poor in general, and worthy of our indignation and resentment.

The Poor Are an Eyesore

When the media does cover the poor, they are often presented through the eyes of the middle class. For example, sometimes the media includes a story about community resistance to a homeless shelter or storekeeper annoyance with panhandlers. Rather than focusing on the plight of the poor, these stories are about middle-class opposition to the poor. Such stories tell us that the poor are an inconvenience and an irritation.

The Poor Have Only Themselves to Blame

In another example of media coverage, we are told that the poor live in a personal and cultural cycle of poverty that hopelessly imprisons them. They routinely center on the Black urban population and focus on perceived personality or cultural traits that doom the poor. While the women in these stories typically exhibit an "attitude" that leads to trouble or a promiscuity that leads to single motherhood, the men possess a need for immediate gratification that leads to drug abuse or an unquenchable greed that leads to the pursuit of fast money. The images that are seared into our mind are sexist, racist, and classist. Census figures reveal that most of the poor are white, not Black or Hispanic, that they live in rural or suburban areas, not urban centers, and hold jobs at least part of the year.[2] Yet, in a fashion that is often framed in an understanding and sympathetic tone, we are told that the poor have inflicted poverty on themselves.

The Poor Are Down on Their Luck

During the Christmas season, the news media sometimes provides us with accounts of poor individuals or families (usually white) who are down on their luck.

These stories are often linked to stories about soup kitchens or other charitable activities and sometimes call for charitable contributions. These "Yule time" stories are as much about the affluent as they are about the poor: they tell us that the affluent in our society are a kind, understanding, giving people—which we are not.* The series of unfortunate circumstances that have led to impoverishment are presumed to be a temporary condition that will improve with time and a change in luck.

Despite appearances, the messages provided by the media are not entirely disparate. With each variation, the media informs us what poverty is not (i.e., systemic and indicative of American society) by informing us what it is. The media tells us that poverty is either an aberration of the American way of life (it doesn't exist, it's just another number, it's unfortunate but temporary) or an end product of the poor themselves (they are a nuisance, do not deserve better, and have brought their predicament upon themselves).

By suggesting that the poor have brought poverty upon themselves, the media is engaging in what William Ryan has called "blaming the victim."[3] The media identifies in what ways the poor are different as a consequence of deprivation, then defines those differences as the cause of poverty itself. Whether blatantly hostile or cloaked in sympathy, the message is that there is something fundamentally wrong with the victims—their hormones, psychological makeup, family environment, community, race, or some combination of these—that accounts for their plight and their failure to lift themselves out of poverty.

But poverty in the United States is systemic. It is a direct result of economic and political policies that deprive people of jobs, adequate wages, or legitimate support. It is neither natural nor inevitable: there is enough wealth in our nation to eliminate poverty if we chose to redistribute existing wealth or income. The plight of the poor is reason enough to make the elimination of poverty the nation's first priority. But poverty also impacts dramatically on the nonpoor. It has a dampening effect on wages in general (by maintaining a reserve army of unemployed and underemployed anxious for any job at any wage) and breeds crime and violence (by maintaining conditions that invite private gain by illegal means and rebellion-like behavior, not entirely unlike the urban riots of the 1960s). Given the extent of poverty in the nation and the impact it has on us all, the media must spin considerable magic to keep the poor and the issue of poverty and its root causes out of the public consciousness.

---

*American households with incomes of less than $10,000 give an average of 5.5 percent of their earning to charity or to a religious organization, while those making more than $100,000 a year give only 2.9 percent. After changes in the 1986 tax code reduced the benefits of charitable giving, taxpayers earning $500,000 or more slashed their average donation by nearly one-third. Furthermore, many of these acts of benevolence do not help the needy. Rather than provide funding to social service agencies that aid the poor, the voluntary contributions of the wealthy go to places and institutions that entertain, inspire, cure, or educate wealthy Americans—art museums, opera houses, theaters, orchestras, ballet companies, private hospitals, and elite universities. (Robert Reich, "Secession of the Successful," *New York Times Magazine*, February 17, 1991, p. 43.)

About Everyone Else

Both the broadcast and the print news media strive to develop a strong sense of "we-ness" in their audience. They seek to speak to and for an audience that is both affluent and like-minded. The media's solidarity with affluence, that is, with the middle and upper class, varies little from one medium to another. Benjamin DeMott points out, for example, that the *New York Times* understands affluence to be intelligence, taste, public spirit, responsibility, and a readiness to rule and "conceives itself as spokesperson for a readership awash in these qualities."[4] Of course, the flip side to creating a sense of "we," or "us," is establishing a perception of the "other." The other relates back to the faceless, amoral, undeserving, and inferior "underclass." Thus, the world according to the news media is divided between the "underclass" and everyone else. Again the messages are often contradictory.

The Wealthy Are Us

Much of the information provided to us by the news media focuses attention on the concerns of a very wealthy and privileged class of people. Although the concerns of a small fraction of the populace, they are presented as though they were the concerns of everyone. For example, while relatively few people actually own stock, the news media devotes an inordinate amount of broadcast time and print space to business news and stock market quotations. Not only do business reports cater to a particular narrow clientele, so do the fashion pages (with $2,000 dresses), wedding announcements, and the obituaries. Even weather and sports news often have a class bias. An all news radio station in New York City, for example, provides regular national ski reports. International news, trade agreements, and domestic policies issues are also reported in terms of their impact on business climate and the business community. Besides being of practical value to the wealthy, such coverage has considerable ideological value. Its message: the concerns of the wealthy are the concerns of us all.

The Wealthy (as a Class) Do Not Exist

While preoccupied with the concerns of the wealthy, the media fails to notice the way in which the rich as a class of people create and shape domestic and foreign policy. Presented as an aggregate of individuals, the wealthy appear without special interests, interconnections, or unity in purpose. Out of public view are the class interests of the wealthy, the interlocking business links, the concerted actions to preserve their class privileges and business interests (by running for public office, supporting political candidates, lobbying, etc.). Corporate lobbying is ignored, taken for granted, or assumed to be in the public interest. (Compare this with the media's portrayal of the "strong arm of labor" in attempting to defeat trade legislation that is harmful to the interests of working people.) It is estimated that two-thirds of the U.S. Senate is composed of millionaires.[5] Having such a preponderance of millionaires in the Senate, however, is perceived to be neither unusual nor antidemocratic; these millionaire senators are assumed to be serving "our" collective interests in governing.

The Wealthy Are Fascinating and Benevolent

The broadcast and print media regularly provide hype for individuals who have achieved "super" success. These stories are usually about celebrities and superstars from the sports and entertainment world. Society pages and gossip columns serve to keep the social elite informed of each others' doings, allow the rest of us to gawk at their excesses, and help to keep the American dream alive. The print media is also fond of feature stories on corporate empire builders. These stories provide an occasional "insider's" view of the private and corporate life of industrialists by suggesting a rags to riches account of corporate success. These stories tell us that corporate success is a series of smart moves, shrewd acquisitions, timely mergers, and well thought out executive suite shuffles. By painting the upper class in a positive light, innocent of any wrongdoing (labor leaders and union organizations usually get the opposite treatment), the media assures us that wealth and power are benevolent. One person's capital accumulation is presumed to be good for all. The elite, then, are portrayed as investment wizards, people of special talent and skill, whom even their victims (workers and consumers) can admire.

The Wealthy Include a Few Bad Apples

On rare occasions, the media will mock selected individuals for their personality flaws. Real estate investor Donald Trump and New York Yankees owner George Steinbrenner, for example, are admonished by the media for deliberately seeking publicity (a very un-upper class thing to do); hotel owner Leona Helmsley was caricatured for her personal cruelties; and junk bond broker Michael Milkin was condemned because he had the audacity to rob the rich. Michael Parenti points out that by treating business wrongdoings as isolated deviations from the socially beneficial system of "responsible capitalism," the media overlooks the features of the system that produce such abuses and the regularity with which they occur. Rather than portraying them as predictable and frequent outcomes of corporate power and the business system, the media treats abuses as if they were isolated and atypical. Presented as an occasional aberration, these incidents serve not to challenge, but to legitimate, the system.[6]

The Middle Class Is Us

By ignoring the poor and blurring the lines between the working people and the upper class, the news media creates a universal middle class. From this perspective, the size of one's income becomes largely irrelevant: what matters is that most of "us" share an intellectual and moral superiority over the disadvantaged. As *Time* magazine once concluded, "Middle America is a state of mind."[7] "We are all middle class," we are told, "and we all share the same concerns": job security, inflation, tax burdens, world peace, the cost of food and housing, health care, clean air and water, and the safety of our streets. While the concerns of the wealthy are quite distinct from those of the middle class (e.g., the wealthy worry about investments, not jobs), the media convinces us that "we [the affluent] are all in this together."

The Middle Class Is a Victim

For the media, "we" the affluent not only stand apart from the "other"—the poor, the working class, the minorities, and their problems—"we" are also victimized by the poor (who drive up the costs of maintaining the welfare roles), minorities (who commit crimes against us), and workers (who are greedy and drive companies out and prices up). Ignored are the subsidies to the rich, the crimes of corporate America, and the policies that wreak havoc on the economic well-being of middle America. Media magic convinces us to fear, more than anything else, being victimized by those less affluent than ourselves.

The Middle Class Is Not a Working Class

The news media clearly distinguishes the middle class (employees) from the working class (i.e., blue collar workers) who are portrayed, at best, as irrelevant, outmoded, and a dying breed. Furthermore, the media will tell us that the hardships faced by blue collar workers are inevitable (due to progress), a result of bad luck (chance circumstances in a particular industry), or a product of their own doing (they priced themselves out of a job). Given the media's presentation of reality, it is hard to believe that manual, supervised, unskilled, and semiskilled workers actually represent more than 50 percent of the adult working population.[8] The working class, instead, is relegated by the media to "the other."

In short, the news media either lionizes the wealthy or treats their interests and those of the middle class as one in the same. But the upper class and the middle class do not share the same interests or worries. Members of the upper class worry about stock dividends (not employment), they profit from inflation and global militarism, their children attend exclusive private schools, they eat and live in a royal fashion, they call on (or are called upon by) personal physicians, they have few consumer problems, they can escape whenever they want from environmental pollution, and they live on streets and travel to other areas under the protection of private police forces.*[9]

---

*The number of private security guards in the United States now exceeds the number of public police officers. (Robert Reich, "Secession of the Successful," *New York Times Magazine*, February 17, 1991, p. 42.)

The wealthy are not only a class with distinct life-styles and interests, they are a ruling class. They receive a disproportionate share of the country's yearly income, own a disproportionate amount of the country's wealth, and contribute a disproportionate number of their members to governmental bodies and decision-making groups—all traits that William Domhoff, in his classic work *Who Rules America*, defined as characteristic of a governing class.[10]

This governing class maintains and manages our political and economic structures in such a way that these structures continue to yield an amazing proportion of our wealth to a minuscule upper class. While the media is not above referring to ruling classes in other countries (we hear, for example, references to Japan's ruling elite),[11] its treatment of the news proceeds as though there were no such ruling class in the United States.

Furthermore, the news media inverts reality so that those who are working class and middle class learn to fear, resent, and blame those below, rather than those above, them in the class structure. We learn to resent welfare, which accounts for only two cents out of every dollar in the federal budget (approximately $10 billion) and provides financial relief for the needy,* but learn little about the $11 billion the federal government spends on individuals with incomes in excess of $100,000 (not needy),[12] or the $17 billion in farm subsidies, or the $214 billion (twenty times the cost of welfare) in interest payments to financial institutions.

Middle-class whites learn to fear African Americans and Latinos, but most violent crime occurs within poor and minority communities and is neither interracial[†] nor interclass. As horrid as such crime is, it should not mask the destruction and violence perpetrated by corporate America. In spite of the fact that 14,000 innocent people are killed on the job each year, 100,000 die prematurely, 400,000 become seriously ill, and 6 million are injured from work-related accidents and diseases, most Americans fear government regulation more than they do unsafe working conditions.

Through the media, middle-class—and even working-class—Americans learn to blame blue collar workers and their unions for declining purchasing power and economic security. But while workers who managed to keep their jobs and their unions struggled to keep up with inflation, the top 1 percent of American families saw their average incomes soar 80 percent in the last decade.[13] Much of the wealth at the top was accumulated as stockholders and corporate executives moved their companies abroad to employ cheaper labor (56 cents per hour in El Salvador) and avoid paying taxes in the United States. Corporate America is a world made up of

---

* A total of $20 billion is spent on welfare when you include all state funding. But the average state funding also comes to only two cents per state dollar.

† In 92 percent of the murders nationwide the assailant and the victim are of the same race (46 percent are white/white, 46 percent are black/black), 5.6 percent are black on white, and 2.4 percent are white on black. (FBI and Bureau of Justic Statistics, 1985–1986, quoted in Raymond S. Franklin, *Shadows of Race and Class*, University of Minnesota Press, Minneapolis, 1991, p. 108.)

ruthless bosses, massive layoffs, favoritism and nepotism, health and safety violations, pension plan losses, union busting, tax evasions, unfair competition, and
price gouging, as well as fast buck deals, financial speculation, and corporate
wheeling and dealing that serve the interests of the corporate elite, but are generally wasteful and destructive to workers and the economy in general.

It is no wonder Americans cannot think straight about class. The mass media
are neither objective, balanced, independent, nor neutral. Those who own and direct the mass media are themselves part of the upper class, and neither they nor
the ruling class in general have to conspire to manipulate public opinion. Their
interest is in preserving the status quo, and their view of society as fair and equitable comes naturally to them. But their ideology dominates our society and justifies what is in reality a perverse social order—one that perpetuates unprecedented
elite privilege and power on the one hand and widespread deprivation on the
other. A mass media that did not have its own class interests in preserving the status quo would acknowledge that inordinate wealth and power undermines democracy and that a "free market" economy can ravage a people and their
communities.

NOTES

1. Martin Lee and Norman Solomon, *Unreliable Sources*, Lyle Stuart (New York,
1990), p. 71. See also Ben Bagdikian, *The Media Monopoly*, Beacon Press (Boston, 1990).

2. Department of Commerce, Bureau of the Census, "Poverty in the United States:
1992," *Current Population Reports, Consumer Income*, Series P60–185, pp. xi, xv, 1.

3. William Ryan, *Blaming the Victim*, Vintage (New York, 1971).

4. Benjamin Demott, *The Imperial Middle*, William Morrow (New York, 1990),
p. 123.

5. Fred Barnes, "The Zillionaires Club," *The New Republic*, January 29, 1990, p. 24.

6. Michael Parenti, *Inventing Reality*, St. Martin's Press (New York, 1986), p. 109.

7. *Time*, January 5, 1979, p. 10.

8. Vincent Navarro, "The Middle Class—A Useful Myth," *The Nation*, March 23,
1992, p. 1.

9. Charles Anderson, *The Political Economy of Social Class*, Prentice Hall
(Englewood Cliffs, N.J., 1974), p. 137.

10. William Domhoff, *Who Rules America*, Prentice Hall (Englewood Cliffs, N.J.,
1967), p. 5.

11. Lee and Solomon, *Unreliable Sources*, p. 179.

12. *Newsweek*, August 10, 1992, p. 57.

13. *Business Week*, June 8, 1992, p. 86.

113

Masked Racism:
Reflections on the
Prison Industrial Complex

Angela Davis

Imprisonment has become the response of first resort to far too many of the social problems that burden people who are ensconced in poverty. These problems often are veiled by being conveniently grouped together under the category "crime" and by the automatic attribution of criminal behavior to people of color. Homelessness, unemployment, drug addiction, mental illness, and illiteracy are only a few of the problems that disappear from public view when the human beings contending with them are relegated to cages.

Prisons thus perform a feat of magic. Or rather the people who continually vote in new prison bonds and tacitly assent to a proliferating network of prisons and jails have been tricked into believing in the magic of imprisonment. But prisons do not disappear problems, they disappear human beings. And the practice of disappearing vast numbers of people from poor, immigrant, and racially marginalized communities has literally become big business.

The seeming effortlessness of magic always conceals an enormous amount of behind-the-scenes work. When prisons disappear human beings in order to convey the illusion of solving social problems, penal infrastructures must be created to accommodate a rapidly swelling population of caged people. Goods and services must be provided to keep imprisoned populations alive. Sometimes these populations must be kept busy and at other times—particularly in repressive super-maximum prisons and in INS detention centers—they must be deprived of virtually all meaningful activity. Vast numbers of handcuffed and shackled people are moved across state borders as they are transferred from one state or federal prison to another.

All this work, which used to be the primary province of government, is now also performed by private corporations, whose links to government in the field of what is euphemistically called "corrections" resonate dangerously with the military industrial complex. The dividends that accrue from investment in the punishment industry, like those that accrue from investment in weapons production, only amount to social destruction. Taking into account the structural similarities and

From *Colorlines* (Fall, 1998).

profitability of business–government linkages in the realms of military production and public punishment, the expanding penal system can now be characterized as a "prison industrial complex."

The Color of Imprisonment

Almost two million people are currently locked up in the immense network of U.S. prisons and jails. More than 70 percent of the imprisoned population are people of color. It is rarely acknowledged that the fastest growing group of prisoners are black women and that Native American prisoners are the largest group per capita. Approximately five million people—including those on probation and parole—are directly under the surveillance of the criminal justice system.

Three decades ago, the imprisoned population was approximately one-eighth its current size. While women still constitute a relatively small percentage of people behind bars, today the number of incarcerated women in California alone is almost twice what the nationwide women's prison population was in 1970. According to Elliott Currie, "[t]he prison has become a looming presence in our society to an extent unparalleled in our history—or that of any other industrial democracy. Short of major wars, mass incarceration has been the most thoroughly implemented government social program of our time."

To deliver up bodies destined for profitable punishment, the political economy of prisons relies on racialized assumptions of criminality—such as images of black welfare mothers reproducing criminal children—and on racist practices in arrest, conviction, and sentencing patterns. Colored bodies constitute the main human raw material in this vast experiment to disappear the major social problems of our time. Once the aura of magic is stripped away from the imprisonment solution, what is revealed is racism, class bias, and the parasitic seduction of capitalist profit. The prison industrial system materially and morally impoverishes its inhabitants and devours the social wealth needed to address the very problems that have led to spiraling numbers of prisoners.

As prisons take up more and more space on the social landscape, other government programs that have previously sought to respond to social needs—such as Temporary Assistance to Needy Families—are being squeezed out of existence. The deterioration of public education, including prioritizing discipline and security over learning in public schools located in poor communities, is directly related to the prison "solution."

Profiting from Prisoners

As prisons proliferate in U.S. society, private capital has become enmeshed in the punishment industry. And precisely because of their profit potential, prisons are becoming increasingly important to the U.S. economy. If the notion of punishment as a source of potentially stupendous profits is disturbing by itself, then the strategic dependence on racist structures and ideologies to render mass punishment palatable and profitable is even more troubling.

Prison privatization is the most obvious instance of capital's current movement toward the prison industry. While government-run prisons are often in gross violation of international human rights standards, private prisons are even less accountable. In March of this year, the Corrections Corporation of America (CCA), the largest U.S. private prison company, claimed 54,944 beds in 68 facilities under contract or development in the U.S., Puerto Rico, the United Kingdom, and Australia. Following the global trend of subjecting more women to public punishment, CCA recently opened a women's prison outside Melbourne. The company recently identified California as its "new frontier."

Wackenhut Corrections Corporation (WCC), the second largest U.S. prison company, claimed contracts and awards to manage 46 facilities in North America, U.K., and Australia. It boasts a total of 30,424 beds as well as contracts for prisoner health care services, transportation, and security.

Currently, the stocks of both CCA and WCC are doing extremely well. Between 1996 and 1997, CCA's revenues increased by 58 percent, from $293 million to $462 million. Its net profit grew from $30.9 million to $53.9 million. WCC raised its revenues from $138 million in 1996 to $210 million in 1997. Unlike public correctional facilities, the vast profits of these private facilities rely on the employment of non-union labor.

The Prison Industrial Complex

But private prison companies are only the most visible component of the increasing corporatization of punishment. Government contracts to build prisons have bolstered the construction industry. The architectural community has identified prison design as a major new niche. Technology developed for the military by companies like Westinghouse are being marketed for use in law enforcement and punishment.

Moreover, corporations that appear to be far removed from the business of punishment are intimately involved in the expansion of the prison industrial complex. Prison construction bonds are one of the many sources of profitable investment for leading financiers such as Merrill Lynch. MCI charges prisoners and their families outrageous prices for the precious telephone calls which are often the only contact prisoners have with the free world.

Many corporations whose products we consume on a daily basis have learned that prison labor power can be as profitable as third world labor power exploited by U.S.-based global corporations. Both relegate formerly unionized workers to joblessness and many even wind up in prison. Some of the companies that use prison labor are IBM, Motorola, Compaq, Texas Instruments, Honeywell, Microsoft, and Boeing. But it is not only the hi-tech industries that reap the profits of prison labor.

Nordstrom department stores sell jeans that are marketed as "Prison Blues," as well as t-shirts and jackets made in Oregon prisons. The advertising slogan for these clothes is "made on the inside to be worn on the outside." Maryland prisoners inspect glass bottles and jars used by Revlon and Pierre Cardin, and schools throughout the world buy graduation caps and gowns made by South Carolina prisoners.

"For private business," write Eve Goldberg and Linda Evans (a political prisoner inside the Federal Correctional Institution at Dublin, California) "prison labor is like a pot of gold. No strikes. No union organizing. No health benefits, unemployment insurance, or workers' compensation to pay. No language barriers, as in foreign countries. New leviathan prisons are being built on thousands of eerie acres of factories inside the walls. Prisoners do data entry for Chevron, make telephone reservations for TWA, raise hogs, shovel manure, make circuit boards, limousines, waterbeds, and lingerie for Victoria's Secret—all at a fraction of the cost of 'free labor.'"

Devouring the Social Wealth

Although prison labor—which ultimately is compensated at a rate far below the minimum wage—is hugely profitable for the private companies that use it, the penal system as a whole does not produce wealth. It devours the social wealth that could be used to subsidize housing for the homeless, to ameliorate public education for poor and racially marginalized communities, to open free drug rehabilitation programs for people who wish to kick their habits, to create a national health care system, to expand programs to combat HIV, to eradicate domestic abuse—and, in the process, to create well-paying jobs for the unemployed.

Since 1984 more than twenty new prisons have opened in California, while only one new campus was added to the California State University system and none to the University of California system. In 1996–97, higher education received only 8.7 percent of the State's General Fund while corrections received 9.6 percent. Now that affirmative action has been declared illegal in California, it is obvious that education is increasingly reserved for certain people, while prisons are reserved for others. Five times as many black men are presently in prison as in four year colleges and universities. This new segregation has dangerous implications for the entire country.

By segregating people labeled as criminals, prison simultaneously fortifies and conceals the structural racism of the U.S. economy. Claims of low unemployment rates—even in black communities—make sense only if one assumes that the vast numbers of people in prison have really disappeared and thus have no legitimate claims to jobs. The numbers of black and Latino men currently incarcerated amount to two percent of the male labor force. According to criminologist David Downes, "[t]reating incarceration as a type of hidden unemployment may raise the jobless rate for men by about one-third, to 8 percent. The effect on the black labor force is greater still, raising the [black] male unemployment rate from 11 percent to 19 percent."

Hidden Agenda

Mass incarceration is not a solution to unemployment, nor is it a solution to the vast array of social problems that are hidden away in a rapidly growing network of prisons and jails. However, the great majority of people have been tricked into believing in the efficacy of imprisonment, even though the historical record clearly demonstrates that prisons do not work. Racism has undermined our ability to create a popular critical discourse to contest the ideological trickery that posits imprisonment as key to public safety. The focus of state policy is rapidly shifting from social welfare to social control.

Black, Latino, Native American, and many Asian youth are portrayed as the purveyors of violence, traffickers of drugs, and as envious of commodities that they have no right to possess. Young black and Latina women are represented as sexually promiscuous and as indiscriminately propagating babies and poverty. Criminality and deviance are racialized. Surveillance is thus focused on communities of color, immigrants, the unemployed, the undereducated, the homeless, and in general on those who have a diminishing claim to social resources. Their claim to social resources continues to diminish in large part because law enforcement and penal measures increasingly devour these resources. The prison industrial complex has thus created a vicious cycle of punishment which only further impoverishes those whose impoverishment is supposedly "solved" by imprisonment.

Therefore, as the emphasis of government policy shifts from social welfare to crime control, racism sinks more deeply into the economic and ideological structures of U.S. society. Meanwhile, conservative crusaders against affirmative action and bilingual education proclaim the end of racism, while their opponents suggest that racism's remnants can be dispelled through dialogue and conversation. But conversations about "race relations" will hardly dismantle a prison industrial complex that thrives on and nourishes the racism hidden within the deep structures of our society.

The emergence of a U.S. prison industrial complex within a context of cascading conservatism marks a new historical moment, whose dangers are unprecedented. But so are its opportunities. Considering the impressive number of grassroots projects that continue to resist the expansion of the punishment industry, it ought to be possible to bring these efforts together to create radical and nationally visible movements that can legitimize anti-capitalist critiques of the prison industrial complex. It ought to be possible to build movements in defense of prisoners' human rights and movements that persuasively argue that what we need is not new prisons, but new health care, housing, education, drug programs, jobs, and education. To safeguard a democratic future, it is possible and necessary to weave together the many and increasing strands of resistance to the prison industrial complex into a powerful movement for social transformation.

Blaming the Victim

William Ryan

Twenty years ago, Zero Mostel used to do a sketch in which he impersonated a Dixiecrat Senator conducting an investigation of the origins of World War II. At the climax of the sketch, the Senator boomed out, in an excruciating mixture of triumph and suspicion, "What was Pearl Harbor *doing* in the Pacific?" This is an extreme example of Blaming the Victim.

Twenty years ago, we could laugh at Zero Mostel's caricature. In recent years, however, the same process has been going on every day in the arena of social problems, public health, anti-poverty programs, and social welfare. A philosopher might analyze this process and prove that, technically, it is comic. But it is hardly ever funny.

Consider some victims. One is the miseducated child in the slum school. He is blamed for his own miseducation. He is said to contain within himself the causes of his inability to read and write well. The shorthand phrase is "cultural deprivation," which, to those in the know, conveys what they allege to be inside information: that the poor child carries a scanty pack of cultural baggage as he enters school. He doesn't know about books and magazines and newspapers, they say. (No books in the home; the mother fails to subscribe to *Readers' Digest*.) They say that if he talks at all—an unlikely event since slum parents don't talk to their children—he certainly doesn't talk correctly. (Lower-class dialect spoken here, or even—God forbid!—Southern Negro.) *(Ici on parle nigra.)* If you can manage to get him to sit in a chair, they say, he squirms and looks out the window. (Impulse-ridden, these kids, motoric rather than verbal.) In a word he is "disadvantaged" and "socially deprived," they say, and this, of course, accounts for his failure (*his* failure, they say) to learn much in school.

Note the similarity to the logic of Zero Mostel's Dixiecrat Senator. What is the culturally deprived child *doing* in the school? What is wrong with the victim? In pursuing this logic, no one remembers to ask questions about the collapsing buildings and torn textbooks, the frightened, insensitive teachers, the six additional desks in the room, the blustering, frightened principals, the relentless segregation, the callous administrator, the irrelevant curriculum, the bigoted or cowardly members of the school board, the insulting history book, the stingy taxpayers, the fairy-tale readers, or the self-serving faculty of the local teachers' college. We are encouraged to confine our attention to the child and to dwell on all his alleged defects. Cultural deprivation becomes an omnibus explanation for the educational disaster area known as the inner-city school. This is Blaming the Victim.

Pointing to the supposedly deviant Negro family as the "fundamental weakness of the Negro community" is another way to blame the victim. Like "cultural deprivation," "Negro family" has become a shorthand phrase with stereotyped connotations of matriarchy, fatherlessness, and pervasive illegitimacy. Growing up in the "crumbling" Negro family is supposed to account for most of the racial evils in America. Insiders have the word, of course, and know that this phrase is supposed to evoke images of growing up with a long-absent or never-present father (replaced from time to time perhaps by a series of transient lovers) and with bossy women ruling the roost, so that the children are irreparably damaged. This refers particularly to the poor, bewildered male children, whose psyches are fatally wounded and who are never, alas, to learn the trick of becoming upright, downright, forthright all-American boys. Is it any wonder the Negroes cannot achieve equality? From such families! And, again, by focusing our attention on the Negro family as the apparent *cause* of racial inequality, our eye is diverted. Racism, discrimination, segregation, and the powerlessness of the ghetto are subtly, but thoroughly, downgraded in importance.

The generic process of Blaming the Victim is applied to almost every American problem. The miserable health care of the poor is explained away on the grounds that the victim has poor motivation and lacks health information. The problems of slum housing are traced to the characteristics of tenants who are labeled as "Southern rural migrants" not yet "acculturated" to life in the big city. The "multiproblem" poor, it is claimed, suffer the psychological effects of impoverishment, the "culture of poverty," and the deviant value system of the lower classes; consequently, though unwittingly, they cause their own troubles. From such a viewpoint, the obvious fact that poverty is primarily an absence of money is easily overlooked or set aside.

The growing number of families receiving welfare are fallaciously linked together with the increased number of illegitimate children as twin results of promiscuity and sexual abandon among members of the lower orders. Every important social problem—crime, mental illness, civil disorder, unemployment—has been analyzed within the framework of the victim-blaming ideology. . . .

I have been listening to the victim-blamers and pondering their thought processes for a number of years. That process is often very subtle. Victim-blaming is cloaked in kindness and concern, and bears all the trappings and statistical furbelows of scientism; it is obscured by a perfumed haze of humanitarianism. In observing the process of Blaming the Victim, one tends to be confused and disoriented because those who practice this art display a deep concern for the victims that is quite genuine. In this way, the new ideology is very different from the open prejudice and reactionary tactics of the old days. Its adherents include sympathetic social scientists with social consciences in good working order, and liberal politicians with a genuine commitment to reform. They are very careful to dissociate themselves from vulgar Calvinism or crude racism; they indignantly condemn any notions of innate wickedness or genetic defect. "The Negro is *not born* inferior," they shout apoplectically. "Force of circumstance," they explain in reasonable tones, "has *made* him inferior." And they dismiss with self-righteous contempt any claims that the poor man in America is plainly unworthy or shiftless or enamored of idleness. No, they say, he is "caught in the cycle of poverty." He is trained to be poor by his culture and his family life, endowed by his environment (perhaps by his ignorant mother's outdated style of toilet training) with those unfortunately unpleasant characteristics that make him ineligible for a passport into the affluent society.

Blaming the Victim is, of course, quite different from old-fashioned conservative ideologies. The latter simply dismissed victims as inferior, genetically defective, or morally unfit; the emphasis is on the intrinsic, even hereditary, defect. The former shifts its emphasis to the environmental causation. The old-fashioned conservative could hold firmly to the belief that the oppressed and the victimized were born that way—"that way" being defective or inadequate in character or ability. The new ideology attributes defect and inadequacy to the malignant nature of poverty, injustice, slum life, and racial difficulties. The stigma that marks the victim and accounts for his victimization is an acquired stigma, a stigma of social, rather than genetic, origin. But the stigma, the defect, the fatal difference—though derived in the past from environmental forces—is still located *within* the victim, inside his skin. With such an elegant formulation, the humanitarian can have it both ways. He can, all at the same time, concentrate his charitable interest on the defects of the victim, condemn the vague social and environmental stresses that produced the defect (some time ago), and ignore the continuing effect of victimizing social forces (right now). It is a brilliant ideology for justifying a perverse form of social action designed to change, not society, as one might expect, but rather society's victim.

As a result, there is a terrifying sameness in the programs that arise from this kind of analysis. In education, we have programs of "compensatory education" to build up the skills and attitudes of the ghetto child, rather than structural changes in the schools. In race relations, we have social engineers who think up ways of "strengthening" the Negro family, rather than methods of eradicating racism. In health care, we develop new programs to provide health information (to correct the supposed ignorance of the poor) and to reach out and discover cases of untreated illness and disability (to compensate for their supposed unwillingness to seek treatment). Meanwhile, the gross inequities of our medical care delivery systems are left completely unchanged. As we might expect, the logical outcome of analyzing social problems in terms of the deficiencies of the victim is the development of programs aimed at correcting those deficiencies. The formula for action becomes extraordinarily simple: change the victim.

All of this happens so smoothly that it seems downright rational. First, identify a social problem. Second, study those affected by the problem and discover in what ways they are different from the rest of us as a consequence of deprivation and injustice. Third, define the differences as the cause of the social problem itself. Finally, of course, assign a government bureaucrat to invent a humanitarian action program to correct the differences.

Now no one in his right mind would quarrel with the assertion that social problems are present in abundance and are readily identifiable. God knows it is true that when hundreds of thousands of poor children drop out of school—or even graduate from school—they are barely literate. After spending some ten thousand hours in the company of professional educators, these children appear to have learned very little. The fact of failure in their education is undisputed. And the racial situation in America is usually acknowledged to be a number one item on the nation's agenda. Despite years of marches, commissions, judicial decisions, and endless legislative remedies, we are confronted with unchanging or even widening racial differences in achievement. In addition, despite our assertions that Americans get the best health care in the world, the poor stubbornly remain unhealthy. They lose more work because of illness, have more carious teeth, lose more babies as a result of both miscarriage and infant death, and die considerably younger than the well-to-do.

The problems are there, and there in great quantities. They make us uneasy. Added together, these disturbing signs reflect inequality and a puzzlingly high level of unalleviated distress in America totally inconsistent with our proclaimed ideals and our enormous wealth. This thread—this rope—of inconsistency stands out so visibly in the fabric of American life, that it is jarring to the eye. And this must be explained, to the satisfaction of our conscience as well as our patriotism. Blaming the Victim is an ideal, almost painless, evasion.

The second step in applying this explanation is to look sympathetically at those who "have" the problem in question, to separate them out and define them in some way as a special group, a group that is *different* from the population in general. This is a crucial and essential step in the process, for that difference is in itself hampering and maladaptive. The Different Ones are seen as less competent, less skilled, less knowing—in short, less human. The ancient Greeks deduced from a single characteristic, a difference in language, that the barbarians—that is, the "babblers" who spoke a strange tongue—were wild, uncivilized, dangerous, rapacious, uneducated, lawless, and, indeed, scarcely more than animals. Automatically labeling strangers as savages, weird and inhuman creatures (thus explaining difference by exaggerating difference) not infrequently justifies mistreatment, enslavement, or even extermination of the Different Ones.

Blaming the Victim depends on a very similar process of identification (carried out, to be sure, in the most kindly, philanthropic, and intellectual manner) whereby the victim of social problems is identified as strange, different—in other words, as a barbarian, a savage. Discovering savages, then, is an essential component of, and prerequisite to, Blaming the Victim, and the art of Savage Discovery is a core skill that must be acquired by all aspiring Victim Blamers. They must learn how to demonstrate that the poor, the black, the ill, the jobless, the slum tenants, are different and strange. They must learn to conduct or interpret the research that shows how "these people" think in different forms, act in different patterns, cling to different values, seek different goals, and learn different truths. Which is to say that they are strangers, barbarians, savages. This is how the distressed and disinherited are redefined in order to make it possible for us to look at society's problems and to attribute their causation to the individuals affected. . . .

Blaming the Victim can take its place in a long series of American ideologies that have rationalized cruelty and injustice.

Slavery, for example, was justified—even praised—on the basis of a complex ideology that showed quite conclusively how useful slavery was to society and how uplifting it was for the slaves.[1] Eminent physicians could be relied upon to provide the biological justification for slavery since after all, they said, the slaves were a separate species—as, for example, cattle are a separate species. No one in his right mind would dream of freeing the cows and fighting to abolish the ownership of cattle. In the view of the average American of 1825, it was important to preserve slavery, not simply because it was in accord with his own group interests (he was not fully aware of that), but because reason and logic showed clearly to the reasonable and intelligent man that slavery was good. In order to persuade a good and moral man to *do* evil, then, it is not necessary first to persuade him to *become* evil. It is only necessary to teach him that he is doing good. No one, in the words of a legendary newspaperman, thinks of himself as a son of a bitch.

In late-nineteenth-century America there flowered another ideology of injustice that seemed rational and just to the decent, progressive person. But Richard Hofstadter's analysis of the phenomenon of Social Darwinism[2] shows clearly its functional role in the preservation of the *status quo*. One can scarcely imagine a better fit than the one between this ideology and the purposes and actions of the robber barons, who descended like piranha fish on the America of this era and picked its bones clean. Their extraordinarily unethical operations netted them not only hundreds of millions of dollars but also, perversely, the adoration of the nation. Behavior that would be, in any more rational land (including today's America), more than enough to have landed them all in jail, was praised as the very model of a captain of modern industry. And the philosophy that justified their thievery was such that John D. Rockefeller could actually stand up and preach it in church. Listen as he speaks in, of all places, Sunday school: "The growth of a large business is merely a survival of the fittest. . . . The American Beauty rose can be produced in the splendor and fragrance which bring cheer to its beholder only by sacrificing the early buds which grow up around it. This is not an evil tendency in business. It is merely the working-out of a law of nature and a law of God."[3]

This was the core of the gospel, adapted analogically from Darwin's writings on evolution. Herbert Spencer and, later, William Graham Sumner and other beginners in the social sciences considered Darwin's work to be directly applicable to social processes: ultimately as a guarantee that life was progressing toward perfection but, in the short run, as a justification for an absolutely uncontrolled laissez-faire economic system. The central concepts of "survival of the fittest," "natural selection," and "gradualism" were exalted in Rockefeller's preaching to the status of laws of God and Nature. Not only did this ideology justify the criminal rapacity of those who rose to the top of the industrial heap, defining them automatically as naturally superior (this was bad enough), but at the same time it also required that those at the bottom of the heap be labeled as patently *unfit*—a label based solely on their position in society. According to the law of natural selection, they should be, in Spencer's judgment, eliminated. "The whole effort of nature is to get rid of such, to clear the world of them and make room for better."

For a generation, Social Darwinism was the orthodox doctrine in the social sciences, such as they were at that time. Opponents of this ideology were shut out of respectable intellectual life. The philosophy that enabled John D. Rockefeller to justify himself self-righteously in front of a class of Sunday school children was not the product of an academic quack or a marginal crackpot philosopher. It came directly from the lectures and books of leading intellectual figures of the time, occupants of professorial chairs at Harvard and Yale. Such is the power of an ideology that so neatly fits the needs of the dominant interests of society.

If one is to think about ideologies in America in 1970, one must be prepared to consider the possibility that a body of ideas that might seem almost self-evident is, in fact, highly distorted and highly selective; one must allow that the inclusion of a specific formulation in every freshman sociology text does not guarantee that the particular formulation represents abstract Truth rather than group interest. It is important not to delude ourselves into thinking that ideological monstrosities were constructed by monsters. They were not; they are not. They are developed through a process that shows every sign of being valid scholarship, complete with tables of numbers, copious footnotes, and scientific terminology. Ideologies are quite often academically and socially respectable and in many instances hold positions of exclusive validity, so that disagreement is considered unrespectable or radical and risks being labeled as irresponsible, unenlightened, or trashy.

Blaming the Victim holds such a position. It is central in the mainstream of contemporary American social thought, and its ideas pervade our most crucial assumptions so thoroughly that they are hardly noticed. Moreover, the fruits of this ideology appear to be fraught with altruism and humanitarianism, so it is hard to believe that it has principally functioned to block social change.

A major pharmaceutical manufacturer, as an act of humanitarian concern, has distributed copies of a large poster warning, "LEAD PAINT CAN KILL!" The poster, featuring a photograph of the face of a charming little girl, goes on to explain that if children *eat* lead paint, it can poison them, they can develop serious symptoms, suffer permanent brain damage, even die. The health department of a major American city has put out a coloring book that provides the same information. While the poster urges parents to prevent their children from eating paint, the coloring book is more vivid. It labels as neglectful and thoughtless the mother who does not keep her infant under constant surveillance to keep it from eating paint chips.

Now, no one would argue against the idea that it is important to spread knowledge about the danger of eating paint in order that parents might act to forestall their children from doing so. But to campaign against lead paint *only* in these terms is destructive and misleading and, in a sense, an effective way to support and agree with slum landlords—who define the problem of lead poisoning in precisely these terms.

This is an example of applying an exceptionalistic solution to a universalistic problem. It is not accurate to say that lead poisoning results from the actions of individual neglectful mothers. Rather, lead poisoning is a social phenomenon supported by a number of social mechanisms, one of the most tragic by-products of the systematic toleration of slum housing. In New Haven, which has the highest reported rate of lead poisoning in the country, several small children have died and many others have incurred irreparable brain damage as a result of eating peeling paint. In several cases, when the landlord failed to make repairs, poisonings have occurred time and again through a succession of tenancies. And the major reason for the landlord's neglect of this problem was that the city agency responsible for enforcing the housing code did nothing to make him correct this dangerous condition.

The cause of the poisoning is the lead in the paint on the walls of the apartment in which the children live. The presence of the lead is illegal. To use lead paint in a residence is illegal; to permit lead paint to be exposed in a residence is illegal. It is not only illegal, it is potentially criminal since the housing code does provide for criminal penalties. The general problem of lead poisoning, then, is more accurately analyzed as the result of a systematic program of lawbreaking by one interest group in the community, with the toleration and encouragement of the public authority charged with enforcing that law. To ignore these continued and repeated law violations, to ignore the fact that the supposed law enforcer actually cooperates in lawbreaking, and then to load a burden of guilt on the mother of a dead or dangerously ill child is an egregious distortion of reality. And to do so *under the guise* of public-spirited and humanitarian service to the community is intolerable.

But this is how Blaming the Victim works. The righteous humanitarian concern displayed by the drug company, with its poster, and the health department, with its coloring book, is a genuine concern, and this is a typical feature of Blaming the Victim. Also typical is the swerving away from the central target that requires systematic change and, instead, focusing in on the individual affected. The ultimate effect is always to distract attention from the basic causes and to leave the primary social injustice untouched. And, most telling, the proposed remedy for the problem is, of course, to work on the victim himself. Prescriptions for cure, as written by the Savage Discovery set, are invariably conceived to revamp and revise the victim, never to change the surrounding circumstances. They want to change his attitudes, alter his values, fill up his cultural deficits, energize his apathetic soul, cure his character defects, train him and polish him and woo him from his savage ways.

Isn't all of this more subtle and sophisticated than such old-fashioned ideologies as Social Darwinism? Doesn't the change from brutal ideas about survival of the fit (and the expiration of the unfit) to kindly concern about characterological defects (brought about by stigmas of social origin) seem like a substantial step forward? Hardly. It is only a substitution of terms. The old, reactionary exceptionalistic formulations are replaced by new progressive, humanitarian exceptionalistic formulations. In education, the outmoded and unacceptable concept of racial or class differences in basic inherited intellectual ability simply gives way to the new notion of cultural deprivation: there is very little functional difference between these two ideas. In taking a look at the phenomenon of poverty, the old concept of unfitness or idleness or laziness is replaced by the newfangled theory of the culture of poverty. In race relations, plain Negro inferiority—which was good enough for old-fashioned conservatives—is pushed aside by fancy conceits about the crumbling Negro family. With regard to illegitimacy, we are not so crass as to concern ourselves with immorality and vice, as in the old days; we settle benignly on the explanation of the "lower-class pattern of sexual behavior," which no one condemns as evil, but which is, in fact, simply a variation of the old explanatory idea. Mental illness is no longer defined as the result of hereditary taint or congenital character flaw; now we have new causal hypotheses regarding the ego-damaging emotional experiences that are supposed to be the inevitable consequence of the deplorable child-rearing practices of the poor.

In each case, of course, we are persuaded to ignore the obvious: the continued blatant discrimination against the Negro, the gross deprivation of contraceptive and adoption services to the poor, the heavy stresses endemic in the life of the poor. And almost all our make-believe liberal programs aimed at correcting our urban problems are off target; they are designed either to change the poor man or to cool him out.

We come finally to the question, Why? It is much easier to understand the process of Blaming the Victim as a way of thinking than it is to understand the motivation for it. Why do Victim Blamers, who are usually good people, blame the victim? The development and application of this ideology, and of all the mythologies associated with Savage Discovery, are readily exposed by careful analysis as hostile acts—one is almost tempted to say acts of war—directed against the disadvantaged, the distressed, the disinherited. It is class warfare in reverse. Yet those who are most fascinated and enchanted by this ideology tend to be progressive, humanitarian, and, in the best sense of the word, charitable persons. They would usually define themselves as moderates or liberals. Why do they pursue this dreadful war against the poor and the oppressed?

Put briefly, the answer can be formulated best in psychological terms—or, at least, I, as a psychologist, am more comfortable with such a formulation. The highly charged psychological problem confronting this hypothetical progressive, charitable person I am talking about is that of reconciling his own self-interest with the promptings of his humanitarian impulses. This psychological process of reconciliation is not worked out in a logical, rational, conscious way; it is a process that takes place far below the level of sharp consciousness, and the solution—Blaming the Victim—is arrived at subconsciously as a compromise that apparently satisfies both his self-interest and his charitable concerns. Let me elaborate.

First, the question of self-interest or, more accurately, class interest. The typical Victim Blamer is a middle-class person who is doing reasonably well in a material way; he has a good job, a good income, a good house, a good car. Basically, he likes the social system pretty much the way it is, at least in broad outline. He likes the two-party political system, though he may be highly skilled in finding a thousand minor flaws in its functioning. He heartily approves of the profit motive as the propelling engine of the economic system despite his awareness that there are abuses of that system, negative side effects, and substantial residual inequalities.

On the other hand, he is acutely aware of poverty, racial discrimination, exploitation, and deprivation, and, moreover, he wants to do something concrete to ameliorate the condition of the poor, the black, and the disadvantaged. This is not an extraneous concern; it is central to his value system to insist on the worth of the individual, the equality of men, and the importance of justice.

What is to be done, then? What intellectual position can he take, and what line of action can he follow that will satisfy both of these important motivations? He quickly and self-consciously rejects two obvious alternatives, which he defines as "extremes." He cannot side with an openly reactionary, repressive position that accepts continued oppression and exploitation as the price of a privileged position for his own class. This is incompatible with his own morality and his basic political principles. He finds the extreme conservative position repugnant.

He is, if anything, more allergic to radicals, however, than he is to reactionaries. He rejects the "extreme" solution of radical social change, and this makes sense since such radical social change threatens his own well-being. A more equitable distribution of income might mean that he would have less—a smaller or older house, with fewer yews or no rhododendrons in the yard, a less enjoyable job, or, at the least, a somewhat smaller salary. If black children and poor children were, in fact, reasonably educated and began to get high S.A.T. scores, they would be competing with *his* children for the scarce places in the entering classes of Harvard, Columbia, Bennington, and Antioch.

So our potential Victim Blamers are in a dilemma. In the words of an old Yiddish proverb, they are trying to dance at two weddings. They are old friends of both brides and fond of both kinds of dancing, and they want to accept both invitations. They cannot bring themselves to attack the system that has been so good to them, but they want so badly to be helpful to the victims of racism and economic injustice.

Their solution is a brilliant compromise. They turn their attention to the victim in his post-victimized state. They want to bind up wounds, inject penicillin, administer morphine, and evacuate the wounded for rehabilitation. They explain what's wrong with the victim in terms of social experiences *in the past*, experiences that have left wounds, defects, paralysis, and disability. And they take the cure of these wounds and the reduction of these disabilities as the first order of business. They want to make the victims less vulnerable, send them back into battle with better weapons, thicker armor, a higher level of morale.

In order to do so effectively, of course, they must analyze the victims carefully, dispassionately, objectively, scientifically, empathetically, mathematically, and hardheadedly, to see what made them so vulnerable in the first place.

What weapons, now, might they have lacked when they went into battle? Job skills? Education?

What armor was lacking that might have warded off their wounds? Better values? Habits of thrift and foresight?

And what might have ravaged their morale? Apathy? Ignorance? Deviant lower-class cultural patterns?

This is the solution of the dilemma, the solution of Blaming the Victim. And those who buy this solution with a sigh of relief are inevitably blinding themselves to the basic causes of the problems being addressed. They are, most crucially, rejecting the possibility of blaming, not the victims, but themselves. They are all unconsciously passing judgments on themselves and bringing in a unanimous verdict of Not Guilty.

If one comes to believe that the culture of poverty produces persons *fated* to be poor, who can find any fault with our corporation-dominated economy? And if the Negro family produces young men *incapable* of achieving equality, let's deal with that first before we go on to the task of changing the pervasive racism that informs and shapes and distorts our every social institution. And if unsatisfactory resolution of one's Oedipus complex accounts for all emotional distress and mental disorder, then by all means let us attend to that and postpone worrying about the pounding day-to-day stresses of life on the bottom rungs that drive so many to drink, dope, and madness.

That is the ideology of Blaming the Victim, the cunning Art of Savage Discovery. The tragic, frightening truth is that it is a mythology that is winning over the best people of our time, the very people who must resist this ideological temptation if we are to achieve nonviolent change in America.

NOTES

1. For a good review of this general ideology, see I. A. Newby, *Jim Crow's Defense* (Baton Rouge: Louisiana State University Press, 1965).

2. Richard Hofstadter, *Social Darwinism in American Thought* (revised ed.; Boston: Beacon Press, 1955).

3. William J. Ghent, *Our Benevolent Feudalism* (New York: The Macmillan Co., 1902), p. 29.

115

Language, Culture, and Reality

Donaldo Macedo and Lillia I. Bartolome

I concluded long ago that they found the color of my skin inhibitory. This color seems to operate as a most disagreeable mirror, and a great deal of one's energy is expended in reassuring white Americans that they do not see what they see.

This is utterly futile, of course, since they do see what they see. And what they see is an appallingly oppressive and bloody history known all over the world. What they see is a disastrous, continuing, present condition which menaces them, and for which they bear an inescapable responsibility. But since in the main they seem to lack the energy to change this condition they would not be reminding of it.

—James Baldwin[1]

As James Baldwin so succinctly points out, many white Americans prefer not to be reminded of the "appallingly oppressive and bloody history" of racism that has characterized the very fabric of U.S. society. In fact many, if not most, white Americans from various ethnic backgrounds would feel extremely uncomfortable if the curriculum in schools incorporated an antiracist pedagogy that asked, "Mirror, mirror on the wall, is everyone welcome in the hall?"

Sadly, in a good number of halls not everyone is welcome. A report published by the National Association of Black Journalists revealed that 32 percent of African-American journalists fear that bringing up issues of race in their articles damages their chances for advancement.[2] This statistic reveals a condition of fear that most likely exists in many forms and many occupations, including teaching. We believe this condition of fear gives rise to a form of censorship that views the aggressive denouncement of racism as worse than the racist act itself.

In this chapter, we argue that . . . one of the most pressing challenges facing educators in the United States is the specter of an "ethnic and cultural war." . . .

Central to the idea of an ethnic and cultural war is the creation of an ideologically coded language that serves at least two fundamental functions: on the one hand, this language veils the racism that characterizes U.S. society, and on the other hand, it insidiously perpetuates both ethnic and racial stereotypes that devalue identities of resistance and struggle. Although the present assault on Latinos is mostly characterized by a form of racism at the level of language, it is important to differentiate between language as racism and the experience of racism. For example, former presidential candidate Patrick Buchanan's call for the end of illegal immigration "even if it means putting the National Guard all along the Southern frontier" constitutes a form of racism at the level of language.[3] This language-based racism has had the effect of licensing institutional discrimination, whereby both documented and undocumented immigrants materially experience the loss of their dignity, the denial of their humanity, and, in many cases, outright violence, as witnessed by the recent cruel beatings of a Mexican man and woman by the border patrol. This incident was captured on videotape, and outraged the Latino/Mexicano communities in the United States, as well as in Mexico, leading to a number of demonstrations in Los Angeles. Terms like "border rats," "wetbacks," "aliens," "illegals," "welfare queens," and "nonwhite hordes" used by the popular press not only dehumanize other cultural beings but also serve to justify the violence perpetuated against subordinate groups. . . .

By deconstructing the cultural conditions that give rise to the present violent assault on undocumented immigrants, affirmative action, African-Americans, and other racial and ethnic groups, we can single out those ideological factors that enable even highly educated individuals to embrace blindly, for example, conservative radio talk-show host Rush Limbaugh's racist tirades designed to demonize and dehumanize ethnic and cultural identities other than his own. Here are some examples:

- Now I got something for you that's true—1992, Tufts University, Boston. This is 24 years ago or 22 years ago. Three-year study of 5,000 coeds, and they used a benchmark of a bra size of 34C. They forward that—now wait! It's true. The larger the bra size, the smaller the IQ.
- Feminism was established so that unattractive women could have easier access to mainstream society.
- There are more American Indians alive today than there were when Columbus arrived or at any other time in history. Does that sound like a record of genocide?
- Taxpaying citizens are not being given access to these welfare and health services that they deserve and desire. But if you're an illegal immigrant and cross the border, you get everything you want.[4]

The racism and high level of xenophobia we are witnessing in our society today are not caused by isolated acts by individuals such as Limbaugh or onetime Louisiana gubernatorial candidate David Duke. Rather, these individuals are representatives of an orchestrated effort by segments of the dominant society to wage a war on the poor and on people who, by virtue of their race, ethnicity, language, and class, are reduced at best to half-citizens, and at worst to a national enemy responsible for all the ills afflicting our society. We need to understand the cultural and historical context that gives rise to over 20 million Limbaugh "ditto heads" who tune in to his weekly radio and television programs.

We need also to understand those ideological elements that inform our policymakers and those individuals who shape public opinion by supporting and rewarding Limbaugh's unapologetic demonizing of other cultural subjects. For example, television commentator Ted Koppel considers him "very smart. He does his homework. He is well informed." Syndicated columnist George Will considers him the "fourth branch of government," and former Secretary of Education William Bennett—the virtue man—describes Limbaugh as "possibly our greatest living American."[5] What remains incomprehensible is why highly educated individuals like Koppel, Will, and Bennett cannot see through Limbaugh's obvious distortions of history and falsification of reality. We posit that the inability to perceive distinctions and falsifications of reality is partly due to the hegemonic forces that promote an acritical education via the fragmentation of bodies of knowledge. Such a process makes it very difficult for students (and the general population) to make connections among historical events so as to gain a more critical understanding of reality. . . .

"Affirmative action" and "welfare" are also code words that license a form of racism via language that assuages the fear of the white working and middle class as they steadily lose ground to the real "affirmative action and welfare" programs designed to further enrich the upper class and big business:

> When the Fed raises the interest rates, it helps big business at the expense of individual home owners. When politicians resist raising the minimum wage, it helps big business send off the working poor. When politicians want liability caps, they defend Big Oil, Ma Bell and her offspring and Detroit gas guzzlers over potential victims of defective products and pollution. As the Gingrich revolution slashes school lunches for the poor, corporations get $1.11 billion in tax breaks, according to Labor secretary Robert Reich.[6]

We also know that even within the context of the present affirmative action policy, the genuine beneficiaries have been white women. Their convenient silence on the present assault on affirmative action makes them complicit in perpetuating the racist myth that

> black people take jobs from white people . . . [which leads] one to conclude that African-Americans are not considered Americans. White men lose jobs to other white men who do not say, they gave my job to an inferior white man! White male competency is assumed. African-Americans, regardless of achievement, are forever on trial.[7]

In other words, Henry Louis Gates Jr.'s prominence as a scholar did not lessen the racism he had to face at Duke University when he taught there. Cornel West's status as a renowned public intellectual did little for him as he watched nine taxis go by and refuse to pick him up in the streets of New York. bell hooks's eminence as a major feminist scholar does not lessen the pain of racism and sexism she endures; her status as an author of many highly acclaimed feminist books still does not provide her with the access to media and magazines enjoyed by many white feminists. As hooks recently pointed out to Naomi Wolf:

> I have written eight feminist books. None of the magazines that have talked about your book, Naomi, have ever talked about my books at all. Now, that's not because there aren't ideas in my books that have universal appeal. It's because the issue that you raised in *The Beauty Myth* is still about beauty. We have to acknowledge that all of us do not have equal access.[8]

hooks's comment denudes the myth created by the anti-affirmative action discourse that "pretends that we live in a colorblind society where individuals are treated according to the American ethic [that] has always held that individual effort and achievement are valued and rewarded."[9] . . .

Tolerance for different racial and ethnic groups as proposed by some white liberals not only constitutes a veil behind which they hide their racism, it also puts them in a compromising racial position. While calling for racial tolerance, a paternalistic term, they often maintain the privilege that is complicit with the dominant ideology. In other words, the call for tolerance never questions the asymmetrical power relations that give them their privilege. Thus, many white liberals willingly call and work for cultural tolerance but are reluctant to confront issues of inequality, power, ethics, race, and ethnicity in a way that could actually lead to social transformation that would make society more democratic and humane and less racist and discriminatory. This form of racism is readily understood by its victims, as observed by Carol Swain, an African-American professor at Princeton University: "White liberals are among the most racist people I know; they're so patronizing towards blacks."[10] . . .

It is against this mean-spirited and racist backdrop that we analyze the controversy over multiculturalism and the role that language plays in the process. In our analysis we do not discuss the way Puerto Ricans dance salsa, how Chicanos celebrate Cinco de Mayo, or how Haitians believe in voodoo. Although the knowledge of such cultural traits is useful, we do not think it prepares us to deal with the tensions and contradictions generated by the coexistence of multicultural groups in a racist society. Instead, we argue that multicultural analyses should not be limited to the study of the "other' in a way that makes the white cultural group invisible and beyond study. White invisibility is achieved partly through the very language we use to structure our discourse on race and ethnicity. For example, both whites and nonwhite racial and ethnic groups use the linguistic construction "people of color" to designate non-white individuals. The hidden assumption is that white is colorless, a proposition that is semantically impossible. By pointing out that white is also a color, we can begin to interrogate the false assumptions that strip white people of their ethnicity. In fact, a thorough understanding of racial and ethnic realities must begin by reinserting both color and ethnicity into the false discourse of colorless whites that contributes to making ethnicity invisible within this concept of whiteness. In addition, it is not necessarily important for us to understand how cultural differences are structured along specific behavior patterns, but it is important to understand instead the antagonism and tensions engendered by cultural differences that coexist asymmetrically in terms of power relations.

Culture is intertwined with language and represents a sizable dimension of its reality, but language is rarely studied as part of our multicultural understanding. In this country we often take for granted that the study of multiculturalism should be done in English only; in addition, we also rarely question the role of the dominant language in the devaluation of the cultural and ethnic groups under study. Put simply, we understand little how the English language can subordinate and alienate members of the cultures we study through English. We need to understand how English masks the web of ideological manipulation that makes white cultural and ethnic groups invisible and outside the realm of study. Hence, language not only produces cultural and social inequalities but is also used by the dominant white ideology to distort and falsify realities. Take the proposition "school choice," which creates the illusion that all parents can equally exercise their democratic right to choose the best schools for their children.

The illusion of choice also reinforces the myth that every American can choose where to live and work. However, for a group of African-Americans who attempted to implement the court-ordered integration of a public housing complex in Vidor, Texas, the myth soon became a nightmare. Despite their efforts to assimilate quietly, they were subjected for months to Ku Klux Klan threats and racial epithets shouted from passing cars. Unable to endure the unremittingly hostile atmosphere, they decided to leave.

The illusion of choice also creates a pedagogy of entrapment that makes it undemocratic to argue against school choice. Thus school choice becomes part of a discourse that brooks no dissension or argument, for to argue against it is to deny democracy. The hidden curriculum of school choice consists of taking precious resources from poor schools that are on the verge of bankruptcy to support private or well-to-do public schools. For example, at the same time that the Brockton, Massachusetts, public schools terminated the contract of 120 teachers due to a draconian budget cut, the system shifted approximately $1 million to support middle-class Brockton students who chose to enroll in the more affluent Avon public schools nearby. Although the Avon schools benefited greatly from the school choice windfall, they did not welcome equally all students from Brockton. When a Brockton special education student decided to defy his rejection by the Avon schools, the principal stood by the door on the first day of class to prevent this student, accompanied by his parents, from entering the school building. This episode provides a glimpse of possible future behavior by the Avon schools if a large number of Brockton's subordinated students pick an Avon school as their school of choice. The school choice discourse also eclipses the more fundamental issue of educational funding inequity. . . .

If we critically deconstruct our seemingly democratic society, we begin to understand how the ideological construction of ethnicity and race has played an important role in the reproduction and reinscription of undemocratic structures and power relations along racial, ethnic, cultural, class, and linguistic lines. Thus, it is imperative that we describe and analyze the historical and social conditions of the United States in order to understand how this ideology produces and reproduces inequalities through invisible institutional mechanisms. Central to these hidden mechanisms, language has played a pivotal role in the production and reproduction of distorted realities.

Language and the Construction of Racism

Given the sophisticated use of language in the social construction of the "other" in dehumanizing cultural subjects, we feel that educators need to become "cultural brokers" to help create a psychologically beneficial pedagogical space for all students. Educators also need to make sure that they do not teach a form of literacy that gives learners a lasting experience of subordination. We need to understand that language is the only effective tool for us to deconstruct the web of ideological manipulation that makes the white cultural and ethnic group invisible and outside the realm of study.

Educators, particularly those working with multilingual and multicultural students, need to understand how discourses, according to linguist Oliver Reboul, are very often anchored in shock words, terms or expressions produced by themselves [which], due to their strong connotations, provoke a reaction no matter what sentence within which they are inserted.[11]

In other words, these terms, expressions, and words have a positive association, almost independent of their meanings. For example, in the present discussion of welfare reform, the word "reform" provokes a positive effect that forces most middle-class white individuals to leave its meaning, in different contexts, unexamined. Who in the white-dominated middle class would oppose reforming a welfare system they believe only benefits lazy individuals living off of those who work hard to pay taxes? Who in this segment of the middle class would oppose reforming what Patrick Buchanan characterizes as a "social catastrophe" and as "Great Society programs not only [responsible] for financial losses but also for the drop in high school test scores, drug problems and a generation of children and youth with no fathers, no faith and no dreams other than the lure of the streets."[12]

Thus, "welfare reform for the poor" represents a positive shock phrase to the majority of white middle-class individuals, who feel put upon by paying high taxes to, in their view, support lazy individuals who are poor because they do not want to work. When one points out that a higher percentage of their taxes goes to support welfare for the rich, the cry is uniform, immediate, and aggressive: there is no room in the United States for incitement of class warfare. When the call is to reform welfare for the rich, the reaction is as swift as it is disingenuous. By changing the context of welfare reform from the poor to the rich, the shock-word impact changes accordingly, from a positive to a negative effect. Let's examine some positions taken by politicians and policymakers with respect to class warfare:

- Alfonse M. D'Amato, Republican senator from New York, set the tone: "There is something that I think is very dangerous taking place in this nation. Let me tell you what it is. It is class warfare under the theory of 'let's get the rich guy, the richest 1 percent.' So we set them up, target them. Those are the people we are going to get."
- William S. Cohen, Republican senator from Maine, put it this way: "We are talking about taxing the rich. Once again, we are engaging in classic class warfare.
- Bob Dole, former Republican senator from Kansas: "I do not know how long we can continue that kind of class warfare."
- Slade Gordon, Republican senator from Washington: "While reducing the budget deficit may be the most important issue before this Congress, the president and his allies in Congress are offering this country what amounts to class warfare. I object to these higher taxes."
- Robert K. Dornan, former Republican representative from California, said: "To sell this program of higher taxes, Clinton and his liberal allies here in the House have turned to the standard liberal theme of class warfare, though they have couched it in terms of 'progressivity,' 'fairness,' and 'equality.'"
- Jim Bunning, Republican representative from Kentucky, labeled the legislation "a historic class warfare scheme."
- Gerald B. H. Solomon, Republican representative from New York, observed: "As young Russians cover Marx's statue in Moscow with flippant slogans such as 'workers of the world, forgive me,' America is awash in the Marx-Leninesque rhetoric of class warfare."[13]

These politicians are correct in stating that we have ongoing class warfare in the United States, but it is actually warfare on the middle class and the poor, not on the rich, as they claim. Since the early 1960s, there has been a progressive change in the tax code that enriches the upper class while eroding the economic base of the middle and lower classes.[14] This transfer of wealth from the poor and middle classes to the upper class has created an enormous gap between a small elite and a growing sea of poverty. For example, 2 percent of the U.S. upper class controls 48 percent of the nation's wealth, while 51 percent of African-American children live in poverty.[15] Upon close examination of organizations benefiting from the present tax code, we soon realize how the policymakers have insistently waged class warfare that benefits large corporations. For example:

- The Chase Manhattan Corporation, based in New York, is the parent company of Chase Manhattan Bank, the global banking institution. For the years 1991 and 1992, Chase reported income before taxes of $1.5 billion. The company paid $25 million in income tax, which represents a tax rate of 1.7 percent. The official corporate tax rate in those years was 34 percent.
- The Ogden Corporation, diversified supplier of aviation, building, and waste management services, reported income before taxes of $217 million. The

company paid less than $200,000 in taxes. Given the rate of $1 being paid for every $1,085 earned by the Ogden corporation, if this were the case for a working class family of four earning $25,000 a year, they would be proportionally responsible for paying approximately $25 in taxes each year.

• While the very rich corporations paid a minuscule percentage of their reported income in taxes, individuals with incomes between $13,000 and $15,000 paid taxes at a rate of 7.2 percent, or four times the Chase rate.[16]

As we can see, the power of ideology is so insidious that the unanalyzed positive association of shock words such as "welfare reform" is often accepted by the very people who are in a position to be adversely affected by such reform. Thus, many working-class white people are misled by the positive illusion of "welfare reform" without realizing that they themselves are, perhaps, one paycheck away form benefiting from the very social safety net they want reformed or destroyed. In an age of institutional downsizing (which is a euphemism for corporate greed and maximization of profit), the economic stability of both the white middle and working classes is fast disappearing, thus creating an even more urgent need to make horizontal the economic oppression that is eating away their once more or less secure economic status. By this, we mean that both the white middle and working classes need a scapegoat in order to blame the "other" for their present economic insecurities.

Unfortunately, the same ideology that anchors its discourse on the positive effect of shock words also prevents us from having access to the subtext containing the opposite meaning of the illusory "reality." It is for this reason that conservative politicians who propose welfare reform as a panacea for all the economic ills of our society will not tolerate a counterresponse that challenges the false assumption that welfare recipients are the cause of the nation's economic problems. For welfare reform to be equally exercised, it would have to include welfare reform for the rich, who are most responsible for exacerbating the already huge gap between themselves and the poor. Since discussion concerning welfare reform for the rich is beyond question, the only way to rationalize support for welfare reform is to stay at the level of the positive effect of the shock word that often obfuscates the reality. . . .

The dominant discourse uses the presence of taboo words such as "class" and "oppression" to dismiss a counterdiscourse that challenges the falsification of reality. Thus, to call for welfare reform for the rich is immediately dismissed as "class warfare," a taboo concept not in keeping with the myth that the United States is a classless society. In fact, the ideological power of this myth is so strong that policymakers, the media, and educators can refer to the "working class" being pressured by foreign imports or a "middle class" overburdened by taxes, while simultaneously denying the existence of class differences in the United States. If in fact we live in a classless society, why do we constantly refer to the existence of the working class versus the middle class? What is omitted from the dominant discourse is the existence of the term "upper class." As a substitute, the dominant discourse creates euphemisms such as "rich," "well-to-do," and "affluent." By closing the link between the working, middle, and upper classes, it would be impossible to sustain the myth that we live in a classless society. Therefore, it is important that the dominant discourse suppress the term "upper class" and, in so doing, deny its existence. . . .

What becomes clear through our discussion is that our "democracy" remains paralyzed by a historical legacy that has bequeathed to us rampant social inequality along the lines of ethnicity and race. . . .

NOTES

1. James Baldwin, *The Price of the Ticket: Collected Nonfiction 1948–1985* (New York: St. Martin's/MAREK), p. 409.

2. Derrick Z. Jackson, "Muted Voices in the Newsroom," *Boston Globe*, September 2, 1993, p. 15.

3. Michael Rezendes, "Declaring 'Cultural War': Buchanan Opens '96 Run," *Boston Globe*, March 21, 1995, p. 1.

4. Steven Randall, Jim Naureckus, and Jeff Cohen, *The Way Things Ought to Be: Rush Limbaugh's Reign of Error* (New York: New Press, 1995), pp. 47–54.

5. Randall et al., *The Way Things Ought to Be*, p. 10.

6. Derrick Jackson, "The Assassination of Affirmative Action," *Boston Globe*, March 22, 1995, p. 13.

7. Ibid.

8. bell hooks, Gloria Steinem, Urvashi Vaid, and Naomi Wolf, "Let's Get Real About Feminism: The Backlash, the Myths, the Movement," *Ms.*, September/October 1993, p. 39.

9. Jackson, "The Assassination of Affirmative Action," p. 13.

10. Peter Applebone, "Goals Unmet, Duke Reveals the Perils in Effort to Increase Black Faculty," *New York Times*, September 19, 1993, p. 1.

11. Oliver Reboul, *Lenguage e Ideologia* (Mexico City: Fondo de Cultura Economica, 1986), p. 116.

12. Adam Pertman, "Buchanan Announces Presidential Candidacy," *Boston Globe*, December 15, 1991, p. 1.

13. Donald I. Bartlett and James B. Steele, *America: Who Really Pays the Taxes?* (New York: Simon & Schuster, 1994), p. 93.

14. Robert Kuttner, "The Rewards of Our Labor Are Increasingly Unequal," *Boston Globe*, September 4, 1995, p. 15.

15. Donaldo Macedo, *Literacies of Power: What Americans Are Not Allowed to Know* (Boulder, CO: Westview Press, 1994), pp. 42–43.

16. Ibid.

Suggestions for Further Reading

Basow, Susan. *Gender: Stereotypes and Roles.* Pacific Grove, CA: Brooks/Cole
Publishing, 1992.

Brumberg, Joan Jacobs. *The Body Project. An Intimate History of American Girls.* New
York: Random House, 1997.

Cole, David. *No Equal Justice: Race and Class in the American Criminal Justice System.*
New York: The New Press, 1999.

Goings, Kenneth W. *Mammy and Uncle Mose: Black Collectibles and American
Stereotyping.* Bloomington: Indiana University Press, 1994.

Harding, S., and M. B. Hintikka. *Discovering Reality: Feminist Perspectives on
Epistemology, Metaphysics, Methodology, and Philosophy of Science.* Boston:
D. Reidel Publishing, 1983.

Holtzman, Linda. *Media Messages: What Film, Television, and Popular Music Teach Us
about Race, Class, Gender, and Sexual Orientation.* Armonk, NY: M.E. Sharp, 2000.

hooks, bell. *Teaching to Transgress: Education as the Practice of Freedom.* New York:
Routledge, 1994.

Kilbourne, Jean. *Deadly Persuasion: Why Women and Girls Must Fight the Addictive
Power of Advertising.* New York: Free Press, 1999.

Kramarae, C., M. Schultz, and W. M. O'Barr, eds. *Language and Power.* Beverly Hills,
CA: Sage Press, 1984.

Lee, Martin A., and Norman Solomon. *Unreliable Sources.* New York: Lyle Stuart, 1990.

Loewen, James. *Lies My Teacher Told Me.* New York: Touchstone Books, 1996.

Mazzocco, Dennis W. *Networks of Power: Corporate TV's Threat to Democracy.* Boston:
South End Press, 1994.

Oakes, J. *Keeping Track: How Schools Structure Inequality.* New Haven, CT: Yale
University Press, 1985.

Orenstein, Peggy. *School Girls.* New York: Doubleday, 1994.

Parenti, Michael. *Inventing Reality.* New York: St. Martin's Press, 1986.

Sadker, Myra, and David Sadker. *Failing at Fairness: How America's Schools Cheat
Girls.* New York: Scribner's, 1994.

Silliman, Jane, and Anannya Bhattacharjee. *Policing the National Body: Race, Gender,
and Criminalization.* Boston: South End, 2002.

Spender, Dale. *Man Made Language,* 2d ed. Boston: Routledge and Kegan Paul, 1985.

Thompson, Becky W. *A Hunger So Wide and So Deep.* Minneapolis: University of
Minnesota Press, 1994.

Wolf, Naomi. *The Beauty Myth.* New York: Doubleday Anchor, 1992.

PART VIII

Making a Difference:
Social Activism

AN ADEQUATE UNDERSTANDING OF THE NATURE and causes of race, class, and gender oppression is a critical first step toward moving beyond them. Solutions to problems are generated, at least in part, by the way we pose them. That is why so much of this book is devoted to defining and analyzing the nature of these systems of oppression. Only when we appreciate the subtle and complex factors that operate together to create a society in which wealth, privilege, and opportunity are unequally divided will we be able to formulate viable proposals for bringing about social change.

What, then, have the selections in this book told us about racism, sexism, heterosexism, and class divisions? First, that there is no single cause. Eliminating these forms of oppression will involve changes at the personal, social, political, and economic levels. It will require us to think differently about ourselves and others and see the world through new categories. We will have to learn to pay close attention to our attitudes and behavior and ask what values and what kinds of relationships are being created and maintained, both consciously and unconsciously, by them. We will have to reevaluate virtually every institution in society and critically appraise the ways in which those institutions, intentionally or unintentionally, privilege some and disadvantage others in the course of what we take to be their normal methods of operation. As we identify the ways in which our society reproduces the forms of inequality and privilege that we have been studying, we will have to act to change them. In short, we must scrutinize every aspect of economic, political, and social life with a view to asking whose interests are served and whose are denied when the world is organized in this way.

As many of the readings in this book make clear, significant and lasting changes in our society will only come about when each of us assumes responsibility for making a difference. Racism, sexism, class inequities, and heterosexism and homophobia are everybody's problems. They undermine the quality of life for all of us, ironically, even for those people who seem, at least in the short run, to profit from them. While the enormity of the work to be done can seem overwhelming, in Selection 116 Andrea Ayvazian suggests that one way to overcome a sense of immobilization is to become an ally of those who are oppressed. According to Ayvazian, "an ally is a member of a dominant group in our society who works to dismantle any form of oppression from which she or he receives the benefit." By acting consciously and deliberately to challenge oppression and to make privilege visible, allies provide role models for us all and demonstrate ways in which each of us can act as a powerful agent of change. Several of the articles that follow provide concrete examples of what this might mean.

A very concrete way that those of us who are white can own the race problem and take steps toward solving it is suggested by Fletcher Blanchard in Selection 117. Blanchard reports on a study he did that showed the importance and value of condemning racist harassment whenever we come upon it. In his study, college students who overheard someone else speak out against racism were much more likely to express strong anti-racist views themselves. He concludes that "each of us can affect others' concern for eliminating racism by taking strong public stands condemning bigotry on campuses." Selection 118 by Michael Bronski expresses a similar concern for the need to stand up to and speak out against anti-gay violence. Bronski maintains that since anti-gay hatred, like all hatred, is learned, violence against lesbian women and gay men will continue until all of us own the problem and act to end it. Some of the strategies Bronski advocates are not turning a deaf ear when people use the term "fag" or tell homophobic jokes, supporting education that includes positive information about lesbians and gays, and providing lesbian and gay friends and relatives with support.

Several of the articles that follow describe specific ways in which college students today are working for social change by organizing against injustice and inequality. Selection 119 tells how students at Rice University decided to take a stand against homophobia and in support of gay, lesbian, bisexual, and transgendered students. Selections 120 and 121 describe the United Students Against Sweatshops campaign, which has been so successful in championing the rights of workers all around the globe. This campaign, which has pitted students against major corporations like Nike and Champion, shows what can happen when students band together to organize their campuses and apply pressure to end exploitation. For more and current information about this campaign go to their website: <www.usasnet.org>. Another important initiative has been student participation in the Taco Bell boycott. Selection 122 talks about the ways in which college students are contributing to this national campaign in support of economic justice for the immigrant farm workers who pick the tomatoes used by the fast-food giant. More information is available at <www.ciw-online.org>. Selection 123 speaks directly to one of the issues underlying these campaigns by arguing that the growing economic inequality that characterizes U.S. society is neither an unavoidable consequence of economic growth, as some would have us believe, nor a necessary prerequisite for that growth, as other argue.

One of the most exciting and successful recent union organizing campaigns has been the drive to organize janitors carried out by Service Employees International Union (SEIU) Local 1877 in Los Angeles. Selection 124 describes the drive in detail and suggests ways in which the tactics it employed can provide models for organizing other sectors of the labor movement and the community. It is followed by an article that takes a look at how community organizations such as People United for a Better Oakland (PUEBLA) and the Laotian Organizing Project (LOP) are making culture and community central to the process as they seek out new organizing paradigms that simultaneously empower and nourish the communities they bring together.

Part VIII of the book and our study ends with a poem by Aurora Levins Morales, "Child of the Americas," which encourages us to look to the future and helps us envision a new paradigm, one that embraces difference and sees in it the basis for creating a new sense of unity.

Interrupting the Cycle of Oppression:
The Role of Allies as Agents of Change

Andrea Ayvazian

Many of us feel overwhelmed when we consider the many forms of systemic oppression that are so pervasive in American society today. We become immobilized, uncertain about what actions we can take to interrupt the cycles of oppression and violence that intrude on our everyday lives. One way to overcome this sense of immobilization is to assume the role of an ally. Learning about this role—one that each and every one of us is capable of assuming—can offer us new ways of behaving and a new source of hope.

Through the years, experience has taught us that isolated and episodic actions—even dramatic, media-grabbing events—rarely produce more than a temporary blip on the screen. What does seem to create real and lasting change is highly-motivated individuals—usually only a handful at first—who are so clear and consistent on an issue that they serve as a heartbeat in a community, steadily sending out waves that touch and change those in their path. These change agents or allies have such a powerful impact because their actions embody the values they profess: their behavior and beliefs are congruent.

What Is an Ally?

An ally is a member of a dominant group in our society who works to dismantle any form of oppression from which she or he receives the benefit. Allied behavior means taking personal responsibility for the changes we know are needed in our society, and so often ignore or leave to others to deal with. Allied behavior is intentional, overt, consistent activity that challenges prevailing patterns of oppression, makes privileges that are so often invisible visible, and facilitates the empowerment of persons targeted by oppression.

From *Fellowship* (January–February 1995). Reprinted with the permission of Rev. Dr. Andrea Ayvazian, Dean of Religious Life, Mount Holyoke College, South Hadley, MA.

I use the term "oppresion" to describe the combination of prejudice plus access to social, political, and economic power on the part of a dominant group. Racism, a core component of oppression, has been defined by David Wellman as a system of advantage based on race. Wellman's definition can be altered slightly to describe every other form of oppression. Hence we can say that sexism is a system of advantage based on gender, that heterosexism is a system of advantge based on sexual orientation, and so on. In each form of oppression there is a dominant group—the one that receives the unearned advantage, benefit, or privilege—and a targeted group—the one that is denied that advantage, benefit, or privilege. We know the litany of dominants: white people, males, Christians, heterosexuals, able-bodied people, those in their middle years, and those who are middle or upper class.

We also know that everyone has multiple social identities. We are all dominant and targeted simultaneously. I, for instance, am simultaneously dominant as a white person and targeted as a woman. A white able-bodied man may be dominant in those categories, but targeted as a Jew or Muslim or as a gay person. Some people are, at some point in their lives, entirely dominant; but if they are, they won't be forever. Even a white, able-bodied, heterosexual, Christian male will literally grow out of his total dominance if he reaches old age.

When we consider the different manifestations of systematic oppression and find ourselves in any of the categories where we are dominant—and therefore receive the unearned advantages that accrue to that position of advantage—we have the potential to be remarkably powerful agents of change as allies. Allies are whites who identify as anti-racists, men who work to dismantle sexism, able-bodied people who are active in the disability rights movement, Christians who combat anti-Semitism and other forms of religious prejudice. Allied behavior usually involves talking to other dominants about their behavior: whites confronting other whites on issues of racism, men organizing with other men to combat sexism, and so on. Allied behavior is clear action aimed at dismantling the oppression of others in areas where you yourself benefit—it is proactive, intentional, and often involves taking a risk.

To tether these principles to everyday reality, just think of the group Parents, Families and Friends of Lesbians and Gays (PFLAG) as the perfect example of allied behavior. PFLAG is an organization of (mainly) heterosexuals who organize support groups and engage in advocacy and education among other heterosexuals around issues of gay and lesbian liberation. PFLAG speakers can be heard in houses of worship, schools, and civic organizations discussing their own commitment to securing gay and lesbian civil rights. Because they are heterosexuals speaking (usually) to other heterosexuals, they often have a significant impact.

The anti-racism trainer Kenneth Jones, an African-American, refers to allied behavior as "being at my back." He has said to me, "Andrea, I know you are at my back on the issue of race equity—you're talking to white people who cannot hear me on this topic, you're out there raising these issues repeatedly, you're organizing with other whites to stand up to racism. And I'm at your back. I'm raising issues of gender equity with men, I am talking to men who cannot hear you, I've made a commitment to combat sexism."

Available to each one of us in the categories where we are dominant is the proud and honorable role of ally: the opportunity to raise hell with others like us and to interrupt the cycle of oppression. Because of our very privilege, we have the potential to stir up good trouble, to challenge the status quo, and to inspire real and lasting change. William Stickland, an aide to Jesse Jackson, once said: "When a critical mass of white people join together, rise up, and shout a thunderous 'No' to racism, we will actually alter the course of history."

Reducing Violence

When I ponder the tremendous change a national network of allies can make in this country, I think not only of issues of equity and empowerment, but also of how our work could lead to diminishing levels of violence in our society. Let us consider for a moment the critical connection between oppression and violence on one hand, and the potential role of allied behavior in combating violence on the other.

A major source of violence in our society is the persistent inequity between dominant and targeted groups. Recall that oppression is kept in place by two factors:

1. Ideology, or the propagation of doctrines that purport to legitimize inequality; and
2. Violence (or the threat of violence) by the dominant group against the targeted group.

The violence associated with each form of systemic oppression noticeably decreases when allies (or dominants) rise up and shout a thunderous "No" to the perpetuation of these inequities. Because members of the dominant group are conferred with considerable social power and privilege, they carry significant authority when confronting perpetrators of violence in their own group—when whites deter other whites from using violence against people of color, when heterosexuals act to prevent gay bashing, and so on.

Research studies have confirmed what observers and allies have been saying for years: that when a woman is the victim of ongoing, violent domestic abuse, it makes no difference to her chances of survival if she has counseling, takes out a restraining order, or learns to fight back. According to the studies, the only factor that statistically increases a woman's chances of survival is if the victimizer himself is exposed to direct and ongoing anti-battering intervention.

These studies have inspired the creation of model mentoring programs in places like Quincy, Massachusetts, Duluth, Minnesota, and New York City—programs in which men prone to violence against women work with other men through a series of organized interventions. The success of these programs has demonstrated that it is actually possible to interrupt and stop the cycle of violence among batterers. In 1992, for instance, the model program in Quincy helped cut the incidence of domestic homicide to zero. The Batterers Anonymous groups, in which men who are former perpetrators work with men who are current batterers, have also had remarkable success in breaking the habit of violence. These groups are allied behavior made manifest; their success in reducing the incidence of violence against women is now statistically proven.

In our society, oppression and violence are woven together: one leads to the other, one justifies the other. Furthermore, members of the dominant group who are not perpetrators of violence often collude, through their silence and inactivity, with those who are. Allied behavior is an effective way of interrupting the cycle of violence by breaking the silence that reinforces the cycle, and by promoting a new set of behavior through modeling and mentoring.

Providing Positive Role Models

Not only does allied behavior contribute to an increase in equity and a decrease in violence, but allies provide positive role models that are sorely needed by today's young people. The role of ally offers young people who are white, male, and in other dominant categories a positive, proactive, and proud identity. Rather than feeling guilty, shameful, and immobilized as the "oppressor," whites and other dominants can assume the important and useful role of social change agent. There have been proud allies and change agents throughout the history of this nation, and there are many alive today who can inspire us with their important work.

I often speak in high school classes and assemblies, and in recent years I have taken to doing a little informal survey from the podium. I ask the students if they can name a famous living white racist. Can they? Yes. They often name David Duke—he ran for President in their lifetime—or they sometimes name Senator Jesse Helms; and when I was in the midwest, they named Marge Schott, the owner of the Cincinnati Reds. It does not take long before a hand shoots up, or someone just calls out one of those names.

Following that little exercise, I ask the students, "Can you name a famous living white anti-racist (or civil rights worker, or someone who fights racism)?" Can they? Not very often. Sometimes there is a whisper or two, but generally the room is very quiet. So, recently, I have been saying: forget the famous part. Just name for me any white person you know in your community, or someone you have heard of, who has taken a stand against racism. Can they? Sometimes. Occasionally someone says "my mom," or "my dad." I have also heard "my rabbi, my teacher, my minister." But not often enough.

I believe that it is difficult for young people to grow up and become something they have never heard of. It is hard for a girl to grow up and become a commercial airline pilot if it has never occurred to her that woman can and do fly jet planes. Similarly, it is hard for young people to grow up and fight racism if they have never met anyone who does.

And there *are* many remarkable role models whom we can claim with pride, and model ourselves after. People like Laura Haviland, who was a conductor on the Underground Railroad and performed unbelievably brave acts while the slave-catchers were right on her trail; Virginia Foster Durr, a southern belle raised with great wealth and privilege who, as an adult, tirelessly drove black workers to and from their jobs during the Montgomery bus boycott; the Rev. James Reeb, who went south during the Mississippi Freedom Summer of 1964 to organize and march; Hodding Carter, Jr., editor and publisher of a newspaper in the Mississippi Delta who used his paper to battle for racial equity and who took considerable heat for his actions. And more: the Grimke sisters, Lucretia Mott, William Lloyd Garrison, John Brown, Viola Liuzzo.

There are also many contemporary anti-racists like Morris Dees, who gave up a lucrative law practice to start the Southern Poverty Law Center and Klan Watch in Alabama and bring white supremacists to trial; Anne Braden, active for decades in the civil rights struggle in Kentucky; Rev. Joseph Barndt, working within the religious community to make individual churches and entire denominations proclaim themselves as anti-racist institutions. And Peggy McIntosh, Judith Katz, and Myles Horton. And so many others. Why don't our young people know these names? If young people knew more about these dedicated allies, perhaps they would be inspired to engage in more anti-racist activities themselves.

Choosing Our Own Roles

We also need to consider our role as allies. In our own communities, would young people, if asked the same questions, call out our names as anti-racists? In areas where we are dominant, is our struggle for equity and justice evident? When we think about our potential role as allies, we need to recall a Quaker expression: "Let your life be your teaching." The Quakers understand that our words carry only so much weight, that it is our actions, our daily behaviors, that tell the true story.

In my own life I struggle with what actions to take, how to make my beliefs and my behaviors congruent. One small step that has had interesting repercussions over the last decade is the fact that my partner (who is male) and I have chosen not to be legally married until gay and lesbian couples can be married and receive the same benefits and legal protection that married heterosexual couples enjoy. A small step, but it has allowed us to talk with folks at the YMCA about their definition of "family" when deciding who qualifies for their "family plan"; to challenge people at Amtrak about why some "family units" receive discounts when traveling together and others do not; and to raise questions in the religious community about who can receive formal sanction for their loving unions and who cannot. These are not earth-shattering steps in the larger picture, but we believe that small steps taken by thousands of people will eventually change the character of our communities.

When we stop colluding and speak out about the unearned privileges we enjoy as members of a dominant group—privileges we have been taught for so long to deny or ignore—we have the potential to undergo and inspire stunning transformation. Consider the words of Gandhi: "As human beings, our greatness lies not so much in being able to remake the world, as in being able to remake ourselves."

In my own community, I have been impressed by the efforts of three middle-aged males who have remade themselves into staunch allies for women. Steven Botkin established the Men's Resource Center in Amherst, Massachusetts twelve years ago and put a commitment to eliminating sexism in its very first mission statement. Another Amherst resident, Michael Burkart, travels nationwide and works with top executives in Fortune 500 companies on the issue of gender equity in their corporations. And Geoff Lobenstine, a social worker who identifies as an anti-sexist male, brings these issues to his work in Holyoke, Massachusetts.

Charlie Parker once said this about music: "Music is your own experience, your thoughts, your wisdom. If you don't live it, it won't come out of your horn." I think the same is true about us in our role as allies—it is our own experience, our thoughts, our wisdom. If we don't live it, it won't come out of our horn.

Preparing for the Long Haul

Now I would be the first to admit that personally and professionally the role of ally is often exhausting. I know that it involves challenges—being an ally is difficult work, and it can often be lonely. We must remember to take care of ourselves along this journey, to sustain our energy and our zest for those ongoing challenges.

We must also remember that it is hard to go it alone: allies need allies. As with any other struggle in our lives, we need supportive people around us to help us to persevere. Other allies will help us take the small, daily steps that will, in time, alter the character of our communities. We know that allied behavior usually consists of small steps and unglamorous work. As Mother Teresa once said: "I don't do any great things. I do small things with great love."

Finally two additional points about us in our role as allies: First, we don't always see the results of our efforts. Sometimes we do, but often we touch and even change lives without ever knowing it. Consequently, we cannot measure our success in quantitative terms. Like waves upon the shore, we are altering the landscape—but exactly how, may be hard to discern.

Doubts inevitably creep up about our effectiveness, about our approach, about the positions we assume or the actions we take. But we move forward, along with the doubts, the uncertainty, and often the lack of visible results. In our office, we have a famous William James quote on the wall to sustain us: "I will act as though what I do makes a difference." And, speaking personally, although my faith gets rattled, I try to act as though what I do does make a difference.

Second, there is no such thing as a perfect ally. Perfection is not our goal. When I asked my colleague Kenneth Jones what stood out for him as the most important characteristic of a strong ally, he said simply: "being consistently conscious." He didn't say "never stumbling," or "never making mistakes." He said:

"being consistently conscious." And so we do our best: taking risks, being smart, making errors, feeling foolish, doing what we believe is right, based on our best judgment at the time. We are imperfect, but we are steady. We are courageous but not faultless. As Lani Guinier said: "It is better to be vaguely right than precisely wrong." If we obsess about looking good instead of doing good, we will get caught in a spiral of ineffective action. Let's not get side-tracked or defeated because we are trying to be perfect.

And so we move ahead, pushing ourselves forward on our growing edge. We know that although none of us are beginners in dealing with issues of oppression and empowerment, none of us are experts either. These issues are too complex, too painful, and too pervasive for us to achieve a state of clarity and closure once and for all. The best we can hope for is to strive each day to be our strongest and clearest selves, transforming the world one individual at a time, one family at a time, one community at a time. May we summon the wisdom to be devoted allies today. May we walk the walk, living as though equity, justice and freedom for all have already arrived.

Like most activists, I carry a dream inside me. As I travel nationwide for my work, I can actually see signs of it becoming true. The dream is that we will create in this country a nonviolent army of allies that will challenge and break the cycle of oppression and usher in a new era of liberation, empowerment, and equity for persons historically targeted by systemic oppression. Within each individual is the potential to effect enormous change. May we move foward, claiming with pride our identities as allies, interrupting the cycle of oppression, and modeling a new way of behaving and believing.

117

Combatting Intentional Bigotry and Inadvertently Racist Acts

Fletcher A. Blanchard

What you say about racial discrimination matters: Your vocal opinions affect what others think and say. A series of experiments that I and my students and colleagues conducted demonstrate that racial prejudice is much more malleable than many researchers, policy makers, and educational leaders believe. In the wake of the verdict in the case of four Los Angeles policemen accused of beating Rodney King and the violence that followed it, the search for ways to lessen the devastating consequences of racism in America has intensified. If we understand that simply overhearing others condemn or condone racial harassment dramatically affects people's reactions to racism, we may be able to help find solutions to tensions and bigotry—both on campuses and in the larger society.

In the experiments we conducted, the first two of which are described in an article in *Psychological Science* (March, 1991), we briefly interviewed students as they walked between classes. In some portions of the experiment, the interviewer also stopped a second person, ostensibly another student but in reality a member of the research team, who offered her programmed opinions first. After hearing someone else condemn racism, college students expressed anti-racist sentiments much more strongly than those who heard someone express equivocal views. However, students who first heard someone condone racism then voiced views that reflected strong acceptance of racism.

The large differences that we observed appeared both when research participants spoke their views publicly and when we measured their opinions more anonymously by asking them to complete a questionaire and return it to the researcher in a sealed envelope. The elasticity of privately held views regarding racism appears to reveal a lack of knowledge about the nature of racism and uncertainty about how institutions and individuals might appropriately respond to expressions of racism.

From *The Chronicle of Higher Education* (May 13, 1992). Reprinted by permission of the author.

I suspect that one of the reasons that opinions about racism are so easily influenced derives from the high level of racial segregation that still characterizes contemporary American society. Indeed, one wonders just how much people's ignorance about racism and lack of contact with other races contributed to the verdict in the King case. Although a recent survey by People for the American Way indicated that many young Americans say they have a friend of another race, most still know little about other racial and ethnic groups.

Public-opinion polls over the last several decades portray largely favorable trends regarding whites' attitudes toward African Americans, but those attitudes and opinions derive from little direct experience. Few white college students have grown up in integrated neighborhoods, attended schools with integrated classrooms, or observed their parents interact in a friendly manner with people of color.

Even fewer of the white students entering college today have had the chance to learn from black teachers, work for black employers, or participate in voluntary activities and organizations where the adult leaders, coaches, or advisers were black. America's campuses constitute the first multiracial social setting encountered by many young people.

As a result, few of the many whites who have reached an honest commitment to egalitarian values have had the opportunity to acquire the full range of interpersonal skills, sensibilities, and knowledge that might allow them to fulfill that commitment. Few, for example, have vicariously experienced the pain felt by a friend who has suffered racial harassment. Few have discovered the ways that everyday language may communicate disrespect for a particular group. Thus the elasticity of reactions to racism appears to reflect the uncertainty that the inexperienced, but well intentioned, bring to their first interracial setting.

Although there has been an alarming increase in racial harassment on campuses and in society at large, the results of opinion polls showing a trend toward more egalitarian racial attitudes among Americans make it difficult to attribute the racist attacks to any increase in racial prejudice among the many. Instead, much of the harassment should be understood to represent open hostility expressed by the strongly prejudiced few. Efforts to reduce racial harassment and enhance tolerance must acknowledge the many who are naive, inexperienced, and often well intentioned, on the one hand, and the few who are genuinely mean spirited, on the other. Strategies that are effective for one group may be less so for the other.

Many colleges and universities are responding to the current wave of racist attacks by creating policies that attempt to define and regulate racial harassment. However, none of the new codes of conduct acknowledges the important differences between the intentional behavior of the committed bigot and the inadvertent behavior of the profoundly inexperienced.

The least controversial variety of code, aimed squarely at the committed bigot, borrows language from federal and state civil-rights statutes and anti-harassment regulations. By narrowly framing the boundaries of unacceptable behavior, this approach provides a basis for punishing some behavior of the mean-spirited few.

Unfortunately, the federal and state regulations that define and bar racial harassment are neither as articulate nor as encompassing as those governing sexual harassment. Until state and federal rules barring racial harassment recognize how seemingly less-odious behaviors can accumulate to produce an atmosphere of intimidation, codes of conduct that rely on them will restrain only the most flagrant forms of attack.

A second approach to regulating racial harassment, aimed squarely at the well-intentioned many, consists of urging civility. Instead of defining the limits of impropriety and barring behavior that oversteps those bounds, civility codes encourage general tolerance and acceptance, leaving it to administrators and adjudicating bodies to apply the rules to particular instances of unacceptable behavior.

These policies rarely offer the specific guidance required by those inexperienced with racism. Little controversy follows the promulgation of such codes. Rather, it more often attends their application to particular instances of objectionable behavior—behavior that falls somewhere between civility and clearly illegal harassment.

A third variety of code attempts to define and forbid a much broader range of impropriety than currently is addressed by federal and most state regulations. The prohibitions often embrace both the intentional behavior of the committed bigot and the careless behavior of those inexperienced with interracial contacts. Although both classes of behavior cause harm, the new policies fail to acknowledge the different motivations of the actors, and thus the need for different remedies.

Most important, it is difficult to write such codes so that they enhance freedom from discrimination but also preserve the broader freedom of speech. These are the policies that have generated the most interesting debate and the most belligerent contention. Some of the opposition has been raised by those who would safeguard the use of racial epithets under the guise of defending First Amendment freedoms. Other opponents have resorted to ridicule and name calling, perhaps to avoid acknowledging the prevalence of racial harassment and bias in our society. The principled portions of the discussion undoubtedly have enhanced both our understanding of the boundaries of free speech and of the causes of contemporary racism.

The principal virtue of all of the codes I have outlined is that each encourages consensus regarding proper conduct. It is this consensus—the shared sense of what is right and what is wrong—that steers social behavior much more effectively than mere rules and regulations. Articulate codes that are widely distributed and discussed can contribute to a consensus that rejects bigotry.

No one of these three strategies for regulating racism is complete, however. The most effective policies must combine elements of all three approaches. The best policies must proscribe illegal racial harassment, thereby providing punishment for the mean-spirited few, as well as prescribe expectations for tolerance and respect, thereby providing guidance for the inexperienced many. The best policies also will step beyond the boundaries of current statutes, recognizing, for example, that racial epithets directed at individuals are intolerable in humane society.

By linking codes of conduct with statements of academic mission, effective policies signal a strong institutional commitment to the protection of civil rights. Yet no code of conduct, no matter how comprehensively it is framed, can create by itself the sort of accepting and respectful communities that we need.

Other forms of attention to the discriminatory consequences of behavior are required if colleges and universities are to become the sort of educational settings where everyone can thrive. The fact that people of color often find themselves numerically underrepresented in academic institutions exaggerates the discomfort and pain that arise out of insensitive acts.

Consider an organization in which 10 percent of the people are black and 90 percent are white. Imagine a department of that organization in which 10 people work, nine of whom are white and one of whom is black. Imagine further that all nine of the whites perceive themselves to be unprejudiced and have adopted a genuine commitment to egalitarian values. If each of those well-intentioned whites makes only one insensitive "mistake" a month, the one black target of the nine naive whites would experience, on average, some hurtful and isolating behavior every third day.

The well-intentioned white is aware of only one insensitive event over the last month—if, in fact, he or she has been informed of that lapse. But the personal experience of the person of color reflects a high rate of discriminatory behavior. Reduce the proportion of African Americans or add an intentional racist and the resulting setting becomes even more intolerable. This imbalance in perceptions of the rate of discrimination and insensitivity exacerbates the potential for misunderstanding.

Until college students bring with them from high school more extensive experience with interracial interaction, massive commitments to remedial education and training will be required to reduce the rate of unintentional harm caused by these "interracially incompetent" people. I suspect that the best educational techniques will take advantage of the positive motivation to "do the right thing" that characterizes most entering students—by emphasizing vivid and concrete examples of the hurtful and harmful behavior of the naive. One-shot "workshops" presented during first-year orientation probably will not be sufficient. Rather, activities or programs that foster the early formation of strong interracial friendships will contribute most to intergroup understanding.

Until inexperienced students master the behaviors that reflect their egalitarian commitments, we must maintain havens for minority students that protect them from intentional harassment and naive disrespect, including cultural centers and organizations for particular minority groups. By also introducing programs and activities that foster formation of strong interracial friendships, it may be possible, over time, to reduce the need for safe havens.

It is solid interracial friendships that help insulate targets of harassment from the most devastating consequences of anonymous racist attacks and exaggerated feelings of isolation. Such friendships also will provide the basis for the sort of interracial learning that has been absent from the experience of many who enter college today.

The research that I described at the outset suggests that each of us can affect others' concern for eliminating racism by taking strong public stands condemning bigotry on campuses. Just as anti-smoking attitudes among non-smokers eventually led to regulations banning smoking in public places, a broad consensus that eschews bigotry surely can reduce the display of intentional bias and inadvertent discriminatory behavior on campuses.

Our research suggests that no one need wait for administrators to take the lead. Each of us can influence each other by criticizing the willful bigotry of the mean-spirited few and gently guiding the well-intentioned efforts of the inexperienced many.

118

Confronting Anti-Gay Violence

Michael Bronski

Several weeks ago I was walking with my lover in a quiet neighborhood in Cambridge, Massachusetts, on our way to a late afternoon movie. We were holding hands in an offhanded sort of way, chatting together, when a group of young teens sitting on a front stoop across the street (the oldest was probably 14, the youngest maybe 12) yelled "faggot"; then they laughed and threw some plastic soda bottles at us before they ran off. We thought for a moment of chasing and confronting them— this didn't seem particularly dangerous and I have always felt that confronting this sort of harassment, if not immediately dangerous, is always better than ignoring it— but they were already a block away and it did not seem worth the time or energy. We went off to the movies, but the incident was deeply disquieting. Gay men and lesbians have always been aware of anti-gay violence. It becomes a way of life, just as it is for many people of color in America and for women making their way through the world everyday. In the past months we have heard—in the mainstream media—that there is a new focus on gay bashing. And the message here is that this new focus will bring about a new understanding and the end to it. Aside from the Matthew Shepard murder in Laramie, Wyoming, by Russell Henderson and Aaron McKinney, both 21, last October other murders of gay people have been deemed newsworthy:

On January 17 Kevin Tryals and Laaron Morris of Galveston, Texas, were found in a burning car on a dead-end road outside of city limits. Both bodies were

ZNet Commentary, April 9, 1999.

severely burned. The medical examiner's office ruled that both men were dead before the car was ignited and that both men died from multiple gunshot wounds. Police have ruled out robbery and are treating the murders as anti-gay violence.

On February 20 the burned remains of Billy Jack Gaither, 39, a factory worker were discovered in Sylacauga, a small town in Alabama. He had been beaten to death (or near death) with an ax handle and thrown onto a stack of tires and set afire. His attackers, 21-year-old Charles Butler and 25-year-old Steven Mullins, claim he made a pass at them.

On March 1, the severed head of Henry Edward Northington, 39, was found on a pathway to a park known as a gay men's cruising spot outside of Alexandria, Virginia. Northington was homeless and gay. No one has been arrested.

On March 12, in Los Angeles, Juan Chavez, 34, pleaded guilty of murdering five gay men by luring them to their homes supposedly for sex and then robbing and strangling them. He also was accused of taking the victims' cars after killing them. He claimed he commited the murders to stop the spread of AIDS.

On March 15 the body of Michael Barber, 56, was discovered in his apartment in Fort Lauderdale, Florida, encased in a zippered plastic bag. He had died of multiple stab wounds. Barber, an ex-Marine, had worked as a gardener in the area. Six months ago Charles Squires, 64, of nearby Wilton Manors, Florida, was found stabbed to death and wrapped in plastic inside his home. Police are treating both as anti-gay crimes.

On March 19, Bradley Davis, 24, of San Francisco, was found bleeding and semiconscious between two parked cars at 12:15 A.M. near 18th and Castro Streets by police officers who were called to the scene. Officers arrested three suspects — Ban Doc Im, 21; Henry Sai Kwong, 19; Thang Cao Truong, 18 — who were seen by witnesses attacking Davis after standing on Castro shouting anti-gay and anti–African American epithets. There is no doubt that since the Shepard murder anti-gay violence has been deemed more newsworthy, while some analysts are claiming that violence against gay, lesbian, and transgendered people is rising. The Triangle Foundation, a gay rights advocacy group in Detroit, documented two Michigan anti-gay murders in 1997 and six in 1998; by March of 1999, they were investigating five. But the reality is that there have always been an enormous number of murders, beatings, attacks, and harassments; what has changed are both the rate of reporting and the attention of the media. Generally speaking, queer commentators and activists see this as a positive trend; it seems to me that increased visibility for homophobic violence is only a first, albeit important, but rather small step. The enormous coverage given to the Shepard murder — and we will see much more once the trial starts — is, in itself, a study of what can go wrong. It is clear that Matthew Shepard's place as a media star was predicated on several factors: his murder was brutal and shocking, and his age, race, good looks, and class status made him the perfect victim for a national media looking for a good story. But will this coverage have any lasting effect on how both the media and public policy deal with anti-gay violence? If Matthew Shepard had been an African American teenage hustler, the story would have been different: there would not have been a story. Are the media simply going to go for the most sensational stories of anti-gay violence: beheadings, public burnings, dead bodies in zippered bags? The only reason the press reported on the Castro Street beating was that it took place in the dead-center of the most famous public gay neighborhood in the world.

Anywhere else it would not be news. In the past three decades U.S. culture has made some significant changes in how some issues about violence and discrimination are perceived and acted upon. Rape (although it still occurs all the time) is now treated more seriously by the police and the courts. The same is true of domestic violence. As recent events in New York have shown, the uphill, and ferociously waged, battle to have police violence against people of color is alive, well, and even making some progress. These changes all came about because of committed, sustained grass-roots organizing, an insistence that the issues be taken seriously—as a moral imperative—and a demand that the popular media both pay attention and act more responsibly. But will this coverage of anti-gay violence engender substantive change? If it has any chance to, it must move beyond simple sentimentalization and pity for "nice" victims: the bulk of reported anti-gay assaults in Manhattan, for instance, are faced by African American and Latino transgendered sex workers. The other thing that has to change is that anti-gay violence cannot continue to be viewed outside of a broader political and social context of the personal lives of heterosexuals. This may be beginning to happen. An editorial in the *St. Louis Dispatch* on March 10 noted "the ideas allowed to fester into the kind of murderous hatred that killed Gaither and Shepard . . . sprouted long before any blows were struck, any triggers were pulled, any fires were set. Like all hatred, anti-gay hatred is learned. Don't turn a deaf ear when your kid calls another child a 'fag' on the playground. Don't laugh at homophobic jokes in the office. Support education that includes positive information on gays and lesbians. Let gay and lesbian acquaintances or friends or relatives know they have your support. To condemn the brutal slayings of these men without examining the routine homophobia in our daily lives would by hypocrisy." I have deep suspicions of the ability of the mainstream media to effect any positive social change. I think of the young men— boys, really—who shouted and threw a bottle at me in the emblematically liberal city of Cambridge. I am old enough to be their grandfather, my lover is old enough to be their father. The men—boys?—accused of killing the "innocent" Matthew Shepard were his age. How do we work on building a common consensus that hating gay people enough to attack them is wrong in a culture that supports, or doesn't care about, the most murderous aspects of U.S. foreign policy? How do we discuss "accepting"—never mind valuing—homosexuality in a country in which the complexity of race is still, for the most part, undiscussable? Gay and lesbian activists have been organizing around violence issues for decades, and to a large degree they have not been taken seriously by many other political, religious, or social institutions. It is one thing to advise that men and women not laugh at fag jokes in the office, but we have to realize that not laughing at—or rebuking the teller of—fag jokes often labels someone a fag himself. One of the main problems in fighting anti-gay prejudice is that the specter of homosexuality is everywhere, implicating anyone who counters the sentiment. The mainstream press's coverage of anti-gay violence may be a beginning of a more complex, fruitful public discourse, but it is only one facet of how the problem is confronted. Gay activists have to begin, or continue, building coalitions with other anti-violence and social action groups. Individuals doing political work on the left also have to take more time and energy in examining the myriad ways sexuality—in all its manifestations—impacts on social, national, and international policies and politics. In the meantime I am still going to hold my lover's hand wherever and whenever I want to. But I am also going to watch my back and be more purposeful in challenging people when faced with harassment or violence. If we had chased and confronted those boys, they might have thought twice before doing this again.

119

Rice Shirts Make More Than Fashion Statement

Ron Nissimov

Responding to controversial comments attributed to Rice University football coach Ken Hatfield, scores of students showed up at Saturday's homecoming game wearing bright yellow T-shirts that said, "I AM NOT HOMOPHOBIC."

"We wanted to show Rice University supports a nondiscrimination policy and also supports gay athletes," said Christel Miller, a sophomore from Los Angeles who is vice president of Pride!, a student organization for gay, lesbian, bisexual and transgender students.

Many Rice students, faculty and alumni were angered by statements attributed to Hatfield in the Nov. 1 issue of *The Chronicle of Higher Education*, a weekly journal of academia. Reporter Jennifer Jacobson paraphrased Hatfield as saying he "probably would think hard" about kicking gay athletes off his team. Hatfield, who is active in the Fellowship of Christian Athletes, was also paraphrased as saying that homosexuality conflicts with his devout Christian beliefs. When asked what he would tell a gay player who comes out, Hatfield was quoted as saying that he would ask, "What happened? What changed since we recruited you? When did this come about?"

Miller said a batch of 100 shirts was sold in one hour Friday, and another batch of 100 was made before Saturday's game. Students distributing the shirts asked for a $2 donation.

"I feel Coach Hatfield has a right to voice his beliefs, but he should not have made the statements in the context of representing the university," said Patrick MacAlpine, a sophomore from Dexter, Mich., who also wore the T-shirt in the student stands on the sunny, windy afternoon.

Not all students felt Hatfield had done anything wrong.

Cordon DeKock, a freshman from Enid, Okla., who was screaming at the visiting University of Hawaii team as a member of the "Rice Rally Club," said the comments "have been blown way out of proportion."

"The coach made comments that were based on his religious beliefs," said DeKock, whose white T-shirt said "Rice Rally Club" on the front and "Beer Me" on the back. "Political correctness is a problem on campus."

Jay Oliphant, a 1981 Rice alumnus who lives in Atlanta, agreed. He bought a yellow T-shirt and cut out the words "NOT HOMOPHOBIC," leaving "I AM" followed by a hole.

"I am a believer in free speech," Oliphant said. "This is classical political correctness run amok. They're taking what should be private and making it public."

But alumnus Jay Grannis of Houston said the problem was precisely that the coach made public statements.

"Hatfield was unwise to say what he did," said Grannis, a 1999 graduate. "As an official of the university, he has to be careful about expressing his personal beliefs if they can be construed as expressing the university's position."

In addition to paying for the T-shirts, Gillis has taken other measures to try to demonstrate that Rice welcomes gay students and athletes, including asking Hatfield to publicly apologize and announcing he would form a presidential advisory committee to explore whether more needs to be done.

After publishing an apology in the weekly journal and telling the *Houston Chronicle* he was incorrectly paraphrased, Hatfield has repeatedly declined to comment on the matter. *The Chronicle of Higher Education* continues to stand by its story.

Sweats and Tears:
A Protest Is Sweeping U.S. Campuses to End the Use of Sweatshops to Produce College-Endorsed Clothes

Simon Birch

It is being dubbed the biggest act of American student unrest since the anti-Vietnam protests of the 1960s. In colleges and universities across the United States students are protesting about the sweatshop factory conditions that they claim are commonplace in the production of university-endorsed clothing.

These factories are found throughout the third world in countries such as Guatemala, Nicaragua and Bangladesh. With more than 220 college and university student groups now members of the umbrella organisation that is coordinating the national campaign, United Students Against Sweatshops, the sweatshop issue is now recognised as the single biggest and fastest-growing campaign within American universities. This year alone university and college students have led 16 separate sit-ins of university buildings.

There is nothing in the UK university system comparable to the American practice of clothing and sports manufacturers providing lucrative sponsorship deals to universities and colleges, something that campaigners cite as one of the main reasons for the campaign's success.

"Students have a more direct relation to sweatshop issues than they do to many other social justice and environmental issues," says Andrew Cornell, a recent graduate from the University of Michigan and sweatshop activist. "By buying clothing and shoes from companies that use sweatshops, students are supporting those companies. People are often more willing to get involved in a campaign that they are tied to personally."

Molly McGrath from the University of Wisconsin sweatshop campaign believes that it is the simplicity of the campaign that has led to its popularity. "A lot of the students involved in the campaign are generally like me, white kids who've never been involved in political or social justice activity before, but who recognise

From *The Guardian (London)* (July 27, 2000) p. 21.

that our clothes shouldn't be made by people who are treated like slaves—it's an easy thing to understand."

Despite being dominated by a number of big-name corporate players, such as Nike and Reebok, the students make it clear that they are not interested in calling for a boycott of any one company.

"This is an industry-wide problem, and is not specific to a handful of companies, which is why this campaign doesn't call for a boycott," says Suzanne Webb from the University of Kentucky sweatshop campaign. "A boycott would only hurt the very people that we are working with."

Instead, the sweatshop campaign is now focusing on two key demands: that universities withdraw their membership of the industry-backed Fair Labor Association and instead sign up with the Workers Rights Consortium (WRC), a body made up of students, university officials, and labour and human rights campaigners.

The reluctance of universities to agree to these demands has led to a number of student occupations of university administration buildings such as the sit-in at the University of Kentucky in April that ended with police arresting students amid protests of heavy-handed tactics on the part of the university and police.

The response from industry has been similarly dramatic. In spring, Nike, the market-leader of the sportswear industry, announced that it was to cancel millions of dollars' worth of sponsorship from three U.S. universities. The decision followed the announcement from Oregon, Michigan and Brown universities that they were to accept the student demands and become members of the WRC.

This move was just the latest in a series of successes for the sweatshop campaign. Apart from placing the issue firmly on the national corporate agenda, the campaign has forced sportswear giants such as Nike to retreat from their previously held position of never revealing the locations of their factories, to publicly listing all the factories that make clothes for five large American universities. Nike has since gone on the PR offensive, with the Nike boss, Phil Knight, personally intervening in the damage-limitation exercise, claiming that:

"We are very, very serious about providing good factory working conditions and continuously improve the working experience for all 500,000 people who make Nike products. We are committed to having the best monitoring and remediation process possible and to be open."

"These claims are baseless," replies Cornell. "Independent monitoring groups find shocking violations of working conditions every time they investigate clothing factories."

Despite these apparent successes, Angela Hale from the British-based anti-sweatshop campaign, Women Working Worldwide, is sceptical about the overall impact of the student campaign. "American campaigners might shout louder than campaigners here in Europe, but whether this means that there's been any change to workers' lives is another matter. What happens in American campuses is not going to change working conditions of people in Thailand. That is going to happen through workers' organisations over there."

However, Hale concedes that the students have played an important role in the debate on sweatshops: "Raising people's awareness is important to make sure people know what's going on. Workers in the South can gain enormous strength and confidence and extra resources through knowing that student actions are taking place across America."

121

United Students Against Sweatshops

Short USAS Description

United Students Against Sweatshops is an international student movement of campuses and individual students fighting for sweatshop-free labor conditions and workers' rights. We define "sweatshop" broadly and recognize that it is not limited to the apparel industry, but everywhere among us. We believe that university standards should be brought in line with those of its students who demand that their school's logo is emblazoned on clothing made in decent working conditions. We have fought for these beliefs by demanding that our universities adopt ethically and legally strong codes of conduct, full public disclosure of company information and truly independent verification systems to ensure that sweatshop conditions are not happening. Ultimately, we are using our power as students to affect the larger industry that thrives in secrecy, exploitation, and the power relations of a flawed system.

Principles of Unity

The principles of unity below have been drafted as an assessment of the spirit and of the issues which bring students on campuses across North America together to create a united youth front against sweatshops.

Hopefully, these principles touch on the underlying consciousness we are all developing, within ourselves as individuals and within our collectives, whether they be local, regional, national, or international.

The abuse of sweatshop labor is among the most blatant examples of the excesses and exploitation of the global economy. We recognize, however, that the term "sweatshop" is not limited to the apparel industry as traditionally conceived; sweatshop conditions exist in the fields, in the prisons, on our campuses, in the power relations of a flawed system.

Thus, we consider all struggles against the systemic problems of the global economy to be directly or by analogy a struggle against sweatshops. Whether a campus group focuses its energies on the apparel industry or on another form of sweatshop, agreement with the principles below will be used as the sole requisite for working under the name of United Students Against Sweatshops.

The Principles

1. We work in solidarity with working people's struggles. In order to best accomplish this and in recognition of the interconnections between local and global struggles, we strive to build relationships with other progressive movements and cooperate in coalition with other groups struggling for justice within all communities—campus, local, regional, and international.

2. We struggle against racism, sexism, homophobia, classism, and other forms of oppression within our society, within our organizations, and within ourselves. Not only are we collectively confronting these prejudices as inherent defects of the global economy which creates sweatshops, but we also recognize the need for individuals to confront the prejudices they have internalized as the result of living and learning in a flawed and oppressive society.

3. We are working in coalition to build a grassroots student movement that challenges corporate power and that fights for economic justice. This coalition is loosely defined; thus we strive to act in coordination with one another to mobilize resources and build a national network while reserving the autonomy of individuals and campuses. We do not impose a single ideological position, practice, or approach; rather, we aim to support one another in a spirit of respect for difference, shared purpose and hope.

4. We strive to act democratically. With the understanding that we live and learn in a state of imperfect government, we attempt to achieve truer democracy in making decisions which affect our collective work. Furthermore, we strive to empower one another as individuals and as a collective through trust, patience, and an open spirit.

The power of these principles to unify us as United Students Against Sweatshops ultimately rests with the individual. Self-evaluation and personal responsibility are critical to the effectiveness of our work. We all must continue to struggle as individuals in order to struggle in concert; thus we strive for compassion and support for one another as we continue this endeavor together.

Brief Description of ABC and ISC

Alliance Building Committee: Standing committee formed at the USAS national conference in August of 2000, open to anyone in USAS. It seeks to form alliances with other groups and people to work together against racism, sexism, homophobia, classism, and other forms of oppression. We must address these issues in a straightforward manner—whether that be within our organizations, within our work, or within ourselves.

International Solidarity Committee: Standing committee formed at the USAS national conference in August of 2000, open to anyone in USAS, to establish ongoing long-term relationships based on trust, and by doing this establish international solidarity deeper than rhetoric. Since we do not know what is best for workers in communities thousands of miles away (or down the street) we will build international relationships to support, not determine, the direction of organizing that is happening all over the world.

122

Students Spend Spring Break Protesting Taco Bell

Michael Critzon

April 08, 2002

Boycott Taco Bell

That is the message from four Student Labor Action Coalition [SLAC] members and CMU students who spent their spring break touring the nation and speaking about Taco Bell with the Coalition of Immokalee Workers.

Immokalee, Fla., is home to the Six L's Packing Company, Inc., where predominantly immigrant farm workers are paid from 35 to 45 cents for every 32-pound bucket of tomatoes they pick. They are paid about $7,500 annually. They don't have health insurance, sick leave, paid holidays or vacations, or a pension.

Taco Bell is a major buyer of Six L's tomatoes, and given its size and economic strength, it has the power to help these workers live a better life, according to the coalition's Web site.

From *Central Michigan Life*, student newspaper at Central Michigan University, Mount Pleasant, Michigan.

Angelo Moreno, Tiffany Ten Eyck, Lovella Hoffert, and Angie Pohlman joined about 75 farm workers from Immokalee and about 30 students from other schools in Chicago to peacefully protest in eight cities en route to Irvine, Calif., the location of Taco Bell's headquarters.

Hoffert, Cadillac junior, said she could see the struggle on the workers' faces as soon as the bus arrived.

"At that moment, I realized why I was there, why we were there fighting for them and why others should be, too," she said. "It was emotional for me to be with them and fight for them."

Pohlman, Saginaw senior, agreed.

"There was a great feeling of togetherness and solidarity especially when we were rallying," she said. "It was the most exhausting and wonderful thing I have ever been a part of."

The group visited Madison, Wis.; Omaha, Neb.; Denver, Col.; Salt Lake City, Utah; San Francisco, Fresno and Los Angeles, Calif. Each city had a meeting point where the group would march to the Taco Bell for the action, which varied from standing in a small area and passing out fliers to chanting, music and speakers.

"Every city had its own feel," said Moreno, Mount Pleasant freshman.

Denver was the first place that the activists realized that Taco Bell had printed out counter fliers for the employees to hand out, which turned out to be full of lies, he said.

"It was a flier war," Moreno said.

Salt Lake City was the only place where they ran into trouble with the police, Moreno said. After waving a car out of line at the drive thru, they were told by a police officer that they could not wave their hands and hold up fliers at the cars because he "saw what it did to the last car," he said.

In Fresno, participants of the tour ran into some people who were quite negative, but that did not stop the group's desire to further educate the public.

"A lot of the people we talked to were surprised," Hoffert said. "We live in this place that if we don't see it, it doesn't happen and it is just too easy to only care about yourself."

The main action was in Irvine where about 2,000 people, according to press counts, attended. They protested for about four hours ending with representatives from the Coalition of Immokalee Workers and Taco Bell meeting to talk about the future of the workers.

The workers wish for Taco Bell to pay 1 cent more for each pound of tomatoes they buy from Six L's. This would nearly double the farm workers' annual pay to about $14,000 and would cost the consumer about one-fourth of a penny more for a Chalupa.

"The meeting was very positive, hopefully laying the groundwork for more dialogue and a real, meaningful solution to the farm workers' problems in the near future," said Greg Asbed, Coalition of Immokalee Workers staff member.

Those on the tour stayed in churches and union buildings. Food was provided at nearly every city the tour stopped by Food Not Bombs, an organization that is dedicated to providing free food at protests and other events.

Food Not Bombs was even on hand in Fresno giving food to people who were entering Taco Bell so they would not go in to buy food, Moreno said.

To get involved with boycotting Taco Bell, go online to www.ciw-online.org, and search for the truth, educating yourself and others.

"We need to rethink the way that we have simplified our lives to the point that human beings are easily exploited, oppressed and killed in the name of profit. It is happening in our fields, in global sweatshops, and all around the world," said Ten Eyck, Shepherd senior. "This is not really boycotting Taco Bell to me; it is about changing my ideologies and my society in a way that human beings will no longer be exploited because it is cost-effective."

SLAC is having a farm worker teach-in at 7 p.m. Tuesday in Moore 105, which will focus on farm workers' struggles and devote time to the tour and the Taco Bell issue.

"Taco Bell's target market is the 18- to 24-year-old demographic. Students have the power to tell Taco Bell how you want them to do business. Use it, they will listen," Asbed said.

Taco Bell representatives could not be reached for comment.

123

Narrowing the Income Gap between Rich and Poor

Michael Hout and Samuel R. Lucas

The growing income gap between rich and poor Americans has become a key issue in this political season. The gap is larger now than at any point in the last 75 years. But a heated political and academic debate is under way about what the numbers mean. Some politicians and commentators try to dismiss income in-

From *The Chronicle of Higher Education* (August 8, 1995). Reprinted by permission of the authors.

equality with a variety of false assertions. They claim that inequality is inevitable because every society has its rich and poor; that it is a reflection of Americans' unequal talents; that it is necessary for economic growth; or that it may be unfortunate but must be tolerated because of the prohibitive expense of initiating government programs to redistribute wealth.

The results of a year-long research project that we and four colleagues in the sociology department at the University of California at Berkeley conducted contradict all of these propositions, as we document in *Inequality by Design: Cracking the Bell Curve Myth*, Princeton University Press (1996). Social inequality is not a force beyond our control.

Recent American history and the experience of several European nations show that economic inequality depends on the choices we make—how we regulate corporations and unions, how we distribute the tax burden, how we finance or do not finance education, and how we set wages. Nor is "taxing and spending" our only option.

Perhaps the most telling argument against the inevitability of our current situation is that not only is the inequality in income between the richest and the poorest in the United States greater now than in the past, but it is also greater than that of any other populous, industrialized country. Workers in such countries also have had to deal with the globalization of trade and the disruptions caused by new technology; yet only workers in the United States have lost so much ground. For example, in 1974 the chief executive officers of American corporations made about $35 for every worker's dollar; in 1995, they made $224 for every worker's dollar. By contrast, the chief executive officers of German corporations make about 21 deutsche marks (about $14) for every one earned by workers. Clearly, different economic choices produce different outcomes.

While every society has its rich and poor, inequality is mainly a matter of degree. In 1974, when the gap between the incomes of the richest and poorest Americans was at a historic low, the top 10 percent of U.S. households had incomes 31 times those of the poorest 10 percent and four times those of median-income households. By 1994, those numbers were 55 times the poorest and six times the median. Not only is inequality growing; its growth is accelerating. Inequality surged between 1991 and 1993 as the most recent recession lowered incomes for all but the richest Americans. Executives killed jobs in ways that would be illegal in Germany and France—for example, shutting down plants in some regions and relocating them in jurisdictions with right-to-work laws. Wall Street rewarded the executives with a mid-recession rally that boosted the value of their stock options.

Viewing inequality as inevitable absolves us of responsibility for reducing it. The current differences among nations mean that Americans need to be activist, not fatalistic, in the face of growing inequality. They also suggest that inequality is not produced by the genetic or other immutable personal characteristics that doom many workers to low wages. In their controversial book *The Bell Curve: The*

Reshaping of American Life by Differences in Intelligence (Free Press, 1994), the political scientist Charles Murray and the late psychologist Richard J. Herrnstein tried to explain the rising inequality of incomes in the United States by claiming that the economy now rewards intelligence more than in the past.

Our reanalysis of their data shows conclusively that the test scores that they relied on to gauge intelligence reflect home environments—particularly parents' socio-economic levels—as well as the quality of the schools people attended. For example, if I.Q. tests measure innate ability, people's scores on them ought to correlate equally well with their educational achievements both before and after the test. But the data used by Mr. Murray and Mr. Herrnstein show that people's scores correlate much more closely with their educational achievements at the time of the test than they do with their subsequent educational achievements. Schools create intelligence; they do not merely certify it. Thus the "intelligence" measured by tests is affected by a person's environment and is not solely the result of inborn characteristics.

Certainly, cognitive skills—though not innate—are important to one's earnings. However, errors and omissions in *The Bell Curve* also exaggerate the role of I.Q. in American inequality. Our reanalysis of the book's data shows that refining and enriching people's social environment makes I.Q. just one variable among many affecting inequality. Would that talent alone decided where a person ended up in society. Being born rich is still at least as much of an advantage as performing well on tests. . . .

Nor are the growing disparities in income an unavoidable negative effect of economic growth. Our review of the latest economic research concludes that such disparities may actually hinder growth. Since 1945, societies that have had greater inequality in incomes between the richest and poorest families have tended to have lower, not higher, subsequent economic growth.

The German and Italian economies grew faster between 1975 and 1989 than did that of the United States, but the gap between the incomes of the richest and the poorest citizens in those countries did not increase. In the United States, the period from 1955 through 1974 was the era of the greatest economic growth in this century, and also the era of the greatest equality of incomes in this century. The richest 5 percent of U.S. households saw their incomes go up rapidly during that period, but their share of total household income fell from 22 percent to 16 percent as the incomes of poor and middle-income households rose even faster.

Greater equality of income between the richest and poorest does not harm productivity, either. In a comparative analysis of Western nations spanning the 1970s and 1980s, the Northwestern University economist Rebecca Blank found that factors including job-security laws (such as tenure laws for workers in some European countries), homeowner subsidies (such as tax deductions for mortgage interest in the United States), health insurance, and public child care did not inhibit the flexibility of businesses to shift resources, for example from one set of priorities or products to another.

Growing inequality of incomes may actually be hurting our economic performance. In a study of more than 100 U.S. businesses, Douglass Cowherd of the Brookings Institution and our Berkeley colleague David Levine found that the smaller the wage gap between managers and workers, the higher the quality of the business's products. Considering how the gap between management compensation and workers' wages has grown in recent years, this analysis suggests that the quality of some companies' products may be suffering.

Do we have to raise taxes and spend on welfare programs to have less inequality of income? Research shows that many social programs can reduce inequality, but it also shows that many countries have low inequality without high spending on social programs. Rates of poverty among children are sensitive indicators of overall inequality. At 22 percent, the proportion of poor children in the United States is higher than that in any other populous, industrial country. Australia and Canada are next, with 14 percent of their children living in poverty—a rate more than 30 percent below that of the United States. The rate of childhood poverty is 10 percent in Britain and Italy, and in the single digits in Germany (7 percent), France (6 percent), and the Netherlands (6 percent).

Some countries achieve their lower rates with expensive social programs, but others don't. Childhood poverty would be substantially higher in France (25 percent) and in Britain (30 percent) if there were no taxes and no welfare programs to redistribute income in those two countries. Their welfare states bring their rates of childhood poverty below that of the United States. But the percentage of children living in poverty already is low before the government transfers any money to poor people in Germany (where the rate is 9 percent before counting the taxes and welfare spending that lower it to 7 percent) and in Italy (12 percent as opposed to the 10 percent after social spending). The rate of childhood poverty is moderate in the Netherlands (14 percent before social programs lower it to 6 percent). Those nations do not need extensive welfare spending to keep children out of poverty, because the economy itself does not generate as much inequality as we see in France, Britain, or the United States.

Germany, Italy, and the Netherlands have less poverty because they have no working poor. They boost the bottom of the income distribution with a minimum wage guaranteeing that full-time workers' children will not be poor. With the current minimum wage of $4.25 per hour, however, an American parent of two can work full time and still fall below the poverty line. Even though Congress has approved a bill raising the minimum wage to $5.25 in September 1997, that will still be true. Indeed, it would be true even if we raised the minimum wage to $6.50 per hour. The continuing debates about the minimum wage in this country have not contradicted this essential point: Young workers and their children are not as poor in countries with higher minimum wages.

Many European countries also use national wage agreements to control inequality. The details differ, but these countries all use some form of collective bargaining that makes management accountable to workers. In Austria and Norway, national associations of employers in different industries bargain with representatives of national unions to determine wages for workers in each sector of the economy. In Germany and Italy, bargaining goes on between unions and employers' associations in each industry or region. The government then routinely extends the terms of these agreements to non-union workers and companies.

In the United States, workers' wages are negotiated with a specific employer, either by individual employees or by a local union. In many jobs, the employer simply offers the job at a preset wage with little or no negotiation. This extremely decentralized system weakens the bargaining power of workers. Research by the Harvard University economist Richard Freeman, reported in *Working Under Different Rules* (Russell Sage Foundation, 1994), shows that the distribution of wages for workers of the same age, education, gender, and occupation is much wider in the United States than in countries with more centralized methods of setting wages.

Unions are the key to more uniform policies for setting wages. They help lower the inequality of income because they typically make management more accountable to workers, particularly when managers try to raise their own pay. The decline of unions in the United States in recent decades has meant that workers have lost the power to claim their share of economic growth. Between 1970 and 1990, the proportion of workers in the private sector belonging to unions dropped from 30 percent to just 11 percent, the lowest rate of union membership in the industrialized world except, possibly, for Japan.

Even as unions were declining, American workers set records in productivity (output per working hour). Between 1949 and 1974, increases in productivity were rewarded by increases in wages. Since 1974, productivity increased 68 percent in manufacturing and 50 percent in the service sector of the economy, but real wages grew less than 10 percent. The gains in productivity fueled both executive compensation—up 600 percent since 1974, according to research by the economic writer Graeff Crystal—and the stock market, where the Dow Jones Industrial Average has risen from 1,500 to more than 5,500 since 1974. Workers have set the table for an American economic feast for over two decades, but they have not received their slice of the growing pie.

The reports about economic inequality keep appearing. Political leaders, with the exception of the Republican Presidential candidate Patrick Buchanan, have been surprisingly passive. The action gap is almost as big as the income gap.

Our review of recent American history and of the actions of our competitors makes it clear that the country need not accept ever-more-extreme income disparities. Nor is the unpopular combination of high taxes and social spending our only remedy. In the past, investments in our schools and colleges helped to equalize opportunity for many citizens. Institutions such as labor unions empowered workers who wanted to claim a share of their own productivity. Today, the economies of countries that have national-incomes policies that include a voice for workers are growing faster than is the economy of the United States, and they are doing a better job of sharing the wealth.

That suggests that the solutions to America's problems of inequality of income are in the classrooms, boardrooms, and workplaces around the country. Washington's role should be to foster opportunity through education and to find ways to bring employers and workers together on an equal footing, so they can solve economic problems directly. For example, we need changes in the policies of the National Labor Relations Board to make it easier to form unions and easier for unions to force employers to engage in binding arbitration over contracts and other disputes.

124

A Clean Sweep:
The SEIU's Organizing Drive for Janitors Shows How Unionization Can Raise Wages

Harold Meyerson

On Friday, April 7, I came upon one method of increasing the income of the working poor that, I confess, had never even occurred to me. The janitors of Service Employees International Union (SEIU) Local 1877, embroiled in a county-wide strike, were marching down Wilshire Boulevard from downtown Los Angeles to tony Century City, roughly an eight-mile walk. Ten years earlier, another such march had culminated in one of the LAPD's periodic riots, when police set upon the marchers in Century City, beating and injuring scores. This time L.A.'s city attorney was in the parade's front row, flanked by a dozen other elected officials, Jesse Jackson, and a host of ministers, priests, and rabbis. But that wasn't all that was different about this march.

As the janitors left downtown, the people on the sidewalks—few of whom had known in advance about the march—started giving them a thumbs-up sign. After a couple of miles, the sidewalk passersby weren't just signaling their support; they were cheering. Then, as the march reached Beverly Hills, people on the sidewalk—first one, then a couple, then a bunch—did something I'd never seen. They

From *The American Prospect* (June 19—July 3, 2000) pp. 24—29.

darted into the street and handed the janitors cash. Spontaneous redistribution—something never before noted in any recorded history of Los Angeles.

Seventeen days later, L.A.'s janitors won themselves a considerable nonspontaneous redistribution: a wage increase of about 26 percent, spread over the next three years. The janitors who work at either end of their April 7 march—downtown or in Century City, areas almost entirely unionized—will see their hourly pay rise from just under $8 to just over $10. (At that rate, it's possible that one parent in a two-working-parent family could afford to work just one job—and actually get some time with his or her kids.) Janitors in other, less unionized parts of town will see an even greater percentage increase.

This, of course, was the far greater miracle: that a union 98 percent of whose members are immigrants—80 percent Central Americans, 55 percent women, and all of them poor—could wrest this kind of settlement from the nation's largest building service contractors and real estate investors. The settlement is a tribute to the spirit and tenacity of the janitors themselves, to the cohesiveness of the L.A. labor movement, and to the manifest strategic smarts of the international union to which the janitors belong, the SEIU. The settlement, so to speak, is the result of a three-level exceptionalism: The local, the central labor council, and the international are each about as good as it gets in the American labor movement today. . . .

Who Organizes?

Initiated in 1985 during John Sweeney's tenure as SEIU president, J for J [Justice for Janitors] has become known throughout the country as one of the most noisy, rambunctious, disruptive—and successful—efforts both to organize and win raises for workers at or near the bottom of the economy. Indeed, one such disruption—a rush-hour sit-down locking one of the bridges across the Potomac, pulled off under the very noses of the police detail assigned to guard the bridge—became a major point of contention between Sweeney and Tom Donahue, who was Sweeney's opponent during the 1995 campaign for the AFL-CIO presidency. The role of labor, Donahue insisted, was to build bridges, not block them. Sweeney countered that he'd built as many bridges as anyone in the labor movement, but there was a time to block bridges, too: when management was recalcitrant. It wasn't nice—it infuriated motorists—but then, the janitors have never depended on the kindness of strangers. More than any other union, the SEIU—under both Sweeney and his successor Andy Stern—has understood that the only real power of the poor is the power to disrupt. And no other union has channeled that disruption in so brilliant and productive a way. . . .

At first glance, the very idea that L.A.'s janitors could sustain and win a strike seemed preposterous. With an average hourly wage of $7.20, they were in no position to have socked away a rainy-day fund. The fact that they were spread across roughly 900 different work sites meant that bonding together as an effective union was anything but easy; it also made setting up effective picket lines very difficult.

(The local has 8,500 members.) The fragmented and byzantine structure of the industry also complicated matters greatly, compelling the union to negotiate up front with 18 different building service contractors while conducting back-channel discussions with a like number of building owners. In this kind of structure, the least wealthy, or most stingy, service contractor could easily gum up a settlement.

The primary asset the janitors brought to their strike, of course, the sine qua non of their victory, was their local, which has taken them a dozen years to rebuild to a position of strength. Up until 1983–1984, Los Angeles, like most nonsouthern U.S. cities, had a unionized janitorial work force (which in Los Angeles was heavily black). In 1983 the local signed a contract with the service contractors providing its members with an hourly wage of $7.32.

At the same time, thousands of Central Americans began moving to Los Angeles, many fleeing the U.S.-backed wars that were raging in their homelands. Building service contractors began discharging their unionized workers and hiring refugees. No other American city experienced quite so wholesale a substitution of one work force for another. None of L.A.'s new janitors made anything like $7.32 an hour. Instead, they made the federal minimum wage—then $3.35 an hour, just 44 percent of the rate set by the union contract. "Almost immediately after the ink was dry on the contract," says Jono Shaffer, who came to L.A. to start up Justice for Janitors a few years later, "the union had to go into renegotiations, dropping wages just to keep some members in the buildings." From 5,000 members in 1978, the local shrank to 1,800 in 1985.

Throughout the mid-1980s, many of SEIU's janitorial locals were under assault from contractors either able to exploit a changing work force or just indulging in the rampant union-busting of the time. In 1985 the union hastily assembled its first, impromptu Justice for Janitors campaign in Pittsburgh, where management was trying to win major givebacks. In 1986 SEIU decided to shore up its position in building services by making J for J a national—and proactive rather than reactive—campaign. After an initial victory in Denver, J for J came to Los Angeles in 1988.

Reorganizing the L.A. local proved particularly arduous. "In a sense," Shaffer recalls, "the new local began on the Olympic Boulevard bus from Century City [home to many high-rises] to Pico Union [home to many janitors], the 2:30 A.M. bus. It was the janitors' private bus; there sure wasn't anyone else on it, and it was the one place where they were together and could talk freely about their work."

By the early 1990s, the janitors had unionized Century City, strengthened their position in downtown, and formed a distinct, statewide janitors' local. With accomplished J for J organizer Mike Garcia as its new president, the local plunged into a series of campaigns organizing janitors in L.A.'s numerous suburbs and edge cities, and persuading the building contractors to recognize the union and agree to the terms of its L.A. master contract. Characteristically, these campaigns combined on-site strikes; pressure from local pols, clerics, and community groups; and the occasional intervention of the buildings' owners on the janitors' behalf. . . .

What It Takes to Organize

. . . The campaign required SEIU to make alliances with community groups and hire a slew of young organizers off campuses and from community-based organizations. This was far from common practice at the time because most unions viewed such groups and organizers as too radical or because organizing was just not a union priority, or for both reasons.

The L.A. janitors' local got more than its share of such organizers, however. Together with members who'd been politically active in their homelands and had led the fight to create a distinct janitors' local, they set about building a union that involved the maximum number of members in its work and decision making. . . . Over the past five years, as the local grew to represent 70 percent of the janitorial work force in L.A.'s class-A office properties, members learned to represent one another in grievances and to lead meetings; they also mastered the arcane structure of their industry. Late this March, with their contract about to expire and talks with employers at an impasse, the union convened a meeting of its 100 or so stewards. There, says Triana Silton, the staffer in charge of J for J in Los Angeles, the union's leaders told the stewards, "If we go out, you folks will have to run the strike." Which, the stewards pledged, they would. . . .

By day, as the newscast helicopters hovered overhead, the janitors (at times numbering well over 1,000) marched down L.A.'s boulevards and threw together rallies with the speed and mobility of Patton's Third Army. (On one occasion, they rustled up 500 members and half of L.A.'s city council on three hours' notice so that Ted Kennedy, passing through town, could endorse the strike.) At sunset, the real work of the strike began as members dispersed to the myriad of office buildings around town. "With so many buildings out, you couldn't possibly have staff at more than a handful," Shaffer says. "At most work sites, the members ran the strike and the picket line and the scab patrols."

In the end, the union pulled roughly half its members onto the streets in its effort to shut down the cleanup of L.A.'s office buildings. The net the janitors strung had plenty of holes in it, but the nighttime cleanings in many of the city's most prominent buildings were incomplete and haphazard, when they happened at all.

Local 1877 had had plenty of practice mobilizing its members. In a city where labor has played the decisive role in election after election over the past four years, the janitors were the most politically active union in town. . . .

The federation brought its own distinct clout to the janitors' strike; combined with the janitors' own efforts, it's no mystery why Local 1877 went into the strike with a statement of support from 48 L.A.-area elected officials or, as the strike unfolded, why it won further statements of support from the county supervisors, both houses of the state legislature, a unanimous city council, and Republican Mayor Richard Riordan. Not since the 1994 earthquake had so many L.A. electeds come together for the same cause.

The intervention that many of these officials made on the janitors' behalf was anything but casual: Council members were arrested for civil disobedience; assembly members sat on the janitors' side of the table during bargaining sessions; congressmen addressed rallies; Ted Kennedy, Dianne Feinstein, and Al Gore came to town and spoke for their cause. Assembly Speaker Antonio Villaraigosa, County Supervisor Zev Yaroslavsky, and the mayor publicly and privately pressured their building-owner buddies to settle.

One factor in generating such singular solidarity among the electeds was apparent on the day of the janitors' march, at the post-primary breakfast that the Los Angeles County Federation of Labor hosted for pols it had helped in the previous month's primary. The breakfast was held in a hotel along the janitors' parade route, so the assembled pols could come outside and bless the janitors as they passed. However, the absence of one pol—nine-term Congressman Marty Martinez—was felt more than the presence of all the others.

In the March primary, the federation had broken with all precedent to oppose Martinez's re-election. Martinez had a career 90 percent AFL-CIO voting record, but he was the most lackadaisical of members, and, worse, he had swapped his vote to the White House (for a freeway extension) during the 1997 fight over fast track, neglecting to notify the unions he was about to switch sides. When state senator Hilda Solis, a stellar pro-labor legislator with wide support, challenged Martinez, the federation endorsed her and poured in an army of volunteers, the greatest number of whom came from the janitors. Solis clobbered Martinez, 69 to 31 percent—and the ghost of poor Marty hung over the breakfast as a grim reminder to all the electeds of the fate that might await them if they spurned the unions' cause.

Adding oomph to the janitors' clout was just one of the federation's endeavors on the janitors' behalf. This year, contracts expire for 300,000 of the 800,000 union members whose locals are federation affiliates, and the federation has turned the local labor movement into a kind of mutual-aid society. Even before the janitors' strike began, it convened a rally of 10,000 members from all the different unions whose contracts were up, and almost all these unions were to provide the janitors with money, food, and bodies in the weeks ahead. Locals that had long been indifferent to such struggles honored the janitors' picket lines this time around. The operating engineers—who maintain elevators, air conditioning systems, and such in office buildings all across town—offered full pay from their own strike fund to any members who didn't cross the janitors' lines. Before the strike, the operating engineers had never given any indication that they cared whether the janitors lived or died.

Solidarity on a Bigger Stage

Nor was the janitors' simply a local strike. The chief building maintenance contractors they were fighting were national, even global, corporations. The companies, Real Estate Investment Trusts (REITs), and pension funds that owned L.A.'s high-rises owned high-rises all across the nation. And accordingly, the janitors' international union had decided to turn their strike into a national one.

What the SEIU had done was line up the expiration dates of its janitorial contracts in most major cities so that, as nearly as possible, they would coincide or at least follow one another in close succession. The L.A. janitors walked first, but within two weeks they were followed by the janitors in Chicago and San Diego, at the same time that New York's janitors settled without a strike. One week after the L.A. strike ended, janitors were slated to strike in Cleveland, and so it goes, one city after another, through October.

The union is merely following the consolidation of the industry. In the 1980s, save in those cities where the unions were exceptionally strong (New York, San Francisco, downtown Chicago), building owners created a protective shield behind which they could deny all responsibility for the union-busting of the Reagan years. They handed over the task of hiring, firing, supervising, and paying the janitors to the hitherto small-scale and local building service industry. (The amounts these contractors agreed to pay the janitors, however, still had to be cleared with the building owners.) In short order, these contractors grew mightily, and soon the industry came to be dominated by such nationwide companies as American Building Maintenance (ABM) and OneSource (until relatively recently, a Danish-based conglomerate called ISS/DESCO Services).

Moreover, the ownership of class-A office properties has also been consolidated in recent years. In the 1980s, most of downtown L.A.'s high-rises were owned by foreign (chiefly Japanese) investors. Today, the city's choice properties are owned primarily by REITs and pension funds—the same REITs and pension funds that own choice properties throughout the nation. According to an April survey in the *Los Angeles Business Journal*, 51 percent of the class-A property on L.A.'s west side—that is, the highest-rent buildings in all of Los Angeles—was owned by pension funds, and another 21 percent by REITs. Moreover, according to figures compiled by the SEIU, the largest class-A property owner in southern California is also the largest in the United States—Chicago-based Equity Investments, which owns 77 million square feet across the country. Another major L.A. real estate owner, Warren "Ned" Spiecker, has 41 million square feet of office property on the West Coast.

When L.A.'s janitors struck, then, SEIU leaders were already talking with these owners and contractors on a national level. "We met with ABM, OneSource, Equity, the major owners in New York and L.A. prior to the contract expirations," says SEIU president Andy Stern. "We made clear that these were integrated, though not common, negotiations. When we sat down with owners and contractors in Chicago or L.A.," Stern continues, "they understood that this wasn't simply a discussion about Chicago or L.A."

So did SEIU's janitors all across the nation. As the date for the first contract expiration neared, the international set up a series of teleconferences among members in different cities, members of one local flew across the country to sit in at the bargaining sessions of another local, and a nationwide solidarity developed among the janitors. (Solidarity is the concept that unions most frequently invoke and most seldom cultivate.) It was this cross-city bond that underlay the threat that the international's leaders conveyed to the owners and contractors: If the local on strike in

L.A. against ABM, say, sent one picket to a building cleaned by ABM in New York, the New York janitors wouldn't clean the building. By the final week of the L.A. strike, ratcheting up the pressure, SEIU put this plan into action. "Members from 1877 [the L.A. local] flew to Seattle, Denver, San Francisco, San Jose, and their pickets were honored," says SEIU Building Service Director Stephen Lerner. "We just did a couple of buildings in each city for one night, but we planned to escalate considerably if the strike had to go into its fourth week."

The international's threat to the nationwide owners and employers worked because, on the management side of the table, size matters. The building owners—for whom the janitors' wages are just a small part of their overall expenses—can bring pressure on the contractors, from whom janitors' wages take a bigger bite. This is why the SEIU prefers to negotiate directly with the owners, which it's able to do only in the cities where it's strongest. . . .

The most astonishing sight in the janitors' strike—and I saw it repeatedly—was of motorists stuck in traffic for 15 or 20 minutes as the janitors marched across an intersection. Time and again, drivers got out of their cars and shook their fists—not in anger, but in clamorous support.

The strike had two immediate effects on the city. First, it pushed the reality of low-wage work smack into everyone's face. (Even L.A.'s TV newscasts—the most substance-free in the land—were compelled to cover the janitors' daily marches and mention the wage rates at which they worked.) Second, the janitors provided the city with its first plausible and visible solution for poverty-wage work: unionization. In middle-class L.A., let alone in upwards-of-middle-class L.A., I've not detected any overwhelming public sentiment to unionize low-wage workers. But the janitors forced Los Angeles to confront its transformation into the national capital of low-wage work on a less theoretical level. Behind the spontaneous cash donations in the streets of Beverly Hills was not only guilt about such manifest poverty in the midst of such manifest plenty, but also a kind of civic relief: At last, somebody was doing something about what Los Angeles had become—a city with a vanishing middle class and an explosion in the number of Angelenos at work for poverty-level wages. . . .

Recipe for Organizing

Francis Calpotura

"She always felt that cooking for members was her way of contributing to the cause," says Louis Jackson as he reminisces about the years that he and his wife, Wilma Jean, spent with People United for a Better Oakland (PUEBLO). "She was most proud of that."

Heaping mounds of homemade macaroni with melted cheese and pounds of meatloaf in tomato sauce with finely chopped onions and chunky garlic were Wilma Jean Jackson's specialties. These were staple dishes at PUEBLO monthly membership meetings. She would arrive two hours before anyone else and bogard the kitchen at the old PUEBLO office on East 21st Street. On those days, Wilma Jean ruled the oven and stove tops.

I was a PUEBLO organizer at the time, and I always tried to get Wilma Jean to do other things. Leadership development is a central organizing goal, and I took pride in my abilities as an organizer. "Wilma Jean, you're such a good cook," I once told her as she stirred a huge pot of boiling water filled halfway with macaroni shells. "How about spicing up our meeting with the police chief next week with your presence? You know how much the Oakland cops have been harassing young black men in your neighborhood. Even your son Clarence was pulled over for no reason at all."

"No, no, no, young man! You're not gonna get me to do anything like that. How many times am I gonna tell you that I don't do stuff like that. Let Gwen, Rita, or the other members do the talking. I cook."

Wilma Jean Jackson passed away last November. In the past few years, I only got to see her during PUEBLO's Annual Dinner Celebrations, dressed to the T, and lugging around big pots of mac and cheese. Born in Oklahoma, Wilma Jean took a cooking job at Kansas State University in Wichita at age 18. In July 1967, her family migrated to Richmond, California where she got her high school diploma. She is survived by her husband Louis, their sons Clarence, Henry, and Paul, and 10 grandchildren. Wilma Jean knew how to cook for a large family.

From *Colorlines* (Winter 2001—2002) pp. 18—20.

Food as Family

"Food is always part of our meetings, retreats, and gatherings," according to Karleen Lloyd, Organizing Director at PUEBLO. "It helps create a feeling of family—sitting around the table, sharing and eating food that we all helped prepare." The food on the PUEBLO table reflects their multicultural membership: corn tamales kneaded by Berta, Vietnamese spring rolls prepared by Mr. Tai, *pansit* (Filipino noodles) cooked by Salud Dacumos, and, at times, Wilma Jean's golden fried chicken.

"Food opens the door for people to interact in a different way," remarks Mayron Payes, Worker Rights Coordinator for the Coalition for Humane Immigrant Rights in Los Angeles (CHIRLA). CHIRLA organizes day laborers, domestic workers and other migrant workers in L.A.'s expanding low-wage industries. Mexicans, Salvadorans, indigenous Oaxacans, and Guatemalans comprise the majority of their membership. "When you involve food in organizing a diverse constituency, 'How do you cook this?' starts the trust-building process. It brings people closer because they want to know about the culture of other communities." You are what you eat.

In the town of Gainesville, Georgia, the Newtown Florist Club has been bringing African Americans together for decades. "We just celebrated our 50th anniversary last November," says a proud Faye Bush, president of Newtown. In its beginnings, Florist Club members went door-to-door asking for donations to buy flowers for families of recently deceased community residents. But in the late 1980s, the Florist Club took to the doors again—this time asking why people were dying and getting ill, and if the 13 polluting industries that surround their neighborhood bore any responsibility. The organization has transformed itself from a mutual assistance association to a social change group.

"We've always had 100 percent black membership since we got started, but that began changing five years ago when we did a Peace March with Hispanic groups in response to racist comments from our mayor. He blamed the increase in violence to black and Hispanic gangs." Since that time, Latino attendance in Club activities has been consistent and increasing.

"Food adds fellowship, especially when you're trying to integrate a new constituency base in your organization," explains Faye. "One day we'll serve soul food in our meetings, and the next we'll have Mexican food. Food is just another way of being able to talk about our life journeys to each other." The Florist Club plans to call their upcoming annual leadership gathering "Taste of the Town" and make the sharing of food, culture, and stories a main emphasis.

Family Tensions

Growth also brings new contradictions to an organization. Karleen Lloyd notices a cultural shift in PUEBLO's food practices as more professionals of color have joined the organization. "It's a class thing," says Karleen. "Recently, we've been hearing comments like, 'People in this organization eat too much. It takes up a lot of time in our meetings.' They want corporate efficiency. But that's not who we are."

Another tension involves money. "Our line item for meetings is huge," laments Grace Kong, lead organizer for the Laotian Organizing Project in Richmond, California. "It adds up. Especially when you're organizing youth. They're always hungry, so you need to feed them to keep them engaged."

Through the years, PUEBLO has substantially increased its line item for food. "We've come to realize that in order to make our organization accessible to low-income and working people—most of whom are women," asserts Karleen of PUEBLO, "we not only have to provide childcare, transportation, and translation services. We also have to make sure there's food at meetings. If not, then we're not serious about bringing them into the organization."

This organizational commitment is reminiscent of the Free Breakfast for School Children Program originated by the Black Panther Party three decades ago in Oakland's poor neighborhoods. Thinking, meeting, and acting are difficult at best when your belly is empty.

Home Coming

Thumsom, Loatian Papaya Salad:
Pound garlic, Laotian chili pepper, salt and MSG with pestle and mortar.
Fold shrimp paste in with other ingredients.
Add shredded green papayas and cherry tomatoes cut in half.
Pour in lime juice, fish sauce, and a heaping spoonful of sugar.
Pound everything together to make a deliciously hot, sour, and sweet salad.
Best eaten in the mid-afternoon to stay cool when the sun is in its full blaze.

The youth leaders of the Laotian Organizing Project (LOP) from Richmond, California, brought their pestles and mortars, cutting board and knives, and an Igloo container full of ingredients to their annual retreat at Lake Tahoe. They remembered their last retreat, when they ate pizza, KFC, and spaghetti for two days. Protests of "We want rice!" rang out during the long drive back. They made a pact that this retreat would be different.

"We spent the first night chopping, pounding, telling stories, and trying to recall how their mothers made delicious *thumsom*," recounts Grace Kong. "It reminded them of their home in Richmond, and of a culture that's familiar." In that moment, home, culture, and the struggle for change were folded into the organization.

LOP's members come from various tribes from the country of Laos: Mien, Khmu, Hmong, and Lao. In their homeland, they were farmers for generations, residing mostly in the Laotian hinterlands. During the Indochina conflicts of the '60s and '70s, the CIA heavily recruited from these communities to fight a counterinsurgency war against the Pathet Lao guerrillas. Uprooted from Laos and resettled in Richmond, these communities maintain homeland practices that affirm their history and continued survival. One of the first LOP community initiatives was the Laotian Community Gardens project. Members planted flowers, tomatoes, eggplants, and chilies—food stuff that reminded them of home. In the Laotian neighborhood of Richmond, front-yard gardens that dot the streets serve as a testament of a community holding on to its culture. . . .

Nourishing the Whole

If you are open to it, the craft of organizing allows you amazing insight into the human condition. And just when you think you've figured everything out, more things come up that slap you around and teach you to be humble.

I learned that organizing is centrally about power—building an organization by recruiting members and marshaling meager resources to win fights. In so doing, we shift the balance of power. I guess I still believe in this basic formulation, but it fails to excite me.

Nor do I think it excites the people we try to organize.

I am in search of a new organizing paradigm, one where culture is central to the enterprise and which considers the organization as a social space to celebrate and transform cultural norms. And the creation of this space is as important as winning on issues.

"At LOP, we don't just get people together to talk about serious issues and plan winning strategies," shares Grace Kong. "It's about nourishing ourselves, having fun, and acknowledging that, even with all the rending experiences we've gone through, we are whole people. Food nourishes the whole."

I regret that I didn't get a chance to fully thank Wilma Jean Jackson and express my appreciation for her singular vision of making those who broke bread with her whole again.

Wilma Jean, Presente!

Child of the Americas

Aurora Levins Morales

I am a child of the Americas,
a light-skinned mestiza of the Caribbean,
a child of many diaspora, born into this continent at a crossroads.

I am a U. S. Puerto Rican Jew,
a product of the ghettos of New York I have never known.
An immigrant and the daughter and granddaughter of immigrants.
I speak English with passion: it's the tongue of my consciousness,
a flashing knife blade of crystal, my tool, my craft.
I am Caribeña, island grown. Spanish is in my flesh,
ripples from my tongue, lodges in my hips:
the langauge of garlic and mangoes,
the singing in my poetry, the flying gestures of my hands.
I am of Latinoamerica, rooted in the history of my continent:
I speak from that body.

I am not african. Africa is in me, but I cannot return.
I am not taína. Taîno is in me, but there is no way back.
I am not european. Europe lives in me, but I have no home there.

I am new. History made me. My first language was spanglish.
I was born at the crossroads
and I am whole.

From Aurora Levins Morales and Rosario Morales, *Getting Home Alive* (Milford, CT: Firebrand Books, 1986).

Suggestions for Further Reading

Colby, A., and W. Damon. *Some Do Care: Contemporary Lives of Moral Commitment.* New York: Free Press, 1992.

Dees, Morris. *A Season of Justice: A Lawyer's Own Story of Victory Over America's Hate Groups.* New York: Touchstone Books, 1991.

Featherstone, Lisa, and the United Students Against Sweatshops. *Students Against Sweatshops: The Making of a Movement.* Praeger, 2002.

Kiang, Peter N. *We Could Shape It: Organizing for Asian Pacific American Student Empowerment.* Boston: University of Massachusetts Press, 1996.

Kivel, Paul. *Uprooting Racism: How White People Can Work for Racial Justice.* New York: New Society Publishers, 1996.

Lynch, James. *Prejudice Reduction in the Schools.* New York: Nichols Publishing, 1987.

Naples, Nancy A., and Karen Bojar, eds. *Teaching Feminist Activism Strategies from the Field.* New York: Routledge, 2002.

Pogrebin, L. C. *Growing Up Free.* New York: Bantam Books, 1981.

Prokosch, Michael, et al. *The Global Activist's Manual: Local Ways to Change the World.* New York: Thunder's Mouth Press/Nation Books, 2002.

Reddy, Maureen T. *Everyday Acts against Racism.* Seattle: Seal Press, 1996.

Rose, Fred. *Coalitions Across the Class Divide: Lessons from the Labor, Peace and Environmental Movements.* Ithaca, NY: Cornell University Press, 2000.

Spring, J. *Deculturalization and the Struggle for Equality: A Brief History of the Education of Dominated Cultures in the U.S.* New York: McGraw-Hill, 1997.

Stoltenberg, Jon. *The End of Manhood: A Book for Men of Conscience.* New York: Dutton, 1993.

Stout, Linda. *Bridging the Class Divide.* Boston: Beacon Press, 1996.

Thompson, Becky. *A Promise and a Way of Life: White Antiracist Activism.* Minneapolis: University of Minnesota Press, 2001.

Index